CHINA

**FODOR'S
TRAVEL PUBLICATIONS**

NEW YORK • TORONTO
LONDON • SYDNEY • AUCKLAND

WWW.FODORS.COM

CONTENTS

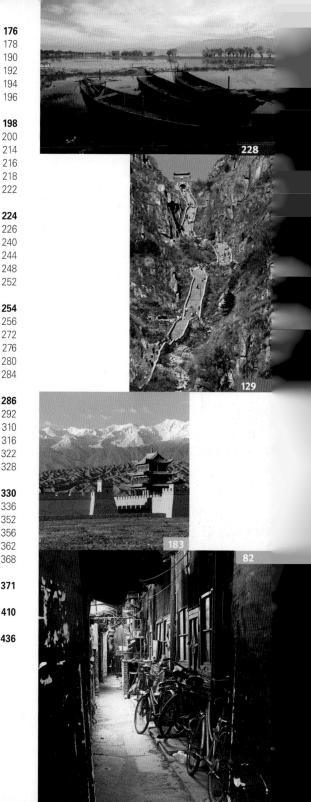

UNDERSTANDING CHINA

Understanding China is an introduction to the country, its geography, economy, history and its people, giving a real insight into the nation. Living China gets under the skin of China today, while The Story of China takes you through the country's past.

The first thing that strikes visitors about China is its immense size. The third-largest country in the world, it is also the most densely populated, with nine out of ten of its 1.3 billion people living on just 30 percent of the land. China's unique civilization has an unbroken history of more than 5,000 years and an astonishingly rich cultural heritage. But what makes modern China so immensely fascinating is that the traditional way of life, based on farming, communal values and the family, exists side by side with a newly emerging, Western-influenced culture that prizes consumerism, innovation and the technology of the digital age. It is this rejuvenated, multi-faceted China that visitors can look forward to discovering.

POLITICS

The People's Republic of China is a Communist state ruled by a single political party. The head of state, currently President Hu Jintao, has wide executive powers. Day-to-day decisions are made by the State Council, which is appointed by China's supreme legislative body, the National People's Congress. Elections, held every five years, are confined to delegates nominated by the Party. China occupies an increasingly prominent role on the world stage and is one of the five members of the Security Council of the United Nations. China's entry into the World Trade Organization in December 2001 was an important landmark in the government's policy of 'opening up,' but has raised concerns in the US and Europe over China's huge foreign trade surplus.

While the Communist Party has espoused economic liberalism, there aren't many signs that the country is heading in a more democratic direction. Criticism of the Party by outsiders is anathema, dissidents are often jailed or sent to labor camps for 're-education,' the media is subject to censorship and there is a heavy security presence in the border regions of Tibet and Xinjiang. But the survival of the regime will ultimately depend on the Party's ability to address a range of environmental, social and demographic issues arising from China's breakneck economic development over the last 25 years. These include corruption at national and local level, the disparity between rich and poor, inadequate health care and education provision, rural unemployment, the appropriation of agricultural land for industrial use and environmental pollution.

TRADITIONAL BELIEFS

Though China is officially atheist, and only 7 percent of the population professes a religion, traditional beliefs are deeply rooted in the national psyche.

Little is known about the life of China's greatest philosopher, Kong Zi (Confucius, c551–479BC). The son of an impoverished nobleman in Shandong province, he is said to have worked as a bookkeeper before founding a school, like his Greek contemporary, Socrates. But his teachings made him enemies, and he spent most of his life wandering the countryside in search of a patron. While Confucius' teachings commend values like moderation, compromise, public duty and reverence for the ancestors, it was his emphasis on filial piety and obedience to authority that later appealed to rulers of the Han dynasty, who turned Confucianism into a cult.

The founder of Taoism, Lao Zi (The Old Master), is a semilegendary figure, credited with a collection of sayings, known as *The Way and its Power* (Daodejing). Taoism is often seen as complementing Confucianism with its emphasis on the contemplative life, on oneness with nature and the renunciation of ambition. But Taoism came to embrace a whole range of traditional beliefs, from magic to medicine—Beijing's White Cloud Temple still has a Taoist clinic. Like Confucianism, Taoism developed from a philosophy into something akin to a religion, with its own priests, deities and temples.

Buddhism entered China from India via the Silk Road in the first century AD. Its more than superficial resemblance to Taoism contributed to its popularity, especially after the Buddhist sutras were translated into Chinese in around 200AD. Eventually, indigenous Buddhist schools emerged, the most noteworthy being Chan or meditative Buddhism, exported to Japan as Zen.

LANGUAGE

The official language of communication in China is *Putonghua* (meaning 'common speech'), known in the West as Mandarin. Derived from Beijing dialect, it is spoken by about 70 percent of the population. Cantonese (*yue*) is spoken widely in Hong Kong, Guangzhou and the far south of China. Other important dialects include Shanghainese (*wu*) and Fujianese (*minbei*). The Tibetan, Uighur and Mongolian peoples all have their own distinct languages.

What makes Chinese unique is its script, which has a history of more than 3,500 years. Over time, the primitive pictographs found on oracle bones dating from the Shang dynasty were combined to communicate more sophisticated concepts and ideas until today's symbols evolved. There are more than 50,000 ideograms but only a fraction is in common usage. As written Chinese uses symbols rather than an alphabet, and does not attempt to recreate the spoken word, it transcends dialect and can be used by all Chinese to communicate.

THE PEOPLE

The majority of the population (around 92 percent) claims descent from the Han, but the Han is only one of 56 major ethnic groups and around 200 minority peoples that constitute the Chinese nation. While the Zhuang, China's largest minority (population 13 million), has its own autonomous region in Guangxi province, it is now virtually indistinguishable from the Han. Also fully integrated are the Manchus, who supplied China with its Qing Dynasty rulers but whose language is now all but extinct. The three dozen minorities in the mountainous regions of southwestern China, such as the Bai, Dai, Naxi and Miao, while assimilated, are officially encouraged to preserve their own culture and dialects.

While the Chinese government promotes the idea that all its peoples live in peace and harmony, sporadic outbreaks of violence and unrest are still reported in Tibet and Xinjiang, where disaffected elements of the population feel they have little in common with the Han. Major rioting in Lhasa, Tibet's provincial capital, resulted in the area being closed to tourism: Restrictions may still apply to foreigners. A series of small-scale attacks, linked to Islamic terrorism, were also reported in Xinjiang during the Beijing Olympic Games in August 2008.

Opposite *The Imperial Summer Palace at Chengde*
Left *Sorting the catch on the floating fish market in Sai Kung town in the New Territories*

I NINGXIA HUIZU ZIZHIQU
2 BEIJING SHI
3 HEBEI
4 TIANJIN SHI
5 SHANGHAI SHI
6 CHONGQING
7 AOMEN (MACAU)
8 XIANGGANG (HONG KONG)

CHINA'S REGIONS

Beijing China's capital and second-largest city, Beijing has a population of around 15 million and the lion's share of the tourist sights. It is also a focus for heavy industry and air pollution is a major problem. The authorities moved some of the worst offenders, the steel-producing Shougang factories in particular, out of the region in time for the 2008 Olympics and there are high hopes that these largely successful temporary efforts will lead to permanent improvements in environmental standards.

The North Northern China, the heartland of Han Chinese culture, is dotted with historic cities. Xi'an, the Zhou dynasty capital for 1,000 years, is the best known, and its terra-cotta warriors remain one of China's most magnificent cultural sights. The hill resort at Chengde was a summer retreat for the Qing emperors during the 18th and 19th centuries, while modern-day Kaifeng and Luoyang saw the rise and fall of no less than 20 dynasties. Confucianism had its origins in the towns of Qufu and Zouxian. The cities in northern China are modernizing rapidly and becoming increasingly cosmopolitan. The area's popular coastal resorts retain a more old-fashioned feel.

The Northeast Northeastern China has been strongly influenced by its Korean, Russian and Japanese neighbors and is culturally and ethnically distinct from the rest of the country. The provinces of Jilin, Heilongjiang and Liaoning offer an interesting mix of cosmopolitan and historic cities and extreme wilderness. The cities of Shenyang and Changchun respectively offer insights into the start and end of

the Qing dynasty. Harbin and Jilin exhibit the region's Russian and Japanese influences, while Dalian shows the confident, fun side of the new, economically prosperous China. Outside the cities are remote lakes, mountains and border towns that speak of humility in the face of awesome terrain and climatic conditions: Summer months in the northeast can be uncomfortably warm, while winter sees some of the planet's lowest temperatures. In an effort to turn past adversity to future profit, the region now offers some very good skiing.

Inner Mongolia and the Silk Road This region encompasses some of China's least developed areas, places that are on the fringe both geographically and culturally. Yet their historical significance in the formation of modern China is considerable. It was via the Silk Road that Buddhism, Islam, knowledge of the West and untold wealth arrived in China. Abandoned forts and former cities, as well as the thriving markets of Turpan and Kashi (Kashgar), are part of this legacy. It was from Inner Mongolia that Ghengis Khan established Asia's greatest empire, one that ruled over all China under his son Kublai Khan. Today the area is interesting for both its geography, which encompasses grasslands, inland deserts and high mountains, and its people, who include the sizable Mongolian, Hui and Uighur minorities as well as peoples of Central Asian ancestry. Nomadic Mongolian culture continues to thrive and traditional pastimes such as singing and horse racing are common.

Sichuan and the Tibetan Plateau Sichuan's name translates as Four Rivers, and comes from the four tributaries of the Yangtze that flow through it. The

Chengdu Plain to the east is a densely populated lowland agricultural region. Most of the province's cities are in this area, including the capital Chengdu, Leshan, Zigong, Neijiang and Nanchong. To Chengdu's west and north, steep forested mountains provide some of the last remaining refuges of the giant panda.

The Tibetan Plateau rises from Sichuan's far west, stretching for some 2,500km (1,563 miles) and encompassing all of Tibet. Known as the Roof of the World and fringed by the Himalayas, its altitude averages over 4,500m (14,764ft). The climate is harsh, although valley areas are farmed in the short growing season. Most Tibetans live in the capital Lhasa, second city Xigaze (Shigatse) and towns such as Gyantze and Zetang (Tsedang), all concentrated in the south.

The Southwest Southwestern provinces Guangxi, Guizhou and Yunnan comprise a wide variety of topography and climate. Guangxi's landscape is famous for the sugarloaf peaks of its limestone karst mountains, notably between Guilin and Yangshuo along the Li River (Li Jiang), but also in other areas and in neighboring Guizhou. Guangxi's capital, Nanning, is in the south. To the north and into Guizhou, mountains have been carved over centuries into series of rice terraces. Numerous ethnic minority villages dot the mountains east of provincial capital Guiyang.

Yunnan is the most diverse region culturally and geographically. Its 26 minority groups live across the province, which ranges from the tropical rainforests of Xishuangbanna to high mountains. The capital Kunming has a mild, springlike climate year round. Jinghong lies close to Burma and Laos. Other key cities are Dali, Xiaguan and, in the northwest, Lijiang and Zhongdian.

South China and the Yangtze The heart of the Guangdong province is mighty Guangzhou (Canton), the Pearl River Delta powerhouse, which vies with Shanghai for the title of China's most dynamic city. The subtropical island province of Hainan Dao (Hainan Island) has been dubbed China's 'Hawaii.' At opposite ends of the Taiwan Straits in the province of Fujian, the port towns of Fuzhou and Xiamen share coastal character. Lushan, in Jiangxi province, is a 'little Switzerland' that has long lured Chinese visitors seeking to escape the summer heat on the plains. Thanks to its storied Xi Hu (West Lake), Zhejiang province's capital Hangzhou is one of the most romantic Chinese cities. Canal-threaded Shaoxing is tranquil. At the coast, the port town of Ningbo is a stepping stone to Putuoshan island's Buddhist mountain.

The Yangtze river cuts through a broad swathe of central China: This emblematic river valley takes in parts of Chongqing Municipality and of Hubei, Hunan, Anhui and Jiangsu provinces. Highlights along its course are Chongqing city, Yellow Mountain (Huangshan), the Three Gorges Dam (San Xia da Ba), Wuhan and, as the river

Above *Qutang Gorge is the smallest of the Three Gorges on the Yangtze River*

gets closer to Shanghai, the cities of Nanjing, Suzhou and Changzhou, along with Lake Tai (Tai Hu) and the Grand Canal (Da Yunhe).

Shanghai With a population of more than 18 million, Shanghai is one of the world's largest cities and is still expanding—nine new satellite towns will be completed by 2010, when the city will host the World Expo. The second-largest cargo port in the world after Singapore, Shanghai is also China's leading business center. While comparatively light on sights, Shanghai has the best nightlife on mainland China and is ideally situated for day trips to Suzhou, Hangzhou and Lake Tai (Tai Hu).

Hong Kong and Macau Hong Kong Island contains the business heart of the former British colony. Its north shore along Victoria Harbour is a forest of high-rise commercial and apartment buildings. Elsewhere there are the cool heights of Victoria Peak, wilderness trails, and busy south-coast beach and harbor resorts.

The densely populated Kowloon Peninsula across Victoria Harbour from Hong Kong Island is noted for its mass-market shopping. It also has good cultural venues, museums and temples. The New Territories are the large and sparsely populated swathe of land between Kowloon and the mainland border. It has a wild, mountainous landscape with remote bays and beaches and the odd, high-rise-studded 'new town'. Of hundreds of Outlying Islands, the main ones are: Lantau, mostly wilderness but with pockets of urban development; Lamma, noted for its alternative lifestyle and seafood restaurants; and laid-back Cheung Chau.

The former Portuguese colony of Macau is centered on densely populated Macau town, which occupies a narrow peninsula attached to the Chinese mainland. Offshore, the quieter islands of Taipa and Coloane have been joined together by land reclamation.

BEST OF CHINA

BEIJING

Beihai Park (▷ 68–69) This park was first laid out by the Mongols and was the site of Kublai Khan's palace.

Forbidden City (▷ 70–77) Six hundred years of Chinese history is contained within the walls of this huge palace.

The Great Wall of China (▷ 93) A monument to human ingenuity, the Great Wall is one of the world's greatest structures.

Lama Temple (▷ 89–90) Wander through the most important Buddhist temple outside Tibet.

Summer Palace (▷ 61–65) China's largest classical garden enchants visitors today just as it delighted the nation's rulers in the past.

Temple of Heaven (▷ 84–88) This ensemble of architectural masterpieces dates from the Ming dynasty.

Tian'anmen Square (▷ 78–81) The sheer scale of the world's largest public square will take your breath away.

THE NORTH

Chengde (▷ 122–123) Chengde's replica of the Potala Palace in Lhasa is a little bit of Tibet in North China.

Datong (▷ 124) Visit the spectacular and vertigo-inducing Hanging Temple at Heng Shan.

Qingdao (Tsingtao; ▷ 126) Sit and drink Tsingtao beer in the former German concession, which is now a prosperous city.

Opposite A section of the Great Wall of China: this watchtower is strategically placed on a hilltop at Simatai

Qufu (▷ 127) Light incense to venerate the great sage at the Temple of Confucius, a 2,500-year-old tradition.
Taishan (▷ 129) Visit the mist-covered peaks of Taishan, China's most sacred mountain for more than 2,000 years.
Xi'an (▷ 132–135) Stroll around the walled city, symbolic eastern end of the historic Silk Road. A trip to see the terra-cotta warriors is a must—marvel at the individual features of the 8,000 clay soldiers set to guard the tomb of China's first Emperor.

THE NORTHEAST

Changbaishan (▷ 153) A pristine reserve of forest, lakes and wildlife on the frontier with North Korea.
Changchun (▷ 153) The Puppet Emperor's Palace was the residence of the 'Last Emperor' Pu Yi under the control of the Japanese.
Dalian (▷ 154) Dine on fresh seafood in Dalian, Northeast China's bustling seaside resort city.
Harbin (▷ 156–158) Home to the astonishing Harbin Ice Festival and some of China's best Russian architecture.
Shenyang (▷ 160–161) The Imperial Palace is second only in size to the Forbidden City in Beijing.
Zhalong Nature Reserve (▷ 159) Take a camera and binoculars to visit this spectacular and fecund wetland reserve and bird sanctuary.

INNER MONGOLIA AND THE SILK ROAD

Dunhuang (▷ 180–181) Visit the astonish-ing Mogao Caves in the deserts of northwestern Gansu.
Jiayuguan (▷ 183) The magnificent restored fortress at the western end of the Great Wall.
Kashi (Kashgar; ▷ 184–185) The Id Kah Mosque is one of the largest in China, and draws great crowds of worshipers to this ancient Uighur town.
Tulufan (Turpan) (▷ 187) Watch the sunset while dining on seedless raisins, fresh Uighur bread and local wine.
Ürümqi (Wulumuqi) (▷ 188) During the summer make the journey to Heavenly Mountains (Tian Shan) and visit a Kazakh yurt.
Xiahe (▷ 189) Site of the Labrang Monastery in southeastern Gansu, the largest Tibetan monastery outside Tibet.

Clockwise from left to right *Beijing's Hall of Prayer for Good Harvests; terra-cotta warriors on display at the Museum of Terra-cotta Warriors and Horses of Qin Shi Huang; Dalian skyline from Labor Park*

UNDERSTANDING CHINA

Left *View over the blue water of Lugu Lake and the mountainous countryside of Yunnan Province*
Below *Red-clad monks blowing horns in the doorway of Labrang Monastery*

THE SOUTHWEST

Lijiang (▷ 234–236) This delightful, ancient cobblestone UNESCO World Heritage-listed town will undoubtedly leave a lasting impression.

Longsheng (▷ 229) The women of the Red Yao tribe who live in this area of terraced mountain rice fields have the longest hair in China.

Lugu Hu (Lugu Lake; ▷ 237) See one of China's last matriarchal societies in this idyllic alpine setting.

Xishuangbanna (▷ 238) Visit Wild Elephant Valley, and if you're lucky you may see a wild jumbo.

SICHUAN AND THE TIBETAN PLATEAU

Chengdu (▷ 202–204) Watch a traditional Sichuan opera performance at an ancient teahouse.

Emeishan (▷ 205) Watch the sun rise from the summit of this Buddhist mountain. You will be rewarded with a stunning vista, often onto a sea of clouds below.

Lhasa (▷ 208–210) The impressive Potala Palace sits in a prominent position atop Red Mountain.

Samye (▷ 211) Visit Tibet's oldest monastery—a superb ancient structure in a remote river valley.

Wolong Nature Reserve (▷ 212) You can watch giant pandas at close quarters in their mountain sanctuary.

SOUTH CHINA AND THE YANGTZE

Chang Jiang (Yangtze River; ▷ 257) A cruise along China's mightiest river remains one of the world's great journeys.

Guangzhou (Canton; ▷ 260–263) See a 2,000-year-old tomb, an important historical find. Shamian Island is a remnant of the city's former European culture.

Hainan Dao (▷ 259) This subtropical island is the best choice for a traditional beach vacation.

Hangzhou (▷ 264–265) Take a cruise on the city's beautiful West Lake (Xi Hu) and visit its pavilions and pagodas.

HONG KONG AND MACAU

Aberdeen (▷ 337) Dine on a floating restaurant in the fishing port of this Hong Kong Island resort.
Kowloon Park (▷ 341) This park's shaded green spaces offer more than just a breath of fresh air.
Lantau Island (▷ 345) Hong Kong's largest island has the Po Lin Monastery and its Tian Tan Buddha.
Macau (▷ 348–351) Largo do Senado (Senate Square) is the handsome heart of the former Portuguese colony.
The Peak (▷ 338) Ride the Peak Tram funicular to a point high above Victoria Harbour for—when there's no intervening veil of cloud—one of the world's finest city views.
Star Ferry (▷ 342) Shuttling between Hong Kong Island and Kowloon, these green-and-white ferryboats have become a much-loved part of the waterfront spectacle.
Tsim Sha Tsui Promenade (▷ 342) A handsome setting for viewing the fascinating harbor panorama and the towers of Hong Kong Island.

Left *Jumbo Floating Restaurant in Aberdeen, Hong Kong is one of the world's largest floating restaurants*
Below *Tian Tan Buddha, Lantau Island, Hong Kong measures 34m (112ft) and is the world's tallest outdoor seated bronze Buddha*

Huangshan (▷ 259) 'Yellow Mountain' offers some quintessentially Chinese craggy vistas.
Nanjing (▷ 266–268) Zijinshan (Purple and Gold Mountain) makes a pleasant escape from furnace-like Nanjing in summer, and has mementos of past glories.
Suzhou (▷ 270) Choosing between Suzhou's fine gardens is not easy, but the 14th-century Forest of Lions Garden (Shizilin Yuan) has the edge in classical grace.
Wuxi and Tai Hu (▷ 271) The great Lake Tai is the star of this show.

SHANGHAI

The Bund (▷ 305) Prepare to be bowled over by the colonial architecture gracing the city's waterfront.
French Concession (▷ 294–297) Spend a day exploring this historic neighborhood, then return after dark to experience some of the city's best nightlife.
Nanjing Lu (▷ 300) Shopaholics will not be able to resist the malls and boutiques lining this shopping street.
Nan Shi (Old Town; ▷ 304) Explore the traditional Shikumen housing projects of the old town, then find out more by visiting the museum in Xintiandi (▷ 300).
Shanghai Museum (▷ 301) Enjoy the pick of China's cultural heritage, all in one purpose-built museum.
Yu Garden (▷ 302–303) A traditional Chinese garden is an unexpected find in this city of skyscrapers.

TOP EXPERIENCES

Attend one of the many international sporting events held in China: Formula One racing, European Tour golf, Master's Cup tennis or one of the marathons—take your pick.

Be amazed by the edibles. Grasshoppers are just one of many delicacies on sale in one of China's night markets.

Bring your camera. You'll need it to capture the celebrations at one of China's many local festivals.

Check out one of China's growing number of winter-sports resorts. The choice ranges from ice-skating and snowboarding to outdoor and indoor skiing.

Cruise along one of China's famous waterways. The spectacular scenery of the Li River (▷ 230–232) was praised by poets of the Tang and Song dynasties.

Eat a typical Chinese breakfast. This could be anything from dim sum (dumplings) in Hong Kong to *mantou* (steamed buns) or congee (rice porridge) in Beijing.

Enjoy a visit to a classical Chinese garden. Take pleasure in the ingenuity that goes into its design. Suzhou (▷ 270) is as good a place to start as any.

Explore one of the less-visited sections of the Great Wall (▷ 93). The views on the hike from Simatai to Jinshanling are breathtaking.

Feast on a traditional Uighur (Xinjiang) lamb barbecue. It's spiced with cumin and chili powder. If you can't get to Kashi (Kashgar), you'll find Uighur restaurants in many of China's big cities.

Follow in the footsteps of countless Buddhist and Taoist pilgrims. Climb one of China's holy mountains.

Go to a martial-arts demonstration. If you can't get to Shaolin (▷ 128), its spiritual home, catch the latest Jet Li movie in Hong Kong.

Join a bicycle tour of Beijing's famous *hutong* (alleys). Get an insight into a fast-disappearing way of life.

Play a round of golf. China has around 1,000 golf courses, many in scenic surroundings.

See a panda in its natural habitat. A good bet is to head to the Wolong Nature Reserve (▷ 212).

Spend the night in a yurt. Join a grassland tour from Hohhot to sample typical Mongolian hospitality (▷ 182).

Take tea in a traditional teahouse. Chengdu (▷ 202–204), Kunming (▷ 233) and Guilin (▷ 230–232) are all capitals of tea-growing provinces.

Visit Qufu, birthplace of Confucius. China's greatest philosopher's birthday is celebrated with a festival at the end of September (▷ 127 and 143).

Watch Beijing opera. In the sumptuous Huguang Guildhall (▷ 104), there's a fascinating museum here too.

Watch the locals practice tai chi. Simply get up early, head for the nearest park.

Above *Yurts and camels at Lake Karakul, Karakoram Highway, Xinjiang Province*
Left *Burning incense at the Yuantong Temple, Kunming*

LIVING CHINA

Often considered to be over-pampered by parents, self-centered, unsociable, reluctant to share and overweight, members of the one child generation have been dubbed 'Little Emperors' by Chinese sociologists. Official estimates put the number of registered only children since the introduction of the one-child policy in 1979 at close to 100 million. The experiences of this unique generation have been profoundly different from those of their parents and grandparents, born in an era of severe food shortages and material deprivation. During the political turmoil of the Cultural Revolution, the survival of the family itself was threatened. While the one-child generation has benefited from rapid economic growth, educational and career opportunities, freedom to travel and to form relationships without interference, there are hidden emotional costs as parents exert huge pressure on their only child to succeed. This comes at a time of predicted demographic imbalance. As China is confronted with a rapidly aging population, a shrinking workforce and an inadequate welfare system, the government is considering relaxing the one-child policy.

Clockwise from left to right *A young boy takes a photograph of his multi-generational family at the park; a cyber room in Shanghai; Li Yuchun, winner of 'Supergirls,' performs in Shanghai*

SPEED DATING

On a Saturday afternoon in October 2005, 5,000 single men and women gathered in Shanghai's Zhongshan Park for the biggest speed-dating event in Chinese history. Today, China's young professionals are intent on finding their own partners, rather than resorting to the traditional matchmaker or *mei po*. But they no longer have time to look for a partner in conventional ways—one civil servant who signed up for Zhongshan Park was too busy to attend and was represented by her mother who photographed hopefuls with a digital camera. Women, who outnumbered men by a ratio of 2:1 at the event, are becoming more discerning in their choice of partners, seeking men with good prospects and, preferably, their own apartment. Moreover, China's 'go-getters' are increasingly reluctant to take on a commitment, putting career before marriage and family.

LI YUCHUN

In August 2005 a 20-year-old music student, Li Yuchun, won a talent contest on a pioneering reality show called 'Supergirls,' created by Hunan satellite TV (and since stopped by the national government). The final attracted an audience of 400 million, the largest ever for a program in China.

Li Yuchun garnered 3.5 million SMS mobile-phone votes from young fans of the show, but what took everyone by surprise was that her performances had been criticized by the judges and that China's new pop heroine was so unlike the usual female stereotype. A self-confessed tomboy who spurned eyeliner and lip-gloss and who sang male songs at audition, Li Yuchun struck a chord with a generation that is seeking new ways to express itself. Since winning the show, she has acquired all the trappings of celebrity, from recording and sponsorship deals to appearing on the cover of *Time Asia* magazine. She even has her own stamps.

CYBER ADDICTS

Brought up by his mother on a run-down housing project in Chengdu, Meng 'RocketBoy' Yang now makes a living from playing computer games. In 2004 he took the cyber world by storm, beating the world online gaming champion in a competition held at the Great Wall. The 24-year-old walked away with 1 million RMB in prize money and a lucrative sponsorship deal with a hardware games developer. Now Meng is spending 12 hours a day in intensive training for the Cyber Professional League World Tour, but laughs off any idea of becoming hooked. Not so lucky are China's estimated 4 to 5 million computer addicts. The government is becoming so concerned about the growing social problem that it has approved the opening of an addiction clinic in Beijing and, with the support of parents and leading Chinese games manufacturers, is introducing legislation aimed at curbing the amount of time players can spend in front of the screen.

MIAN MIAN

Condemned in 2000 as 'a poster child for spiritual pollution,' writer Mian Mian has, with the publication of her second novel, gained a degree of respectability as the spokesperson of her generation. Born into a middle-class Shanghainese family, Mian Mian dropped out of school before leaving home for Shenzhen, where she threw herself into a life of experimental drug-taking and promiscuous sex, inspired by her idols, 60s band The Doors. Rescued by her father, she emerged from treatment for heroin addiction to write a thinly disguised autobiographical novel, *Candy*, which so outraged the authorities that former president Jiang Zemin is said to have taken a personal hand in banning it. Her second novel, *Panda Sex*, is less controversial and deals with the search for a stable relationship in a rapidly changing society.

Some say it will take approximately 20 years, others twice that. But one thing forecasters agree on is that, barring unforeseen circumstances, China will emerge as the world's leading economic superpower. Over the last 20 years, the Chinese economy has grown at an average annual rate of nearly 10 percent. Industrial output rose 16.4 percent in the first quarter of 2008, according to the National Bureau of Statistics, consolidating China's position as the world's manufacturing workshop. 'Made in China' is stamped on everything from televisions to cell phones, shoes to automobiles, computer software to toys. And by exporting its goods abroad, China has boosted its foreign currency reserves (the highest in the world) to record levels. Up to now the trading surplus has been mainly due to foreign investment, but China is turning this around—Chinese companies have become key stakeholders in many major western companies and won huge construction contracts in parts of the developing world, notably Africa. However, with China's stock market enduring a torrid time in 2008, and signs that the property bubble is bursting, there may still be trouble ahead.

Clockwise from left to right *New buildings going up in the southern provincial city of Shenzhen; the dramatic Lippo Building in Hong Kong; textile workers in Shenzhen*

THE ENVIRONMENT

On November 13, 2005 an explosion at the Jilin petrochemical plant, in northern China, released more than 100 tons of benzene, nitric acid and aniline dye into the Songhua River. Five people died and more than 70 were injured in the blast. Eleven days later a toxic slick 80km (50 miles) long reached Harbin (population 3.5 million). The authorities, reluctant to acknowledge the seriousness of the event, did not notify the State Environmental Protection Agency until five days after the blast. China's Ministry for Water Resources says that 300 million people drink contaminated water every day, while factories dump sewage and waste into waterways. In 2006 China's ruling State Council decided to make water quality a priority. The government will compel enterprises to improve emissions treatment facilities at their plants or face draconian fines.

GUANGDONG

With a population of 92 million, Guangdong is one of China's wealthiest provinces and experienced the fastest economic growth in the country. At its heart are Shenzhen and the Pearl River Delta Economic Zone. Enterprises here produce 90 percent of the world's computer keyboards and mouses and 70 percent of computer screens. Another of Guangdong's rapidly growing cities, Dongguan, is home to several overseas companies, including Siemens, Nokia and Duracell, as well as to the world's largest shoe factory, Yue Yua. However a slowdown in Guangdong's factories in 2008 is a harbinger of the challenges facing much of China as it attempts to follow Japan, South Korea and Taiwan's example and diversify from manufacturing into services. Domestic inflation, the rising value of the RMB and new labor laws have made Guangdong a less ideal place for cheap mass production and there is some evidence that companies are moving elsewhere.

THE RICH LIST

The entry-level bank balance for those hoping to break into China's Rich List has soared in recent years. At the last count, in late 2007, those with US$1 billion could barely break into the top 100. The majority of China's rich are self-made entrepreneurs in their 30s or 40s who got their big break during the economic experiments of the 1980s and 1990s. However, the richest person in China was a 26-year-old called Yang Huiyan, whose assets were valued at US$17.5 billion. Yang was bequeathed a 59.5 percent stake in her father's development company, Country Garden, and her shares rose sharply after the company listed on the Hong Kong stock exchange in April 2007. However, 18 months later her shares were worth less than half of their original value. With property prices falling across China, and the country's stock market down nearly 300 percent, the old-school entrepreneurs will likely rise back to the top of China's Rich List.

THE NEW CONSUMERS

Beijing's Golden Resources Shopping Mall has more than 1,000 retail outlets, 230 escalators and parking for 10,000 cars. For a few short months in 2004 it was the largest shopping mall in the world. But no longer. In 2005 it was overtaken by the South China Mall in Dongguan. However China's fearless new developers are discovering that biggest does not always mean best. The South China Mall was built to house 1,500 stores and accommodate 70,000 visitors every day. Its gilded interiors included giant replicas of European monuments, a 25m (82ft) Arc de Triomphe among them. And yet, at the time of writing, the mall is famous not for its size, or shopping opportunities, but for the fact that it is deserted, with barely a dozen functioning stores.

In the end, it was difficult to believe there had ever been any doubt. For four years, the world wondered whether China could build on its success in Athens and pip its great sporting rival on the medal table at its own Olympiad. As it turned out, the competition wasn't even close. China led the way from the first day to the last of the 2008 Beijing Games, taking 51 gold medals to the USA's 36. Success can be attributed to the General State Sports Administration, which runs Chinese sports with the efficiency and single-mindedness of a military operation, cultivating a strong sense of national pride along the way. From the age of five promising children are identified and sent to one of 3,000 dedicated sports schools, which churn out 100,000 superbly trained athletes every year. Those who have won glory at the recent Games can look forward to lucrative sponsorship deals, raising the question of which is more important to aspiring athletes: national glory or making a living in an increasingly wealth-obsessed society.

Above *Beijing's now-famous 'Bird's Nest' stadium*

YAO MING

He has a huge international following and is one of the best-known faces in China. Born in Shanghai in 1980 to parents who were both outstanding basketball players, Yao Ming is a typical product of China's sports establishment. After entering the Shanghai Sports Academy at the age of 12, he was subjected to rigorous training. In 1997, Yao joined the Shanghai Sharks and embarked on a professional career. He may have gone relatively unnoticed had sports clothing giant Nike not shown an interest in sponsoring the Sharks.

Yao was invited to visit the United States and in 2002 signed a four-year contract with the Houston Rockets worth $17.8 million. Today the 2.26m-tall (7ft 5in) multimillionaire is an advertiser's dream, with a long list of endorsements. His failure to win Olympic gold in 2008 is unlikely to have dented his astonishing popularity one bit.

A CAUTIONARY TALE

With film-star looks, the media hanging on his every word, and an Olympic gold medal at the 2004 games, 24-year-old diving champion Tian Liang seemed to have it all. Things began to go wrong after Tian failed to report for training after a two-month break, complaining of exhaustion. The swimming authorities allowed him an extended leave of absence. But reports were soon circulating that instead of recuperating, he was negotiating a singing career with an entertainment corporation. His name was also romantically linked with diving gold medallist, Guo Jingjing, herself rarely out of the headlines. Tian then made the fatal error of being in Malaysia for a photo shoot when fellow sporting celebrities were raising money for China's tsunami disaster fund. When he returned to the training camp in January 2005 he was shown the door and, despite great efforts to regain his place, missed out on the 2008 Olympic Games.

SUPER LEAGUE

When defending soccer champions Shenzhen Jianlibao went nine games without a win in 2005, the coach was fired and Shenzhen won the next game. On the face of it an unremarkable story, but the row was symptomatic of a deep-seated malaise. In 2004 the Chinese FA, which has run the game since 1924, set up a Super League—with disastrous results. Within weeks two matches were abandoned when teams walked off the pitch to protest at refereeing decisions and seven clubs threatened to pull out of the league altogether. The chairmen blamed the FA for problems including allegations of match fixing, betting scandals, drug use, financial incompetence and crowd trouble. The league's prestige hasn't been helped by the dismal performance of the national team in recent World Cup qualifying matches and at the 2008 games. In a climate of national success, players were dumped out of the tournament in the first round.

CRICKET MATCHES

In August 2004 police broke up an illegal betting ring in Hong Kong, arresting 115 people. The criminals were not gambling on horse racing or the outcome of soccer matches, but on crickets. These chirruping insects have been prized for their combative skills since the Song dynasty. Today farmers in Shandong province (prime cricket-raising country) can make a living from the sale of crickets alone—a specimen in peak condition can fetch up to 10,000 RMB on the open market. On fight days the contestants are weighed, then their feelers are tickled with a brush to stimulate them. Bouts take place in plastic tubs and are usually over in a couple of minutes when one of the contestants scuttles off.

Below *A local team practising rowing for the annual Dragon Boat Race Festival of Hong Kong*

As Communist ideology loses influence, China's traditional celebrations have enjoyed a recent resurgence. In 2008, China reduced the length of its Labor Day break and made three of its most cherished festivals—Tomb Sweeping Day, the Dragon Boat Festival and Mid-Autumn Festival—national holidays. However, as in the West many in China worry that ancient traditions have been commercialized in the nation's recent economic revival. A poll of Shanghai residents found that only one in three respondents enjoyed the New Year festivities, even though the city government recently relaxed a ban on fireworks for the first time in a decade. The pressure of work may have influenced the result. An increasing number of young professionals are failing to make it home for the annual reunion, and prefer to cook traditional dishes ready-made from the frozen shelves of supermarkets. For children too, New Year is no longer the special occasion it once was. While a generation ago Spring Festival was the one time in the year when youngsters wore new clothes and were given a red envelope, or *hongbao*, containing money for small treats, today many expect computer games or designer fashions.

Clockwise from left to right *Martial arts training in Shaolin; a calligrapher at work; exercising with fans in a park in Beijing*

MARTIAL ARTS

Hong Kong action-movie director Yuen Wo-Ping claims it will be difficult, if not impossible, to find a future martial arts star with the charisma of Bruce Lee or Jackie Chan as children today are unwilling to put in the hard work. But martial arts (*wushu* in Chinese) is flourishing independently of the Kung Fu industry. A 20-part TV series on the subject followed enthusiasts all over China. The spiritual home of martial arts is Shaolin Temple in Henan province (▷ 128). The monks are not allowed to teach within the monastery, so a new training center has opened nearby. In 2006 Shaolin collaborated with a Shenzhen TV station to produce a reality show where a new *wushu* superstar was unearthed. Participants came from the US, Europe and Australia, but China's own Gu Shangwei was eventually declared the champion and took his place, not as a revered Shaolin master, but as the latest star of a TV series.

A DYING ART

Lin Jianguo, a former student of the Shanghai Arts and Crafts Institute, tours secondary schools teaching calligraphy. He finds the students generally ill informed, but believes they are keen to learn. But the evidence suggests that Lin is swimming against the tide. Calligraphy, if it appears at all on school curriculums beyond primary level, is almost invariably an optional subject, which fails to claim the students' attention. The widespread growth in the use of Pinyin (the romanized form of Chinese characters) in computer programs, graphic design software and text messaging poses a much greater threat, not only to calligraphy as an art form but to the written language itself. A survey conducted by a Guangzhou-based magazine found that 35 percent of respondents born in the early 1990s were unable to name even one of the four *wenfangsibao*—the brush, ink stick, paper and ink slab essential to the practice of calligraphy.

MINORITY LANGUAGE

In a border region of southwest China, He Shujie is helping to preserve the culture of the Naxis, one of China's ethnic minorities. He is a custodian of the unique Dongba language. It is composed of more than 1,500 pictographs, the only hieroglyphic language still in use today. In 2003, the 1,000-year-old classics of Naxi literature, including their creation story, were added to UNESCO's 'Memory of the World' list, a decision which may have saved the language from extinction. In the same year a paper mill was set up in Lijiang, Yunnan province, to train young people in the Naxi art of papermaking by hand, a tradition that all but disappeared in the 1950s. A shop in the front hall promotes Dongba culture, selling books and a recently compiled Dongba dictionary. Visitors to the workshop are encouraged to try their hand at making paper using the indigenous stringbush bark and He Shujie is on hand to inscribe pictographs on the finished product.

PARK LIFE

On Wednesday mornings an ad hoc choral society, mostly of women in their 40s and 50s, gathers near the south gate of Beijing's Jingshan Park for a rendition of old favorites from the Maoist era. They are not making a political statement. This was the music they grew up with. In Kunming's Green Lake Park, more than 2,100km (1,300 miles) away, amateur musicians from all walks of life meet on Sunday afternoons to perform patriotic songs and folk dances for an appreciative audience of casual onlookers. Within earshot people are sitting down to play Chinese chess or mahjong, working out to tai chi, or practicing the ancient art of kite flying. There is no better place for keeping traditions alive than a Chinese park.

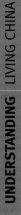

'Medicine and food are one and the same,' said the Yellow Emperor, Huang Di, in *Nei Jing*, China's first *materia medica*, compiled around 2600BC. According to traditional Chinese medicine (TCM), food is not only nutritious, but a means of preventing and treating illnesses and of maintaining a balance between yin and yang. One important source of nutrition praised by the Yellow Emperor was congee—many people still start the day with this rice porridge. But this is as far as healthy eating goes for an increasing number of Chinese people in stressful occupations where time is at a premium. Surveys have revealed a growing tendency among office workers to snack, or resort to fast food rather than follow a balanced diet. It's enough to make the Yellow Emperor turn in his grave.

OBESITY

Every summer China Central TV sponsors a weight-loss camp for children and teenagers. Obesity is on the increase—government reports suggest that as many as one in three of China's city dwellers may be overweight. Compare this with one in five in the early 1990s. The resulting strain on an already deteriorating health service, coupled with the potential cost to the economy in terms of days lost at work, is giving food for thought to Chinese health officials, dieticians and educators. The root cause, already familiar in Western societies, is a more pressured lifestyle encouraging poor dietary habits and lack of regular exercise. At the same time the nation is developing a craving for fast food. McDonald's and KFC entered the Chinese market in the 1980s and can be found across Chinese cities large and small.

Above *Enjoying the atmosphere at a terrace bar in Beijing*

THE STORY OF CHINA

Archeologists in Yunnan province have found evidence of our earliest ancestors dating back 1.7 million years. *Homo sapiens* arrived on the scene some 200,000 years ago, while finds at Erlitou, near Luoyang, confirm the existence of the Xia, China's first dynasty (*c*2000BC). Chinese recorded history really begins with the Shang (*c*1600–*c*1100BC), who occupied a swathe of territory along the Yellow River. They practiced ancestor worship, developed a pictographic language and produced superb bronzeware ritual vessels. The Shang made way for the Zhou. Zhou rule was feudal in nature, the king relying on vassals to govern the more distant regions. In 771BC the Zhou were driven from their western capital, Xian, to Luoyang in the east. Zhou rule disintegrated over the following centuries as rival kingdoms struggled for supremacy. The great philosopher Confucius (551–479BC) lived during this period of internecine strife. It was Qin Shi Huang, self-styled First Emperor, who succeeded in uniting China for the first time in 221BC. The Han dynasty, which replaced the Qin in 206BC, gave China more than four centuries of stability, but the empire eventually fragmented into warring states.

Clockwise from left to right *Rows of terra-cotta warriors, Xi'an; ancient cave monastery at the Thousand Buddha Caves near Kizil; a painting of Confucius at the Confucian Temple in Suzhou*

MIGHTY QIN

He was the emperor who unified China, who commissioned the Terracotta Army (▷ 135) to accompany him into the afterlife and who inspired the building of the Great Wall. But when he died in 210BC, aged 49, Qin Shi Huang was still seeking the one thing that eluded him—the elixir that would guarantee immortality. Born Ying Zheng, he became ruler of the Qin kingdom at the age of 13, though power was initially in the hands of his mother and the prime minister, Lu Buwei. Ying Zheng first revealed the ruthless side of his character in 237BC, when he put down a palace coup, banished his mother from court and forced minister Lu to commit suicide. He then turned his attention on his neighbors, defeating them in a series of whirlwind campaigns that left him master of China after just nine years. But Qin's self-aggrandizing projects brought the empire to the point of bankruptcy and his dynasty, instead of lasting for 10,000 generations as he had hoped, ended in chaos only four years after his death.

BONE WRITING

In 1899, Wang Yirong, an official in the Qing government, fell ill with malaria. A pharmacist recommended a medicine containing ground-up turtle shells. As he prepared the concoction Wang noticed unusual markings on a shell. He began collecting them and noting down what he came to realize were inscriptions. The source of the shells was traced to Anyang in Henan province, but it was not until 1928, after excavations in the area, that the full significance of Wang's discovery became apparent. The farmers who supplied the shells had been ploughing up the site of a capital of the Shang dynasty. The shells had been used for divination—the inscriptions were questions for the oracle and recorded replies. Archeologists identified more than 4,500 different characters and established a direct link between the Shang pictograms and modern Chinese script. Sadly, Wang Yirong did not live to see the results of his discovery—he committed suicide after getting caught up in the Boxer Rebellion in 1900 (▷ 30).

PEKING MAN

In December 1929 an international team of scientists unearthed a near-complete fossilized human skull beneath a limestone cliff in Zhoukoudian, about 48km (30 miles) from Beijing. It belonged to an early ancestor, *Homo erectus*, and had been lying in the ground for at least 350,000 years. Excavations continued but then in 1937 came war with Japan; work was suspended and the fossils were eventually packed into crates and handed over to US marines who were charged with taking them to safety. On the following day, however, the Japanese attacked Pearl Harbor, the marines were taken prisoner and the precious consignment of bones disappeared without trace.

SIMA QIAN

For Grand Astrologer Sima Qian (*c*145–86BC), condemned by Emperor Wudi for speaking out on behalf of a general who had fallen from favor, the choice was between suicide and castration. Most men would have chosen suicide, but Sima Qian had embarked on an extraordinary project started by his father and so succumbed to the knife. When the project was completed, *Records of the Historian* ran to 130 chapters and was the first comprehensive history of China. Much more than a narrative, it includes chronologies; treatises on music, religious ritual and economics; and vivid biographies of the famous, including courtiers, generals, politicians and emperors. His book served as an inspiration for generations of historians and is still an essential work of reference on the Qin and Han dynasties.

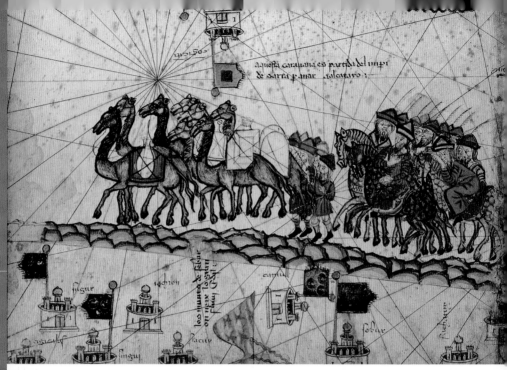

China was reunited by the Sui (AD581–618), but it was under the Tang (AD618–907) and Song (960–1279) that the country enjoyed a golden age. Silk and porcelain were exported via the Silk Road, boosting foreign trade. The ruling elite enjoyed printed books on geography, architecture and medicine, superb paintings and the work of some of the world's finest craftsmen. The population doubled to 120 million as urban metropolises like Kaifeng and Hangzhou grew up alongside Chang'an (modern-day Xi'an), the world's largest city. An imperial civil service was created, based on merit and administered by trained bureaucrats. Buddhism flourished alongside Confucianism and Taoism. Yet throughout the Song period, the empire was under pressure from northern barbarian tribes. The Mongols emerged victorious when Ghengis Khan's cavalry swept across the Chinese frontier, taking all before them. By 1279 Khan's grandson, Kublai Khan, had established his own dynasty, the Yuan ('The Beginning'), with its capital at Beijing. The Mongols were resented as invaders and because their customs, dress, language and religion were alien. Still, their rule was not especially harsh—links with the outside world remained open and Kublai Khan was tolerant of other philosophies.

Clockwise from left to right *A Catalan map showing Marco Polo, 1254–1324, traveling in caravan with his brothers along the Silk Road; the Grand Buddha at Leshan; a painted mural in the caves of Mogao*

GRAND CANAL

In AD605 Emperor Yang Di ordered the construction of what is still the longest canal in the world. More than 1 million laborers worked on the project, up to 40 percent of whom died from overwork, hunger or disease. Incredibly, the canal, extending to more than 1,800km (1,100 miles), was completed in less than six years. It joined China's two great waterways, the Yangtze and Yellow rivers, giving northern China access to the fertile rice fields of the south. All traffic halted when Yang Di made his annual tours of inspection, sailing in a flotilla of 'dragon boats,' four floors high and decorated with lanterns and pennants. Vast quantities of unwanted food and drink were dumped overboard. Yang Di's extravagance was his undoing—in AD616 he was assassinated.

LOVE STORY

Emperor Xuan Zhong (reigned 713–755) was already getting on in years when the young and beautiful concubine Yang Guifei caught his eye—a fatal attraction as it turned out. For the emperor became so besotted that he neglected his official duties entirely, preferring to idle his time away in her company. But their idyll was not to last. Yang Guifei made the fatal error of adopting the powerful general An Lushan as her favorite. This over-mighty subject turned traitor and launched a rebellion that would tear the country apart. As the emperor and his entourage fled the capital, his ministers forced Yang Guifei to commit suicide. Overcome by grief, Xuan Zhong fell into despair and later abdicated. Their love affair was immortalized in one of Bai Juyi's most famous poems, *Song of Everlasting Sorrow*.

HIGH FLYER

Bai Juyi (772–846) was not only a famous poet but an important government official who rose from humble origins to become governor of Suzhou. He owed his success to one of China's most famous institutions, the Imperial Civil Service Examinations, known as 'the ladder to the clouds.' Climbing the ladder was done in stages and might take as long as 10 years.

For the examinations, candidates had to provide their own candles, writing materials and food and were body searched before entering a cubicle approximately 2m (6ft) long and 1m (3ft) wide, where they remained for the duration of the exam (usually 24 hours). As a further precaution against cheating, the candidate selected a question at random by shooting an arrow at the list of subjects. The answers were then transcribed by the Bureau of Examination Copyists to guarantee the anonymity of the scripts. Outstanding applicants like Bai Juyi were invited to the palace for a final exam on the Confucian classics, overseen by the emperor himself.

TALL STORY?

Marco Polo's *Description of the World* was the most popular travelogue of its day and an international best-seller. It was also the first insiders' account of China (Cathay) written by a Westerner and what a tale it told. According to Marco's account, he was received by Kublai Kahn himself, no less, in the legendary summer palace of Shang Du (Xanadu) and made such an impression that he was entrusted with numerous diplomatic missions, and even served as governor of Yangzhou. But many scholars now doubt whether Marco Polo (1254–1324) ever set foot in China. Why, they argue, is there no mention of him in the Imperial Archives if he was a senior government official? Also puzzling is that this usually keen-eyed observer fails to comment on local customs like foot binding, the use of chopsticks or the habit of drinking tea. Yet intriguingly, evidence has come to light that confirms that there was a flourishing Italian trading community in Hangzhou at this time. Maybe Marco Polo was telling the truth after all.

CHINA UNDER THE MING AND QING

In 1368 the peasant general Zhu Yuanzhang overthrew the Mongols, ushering in the Ming dynasty and a long period of stability and prosperity. Major construction projects included the Great Wall and the Forbidden City. The greatest Ming emperor, Yongle, commissioned voyages of discovery. A rebellion in 1644 let in the Manchus, who established China's last dynasty, the Qing. While the Qing produced outstanding rulers like Kangxi and Qianlong, this period marks the onset of decline. Western powers had sought trading concessions since the 18th century and China's defeat in the Opium Wars gave foreigners a foothold. As industrialization took root on the eastern seaboard, social unrest grew. Sporadic unrest, culminating in the Boxer Rebellion (1898–1901), an uprising by secret societies in Shandong province directed against foreigners, coalesced with movements for modernization and reform, reaching the court in 1898. But the conservative advisors of Dowager Empress Cixi, the power behind the throne, opposed change. Limited reforms, around the time of Cixi's death in 1908, were too little, too late.

Clockwise from left to right *Boats on display in the Hong Kong Maritime Museum; a statue in the Dragon King Temple in Beijing; ancient armillary sphere*

THE EUNUCH ADMIRAL

Ma Sanbao was just 11 when, in 1382, Ming troops mopping up Mongol resistance in Yunnan province removed him from his family. He was taken to Beijing, where he was castrated and served a prince. The prince became Emperor Yongle and Ma's career blossomed. He was renamed Zheng He and in 1405, as Grand Admiral of the western seas, he led the first of seven expeditions. His fleet was three times the size of the Spanish Armada and comprised more than 300 vessels, including 62 'treasure ships.' On board were 26,000 men, 300 commanding officers and 180 doctors and medics. The flagship was four times the size of Columbus's *Santa Maria*. The expeditionary force roamed as far as Indonesia, India, the Persian Gulf, the Red Sea and east Africa. Following Zheng He's death in 1433, the xenophobes at court prevailed and his charts and records were burned.

KIDNAPPED

Under surveillance from the moment of his arrival in England in October 1896, Sun Yat-sen was bundled into a cab on a London street and taken to the Chinese Legation. There he was held for 12 days under guard and with the windows nailed shut. He expected deportation and execution, but managed to smuggle out a note to an old doctor friend, James Cantlie, who took the matter up with the press and eventually secured his release. The incident brought this hitherto obscure revolutionary celebrity status and invaluable publicity. Born in Cuiheng in southern China in 1866, Sun was educated in a Hawaiian missionary school. He studied medicine in Hong Kong, but became mixed up in the revolutionary movement, founding the Revive China Society in 1894. In the following year he instigated his first attempted insurrections in southern China and was on the run when he was seized in London.

HEAVENLY KINGDOM

Rebels drowned in the city moat, hanged themselves from trees in the palace gardens or set themselves alight rather than surrender —the victorious Qing general estimated the number of dead in Nanjing at 100,000. The leader of the Taiping Rebellion, which lasted from 1850 to 1861 and claimed more than 20 million lives, had committed suicide a month earlier. Hong Xiu Quan was a former village schoolteacher from Guangxi province. After repeatedly failing the civil service exams, he read a protestant missionary tract and converted to Christianity. Susceptible to visions he convinced himself that he was the younger brother of Jesus Christ and had to rid China of the Manchus and establish a Heavenly Kingdom of Peace (Taiping). For years the Taiping had the Qing army on the run, but when they made the error of attacking Shanghai, the foreign community rallied and a force of irregulars under General Charles Gordon joined with the Chinese army in putting down the rebellion.

DRUG BUST

A marble bas-relief on the Monument to the People's Heroes in Beijing (▷ 81) commemorates a famous episode of resistance to the colonial powers. On June 3, 1839, imperial Commissioner Lin Zexu supervised the destruction of a consignment of 1,200 tons of opium on a beach near Humen (Guangdong province). For decades, Western traders in Canton and Macau had ignored the government monopoly on opium—designed to limit consumption—by smuggling in huge quantities of the drug from India. The British government protested Commissioner Lin's actions and blockaded Guangzhou, the prelude to the First Opium War. It ended with the infamous Treaty of Nanking, whereby the Chinese were forced to pay an indemnity for the destruction of the opium and to cover the cost of the war.

一代天骄——毛泽东

YI DAI TIAN JIAO —— MAO ZE DONG

In 1911 a rash of mutinies and armed uprisings led to the abdication of Emperor Puyi and the end of the imperial regime. The following year, Sun Yat-sen was elected provisional President of the Republic of China. But his Guomindang (Nationalist) Party supporters were betrayed by former Qing general Yuan Shikai, who established a dictatorship. Yuan's death in 1916 left a power vacuum, which was filled by warlord generals. When Sun Yat-sen died in 1925 Chiang Kaishek, his brother-in-law, emerged as the Guomindang's strongman. In 1927, after setting up government in Nanjing, Chiang ruthlessly suppressed the Chinese Communist Party, whose members in 1934, led by Mao Zedong, embarked on the retreat known as the Long March. Meanwhile, Japan had taken advantage of China's weakness and invaded Manchuria, leading to war in 1937. Following Japan's defeat in 1945, civil war erupted between Communists and Nationalists. While the latter had military superiority, the Communists proved to be better strategists and by October 1949, Mao was master of Beijing. Chiang Kaishek and his supporters fled to Taiwan, where they established a rival Nationalist regime.

Clockwise from left to right *Revolutionary poster of Mao Zedong; the last emperor, Puyi, in 1934; a tapestry showing Mao Zedong and colleagues on the Long March*

LONG MARCH

In the summer of 1936, Mao Zedong gave the first official account of what became known as the Long March to the American reporter Edgar Snow. It was an epic tale of incredible courage and endurance, of triumph in the face of adversity. For 369 days Mao and his 100,000 followers trekked across 18 mountain ranges, 24 rivers and 12 provinces, walking 12,500km (8,000 miles). Harried and strafed from the air by Nationalist forces, they were reduced to fewer than 10,000 by the time they reached northern Shanxi in October 1935.

Today, more than 70 years later, skeptics outside China question Mao's account. Some say that the pursuit of the Communists was halfhearted, others point out that Mao was aware of his enemy's movements in advance thanks to code-breakers. More controversially, in the 2005 biography *Mao: The Unknown Story* by Jung Chang and Jon Halliday, doubts have been raised about whether the Battle of Dadu River (▷ Luding, 206), ever took place.

RAPE OF NANJING

In 1946 Japanese general Matsui Iwane was arraigned before the international war crimes tribunal in Tokyo and charged with direct responsibility for the single worst atrocity of the Second Sino-Japanese War. Between December 1937 and January 1938 his troops massacred up to 350,000 unarmed people following the military occupation of Nanjing. Some of the victims were buried alive, others used for bayonet practice. At least 20,000 women—the youngest aged 8, the oldest more than 70—were raped before being killed or forced into prostitution. It is still not clear whether the killing spree was spontaneous or part of a policy to deter resistance in other Chinese cities. The Nanjing *Datusha* (Great Nanjing Massacre) remains a stumbling block in relations between China and Japan. In 2005 violent demonstrations broke out in several Chinese cities after it became known that the Japanese Ministry of Education had approved secondary school textbooks dismissing the massacre as an 'incident.'

BIG-EARED DU

Chiang Kaishek would never have emerged as the master of Nationalist China without the help of Shanghai's notorious underworld figure, Du Yuesheng. 'Big-eared Du' controled drug-dealing, prostitution and extortion rackets. As Chiang Kaishek's troops were poised to enter Shanghai, the two men struck a deal, Du promising to provide the muscle to break the Communists' hold on the city in return for a free run of the narcotics business. Du and his gangland associates formed militias and stockpiled weapons. On April 12, 1927, Du's men joined with the Nationalist forces to launch a reign of terror that left at least 5,000 dead in Shanghai. The gangster prospered under Chiang's patronage. He went legitimate, becoming a director of the Bank of China and, irony of ironies, of Shanghai's Opium Suppression Bureau.

KILLING FIELDS

Human life was cheap in northeast China's Shandong province during the 1920s and 1930s. For years the province had been the virtual fiefdom of warlord General Zhang Zongchang, a heavy-drinking former peasant, described by the last emperor, Puyi, as a 'monster,' whose forces dispatched opponents by splitting their skulls open with swords. An eyewitness reported that Shandong was in a virtual state of anarchy at the time, with kidnappings, rapes and murders taking place in broad daylight, while marauding bands set villages alight, depriving the inhabitants of food and shelter for days on end. The situation deteriorated further when war broke out between China and Japan and Shandong was invaded. The horror of those times is vividly recreated in Mo Yan's novel, *Red Sorghum*, made into a movie in 1987 by the distinguished director Zhang Yimou.

COMMUNIST CHINA

The Communists inherited a country devastated by civil war with agriculture in ruins, factories at a standstill, communications disrupted and inflation rampant. But there was a mood of optimism as the Party set about redistributing the land and getting industry back on its feet. In 1958, Mao embarked on the Great Leap Forward, a disastrous socio-economic experiment which ended in famine and the deaths of up to 30 million people. Mao's hold on power was threatened but his supporters hit back during the Cultural Revolution (1966–76). What started as a campaign to invigorate the Party and country quickly descended into anarchy, with purges, witch hunts, factional infighting, ideological warfare and the public humiliation of intellectuals and officials. Among the 700,000 victims was Deng Xiaoping, who survived to lead China following Mao's death in 1976. Two years later Deng embarked on the economic reforms that are still continuing today.

LIN BIAO

The *Quotations from Chairman Mao*, the 'little red book' waved ecstatically by Red Guards during rallies on Tian'anmen Square, was the brainchild of Defense Minister Lin Biao. Lin fought alongside Mao during the civil war, emerging as one of the Red Army's most brilliant strategists. By 1966 he was Mao's deputy and chosen successor. But as the power of the People's Revolutionary Army increased during the Cultural Revolution, Mao saw Lin as a threat and his star began to wane. In desperation he planned to assassinate Mao and seize power. But the plot was uncovered in September 1971 and Lin Biao was never seen again. A year later it was announced that the plane taking him out of the country had crashed, killing everyone on board.

Above *Chinese leader Deng Xiaoping (left) at a party conference, with the then Communist Party chief Zhao Ziyang, who was later deposed*

ON THE MOVE

On the Move gives you detailed advice and information about the various options for traveling to China before explaining the best ways to get around the country once you are there. Handy tips help you with everything from buying tickets to renting a car.

ARRIVING BY AIR

China's main international airports are Beijing, Shanghai and Hong Kong. Numerous flights operate from Europe, North America, Asia and Australia. Scheduled international flights also serve other airports, notably Chengdu, Shenyang, Guangzhou and Macau, plus others including Xi'an, Shenzhen, Nanjing and Kunming. Demand is high on many routes, so flights need to be booked well in advance. The highest demand, and when tickets are most expensive, is the summer peak and around the major Chinese holiday periods of Spring Festival (Chinese New Year to late January or early February), Labor Day (May 1) and National Day (October 1).

AIRLINES

International services are operated by China's three main airlines—flag-carrier Air China, China Eastern Airlines and China Southern Airlines. Many major international airlines fly to China. They include British Airways, Virgin Atlantic, Air France, Finnair, KLM, Lufthansa, American Airlines, United Airlines, Emirates, Singapore Airlines, Thai Airways International, JAL and Qantas.

AIRPORTS

Beijing Capital International Airport (PEK) is 25km (16 miles) northeast of central Beijing. It is dominated by the gargantuan new Terminal 3 building, opened in

GETTING INTO TOWN FROM THE AIRPORT

AIRPORT	BEIJING (PEK)	HONG KONG (HKG)
DISTANCE TO CITY	25km (16 miles)	20km (12.5 miles)
TAXI	Taxi stands outside arrivals areas of Terminals 1 and 2 and in transport center at Terminal 3. Show driver the hotel name in Chinese characters. Most speak no English. Price: around 100RMB. Journey time: 40–60 min. Capital Taxi Co: tel 010 6406 5088 for an expensive chauffeur service	Taxi stands in Ground Transportation Centre outside arrivals hall—three lines for urban taxis (red), New Territories taxis (green) and Lantau taxis (blue). Price: around HK$340 (to Central). Journey time: 45 min. Transport Department enquiries hotline: tel (00852) 2804 2600
BUS	Five routes from Beijing's Capital Airport serve different areas of the city with stops at some major hotels. Routes include Fangzhuang for the World Trade Centre and Xidan, which is on Changan Avenue, close to Tian'anmen Square and Wanfujing Street. Buses leave from outside both terminals. Frequency is every 10–30 min depending on route, and buses run from 7am until the last flight to Xidan. Journey times to the city dependent on number of stops and traffic, but generally at least 60 min. Buy tickets from booths just outside the terminals, next to bus stops. Price: 16–20RMB. 24-hour Airport Bus hotline: tel 010 6459 4375; www.bcia.com.cn	Airbus services to Hong Kong and the New Territories leave from GTC outside arrivals every 15–30 min from 6am. Pay at GTC or on bus. Price: HK$17–28. Airbus: tel (00852) 2261 2791; www.kmb.hk. Cityflyer has five routes to Kowloon and Hong Kong at frequent intervals from 6am. Pay at GTC or on bus. Price: about HK$40 (Central). Cityflyer: tel (00852) 2873 0818; www.citybus.com.hk. The Airport-Mainland Coach Station (7am–11pm) has mainland routes including Shenzhen and Guangzhou. Price: around HK$250 (Guangzhou). China Travel Tours Transportation Services: tel (00852) 2261 2472; http://ctsbus.hkcts.com
TRAIN	The new Airport Express rail link opened just prior to the Beijing Olympic Games. It runs between terminals 2 and 3 and Dongzhimen. The driverless trains run on a 27.3km (16 mile) track and take around 18 minutes. Dongzhimen is busy and tricky to navigate, so consider taking a taxi or a shuttle bus if you are travelling with lots of luggage.	Airport Express: tel (00852) 2881 8888;www.mtr.com.hk. Fast direct trains go to Hong Kong Island via Kowloon every 10 min 5.15am–1.15am with free shuttle bus link to major hotels. Price: about HK$90 Kowloon, HK$100 Hong Kong Island (Central). Journey time: 24 min (Central)
CAR	No car rental desks at the airport. Jinri Xin'gai'nian Car Rental: tel 010 6457 5566 (location nearby). Shouqi Car Rental: tel 010 6232 8701 (location nearby). Avis: tel 010 8406 3343; www.avischina.com (location in city, chauffeured vehicles and self-drive)	No car rental desks at the airport. Limousine counters in GTC. Intercontinental Hire Cars: tel (00852) 2261 2188. Parklane Limousine Service: tel (00852) 2261 0303; www.hongkonglimo.com

Left *Dunhuang Airport is one of the several airports in China that have been expanded and modernized*

2008. This is the largest terminal in the world, and the main hub for the majority of international flights from Europe, North America and Australia. With a capacity for 82 million passengers per year, Beijing Capital International Airport is likely to become one of the busiest airports in the world, though the sheer size of its three terminals means there's little danger of overcrowding. Terminal 3 is home to national carrier Air China, and is the base for most of the major national airlines that fly into Beijing. Terminal 2 is home to China Eastern, as well as several international carriers (KLM included). Terminal 1 was renovated in 2004, and serves mainly as a base for China Southern. It's possible to walk between terminals 1 and 2, though there are free shuttle buses between all three terminals approximately every seven minutes.

Terminal 3 is split into three sections. The main terminal building is 3C and home to most domestic carriers. The two satellite concourses, 3D and 3E are the base for international carriers (note that there is no A or B section, due to fears of confusion with the existing two terminals). There are four floors, with arrivals on the second floor and departures on the fourth floor. Both have major information centers and a liberal scattering of banks and 24-hour ATMs. The Baggage Enquiry Counter is on the second floor, as is the First Aid clinic. Roving Service Ambassadors can be found on the second and fourth floors, offering assistance. The huge food court containing more than 70 food outlets, can be found on the mezzanine level above the fourth floor. There is a host of other services, including coffee shops, postal centers and beauty salons.

A huge new transportation center is located at the front of Terminal 3 and has three dedicated lanes for airport buses, taxies and private

SHANGHAI-PUDONG (PVG)
40km (25 miles)

Taxi stands outside arrivals hall of both terminals. Have your destination written in Chinese, and ensure the meter is switched on for the journey. Ignore unofficial taxi touts in and just outside the arrivals hall.
Price: around 150RMB. Journey time: 25–40 min.
Dazhong Taxi Service Co: tel 021 96822

Seven Airport Bus routes operate between Pudong Airport's two terminals and different parts of Shanghai 7am–11pm, as well as one to Hongqiao Airport for other domestic connections. Buses leave at 10–30 min intervals from outside the arrivals hall. Routes include line 2 to the City Air Terminal at Jingan Temple and line 5 to Shanghai Railway Station. Line 3 to Galaxy Hotel and line 6 to Zhongshan Park both stop at Longyang Road and connect to the metro (line 2). Buy tickets on board the bus. Price: 16–20RMB (30RMB or so to Hongqiao).
Journey time: 40–50min. Note that shuttle buses visit terminal 1 first and travelers at terminal 2 may not get a seat at busy times.
Airport Bus: www.shanghaiairport.com/en

Maglev: tel 021 2890 7777; www.smtdc.com
Trains on the high-speed magnetic levitation line operate every 15 min 7am–9pm to Longyang Road metro station, connecting to metro line 2.
Approximate price: 50RMB one-way, 80RMB round-trip (passengers with current day's flight ticket get 20 percent discount).
Journey time: 8 min
Car rental desks in the international arrivals area.
Avis (tel 021 6834 6668) has self-drive vehicles and cars with drivers: www.avischina.com
Shanghai Bashi & Airport Bus Vehicle Rental Co:
tel 021 6835 5556

vehicles. There are five main bus routes into the city center. Tickets should be purchased on board and cost 16RMB. A new light-rail line has been constructed between Dongzhimen, in the east of central Beijing, and the airport. Terminals 2 and 3 each have their own dedicated station. The travel time from Terminal 3 to Dongzhimen is about 18 minutes and tickets cost around 30RMB or so. The Beijing Capital International Airport passenger information hotline is 010 6454 1100, with a dedicated English-language service available. Buses go to Beijing from outside both terminals.

Hong Kong International Airport

(HKG), also known as Chek Lap Kok, on Lantau Island, opened in 1998. Automated trains shuttle between the East Hall and West Hall. The airport has been designed with visitors with disabilities in mind with wheelchair-accessible toilets and walkways, escalators, and elevators have audible signals and Braille signs.

There are multimedia information booths, and a customer services booth (tel 00852 2181 0000) is in the Check-in Hall. The terminal

Below *Airport Express MTR train links Hong Kong International Airport to the city center in 24 minutes*

has 24-hour help phones. Visitor information counters (hotline tel 00852 2508 1234), in the transfer area and at Buffer Halls A and B, offer tourist brochures and access to the Hong Kong Tourism Board website. Baggage carts are free and there are porters.

Left luggage (daily 5.30am–1.30am) is on Arrivals level 5. Level 6 in departures has a children's play area and a hair and beauty salon. A clinic (tel 00852 2261 2626) is on level 6 in room 6T009. Lost and found (tel 00852 2182 2018, daily 8am–11pm) is in room 6T056.

HKIA has 40 food and drink outlets and 60 shops in the East Hall and beyond security in the West Hall. Duty-free items can be ordered on level 7 in the Check-in Hall. Duty-free shops are airside in departures and arrivals. A Bank of China branch is in the Check-in Hall, while HSBC has one in Arrivals on level 5. Currency exchange offices and machines are throughout the airport, as are ATMs. Three post offices are by check-in and in the departure areas.

Airbus and Cityflyer airport buses, the Airport Express train, taxis

USEFUL CONTACTS

AIRPORTS

Beijing	www.bcia.com.cn
Shanghai	www.shanghaiairport.com
Hong Kong	www.hongkongairport.com
Macau	www.macau-airport.gov.mo
Chengdu	www.cdairport.com
Guangzhou	www.baiyunairport.com

AIRLINES

Air China	4008 100 999*	www.airchina.com.cn/en/index.jsp
China Southern Airlines	020 8613 3399	www.cs-air.com/cn
China Eastern Airlines	021 95108	www.ce-air.com
Hainan Airlines	0898 950718	www.hnair.com
Cathay Pacific Airways	(00852) 2747 1888	www.cathaypacific.com
British Airways	010 8511 5599	www.ba.com
Virgin Atlantic	021 5353 4600	www.virgin-atlantic.com
Lufthansa	4008 868 868*	www.lufthansa.com
Air France	4008 808 808*	www.airfrance.com
KLM	4008 808 222*	www.klm.com
American Airlines	010 5879 7600	www.aa.com
United Airlines	(00852) 2122 8256	www.unitedairlines.com
Finnair	010 6512 7180	www.finnair.com
Singapore Airlines	010 6505 2233	www.singaporeair.com
Thai Airways International	010 8515 0088	www.thaiair.com
Emirates	021 3222 9999	www.emirates.com
JAL	4008 88 0808*	www.jal.co.jp
Qantas	800 819 0089*	www.qantas.com.au

* = numbers that can only be called from within China

TRAINS

Ministry of Railways	www.chinamor.cn.net (in Chinese)
Mass Transit Railway Corporation	www.mtr.com.hk
(Hong Kong Metro and trains to mainland)	
Travel China Guide (rail timetable)	www.travelchinaguide.com/china-trains
(rail and tour booking service by China Travel Service)	

CAR RENTAL

Avis	www.avischina.com

and limousines depart from the Ground Transportation Centre. Ferry transfers to the mainland and Macau are accessed via the Ferry Transfer Desk on level 5 in East Hall Arrivals. Hong Kong's Rehabus bus service (tel 00852 8100 8655) for visitors with disabilities serves HKIA.

TurboJet Sea Express (www. turbojetseaexpress.com) operates fast ferry services from HKIA SkyPier to Macau (seven per day, 45 min, adult HK$215, child (2–12) HK$160) and Shenzhen Airport (four per day, 40 min, adult HK$295, child HK$225). CKS (www.cksp.com.hk) operates a similar service from HKIA SkyPier to Shenzhen/Shekou (hourly, 30 min, adult HK$220, child HK$120), Humen/Taiping (six per day, 60 min, adult HK$290, child HK$160), and Zhongshan (daily, 70 min, adult HK$250, child HK$133). Buy tickets for both services from Ferry Transfer Desk, level 5, HKIA.

Shanghai Pudong International Airport (PVG) opened in 1999 40km (25miles) east of the city centre. A second, parallel terminal was added in 2008. Departures are on the upper level and arrivals on the lower level, with the middle mezzanine level dedicated to restaurants.

Ctrip, one of China's most reliable online travel aggregators, has booths in both terminals and there are several local banks, including the Bank of China. Bank counters open from 9am until approximately 8.30pm and exchange rates are generally better than anything you'll find back home. Both terminals have Chinese restaurants, while there's a KFC in the Maglev building, between the two terminals.

The excellent budget Hotel 168 provides respite for those in need of rest. Free Wi-Fi access is available throughout both terminals. There are free shuttle buses that travel between two terminals from 6am to 9pm, departing at 10-minute intervals, and three hallways for visitors to walk between the two terminals. It should take less than 10 minutes if you have light luggage. Transport to the city is by shuttle

Above *The 1,300km (800-mile) Karakoram Highway links Kashi (Kashkar) in China with Islamabad in Pakistan*

bus and taxi from outside either terminal and the Maglev, the fastest commercial passenger train in the world, which runs to the Longyang Lu subway station in the east of the city center at speeds of 431kph (267mph). The 30km (19mile) journey takes 8 minutes and a single ticket costs 50RMB.

ARRIVING OVERLAND
China shares boundaries with 14 countries: Afghanistan, Bhutan, Burma (Myanmar), India, Kazakhstan, Kyrgyzstan, Laos, Mongolia, Nepal, North Korea, Pakistan, Russia, Tajikistan and Vietnam. Some border crossing points are closed or not accessible to foreign tourists. But you can enter China from most adjacent countries, including by train from Vietnam and Kazakhstan (Almaty–Ürümqi) and on the Trans-Siberian Railway via Mongolia and Russia.

MAIN ENTRY POINTS

Vietnam Twice-weekly train service (Tue, Fri, 6.30pm) runs from Hanoi to Beijing. The train goes to Dong Dang, where the journey resumes on a Chinese express train after customs and passport control. The whole journey takes about 43 hours.

The Vietnam section is operated by Vietnam Railways (www.vr.com. vn). Other trains also run to Dong Dang, about 3km (2 miles) from the Friendship Pass border point at Huu Nghi (Youyi Guan). Trains also run from Hanoi to another border gate with Yunnan at Lao Cai. Direct service no longer goes to Kunming, but you can get sleeper buses there from Hekou, near the border.

Nepal The Friendship Highway from Kathmandu to Tibet crosses the border near the Nepali town of Zhangmu. You need a Tibetan Tourism Bureau permit, which requires visitors to be on a tour. Book a tour before leaving home,

or join one when you are in Kathmandu. Travel restrictions currently apply to all independent travel to Tibet from China by foreigners; please check the current situation before planning your trip.

Russia Most visitors from Russia enter at Manzhouli, in Inner Mongolia, on the Trans-Manchurian branch of the Trans-Siberian Railway going to Beijing via Harbin. It takes just over six days from Moscow.

Mongolia The Trans-Mongolian enters China's Inner Mongolia at Erenhot and goes via the Mongolian capital, Ulan Bator. From Moscow it takes six days.

Laos The road to the Laotian border town of Boten improves on the Chinese side. Get buses from Mohan, just across the border in Xishuangbanna region, and then on to the city of Mengla for a sleeper bus service.

ARRIVING BY SEA

China is well-served by ferries from neighboring countries. A weekly passenger and cargo service by the Shanghai Ferry Company (tel 021 6537 5111, www.shanghai-ferry.co.jp) sails between Osaka in Japan and Shanghai. Weekly sailings alternating between Kobe and Osaka to Shanghai are operated by the China Japan International Ferry Company (tel 021 6325 7642). A passenger service from Kobe to Tianjin operates every week by China Express Line (tel 022 2420 5777, www.celkobe.co.jp). All Japanese sailings take two days.

Regular services operate from South Korea's Incheon to Dandong, Dalian, Tianjin, Yantai, Weihai and Qingdao.

Above *This ferry boat in Aberdeen harbor, Hong Kong, is one of many similar services that provide vital transportation links around the province*

BY AIR

Flying is an excellent way to travel around China, especially over longer distances. The aviation industry has undergone a revolution, and poor safety records and chaotic airports are long gone. Now, the latest aircraft are used, and many airports have modern terminals. Delays are still common, although most flights are more or less on time. Extensive route networks operated by China's three main airlines and smaller carriers provide lots of choice for travel: There are nearly 200 airports with regular flights.

BY TRAIN

China's vast rail network is also seeing major investment. The world's highest railway line, a 1,142km (714-mile) engineering marvel linking Golmud in Qinghai with the Tibetan capital, Lhasa, opened in 2006.

Trains now travel direct to Lhasa from Beijing, Xi'an, Chengdu, Chongqing and Guangzhou. A high-speed link to rival Japan's bullet train is being built between Beijing and Shanghai, and Shanghai's magnetic levitation train seems set to be extended all the way to Hangzhou. Chinese trains have four classes of travel: soft seat and hard seat, and soft and hard sleepers on long-distance trains.

Hard sleepers are quite acceptable but offer little privacy, with open-plan cars typically having six-berth bays in two lots of triple bunks. Soft sleepers generally have four-berth compartments. The most modern trains also have deluxe compartments with two single beds, TV screens and a private toilet and washroom. Sleeper trains generally include restaurant cars, and where stops are made you can buy food at stations. Train tickets are notoriously hard to get hold of and cannot be purchased more than a few days before the intended date of travel. Some major stations have ticket offices for foreigners. Buying through an agency or hotel concierge is more expensive but removes a major hassle factor.

BY CAR

Self-drive car rental is not an option for visitors because of the requirement to get a Chinese driver's license, which requires residency status. You can rent a car with a driver if you want to avoid a group tour or using public transportation. English-speaking drivers often act as guides.

BY BUS

Bus routes link towns and cities throughout China, with longer routes operated by sleeper buses.

However, conditions can be cramped and journeys are unlikely to be as pleasant as in sleeping cars on trains. Urban buses are plentiful but are often difficult and uncomfortable to use. Signs may be in Chinese only and crowds can be overwhelming.

BY TAXI

Taxis are plentiful, but drivers are unlikely to speak English. Ask hotel staff to tell the driver your destination, and have a card with the hotel name in Chinese to show when you return.

BY METRO

Six major cities have underground metro systems with several more operating overground 'light rail' networks. They are user-friendly with signs and route maps in English as well as Chinese, and are inexpensive.

WALKING AND BICYCLING

Walking is a good way to explore if you have a decent map and are careful when crossing roads. Aggressive driving makes urban cycling risky but renting a bicycle in rural parts is a great option for seeing the country.

Above Bus depot at the Huanggang border crossing near the southern provincial city of Shenzhen

DOMESTIC FLIGHTS

With China covering such a huge area, flying is the best way to see different parts of the country in a short time. Beijing is the country's largest hub, but there are other major hubs at cities such as Shanghai, Guangzhou, Chengdu, Xi'an, Hangzhou, Shenyang, Chongqing and Ürümqi (Wulumuqi). Many flights also go from Hong Kong to mainland China destinations.

BAGGAGE ALLOWANCE FOR DOMESTIC FLIGHTS	
Hold luggage	First class 40kg (88lb)
	Business class 30kg (66lb)
	Economy class 20kg (44lb)
Carry-on luggage	Two bags per passenger in first class and one bag in business and economy classes, the total weight not exceeding 5kg (11lb)
Allowances can change, so always check before you travel	

China's domestic airline scene has undergone consolidation, and a number of small carriers have been taken over by the three state-owned major players: Air China, China Southern Airlines and China Eastern Airlines. They and their subsidiaries now operate the bulk of flights around China. Of other carriers, the largest is Hainan Airlines. The former state-controled aviation monopoly has now been opened up to the private sector, and new ventures include Shanghai's Spring Airlines and Yunnan's Lucky Air. Hong Kong's Dragonair is now part of Cathay Pacific.

DOMESTIC AIRLINES

Air China, the national flag carrier and official airline of the Beijing Olympics, is actually China's second-largest airline. Its major hub is Beijing and it has secondary hubs in five other cities, including Chengdu

and Chongqing. It operates about 60 domestic routes.
» Central reservations: tel 4008 100 999; www. airchina.com.cn/index.jsp

China Southern Airlines is the largest airline in China. Its fleet of 600 aircraft serves 142 cities throughout China from its main hub at Guangzhou's Baiyun International Airport and other hubs, including Beijing, Wuhan and Xiamen.
» Central reservations: tel 020 8613 3399; www.cs-air.com/en

China Eastern Airlines is based in Shanghai and has hubs at the city's Hongqiao and Pudong International airports, as well as Xi'an, Kunming and Wuhan. From Shanghai it has daily flights to Beijing, Hong Kong and Guangzhou, Kunming and Shenzhen, plus many other flights.
» Central reservations: tel 021 95108.

Hainan Airlines is China's fourth-largest airline and is based at Haikou on the island of Hainan. It also has hubs at Ningbo and Xi'an and serves more than 50 domestic destinations.
» Central reservations: tel 0898 950718, freephone 800 876 8999; www.hnair.com

PRICES

One-way fares between Beijing and Shanghai are around 1,130RMB, while a flight from Chengdu to Lhasa is about 1,200RMB. Fares are often discounted out of season. Business-class fares are usually an extra 30 percent and first class an extra 50 percent. Children under 12 and infants under two pay 50 percent and 10 percent respectively. A 50RMB airport construction fee is absorbed in the price of the ticket.

BUYING TICKETS

Buying airline tickets in China has become easier in recent years, though many of the major airlines still have poor websites and make it difficult to use international credit cards when buying tickets. The main improvement has come with online aggregators, Ctrip (www.ctrip.com) being the most successful. These have excellent English-language sites and allow use of the likes of Visa, Amex and Mastercard.

Left *With distances within China being so large, domestic flights can save you time*

TRAINS

China's extensive railway system is undergoing an ambitious expansion: New high-speed shuttles between nearby cities have slashed traveling times, particularly the Beijing–Tianjin; Shanghai–Nanjing and Guangzhou–Shenzhen routes. The world's highest railway links Tibet with the rest of China and will be extended beyond Lhasa. Other plans include a high-speed railway line between Beijing and Shanghai reducing the journey time to five hours, and a second Maglev rail service, connecting Shanghai with Hangzhou in 30 minutes.

Train travel in China is punctual, good value and comfortable, especially on its newer express trains. It is the country's key mode of transportation and is one of the world's busiest railway systems. You should avoid travel in China's three holiday periods. The busiest time for travel is the Spring Festival (Chinese New Year). The busy period extends for 40 days.

Each train type usually has a letter, followed by one or more numbers. Suburban trains are designated S, while those operating purely within one railway bureau's region have the letter N. To travel longer distances, use trains with codes K (fast), T (express) and Z (limited or nonstop express). All are usually air-conditioned, while Z-class trains have individual controls in compartments. The train numbers indicate the direction. Odd numbers are those from Beijing or heading north or west elsewhere; trains bound for Beijing or going south or east are even.

Local trains usually only have hard seats (*Yingzuo*, or YZ), the

Above *The Shanghai metro is modern and clean*

APPROXIMATE TRAIN PRICES							
	HARD SEAT	SOFT SEAT	HARD SLEEPER			SOFT SLEEPER	
			top	middle	bottom	top	bottom
Beijing–Shanghai	180	300	310	320	330	480	500
Beijing–Xi'an	160	250	270	280	290	420	430
Shanghai–Hangzhou	35	50	n/a	n/a	n/a	n/a	n/a
Shanghai–Guangzhou	210	340	360	370	380	560	590
Guangzhou–Hong Kong	30	45	n/a	n/a	n/a	n/a	n/a
Beijing–Lhasa*	400	n/a	n/a	n/a	820	n/a	1,300
Chengdu–Lhasa*	340	n/a	n/a	n/a	720	n/a	1,150
Kunming–Chengdu	150	230	250	260	270	390	400
Unit: Chinese RMB. * = Tibet permit required. Travel must be part of an official tour							

rail equivalent of economy, while regional trains also have more comfortable soft seats (*Ruanzuo*, or *RZ*).

Long-distance trains also have hard sleeper (*Yingwo*, or *YW*) and soft sleeper (*Ruanwo*, or *RW*) classes. Despite the name, hard sleepers do have proper mattresses with reasonable bedding, but in bays with two tiers of three bunks open to the passageway as opposed to closed compartments with four beds in soft sleepers. Newer trains have two-bed compartments as well.

The new Z-class trains from Beijing to Shanghai, Hong Kong and Xi'an are comfortable and have good facilities, and restaurant cars have menus in English. Several trains a day travel from Beijing to both Shanghai and Xi'an. Hong Kong trains from Beijing operate every other day.

TICKETS AND PRICING

Upper sleeping berths are cheaper. Children below 1.1m (3.8ft) go free; those below 1.4m (4.5ft) pay half price. Buy tickets from stations. Major city stations have special ticket offices for foreigners. Tickets for Z-class trains can be bought 20 days ahead, but for other long-distance trains, as little as four days ahead. Hotels will buy tickets for guests, adding a service fee. Travel agencies will also arrange tickets, with a mark-up of 25–30 percent. Online agencies include www.chinatripadvisor.com (tel 0559 231 9660), which is operated by the Huangshan, Anhui, branch of China Travel Service Train schedules can be found at www.travelchinaguide.com/china-trains/.

SPECIAL ROUTES
Qinghai–Tibet Railway
The 1,142km (714-mile) line between Golmud and Lhasa opened in July 2006, connecting Tibet with China by rail. The world's highest railway, it uses special cars with oxygen tubes for passengers to alleviate high-altitude sickness. Most of the line is above 4,000m (13,123ft) and the highest point is at 5,072m (16,640ft).

The line opened with passenger services to Lhasa from Beijing, Shanghai, Guangzhou, Chengdu and Chongqing, with Xi'an and Lanzhou being among the major stops en route. The Beijing to Lhasa route (4,064km/2,540 miles), takes 48 hours and costs 1,262RMB in a lower-berth soft sleeper.

Trains are air-conditioned and have hard and soft sleepers, a dining car and bar. An information display gives speed, temperature and altitude. A Passenger Health Registration Card is needed and is available when buying your ticket.

Trans-Siberian Express
Two branches operate weekly between Moscow and Beijing. The Trans-Mongolian branch goes via Mongolia and the Gobi Desert. Deluxe two-berth compartments have a wash-room, which includes a shared shower.

The Trans-Manchurian route via Harbin uses Russian rolling stock with two-berth first-class and four-berth second-class cars. Both journeys take about six days.

Hong Kong–Guangzhou
Hong Kong's MTR Corporation (www.mtr.com.hk) operates a regular service between Guangzhou and Hong Kong. Its trains have both premium and first-class cars. Trains operated by the mainland rail authority include the all-premium Xinshisu train and semi-high-speed trains. The fastest trains take just over 90 minutes.

Left *A view of the interior of a railcar on the Kowloon and Canton Railway, Hong Kong*

BY ROAD

China's expanding long-distance highway network makes road travel around the country a viable alternative to rail or air. Long-distance sleeper buses operate between many cities and towns. Self-drive car rental is limited, but you can rent a car and driver for excursions or to travel around remote areas.

LONG-DISTANCE BUSES

Buses offer a cheap form of long-distance travel, although sleeper bus prices often match those of hard sleepers on trains. It is an alternative to more expensive flights to far-flung cities and towns. With no national network of bus services, getting information on routes and booking journeys is not easy. Major cities have several bus stations operating long-distance routes. Beijing alone has 19 stations with routes to other cities. Major termini include Zhaogongkou (tel 010 6772 9491), Bawangfen (tel 010 8771 8844) and Liuliqiao (tel 010 8383 1717). Note that tickets can normally be purchased a few days in advance but not during busy festival periods.

There is no set standard of bus and some are more luxurious than others. There is generally one on-board toilet. Bunk beds are typically arranged in three rows. They are small, even by Chinese standards. Smoking, spitting, erratic driving and blaring horns may well make journeys unpleasant endurance tests. There may also be frequent stops for food, toilets and fuel, as well as for traffic jams. Car ownership in China over recent years has rocketed so much that jams are frequent in towns and cities.

DRIVING

Self-drive car rental in China is not an option for vacation visitors because of restrictions. International drivers' licenses are not accepted and a temporary Chinese one requires a minimum three-month residency permit and you must pass a test and have a medical examination.

Right *Traffic signs in major cities show both Chinese characters and their Pinyin equivalent*

Roads are also daunting, given the generally poor standard of driving and mobile hazards such as mini-tractors, hand carts, bicycles and fume-belching trucks. Rural areas may also have road signage only in Chinese characters.

Of the major international rental companies, only Avis (www.avischina.com) has entered the market, through a joint venture with Anjun Car Rental Company. It has locations in five major cities including Shanghai, where rental is available at both Pudong and Hongqiao airports, and Beijing, which has a rental booth in Terminal 2 of the Beijing Capital International Airport and one downtown location.

CHAUFFEURED CARS

For visitors, renting a car with a driver is the only realistic option for independent travel. You can book them through travel agencies and through hotels in China. For longer journeys in remote areas, booking well beforehand through a reputable company is advised.

Avis rents chauffeured cars, which will meet clients at airports. One day's rental of a Volkswagen Santana or similar with a driver costs 530RMB. That compares with around 400RMB per day for self-drive rental, including local taxes and fees plus basic insurance. Clients are given an information booklet with helpful hints and phrases.

LONG-DISTANCE BUS ROUTES

ROUTE	DURATION (HOURS)	DISTANCE	APPROXIMATE PRICE (RMB)
Shanghai–Suzhou	1.5	100km (62.5 miles)	35
Shanghai–Hangzhou	3	176km (110 miles)	60
Shanghai–Nanjing	5	306km (191 miles)	90
Shanghai–Beijing	15	1,262km (789 miles)	320
Beijing–Chengde	3.5	240km (150 miles)	50
Beijing–Shenyang	8	750km (469 miles)	165
Beijing–Qingdao	8	719km (449 miles)	170
Beijing–Wuhan	10	1,100km (688 miles)	230

Beijing's main sights are spread out. Central attractions such as Tian'anmen Square, the Forbidden City and the shopping street Wanfujing are accessible by subway. Other sights can only be reached by bus, taxi or rented vehicles.

BY METRO

Built for military use in the 1960s, Beijing's metro (www.explorebj. com) is the oldest in China and, until recently, had a fairly limited city center scope. However, a huge expansion ahead of the Olympic Games has made the network the second largest in China (behind Shanghai). Three new lines were opened in July 2008, just three weeks before the start of the Games, and there are plans to expand the network to 19 lines and 561km (348 miles) of tracks by 2020.
» Metro map ▷ 59.
» First trains usually begin running shortly after 5am and continue until around 11pm.
» The Beijing metro currently charges a flat fare of 2RMB for travel between any two stations, on any lines—including transfers. The Airport Express charges 25RMB for a single journey. Automated ticket turnstiles have been introduced on all lines.
» The Beijing Municipal Administration and Communications Card, a monthly smart card known as the *yikatong* (one-card pass), can be purchased from most metro stations and used to store credit that can be used on the metro, buses and taxi. A 20RMB deposit is required.

BY BUS

Beijing's huge bus network was improved in the run up to the Beijing Games. Around 10,000 of the creaking old buses, once ubiquitous on the city streets, have been replaced and Beijing now claims the world's biggest natural-gas-powered fleet. Fares cost just 1RMB. It's still tricky to get your bearings with signs on bus stops and on buses in Chinese only, or—at best—pinyin.

The largest bus operator is the Beijing Bus Company (helpline tel 010 96166; www.bjbus.com).

BY TAXI

The fare is 2RMB per kilometer after the first 3km (2 miles), with a minimum charge of 10RMB during the day and 11RMB after 11pm. Rates increase by 50 percent after the first 15km (9 miles). Rates are displayed on rear windows. Taxis can be hailed in the street and also wait at stands outside the airport, stations and some tourist attractions. Have the name of your destination and your hotel written in Chinese.
» A 'For Hire' sign is illuminated when the meter is off. Ensure the meter is switched on at the start of the journey. Tipping is not the norm.
» The biggest taxi company in Beijing is the Capital Taxi Co (▷ 36).

BY CAR

You can rent a vehicle with a driver in Beijing. Hotels or travel agencies will arrange chauffeured car rental.
» Avis has an airport booth by gate 11 in the domestic arrivals of Terminal 2 (Mon–Fri 9–4.30; tel 010 6458 4554) and a downtown location (Mon–Sun 8.30–5; tel 010 8406 3343; www.avischina.com). One day's rental for an intermediate car with driver costs around 800RMB.

BY BICYCLE

Major roads have dedicated bicycle lanes but these are very busy during rush hour.
» Beijing Kingdom Bicycle Rentals Co (tel 133 8140 0738; www. bicyclekingdom.com) rents bicycles by the day or longer.

Left *Rickshaws and their drivers near Drum Square, Beijing*
Opposite *A busy street in Shanghai*

ON THE MOVE | GETTING AROUND

GETTING AROUND SHANGHAI

China's most extensive subway system, the Shanghai metro includes underground lines and elevated tracks. Expansion has helped to ease pressure but overcrowding remains a problem. The high-speed Maglev (magnetic levitation) line links the metro to Pudong International Airport. There are more than 1,000 bus routes.

BY METRO

Shanghai's super-slick metro is the largest in China. There are eight lines that cover most key parts of the city, with more under construction. Ticket prices are calculated according to distance, ranging from 3RMB for journeys under 6km (4 miles), to a maximum of 8RMB. Station ticket attendants are unlikely to speak English but you can buy tickets by value rather than destination at the counters. Automatic ticket machines give change. Alternatively, pick up a *jiaotongka* (Shanghai Transportation Card) which can be used to pay for subway journeys, as well as buses and taxis. The card requires a 20RMB deposit and can be recharged anytime. You can buy the card at most metro stations.
» Metro map ▷ 291
» Trains run every few minutes from approximately 5.30am until 11pm on lines 1 and 2, though trains finish before 10pm on other routes.
» Shanghai's metro can be horrifically crowded, especially on weekday mornings and during most of the weekend.
» Several of Shanghai's major tourist sights are not served by the subway (the Bund, Yuyuan, M50, Jade Buddha Temple, for example)

and neither international airport is currently connected.

BY BUS

Buses are mostly used by locals. Signs can be confusing, and information is all in Chinese other than the bus number and route start and end times.
» Fares start at 1RMB for non air-conditioned buses and 2RMB for buses with air-conditioning. Some routes are flat fare and require exact change. Other routes charge by stages, with prices up to 6RMB.

BY TAXI

Shanghai taxi drivers are among the most professional and reliable in China. However, English is rarely spoken so carry your hotel name and destination in Chinese characters. The meter should be used at all times and drivers cannot refuse a fare. The driver's name, photograph and registration number should also be displayed prominently in the front of the vehicle. If there is any argument or confusion at the end of a journey, note the complaints number and ask the driver for a *'fa piao'*. These printed receipts give details of your journey.
» The largest taxi operator, Dazhong Taxi Service Co. (tel 021 96822),

uses turquoise vehicles but other reputable companies have yellow, green, white, blue or red taxis.
» The flag fare is 11RMB and covers a basic distance of 3km (2 miles), with each additional kilometer costing 2.1RMB. The flag fares goes up to 14RMB after 11pm, and the distance price also goes up at night, or on journeys above 10km (6 miles). Drivers will not expect tips.
» Taxis wait at official stands but are usually hailed on the street. It can be nigh-on impossible to find a taxi in poor weather in Shanghai. Similarly, Friday afternoons are difficult.

BY CAR

Cars can be rented with drivers. Avis China has locations in Shanghai, including at airports; open 8–8 (head office tel 021 6241 0215; www.avischina.com). A car with driver costs around 800RMB per day. Hotels and travel agencies will also arrange cars with drivers.

BY BICYCLE

Bicycling is dangerous and bicycles have been banned from many major arteries.

BY FERRY

Ferries cross the Huangpu River 6am–11.30pm (1–4RMB round-trip).

GETTING AROUND OTHER MAJOR CITIES

Cities across China are investing in mass transit systems. Besides Beijing and Shanghai, Hong Kong and Guangzhou have major networks. New smaller subways have opened in Guangzhou, Tianjin, Wuhan, Shenzhen and Nanjing. Chongqing has a monorail, and both Changchun and Dalian have light railways and existing tram systems. Chengdu will have a single-line subway by 2010. Others are planned for Hangzhou, Harbin, Qingdao, Shenyang and Xi'an.

HONG KONG

» Hong Kong has an extensive transportation system. Octopus electronic ticket cards can be used on the Mass Transit Railway (MTR), Airport Express train, light rail, buses, ferries, Peak Tram and most taxis. They cost about HK$150 for adults and HK$70 for children aged 3–11 and over-65s, including a refundable HK$50 deposit, though a HK$7 fee is charged if the card is returned within three months. Available from shops and MTR and KCR stations, they can be topped up at vendors and by some ATMs.

» The MTR (24-hour hotline 00852 2881 8888; www.mtr.com.hk) opened in 1979 and is one of the world's 10 most heavily used transit systems. It has expanded hugely in recent years and, aside from the Airport Express, there are now a total of 10 lines that serve Hong Kong Island, Kowloon, Lantau Island (including a spur line to Disneyland Resort) and the New Territories (including new lines to the far east and west of this largely rural area). Trains run every 2–5 minutes from 6am to 1am on the busiest lines. The last train to the mainland border departs around 11pm.

» In 2007 the MTR merged with the Kowloon-Canton Railway (KCR) company, previously responsible for the overland route to the mainland border. This key route is now known as the East Rail Line, and splits after the Sanshui to meet both of the major customs ports with the mainland city of Shenzhen.

One-way MTR tickets cost HK$4–39, or HK$3–19.5 for children and over-65s. An MTR 1-Day Pass allows 24 hours of unlimited rides and costs HK$50. A 3-Day Hong Kong Transport Pass is useful for short-stay visitors, entitling them to one ride on the Airport Express train and shuttle bus plus three days' unlimited MTR travel.

» Hong Kong's venerable trams (www.hktramways.com) run along Hong Kong Island's northern shoreline between 5.10am and midnight. The HK$2 fare (HK$1 for children under 12 or over-65s) is fixed, with exact money required.

» Buses run throughout Hong Kong Island, Kowloon and the New Territories. Destinations are displayed in English and Chinese. Fares start at HK$1.20 and exact change is required.

» Urban taxis are red, New Territories taxis are green and Lantau Island taxis are blue. The base price is HK$15 for urban taxis and HK$1.40 per 0.2km after the first 2km (1.25 miles). Other taxis are slightly cheaper. Tolls and luggage handling are extra. Round fares up to the nearest HK dollar as a tip.

» The Star Ferry (www.starferry.com.hk) service across Victoria Harbour between Hong Kong Island and Kowloon costs HK$2.20–5.30 for an upper deck seat, depending on the route. Ferries run Mon–Sat 7.20am–11pm, Sun 7.40am–11pm.

GUANGZHOU

» Guangdong capital Guangzhou (Canton) gained its first subway line in 1999. The Guangzhou metro (tel 020 8328 9033; www.gzmtr.com/en) now has four lines. Three new lines are due to be open by 2010. The Guangfo Line subway will run to Foshan City and the Guangzhou Line light rail will link to nearby cities. A light rail line will also serve Baiyun International Airport.

» Trains run daily 6am–11.30pm, with 4–5 minute intervals at peak times. Fares range from 2RMB to 8RMB. The Yang Cheng Tong electronic card can be used for metro, buses, ferries and taxis. It costs 80RMB, including a 30RMB refundable deposit.

» Red, blue and yellow taxis are operated by the city's three major taxi companies. Green taxis are run by smaller operators, and drivers may be from rural areas. Fares start at 8RMB and are the same day or night. A 1RMB 'fuel surcharge' is added to the total cost.

NANJING

» Nanjing metro's single line opened in 2005. Line 1 runs from Maigaoqiao to Olympic Stadium via Nanjing Railway Station. Line 3, the next line under construction will open in stages.

» Trains run every 3–7 minutes from 6.30am up to 11pm at weekends. Fares cost 2–4RMB. The system uses electronic tickets. There is a 15kg (33lb) weight limit, as well as size limits for bags.

WUHAN

» Wuhan's part-elevated, driverless metro system opened in 2004. The initial section of Line 1 from Huangpu to Zongguan is being extended, with the number of stations rising from 10 to 26. Another two lines are planned by 2010.

» Four-car trains run 6.30am–10pm at intervals of 6–10 minutes. Fares are 1.5–2RMB and tickets are electronic.

» Taxi fares start at 8RMB for the first 3km (2 miles). Buses cost from 1RMB. Routes 401 and 402 tour the city's main scenic spots.

TIANJIN

» Tianjin first opened its metro in 1984. Line 1 has been extended to run from Liuyuan to Shuanglin. Several new lines are planned.

» Trains run 9–9, every 7–8 minutes at peak periods. Fares are 2–5RMB.

» The Binhai Line (www.ctbmt.cn), a light rail mass transit commuter line, links downtown with the Tianjin Economic Development Area (TEDA) and runs for almost 46km (29 miles). Trains operate 6.30am–9.30pm and fares are 2–6RMB.

CHONGQING

» On the first elevated monorail line of the metro (www.cqmetro.cn), the trip between Jiachangkou and Xinshancun takes 34 minutes.

Two underground lines should be completed by 2011.

» Fares are 1–4RMB. Trains operate 7am–10pm, at 8–12 minute intervals.

SHENZHEN

» Two lines (the east–west Line 1 and north–south Line 4), with 19 stations, currently operate on the Shenzhen Subway. Both passenger border posts with Hong Kong are connected to the network. Extensions to both lines and three more lines will be added by 2010.

» Trains run 6.10am–11.40pm. Fares are 2–5RMB. You can use one-way tickets or a TransCard electronic ticket (90RMB, including 40RMB refundable deposit). It also covers buses, minibuses and some taxis.

Opposite *A jetfoil in Hong Kong*
Below *An underground subway in Xi'an*

China has traditionally catered poorly to visitors with disabilities, although thanks to surging urban redevelopment and huge investment in its transportation infrastructure, facilities have improved. Many places still present a challenge, however, and much of China remains wheelchair-unfriendly. China still lags behind many countries in its attitude to disability.

It was hoped that the Beijing Olympics—the Paralympics in particular—would be a catalyst for improving disability access in China. Certainly the new developments all feature wheelchair ramps or lifts and international-standard facilities. However, even during the Games Chinese media reported countless examples of tactile paths being blocked, either with private bicycles or stalls, or government-installed signposts or bins. With crowded roads, poor driving standards and a general lack of consideration for the mobility impaired, the street remains a relatively dangerous place for visitors with disabilities.

AIR TRAVEL

China's major international airports provide many features to help the less able, including tactile paths, wheelchair-accessible toilets, wheelchair-height telephones, Braille signs and elevator buttons, and audible warnings. The terminal shuttle train at Hong Kong International Airport takes wheelchairs, while Terminal 3 at Beijing's Capital International Airport has been designed to reduce walking distances.

Airlines provide wheelchairs on departure and arrival, and will carry passengers' wheelchairs. Guide dogs fly free of charge. Passengers with special requirements should contact the airline at least 72 hours before their flight.

TRAINS

Space is very tight in sleeper train passageways and compartments. Newer express trains have deluxe soft sleeper compartments. Some have a private toilet. The new Lhasa trains have at least one wheelchair-accessible toilet. Hong Kong's MTR and KCR systems have wheelchair-accessible stations on several lines. Stations have tactile layout maps and guide paths, Braille on ticket machines and signs, and audible escalator and gate signals. Some stations have elevators and some new subway lines can also accommodate wheelchairs.

BUSES

Most buses in China are not easily accessed by wheelchairs. Hong

USEFUL CONTACTS

Beijing Xinhua International Tours
tel 010 6716 0201 ext 1006/1007
www.tour-beijing.com
Beijing-based tour operator which offers pre-planned or custom tours for people with disabilities.

MTR tel (00852) 2881 8888 www.mtr.com.hk
Website giving details of Hong Kong's Mass Transit Railway stations and lines, including facilities for people with disabilities.

The Hong Kong Society for Rehabilitation
tel (00852) 2817 8154
www.rehabsociety.org.hk/Rehabus.470.0.html
Operates the Rehabus buses for wheelchair-users with dial-a-ride service, airport pick-ups and sightseeing tours.

Kong's Rehabus service has a fleet of buses equipped with hydraulic tail lifts, wheelchair restraints and handrails.

Visitors can book buses in advance for travel between the airport and hotel or for sightseeing.

AROUND TOWN

Beijing's government has added tactile paths and lowered curbs, and access ramps to many buildings. However, paths can be blocked by obstructions. Many older towns have cobbled streets. Even where buildings have entrance ramps, interiors are often not wheelchair-friendly. New shopping malls cater to those with disabilities, but many shops and restaurants do not.

HOTELS

Large hotels are usually well geared up, with wheelchair ramps, Braille-equipped elevators and dedicated rooms with extra space and accessible toilets.

REGIONS

This chapter is divided into nine regions of China (▷ 8–9). Places of interest are listed alphabetically in each region, except in Beijing and Shanghai where places of interest are ordered from west to east across the city.

China's Regions 52–370

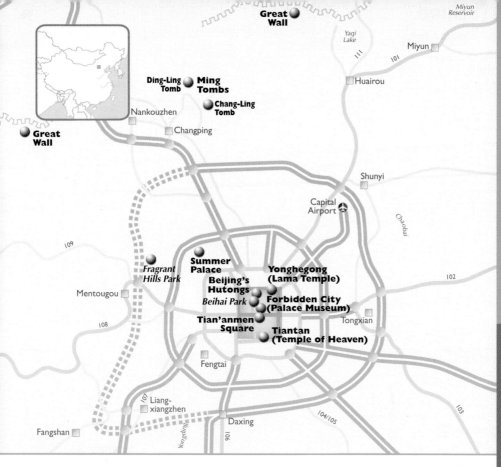

Great Wall

Miyun Reservoir

Yaqi Lake

Miyun

Great Wall

Ding-Ling Tomb

Ming Tombs

Chang-Ling Tomb

Nankouzhen

Huairou

Changping

Shunyi

Capital Airport

Chaobai

109

Fragrant Hills Park

Summer Palace

Yonghegong (Lama Temple)

102

Beijing's Hutongs

Mentougou

Beihai Park

Forbidden City (Palace Museum)

Tian'anmen Square

Tongxian

108

Tiantan (Temple of Heaven)

Fengtai

107

Liang-xiangzhen

Daxing

104/105

103

Fangshan

Yongding

906

BEIJING

If China's enormous landmass resembles a rooster, Beijing is appropriately located right on the bird's jugular. Capital of the vast country for most of the past 800 years, Beijing has been the pressure point for much historical drama, from Kublai Khan's Mongol marauders to mass rallies, by way of 600 years of imperial pomp. For most of the last quarter century, however, Beijing had been unable to compete with the urban revolutions taking place in the likes of Shanghai or Shenzhen. Then the Olympics happened. The move from graying Soviet-style bastion of communist power to effervescent global icon has been breathtaking.

The 2008 Games bequeathed Beijing with a series of new landmark buildings, and gave the city a new sheen and its people a sense of confidence. Some of the city's charming *hutong* alleys were sacrificed to make way for trendy new office and residential developments, but Beijing's yin-yang balance remains. The historic sights and cultural attractions make Beijing the best place to conjure the 'costume-drama' China of the movies, but it's also the ultimate expression of modern Chinese zest. The huge new Norman Foster-designed airport terminal paves the way for Beijing to become China's busiest transportation hub, and the city is now second only to Shanghai in financial terms. Historic stereotypes paint Beijingers as yokels, but there's a new go-getting spirit, even if the people retain an easy-going nature and a love of all-day tea-house conversation.

Unusually for a major conurbation, Beijing lies close to neither river nor sea. With development unconstrained by natural obstructions, the city has sprawled. Beijing takes time to navigate, but its size is mitigated by orderliness. The road network has the look of a spider's web, structured around wide boulevards and a series of giant ring roads that radiate out from the Forbidden City.

Ditan Park

Andingmen

Andingmendongbin

Yonghegong
Lama Temple

ANDINGMENDONG DAJIE

Wudaoying Hutong

Houxiaojia Hutong
Qianxiaojia Hutong

Guozijian
Imperial
Academy

Yonghegong
(Lama Temple)

Qinglong Hutong

Beiguanting
Hutong

Huayuan
Xiang

Lingguang
Xiang

Yongcheng
Hutong
Chaibang
Hutong

Yongkang Hutong

Dage Xiang

Janchang Hutong

Bailin
Temple

Paojutou Tiao

Paoju Hutong

Temple of
Confucius

Guozijian Jie

Theniandian Hutong

Beixin Hutong

Houyongkang
Hutong

Xiejia Hutong

Fangjia Hutong

Qianyongkang Hutong

Fensiting Hutong

Beixinqiao 3 Tiao

Caoyuan Hutong

Nanguan
Park

Xiyangguan
Hutong

Dongyangguan
Hutong

Dongzhimen

Jiaodaokoubei 3 Tiao

Xigong Jie

Xiaojuerhutong
Hutong

Dongsi Jie

Jiaodaokoubei 2 Tiao

Beixinqiao Tiao

Xishoupa
Hutong

Dongshoupa
Hutong

XIANHETUAN LU

DAJIE

Jiaodaokoubeitou Tiao

Beixinqiao

DONGZHIMEN
BUS TERMINAL

JIAODAOKOUDONG DAJIE

DONGZHIMENNEI DAJIE

Dashanzi Art
District

Tu'er Hutong

Shique Hutong

Daju Hutong

Beixincang Hutong

Ju'er Hutong

Xiang'er Hutong

Xintaicang Hutong

Cangjiadao

Houyuan'ensi Hutong

Taixing Hutong

Xiguan Hutong

Dongsi 14 Tiao

Qinlao Hutong

Dongwang Hutong

Baimicang Hutong

Dongsi 13 Tiao

Haiyuncang Hutong

Beibingmasi Hutong

Wen Tianxiang
Temple Fuxue Hutong

Xinsi Hutong

Menlou Hutong

Songnian Hutong

Dongsishitiao

Dongmianhua Hutong

DONGCHENG

Dongsi 12 Tiao

Nansongnian Hutong

Banchang Hutong

Zhangzizhonglu

Dongsi 11 Tiao

Beimencang Hutong

Chaodou Hutong

DAJIE

ZHANGZIZHONG LU

DONGSI 10 TIAO

Liboying Hutong

Xiezuo Hutong

Dongsi 9 Tiao

Shaniao Hutong

Wangzhima Hutong

Dongsi 8 Tiao

Xiangyang Hutong

Weijia Hutong

Dongsi 7 Tiao

Shijinhuayuan Hutong

Dongsi 6 Tiao

Nanmencang Hutong

National
Art Museum
of China

Yuqun Hutong

Qianliang Hutong

Dongsi 5 Tiao

Dongsi 4 Tiao

Longfusi Jie

Dongsi 3 Tiao

Dongsi

Dongsi 2 Tiao

Fu Wangfu

DONGSIXI DAJIE

Shaojiu Hutong

Chaoyangmen

CHAOYANGMENNEI DAJIE

WUSI DAJIE

Cuihua Hutong

Beizhugan Hutong

Dongchang Hutong

Duofu Xiang

Zhugan Hutong

Dongsi
Mosque

Qianchaomian Hutong

Qianguaibang Hutong

Nanzhugan Hutong

Baofang Hutong

Lishi Hutong

Capital
Theatre

Dengcao Hutong

Hutong

Xinxian
Hutong

Daboge Hutong

Yanle

Hongyan
Hutong

Bensi Hutong

Neiwubu Jie

Dafangjia Hutong

Dengshikouxi Jie

Dengshikou Dajie

Shijia Hutong

Lumicanghou Xiang

Zhihua
Temple

Dengshikou

Baishu Hutong

Ganmian Hutong

Lumicang Hutong

Shaojiu Hutong

Xitangzi Hutong

Xishicao Hutong

Dongshicao Hutong

Xiaoyabao

Xila Hutong

Ganyu Hutong

Sui'anbo Hutong

Dayabao Hutong

Yabao Lu

Dong'anmen Dajie

Jinyu Hutong

Pudu
Temple

Caichang Hutong

Hongxing Hutong

Meizha Hutong

Dongtangzi Hutong

57

Zhaotangzi
Hutong

Daruanfu Hutong

Beishuaifu Hutong

Waijiaobu Jie

Dayangyibin Hutong

Guanghua Lu

Qiantianshuijing
Hutong

Shuaifuyuan
Hutong

Xizongbu Hutong

Dongzongbu Hutong

D

E

F

Xinkailu Hutong

Dingyin Hutong

Congyuantou Tiao

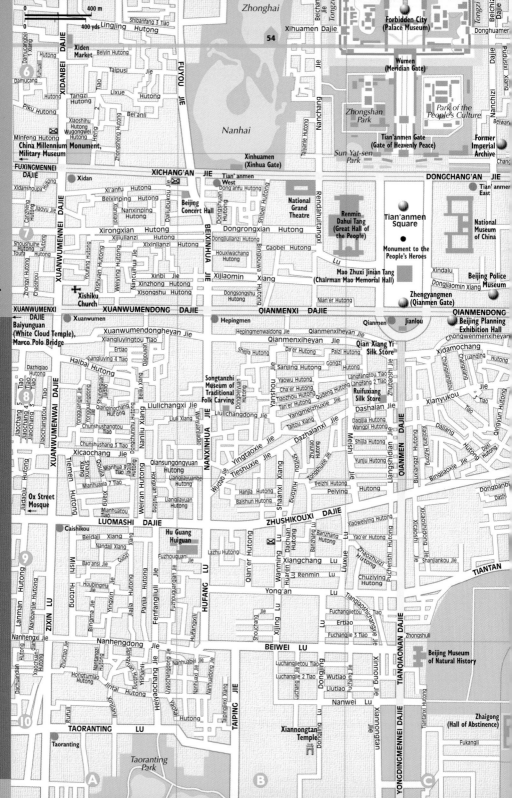

Zhonghai

400 m

400 yds

Lingling Hutong

Shibanfang 3 Tiao

Beichang Jie

Tongzi

Xihuamen Dajie

Chang... Jie

Forbidden City (Palace Museum)

Tongzi

Beichizi Dajie

Donghuamer...

6

Damucangdian Xiang

Beiyin Hutong

Xiden Market

Taipusi Jie

Damucang

Xinhuai

Minfeng Hutong

Piku Hutong

Xiaoshihu Hutong

Wuqongwei Hutong

Tangzi Hutong

Lixue Hutong

Bei'anli

China Millennium Monument, Military Museum

Wumen (Meridian Gate)

Nanchang

Taiyanie Hutong

Zhongshan Park

Park of the People's Culture

Belwan

Nanchizi

Nanhai

Fuxingmennei Dajie

Xinhuamen

Xinhua Gate

Tian'anmen Gate (Gate of Heavenly Peace)

Chang...

Former Imperial Archive

Sun Yat-sen Park

Xichang'an Jie

Xidanshoupa

Xidan

Canzhang Xiang

Jiaoyu Jie

Xi'anfu Hutong

Beixinping Hutong

Nanxinping Hutong

Tian'anmen West

Dong'anfu Hutong

Shibei Hutong

Beijing Concert Hall

National Grand Theatre (Xinhua) Hall

Rendahuitangxi

Renmin Dahui Tang (Great Hall of the People)

Dongchang'an Jie

Tian'anmen East

National Museum of China

7

Shoushuhe Hutong

Zhongyi Hutong

Toufa

Xirongxian Hutong

Xijiulianzi

Xixinlianzi Hutong

Youdang Hutong

Nancuihua Jie

Weiying

Dongrongxian Hutong

Donglilullanzi Hutong

Houxiwachang Hutong

Gaobei Hutong

Tian'anmen Square

Monument to the People's Heroes

Xinbi Hutong

Xinzhong Hutong

Xisongshu Hutong

Xijiaomin Xiang

Dongsongshu Hutong

Nian'er Hutong

Dongjiaomin Xiang

Xindalu

Mao Zhuxi Jinian Tang (Chairman Mao Memorial Hall)

Zhengyangmen (Qianmen Gate)

Beijing Police Museum

Xuanwumenxi Dajie

Xuanwumen

Xuanwumendong Dajie

Qianmenxi Dajie

Qianmendong

Baiyunguan (White Cloud Temple), Marco Polo Bridge

Hepingmen

Hepingmenwaidong Jie

Qianmenxiheyan Jie

Qianmenxiheyan Jie

Qianmen

Qianmenxiheyan

Beijing Planning Exhibition Hall

Chongwenmenxiheyan

8

Xianluyingtou Tiao

Ertiao

Langluying 4 Tiao

Dazhiqiao

...Tiao

Jiaochang 3 4 5 Tiao

Haibai Hutong

Shejia Hutong

Da'er Hutong

Paizi Hutong

Langfangtou Tiao

Langfang 2 Tiao

Qian Xiang Yi Silk Store

Gongzi

Qian Xiang Yi Silk Store

Ruifuxiang Silk Store

Xidamochang

Chuanganglang

Guanging

Jie

Xianyukou

Songtanzhi Museum of Traditional Folk Carving

Sanjing Hutong

Yaowu Hutong

Cha'er Hutong

Tiaozhou Hutong

Tan'er Hutong

Qudeng Hutong

Yangmeizhuxie Jie

Taitou Xiang

Dashalan

Dashilan Jie

Dajiia Hutong

Wangpi Hutong

Dailiang

3 Tiao

Daxi Hutong

Xuanwumenwai Dajie

Tiemen

Xicaochang Jie

Qiansungongyuan Hutong

Liuli Xiang

Liulichangxi Jie

Liulichangdong Jie

Liangjiayuanbei Hutong

Shitou

Zhumati

Zhongxuxie Jie

Meishi

Shijia Hutong

Yunju Hutong

Peizhi Hutong

Peiying

Hutong

Buxiangzi Hutong

Binglaoxie Jie

Qinglong Hutong

Ox Street Mosque

Manhua 7 Tiao

Liangjiayuan Hutong

Hanjia Hutong

Baishun Hutong

Dongbanbi

Dashi

Xiaoshidiao Jie

Luomashi Dajie

Zhushikouxi Dajie

Xiaowelying Hutong

Yao'er Hutong

shanjiankou Jie

Tiantan

Caishikou

Beidaji Xiang

Nandaji Xiang

Bao'ansi Jie

Hu Guang Huiguan

Lazhu Hutong

Dachuan Hutong

Banzhang Hutong

Zhaozhuizi Hutong

Chuziying Hutong

Pucheshi Hutong

9

Houbingma Jie

Fuzhouguan

Qian'er Hutong

Xiangchang Lu

Huaren Jie

Renmin

Liuxue Lu

Jinxinx

Bingma Hutong

Jiala Hutong

Panla Hutong

Fenfangliuli

Fuzhouguangxin Hutong

Fuzhouganjian Jie

Wanming Lu

Yong'an Lu

Tianqiaoshizhangjie Jie

Fuchangjie Lu

Ertiao

Fuchangjie 3 Tiao

Zhongshuli

Nanhengxi Jie

Nanhengdong Jie

Shouchang Xijing

Xixing

Beiwei Lu

Luchangjietou Tiao

Luchangjie 2 Tiao

Xinnong Lu

Wutiao

Liutiao

Beijing Museum of Natural History

10

Rufuli

Xiaochan...dian

Nantang...dian

Zhucan Jie

Hongtumiao Hutong

Heyaochang Jie

Jintai Hutong

Nanhuabei Jie

Nanhuaxi Jie

Nanhuadong Jie

Taipingliey Xiang

Yaoba Hutong

Xinnong Jie

Nanwei Lu

Xiannongtan Jie

Tianxi Hutong

Zhaigong (Hall of Abstinence)

Taoranting Lu

Taiping Jie

Xiannongtan Temple

Yongdingmennei Dajie

Fukangli

Taoranting

Taoranting Park

A

B

C

Shaojiu Hutong
Xila Hutong
Dong'anmen Dajie
Canyu Hutong
Jinyu Hutong
Xitangzi Hutong
Ganmian Hutong
Xishicao Hutong
Dongshicao Hutong
Sul'anbo Hutong
Hongxing Hutong
Lumicang Hutong
Xiaoyabao Hutong
Dayabao Hutong
Yabao Lu

Pudu Temple
Caichang Hutong
Daruanfu Hutong
Datianshuijing Hutong
Meizha Hutong
Beishuaifu Hutong
Dongtangzi Hutong
Waijiaobu Jie
Zhaotangzi Hutong
Dayangyibin Hutong
Dongzongbu Hutong

Shuaifuyuan Hutong
Xizongbu Hutong
Xinkailu Hutong
Dingyin Hutong
Congyuantou Tiao

Dongdan 3 Tiao
Nanguanchang Hutong
Dongdan 2 Tiao
Beijige 4 Tiao
Beijige 3 Tiao
Beijige 2 Tiao
Beijigetou Hutong
Xifenglou Hutong

Jianguomen

JIANGUOMENNEI DAJIE

Wangfujing
Dongdan
Dongdan Park
Xibiaobei Hutong
Maxian Hutong
Xianyu Xiang
Beijingzhan 3 Xiang
Dongbiaobei Hutong
Huangtudayuan
Laoqianju

Guanxiangtai (Ancient Observatory)

Taijichangtou Tiao
Taijichang 2 Tiao
Taijichang 3 Tiao
Suzhou Hutong
Nanbabao Hutong
Hutong

BEIJINGZHANDONG JIE

Zhengyi Lu
Dahua
Chuanban
Hougou Hutong
Rougou Hutong

BEIJING RAILWAY STATION
Beijing Railway Station

Chout Hutong
Kuijiachang Hutong

Dongjiaomin Xiang

DAJIE
CHONGWENMENXI DAJIE
Chongwenmendongshuncheng Jie

Dongbianmen Tower

Ming Walls Cultural Relics Park

Qianmennanhe'an Jie
Dongdamochang
Xiyue Hutong
Jinmao Hutong
Dougu Hutong

Chongwenmen
Chongwenmendongheyan
Huashishangtou Tiao
Shang 2 Tiao
Shang 3 Tiao
Huashishang 4 Tiao

Donghouheyan
Huashizhongtou Tiao
Huashizhong 2 Tiao
Huashizhong 3 Tiao
Huashizhong 4 Tiao

Huashixiatou Tiao
Huashixia 2 Tiao
Huashixia 3 Tiao
Dong 4 Tiao

CHONGWENMENDONG DAJIE

Xixinglong Jie
Chongwenmencheng
Dongxinglong Jie
Xihuashi Dajie
Donghuashi Dajie

Caochangcheng Hutong
Hebochangxi
Dongchashi Hutong
Shantang Hutong
Shanhu Hutong
Gaoying Hutong
Xanghuan Hutong

Shoupa Hutong
Ganoyi Hutong
Yingzi Hutong
Jingzi Hutong
Jiankang Jie

Shangtangzi Hutong
Dongdecao Hutong
Zhuying Hutong
Xiatangzi Hutong
Xiatangdao Hutong
Zhongguoqiang Hutong
Tianlongdongli

Beijiaowen Hutong
Baiqiaotou Tiao
Donghuashixie Jie
Santiao
Baiqiao Dajie

ZHUSHIKOUDONG DAJIE
Jinxiutou Tiao
Ertiao
Santiao
Qinghua Jie

GUANGQUMENNEI DAJIE

Ciqikou
Mawelmao Hutong
Donglishiying Hutong
Xiangle Hutong

CHONGWEN
Dongxiaoshi
Xixiaoshi
Xiyuanzi
Longxugou Lu

Xitang Jie
Shatushan Jie
Dongtang Jie
Dongbi Jie
Congdianxi Jie
Sixiang

Ximi Xiang
Yangcao Jie
Yangding Hutong

Peixin Jie

XINGFU DAJIE

Xizhaosizhong Jie

Xingfu Xiang
Xingfubeili
Anhuabeili
Anhuananli
Annabei

Xingfu Lu

LU
TIANTAN LU

Fahuasi
Tiyuguanxi Lu
Yingfangxi Jie
Bigan Hutong
Juzhang Hutong
Beigangzi
Nangangzi Jie

Wenzhang Hutong

Fuguang Lu

Guangmingxi Lu
Guangmingzhong Jie
Ertiao

Double Ring Longevity Pavilion

Honggizo Market

Tiantandongmen
TIYUGUAN LU
Yingfangnan Jie
Nangangzi Jie

GUANGMING LU

Chinese Rose Garden

Qi'niandian (Qinian Hall)

TIANTANDONG LU
TIYUGUANXI LU

LONGTAN LU
Xingfu Dajie
Longtan Jie
Bateo
Qitiao
Liutiao
Wutiao

Tiantan Park (Temple of Heaven)

Huangqiong Yu (Imperial Vault of Heaven)

Beijing Amusement Park

Yuandushi Temple

D   E   F

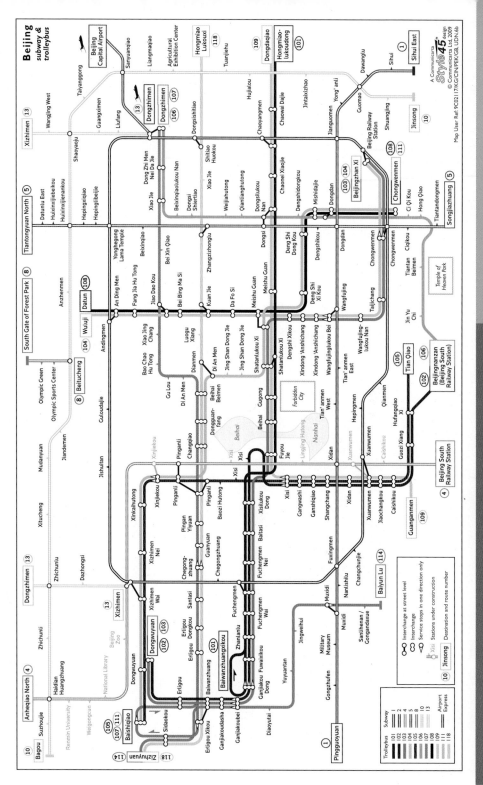

Beijing
subway &
trolleybus

A Communicarta
sty/e45 design
© Communicarta Ltd. 2009
Map User Ref: 9CO2117/KGf/CIN/PEK/GB, UDN/6b

INTRODUCTION

The favorite retreat of Qing dynasty emperors, the Summer Palace is China's largest imperial garden with classical landscape design; it is a UNESCO World Heritage Site attracting 6 million visitors a year.

Most visitors enter the Summer Palace (Yiheyuan) through the East Gate, where the main parking area and bus station are located. Ahead are the buildings of the former imperial court, including the splendid theater in the Garden of Virtue and Harmony and the private apartments of Dowager Empress Cixi and Emperor Guangxu. The celebrated Long Corridor skirts Kunming Lake. Pleasure cruises depart from the jetty near the *qingyanfang* (marble boat), or you can rent a rowboat or motorboat. To the rear of the lake is Longevity Hill, with more temples and palaces and spectacular views of the palace grounds. Suzhou Street, a recreated Ming dynasty shopping street, is of limited appeal—give it a miss if time is short.

Records indicate that there was a royal retreat on this site as early as the 13th century. In 1750 Emperor Qianlong, inspired by a visit to West Lake in Hangzhou, ordered the construction of the 'Garden of Clear Ripples,' the predecessor of the present palace, dedicating it to his mother. Ten thousand laborers were employed on the project, which took 14 years to complete. In 1860 Anglo-French forces burned the palace to the ground during the Second Opium War (▷ 30–31). The Dowager Empress Cixi paid for the rebuilding by diverting funds intended for the Imperial Navy through a spurious Naval Academy on Kunming Lake. She also gave the palace its present name, Garden of Peace and Harmony (Yiheyuan), in 1898, just two years before it was ransacked and destroyed for a second time by the Eight Western Powers, in retaliation for her covert support of the Boxer Rebellion (▷ 30). The palace was declared state property after the Communist Revolution in 1949 and opened to the public.

INFORMATION

✚ Off map 54 A1 ✉ Yiheyuan Lu, Haidian District ☎ 010 6288 1144
🕓 Apr 1–end Oct daily 6.30–6; Nov 1–end Mar daily 7–5 👜 Through ticket for all sights: adult 60RMB Apr 1–end Oct, 50RMB Nov 1–end Mar. Gate Ticket: 30RMB Apr 1–end Oct, 20RMB Nov 1–end Mar. Additional charges for some sites. Child under 1.2m (4ft) half price 🍴 Restaurant in Pavilion of Listening to Orioles (Imperial-style cuisine), tel 010 6288 1955/1608
🚇 Xizhimen and minibus 375 🚌 301, 303, 304, 332, 333, 346, 808, 826, 904
👜 Tour guides, audio guides, guidebooks available from all gates

Opposite *Changlang (Long Corridor) is a shaded walkway*
Above *A pleasure boat on Kunming Lake waiting for passengers*

TIPS

» The imperial family usually traveled to the Summer Palace by boat. Visitors can get a sense of that experience by taking the boat from Yuyuantan Park (summer only).

» The Summer Palace receives up to 100,000 visitors a day so crowds are to be expected. To avoid the worst of the crush, take a boat out on to the lake, or picnic on the grassy shoreline to the west, beyond Jade Belt Bridge.

» Buying the inexpensive Gate Ticket (which covers entrance to the grounds only) can be a false economy as it excludes admission to the Garden of Virtue and Harmony and the Tower of Buddhist Incense, two sights well worth seeing.

» The subway linking the city center with the Summer Palace had been completed at the time of writing but was yet to open. It is due to be unveiled in 2009 and will be by far the easiest way to visit.

Below A pavilion in the Garden of Harmonious Pleasures

WHAT TO SEE

HALL OF BENEVOLENT LONGEVITY

Effectively the seat of government during the last years of the imperial regime, it was here that the Dowager Empress Cixi dealt with affairs of state and gave audiences to foreign diplomats (wives were received more informally in the Hall of Joyful Longevity). Most of the furnishings are 19th century, including the exquisite screen behind the throne, made from red sandalwood and carved with protective dragons. Each of the 226 glass panels is engraved with a Chinese character indicating longevity. During the early years of Emperor Guangxu's reign, Cixi would sit behind the screen and offer him advice; later she dispensed with the charade and occupied the throne herself. The hall takes its name from a saying of Confucius: 'He who rules benevolently will enjoy a long life.' In the forecourt, look out for the fearsome bronze statue of a kylin, a mythological beast with a dragon's head, a lion's tail and the antlers of a deer. It was said to offer protection from fire.

GARDEN OF VIRTUE AND HARMONY

A 'must see' to the north of the Hall of Benevolent Longevity (look for the separate turnstile and the ticket sellers in period costume) is the Dowager Empress' private theater, built in 1894 to mark her approaching 60th birthday. The stage is a huge three-tiered structure, 21m (69ft) high and 27m (88.5ft) wide. The floors and ceilings were fitted with winches and trapdoors for special effects, while underneath ponds were constructed to improve the acoustics. Cixi, a Beijing opera buff, watched the performances from a carved seat in the Hall of Nurtured Joy opposite. The Dressing House contains a small exhibition of costumes, props and other theatrical paraphernalia; here too is Cixi's Mercedes-Benz, the first car to be imported into China. It was a present from the warlord and subsequent dictator Yuan Shikai.

HALL OF JOYFUL LONGEVITY

The Hall of Joyful Longevity, the lakeside residence of the Dowager Empress from 1889 to 1908, served as bedroom, dressing room, dining room and reception area. The blue porcelain dishes on either side of the carved dining table were filled with fruit to add fragrance when Cixi was entertaining visitors. Copper incense burners performed the same function. The central chandelier was imported from Germany and fitted with electric lights, the first in China. Visitors can peer in at the opulent interiors of the flanking chambers to see many of Cixi's personal belongings—look out for the exquisite marble clock on her night table. In the Hall of Forever Longevity next door is a small exhibition devoted to the palace eunuchs who attended her.

HALL OF JADE RIPPLES

The Hall of Jade Ripples was the palace of the Emperor Guangxu and his consort. It was here, in 1898, that he and his reform-minded advisors planned the decrees aimed at modernization and bringing China into the international mainstream. This 100 Days movement ended abruptly when Cixi discovered what was afoot. Six of the Emperor's associates were beheaded without further ado, while Guangxu himself was placed under house arrest for the last 10 years of his life. To prevent escape a perimeter wall was erected and all rear exits to his apartments sealed. Guangxu's bedroom and study have been preserved as he left them and serve as a poignant commentary on his thwarted ambitions. Among his possessions is a rosewood desk, the glass top painted with landscapes in a mixture of Asian and Western styles.

LONG CORRIDOR

The longest structure of its kind in the world (728m/ 2,277ft), the covered walkway at the foot of Longevity Hill is simply breathtaking. Each of its 273

bays opens like a window onto Kunming Lake with spectacular views, but it is the artwork, restored in 2004 at a cost of 100 million RMB ($12.7 million) that is the main draw. Every frame, cross-beam and ceiling panel is embellished with paintings, so that strolling along the corridor feels like visiting an art gallery. Take your time to enjoy the landscapes, mythological scenes, flora and fauna as they unfold before you, more than 8,000 miniature works of art in all.

KUNMING LAKE

Conceived as a counterpoint to Longevity Hill, Kunming Lake covers more than three quarters of the total area of the park. Dikes were built to divide it into three distinct entities, each with its own manmade island. Near the jetty west of Longevity Hill is the *Qingyanfang*, the 36m-long (118ft) marble paddle-steamer commissioned by Cixi in 1893. South of the Hall of Benevolent Longevity is the beautifully proportioned Seventeen-Arch-Bridge, its pilasters decorated with 544 stone lions, each carved with its own distinctive features. The bridge is guarded by a bronze ox (a long-established, potent symbol in China to ward off floods) and connects the aptly named Spacious Pavilion with Southern Lake Island, a verdant hideaway shrouded with pines and cypresses. Emperors came here to worship in the Dragon King Temple. Visitors can cross Kunming Lake by ferry or take one of the wooded paths around the perimeter.

Above *The corridor and courtyard of the Hall of Jade Ripples*

LONGEVITY HILL

This manmade hill harmonizes with the mountains to the northwest of Beijing, while its temples and palaces, grouped in ascending tiers, provide a majestic backdrop to the lake below. The ascent begins beyond the two ceremonial gateways at a point roughly halfway along the Long Corridor. Directly ahead is the double courtyard of the Hall of Dispelling Clouds. One of the few buildings to escape destruction by foreign armies, it was used just once a year to celebrate the birthday of the Empress, a tradition begun in Emperor Qianlong's day and culminating in 1904 with the 70th anniversary of Cixi's birth. Most of the objects displayed are birthday gifts, including an arresting oil painting of the Dowager Empress by Dutch-American artist Hubert Vos. Longevity Hill's principal landmark, the 41m-high (135ft) Tower of Buddhist Incense, is well worth the climb for the superb views across the lake.

MORE TO SEE

GARDEN OF HARMONIOUS INTERESTS

This delightful garden was laid out in the 18th century at the behest of Emperor Qianlong. It was designed to reflect the changing seasons, with lotus blossoms to the fore in summer, weeping willows in autumn and snowfall in winter. Of the eight scenic viewpoints, don't miss Know-the-Fish Bridge and Jade Violin Gorge, where the water splashing on the rocks is meant to imitate the sound of music.

WANCHENG GALLERY

The palace's priceless collection of artistic treasures is on view in the exhibition halls of the Courtyard of Literary Prosperity (turn left at the main palace entrance). The displays include gold- and silverware, bronzes, jade, porcelain, jewelry and furniture. Also worth seeing is the exhibition on daily life in the Qing Court. Separate admission charge: adult 20RMB, child under 1.2m (4ft) free.

Below *The Seventeen-Arch-Bridge over Kunming Lake*

KEEPING IT IN THE FAMILY

Yelu Chucai (1189–1243), chief minister of Mongol ruler Genghis Khan, and his son Yelu Zhu (1230–85) are buried in a pavilion on the shores of Kunming Lake. These tombs confirm that the site had been occupied off and on for at least eight centuries.

POWER BEHIND THE THRONE

Cixi's rise to power owed much to the fact that she alone of the Emperor Xianfeng's concubines provided him with a male heir. When the emperor died unexpectedly in 1861, Cixi was appointed regent for his five-year old successor, Tongzhi, and later, for her nephew, Guangxu. Skillful political maneuvering (and a degree of ruthlessness) enabled her to hold on to the reins of power until her death in 1908. Rightly or wrongly, Cixi's name has become synonymous with the corruption and decline of the Qing dynasty, which finally petered out just a few years after her death. Her support of the Boxer Rebellion (▷ 30) provoked the anger of the Eight Western Powers and led to the destruction of the Forbidden City and the Summer Palace.

Above *Rooftops and view across Kunming Lake with the Seventeen-Arch-Bridge and skyscrapers of Beijing in the distance*

Above *The ruins of the Oceanic Banquet Hall in the grounds of the Old Summer Palace*

OLD SUMMER PALACE

Yuanmingyuan (the Garden of Perfection and Brightness) was a popular royal summer retreat as far back as the 15th century. In 1723 Emperor Yongzheng began the ambitious building that would eventually earn the palace its reputation as 'the Chinese Versailles.' Jesuit missionary architects created a wonderland of baroque and rococo palaces, pavilions, gazebos and follies, while the grounds were modeled on the gardens of southern China. During the Second Opium War British and French forces destroyed the buildings and looted the contents. Models give visitors an idea of what the palace must once have looked like. The grounds have been re-landscaped and are a good place to head for a picnic.

🚇 Off map 54 A1 ✉ 28 Qinghua Xila, Haidian District (2km/1mile east of the Summer Palace) ☎ 010 6262 8501 🕐 Apr–end Oct daily 7–6.30; Nov–end Mar daily 7–5.30 💰 Combined ticket (palace museum and park): adult 25RMB. Park only: adult 10RMB. Child under 1.2m (4ft) free

🚇 Xizhimen, then minibus 375 🍴 Snack stands/cafeteria may be closed in winter ❓ To reach the ruins from the main gate takes at least 25 minutes on foot. Take one of the motorized buggies to get there more quickly

CHINA MILLENNIUM MONUMENT

www.bj2000.org.cn (in Chinese)
What at first looks like an enormous futuristic sculpture is actually a revolving sundial, 28m (92ft) high and 85m (279ft) in diameter. The monument opened in October 2000 to mark National Day and was designed with the Temple of Heaven and other ancient altars as astrological reference points. It also functions as an open-air stage and incorporates an art museum and a multi-media exhibition hall. Climb the steps to the needle for panoramic views of Beijing.

🚇 Off map 56 A7 ✉ 9A Fuxing Lu, Haidian District ☎ 010 6851 3322 🕐 Monument: 9–6. Art Museum: Apr 15–Oct 7 daily 8–6; Oct 8–Apr 14 daily 9–5 💰 Monument (with Art Museum): adult 30RMB, child under 1.2m (4ft) free 🍴 Café in Monument opens irregularly; cafés/refreshment stands in park ❓ The art museum puts on temporary exhibitions and international shows

MILITARY MUSEUM

The Military Museum (Junshibowuguan), a monument to the achievements of the Chinese People's Liberation Army, is a huge building. In the echoing vestibule are more-than-life-size statues of military strategists, among paintings of battle scenes. The vaulted first-floor Weapons Hall has an impressive array of military hardware, from tanks and jet fighters to satellites and missile launchers. On the third floor is the Hall of Ancient Wars with an array of replica weapons. Before you leave, visit the excellent museum shop.

🚇 Off map 56 A7 ✉ 9 Fuxing Lu, Haidian District ☎ 010 6686 6244 🕐 Daily 8–5.30 💰 Adult 20RMB, child under 1.2m (4ft) free. Extra 5RMB to see frigate 🚇 Junshibowuguan 🍴 Cafeteria

WHITE CLOUD TEMPLE

The oldest Taoist temple in Beijing, the White Cloud Temple (Baiyungan) was founded in the Tang dynasty (8th century). The Taoist religion (an offshoot of the philosophy) worships a host of divinities, chief among them the founder, Lao Zi. The largest prayer hall commemorates the sage, Founder Qiu. Perhaps the finest artwork in the temple is *Founder Qiu's Visit to the West*. Look out too for stone carvings of Taoist symbols.

✚ Off map 56 A7 ✉ 6 Baiyunguan Jie, Xibianmenwai, Xuanwu District ☎ 010 6346 3531 🕐 Daily 8.30–4 ✋ Adult 10RMB, child under 1.2m (4ft) free 🚇 Nanlishi Lu

OX STREET MOSQUE

Beijing's oldest mosque was founded in AD996. There are still halal markets on Ox Street. You may be surprised by the architecture of the mosque, which appears to differ little from a typical temple. On closer inspection, however, you will find verses from the Koran and other Arabic motifs on the capitals and pillars.

✚ Off map 56 A9 ✉ 18 Niujie, Xuanwu District ☎ 010 6353 2564 🕐 Daily 7–7. Non-Muslims are excluded from the Prayer Hall during services ✋ Adult 10RMB (free for Muslims), child under 11 years free 🚇 Changchunjie, then bus 10 🍴 *Halal* restaurants on Niujie ❓ Visitors must dress appropriately (no shorts, short skirts or sleeveless shirts and blouses)

ANCIENT COIN MUSEUM

Take a fascinating tour of the 4,000-year history of Chinese currency. The exhibition, in a Ming dynasty watchtower, occupies rooms around the main courtyard. An additional exhibition of ancient military equipment is on the second level but requires an additional 10RMB. Captions and explanations in English describe the technology of coin production before introducing the earliest exhibits. Coins were made from seashells, bone and jade before the currency was unified under the Han (2nd century BC). The Deshengmen Tower is also home to the Beijing East Gallery, which you can visit en route to the top for panoramic views of the city.

✚ 54 A1 ✉ Deshengmen Jian Lou Bei'erhuan Zhong Lu, Xicheng District ☎ 010 6201 8073 🕐 Tue–Sun 9–4 ✋ Adult 10RMB, child under 1.2m (4ft) free 🚇 Jishuitan, then walk east 🍴 Snacks and beverages sold on roof of tower

FORMER RESIDENCE OF SONG QINGLING

This rambling Qing dynasty mansion was built in the 19th century for Prince Chun, the father of Puyi, China's last emperor. In 1963 the Communist government presented it to Song Qingling (1893–1981), wife of the first President of the Republic, Sun Yat-sen; she lived here until her death 18 years later. Song Qingling was educated in Shanghai and the United States before returning to China and marrying Sun in 1915. During the Civil War she was a fierce critic of her brother-in-law, the Nationalist leader Chiang Kaishek (▷ 32), and remained loyal to the Communists. After the Revolution she was awarded the honorary title of Vice-President. An exhibition chronicles her life, while several rooms remain as she left them.

✚ 54 B1 ✉ 46 Houhaibeiyan, Xicheng District ☎ 010 6404 4205 🕐 Apr 1–Oct 31 daily 9–5; Nov 1–Mar 31 daily 9–4 ✋ Adult 20RMB, child under 1.2m (4ft) free 🚇 5, 305 🍴 Cafés in nearby Houhai

GONGWANGFU (PRINCE GONG'S RESIDENCE)

This 18th century *siheyuan* (▷ 82) mansion re-opened, after a two-year restoration, in 2008. Its most famous occupant, Prince Gong (1832–98), helped persuade Great Britain to assist in suppressing the Taiping Rebellion in 1861 (▷ 31), saving the Qing dynasty from collapse. You will need a guide to tour the house, as there are few explanations in English. Or settle for the tranquil classical Chinese garden, with its elaborate gateways, shady pavilions, rock gardens and carp ponds. If you can, join a group tour and visit the Prince's Grand Theatre for a performance of Beijing opera.

✚ 54 B2 ✉ 14 Liuyin Jie/ Qianhaixi Jie, Xicheng District ☎ 010 6616 8149 🕐 Daily 8–5 ✋ Adult 20RMB, child under 1.2m (4ft) free 🚇 107, 111, 118 🍴 Sichuan Fandian restaurant on Liuyin Jie ❓ Guided tours available from entrance. Daily acrobatic shows

Below *The lovely garden of the Former Residence of Song Qingling*

INFORMATION

54 B4   1 Wenjin Jie, Xicheng District   010 6403 1102   Park: Jun–end Aug daily 6am–8pm; Sep–end Oct and Apr–end May daily 6am–9pm; Nov–end Mar daily 6.30am–8pm. Sights: daily 9–4   Park only: adult Apr–end Oct 10RMB; Nov–end Mar 5RMB, child under 1.2m (4ft) free. Park and access to all sights: adult 20RMB, child under 1.2m (4ft) free   5, 13, 101, 103, 107, 109, 111   Fangshan Restaurant   Kiosks in the park

INTRODUCTION

Prized by Beijingers for its fabulous classical gardens, historic pavilions and open spaces, Beihai Gongyuan (Beihai Park) is the city's largest park, older still than the Forbidden City.

The main entrance is on Wenjin Jie and leads directly to the main points of interest, Round City and Jade Island. A ferry will take you from the island to the classical Chinese gardens behind the Five-Dragon Pavilion that are also worth seeing. North Lake takes up more than half the area of the park, and is its other main attraction. Rowboats and duck-shaped paddleboats are available for rent from the dock near Round City. Before setting off to explore the park, get your bearings from the ceramic tile map by the East Gate.

Kublai Khan, founder of the Yuan dynasty in 1271, built a palace on Jade Island, the heart of his new capital, Dadu. The grounds included a huge tract of open land to the south, still known as Zhongnanhai (literally meaning 'middle-south lake'). The building of pavilions, temples and gardens continued throughout the Ming and Qing dynasties, notably under the Emperor Qianlong (1736–96). Beihai was opened to the public in 1925 but not Zhongnanhai, and became the seat of government under Mao Zedong and his successors.

WHAT TO SEE

JADE ISLAND (QIONG DAO)

Dominating Jade Island is the White Dagoba (Baita), Beihai's most famous monument and the focal point of the Yong'ansi (Temple of Eternal Peace). Resembling a giant hand-bell, the 36m-high (130ft) Tibetan shrine to Buddha was built to honor the first Dalai Lama to visit China in 1651. It was badly damaged by an earthquake 90 years later, and rebuilt. Visitors are not allowed inside but can climb the hill for fabulous views of Jingshan Park and Zhongnanhai, the area of land to the south of the park.

Above *The Five-Dragon Pavilion was built in the Ming dynasty at Beihai Park in Beijing*

ROUND CITY

Near the main entrance to Beihai Park is an artificial island formed from earth excavated from the lake. The pavilion in the courtyard was built to exhibit Beihai's most precious relic, the jar crafted from a single block of jade and weighing 3.5 tons that was presented to Kublai Khan in 1265. Emperors of the Ming and Qing dynasties watched fireworks from the Hall of Receiving Light, where pride of place belongs to the jade Buddha presented by the rulers of Burma (Myanmar) to the Dowager Empress Cixi. Some pines and cypresses in Round City are up to 800 years old.

MIND-CULTIVATING STUDY

The gardens at the northern end of the park were laid out in the 18th century during the reign of Emperor Qianlong. Do not miss the Mind-Cultivating Study (Jingxinzai), intended, as the name suggests, for contemplation and quiet seclusion. Imitating a classical Chinese landscape painting, its twisting paths meander through woods and rock gardens, lily ponds and streams, gazebos and painted corridors. Also worth seeking out is the Sukhvati garden, presented by Qianlong to his mother on her birthday in 1770. Here is the largest square pavilion in China and a fabulous sculptural representation of the Buddhist-inspired Western Paradise legend, for which the temple is named.

MORE TO SEE

YONG'ANSI

In their enthusiasm to see the White Dagoba, many visitors to Jade Island overlook the Temple of Eternal Peace itself. Painstakingly restored during the 1990s, the splendid halls, grouped in terraces on the hillside, contain prayer wheels and other objects of religious ritual, dazzling artwork and an array of Buddhas (the grinning Matreya Buddha in the Zhengjue Hall is the pick of the bunch). The ceramic dragons which decorate the roofs of the temple are best appreciated from the Lookout Pavilion on the second terrace.

NINE-DRAGON SCREEN

In the northwest corner of the park is the famous Nine-Dragon Screen. One of only four in China (there is another in the Forbidden City, ▷ 77), it was designed during the Ming dynasty to ward off evil spirits and is composed of more than 400 glazed tiles. Down by the jetty is the Five-Dragon Pavilion, where emperors came to fish or camp out.

TIPS

» Founded in 1925, the Fangshan Restaurant in the Hall of Rippling Waters (tel 010 6401 1889; daily 11–1.30, 5–8) serves imperial cuisine, including recipes prepared for the Dowager Empress Cixi in the 19th century. To get there from the main entrance, cross to Jade Island and follow the path to the right along the painted corridor.

» From Tian'anmen Square, hop on the No. 5 bus near Tiananmenxi metro and it will take you to the park's main gate.

From left to right *Strolling down a tree-lined path in Beihai Park; the White Dagoba on Jade Island*

INFORMATION

www.dpm.org.cn

54 C5 ⊠ Xichang'an Jie, Dongcheng District ☎ 010 8511 7311 Apr 16 –end Oct daily 8.30–5; Oct–end Apr daily 8.30–4.30. Adult 60RMB Apr 16–Oct 15, 40RMB Oct 16–Apr 15, child under 1.2m (4ft) free, additional charges for some exhibitions Tiananmenxi, Tiananmendong Starbucks; Emperor's Kitchen canteen in Exhibition Area Visitor Information office, shop, post office, Olympics souvenir stand and toilets in the Exhibition Area (east side)

Above *View of Senwu gate and the red and golden rooftops of the Forbidden City*
Opposite *The Hall of Supreme Harmony (Taihedian)*

INTRODUCTION

The Forbidden City was the residence of emperors and the center of Chinese civilization for more than 500 years. The Palace Museum (Gugong) is China's most popular tourist attraction.

The main entrance to the Forbidden City, a UNESCO World Heritage Site, is through the Tian'anmen Gate (beneath the portrait of Mao Zedong). The ticket office is on your left, just in front of the Meridian Gate. The most important sights lie on a straight-line axis as far as the gardens and the north exit at the Gate of Military Prowess (opposite Jingshan Park). Most of the exhibition halls are to the east (follow the signs in front of the Gate of Heavenly Purity). Also here is the best stocked of the museum shops, a visitor information center and toilets. The halls to the east and west of the main route are generally less congested and there are better opportunities to see interiors close up. Peace and quiet are at a premium anywhere in the Forbidden City; your best bet is the Emperor Qianlong's garden on the east side. An ambitious $185 million restoration program will not be completed until 2020, so some disruption is to be expected.

The Forbidden City was built between 1406 and 1420, during the reign of the Ming emperor Yongle. Its construction was a stupendous undertaking, involving one million laborers, 100,000 craftsmen, and vast quantities of building materials. On completion it was the largest palace complex in the world, covering a total area of 720,000sq m (856,800sq yards). Fires wreaked havoc on countless occasions, the first only 100 days after Emperor Yongle moved in. Further destruction occurred in 1644, when the Manchus descended on the city, but over the following 150 years, the Qing rulers more

than made amends, restoring and refurbishing the existing halls and palaces while undertaking an ambitious building program of their own. In 1900, when the Forbidden City was occupied by the Eight Nation Alliance during the Boxer Rebellion (▷ 30), Emperor Guangxu and the Dowager Empress Cixi were forced to flee; they returned a year later. The last Qing emperor, Puyi, was finally driven out in 1924 and the following year the Forbidden City opened its doors to the public as the Palace Museum.

WHAT TO SEE

HALL OF SUPREME HARMONY (TAIHEDIAN)

Beyond the Meridian Gate visitors enter the vast Outer Court, in imperial times the main reception area and the center of the palace administration. The Taihedian (Hall of Supreme Harmony), the largest and most important building here, was reserved for major ceremonies and rituals, such as coronations, royal weddings, birthdays and the Chinese New Year. It is still the largest timber structure in China and the columns supporting the roof, each carved from a single tree trunk, are decorated with dragons, as is the coffered ceiling and the screen behind the gilded sandalwood throne. Tung oil was used to add lustre to the polish on the floor tiles, actually made of gold. On the veranda you can see some of the bells and chime stones that rang out as the emperor ascended the throne. The Hall is raised on a three-tiered marble terrace to add grandeur and increase visibility. The central ramp was for the emperor's exclusive use. To the right is a sundial, symbolizing the continuity of empire, while the copper grain measure, on the left, signifies justice and impartiality. Placed at intervals along the platform are 18 incense burners, one for each of China's provinces. The bronze cranes and tortoises, symbols of longevity, performed the same function, while the huge iron vats were for storing water in case of fire.

Above left to right *A bronze lioness guarding the Gate of Supreme Harmony; the Dragon Throne in the Hall of Supreme Harmony*

HALL OF MIDDLE HARMONY (ZHONGHEDIAN)

The Hall of Middle Harmony, the smallest of the three halls in the Outer Court, was the emperor's robing room. At other times, it served as an office and was used for routine audiences. On either side of the satin-covered throne are incense burners shaped like mythical beasts. These *luduan*, said to speak in tongues and to travel unimagined distances in a single day, hinted at the emperor's divine powers. The sedan chairs were for daily use; those used on ceremonial occasions were much grander.

HALL OF PRESERVING HARMONY (BAOHE)

Until the 18th century this magnificent building in the Outer Court served as a banqueting hall. Under the Emperor Yongzheng its function changed and it provided a suitably awesome setting for the final stages of the imperial civil service examinations. The emperor alone arbitrated, as the nerve-wracked candidates were subjected to a thorough grilling on the Confucian classics by the resident palace scholars. The marble 'dragon walk' leading down from the terrace at the back of the hall is not only a stunning work of art, but a major feat of engineering. It took 20,000 men and 1,000 horses a month to move the 180-ton block of marble 50km (31 miles) from the quarry to its permanent home. Wells were dug by the roadside so that icy water could be poured over the surface to smooth the way.

TIPS

» The living quarters of the Qing emperors, notably the Hall of Mental Cultivation on the east side and the Palace of Gathering Excellence on the west side, are worth tracking down if you are interested in 18th- and 19th-century decor and furnishings.

» Consult the website www.dpm.org.cn or ask at the visitors' office about the Forbidden City's temporary exhibitions, which are usually worth seeing.

» A guided tour is pricy (at least 250RMB). Better value is the audio guide.

Below *The grand marble terracing outside the Hall of Middle Harmony and the Hall of Preserving Harmony*

PALACES OF THE INNER COURTYARD

Pass through the Gate of Heavenly Purity to enter the private domain of China's Ming dynasty rulers (the Qing preferred the palaces to the east and west). The Palace of Heavenly Purity was where the emperor retired for the night, where he was laid out in state after his death and where the casket containing the name of his chosen successor was concealed. A drama unfolded here in 1542, when one of Emperor Jiaqing's concubines, driven to despair by his sadistic beatings, led a conspiracy to murder him in his sleep. The young women tried to throttle him with a silk cord but the knot slipped and he woke up. With typical savagery, Jiaqing ordered the public execution and dismemberment of all sixteen conspirators.

The neighboring Hall of Union and Peace served as the empress' throne room while the Palace of Earthly Tranquility was where the Ming empresses had their sleeping quarters. Under the Qing these rooms were used only on wedding nights and honeymoons. The wedding chamber itself is decked out in red, considered lucky in China, and the silk curtains around the bed are embroidered with figures of children at play. Note the Chinese character for 'double happiness' on the doors, still associated with weddings today. The palace also served as a shrine to the Buddhist kitchen god Tsao Chun, revered by Qing emperors. On the 23rd day of the 12th lunar month, when it was believed that the god flew to heaven to report on the state of the nation, the emperor would offer sacrifice here to the noisy accompaniment of fireworks, drums and raucous singing.

IMPERIAL GARDEN

The palace garden comes as a surprise, being refreshingly intimate in scale and more reminiscent of the private retreat of a Ming dynasty nobleman than of an emperor. The focal point is the Hall of Imperial Peace, a temple dedicated to the Taoist water-god Zhenwu, who offered protection against fire, a perennial hazard in the palace. Equally captivating are the Pavilion of Ten Thousand Springs, with its exquisite ceiling and painted eaves, and the Hill of Accumulated Beauty, a miniature mountain surmounted by a delightful pavilion. From this vantage point, concubines could peer over the wall to snatch a glimpse of life outside the restrictions and confines of the Forbidden City. Before you leave the gardens, take a closer look at the pavement mosaics depicting Chinese folk tales and scenes from nature.

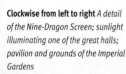

Clockwise from left to right *A detail of the Nine-Dragon Screen; sunlight illuminating one of the great halls; pavilion and grounds of the Imperial Gardens*

PALACE OF ETERNAL HARMONY

Here you will find one of the palace museum's most diverting exhibitions, on the daily life of concubines in the Qing dynasty. The collection of personal effects includes everything from ceremonial robes and headdresses to snuff bottles and spittoons. You can see samples of their embroidery, the lacquered teapots they entertained with and Chinese chess sets for whiling away the time. Among the highlights are a sedan chair and bed belonging to the Concubine Jin, a favorite of Emperor Guangxu. The emperors' concubines were selected every three years from girls aged between 13 and 17 exclusively from families in Manchuria, the emperors' homeland (it was forbidden for Qing dynasty emperors to take a Han Chinese wife). They were divided into eight ranks, from Imperial Honorable to Concubine-in-waiting but, as the exhibition makes clear, all lived a privileged life, even after child-bearing age, when the majority were retired.

HALL OF ANCESTOR WORSHIP

As the name suggests, this magnificent hall, with a stunning painted ceiling worth seeing in its own right, is where the emperor offered ritual sacrifices to his ancestors. It now houses the Clock Gallery, one of the Palace Museum's most popular exhibitions. There are more than 1,000 timepieces on display, the majority from China, Great Britain and France. Clocks were produced in the imperial workshops of the Forbidden City, in Suzhou and in Guangzhou, where mechanical clocks were introduced into China. Among the eye-catching exhibits is an ingeniously contrived Chinese water clock (the largest in the country) commissioned by Emperor Jiaqing in 1799. For most visitors, though, it is not size that impresses but the exquisite workmanship of the artisans.

Above *The Dragon Walkway leads to the Gate of Heavenly Purity*

On these incredibly elaborate timepieces butterflies flutter their wings, lotus buds burst forth, waterfalls flow and monkeys perform the kowtow. Demonstrations are held twice daily, usually at 11am and 4pm; if you are not around at these times, stay to watch the film, which shows a selection of clocks strutting their stuff. The commentary is in Chinese only but most of what you see is self-explanatory.

MORE TO SEE

THE TREASURE HALLS
Three large halls on the eastern side of the Forbidden City display a mere fraction of the palace's priceless collection of artistic treasures, including gold and silverware, jewelry, porcelain, jade carvings, costumes and royal regalia. Among the exhibits are an imperial seal weighing an astonishing 17kg (37.5 lbs), a 1.4m-high (4.5ft) tower containing 150kg (330 lbs) of gold, made to hold the hair of Emperor Qianlong's mother, and the Phoenix Crown worn by Emperor Wanli's wife Xiaoduan (1573–1620), inlaid with 5,000 pearls and 150 precious stones.

NINE-DRAGON SCREEN
This stunning work of art from the reign of the Emperor Qianlong (1736–95), 31m (101ft) long and 6m (19.5ft) high, was made using 270 glazed bricks. The nine imperial dragons are depicted splashing through a foamy sea. The screen served a dual purpose, providing the emperor with a degree of privacy while also fending off evil spirits who, it was thought, could only travel in straight lines.

PAVILION OF SPREADING RIGHTEOUSNESS
In this pavilion, west of the Hall of Supreme Harmony, is a trailblazing exhibition on Court Ritual and Music in the Qing dynasty. For the first time, you get to hear what the music played on occasions like the winter solstice actually sounded like (the performances have been painstakingly reconstructed from books and court manuals).

MERIDIAN GATE
The Meridian Gate (Wumen) was the most important of the four entrances to the Forbidden City. Here the emperor reviewed his troops, passed judgment on prisoners of war, and presented the New Year calendar to his officials. Today the hall is used for exhibitions and you can climb the tower.

ZHENFEI'S WELL
The daughter of a court official, Zhenfei became Emperor Guangxu's favorite wife. Pretty, vivacious and ambitious, she got on the wrong side of the Dowager Empress Cixi by meddling in politics. When the Boxer Rebellion broke out, Cixi decided to flee Beijing and insisted on taking the Emperor with her. Furious with Zhenfei for standing in her way (so the story goes), Cixi ordered her eunuchs to get rid of her. She was drowned in the well that now bears her name.

FENG SHUI
The Forbidden City was laid out according to the principles of *feng shui*—a belief that buildings can be arranged to maximize the flow of chi or positive life energy, bringing good luck. The palace was aligned on a north–south axis with the polar star, thought to be the heart of the universe. The ground plan is in the shape of a square to represent the earth, with the emperor at the center. To meet another requirement, 'mountain behind, water in front,' a moat was dug and an artificial hill created in Jingshan Park. All these cosmological calculations seemed to count for nothing when the three main halls burned down in 1421.

TIAN'ANMEN SQUARE

Above *The Monument to the People's Heroes, illuminated at night*

INFORMATION
✚ 56 C7

INTRODUCTION

The largest public square in the world, Tian'anmen is usually filled with Chinese visitors to the sights, including the Tian'anmen Gate, Mao Zedong's mausoleum and the National Museum.

Tian'anmen Square (*Tian'anmen guangchang*) is vast: 800m (2,400ft) long and 500m (1,650ft) wide. Allow half a day to see all the sights. Remember when scheduling your visit that the Chairman Mao Memorial Hall is closed Mondays and every day from 11–2. The square is served by two metro stations, Tiananmenxi (west) and Tiananmendong (east). Both stations close during public holidays to ease congestion. There is also a metro station to the south of the square at Qianmen. Traffic flows freely around the perimeter of the square but parking can be a nightmare; the situation will ease with the opening of underground parking areas in around 2009 at the National Theatre and National Museum. There are no restaurants on the square but snacks are available from street carts or from the supermarket in Tian'anmen Shopping Center.

Tian'anmen Square has a short but eventful history. It was laid out in the 1950s as a symbol of Communist power and to mark the coming of age of the Chinese people. During the Cultural Revolution (1966–76), the square was the focus of mass rallies of up to a million Red Guards, chanting Mao's name and waving the 'little red book.' The economic liberalizations of Mao's successor Deng Xiaoping encouraged hopes for democratic reforms, but when these were not realized students took to the streets. In June 1989, following a three-month standoff, the tanks moved in, leading to the death of hundreds, possibly thousands, of protestors in the notorious Tian'anmen Square Massacre.

TIP
» Zhengyangmen Gate (daily 8.30–4), at the southern end of Tian'anmen Square, rivals the Gate of Heavenly Peace as a vantage point and is less expensive and less busy (lines are a rarity). Inside is an interesting exhibition of old photographs of Beijing and a shop selling souvenirs.

WHAT TO SEE

GATE OF HEAVENLY PEACE

At the northern end of Tian'anmen Square is the Gate of Heavenly Peace, from which the square takes its name. Access to the Forbidden City was so restricted in imperial times that even ministers had to wait outside on their knees while the emperor's edicts were lowered to them in a golden phoenix. It was from the podium above the entrance to the Gate that Chairman Mao announced the founding of the Communist State on October 1, 1949. A giant portrait of Mao (his image is rarely seen publicly today except on banknotes and in schools) still hangs here. The slogans on either side read 'Long live the Unity of the People of the World' and 'Long live the People's Republic of China.' In front of the gate, five marble bridges span Golden Water Stream (the palace moat). Also notice the two *huabiao*, decorative columns with dragon reliefs and *hou* squatting on the top. These mythological beasts were said to watch over the emperor when traveling and to call him back if he spent too long away from his duties.

✚ 56 C6 ✉ Chang'an Dajie, Dongcheng District ☎ 010 6309 5630 ◉ Mar–end Oct daily 8.30–4.30; Nov–end Feb daily 8.30–4 💰 Adult 15RMB, child under 1.2m (4ft) free. Ticket office on north side of gate, where bags should be deposited Ⓜ Tiananmendong

From left to right *The Arrow Tower on the Qianmen (Qian Gate); portrait of Mao Zedong at Tian'anmen Gate*

NATIONAL MUSEUM OF CHINA

www.nationalmuseum.cn

In 2007 work began on a 1.8 billion RMB ($217.7 million) revamp of the building dominating the eastern side of the square (formerly known as the Museum of Chinese History). By 2010, the new facilities will include 24 exhibition halls, a digital cinema, shops, research facilities and an underground parking area. The museum's fabulous collection of historical and cultural treasures is also in the process of reorganization but the rotating exhibition of pottery, porcelain, jade, bronzes, stone carving, lacquerware and burial armor is definitely worth seeing, as are the special exhibitions. The Wax Museum, with figures of Chinese celebrities such as actor Jackie Chan and basketball superstar Yao Ming (▷ 20–21), is of limited appeal to foreigners.

✚ 56 C7 ✉ 16 Dongchang'an Jie, Dongcheng District ☎ 010 6513 2801 (English service) 🕐 Jul 1–end August and public holidays daily 8–6 (last ticket 5); Sep–Jun daily 8.30–4.30 (last ticket 3.30). Major renovations are currently taking place. The museum was closed at the time of writing but due to re-open in 2010 💷 Adult 30RMB, child under 1.2m (4ft) free 🚇 Tiananmendong ❓ Visitors must leave bags with attendants before entering the building 🎧 Audio guide; volunteer guides currently being trained, will offer free tours

GREAT HALL OF THE PEOPLE (RENMIN DAHUI TANG)

Opposite the National Museum is the Great Hall of the People—home to the National People's Congress, China's highest legislative body. Amazingly it was completed in only 10 months, in 1959. The scale is truly monumental, the total floor area of 170,000sq m (203,000sq yards) exceeding that of the Forbidden City. Each of the 34 reception halls is designed to impress, with gilded marble pillars, crystal chandeliers and huge painted murals depicting China's cities and regions. In these lavish surroundings the country's political leaders entertain foreign heads of state. The guided tour includes the 5,000-seat banqueting hall, where President Nixon was fêted on his historic visit to China in 1972, and the Grand Theatre, where the Communist Party meets when in session. Note the red star on the ceiling, illuminated with 500 bulbs.

✚ 56 C7 ✉ Tian'anmen Square, Xuanwu District ☎ 010 6309 6156 🕐 Daily 8–4. Closed occasionally for government meetings, so phone ahead 💷 Adult 30RMB, child under 1.2m (4ft) free 🚇 Tiananmenxi 🎧 Guided tour available. You can visit the Great Hall on your own if, as is often the case, there is no English-speaking guide on hand

Below *Detail of the Revolutionary Statue that flanks the Chairman Mao Memorial Hall*

MONUMENT TO THE PEOPLE'S HEROES

The 38m-high (125ft) granite and marble column honors the dead of the Chinese revolution. Work on the project began immediately after the Communist takeover but dragged on until 1958. Around the column are quotes by Mao Zedong and the Prime Minister of the day, Zhou Enlai. Mao's is pithier and reads simply: 'Eternal Glory to the Nations' Heroes.' The bas-reliefs on the base record important events in the revolutionary struggle. One shows Chinese sailors setting fire to a consignment of opium brought in by the British in 1839, the incident that sparked off the First Opium War (▷ 31).

CHAIRMAN MAO MEMORIAL HALL

At the southern end of the square is the mausoleum of Mao Zedong, the 'Great Helmsman' as he was known in China. The Memorial Hall was built with volunteer labor and finished in record time—just a year after Mao's death in September 1976. Outside, a steady stream of visitors joins the orderly line as a voice from a loudspeaker gives instructions on etiquette. An atmosphere of hushed reverence pervades once you pass from the anteroom, with its heroic statue of the founder of modern China, into the dimly lit funeral hall, where the body lies preserved in its crystal coffin. Photographs are not allowed—you should leave your camera and bags in the office before you buy your ticket.
🕂 56 C7 ✉ Tian'anmen Square, Dongcheng District ☎ 010 6513 2277 🕓 Tue–Sun 8–12 🖐 Free but 10RMB charge for camera and bags, which must be deposited in office Ⓠ Qianmen

MORE TO SEE

NATIONAL CENTRE FOR THE PERFORMING ARTS

The National Grand Theatre on Xichang'an Jie is easily identified by its laminated glass and titanium roof, and is clearly visible from Tian'anmen Square. It is surrounded by a manmade lake and will boast an opera house, concert hall and a theater. Nicknamed the 'giant egg,' it has generated controversy for appearing out of step with its surroundings. It was designed by French architect Paul Andreu and built at a cost of 3.6 billion RMB—four times that of the Lincoln Center in New York.

Above *Tian'anmen Gate, with fan-shape water fountains*

AREAS WITH OLD OR ESPECIALLY WELL-PRESERVED *HUTONG*:

✛ 54 C2 ✉ Drum and Bell Towers (▷ right)

✛ 54 B–C2 ✉ Qianhai-Houhai

✛ Off map at 54 A3 ✉ North and south of Fuchengmennei Dajie

✛ 55 C2 ✉ Nanluoguxiang area

✛ 55 D1 ✉ West of the Temple of Confucius (▷ 91)

HUTONG

Stroll through these centuries-old alleyways for a fascinating insight into a communal lifestyle that is fast disappearing.

The word *hutong* dates back to the Yuan dynasty (13th century) and is derived from the Mongolian for 'well,' the traditional focal point of the village. By 1949 there were nearly 6,000 of these rambling lanes. The names often reveal something about their past: *liulichang* (tilemakers' alley), *lurou* (donkey-meat alley), *zaoshou* (date-tree alley). Some are truly labyrinthine, while others are tiny—only 10m (11 yards) long and as little as 40cm (15.5in) wide. During the Ming and Qing dynasties imposing residences called *siheyuan* ('four-sided courtyards') were built between the *hutong* for merchants, noblemen or high-ranking officials. Details, such as elaborately carved hitching posts and door piers, or ornamental brickwork, indicated the status of the original occupant.

LOOKING TO TOMORROW

The walled gardens survived until the Communist era, when most were subdivided to meet the growing demand for inexpensive communal housing. The future of the *hutong* and *siheyuan* is uncertain. Some courtyard houses, such as Gongwangfu (▷ 67), have been preserved as cultural monuments, while others are being restored and adapted for private or commercial use (an increasing number are hotels). While many residents complain about unsanitary conditions and overcrowding, others value the sense of community and comparative peace, typical features of *hutong* life.

Above *The courtyard of a house in the Doufuchi Hutong district*

BEIJING PLANNING EXHIBITION HALL

This vast exhibition space provides a fascinating insight into what the urban planners have in store for Beijing over the next few years. Head to the third floor and focus on the amazing 1:750 scale model of the city. The theme is the transformation of Beijing, with a virtual tour of the Forbidden City through its 500-year history and a photographic exhibition on the conservation of *hutong* and courtyard houses. The fourth floor showcases landmarks like Herzog and de Meuron's 91,000-seater Olympic Stadium, Rem Koolhaas's gravity-challenging CCTV building, and Sir Norman Foster's airport extension, the largest single construction project in the world.
✚ 56 C8 ✉ 20 Qianmendong Dajie, Chongwen District ☎ 010 6702 4559 🕓 Tue–Sun 9–5 (last tickets sold at 4) 💷 Adult 30RMB, child under 1.2m (4ft) free. Additional charge (10RMB) for 3D film theater, in Chinese and English 🚇 Qianmen

BEIJING POLICE MUSEUM

One of Beijing's more unusual museums occupies the imposing former premises of the National City Bank of New York. Behind the classical portico are four floors of exhibits, dating back to the Han dynasty and covering every aspect of police work. The intriguing historical displays include topics like 'Smashing Kuomintang Subversion' and the Cultural Revolution, denounced with surprising candor as a catastrophe. Among the 8,000 exhibits is a Jing dynasty tomb of a criminal and a bamboo chest cooler worn by a traffic policeman in the 1960s. There is also a video shooting range on the top floor.
✚ 56 C7 ✉ 36 Dongjiaomin Xiang, Dongcheng District ☎ 010 8522 5018 🕓 Tue–Sun 9–4 💷 Adult 5RMB, child free, student free. 20RMB for 2 laser bullets on shooting range, plus cartoon key ring 🚇 Qianmen, Tiananmendong ❓ Exhibits are labeled in English

Above *A poster displayed in the Wanfung Gallery*

DRUM AND BELL TOWERS

These massive structures, 3km (1.8 miles) due north of the Forbidden City, were Beijing's timekeepers for more than 600 years. The Zhonglou (Bell Tower) is from the Yuan dynasty (1272) and was last rebuilt in 1747. Follow the signs and prepare for a tough climb to the gallery on the second floor (the steps are steep and widely spaced). The bronze bell, cast during the Ming dynasty, is the largest in China, weighs 63 tons, and can be heard up to 20km (12 miles) away. On a clear day you can see as far. The Gulou (Drum Tower) was rebuilt at the same time as the Bell Tower and is similarly decorated with green and yellow glazed tiles. There are 24 drums, one for each hour. At the time of writing the towers were closed with no date set for reopening.
✚ 54 C2 ✉ 9 Zhonggulou Dajie/Di'anmen Dajie ☎ 010 6401 2674 🕓 Apr–Sep daily 9–5.30; Oct–Mar daily 9–5 💷 Drum Tower: 20RMB. Bell Tower: adult 15RMB, child under 1.2m (4ft) free 🚇 Guloudajie, then follow signs south on Jiugulou Dajie 🍴 Café below Bell Tower ❓ The second-floor gallery of the Drum Tower has a small exhibition on the history of timekeeping in China

FORMER IMPERIAL ARCHIVE

Visitors often overlook the Former Imperial Archive (*Huangshicheng*), a magnificent building east of the Forbidden City. The Imperial Archive was a storehouse for all kinds of official documents, from imperial edicts and public records to generals' seals and the imperial genealogy—set out in a 1m-thick (3ft) tome known as the 'Jade Book.' The building, dating from 1534–36, is older than many in the Forbidden City itself.
✚ 56 C6 ✉ 136 Nanchizi Dajie, Dongcheng District 🕓 Tue–Sun 9–4 💷 Free 🚇 Tiananmendong

NATIONAL ART MUSEUM OF CHINA (NAMOC)

www.namoc.org (Chinese only)
A striking contemporary building with a ceramic-tiled Chinese roof, NAMOC reopened in 2003 after an overhaul. The permanent exhibition consists largely of representational art—portraits, landscapes and everyday scenes—but you will find work by more radical artists alongside traditional ink painting, printing and calligraphy. Check English-language newspapers and listings magazines for news about visiting international exhibitions, which are generally outstanding.
✚ 55 D4 ✉ 1 Wusi Dajie, Dongcheng District ☎ 010 6400 6326 🕓 Daily 9–5 (last ticket 4pm) 💷 Adult 20RMB, child free, student under 17 free 🚌 101, 104, 108 🛍 Shop sells postcards and replica astronomical instruments

TEMPLE OF HEAVEN

INFORMATION

57 D10 Tiantandong Lu, Chongwen District 010 6702 8866 Temple buildings: Apr–end Oct daily 8–5.30 (last ticket 5); Nov–end Mar daily 8–5 (last ticket sold at 4.30). Park: 6am–9pm (last ticket sold at 8) Adult 35RMB (high season), 30RMB (low season). Additional charge to see Divine Music Office (10RMB). Park only, 15RMB. No concessions Tiantan Dongmen Chongwenmen, then 38 or 60 bus, Qianmen, then 120 bus Chinese restaurant near West Gate Audio guide available

Above *A view of the Imperial Vault of Heaven*

Opposite *Detail of carving on the Hall of Prayer for Good Harvest*

INTRODUCTION

The Temple of Heaven (Tiantan) represents the high point of Ming-dynasty architecture. No other monument captures the grandeur and mystique of imperial temple ritual so successfully.

The Temple of Heaven is one of the best-preserved temple complexes in China and is a UNESCO World Heritage Site. The 273ha (675-acre) site is larger in area than the Forbidden City and includes a landscaped park. While all points of interest are accessible on foot, there is a fair amount of walking so allow two to three hours for a visit. To gain a proper appreciation of the overall design, follow the route south to north, starting with the Circular Mound Altar.

The Temple of Heaven was founded at the same time as the Forbidden City (1420), in the reign of the Emperor Yongle. Its present appearance dates from the 16th century, when the layout was altered to accommodate a host of new buildings, including a new Circular Mound Altar. In the 18th century, Emperor Qianlong ordered a program of repair and reconstruction, when the grounds were further enlarged. In 1889 the Hall of Prayer for Good Harvests was struck by lightning and badly damaged. It was immediately rebuilt, following the original construction methods but using timber from Oregon firs. The Temple of Heaven was last used for religious worship in 1914 by the dictator Yuan Shikai (▷ 32), who sought, in vain, to legitimize his regime.

WHAT TO SEE

HALL OF PRAYER FOR GOOD HARVESTS

The emperor came here to give thanks to Heaven at the summer and winter solstices, and again on the 15th day of the first lunar month to pray for a good harvest. This architectural masterpiece was constructed without using nails or cement. Before entering, look at the stone carvings on the balustrade, then at the magnificent three-tiered roof, decorated with more than 50,000 blue-glazed tiles. Your eyes may need time to adjust to the sumptuous interior. The pillars supporting the ceiling have symbolic meaning: The four central columns, resplendent with lotus motifs, represent the seasons, the outer pillars the months of the year and the 12 watches of the day, marked at two-hourly intervals by the beating of a drum at the Drum Tower. Look for the golden dragon sculpture on the *zaojing* (coffered ceiling).

IMPERIAL VAULT OF HEAVEN

Connected to the Hall of Prayer for Good Harvests by the 360m-long (1,180ft) bridge known as the Red Stairway, this beautifully proportioned octagonal building was where the emperor consulted the tablets of his ancestors before climbing the steps of the Circular Mound Altar to offer sacrifice. Inside, the highlight again is the *zaojing* (coffered ceiling), carved and painted with emblematic dragons and phoenixes in green, blue and golden hues. Enclosing the building is the Echo Wall. Speak into it and your voice carries to a distant point along the wall. These properties were designed to enhance the mysterious aura of the place. Test this on the Triple Sounds Stones nearby that, on clapping or shouting, produce an additional echo with each step.

Above *The ornate interior of the Imperial Vault of Heaven*

CIRCULAR MOUND ALTAR

The most sacred place in the temple complex, this vast three-tiered marble terrace represents Man, Earth and Heaven. Here the emperor prayed and offered sacrifice before consulting with Heaven on how best to conduct affairs of state. The emperor (the 'Son of Heaven') stood on the raised slab at the center of the uppermost tier, the middle of the earth according to Chinese cosmology. The design of the altar is formulated on the number nine, thought to be heavenly and therefore closest to perfection. The marble slabs on each terrace are arranged in nine concentric circles, each circle comprising nine stones or multiples of nine. Even the staircases and balustrades are arranged with this scheme in mind.

WESTERN AND EASTERN ANNEX HALLS

An absorbing exhibition on the temple ceremonies can be found in these two buildings outside the Hall of Prayer for Good Harvests. Ming-era paintings depict the procession of the Imperial entourage from the Forbidden City. The emperor was carried in a canopied sedan made of jade and was accompanied by some 2,000 people, including members of the imperial family, ministers, courtiers, dancers and musicians, a guard of honor and a magnificently caparisoned escort of elephants. No member of the public could enjoy the spectacle, however, as to set eyes on the emperor at such a moment would have been sacrilegious. The exhibition includes exquisitely fashioned ritual objects from the Ming and Qing dynasties and an intriguing collection of drums, bells, gongs and other musical instruments used in the ceremonies. The temple had its own music and dance academy, the Divine Music Office (west of the Fasting Palace). The building has now been restored and is also used for exhibitions and occasional performances of ancient music.

MORE TO SEE
FASTING PALACE

Enclosed within its own wall on the west side of the park, the 40,000sq m (47,600sq yard) Fasting Palace contains the Hall of Abstinence, where the emperor fasted before offering sacrifice at the Winter Solstice, as well as 18th-century royal apartments and a Ming dynasty bell tower and bell.

TIPS

» Come early to see the locals practice tai chi, play Chinese chess and form impromptu music clubs.

» The busiest times to visit are on weekends, especially Sundays, and on national holidays.

Below *A view of the Imperial Vault of Heaven*

LAMA TEMPLE

INTRODUCTION

The Lama Temple (Yonghegong) is one of the most important Lama Buddhist temples outside Tibet. Its star attraction is the world's largest statue of the Buddha carved from a single block of wood.

Entering from Yonghegong Dajie, visitors pass through a series of ceremonial archways to the ticket office and garden. Postcards and souvenirs are on sale here, as well as a useful audio guide and CDs of Buddhist chants and sacred music. Follow the central path—the route once reserved for emperors—and you will arrive at the first of the five main prayer halls. It is the small details here that make a visit truly rewarding. Look out for carved lions, bronze *mandala* (circular symbols of the universe), incense burners, screen walls, murals, wood carvings and tapestries.

The temple has been a lamasery for Tibetan and Mongolian Buddhist monks since 1744 but its origins go back another half century. It was built in 1694 as the residence of the fourth son of Emperor Kangxi. Work on transforming the palace into a monastery began shortly after his succession in 1735, as it would have been unthinkable for the palace of a Son of Heaven to be put to any other secular use. Emperor Yongzheng's successor, Qianlong, was the first ruler to use the temple for intelligence gathering on separatist activities in Tibet and Mongolia. Lama Temple was closed down by the Communists but emerged unscathed from the Cultural Revolution due to the personal intervention of the Prime Minister, Zhou Enlai. It resumed its functions as a working monastery in 1981 and continues to advertise the government's stated policy of religious tolerance.

INFORMATION

✚ 55 E1 ✉ 12 Yonghegong Dajie, Dongcheng District ☎ 010 6404 4499 🕐 Apr 1–Oct 31 daily 9–5 (last ticket 4.30); Nov 1–Mar 31 daily 9–4.30 (last ticket 4) 💰 Adult 25RMB, child under 1.2m (4ft) free 🚇 Yonghegong ❓ Audio guide, guided tours available

Opposite *Detail of the decorative, carved and brightly painted archway at the entrance to the Lama Temple*
Above *The entrance gateway to the Lama Temple*

» The Lama Temple is best enjoyed at a leisurely pace, as the grounds are quite extensive. Allow at least 1 hour for a visit.
» Avoid the temple during Chinese national festivals.

WHAT TO SEE

HALL OF HEAVENLY KINGS

The first hall used to be known as Gate of Harmony (Yonghemen), as it was the ceremonial gateway to the original palace. Inside is a shrine to the Maitreya Buddha, represented here as a genial-looking Bodhisattva (a divinity worthy of Nirvana who remains among men to help them attain spiritual perfection). Flanking the Maitreya are the four 'heavenly kings' who rule over the earth, one for each point of the compass. They hold the symbols of their divine power: an umbrella, a sword, a *pipa* (a kind of lute) and a water snake.

HALL OF THE WHEEL OF LAW

The overseeing presence in the fourth hall is Tsong Khapa (1357–1419), founder of the Yellow Hat sect of Tibetan Buddhism to which Lama Temple belongs. A mesmerizing gilded copper statue of the saint occupies center stage, while frescoes on the walls depict key moments from his life. Take a closer look behind the image at the *Mountain of 500 Arhats*, a sculpture with figures of Buddha's disciples made from gold, silver, iron, copper and tin. On the left side of the hall, under glass, is a *mandala* sand painting.

PAVILION OF TEN THOUSAND BLESSINGS

The 26m-high (85ft) statue of the Maitreya Buddha was presented to Emperor Qianlong by the Dalai Lama in 1750. Amazingly, it was hewn from the trunk of a single sandalwood tree and took three years to transport from its original home in Nepal. Anyone skeptical about the measurements (and the statue's independently attested claim to be the largest of its kind in the world) should bear in mind that the lower portion (about 8m/26ft) is concealed beneath the floor.

MORE TO SEE

On leaving the Hall of Heavenly Kings stop for a moment to admire one of the temple's many treasures. Mounted on an intricately carved marble base, the bronze cauldron, or *ding*, was used in Buddhist ritual for burning incense. An inscription records that it was cast 'in the 12th year of Emperor Qianlong (1747).'

Below *A woman with incense praying at the Lama Temple*
Opposite *Flowers in the Ming Walls Cultural Relics Park*

TEMPLE OF CONFUCIUS

Founded in 1302, the temple (Kong Miao), honoring China's famous sage, was an important part of the social fabric from its inception. The moral teachings of Confucius (551–479BC) prized traditional values like moderation, filial piety and respect for one's superiors, and were the mainstay of the imperial regime.

The focal point is the Hall of Great Achievements, where emperors offered sacrifice and invoked the spirit of Confucius, who is commemorated by a plain wooden tablet.

To the left of the courtyard behind the hall are 189 stone tablets containing all 13 of the Confucian classics, some 630,000 characters in all. They were carved by a single craftsman in a decade. The names of the successful candidates in the imperial civil service examinations (1466–1904) are engraved on 198 stelae in the front courtyard. Next door is the Imperial College (Guozijian), where civil servants were prepared for the grueling round of exams that paved the way to a senior post at court.

🚇 55 E1 ✉ 13 Guozijian Jie, Dongcheng District ☎ 010 8401 1977 🕐 Daily 8.30–5 ✋ Adult 10RMB, child under 1.2m (4ft) free 🚇 Yonghegong

MING WALLS CULTURAL RELICS PARK

www.redgategallery.com

This restored section of the Ming dynasty city wall follows the course of Chongwenmendong Dajie for 1.5km (1 mile). Built in 1436, it has impressive dimensions: 11m (36ft) high, 15m (50ft) wide at the top and 18m (59ft) at the base. The park, actually an immaculately tended grass verge with shrubs and flowerbeds, opened to the public in 2002. The arch at the eastern end dates from 1915 and formed part of the suburban railway that girdled the city. Adjacent is the massive Dongbianmen watchtower, used to defend the city, with 144 window-size apertures for firing arrows. The tower last saw action during the Boxer Rebellion (▷ 30) in 1900, when it was bombarded, then briefly occupied by the Eight Western Powers. The Red Gate Gallery, a commercial venture founded in 1991 by Australian art historian Brian Wallace to promote cutting-edge local artists, occupies the first and fourth floors. On the third floor is a quirky exhibition on the history of the Chongwen area.

🚇 57 F7 ✉ Chongwenmen-dong Dajie, Chongwen District ☎ Dongbianmen Tower: 010 6527 0574. Red Gate Gallery: 010 6525

1005/6582 4861 🕐 Tower: daily 8–5.30 (last ticket 5). Gallery: daily 10–5 🚌 10, 43, 44 ✋ Tower: adult 10RMB, child under 1.2m (4ft) free 🚇 Chongwenmen

GUANXIANGTAI (ANCIENT OBSERVATORY)

The observatory is one of the world's oldest. Founded during the Yuan dynasty, it moved to its present home in a corner tower of the Ming Wall in 1437. The somewhat lackluster displays in the rooms off the courtyard provide background information on Chinese astronomy. The exhibits to look out for are a 4,500-year-old pottery jar with pictograms representing the sun in its various aspects, and a Song dynasty chart mapping more than 1,400 stars. The highlight is the collection of 17th- and 18th-century astronomical instruments on the roof. They were built with the help of Jesuit missionaries. The beautifully carved 1673 armillary sphere was used to determine the movement of celestial bodies.

🚇 57 F7 ✉ 2 Dongbiaobei Hutong/Jianguomennei Dajie, Dongcheng District ☎ 010 6524 2202 🕐 Tue–Sun 9–4.30 ✋ Adult 10RMB, child under 1.2m (4ft) free 🚇 Jianguomen 🏬 Shop sells postcards and replica astronomical instruments

INFORMATION

✚ Off map ✉ Shisanling, Changping County (about 48km/30 miles northwest of Beijing) ☎ Changling: 010 6076 1888. Dingling: 010 6076 1424 🕙 Daily 8–5 🚌 Tour bus from Qianmen or Beijing Railway Station. Tours include a visit to the Great Wall at Badaling or Juyongguan (▷ 93) 💰 Changling: Apr 1–end Oct 45RMB; Nov 1–end Mar 30RMB. Dingling: high season 65RMB, low season 45RMB ❓ Audio guide at Dingling 🍴 Restaurants in Changling and Dingling reception areas

TIP

» Public tour buses operate throughout the day.

MING TOMBS

Shisanling is the last resting place of 13 Ming dynasty rulers. Mysterious stone sculptures line the processional route known as the Spirit Way.

THE SPIRIT WAY

The monumental approach road to Emperor Yongle's tomb was laid out in the 15th century and is more than 7km (3 miles) long. The significance of the six pairs of animal sculptures, spaced regularly along the route, is a mystery; some scholars have suggested they form a guard of honor. Among the camels, elephants and horses are mythical beasts like the *kilin*, a fearsome creature with horns and dragon's scales. Beyond this impressive line-up are 12 more statues, this time representing generals and court officials. In 1540 a marble Memorial Arch was erected at the start of the Spirit Way. It ranks among the finest examples of stone carving of the Ming period.

THE TOMBS

The 13 mausoleums are distributed over an area of nearly 40sq km (30sq miles). Each is a palace in its own right, laid out according to the rules of *feng shui* to placate the emperor's ancestors. Changling, Emperor Yongle's mausoleum, is the largest and was completed in 1427. The Hall of Heavenly Favours in front of the burial vault was intended for sacrifice. It is supported by 32 massive pillars of *nannu*, a hardwood, also used in the palaces of the Forbidden City. Here, though, the columns are unpainted. Visitors to Dingling, the necropolis of Emperor Wanli (1563–1620), are shown his Underground Palace, a maze of passages and echoing stone vaults. The tomb was excavated in 1956 and some of the treasures are on show in the museum.

THE GREAT WALL

A trip to the Great Wall is an unforgettable experience. The sweeping views from the parapets are breathtaking.

TAIZU'S WALL

When Emperor Qin Shi Huang (▷ 26–27) unified China in the 3rd century BC, he made the momentous decision to transform the piecemeal defenses of the northern frontier into the 'Wall of Ten Thousand Miles' visitors see today. Conscious of the vulnerability of the capital, the first Ming emperor ordered an overhaul of the 600km (360-mile) stretch protecting Beijing and work continued until well into the 16th century. The existing ramparts were extended to the Yellow Sea and widened for up to five horses (or 10 soldiers) to pass abreast. New watchtowers and blockhouses were erected and an early-warning system of torches and smoke signals put in place. The improved wall survived into the Qing period, when it was finally allowed to fall into disrepair.

VISITING THE WALL

Four restored sections of the wall, at Badaling, Juyongguan, Mutianyu and Simatai, can be reached comfortably in a day trip from Beijing. All four were built near strategic mountain passes, up to 1,000m (3,280ft) above sea level. Badaling is the most accessible section of wall from Beijing but also the most congested and commercialized. Some bus tours now stop at the recently restored Juyongguan Great Wall nearby. At Mutianyu the scenery is spectacular but the steps from the gate are steep so you should consider taking the chairlift (35RMB) or gondola (50RMB). Simatai (110km/ 66 miles northeast of Beijing), is less crowded and restoration has been kept to a minimum, leaving more of the original wall exposed. The steps are uneven and there are fewer barriers, so this is no place for vertigo sufferers.

INFORMATION

Badaling and Juyongguan, Yanqing county

✉ 70km (42 miles) northwest of Beijing ☎ 010 6912 2222/6977 1665 🕐 Badaling: daily 7.30–5.30. Juyongguan: core hours 8.30–4 🚇 Deshengmen, then bus 1919 or go to Qianmen tourist bus ✋ Adult 45RMB (40 RMB in winter), child under 1.2m (4ft) free

Mutianyu, Huairou County

✉ 90km (54 miles) northeast of Beijing ☎ 010 6162 6505/6162 6022 🕐 Apr–end Oct daily 6.30–6.30; Nov–end Mar daily 7–5.30 🚌 Bus 936 from Dongzhimen Bus Station ✋ Adult 40RMB, child under 1.2m (4ft) free; cable car 90RMB

Simatai, Miyun County

🕐 Daily 8–5 ✋ Adult 40 RMB, child under 1.2m (4ft) free

Below *The Great Wall at Simatai is only partially reconstructed*

INFORMATION

TIPS

» Buses drop visitors outside the East Gate. To get to Azure Clouds Temple from here, take Biyunsi Lu and follow the signs. Other attractions, including Shuangqing Villa (Mao Zedong's headquarters at the end of the Civil War) are also signposted.

» The atrium and garden of the Fragrant Hills Hotel (designed by I.M. Pei) are good places for a drink. To get there, follow the signs to Xiangshan Hotel.

Below *A bridge and lake in Fragrant Hills Park*

FRAGRANT HILLS

Praised by the Chinese in autumn when the leaves of the smoke trees turn red, Fragrant Hills (Xiangshan) is a place of scenic beauty all year.

FRAGRANT HILLS PARK

A 12th-century imperial hunting retreat, Fragrant Hills was landscaped with pavilions, lakes and teahouses during the reign of Emperor Qianlong. The 160ha (395-acre) park opened to the public in 1956 and was an immediate hit. Incense Burner Peak is the highest point at 557m (1,827ft). You can trek there in about an hour, returning by cable car. Just inside the northern gate is Azure Clouds Temple, a must-see for its stunning architecture. It was built as a nunnery in 1331 and most of the halls date from the Ming dynasty. Two fierce deities, Heng (Dragon) and Ha (Tiger), guard Mountain Gate Hall, warding off evil spirits. The temple is famous for its stupas (tiered towers) but don't overlook the carp ponds, fountains and 500-year-old cypresses on your way to the Hall of Lokapalas and its 500 life-size effigies of Buddha's disciples.
☎ 010 6259 1155 🕐 Park: daily 6am–6.30pm. Azure Clouds Temple: Mar–end Nov daily 8–5; Dec–end Feb daily 8.30–4 💰 Park: adult 10RMB Apr to mid-Nov; 5RMB mid-Nov to end Mar, child under 1.2m (4ft) free. Azure Clouds Temple: adult 10RMB, child under 1.2m (4ft) free

BOTANICAL GARDENS

This delightful garden is built around a Ming dynasty temple, Wofo Si, where the star attraction is a 5m-long (17ft) recumbent statue of the Sakyamuni Buddha, weighing 54 tons. Paths lead to the arboretum and the formal gardens, or you can take a tour of the conservatory (extra charge) and hothouses, where more than 3,000 varieties of plants and trees are cultivated.
☎ 010 6259 1283 🕐 Daily 6am–9pm (last ticket 7) 💰 Adult 10RMB Apr–end May; 5RMB Jun–end Mar, child under 1.2m (4ft) free

MARCO POLO BRIDGE

Marco Polo Bridge (Lugouqiao), a landmark in the southwest of Beijing, was built in 1192, when it was known as the 'bridge over the reed moat.' The location has long been admired: there are stele near the bridge with inscriptions written by Emperor Qianlong in 1751 singing the praises of Lugouqiao as a beauty spot.

The bridge was restored in the 17th century, when two of its eleven arches were swept away during a flood. There is no evidence that the famous Venetian traveler ever visited (▷ 29) but he did write a description of the bridge in his travelogue. In 1937 the war with Japan began here when shots were exchanged across the Yongding River, an episode that entered the history books as the 'Marco Polo incident.'

Most visitors come here today to photograph the marble lions decorating the parapets of the bridge. There are nearly 500 of these sculptures, and no two are identical in expression and attitude.

Afterward you can haggle with the souvenir sellers over the price of a replica or have your picture taken with a camel (echoes of the Silk Road). The 17th-century walls and gate towers of the former village were restored in 2002 and the main street is now lined with restaurants, galleries and stores.

✚ Off map ✉ Bridge: 77 Lugouqiaochengnan Jie, Wangping, Fengtai District. Memorial Hall: 101 Wanpingcheng, Fengtai District ☎ Bridge: 010 8389 4614. Memorial Hall: 010 8389 2355, ext 281 🕐 Bridge: May–Oct 7 daily 7–7; Oct 8–end Apr daily 8–5. Memorial Hall: Tue–Sun 9–4 ✋ Bridge: adult 20RMB. Memorial Hall: free 🚇 Babaoshan, then taxi or buses 309, 339 🍴 Cafés in Wangping

DASHANZI ART DISTRICT

www.artseasons.com.sg
www.3818coolgallery.com
www.798space.com
www.timezone8.com

Once-derelict factories in a northeastern suburb of Beijing have been given a new lease of life as studios, galleries, workshops, cafés and restaurants. The spacious, well-lit interiors make ideal exhibition spaces. Dashanzi took off during the 1990s, when Chinese avant-garde artists began attracting attention. Today modern art is big business and Dashanzi continues to thrive. The main entrance is behind a line of buildings on Jiuxianqiao Lu.

Once inside, an English-language gallery guide and helpful signs point the way. Start with the big players before investigating the smaller lofts. One to look out for in particular is Timezone 8 Bookstore, which specializes in books on modern art and photography and has an exhibition space showing works by international, as well as Chinese, artists.

✚ Off map ✉ 2/4 Jiuxianqiao Lu, 798-Dashanzi (exit off airport expressway) 🕐 Daily 10–6 (approximate hours); many galleries close on Mon 🚇 Dongzhimen, then bus 915, 918, 934 from Dongzhimen bus station ✋ Free 🍴 Vincent's Creperie

Above *Children walking across Marco Polo Bridge*

WALK

QIANMEN AND DAZHALAN

In the days when the Forbidden City was off limits to ordinary Beijingers, Qianmen was the main commercial and residential quarter—many street names recall the trades once practiced here. Qianmen's formerly unenviable reputation as a red-light district dates back to the Ming dynasty, when it harbored gamblers and drug addicts as well as prostitutes. Most of Qianmen's theaters have long since disappeared—one notable survivor is the fabulous Guildhall.

THE WALK

Distance: 4km (2.5 miles)
Allow: 2 hours
Start: Tian'anmen Square
✚ 56 C7
End: Hepingmen metro station
✚ 56 B8

HOW TO GET THERE

Take the metro to Tiananmendong (line 1), then the China National Museum exit to Tian'anmen Square.

★ Tian'anmen Square is one of the world's most famous public spaces (▷ 78–81).

Walk along the eastern side of the square, passing the museum and Tian'anmen Shopping Center. On your left is Dongjiaomin Xiang, a leafy street where the foreign legations of Western powers were situated in late imperial times. Cross the road to Zhengyangmen Gate and climb the tower for views of Tian'anmen and the Forbidden City.

❶ Part of the Ming defenses, Zhengyangmen Gate was originally joined to the equally massive Arrow Tower (Jianlou) by a wall. Inside is an exhibition of photographs of old Beijing, with scale models of the gates. From here you can also see the clock tower of The Station, another local landmark. At the beginning of the 20th century a railroad followed the line of the city wall. It served as a terminus until Beijing Railway Station opened in 1959. The Station was refurbished in the 1990s as a shopping mall.

Take the pedestrian underpass to cross busy Qianmendong Dajie. Pass the metro station entrance and re-emerge at street level on the newly restored and pedestrianized Qianmen Dajie. After a multi-million dollar facelift, the street now resembles its 1920s and 30s commercial heyday.

❷ One of several Western-style buildings to survive on Qianmen Dajie is the elegant Qian Xiang Yi silk store, founded in 1830 (note the wrought-iron balustrade). Just beyond the *pailou* (ceremonial arch), look out for Qianshi *hutong*, only 44cm (17in) at its narrowest point. Qianmen Dajie is also famous for its neighborhood restaurants. Diyi lou (No. 83) specializes in steamed dumplings, while Quanjude (No. 32) is *the* home of Beijing duck.

Coming up on your right is an iron arch and the sign 'Welcome to Dazhalan.' Turn onto this street. Detour first left on to Liangshidian Jie to see the famous Liubiju pickle shop. Return to Dashalan Jie.

❸ This lively commercial street dates back to the Ming dynasty. The name, which means 'Big Railings Street,' comes from the wooden barriers that sealed off the *hutong* at night to prevent crime. At No. 5 is the imposing marble frontage of the Ruifuxiang silk store, in business for more than 120 years. No. 7 is the Ten Fu tea emporium, which offers tastings and a free lesson on the tea ceremony. Portraits of Mao Zedong and other Communist worthies decorate the shopfront of the Xinhua bookstore (No. 11). The Tongrentang pharmacy (No. 24) is a leading producer of traditional Chinese medicine.

At the end of the pedestrian-only area, follow Dazhalanxi Jie, which becomes Tieshuxie Jie before emerging on Nanxinhua Jie. Turn left, cross Luomashi Dajie and on your right is the Huguang Guildhall.

❹ The Guildhall (Huiguan) was built in 1807 as an inn for candidates sitting the imperial exams. They were entertained in the evenings by performances of Beijing opera—the traditional stage and auditorium is still in use today and worth seeing, as is the opera museum.

Leave the Guildhall and retrace your steps to Nanxinhua Jie. Walk in a northerly direction to Liulichang, which crosses Nanxinhua Jie.

❺ Artisans and craftsmen sold their wares on Liulichang during the Ming dynasty, when the workshops manufactured tiles for the Forbidden City. Today the street has been restored as an antiques market, many of the shops specializing in painting, calligraphy and seals. On Liulichangdong Jie (No. 14) don't miss Songtanzhi Museum of Traditional Folk Carving, which showcases Li Song Tang's fabulous collection of stone and wood sculptures. There are several teahouses on the street.

Return to Nanxinhua Jie and head north to Hepingmen metro station.

WHEN TO GO
It is best to do this walk during the day: Not all of the streets are well lit.

PLACES TO VISIT
GUILDHALL OPERA MUSEUM
✉ 3 Hufang Lu ☎ 010 6351 8284
🕐 Daily 9–7.30, when performances begin
🎫 Museum: 10RMB. Performances: from 120RMB

SONGTANZHI MUSEUM OF TRADITIONAL FOLK CARVING
✉ 14 Luilichangdong Jie 14 🕐 Tue–Sun 9–6 🎫 Adult 20RMB, child under 1.2m (4ft) free

WHERE TO EAT
QUANJUDE
✉ 32 Qianmen Dajie ☎ 010 6511 2418
🕐 Daily 11–1.30, 4.30–8

Opposite *Take plenty of time to explore the silk store on Dashalan Jie*

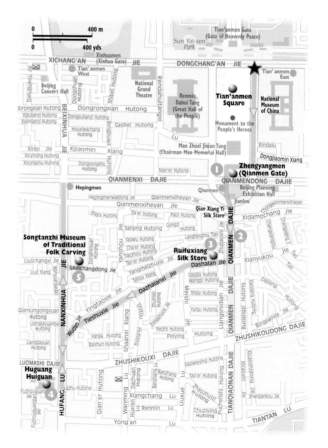

REGIONS BEIJING • WALK

JINGSHAN AND BEIHAI PARKS

Beijing is blessed with an abundance of green spaces. This walk introduces two parks with royal associations. Jingshan Park was once a hunting ground, while Beihai, with its classical Chinese gardens, was where Ming and Qing emperors came to contemplate nature or mull over pressing affairs of state. Beijingers are fond of both parks—you will see them practicing tai chi, polishing their ballroom-dancing skills, or simply relaxing in the company of family and friends.

THE WALK

Distance: 4km (2.5 miles)
Allow: 1.5 hours
Start: Shenwu Gate ✚ 54 C4
End: Dianmennei Dajie ✚ 54 C3

HOW TO GET THERE

Take metro line 1 to Tiananmendong, the station at the north-eastern corner of Tian'anmen Square, then take either bus 3 or 58 (or a taxi) to the southern gate of Jingshan Park.

★ The walk starts outside the northern Shenwu Gate of the Forbidden City. Enter Jingshan Park, passing through the ceremonial gate tower, now a teahouse.

❶ When the moat around the Forbidden City was dug out in the 15th century, the excavated earth was used to make Jingshan Hill. Conceived with *feng shui* in mind, its main purpose was to block the path of evil spirits; more practically it offered protection from bitter northerly winds. When the emperor died, his coffin was carried to Jingshan before interment in the Ming Tombs (▷ 92). Before you begin climbing the hill, follow the signs pointing out the tree where

the last Ming emperor hanged himself in 1644 to avoid capture by Qing loyalists. Continue through the pines and cypresses to the Pavilion of Everlasting Spring at the summit. Take the path down to the west gate. Cross Jingshanxi Jie and continue down Doushanmen Jie through the gate into Beihai Park (▷ 68–69).

Begin your exploration of the park by crossing the bridge to Jade Island and following the path to the right. This will take you past the famous Fangshan Restaurant in the Hall of Rippling Waters, to the Yong'an Si

Temple (▷ 71). Leave the island by the 13th-century Yong'an Bridge to the south. On the other side of the bridge is Round City.

❷ Some of the trees in Round City (▷ 69), pines and cypresses for the most part, are hundreds of years old. The oldest—to the right of the terrace—is a pine planted in the 12th century during the Jin dynasty. It was a custom in imperial times for the emperor to confer titles on trees deemed to have performed a specific service. Emperor Qianlong ennobled one of the pines here for providing shade on a particularly hot summer's day.

From Round City follow the path to the east of Beihai Lake, passing the former Imperial Boathouse. Traveling across the lake by boat was (and still is) one of the great pleasures of Beihai. In the past, tea would have been served to guests as they admired the view. The path skirts Beihai Kindergarten and the Altar of Silkworms. In this shrine, built in the reign of Emperor Qianlong, mulberry leaves were

Above *The Five-Dragon Pavilion*
Opposite *The view across the city skyline over Beihai Lake and Park*

examined for quality under a statue of the goddess of sericulture, His Ling-Shih, before being fed to the imperial silkworms. Continue on the path past the north gate, and you will arrive at Qing-dynasty Buddhist temples.

❸ The focal point is the Mind-Cultivating Study (▷ 69), arguably the most beautiful of Beihai's gardens. Emperor Qianlong had it specially landscaped in the 18th

century for the enjoyment of his sons. The garden was a special favorite of Dowager Empress Cixi, who ordered the building of a narrow-gauge rail link with the Forbidden City.

Leave the garden, following the signs to the Nine-Dragon Screen; then head south toward the lake.

❹ At the water's edge is the Five-Dragon Pavilion, floating summerhouses linked by bridges. The emperors would come here to fish, to be entertained by firework displays over the lake, or simply to bask in the moonlight. This can still be a tranquil spot, so you may like to take a breather before moving on.

Return to the north gate and turn right onto Di'anmenxi Dajie. On the corner of Di'anmennei Dajie, pick up the number 5 bus to Tian'anmen Square and Tiananmenxi metro (line 1).

PLACE TO VISIT
JINGSHAN PARK
🕐 Core hours 6am–8pm ✋ Adult 2RMB, child under 1.2m (4ft) free

WHERE TO EAT
FANGSHAN RESTAURANT
Enjoy imperial-style cuisine in a Ming pavilion overlooking the lake.
✉ 1 Wenjin Jie ☎ 010 6401 1889
🕐 11–1.30, 5–8

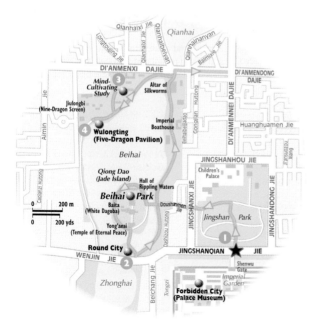

WALK

THE *HUTONG* OF SHICHAHAI

This walk guides you through a part of Beijing famous for its *hutong* and courtyard houses. You can visit the Drum and Bell towers that once kept time for the whole city and take a relaxing stroll along the banks of the Shichahai lakes, created by China's Mongol rulers in the 13th century. Finish with a relaxing drink, taking in the view from one of Houhai's many café terraces.

THE WALK

Distance: 6.5km (4 miles)
Allow: 3 hours
Start: Jiugulou Dajie ✚ 54 C1
End: Guloudajie metro station ✚ 54 C1

HOW TO GET THERE

Take metro line 2 to Guloudajie. Leave the metro and cross Deshengmendong Dajie to Jiugulou Dajie.

★ Jiugulou Dajie was spruced up in 2005 as part of a *hutong* conservation project. Walk down the right-hand side of the road, then turn right into Xiaoshiqiao Hutong, where a sign will point you in the direction of the Bamboo Garden Hotel.

❶ This converted *siheyuan* (courtyard residence) dates from the Qing dynasty. The previous owners include a eunuch in the entourage of the Dowager Empress Cixi. The imposing carved stone gateway indicates its former importance. If you continue along the *hutong*, then bear left into Xinkai Hutong, you will arrive at the childhood home of the renowned conductor Seiji Ozawa. He lived here for five years (1936–41) before his parents returned to Japan. In 2002 he buried part of his mother's ashes under a tree in the garden.

At the end of Xinkai Hutong is Gulouxi Dajie. Cross this main road here and turn right. Carry on walking until you see the Former Residence of Song Qingling appearing on your left (▷ 67). Leave the grounds and stroll down Houhaibeiyan, a tranquil spot lined with willow trees and popular with fishermen. Head toward the Silver Ingot Bridge, where you will probably want to stop to take photographs. On a clear day you can see as far as Fragrant Hills (Xiangshan; ▷ 94).

2 Sometimes referred to as Beijing's 'lake district,' Shichahai comprises three man-made waterways: Qianhai (Front Lake), Houhai (Back Lake) and Xihai (West Lake). All three date from the Yuan dynasty (13th century) and once marked the northern end of the Grand Canal. Barges filled with grain, silver or silks would be unloaded here after making the 1,600km (1,000-mile) journey from Hangzhou province. The word Shichahai (Ten Buddhist Temple Sea) refers not only to the lakes but also to the temples and nunneries that once flourished here.

Cross Silver Ingot Bridge to Houhai and follow the embankment to your left.

3 Houhai's waterfront bars and cafés draw large crowds on warm summer evenings, when many stay open into the small hours, but

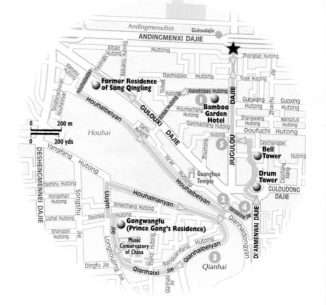

Opposite The gardens at the Former Residence of Song Qingling
Below *The drum in the Drum Tower is beaten four times a day*

are far less busy at other times of the year.

Ignore the left fork and follow the road as it curves to the right. Continue past the Music Conservatory and into Liuyin Jie. At the intersection of Qianhaix Jie is the Guzhenhuang Cantonese restaurant, which specializes in seafood banquets. On your right, after about 200m (220 yards) you will see signs for Prince Gong's Residence (▷ 67). On leaving the mansion, turn right onto Liuyin Jie. At the end of the street turn right again onto Houhainanyan and return to Silver Ingot Bridge. Cross the lake, turn right onto Yandaixie Jie.

4 Yandai Jie (Tobacco Pouch Street) was a market during the Ming dynasty, when it was convenient for the Grand Canal Dock. Today, bars alternate with small boutiques and craft shops, refurbished in traditional style. The bar at No. 37 is a former Taoist Temple (note the triple-arched stone doorway).

At the end of the street take the steps down to Di'anmenwai Dajie. Then turn left and cross Guloudong Dajie to the Drum and Bell towers (▷ 83). Leave by Lingdang Hutong to the west of the Bell Tower and turn right on to Jiugulou Dajie.

5 Life may seem picturesque in the *hutong* to the right and left of Jiugulou Dajie, but the reality is that many of the roofs leak, the only form of heating is a stove and residents often live four to five to a room, sharing an outdoor toilet.

Continue along Jiugulou Dajie, passing the Beijing-USA College of English on your way back to Guloudajie metro.

WHEN TO GO
This walk is ideal for the afternoon or early evening.

WHERE TO EAT
Choose one of the numerous cafés and terrace bars overlooking the banks of Houhai.

WHAT TO DO

SHOPPING

BANNERMAN TANG

This delightful store, near the Temple of Confucius (▷ 91), sells mostly handmade toys and crafts. It's a great place to shop for unusual souvenirs, painted snuff bottles, shadow puppets, clay dolls, kites and Beijing opera masks and the like.

✉ 38 Guozijian Jie, Dongcheng District ☎ 010 8404 7179 ⏰ Daily 9–7 🚇 Andingmen

CHINA WORLD

This huge shopping mall in the heart of the Central Business District is primarily for those hooked on top designer brands, from Cerruti and Louis Vuitton to Cartier and Prada. The amenities include a fitness center and an ice-skating rink.

✉ 1 Jianguomenwai Dajie, Chaoyang District ☎ 010 6505 2288 ⏰ Daily, usually 10–9.30 🚇 Guomao

FOREIGN LANGUAGES BOOKSTORE

China's largest bookstore has a wide selection of titles covering most aspects of life in the country, plus phrase books, English-language fiction, travel and children's books, listings magazines and greeting cards.

✉ 235 Wangfujing Dajie, Dongcheng District ☎ 010 6512 6903 ⏰ Daily 9–9 🚇 Wangfujing

HONGQIAO MARKET

While this market sells everything from antique clocks to furniture, it is best known for its freshwater pearl outlets, which you will find on the third and fourth floors. A good place to start is Fanghua Pearls (No. 4318, 4th floor), where their resident experts will answer your questions.

✉ Tiantan Donglu, Chongwen District ☎ 010 6713 3354 ⏰ Daily 8.30–7 🚇 Chongwomen, then bus 39 or 43

LILY STORE

This innovative Sanlitun jeweler fashions highly original rings, bangles and pendants from pear wood, silver and coral. You'll find her store in the Nali Mini Mall (take the first right after the crossing with Gonti Beilu).

✉ No. 10 Sanlitun Nali Mini Mall, 45–47 Sanlitun Lu, Chaoyang District ☎ 010 6413 1160 ⏰ Daily 11–9 🚌 110, 120

LIULICHANG MARKET

This famous old street, southwest of Tian'anmen Square is choc-full of attractive stores selling Chinese paintings, calligraphy, books, tea and its famously elaborate

Above *Crowds of people at various stalls in Wanfujing Snack Street*

paraphernalia and (mostly fake) antiques. The street was rebuilt in the 1980s in the style of a Qing dynasty market and, if nothing else, it makes for a pleasant stroll. There are two sections, east and west of Nanxinhua Jie

✉ Liulichang Dongjie-Liulichang Xjie, Xuanwu District ⏰ Daily 9–6 🚇 Hepingmen

LIULIGONGFANG

www.liuli.com

Winner of the Design for Asia Award in 2005, Liuligongfang uses a glass-making technique dating back to the Han dynasty to produce exquisite vases, goblets and figurines.

✉ Yansha Plaza (Lufthansa Center), 1F, 52 Liangmaqiao Lu, Chaoyang District ☎ 010 8448 3517 ⏰ Daily 9.30am–10pm 🚌 707, 757

MALIANDAO TEA STREET

Every tea-producing region of China is represented on this fascinating theme street, with more than 600 stores and wholesale markets. Expect to pay around 200RMB per *jin* (0.5kg/1 lb) for a quality tea like Longjing from Hangzhou's West Lake (Xihu). You might also like to try tea-flavored dumplings, the specialty of Songyuan Teahouse, on the third floor of the Tea City mall.

✉ Maliandao Lu, Xuanwun District ☎ No phone 🕐 Daily 8.30–6 🚌 6, 42, 46, 340 on Guang'an Lu

ORIENTAL PLAZA

www.orientalplaza.com

Conveniently situated on the corner of Wangfujing shopping street and only five minutes from Tian'anmen Square, Oriental Plaza can make a good claim to be the city's premier mall. Apart from top designer names and fashion boutiques, you'll find beauty salons, an organic tea shop, restaurants and fast-food eateries, a CRC supermarket and a pharmacy. You can also entertain the children at Sony ExploraScience (▷ 107).

✉ 1 Dongchang'an Jie, Dongcheng District ☎ 010 8518 6363 🕐 May–end Sep daily 10–10; Oct–end Apr daily 9.30–9.30 🚇 Wangfujing

PANJIAYUAN MARKET

Around 4,000 antiques dealers set out their wares in this enormous market, which is a fascinating place. Sift through the curios and family heirlooms and you may find a real bargain, although few of the items on sale are genuine antiques.

✉ Panjiayuan Qiao, Chaoyang District ☎ 010 6775 2405 🕐 Mon–Fri 8–6, Sat, Sun 4.30am–6pm 🚌 35, 41

QIANMEN CARPET

www.carpetrealm.com

Beijing's leading antique carpet dealer will show you a fabulous collection of rugs and carpets from Tibet, Xinjiang and Mongolia, all handmade and colored using natural dyes. The building is interesting in its own right—in the 1960s it was an underground air-raid shelter.

✉ 1F Building 3, Tiantan Mansion, 59 Xingfu Dajie, Chongwen District ☎ 010 6715 1687 🕐 Daily 9.30–5.30 🚌 6, 8, 35, 41, 60

QIANMEN COMMERCIAL STREET

After an expensive and controversial 15-month renovation project, the Qianmen Commercial Street,

immediately south of Tian'anmen Square, re-opened to the public one day before the 2008 Beijing Games began. It's now a wide, 840m-long (900-yard) boulevard of old-but-new Beijing, lined with replica Qing-era grey brick buildings, bird-cage street lamps, and trams running the length of the street. Despite efforts to encourage its commercial past, it's more a place for tourists to take pictures than to shop. However, turn right (west) into Dazhalan for heaps of small hawker stores.

✉ Qianmen Dajie, Xuanwu District 🚇 Qianmen

RUIFUXIANG SILK AND COTTON FABRICS SHOP

This venerable emporium (look for the storks decorating the front of the building) has been around for more than 120 years and has occupied these premises since 1893. There are more than 10,000 bales of fabric on sale, notably Shandong raw silk, cotton and brocade in myriad colors, textures and patterns.

✉ 5 Dazhalan Jie, Xuanwu District ☎ 010 6303 5312 🕐 Daily 9am–10pm 🚇 Qianmen

SILK MARKET PLAZA

On the northern side of Jianguomen Waidajie, just to the east of Yong'anli metro stop, is one of Beijing's most popular malls. Recent high profile lawsuits may have stemmed the flow of fake goods but the ending of the 2008 Games will likely permit a bit of the old commercial chicanery to return to this quintessential Beijing shopping venue.

✉ Xiushui Dongjie, Chaoyang District ☎ 010 5169 8800 🕐 Daily 9–9 🚇 Yong'anli

SILK STREET

The famous Xiushui outdoor silk market closed in 2004 to be replaced by this modern nine-floor mall. While it has lost a lot of its character, the number of stalls has doubled to more than 1,500 and there are still great bargains here, so haggle like mad. Apart from silk and cashmere, you'll find carpets, bags

and suitcases, jewelry and souvenirs. There's also a supermarket, an ATM and a restaurant.

✉ 8 Xiushuidong Jie, Chaoyang District ☎ 010 5169 8800 🕐 Daily 9.30–9.30 🚇 Yong An Li

SUN DONG AN PLAZA

www.sda.com.cn

Many people find this airy, spacious and sensitively designed mall easier to negotiate than its neighbor, Oriental Plaza. Arranged on seven floors under a glass roof, it's a useful mix of chain stores, shops selling audio and video equipment and fast-food vendors. There's also an eight-screen Cineplex.

✉ 138 Wangfujing Dajie, Dongcheng District ☎ 010 5817 6688 🕐 Mon–Thu 9–9, Fri, Sat 9–10 🚇 Wangfujing

TIMEZONE 8 BOOKSTORE

www.timezone8.com

Browse the books on contemporary Chinese art, then visit the adjoining art gallery (▷ 95) and coffee shop.

✉ 4 Jiuxianqiao Lu, Chaoyang District ☎ 010 8456 0336 🕐 Daily 9–9 🚇 Dongzhimen, then bus 401, 418, 909

WANGFUJING MUSICAL INSTRUMENT CITY

Steer your way through the electric guitars and drum kits to check out the traditional Chinese musical instruments, including *erhu* (fiddles) and *guzheng* (zithers).

✉ Lisheng Sports Shopping Mall, 201 Wangfujing Dajie, Dongcheng District ☎ 010 6513 5190 🕐 Daily 9–9 🚇 Wangfujing

XINDE LU CHINESE CLOTHING STORE

While you're visiting the Drum and Bell towers (▷ 83) try to find time to call in at this fabulous bespoke clothing store, which specializes in reproducing Chinese fashions of the pre-revolutionary era. Everything you see here is hand sewn and embroidered by the owner.

✉ 198 Gulou Dongdajie, Dongcheng District ☎ 010 6402 6769 🕐 Daily 9–6 🚇 Guloudajie

ENTERTAINMENT

BANANA
www.clubzone.cn (for tickets)
At this hot and steamy disco with a pulsating beat, the big draw is the visiting international DJs. For a change of scene, check out the quieter lounge on the second floor, where local DJs play what pleases them.
✉ Scitech Hotel, 22 Jianguomenwai Dajie, Chaoyang District ☎ 010 6528 3636 🕐 Nightly 8.30pm–4.30 ✋ Cover charge 20–40RMB, prices rise when star DJs perform 🚇 Jianguomen

BED TAPAS AND BAR
This trendy place near the Drum and Bell towers is run by the same team as Café Sambal (▷ 109). The warren of rooms off the main bar, furnished with wooden Chinese beds and little else, lead eventually to a small courtyard. During the week Bed Bar is a good place to chill and snack on tapas, but it's packed on Friday and Saturday nights.
✉ 17 Zhangwang Hutong, Dongcheng District ☎ 010 8400 1554 🕐 Daily 3pm–2am 🚇 Guloudajie

BEIJING CONCERT HALL
The city's main venue for traditional Chinese and classical Western music has a 1,100-seat auditorium. The China National Symphony Orchestra, the Beijing Philharmonic Orchestra, the China Traditional Music Ensemble and the Oriental Song and Dance Troupe give regular concerts.
✉ 1 Beixinhua Jie, Xicheng District ☎ 010 6605 7006 🕐 All year. Performances usually start at 7.30pm ✋ 10–1,500RMB, depending on artists performing 🚇 Xidan

CD JAZZ CLUB
You'll find this increasingly popular jazz venue near the main entrance of the Agricultural Exhibition Hall. It belongs to local rock musician Liu Yuan, who performs here with his own band on weekends. Other rock and jazz outfits guest here during the week.
✉ 16 Dongsanhuan Beilu (East 3rd Ring Road), Chaoyang District ☎ 010 6506 8288 🕐 Daily 5pm–2am ✋ Free 🚇 Dongzhimen, then buses 110, 117, 120 on Dongzhimenwai Dajie

CENTRO BAR
Arguably Beijing's most hip cocktail bar, laid-back Centro has won numerous plaudits for its deliciously concocted drinks and mellow live music. Sip your cocktail at the bar or relax in one of the screened-off lounges while the resident jazz band provides the entertainment. There is an excellent selection of wines.
✉ 1/F Kerry Center Hotel, 1 Guanghua Lu, Chaoyang District ☎ 010 6561 8833, ext 42 🕐 24 hours ✋ Free 🚍 9, 107, 730, 801

CHAOYANG THEATRE
Shows by the famed China Acrobatic Troupe are held in this theater. This is also a regular venue for magic shows and Beijing Opera performances.
✉ 36 Dongsanhuan Beilu, Chaoyang District ☎ 010 6507 2421/5409 8849 🕐 Daily. Performances 5.15–6.15pm and 7.15–8.30pm ✋ 180–680RMB 🚇 Chaoyangmen, then bus 101 🚍 9, 113, 402, 405, 801

CHERRY LANE CINEMA
www.cherrylanemovies.com.cn
The cinema screens classic and contemporary Chinese films with English subtitles.
✉ 3 Zhangzizhong, Ping'an Dadao, Xicheng District ☎ 010 6404 2711 🕐 Movies Sun 8pm ✋ 50RMB, including snacks 🚇 Zhangzizhonglu

CLUB FOOTBALL CENTRE
The pub in the Red House Hotel really comes alive whenever they're screening British and European soccer matches or NBA and NFL football games. It's a place to make friends over a game of darts or pool. Pub food is available.
✉ 10 Chunxiu Lu, Chaoyang District ☎ 010 6417 0497 🕐 Mon–Thu 11am–midnight, Fri–Sun 11am–12.30am 🚍 117

FORBIDDEN CITY CONCERT HALL
www.fcchoj.com (Chinese only)
This modern concert hall is in Zhongshan Park, to the northwest side of Tian'anmen Square. It serves as an alternative venue to the Beijing Concert Hall in staging concerts of traditional Chinese and Western classical music.
✉ Inside Zhongshan Park, Xicheng District ☎ 010 6559 8285 🕐 All year. Phone for tickets or pick them up from the box office in the Friendship Store on Jianguomenwai Dajie ✋ Between 50–1,800RMB, depending on artists performing 🚇 Tiananmenxi

HUGUANG GUILDHALL
You can enjoy spirited nightly performances of traditional Beijing Opera excerpts in this gorgeous 19th-century theater. Tea and snacks are served and there is a small opera museum here too.
✉ 3 Hufangqiao Lu, Xuanwu District ☎ 010 6351 8284/6352 9134 🕐 Daily. Performances 7.30–8.30pm approximately ✋ Adult/child 180–680RMB 🚇 Hepingmen, then bus 7, 14, 15

LAO SHE TEAHOUSE
www.laosheteahouse.com
Look for the white lions and red banners outside the entrance to this well-known theater. The small auditorium on the third floor stages touristy shows that combine Beijing Opera with slapstick, magic and acrobatics.
✉ Building 3, Zhengyang Shichang, Qianmen Xidajie, Xuanwu District ☎ 010 6303 6830/6302 1717 🕐 Daily. Performances 7.50–9.20pm ✋ 180–380RMB 🚇 Qianmen

LIYUAN THEATRE
www.qianmenhotel.com
The theater in the Jianguo Qianmen Hotel stages nightly shows of Beijing Opera excerpts to tea-sipping, mainly foreign, audiences. After the performance you can look around the actors' make-up room and take a group photo if you wish.
✉ 175 Yong'an Lu, Xuanwu District ☎ 010 8315 7297, hotline 6301 6688/8860 🕐 Daily 7.30am–8.40pm. Performances 7.30pm ✋ Adult/child 200–580RMB 🚇 Hepingmen, then bus 14, 15 25

MAO LIVEHOUSE

www.maolive.com

MAO has quickly become the capital's premier live music venue, with a slightly postmodern iron-riveted facade and a quirky performance area, primed with one of Beijing's meanest sound systems. Fashioned from an old cinema, the auditorium rises away from the stage, offering the choice between the pit and a high view. The music is mostly indie and rock, while there's a sectioned-off bar area for when the music gets too intense.

✉ 111 Gulou Dongdajie, Dongcheng District ☎ 010 6402 5080 🕐 Daily 4pm–late 🚇 Guloudajie

NANLUOGUXIANG

This charming *hutong* alley is more than eight centuries old but is the current darling of Beijing's bohemian set after a wholesale makeover in the last few years. Lining this kilometer-long (0.6 mile) strip are a succession of hip Wi-Fi café hangouts, chill-out bars and essential shops. It's good for lazing away an afternoon in atmospheric surrounds, or a sociable night out. For loud partying, opt instead for Sanlitun—Beijing's more famous but definitely less charming bar strip.

✉ Between Gulou Dongdajie and Di'anmen Dajie, Dongcheng District 🚇 Andingmen

NATIONAL CENTRE FOR THE PERFORMING ARTS

www.chncpa.org

Up there with the 'Bird's Nest' National Stadium for architectural wizardry, the NCPA cost RMB3.2 billion to build and resembles a giant egg floating in a lake of water. Inside is a stunning, 2,398-seat opera house, a fractionally smaller concert hall and a state-of-the-art theater and concert hall, all reachable by first taking the glass tunnel that runs underneath the lake. Admission by performance ticket only but whatever may be on, it's worth going, just for the experience of this magnificent new building.

✉ 2 Chang'an Xijie ☎ 010 6655 0000 🚇 Tiananmenxi

PASS BY BAR

www.passbybar.com

The photos of weathered Tibetan types lend a frontier-town feel to this café-bar, popular with visiting backpackers but also patronized by locals.

There's a useful shop selling books, maps and postcards, while the adjoining restaurant serves mainstream Western meals, including snacks and salads.

✉ 108 Nanluogu Xiang, Dongcheng District ☎ 010 8403 8004 🕐 Daily 9am–2am 🚇 Andingmen

POLY THEATRE

This large theater complex, just across the road from the Swissotel, is a venue for performances by the National Ballet of China and also hosts dramas and the occasional musical.

✉ Poly Plaza, 14 Dongzhimen Nandajie, Dongcheng District ☎ 010 6506 5343 🕐 Performances 7.30pm 💰 Adult/child 80–1,800RMB 🚇 Dongsishitiao

RED MOON

Red velvet predominates in this plush cocktail lounge, where the barman serves a mean Martini as well as quality wines and spirits. There's also a cigar lounge and sushi bar. Lunch is served 11.30–2.30 on weekdays.

✉ 1F Grand Hyatt Hotel, Beijing Oriental Plaza, 1 Dong Chang'an Dajie, Doncheng District ☎ 010 6510 9366 🕐 Mon–Fri 11.30am–2am, Sat 5pm–2am, Sun 5pm–1am 🚇 Wangfujing

RED THEATRE

www.chunyi-kungfu.com
www.heaven-creation.com

The much-praised, highly dynamic interpretation *Chun Yi: The Legend of Kung Fu* plays to packed houses and toured the US in 2006. Look forward to an action-packed evening of martial arts, ballet, modern dance and acrobatics.

✉ 44 Xingfu Dajie, Chongwen District ☎ 010 6714 2473/6710 3671 🕐 Daily. Performances 7.30pm 💰 Adult 180–680RMB, child under 1.2m (4ft) half price 🚌 8

Above *Inside the Pass By Bar*

STAR CITY/ORIENTAL PLAZA MULTIPLEX

In the basement of the shopping mall, this cinema shows the odd English-language film along with Chinese movies with English subtitles.

✉ Oriental Plaza, 1 Dongchang'an Jie (corner of Wangfujing), Dongcheng District ☎ 010 8518 5399 🕐 Mon–Sat 10.45–9.30, Sun 12.30–9.30 💰 Adult 15–50RMB, child 10–25RMB 🚇 Wangfujing

SUZIE WONG'S

www.suziewong.com.cn

Packed every weekend until late, this modern twist on the classical opium den has a fantastic roof deck and some of the wildest parties in town. Jazz and salsa mix with house music, and there are different themes every night. One for the singles crowd.

✉ 1A Nongzhanguan Nanlu, West Gate Chaoyang Park ☎ 010 6590 3377 🕐 Daily 7pm–4am 🚇 National Agricultural Exhibition Center

SPORTS AND ACTIVITIES

BEIJING GOLF CLUB

www.beijinggolfclub.com

This tournament-standard golf course in a pleasant forested setting has a practice course, driving range and restaurant.

✉ On the east bank of Chaobai River, Shunyi District (35km/21 miles). Take the Mapo turnoff on the airport expressway and follow the signs ☎ 010 8947 0245 🕐 Daily 7–7 ✋ Nonmembers, Mon–Fri 800RMB, weekends 1,200RMB, plus 200RMB green fees

BEIJING HIKERS
www.beijinghikers.com
Beijing Hikers organizes overnight and weekend hikes in the countryside, visiting popular sites like the Ming Tombs, but also less well-known locations.
☎ 13910025516 (mobile) 🕐 Book in advance ✋ Adult 200RMB, child aged under 12 150RMB for a weekend hike

BEIJING INTERNATIONAL GOLF CLUB
This Japanese-designed course has a wonderful location in the Valley of the Ming Tombs.
✉ Northwest of the Ming Tombs reservoir, heading toward the Shisanling Memorial, Changping District (35km/21 miles) from Beijing ☎ 010 6076 2288 🕐 Feb 25–Dec 3 7–7 (last tee time 2pm); Dec 4–Feb 24 9–4 (last tee time 12). ✋ Nonmembers, Mon–Fri: men 800RMB, women 450RMB. Nonmembers, weekends: 1,400RMB. For all, 200RMB green fees

BEIJING MARATHON
▷ 107

CHINA WORLD FITNESS CENTRE
This fitness center is a real bargain, considering that the facilities include a 20m (65ft) swimming pool, sauna, Jacuzzi and squash courts.
✉ China World Trade Centre, 1 Jianguomenwai Dajie, Chaoyang District ☎ 010 6505 2266 🕐 Daily 6–11 ✋ Adult 200RMB per session, child 80RMB 🚇 Guomao

CLUB FOOTBALL CENTRE
▷ 104)

LE COOL ICE RINK
www.lecoolicerink.com
You'll find this indoor rink in Tower 2 of the China World Trade Centre shopping mall. Private lessons are also available.

✉ China World Trade Centre, 1 Jianguomenwai Dajie, Chaoyang District ☎ 010 6505 5776 🕐 Daily 10–10 ✋ Adult/child 30–50RMB per 1.5 hour session (including skate rental) 🚇 Guomao

NATIONAL STADIUM
The Beijing Games left the capital with a whole string of new world-class sporting venues that will be used for future meets. The best of them is by far the biggest. The building known simply as 'Bird's Nest' throughout the Games cost around RMB3.5 billion to build and seats approximately 91,000 spectators. If you do happen to be in town during a major event, seize the opportunity to enjoy one of the world's great arenas.
✉ Olympic Green (southeast corner), Haidian District 🚇 Olympic Green

QIAOBO ICE AND SNOW WORLD
www.qbski.com (Chinese only)
This huge indoor skiing facility was built by Tsinghua Sports University with Canadian help. There are two slopes: one (150m/492ft) for beginners, the other (260m/852ft) for advanced skiers.
✉ Chaobai River National Forest Park, Shunyi District ☎ 010 8497 2568 🕐 Daily 9am–10pm ✋ Adult/child Mon–Fri 150RMB an hour, 30RMB for extra hour, Sat, Sun 180RMB an hour, 50RMB for extra hour. 2-hour package including equipment, sauna, locker and a meal 280RMB; 4-hour package 380RMB 🚗 Take the Mapo turnoff from the airport expressway

WORKERS' STADIUM
This 72,000-seat stadium is home to Beijing Xiandai soccer club (formerly Hyundai Guo An). Tickets are available from the north gate.
✉ Gonti Beilu, Chaoyang District ☎ 010 6551 6590 🕐 Reopens early 2008 🚌 113, 115, 118

HEALTH AND BEAUTY
BODHI THERAPEUTIC RETREAT
www.bodhi.com.cn
While this is a Thai establishment, the treatments include Chinese body massage and reflexology and the

Thai staff are trained by a doctor specializing in Traditional Chinese Medicine. Sessions are available at reduced rates before 5pm Monday to Thursday.
✉ 17 Gonti Beilu, Chaoyang District ☎ 010 6417 9595 🕐 Daily 11am–12.30am ✋ From 158RMB per hour 🚌 113

ORIENTAL TAIPAN
www.taipan.com.cn
The highly affordable treatments in this branch of the Hong Kong-based chain include reflexology (with a hot herbal bath), manicure, pedicure, hot-stone aromatherapy and ear-candling.
✉ Basement, 1 Xindong Lu, Chaoyang District ☎ 010 8532 2177 🕐 Daily 11am–12.30am ✋ 168RMB for 90 minutes 🚌 24, 110, 120, 413, 418

FOR CHILDREN
BEIJING ZOO
www.bjzoo.com (Chinese only)
Beijing Zoo has been revamped as a result of the 2008 Olympic Games and the often woeful conditions in which animals were kept has been improved. The panda house is the obvious attraction here—visit during the week if you can, as the zoo is crowded on weekends and on holidays.
✉ 137 Xizhimenwai Dajie, Xicheng District ☎ 010 6831 4411/6839 0274 🕐 Daily 7.30–7 ✋ Adult 15RMB, child 13RMB, child under 1.2m (4ft) free. Additional charge for panda house 5RMB 🚇 Beijing Zoo 🍴 Refreshment points in zoo

BLUE ZOO BEIJING
www.bluezoo.com.cn (Chinese only)
Cleverly concealed beneath the lake in the Workers' Stadium, this rival (and superior) aquarium to the one in Beijing Zoo has proved popular with youngsters since it opened back in 1997.
The creatures of the deep include the usual suspects—stingrays, eels, seahorses, starfish and of course sharks. Fish feeding takes place twice daily.
✉ Gonti Nanlu (enter from south gate of Workers' Stadium), Chaoyang District ☎ 010 6591 3397 🕐 Dec–end Feb

8.30–6.30; Mar–end Nov 8–8 👐 Adult 75RMB, child 50RMB, child under 1m (3.25ft) free 🚌 113, 117, 403 ⬜ Refreshment points in zoo

CHINA PUPPET THEATRE
Shadow and hand puppets are used expertly here to tell traditional folk tales.
✉ 1A, Area 1, Anhua Xili Beisanhuan Lu, Chaoyang District ☎ 6425 4847 🕐 Sat, Sun 10.30–11.30am, 2–3pm 👐 100–680RMB 🚌 207, 302, 379

SONY EXPLORASCIENCE
www.explorascience.com.cn
There are enough gadgets and pieces of technological wizardry here to keep the kids amused for a couple of hours. Of the numerous interactive displays and exhibits, the robotic dogs win hands down. English-speaking guides are on hand to help and each visitor gets a personalized photo as a record.
✉ Inside Chaoyang Park, 1 Chaoyang Gongyuan Nanlu, Chaoyang District ☎ 010 6501 8800 🕐 Mon–Fri 9.30–5.30, Sat, Sun 9–6.30. Closed 2nd Mon and Tue of each month 👐 Adult 30RMB, child under 6 years free 🚇 Bawangfen ⬜ Cafés in Oriental Plaza Shopping Mall

YUYUANTAN PARK
A five-minute walk from the China Millennium Monument, Yuyuantan ranks as one of Beijing's best parks and is a great place to rest your feet, stroll or entertain the children. Signs in English point you in the direction of the various attractions, which include a classical Chinese garden, a boating lake, children's play areas and a water park. Boats also leave from here for the Summer Palace in high season.
✉ Fuxingmenwai Dajie, Haidian District ☎ 010 8865 3711 🕐 Jun–end Aug daily 6am–9.30pm; Sep–end Oct daily 6am–8.30pm; Nov–end Mar daily 6.30am–7pm; Apr–end May daily 6am–8.30pm (all closing times are for the sale of last tickets—gardens will remain open for approximately one hour after this time) 👐 Adult 2RMB, child under 1.2m (4ft) free 🚇 Junshibowuguan ⬜ Cafés and kiosks in the park

FESTIVALS AND EVENTS

JANUARY/FEBRUARY
CHINESE NEW YEAR
www.chinaorg.cn/english/travel
Chinese New Year is the season of temple fairs in Beijing. The most important takes place on the 16th-century grounds of Ditan (Temple of Earth) Park, where in the past emperors offered sacrifices to heaven.

This rite is re-enacted as the climax to an exciting week-long celebration that includes food and drink, parades, competitions and other fun and games.
✉ Ditan Park, Andingmenwai Dajie, Dongcheng District, and temples throughout the city ☎ 010 6421 4657 🚇 Yonghegong

MAY
INTERNATIONAL LABOR DAY
The start of a major week-long national holiday is marked by floral displays and parades in the main square. Note that the Tian'anmen Square metro stations close for this holiday.
✉ Tian'anmen Square 🕐 May 1 🚇 Wangfujing

MIDI MUSIC FESTIVAL
www.midischool.com.cn
Sponsored by the MIDI School of Contemporary Music, this is the nearest China gets to a Western-style rock and pop festival. More than 40 bands, including some from overseas, take part each year in this four-day event.
✉ Haidian Park, Haidian District ☎ 010 6259 0101 🚇 Xizhimen, then bus 904

SEPTEMBER/OCTOBER
DASHANZI INTERNATIONAL ARTS FESTIVAL
www.diaf.org
Three weeks of avant-garde cultural happenings in Dashanzi Art District (▷ 95). There's so much to see and do, from performance art, design, music installation, documentary film, exhibitions, dance to experimental theater. Around 500 Chinese and 100 overseas artists took part in the festival in 2006.
✉ 4 Jiuxianqiao Lu, Chaoyang District ☎ 010 6438 2797 🚇 Dongzhimen, then bus 915, 918, 934

OCTOBER
NATIONAL DAY
Millions converge on the main square to watch the annual celebrations marking the founding of the Republic in 1949. There is much patriotic flag waving and applauding the bands. The Tian'anmen Square metro stations close for this holiday.
✉ Tian'anmen Square 🕐 1 Oct 🚇 Wangfujing

BEIJING MARATHON
www.beijing-marathon.com
Around 15,000 runners from China and overseas take part in the race, which runs from Tian'anmen Square to the Olympic Stadium. A mini marathon and fun runs take place at the same time.
✉ Tian'anmen Square ☎ 010 8525 1888/8503 🚇 Tiananmenxi, Tiananmendong

BEIJING INTERNATIONAL MUSIC FESTIVAL
www.bmf.org.cn
Top Chinese performers join distinguished international celebrities for this annual classical music festival. It is held in concert venues throughout the city. Previous guest artists have included the Berlin Philharmonic Orchestra, the Eroica Trio, the flautist James Galway and the cellist Yo Yo Ma.
✉ Beijing Concert Hall and other venues ☎ 010 6593 0299 (ticket office), 010 6406 8888 (English hotline) 🚇 Tiananmenxi, Tiananmendong

PRICES AND SYMBOLS

The restaurants are listed alphabetically. The prices are for a two-course lunch (L) and a three-course à la carte dinner (D) for one person, without drinks. The wine price is for the least expensive bottle. All the restaurants listed accept credit cards unless otherwise stated.

For a key to the symbols, ▷ 2.

ALAMEDA

Tucked away behind Sanlitun bar street, by Nali Market, Alameda tantalizes the taste buds with a menu of classic Brazilian dishes including specialties like *feijoada* (smoked meat stew). Always make a reservation here because it's a tight squeeze beneath the narrow glass-roofed dining area, which shows off the leafy garden to best effect during daylight hours.

✉ Entrance beside 42 Sanlitun Bei Jie, Chaoyang District ☎ 010 6417 8084
🕐 Daily 12–3, 6–11 🖐 L 60RMB, D 158RMB (plus 38RMB for dessert), Wine 198RMB 🚌 115

BA GUO BU YI

The carved wooden decor in this traditional Sichuanese restaurant is reminiscent of a Qing dynasty inn. The discreet dining spaces are grouped around three sides of an enclosed courtyard. On the fourth side is a stage where guests are treated to occasional live extracts of Chengdu opera. The extensive English-language picture menu ranges from standards like *mapo dofu* (braised pork with tofu) to more exotic dishes such as sharks' lips and braised bullfrog in a glazed pot. Service can be a bit slow.

✉ 89 Di'anmen Dongdajie, Dongcheng District ☎ 010 6400 8888 🕐 Daily 11.15–2, 5–9.30 🖐 L and D 110RMB, Wine 188RMB 🚌 13, 42, 58, 60

BELLAGIO

www.bellagiocafe.com.cn
In a quiet part of Sanlitun, this Taiwanese-owned restaurant attracts a regular clientele of exuberant, trendy young diners. They appreciate both the moderate prices and the wide sweep of the menu, which ranges from Chongqing fried chicken and Taiwanese sautéed beef to Hakka stir-fry. The fashionable interior includes marble-topped tables, velvet seating and strings of glittering metal baubles. Bellagio is always crowded so it's wise to reserve in advance.

✉ 6 Gongrentiyuchang Xilu, Chaoyang District ☎ 010 6551 3533 🕐 Daily 11am–5am 🖐 L and D 80RMB, Wine 199RMB 🚌 113, 115, 118, 823

BERENA'S BISTRO

Attractively priced Sichuan cooking is the main draw of this popular Sanlitun restaurant, which has long been a favorite with expats. Friendly English-speaking staff serve generous portions of tea-smoked duck, sautéed sliced fish with sweet-and-sour sauce, and beef in oyster sauce. It's an informal and relaxed setting, and the playful interior decor includes a birdcage

Opposite The interior of Ba Guo Bu Yi restaurant in Beijing is designed to look like it was created in the Qing dynasty

suspended from the ceiling, opera masks, strings of garlic and red lanterns.

✉ 35 Haoyun Jie (Bar Street), Zaoying Lu, Chaoyang District ☎ 010 6592 2628 🕒 Daily 11–11 🖐 L and D 120RMB, Wine 160RMB 🚌 112, 117, 403

BE THERE OR BE SQUARE

A reliable place when you're shopping in the mall. Be There Or Be Square serves up a variety of mainstream Cantonese dishes in a clean, fast-food environment. Try the home-made stewed mince pork or the wok-fried pork spare ribs, finishing off with a yogurt or pastry. Smoking and nonsmoking sections are available.

✉ Basement, Capital Epoch Plaza, Xicheng District ☎ 010 8391 4078 🕒 Daily 9.30–9.30 🖐 L and D 70RMB
🚇 Xidan

BIANYIFANG

This Qianmen duck restaurant was founded in 1416, which makes it even older than the Forbidden City. What also makes Bianyifang special is that the duck here is cooked using a closed oven, with straw rather than wood as fuel. When the time comes for the chef to carve the duck at your table, the meat will be especially succulent, tender and juicy. Wine is not served.

✉ A2, Chongwenmen Waidajie, Chongwen District ☎ 010 6712 0505 🕒 Daily 11–10
🖐 L and D 188RMB (whole duck), 94RMB (half duck) 🚇 Chongwenmen

BRASSERIE FLO

www.flo.com.cn

The Beijing branch of this well-known French chain has won plaudits for its outstanding French cooking, fine wines and impeccable service. The menu reads like a roll call of classic French dishes: snails in garlic butter, *terrine de foie gras, steak au poivre, tarte au citron*. The oysters are flown in weekly from France. The restaurant has a terrace

and a special playroom for children, which is supervised on weekends.

✉ 2F Rainbow Plaza, 16 Dong Sanhuan Beilu, Chaoyang District ☎ 010 6595 5135 🕒 Daily 11–2.30, 6–11 🖐 L and D 200–300RMB, Wine 220RMB 🚌 671, 718, 801

CAFÉ SAMBAL

This delightful Malaysian restaurant is in a tastefully restored courtyard house in a *hutong* near the Bell Tower. The setting is informal, with bare walls, wooden tables and comfortable settees, and is perfect for a romantic dinner. Try the satay chicken to start, then move on to the highly spiced beef rendang or, alternatively, the deep-fried *pomfret* (a fish) with chili sauce.

✉ 43 Doufuchi Hutong, off Jiugulou Dajie, Xicheng District ☎ 010 6400 4875 🕒 12–12 daily 🖐 L 80RMB (one course), D 110RMB, Wine 180RMB 🚇 Guloudajie

CD CAFÉ

This informal Italian restaurant is the latest addition to Beijing's longest established jazz club. Dine in the pleasant surroundings of the winter garden from a menu that includes home-made pasta dishes, pizzas cooked on a wood-fired oven, steaks and seafood. The jazz sessions on Thursday, Friday and Saturday evenings continue until 2am.

✉ 16 Dongsanhuan Dajie, Chaoyang District ☎ 010 6506 8288 🕒 Daily 4pm–3am 🖐 L and D 100RMB, Wine 260RMB 🚌 215, 420, 718, 815

THE COURTYARD

www.courtyardbeijing.com

For a truly unforgettable experience, reserve a window table in this restaurant overlooking the moat of the Forbidden City. Acclaimed when it first opened in 1997, The CourtYard continues to impress with its refined international fusion cuisine with Asian touches. Perhaps start with an appetizer of braised rabbit and vegetable terrine, followed by cashew nut-crusted lamb chops Xinjiang-style. The interior is minimalist chic with stark white walls and discreet

spotlighting. After dinner, you can relax in the cigar lounge, or look over the contemporary art in the CourtYard Gallery.

✉ 95 Donghuamen Dajie, Dongcheng District ☎ 010 6526 8883 🕒 Daily 6pm–10pm 🖐 L and D 450RMB, plus 15 percent, Wine 300RMB 🚇 Tiananmendong

DING DING XIANG

Though there is nothing special about the ambience or surroundings of this restaurant, it's popular with Beijingers for its hot pot—so popular in fact that you may find yourself lining up at the door for a table. You can customize your meal by choosing your own meat and vegetable ingredients (a vegetarian broth is available). Each dish comes with the restaurant's signature dipping sauce, *jinpai tiaoliao*, made with sesame.

✉ 14 Dongzhong Jie, Dongcheng District ☎ 010 6417 2546 🕒 Daily 11–11 🖐 L and D hot pot for 2 people 300RMB, Wine 80RMB 🚇 Dongzhimen

DRUM AND GONG

www.luogu.net

Set in one of Beijing's most charming *hutong*, this friendly restaurant serves a cuisine described by the English owner as Asian fusion, but which was originally inspired by spicy Sichuan cooking. All dishes have detailed English and French descriptions and the wines are surprisingly affordable. Drum and Gong is becoming increasingly known for its collection of world music and for its Tuesday jam sessions (9.30pm–midnight). Reserve in advance if you want a table on the garden patio.

✉ 104 Nanluogu Xiang, Dongcheng District ☎ 010 8402 4729 🕒 Daily 10am–midnight 🖐 L and D 50–100RMB, Wine 88RMB 🚌 13, 18, 107, 108

DURTY NELLIE'S

A popular hangout of locals and expats alike, this Irish bar has migrated from a currently derelict area of Sanlitun. It has all the usual Celtic trappings—Guinness on draft, portraits of Oscar Wilde, a menu that includes Irish stew, as well as pool tables and dart boards. The small parlors are suited to quiet conversation, while the back room serves as a stage for the occasional live cover band.

✉ 1F Liangmaqiao Flower Market, B8 Dongsanhuan Beilu, Chaoyang District ☎ 010 6593 5050 ⏱ Sun–Thu 10am–1.30am, Fri, Sat 10am–2.30am ✋ From 50RMB 🚌 52, 402, 420, 701, 757

DONG LAI SHUN

This Muslim hot pot restaurant on Wangfujing Dajie has plenty of honest halal mutton and fragrant bubbling broths. As with all hot pot restaurants, raw food is bought to the table and it's up to the diner to dunk it in the tank—here, wonderfully old-fashioned coal-burning copper installations. This is probably the best located and most atmospheric hot pot option in Beijing. The restaurant is always busy with locals and offers great insight into the cozy feasting traditions of Beijingers, especially in winter.

✉ 5F, Xindong'an Guangchang, Wangfujing Dajie, Dongcheng District ☎ 010 6528 0932 ⏱ Daily 11–9.30 ✋ L and D 80–100RMB, Wine 68RMB 🚇 Wangfujing

FAMILY LI RESTAURANT

In an obscure *hutong* in the Houhai Lake area, the Li family restaurant preserves a culinary tradition going back to the Qing dynasty, and not just any culinary tradition—the present owner, now in his 80s is a direct descendant of General Li Shunqing, Chief of the Palace Guard, whose responsibilities extended to the imperial kitchens. General Li committed numerous old recipes to memory and his relatives eventually opened this restaurant in the 1980s. The menu includes such refined dishes as well-stewed superior sharks' fin with duck meat. It is best to reserve ahead.

✉ 11 Yangfang Hutong Deshengmennei Dajie, Xicheng District ☎ 010 6618 0107 ⏱ Daily 11am–1.30 ✋ L and D Set menus from 230–2000RMB, Wine 100RMB 🚇 Jishuitan

FANGSHAN

www.fangshanfanzhuang.com.cn
At Fangshan you have an opportunity to dine out on some of the recipes created in the imperial kitchens for the Dowager Empress Cixi. The restaurant was founded in 1925 and enjoys a superb site in the Ming dynasty Hall of Rippling Waters in Beihai Park. Reserve ahead if you want a table overlooking the lake, though you may be disappointed as group reservations are often made weeks in advance. The set menus change from time to time and are drawn from a total of 800 court dishes.

✉ 1 Wenjin Jie, Beihai Park, Xicheng District ☎ 010 6401 1889 ⏱ Daily 11–1.30, 5–8 ✋ L and D set menus 150RMB, 200RMB, 250RMB, 300RMB per person, Wine 300RMB 🚌 5

FISH NATION

www.fishnation.cn
Fish Nation began as a tiny fish-and-chip shop in a Sanlitun backstreet where there was barely enough room for a couple of tables. In 2005 it expanded to these salubrious premises at the Di'anmendong Dajie end of Nanluogu Xiang, where framed Chinese paintings and candlelit tables make for a sophisticated vibe. English visitors may look no further than the cod in beer batter with chips, but the chef also makes a mean pizza and can rustle up Aussie beef sausages and calamari on demand. British breakfasts are served before 4pm.

✉ 31 Nanluogu Xiang, Dongcheng District ☎ 010 6401 3249 ⏱ Daily 9.30am–1.30am ✋ L and D 90RMB, Wine 100RMB 🚌 13, 42, 113

GONGDELIN

This Qianmen restaurant, just north of the Temple of Heaven, was founded in 1922 and is a useful standby for vegetarians. In line with local custom, the bean-curd-based dishes are dressed up to resemble meat and fish. The yellow croaker in sweet-and-sour sauce, for example, turns out to be made from mashed potato. Food doesn't come much

more inexpensive than this, but the surroundings and service are nothing to write home about. No wine is served.

✉ 158 Qianmen Nandajie, Chongwen District ☎ 010 6511 2542 ⏱ Daily 11–9 ✋ L and D from 38RMB 🚌 9, 44, 110, 723, 729

GRANDMA'S KITCHEN

American home-style cooking is the stock in trade of this friendly diner near the US embassy. The check tablecloths and blue chairs give the place a homey feel. Though you'll find the meatloaf or the Texas burger a meal in itself, try to save room for one of the desserts—choose from cheesecake, apple pie or blueberry pancake.

✉ 11a Xiushui Nanjie, Jianguomenwai, Chaoyang District ☎ 010 6503 2893 ⏱ Daily 7.30pm–11pm ✋ D 80–120RMB, Wine 170RMB 🚇 Jianguomen

GREEN T HOUSE

www.green-t-house.com
So self-consciously exclusive that you must ring a doorbell to enter, the Green T House has a designer-white decor, complemented by mirrored tables and abstract sculptures, and equally high-brow Chinese 'concept' dishes. You pay as much for the for ambience as the food, but there's no better place to see the movers and shakers of the New Beijing.

✉ 6 Gongti Xilu, Sanlitun, Chaoyang District ☎ 010 6552 8310 ⏱ Daily 11.30–2.30, 6–11.30 ✋ L and D 400–500RMB, Wine 390RMB

HATSUNE

The menu at this Japanese restaurant, owned by a Chinese-American, includes a wide range of sashimi, tempura and grilled fish, but it is the chef's creative touch with the sushi that makes this place truly memorable. Both the California roll (crab and avocado) and the 119 roll (tuna in a spicy sauce) can be recommended. There is also a good selection of *sake*.

✉ 2F Heqiao Building C, 8A Guanghua Donglu, Chaoyang District ☎ 010 6581

3939 🌐 Daily 11.30–2, 5.30–10 🖐 L and
D 100–200RMB, Wine (*sake*) 400RMB
🚌 9, 28 37, 402

INDIAN KITCHEN

Much-frequented by Indian
businessmen and their guests—
always a good sign—this Sanlitun
restaurant consistently lives up to its
reputation as one of the best places
to eat curry in the city. While the
menu leans toward southern India,
with dishes like *potato masala dosa*,
yellow dahl butter-fry and mutton
Madras, tandoori meat dishes and
breads are also well represented.
If in doubt, try one of the specials
or chef's recommendations. The
weekday lunch buffet is good value.
✉ 2F, 2, Sanlitun Beixiao Jie, Chaoyang
District 🕿 010 6462 7255 🌐 Daily
11.30–2.30, 5.30–11 🖐 L 40RMB,
D 100RMB, Wine 170RMB 🚌 110, 120, 208

JIN DING XUAN

Always busy, the Ditan Park branch
of this popular Cantonese chain
specializes in dim sum, brought
to your table in steaming bamboo
baskets. Fill up on spring rolls,
barbecued pork buns, chicken's
feet or Shanghainese *xiao long bao*
(pork dumplings), or select from the
comprehensive menu of southern
dishes. The interior is old-style
Chinese with plenty of laquer and
red lanterns.
✉ 77 Hepingli Xijie, Dongcheng District
🕿 010 6429 6888 🌐 Daily 24 hours
🖐 L and D 90RMB, Wine 80RMB
🚇 Yonghegong

KAOROU JI

This Muslim restaurant in the
beautiful Houhai Lake area has been
around for more than a century,
although these premises are not
particularly old. The menu (in English
with pictures of some dishes)
includes specialties like fried duck
shashlik (kabob), mutton with dried
apricot, stewed camel in pear and
roast duck (complete with head).
The green-uniformed staff speak
little English but are friendly and
helpful. Make advance reservations
for one of the tables on the balcony
(summer only).
✉ 14 Qianhai Dongyan, Xicheng District
🕿 010 6404 2554 🌐 Daily 11–2, 5–11
🖐 L and D 75RMB, plus 10–30RMB for tea,
Wine 138RMB 🚌 5, 60, 107, 124

LEGATION QUARTER

www.legationquarter.com
The capital's most high-profile new
'lifestyle' development is anchored
by a super-trendy multi-zone drinking
and dining complex. Featuring a
gorgeous Japanese restaurant, a
Spanish tapas bar with outdoor
terrace, and a North African theme
chill-out bar on the rooftop, a variety
of upscale tastes are catered to.
Dress up nicely, and prepare to flex
some plastic.
✉ 23 Qianmen, Qianmen Dongdajie,
Dongcheng District 🕿 010 6559 6266
🌐 Daily 12–2.30, 6–11 (Japanese
restaurant only open evenings) 🖐 L and
D 400RMB (700 RMB Japanese), Wine
300–400RMB 🚇 Qianmen

LI QUN

The owner of this tiny duck
restaurant, in a rundown Qianmen
courtyard house, left Quanjude
(▷ 113) to open this family
business. The birds are raised on a
farm in Shunyi and delivered here
daily, where they are roasted in a
wood-fired oven—you can watch
the process (and enjoy the aroma)
while you wait. The roasted duck is
served at your table with the
traditional accompaniment of
pancakes, plum sauce and sliced
scallions. Reservations are essential
and you need to allow 45 minutes to
an hour for the duck to cook.
Because of the size and popularity

Left *Fangshan restaurant has an opulent
interior*

of the restaurant, a time limit is placed on each table.

✉ 11 Beixiangfeng, Zhengyi Lu, Chongwen District ☎ 010 6705 5578 ⏰ Daily 10–10 🍴 L and D 200RMB, Wine 158RMB 🚇 Qianmen

MEI FU

This elegant restaurant in a *hutong* near Prince Gong's Residence is dedicated to the memory of the legendary Beijing opera star Mei Lanfang. Guests are treated to muted recordings of his performances while dining from one of several set menus, including dishes favored by the singer himself. The setting is a beautifully restored courtyard house—specify when you make a reservation if you want a room with a view.

✉ 24 Daxiangfeng Hutong, Xicheng District ☎ 010 6612 6847 ⏰ Daily 11.30–1.30, 6–9 🍴 L and D minimum 500RMB per person, Wine 400RMB 🚌 5, 60, 107, 124

METRO RESTAURANT

In a residential part of Sanlitun, west of the Workers' Stadium, Metro Café serves sophisticated Italian cuisine to a discerning clientele of businessmen and embassy staff. Among the appetizers are Florentine pancakes, filled with field mushrooms, ricotta cheese and spinach.

There is a choice of 40 sauces to accompany the fresh pasta dishes, while mains include rabbit cooked with *pao* peppers, or mutton with cumin roasted on an iron plate. The restrained lighting, framed paintings, wooden cabinets and banquettes are reminiscent of an English gentleman's club.

✉ 9 Gongrentiyuchang Xilu, Chaoyang District ☎ 010 6552 7828 ⏰ Mon–Fri 11.30–2, 5.30–10, Sat, Sun 11.30–10 🍴 L and D 230RMB, Wine 150RMB 🚌 112, 117, 403

NAM NAM

Next to Friendship Store, this artfully designed Sanlitun dining space evokes a French colonial villa and is the perfect setting to enjoy the well-executed Vietnamese cuisine. The spring rolls melt in the mouth, while the spicy fish has just the right combination of herbs. Waitresses wear the traditional *ao dai* (long dress worn over trousers). Nam Nam is a good choice to enjoy a romantic dinner for two.

✉ 7 Sanlitun Beilu, Chaoyang District ☎ 010 6468 6053 ⏰ Daily 10.30–10.30 🍴 L and D 100–200RMB, Wine 170RMB

PASS BY BAR

www.passbybar.com

At the Gulou Dongdajie end of Nanluogu Xiang, Beijing's classiest bar and restaurant street, Pass By is a great place to relax after a day's sightseeing. Sit back and enjoy a pizza, a plate of pasta, or a US-imported Angus sirloin steak, accompanied by a bottle of the reasonably priced Californian wine.

✉ 108 Nanluogu Xiang, Dongcheng District ☎ 010 8403 8004 ⏰ Daily 10am–2am 🍴 D 125RMB, Wine 180RMB 🚌 118, 104

PURE LOTUS

This much talked about vegan Buddhist restaurant inside the Agricultural Exhibition Hall has won praise from locals and visitors alike for its beautifully presented

Below *Relaxing in the Pass By Bar on Nanluogu Xiang*

dishes. Only the freshest produce is used—the mushrooms, lotuses and other vegetables come direct from Wutai Mountain, no less. Choose from the extensive English-language menu, which includes everything from pumpkin soup to meatless sausage and baked mushrooms. No garlic, onions or other stimulants are used in the preparation, in line with Buddhist principles.

✉ In the courtyard of the Tongguang Building, Chaoyang District ☎ 010 6592 3627 🕐 Daily 11–11 🍴 L and D 200RMB, no alcohol 🚌 9, 52, 402

QUANJUDE

Founded in 1864, Quanjude is famous as the home of Beijing duck. Farmed locally, the birds are roasted over an open fire, where fruit-tree wood gives them their special fragrance.

You might start with minced duck-meat soup with mushrooms and butter and—if you have room for a dessert—there are dumplings with sweet potato meat cake. No need to make a reservation as the vast dining rooms can accommodate 2,000 people, more-or-less exclusively foreign visitors.

✉ 14 Qianmen Xidajie, Xuanwu District ☎ 010 6302 3062 🕐 Daily 11–2, 4.30–9 🍴 L and D 228RMB (whole duck), Wine 90RMB 🚇 Hepingmen

RED CAPITAL CLUB

www.redcapitalclub.com.cn

In a once-exclusive neighborhood, where Maoist-era officials had their homes, Red Capital Club's courtyard restaurant serves what are reputed to have been the favorite dishes of Communist leaders.

Guests can sit in chairs previously used by members of the political elite while they enjoy Deng Xiaoping Spicy Chicken, Chairman Mao Vegetarian Bean Curd Wrap or Zhou Enlai Asparagus. You will know you've arrived here when you see the vintage limo sporting a red flag.

✉ 66 Dongsi Jiutiao, Dongcheng District ☎ 010 8401 6152, reservations 010 8401 8886 🕐 Daily 6pm–11pm 🍴 L and D from 300RMB, Wine 300RMB 🚇 Dongsishitiao

SERVE THE PEOPLE

'Serve the People wholeheartedly' was Chairman Mao's instruction and this Sanlitun eatery does just that, consistently wowing customers with pleasingly presented and attractively priced Thai dishes. Try one of the red or green curries as a main course, with a coconut chicken soup or papaya salad to start. There is seating on the terrace in the summer.

✉ 1 Sanlitun Xiwujie, Chaoyang District ☎ 010 8454 4580 🕐 Daily 10.30–10.30 🍴 L and D 150RMB, Wine 160RMB 🚌 110, 120, 208

SOUTH SILK ROAD

This trendy restaurant serves Yunnanese folk dishes which have been given an urban twist. It's located in a contemporary space with a glass floor and is owned by painter Fang Lijun, whose artwork graces the walls. The specialties include the essential fried goats' cheese, sausages with cayenne pepper and Sichuan peppercorn, cross-the-bridge noodles, and crispy potato fritters. The famous rice wine is also a must.

✉ No. 12–13, 19A Hehua Shichang (Lotus Lane), Qianhai Xiyan, Xicheng District ☎ 010 6615 5515 🕐 Daily 11.30am–midnight 🍴 L 150RMB and D 200RMB, Wine 98RMB

TEAHOUSE OF FAMILY FU

In a pavilion overlooking Houhai Lake, this is one of only a few traditional teahouses in the city. The owner has furnished the several rooms with tasteful Ming and Qing dynasty reproductions and there are occasional performances of classical Chinese music. Snacks are provided free of charge.

✉ Deshengmen Neidaijie (no number), Dongcheng District ☎ 010 6616 0725 🕐 Daily 10am–midnight 🍴 From 38RMB per pot. L 150RMB, D 260RMB 🚇 Jishuitan

TRAKTIRR

Beijing's Russian community has spawned a number of interesting restaurants—this one beside Nanguan Park may offer the best

value for money. The Russian name summons up images of a country inn where plain, nourishing home cooking is to be expected. In this respect Traktirr does not disappoint. Expect hearty helpings of classic dishes like *pelmeni* (pork dumplings served with sour cream) and chicken Kiev.

✉ Nos 5–15, Dongzhimennei Dajie, Dongcheng District ☎ 010 6403 1896 🕐 Daily 10am–midnight 🍴 L and D 80RMB, Wine 68RMB 🚇 Dongzhimen

THE TREE

www.treebeijing.com

The aroma of thin-crust pizzas baked in a wood-fired oven greets you at this convivial Sanlitun pub restaurant. Enjoy reasonably priced meals and great Belgian beers in its cavernous interior. Reserve in advance on weekends or you might have to wait for a table.

✉ 43 Bei Sanlitun Jie ☎ 010 6415 1954 🕐 Sun–Thu 10.30am–2am, Fri, Sat 10.30am–4am 🍴 L and D 115RMB, Wine 150RMB 🚌 115

VINCENT CAFÉ

The French owner of this rustic-style café in Dashanzi Art District hails from Brittany, where the regional specialties are crêpes and *galettes* (savory buckwheat pancakes). Order from an extensive list of fillings, including egg, mushroom and Norwegian salmon. If you have room, finish your meal with the house dessert—apple crêpe, flambéed in Calvados.

✉ 2 Jiuxianqiao Beilu, Chaoyang District ☎ 010 8456 4823 🕐 Daily 11am–6.30pm 🍴 L and D 60RMB, Wine 100RMB 🚇 Dongzhimen, then 20-minute bus journey from Dongzhimen bus station on 909

XIAO XIN

Typical of the new breed of trendy cafés springing up on this renovated *hutong*, Xiao Xin is special because of its mouthwatering cakes and pastries, dreamed up by the owner himself.

✉ 103 Nanluogu Xiang, Dongcheng District ☎ 010 6403 6956 🕐 Daily 11am–1.30am 🍴 Pastries from 20RMB 🚌 104, 118

STAYING

PRICES AND SYMBOLS

Prices are for a double room for one night, unless otherwise stated. Breakfast is included unless noted otherwise. All the hotels listed accept credit cards unless otherwise stated. Note that rates vary widely throughout the year.

For a key to the symbols, ▷ 2.

THE AMAN AT SUMMER PALACE

www.amanresorts.com
After a lengthy search for a home in mainland China, Aman—one of the world's top luxury hoteliers—plumped for this spot adjacent to the East Gate of the Summer Palace. The rooms and suites are contained within a series of century-old dwellings, originally reserved for palace guests awaiting an audience with the Empress Dowager Cixi. The architecture and design borrows ideas from its palatial neighbor: Suites surround

a courtyard featuring an intricate latticework of pathways, separating formal gardens and trees. Floors are finished in polished Jin clay tiles and the ceilings are open to exposed wooden roof beams. As always at Aman, the spa is a big draw.
✉ 15 Gongmenqian Lu, Summer Palace, Haidian District ☎ 010 5987 9999
🖐 3,300–4,800 RMB 🚪 43 ⛵ 🍸 ♿

BAMBOO GARDEN HOTEL

www.bbgh.com.cn
This beautifully restored, rambling courtyard mansion is in a quiet hutong only five minutes' walk from the metro and not far from the Drum and Bell towers. It's worth paying extra for a room with a veranda overlooking the garden (▷ picture above); ask when making a reservation. The staff are welcoming and used to dealing with foreign visitors. There are two

Chinese restaurants, a café and bar and a spa.
✉ 24 Xiaoshiqiao Hutong (off Jiugulou Dajie), Xicheng District ☎ 010 6403 2229, ext 236/238 🌐 All year
🖐 880RMB, excluding breakfast 🚪 40 ♿ 🚇 Guloudajie

BEIJING COURTOTEL

www.beijingcourtel.com
A new mid-range hotel crafted from a traditional courtyard dwelling. The seven room categories range in size and value, with the cheapest online rates going for just over 400RMB. All come with touches like personal DVD players, Wi-Fi and power showers, and there are cool designer touches in the public areas. The Bell and Drum towers are a short distance away.
✉ 8 Courtyard, Andingmen Xijie, Dongcheng District ☎ 010 6407 6799
🖐 420–1,200RMB 🚪 23 🚇 Andingmen ♿

Opposite A shaded pergola leading into the gardens of Beijing's Bamboo Garden Hotel

BEIJING RAFFLES HOTEL
www.beijing.raffles.com

Beijing's oldest hotel, occupying a prime downtown site, on the corner of Wangfujing shopping street and only one metro stop from Tian'anmen Square, was taken over and refurbished by the Raffles chain in 2006. Sadly, no rooms overlook the Forbidden City. However, some of the hotel's original features have been resurrected, notably the stunning dance floor, complete with grand piano, dating from 1924 (now in the JAAN restaurant). In East 33 restaurant, chefs at the cooking stations serve up a mix of Western and Asian cuisines. Other facilities include squash and tennis courts.

✉ 33 Chang'an Dongjie, Dongcheng District ☎ 010 6526 3388 🕐 All year ✋ 1,688–3,000RMB, excluding breakfast 🚪 171 🔲 🔳 ➿ Indoor 🚇 Wangfujing

CHINA WORLD
www.shangri-la.com

In the China World Trade Center, about 4km (2.5 miles) east of the Forbidden City, this luxury hotel (part of the Shangri-La chain) regularly wins awards for its superb facilities, geared especially to business customers. Nadama, the pick of the restaurants, serves Japanese cuisine, but you should also check out the funky Aria wine bar, where you can enjoy modern international dishes while listening to live jazz.

✉ China World Trade Centre, 1 Jianguomenwai Dajie, Chaoyang District ☎ 010 6505 2266 🕐 All year ✋ 1,080–3,200RMB 🚪 716 🔲 🔳 ➿ Indoor 🚇 Guomao

COMFORT INN
www.choicehotels.com

This hotel, in a streamlined modern tower, is convenient for Sanlitun bar street and local restaurants like Serve the People (▷ 113). Geared to leisure as well as business travelers, the rooms are clean and comfortable (some nonsmoking rooms and rooms for travelers with

disabilities are available). The price includes a Continental breakfast in the hotel restaurant. There is a small swimming pool on the roof and bicycle rental is available.

✉ 6 Gonti Beilu, Chaoyang District ☎ 010 8523 5522 🕐 All year ✋ 800RMB (no discounts) 🚪 96 🔲 ➿ Indoor 🚇 113 🚇 Nongzhanguan

HOTEL COTE COUR SL
www.hotelcotecoursl.com

This new 14-room property reflects a growing taste for traditional courtyard architecture among visitors to Beijing. It's hidden down a historically protected *hutong* alley wonderfully situated for the city's central sights (Wangfujing is easily walkable). Though light on facilities, the hotel's interiors are beautiful and the rooms have been carefully restored and painstakingly decorated with glass mosaic tiles and antiques in every corner.

✉ 70 Yanyue Hutong, Chengdong District ☎ 010 6512 8020 🕐 All year ✋ 1,295–1,800RMB 🚪 14 🚇 Dengshikou 🔲

DONG SI SUPER 8 HOTEL

Around 15 minutes' walk from Chaoyangmen metro station, this budget hotel is not especially convenient for the sights, but represents good value for the money. The staff are friendly and helpful and all rooms have satellite TV and free internet access. Facilities include a business center, function room and beauty salon, while the restaurant specializes in Beijing cuisine and dim sum.

✉ 137 Dongsi Wutiao, Dongcheng District ☎ 010 6406 5688 🕐 All year ✋ 358–600RMB, excluding breakfast 🚪 110 🔲 🚇 Chaoyangmen

EMPEROR HOTEL
www.designhotels.com

A taste of New York-style design cool in the heart of Beijing. The Emperor is on a quiet, tree-lined avenue a short walk from the Forbidden City and Tian'anmen Square, nestled amongst traditional temples and houses. The facade looks classically Chinese but the

interiors have a distinctly cutting-edge design. The 55 rooms and nine suites are relentlessly modern—think white walls, beige woods and giant flatscreen TVs—but comes sprinkled with traditional symbolic touches. The restaurant and bar are both fantastic, the latter featuring a superb rooftop area with views of Beijing's ancient low-rise skyline.

✉ 33 Qihelou Jie, Xicheng District ☎ 010 6526 5566 🕐 All year ✋ 1,388–1,900RMB 🚪 55 🚇 Tian'anmenxi 🔳 🔲

FRAGRANT HILLS HOTEL

Designed by architect I.M. Pei, whose award-winning designs include the Bank of China Tower in Hong Kong, this hotel is set in a landscaped park and has a vast glass-roofed atrium-lounge, which doubles as a greenhouse. Rooms are clean, airy and on the generous side and have views overlooking the park. The hotel currently caters mainly to Chinese and Japanese visitors and the staff, while friendly and helpful, speak little English. However, this situation is likely to change as word gets around. One to watch!

✉ Fragrant Hills Park, Haidian District ☎ 010 6259 1166 🕐 All year ✋ 800–1,400RMB, excluding breakfast 🚪 286 🔲 🔳 ➿ Indoor 🚇 634 to east gate then walk, bearing left and following signs to hotel (Xiang Shan Hotel) 🚇 Fragrant Hills turn off 5th ring road. Taxi 70RMB

GUO MAO SUPER 8 HOTEL

Since opening in 2006, this hotel on the edge of the Central Business District has proved a popular budget alternative to its sister hotel Dong Si Super 8 (▷ left). It's close to the Shuangjing metro station and it is only a short hop by bus to the great shopping and leisure facilities in the World Trade Centre. Rooms are a reasonable price for the size and the restaurant serves a Western-style buffet breakfast. English-speaking desk staff.

✉ 18 Shuangjing Beili, Chaoyang District ☎ 010 6776 3388 🕐 All year ✋ 388–700RMB 🚪 79 🔲 🚇 Shuangjing (under construction) 🚇 37

HAOYUAN HOTEL

www.haoyuanhotel.com

This beautifully restored courtyard house, faithfully refurbished in Ming-dynasty style, is in a quiet *hutong* east of Wangfujing shopping street. The standard rooms are on the small side and you may be tempted to splurge on one of the guest rooms in the east and west wings, which are furnished with canopied beds, carved rosewood cabinets and folding screens and decorated with Chinese paintings and porcelain vases. The restaurant serves imperial court dishes as well as Western cuisine.

✉ 53 Shijia Hutong, Dongcheng District ☎ 010 6512 5557 ⑥ All year ⛏ 470–585RMB ① 19 ⑤ ⑨ Wangfujing, Dengshikou (under construction)

JIANGUO GARDEN HOTEL

Often overlooked, this large Chinese-run hotel is just a couple of minutes' walk from the metro and only 10 minutes from Tian'anmen Square and the Forbidden City. While the sprawling public areas are rather smoky and some of the rooms a bit stuffy, the hotel represents good value, especially as you can often negotiate a discount or upgrade. The buffet breakfast includes Western and Chinese dishes and the restaurants serve Hakka Chinese and Muslim specialties.

✉ 17 Jianguomennei Dajie, Dongcheng District ☎ 010 6528 6666 ⑥ All year ⛏ 1,200–1,700RMB ① 380, 70 nonsmoking rooms ⑤ ⑨ ⛵ Indoor ⑨ Dongdan

HOTEL KAPOK

www.hotelkapok.com

Part of a mini Chinese chain of affordable boutique hotels, Hotel Kapok has a great location, in the former Legation Quarter just east of the Forbidden City. Rooms are small but don't feel overly cramped thanks to the lattice dividers and modern furnishings, which leans heavily on whitewashed walls and earthy, rustic colors. Facilities are simple but the location overcomes all complaints—especially given the

fairly reasonable room tariffs.

✉ 6 Donghuamen Dajie, Dongcheng District ☎ 010 6525 9988 ⑥ All year ⛏ 800–1,400RMB ① 89 ⑨ Tian'anmendong ⑦ ⑤

KERRY CENTER

www.shangri-la.com

This modern luxury hotel is in the heart of the Central Business District. The rooms are all you would expect, but it is the facilities that are outstanding. They include a shopping mall, one of the best cocktail bars in the city (Centro), the Horizon Chinese restaurant (with a play area for children) and indoor tennis and squash courts.

✉ 1 Guanghua Lu, Chaoyang District ☎ 010 6561 8833 ⑥ All year ⛏ 988–1,900RMB, excluding breakfast ① 487 ⑤ ⑦ ⛵ Indoor and children's ⑨ Guanghualu

LÜSONGYUAN HOTEL

In an ancient *hutong* just north of the Forbidden City, this tastefully converted courtyard mansion has rooms in various categories, most of which are furnished in Ming-dynasty style and overlook the garden. The restaurant serves Beijing and northern Chinese cuisine. You can also organize a pedicab tour of the *hutong* of the Houhai District from the hotel.

✉ 22 Banchang Hutong, Doncheng District ☎ 010 6404 0436 ⑥ All year ⛏ 398–850RMB, excluding breakfast ① 58 ⑤ ⑨ 104

PEKING DOWNTOWN BACKPACKERS ACCOMMODATION

If you like meeting fellow travelers and are looking for accommodations that are easy on the wallet, this hostel is for you. Nanluogu Xiang is a rambling *hutong* lined with trendy bars and restaurants and there are more in the Houhai Lake area nearby. Private rooms have their own shower. Hostel services include laundry, bicycle rental, internet access and book exchange. Airport pickup is available for the cost of the toll charge (20RMB) if you are

staying at least four nights.

✉ 85 Nanluogu Xiang, Dongcheng District ☎ 010 8400 2429 ⑥ All year ⛏ 190–390RMB ① 17 ⑤ ⑨ 204

PENINSULA

www.beijing.peninsula.com

The Ming-dynasty-style entrance of Peninsula, one of Beijing's most expensive and luxurious hotels, sits rather uneasily with the strikingly modern marble and glass lobby, where you will find an arcade of designer boutiques. Rooms and suites have marble bathrooms and plasma TVs, but the conservative furnishings verge on the bland. The Jing restaurant, on the other hand, has won praise for its elegant fusion cooking and open-plan kitchen, where you can watch the chefs at work. The hotel can arrange trips to unrestored sections of the Great Wall and rickshaw tours of the *hutong* led by a university professor.

✉ 8 Jinyu Hutong, Dongcheng District ☎ 010 8516 2888 ⑥ All year ⛏ 2,050–3,700RMB, excluding breakfast ① 525 ⑤ ⑦ ⛵ Indoor ⑨ Wangfujing. Airport transfer via Rolls Royce ($200 round trip)

QIANMEN JIANGUO HOTEL

www.qianmenhotel.com

Even if you do not stay in this 1950s-era hotel, where the lavish reception area sets the rather formal tone, you may call in to see a Beijing Opera performance in the Liyan Theatre (▷ 104) or feast on Qianmen roast duck in the Songhe Restaurant. The hotel is near the renovated Qianmen shopping street and not too far from the Temple of Heaven. The rooms are spacious and airy, while the amenities include a sauna, massage and beauty center.

✉ 175 Yongan Lu, Xuanwu District ☎ 010 6301 6688 ⛏ 680–1,078RMB ① 410 (6th floor nonsmoking) ⑤ ⑨ 23

QING ZHU YUAN HOTEL

If Peking Downtown Backpackers (▷ left) is full, this Chinese-run hostel is a decent alternative, although prices are a little higher. It's on the same *hutong*, with access to

the same local bars, restaurants and nightlife.

✉ 113 Nanluogu Xiang, Dongcheng District ☎ 010 6401 3961 🕐 All year ✋ 260–480RMB with bathroom ⓘ 14 🔣 🛏 118

QOMOLANGMA HOTEL

www.qomolangmahotel.com

Qomolangma—the Tibetan name for Mount Everest—is in a former Qing dynasty temple, which retains many original features. It's on the edge of an attractive neighborhood where the sights include the Drum and Bell towers and Houhai Lake. The simply furnished rooms are a decent size and have satellite TV. The restaurant serves regional Chinese and Tibetan dishes.

✉ 149 Gulouxi Dajie, Xicheng District ☎ 010 6401 8822 🕐 All year ✋ 620–1,100RMB ⓘ 74 🔣 🍴 🚇 Guloudajie

RED CAPITAL CLUB RESIDENCE

www.redcapitalclub.com.cn

'Mao chic' is how the American

owner describes the quirky interiors of this boutique hotel. Antique wooden beds, furniture from the offices of former Communist officials, birdcages and goldfish bowls decorate the 200-year-old courtyard house. Below the trapdoor in the courtyard is an old bomb shelter, now a wine bar. There are only five suites so reservations are necessary. The hotel is unmarked: Look for the red door with the number 9.

✉ 9 Dongsi Liutiao, Dongcheng District ☎ 010 6402 7150 🕐 All year ✋ 1,539–2,200RMB, excluding breakfast ⓘ 5 🔣 🛏 24

RITZ-CARLTON FINANCIAL STREET

www.ritzcarlton.com

The luxury Ritz-Carlton brand now has two hotels in Beijing. This is the older of the two but it's more useful for leisure travelers, situated approximately 1km (0.6 mile) west of Tian'anmen Square.

The sparkling glass and chrome exterior is typical of Beijing's new crop of modern development projects, while guests can expect the usual supreme Ritz-Carlton standards of service. With 253 rooms and suites, it's not as big as some of Beijing's other five-star hotels. The spa and restaurants are destinations in their own right.

✉ 83A Jianguo Lu Chaoyang District ☎ 010 5908 8888 🕐 All year ✋ 1,800–2,500RMB ⓘ 253 🏊 🍴 🔣 🚇 Xuanwumen

TANRUI INN

This small hotel is a good budget option near Wangfujing shopping street. The rooms are tastefully decorated.

✉ 15 Baishu Hutong, Dongcheng District ☎ 010 6526 6699 🕐 All year ✋ 458–644RMB ⓘ 60 🔣 🍴 🏊 Indoor 🚇 Dengshikou

Above *The peaceful courtyard of the Lüsongyuan Hotel*

THE NORTH

The northern hinterlands have been largely forgotten in China's 21st-century tourist revamp. The Chinese call this land Zhongyuan, 'the middle plains'. It's the home of the Yellow River basin, the area from which a cohesive Chinese civilization emerged way back in the mists of time. Five of the eight ancient capitals—Luoyang, Anyang, Kaifeng, Zhengzhou and Xi'an—are located here and archeologists continue to make startling finds. Despite its illustrious history and massive population, the area has little modern renown. Its cities tend to be marked by heavy industry. Thanks to the coal-fired power stations, so are the skies.

Bucking this slightly dreary trend is China's longest standing capital city, Xi'an. As the terminus of the Silk Road, Chang'an (as it was previously known) marked the collision point of the East and West. The city was studded with palaces, mosques and marketplaces. Strange foreign faces mingled with the Chinese aristocracy and in its day, it rivaled Constantinople or Rome for glamour and grandeur. The world-famous Terra-cotta Warriors attraction now pulls in a similarly global crowd. Another exception is the oft-sunny coastal province of Shandong, birthplace of Chinese scholar, Confucius, and home to one of China's most revered mountains, Taishan, as well as a string of fast-developing beach resorts.

The northern fringes of this region contain dramatic mountains and large tracts of the Great Wall, though the deceptively flat central plains disguise earth-shattering natural forces. The deadliest earthquake of the 20th century occurred at Tangshan, Hubei province, in 1976 when an earthquake killed at least 240,000 people. Catastrophic flooding of the fabled Yellow River killed around a million in 1887. These days, in certain seasons, the river resembles little more than a dribble.

BEIDAIHE

Beidaihe is North China's leading beach resort, drawing millions of local visitors during the summer. Stretching along 10km (6 miles) of coastline, the three beaches have clean, fine sand and the sea is ideal for swimming. The town has a slightly dated atmosphere, enhanced in part by the many early 20th-century European villas. Nearby Lianfeng Mountain offers good views as well as very pleasant walking.

✚ 423 S7 ▣ Beidaihe train station. Trains from Beijing (3–5 hours). The station is 15km (9 miles) west of town, a 15–20RMB trip by taxi ▣ Service from Beijing takes 3 hours

CHENGDE

▷ 122–123

GONGYI

Midway between Zhengzhou and Luoyang, Gongyi is notable for its Buddhist caves and imperial tombs. The Buddhist caves (daily 8.30–6) date back to the northern Wei dynasty, and were commissioned in the 5th century by Emperor Xiaowen. The complex includes five caves holding more than 7,000 Buddhist statues in more than 200 shrines. The most striking sights, though, are three large bas-relief Buddha images carved into the rock face. The caves are about 15km (9 miles) north of town. The Song Tombs (daily 8.30–5) enshrine seven of the nine northern Song emperors, as well as members of the imperial family and top officials. Most of the 10th- and 11th-century tombs are now ruins, but the avenues leading up to the mausoleums are lined with around 700 stone statues of animals, officials, mandarins and slaves. Yongzhao and Yongding mausoleums, two of the Song

Opposite *Rock formations of Huashan (Flowering Mountain), one of China's sacred mountains of Taoist significance, in the Shaanxi Province*

Above *The attractive entrance to Rich Kang Manor in Kangdian County, Gongyi*

Tombs, have both been restored and are open to the public.

✚ 417 Q9 ▣ From Luoyang and Zhengzhou

HUASHAN

Huashan, 120km (74 miles) east of Xi'an, is the most westerly cluster of the Five Great Mountains (Wuyue) sacred to Taoism. The mountain has five peaks, the highest of which is South Peak (Nan Feng) at 2,160m (7,085ft). There are three ways up the mountain: a 10-minute cable car trip (60RMB one way) to the 1,600m (5,248ft) North Peak (Bei Feng); via a challenging footpath, which follows the same line as the cable car; the most popular route begins at Jade Fountain Temple (20RMB) at the northern foot of the mountain. It is a 6km (3.5-mile) climb, taking between 3 and 4 hours, to the North Peak. From the North Peak you can cross the Green Dragon Ridge (Canglong Feng) before climbing to the other peaks.

✚ 417 P10 ▣ Mengyuan Train Station. The train station is on the Xi'an–Luoyang line, 15km (9 miles) east of Huashan. Trains from Xi'an (2–3 hours) ▣ From Xi'an (2 hours)

JINAN

The capital of Shandong province, Jinan is a major trading town and transportation hub. The exhibits at Shandong Provincial Museum (Tue–Sun 9–12, 1–5) include imperial porcelain, Buddhist statues and prehistoric finds from nearby Longshan. At the Baotu Spring Park (Baotu Quan Gongyuan) you can see some of the famous springs, and also visit the Li Qingzhao Memorial Hall, dedicated to the most renowned female Song dynasty poet (daily 7–6).

✚ 422 R8 ℹ Tourist information office ✉ 78 Wen Hua Donglu, ☎ 0531 296 0760 ▣ Jinan Main Train Station. Trains from Beijing (4–6 hours), Shanghai (9–14 hours) and other cities ▣ From Beijing, Qingdao and Weihai

INFORMATION

www.cncdt.com

🕂 422 R6 🛈 Chengde Information Centre ☎ 0314 205 1023 ⊕ Daily 8–5 🚊 Chengde Train Station. Express trains from Beijing take 4 hours

Above *A view of the temple roofs of Puning Si*

INTRODUCTION

Chengde was the main summer retreat of the Qing Emperors during the 18th and 19th centuries. The town has China's largest imperial garden and impressive Han and minority-style temples.

Chengde (a UNESCO World Heritage Site) sits in a valley by the Wulie River (Wulie He) about 250km (156 miles) northeast of Beijing. The town itself lies to the south of the park that houses the former imperial palace. In the hills to the north and east are eight 18th-century temples. These sites are quite spread out, so tour them by minibus. For those with more time and energy, bicycles are a great way to explore the temples.

Construction of the summer palace at Jehol (the old name for Chengde) began in 1703. It effectively became the seat of government during the summer months throughout the 18th century. The popularity of the palace waned in the early 19th century, but Emperor Xianfeng's court moved here again after the Second Opium War and the subsequent occupation of Beijing in 1860. Much of Chengde's heritage and architecture was lost during the 1960s, and there are efforts to restore some of the more dilapidated temples.

WHAT TO SEE

IMPERIAL SUMMER PALACE

The Qing emperor Kangxi's original plan called for the creation of 36 scenic spots within the 560ha (1,380-acre) walled park. Toward the end of the 18th century, Emperor Qianlong ordered the construction of 36 more. Today the park is a refreshing place to experience the lakes, hills and forests. After entering the main gate you'll see the Front Palace, which houses a collection of Qing imperial artifacts.

🕐 Mid-Apr to mid-Oct daily 7–5.30; mid-Oct to mid-Apr daily 7–4.30 ✋ Adult 90RMB summer, 60RMB winter, child free

EIGHT OUTER TEMPLES

Beyond the palace walls, in the hills to the north and east, the Eight Outer Temples (Wai Ba Miao Putuozongcheng Zhimiao), dating from the latter half of the 18th century, show a variety of Han, Mongolian and Tibetan architectural styles. Putuozongcheng (daily 8–6), the largest temple, is a small replica of the Potala Palace in the Tibetan capital Lhasa and contains traditional Tibetan Buddhism items. The temple compound stretches up the slope of a hill, with the imposing main hall at the top. In the valley to the east, Xumifushou Zhimiao (daily 8–5.30) also shows considerable Tibetan influence. The highlight of the Puning Si (daily 8–5.30), which commemorates the suppression of a Mongol uprising, is a 22m-high (71ft) statue of Guanyin, the Buddhist Goddess of Mercy, fashioned out of wood and covered in gold in the imposing Mahayana Hall at the rear of the complex.

MORE TO SEE

GUANDI TEMPLE

This Taoist temple (daily 8–5.30) close to the main palace gate contains murals and statues of Taoist deities and Confucius. The temple is dedicated to the Guandi, the God of War. His statue is in the main hall.

Below *Water Heart Pavilions (Chui Xin Xie) at the Imperial Summer Palace*

INFORMATION
✚ 417 Q7 ℹ CITS, 21 Yingbin Donglu,
☎ 0352 510 2265 🕐 Daily 8.30–6
🚆 Datong Train Station. Express trains
from Beijing (6–7 hours)

TIP

» The easiest way to see the Yungang
Caves and the Hanging Temple is
on one of the CITS tours available from
Datong.

DATONG

This former capital has an historic walled central area. It is a base for
excursions to the Yungang Caves (Yungang Shiku) and the Hanging Temple
(Xuankongsi).

Datong was capital of the Wei dynasty (AD386–534) and later of the
Liao dynasty (907–1125). The central walled district of the city is quite well
preserved, and the old temples of Huayan and Shanhua can be visited on foot.
Huayan contains one of the country's largest Buddhist halls, with an elaborately
painted ceiling and five Ming-era Buddha statues. Shanhua dates back to the
Tang dynasty, but was entirely rebuilt in the 12th century. There are many
Buddhist statues and murals in the main hall.

YUNGANG CAVES

The main draw are the Yungang Caves (Yungang Shiku; daily 8–5), 16km
(10 miles) to the west of the city. The caves and statuary were carved into
the sandstone cliffs mainly during the 5th-century Wei dynasty. The string
of caves, grottoes and niches stretches for more than 1km (0.5 miles) and
contains more than 50,000 carved Buddha images and religious figures.
Highlights include the huge seated Buddha in Cave 5, the stone pagoda and
carved frescos recounting the life of the Buddha in Cave 6, and the wooden
temple facade protecting this pair of caves.

HANGING TEMPLE

The Hanging Temple (Xuankongsi; daily 7–7), 60km (37 miles) southeast of
Datong, was built by the Wei dynasty over 1,400 years ago, though the present
structures are mainly Qing era. Constructed on the side of a cliff, the temple
halls are caves in the rock face covered by wooden facades supported by
slender pillars balanced on ledges below. A series of bridges and walkways
connect the halls.

Below *Carvings in Cave 20, one of the
caves at Yungang*

JIXIAN

The main sight in this small county town 90km (56 miles) east of Beijing is Dule Temple, a Tang dynasty complex with a very old wooden pavilion containing a 16m-high (52ft) clay sculpture of Guanyin, the Goddess of Mercy. A short distance to the north of town is Yellow Cliff Pass (Huangyaguan), a 3km (1.8-mile) section of the Great Wall restored in the 1980s. This stretch passes through a particularly mountainous landscape, following the contours of a steep ridge. Yellow Cliff Pass includes 20 towers, among them the Phoenix Tower, the largest remaining anywhere on the wall. There is a museum and stelae with calligrapic inscriptions.

✚ 422 R7 🚉 Jixian Train Station. Trains from Beijing (2 hours) and Tianjin (3 hours); 🚌 Buses from Beijing (2 hours) and Tianjin (2.5 hours)

KAIFENG

The capital city of no less than seven dynasties, Kaifeng is today a pleasant, culturally rich, low-rise city that has resisted the rush to modernity seen in similar cities. The old walled city contains several large lakes, as well as most of the main sights. The Prime Minister's Temple (daily 8–6), built in AD555, was a very important northern Song temple. It was rebuilt in the 18th century and houses a magnificent 6m-tall (19.5ft) gilded wooden statue of Guanyin, carved from a single tree. The Shanshan'gan Guild Hall (daily 8.30–6) is a carefully restored example of Qing-era domestic architecture on a grand scale. In the northeast corner of the city walls, the Iron Pagoda (daily 8–6) is actually made of brick. The covering shiny brown tiles give it a distinctive hue. The 50m (54-yard) climb to the top is worthwhile for the view. The Fan Pagoda, to the southeast of the city wall, is a northern Song structure from AD977. Adjacent Yuwangtai Park (Yuwangtai Gongyuan) was a gathering place for musicians in the Tang dynasty.

✚ 424 Q9 ℹ️ CITS, 98 Yingbin Lu ☎ 0378 398 4593 🕐 Daily 8–6 🚉 Kaifeng Train Station. Trains from Xi'an (10 hours), Shanghai (12 hours) and Zhengzhou (1 hour)

LAOSHAN

This range of mountains overlooking the sea has been an important Taoist center for more than 2,000 years. The Great Purity Palace dates from the early northern Song dynasty (AD960–1127), when it was used by the emperor for Taoist rituals. From here you can take a cable car halfway up the mountain or walk to the summit. Along the way are shrines, caves and inscriptions, though the real interest lies in the scenery and the views.

✚ 423 T8 🚌 From Qingdao (1–2 hours)

LUOYANG

Luoyang was an imperial capital for nine dynasties from the 8th century BC through the 10th century AD. Some of the city's former glory is on display in the Luoyang Museum and the Luoyang Museum of Ancient Tombs. Dating from AD68, the White Horse Temple to the east was China's first Buddhist temple. However, the main attraction is undoubtedly the Longmen Caves (daily 6–8), 15km (9 miles) south of town. These northern Wei Buddhist caves line both sides of the Yi River and contain more than 100,000 carvings of Buddha-related figures. You can take a shuttle bus from Longmen to the nearby Shaolin Temple (daily 11.30am).

✚ 417 Q9 🚉 Luoyan Train Station. Trains from Xi'an (6 hours), Shanghai (14 hours) and Beijing (8–10 hours) 🚌 From Zhengzhou, Shaolin and Kaifeng

Above *Exterior of the 13-tiered Iron Pagoda in Kaifeng*
Below *The Longmen Caves are located near Luoyang*

QINGDAO (TSINGTAO)

With its Bavarian-style architecture and seaside atmosphere, this port city offers visitors a refreshing change of pace.

Qingdao was a quiet fishing village until 1897, when Germany extracted a concession here from the ruling Manchu government granting Germany the right to rule the town for 99 years. This was obtained by a combination of military pressure and diplomacy after two German priests were killed by Society for Peace and Justice rebels (known as the Boxers, ▷ 30). Before the arrival of the Japanese in 1914 the Germans built a Bavarian-style town on this stretch of Shandong coastline. Today Qingdao is a clean, modern city, popular for its beaches, but its early 20th-century history is well preserved.

GERMAN CONCESSION

Most of the sights in the German Concession can easily be visited on foot. St. Michael's Catholic Cathedral reopened in the 1980s after it was damaged in the Cultural Revolution. Its twin spires tower over steep cobbled lanes, while the interior is richly decorated. The nearby Protestant Cathedral, though simpler in design, is just as evocative, and has a tall clock tower. Across Xinhaoshan Park to the east is the Qingdao Ying Binguan, a sprawling Bavarian-style castle built as the German Governor's Residence.

PARKS AND BEACHES

The beaches in the bays along Qingdao's coast were very popular among tourists even before they were given worldwide publicity in 2008 when they played host to sailors and spectators attending the Olympic Games. Number 2 and Number 3 beaches are quieter and more attractive than the main beach closer to the German Concession. A visit to these beaches can be combined with a walk in Zhongshan and Taipingshan parks. In the latter is the TV Tower. Go to the top for great views across the city.

Above *The large residence of the former German Governor of Qingdao*

QUFU

The origins of Confucianism and China's largest traditional mansion lie at the heart of this compact city.

As the birthplace of Confucius, China's most influential philosopher, and home to his descendants, the Kong clan, for 77 generations, Qufu is revered by Chinese, Koreans and Japanese. The Kong clan were the most powerful family in the country from shortly after Confucius's death until they fled the approach of Communism in 1948, and their legacy can be felt everywhere in the city.

TEMPLE OF CONFUCIUS

The Temple of Confucius (Kong Miao, Mar–end Nov daily 8–5.30, Dec–end Feb daily 8–5) occupies much of central Qufu. Originally a small pavilion where Confucius taught his students, the complex was expanded in the centuries following the sage's death in 479BC. A series of gates and courtyards containing stelae pavilions brings you to the heart of the complex. Here you'll find the Apricot Pavilion, marking the place where Confucius used to teach, and the Dacheng Hall, a magnificent 32m-tall (105ft) hall used by imperial visitors to leave offerings to Confucius.

KONG MANSION AND CONFUCIAN FOREST

The Kong Family Mansion (Kong Fu, Mar–end Nov daily 8–5.30, Dec–end Feb daily 8–5), next to the temple, was the sprawling home of the descendants of Confucius. The vast complex contains a mix of administrative, residential and devotional buildings, with a shady garden at the back. About 1.5km (1 mile) north of the temple and mansion is the Confucian Forest (Kong Lin, daily 7.30–6), the burial place of Confucius and his family. The approach to the simple tomb of Confucius is lined with stone statuary more usually seen at imperial tombs. Electric buggies are available for transportation within the park.

INFORMATION

✠ 424 R9 ℹ CITS, 36 Hongdao Lu
☎ 0537 449 5491 🕐 Daily 8.30–5
🚆 Yanzhou Train Station. The station is 16km (10 miles) from town 🚌 From Tai'an (1 hour), Jinan (2–3 hours) and Qingdao (7 hours) 🖐 Entrance to all three main attractions 150RMB

Below *The Archway of Zhushui Bridge in Confucius Forest*

PINGYAO

Pingyao is a well-preserved traditional Chinese city. The city wall dates back to the Ming dynasty and is 12m (39ft) high and 6km (3.75 miles) long, with watchtowers every 50m (54 yards). Inside the walls, the streets are lined with traditional Ming and Qing commercial and residential buildings. The Bell Tower, close to the center, is the tallest building. Round the corner, the Rishengchang Museum (May–end Sep daily 8–7, Oct–end Apr 8–6) occupies the site of China's first commercial bank. The extensive exhibits relate to the history of banking, a major source of the city's early prosperity.

🔲 417 P8 👤 Adult 120RMB, child free (a ticket covering all attractions in the city) 🚂 Pingyao Train Station. Trains from Taiyuan (2 hours)

QINGDAO (TSINGTAO)

▷ 101

SHANHAIGUAN

Up the coast from Beidaihe, Shanhaiguan is where the Great Wall meets the sea. The East Gate (Apr–end Sep daily 7–6, Oct–end Mar daily 7.30–5.30) of the town sits on a substantial stretch of wall. Below the eave of the imposing gatehouse is the inscription 'First Pass Under Heaven.' A short distance down the street, the Great Wall Museum (open as East Gate) has photographs of the Wall and displays of weapons and tools. Old Dragon Head (open as East Gate), 4km (2.5 miles) south of town, is the point where the Great Wall ends, jutting out into the sea. Though a modern reconstruction of the wall, this is an evocative place with good views. At Jiao Shan (May–end Oct daily 7.30–5.30, Nov–end Apr daily 8–4), 4km (2.5 miles) north of town, the Great Wall makes its first mountain ascent. There is a cable car (20RMB one-way) for those who prefer to avoid the quite strenuous walk to the top.

🔲 423 S7 🚂 Shanhaiguan Train Station. Trains from Beijing (3–5 hours)

Above *Pagodas and tombs, some of which date back as far as the Tang dynasty, at Stupa Forest, close to Shaolin*

SHAOLIN

Renowned as the birthplace of Chinese martial arts, Shaolin Temple (daily 8–6) is on the western edge of Song Shan Mountain, the central mountain of Taoism's five sacred peaks. The temple was established in AD497, and local legend claims that Shaolin Boxing was developed here in the mid-6th century by Bodhidharma, a south Asian ascetic and the founder of Zen Buddhism. The temple's numerous halls are decorated with frescos of martial arts practitioners and statues depicting boxing moves. In the Qian Fo hall you can see where the Shaolin monks have practiced their moves for several centuries. Near the main temple buildings, the Stupa Forest is a collection of several hundred brick pagodas commemorating famous monks. There is now a shuttle bus to the nearby Longmen Grotto (daily 3pm).

🔲 417 Q9 🚌 From Luoyang and Zhengzhou via Dengfeng

SHIJIAZHUANG

The Hebei Provincial Museum (Tue–Sun 9–5) has interesting pottery and items from Han tombs, but most attractions lie out of town. Zhengding (60RMB day-pass), 18km (11 miles) to the north, is an ancient walled town with magnificent Song and Tang dynasty temple architecture. The Dafo Si Temple (daily 8–5.30) houses a huge Guanyin statue that is more than 1,000 years old. The Kaiyuan Temple and Tianning Temple both have classic brick Tang-era pagodas. Some 40km (25 miles) southeast of Shijiazhuang, the Zhaozhou Bridge (20RMB day-pass) is the oldest bridge in China, built more than 1,400 years ago.

🔲 422 Q8 🚂 Shijiazhuang Train Station. Trains from Beijing (2–3 hours) ✈ From Beijing and several major cities

TAI'AN AND TAISHAN

Taishan, China's most sacred mountain, has long been a place of pilgrimage for the Chinese, from Confucius through to Mao Zedong.

At the heart of Shandong province, Taishan is the holiest of China's five sacred Taoist mountains, intimately related to the country's creation myth. Since earliest times it has been a an important place, and Chinese visitors continue to climb the mountain in droves. At the foot of the mountain is the town of Tai'an, the starting point for your ascent.

DAI TEMPLE

In the center of Tai'an, the Dai Temple (Dai Miao; daily 8–6) is dedicated to the god of the mountain. The huge main hall contains a fresco of the god bearing the visage of the Song Emperor Zhenzong. Many pilgrims pay their respects at this temple before climbing the mountain.

ASCENDING TAISHAN

Two routes lead up the first half of the mountain, converging at the Midway Gate to Heaven. Most people choose to ascend along the Central Route, passing the Red Gate Palace, the first of several temples dedicated to the Princess of the Azure Clouds. The Western Route, which is very scenic and closely follows a road plied by minibuses, is a popular descent. From the Midway Gate to Heaven, the route gets steeper, particularly along the section known as the Path of Eighteen Bends leading up to the South Gate to Heaven, though you can also take a cable car up this part of the mountain. The highest point, 1,545m (5,067ft) above sea level, is a short distance farther up, and here you will find the Jade Emperor Temple.

INFORMATION

✚ Tai'an 422 R9 ✚ Taishan 422 R8
ℹ CITS, 158 Hushan Lu ☎ 0538 822 8797 ◑ Daily 8.30–5.30 💰 127RMB Mar–end Nov; 100RMB Dec–end Feb
🚉 Tai'an Train Station. Trains from Beijing, Jinan, Shanghai and Qingdao
🚌 Regular buses from Jinan and Qufu

TIPS

» A full ascent and descent of the mountain on foot can take around 8–9 hours. The trip can be done more quickly (and less strenuously) using a combination of minibus and cable car (bus round-trip 38RMB).
» Do take some warm clothing. The weather on the mountain changes quickly, and it can be cold outside of the summer months.

Above *People climbing the 6,239 steps to the shrine of Taishan*

129

TAIYUAN

The provincial capital of Shanxi, Taiyuan dates from the 5th century BC, when it was capital of the Zhao kingdom. Today it is an industrial town with interesting temples. The Chongshan Buddhist Temple (daily 8–5) was established in the 7th century, though the current buildings are 14th century. The main hall contains an imposing Guanyin statue, along with ancient Buddhist scriptures. The Twin Pagoda Temple (Apr–end Oct daily 8–6, Nov–end Mar daily 9–5) has two 13-floor octagonal brick pagodas. About 25km (15 miles) southwest, the Jinci Temple (May–end Sep daily 8.30–6, Oct–end Apr daily 8–5) is a Buddhist shrine founded in 1023. A canal runs through the temple, over which a bridge leads you to a terrace with some ancient iron statues. The Shengmu Hall is an old wooden building with Song period clay figures.

➕ 417 Q8 🚆 Taiyuan Train Station. Trains from Beijing (8–10 hours) ✈ Daily flights from Beijing, Guangzhou and Xi'an

TIANJIN

Tianjin has long been a major port and is one of China's largest cities. During the 19th century, trade concessions were granted to several European nations, and the impressive buildings they erected are a main attraction, particularly along Jiefang Bei Lu. Other noted concession buildings include the Wanghailou Church and the Xi Kai Cathedral, with its distinctive domes. Beyond the concessions, the Dabei Temple (daily 8–5) is a revered Buddhist complex with a vast array of statues inside and a large market selling devotional items outside. The nearby Tianhou Temple (daily 8.30–5) is dedicated to Mazu, the Sea Goddess, and has some lively displays.

➕ 422 R7 ℹ CITS, 22 Yuoyi Lu

☎ 0222 810 9988 ⏰ Mon–Fri 8.30–6.30 🚆 Tianjin Main Train Station. There are three stations. Trains from Beijing (1.5–2 hours) arrive at the Main Train Station ✈ Binhai International Airport, tel 022 2490 2929, 15km (9 miles) east of town

WUTAISHAN

Wutaishan is one of four mountain ranges considered sacred in Chinese Buddhism. Nestled in a small valley among the five peaks that make up Wutaishan is the quiet village of Taihuai. Here you'll find around 15 of the more than 30 temples on the mountain. Tayuan Temple (daily 8–6) stands out, with its 50m-tall (164ft) Ming pagoda. Farther up the valley is the large Xiantong Temple (daily 8–6), notable for a bronze hall containing thousands of Buddha images, and the Pusading Temple (daily 8–6), perched at the top of 108 steps, which offers a good view across the valley.

➕ 422 Q7 ℹ CITS, 18 Mingqing Street, Taihuai ☎ 0350 654 3218 ⏰ 24 hours ✋ Adult 100RMB, plus 68RMB for unlimited use of the mountain shuttle buses, child free 🚌 From Datong (5–6 hours) and Taiyuan (4–5 hours)

XI'AN

▷ 132–135

YAN'AN

Between 1936 and 1947, following the Long March (▷ 33), Yan'an was the headquarters of the Chinese Communist Party. Close to the center of town, the Fenghuangshan Revolution Headquarters (daily 8–5.30) was an early Party base.

To the northwest, the Yangjialing Revolution Headquarters Site (daily, variable hours) was the venue for several important central committee meetings. The nearby caves served as homes and workplaces for Party leaders.

➕ 417 N9 🚆 Yan'an Train Station. Trains from Xi'an (7–8 hours) 🚌 Services from Xi'an (6–9 hours) ✈ Flights from Beijing and Xi'an

Left *Big White Pagoda at Wutai Mountains (Wutaishan)*

YANTAI

On the northern Shandong coast, the deep sea port of Yantai was known as Chefoo to Westerners in the 19th century. Though to a degree overshadowed by Qingdao to the south, Yantai saw British, German, American and Japanese concerns established during the 19th and early 20th centuries. Well-restored architecture from this period can be seen in the Yantai Hill Park (daily 8–5) on a hill overlooking the sea.

The Yantai Museum (daily 8.30–11.30, 1–5) is interesting on account of its architecture more than its exhibits. The main hall is dedicated to Tianhou (Mazu), the Empress of Heaven and protector of Seafarers, and was commissioned by sailors from Fujian who sheltered here during a storm. It was built by craftsmen in the southern provinces of Fujian and Guangdong and shipped here in pieces.

Along the coast are several beaches which are becoming increasingly popular with Chinese visitors seeking a quiet vacation.
✚ 423 T8 ℹ Yantai Tourist Information & Service Centre ✉ 32 Hai'an Lu ☎ 0535 663 3222 🕐 Daily 8.30–5.30 🚉 Yantai Train Station. Trains from Beijing, Jinan, Qingdao, Shanghai and Xi'an 🚢 Boats to Dalian (4–7 hours) ✈ Flights from Beijing, Guangzhou and Shanghai

YULIN

Yulin, in the north of Shaanxi province, bordering the Inner Mongolian desert, is a small, remote town, formerly a garrison on the Great Wall. Most of the original Ming city walls are still standing, surrounding a grid of narrow streets lined with traditional houses built around small courtyards. In the middle of town is a traditional Bell Tower.
✚ 417 P8 🚉 Yulin Train Station. Trains from Xi'an (13 hours) 🚌 Services from Yan'an (7 hours) ✈ Flights from Xi'an

ZHENGZHOU

Zhengzhou is the capital of Henan province. The Shang-dynasty City Wall Ruins, to the southeast of town, reveal that there has been a town here since at least 1100BC. More remnants of the city's history can be seen in the Henan Museum (May–end Sep daily 9–6, Oct–end Apr daily 9–5.30), to the north of town. This large museum, housed in a distinctive pyramid-shaped building, has well-captioned exhibits including Shang and Zhou bronze artifacts, ancient stone and jade carvings, and a number of artworks from the Ming and Qing dynasties. There is also an interesting display of dinosaur fossils and eggs found in the region.

You can visit Yellow River Park (Huang He Jingqu, daily 8–10), about 25km (15 miles) north of town, for views of the river near the spot where Nationalist leader Chiang Kaishek breached a dike to repel the approaching Japanese troops in 1938, accidentally killing almost 1 million Chinese people.
✚ 424 Q9 🚉 Zhengzhou Train Station. Connections by rail to most cities, Beijing (6–7 hours) ✈ Daily flights from Beijing, Guilin and Shanghai, regular flights to other cities

ZOUXIAN

Zouxian was the birthplace of the itinerant philosopher Mencius (372–289BC), one of the early proponents and interpreters of Confucianism (Confucius was born in nearby Qufu). He was later known as the Second Sage.

The main sights in this quiet town are the Mencius Temple (daily 8–6), which consists of five spacious courtyards surrounded by 64 halls, and the adjacent Mencius Mansion. Both are to be found in the southern part of town.
✚ 424 R9 🚉 Zouxian Train Station 🚌 Services from Qufu ❓ Trains from Yanzhou

Above *The stone figure of a water god set high above the Huang He (Yellow River)*

INTRODUCTION

As the imperial capital for more than 1,000 years, Xi'an was the heart of ancient China. The old walled city has plenty of interest, while outside are the Terra-cotta Warriors and imperial tombs.

In central Shaanxi province, Xi'an and the surrounding attractions cover a large area. While it's possible to explore most of the sights in and around the walled city on foot, to get the most out of your visit you'll need to take one or more of the tours offered by hotels and agencies throughout the city. The tours to the east of town include the major sights, including the Terra-cotta Warriors, Banpo Neolithic Village and Huaqing Pool.

The Zhou dynasty had its capital in this area from the 11th century BC onward. In 221BC Qin Shi Huang unified China and situated his capital at nearby Xianyang. Then, in 202BC, the founding emperor of the Han dynasty established his capital at Chang'an, on the site of modern day Xi'an. All told, the city has been an imperial capital for more than 1,000 years, spanning 13 dynasties. Its most glorious period was during the Sui and Tang dynasties, when it was the largest city in the world, a place of immense wealth and cosmopolitan culture because of its location at the terminus of the Silk Road.

INFORMATION

✚ 417 N10 ℹ️ Tourist Information Centre ✉️ Xi'an Railway Station (next to Jiefang Hotel) ☎ 029 8745 3872 🕐 24 hours 🚉 Xi'an Train Station. Connections to most major cities, including Beijing (14–18 hours) and Shanghai (20–24 hours) ✈ Xiguan Airport serves all major Chinese cities, as well as international destinations throughout Asia

Opposite *A detail of the warrior statues shows the individuality of each figure*
Above *Performers at the Tomb of Qin Shi Huang*

WHAT TO SEE

OLD CITY

Xian's city walls (Apr–end Oct daily 7.30–9.30; Nov–end Mar daily 8–6) stand 12m (39ft) high and stretch for 14km (8.5 miles) around the old city. At the South Gate you can climb up and walk along these huge Ming dynasty fortifications, or take an electric tram ride (50RMB). Just inside this gate, the Forest of Stelae Museum (daily 8–6) contains a collection of more than 1,000 inscribed stone tablets, some of which offer glimpses into the glorious history of Xi'an. The Bell Tower (Apr–end Oct daily 8.30–9.30; Nov–end Mar daily 8.30–5.30), built in 1384, dominates the intersection near the center of the walled city, and hosts musical performances most afternoons. The companion Drum Tower (Apr–end Oct daily 8.30–9.30; Nov–end Mar daily 8.30–5.30) is nearby and stands on the edge of the Hui Muslim quarter, where you can visit the attractive gardens of the Great Mosque (daily 8–8.30).

PAGODAS

About 1km (0.6 miles) southwest of the South Gate, the Little Goose Pagoda (Xiaoyan Ta, daily 9–5) rises 43m (141ft) in a series of 15 terraces. You can climb to the top of this refined Tang-era structure for views across the city. The taller Big Goose Pagoda (Dayan Ta, daily 8.30–6) stands about 2.5km (1.5 miles) to the southeast in what was the Temple of Maternal Grace (Da Ci'en Si). The 64m-high (210ft) structure was built in AD652 to house Buddhist scriptures from India.

SHAANXI HISTORY MUSEUM

Opened in 1991 and housed in a huge Tang-style building, the Shaanxi History Museum (Shanxi Lishi Bowuguan) has a collection of around 370,000 pieces covering prehistory through to the Qing dynasty. The exhibits are well-presented with English and Chinese labels, and are arranged chronologically. Highlights on the first floor, which covers neolithic finds and early dynastic history, include an engraved Shang tripod cooking pot, Zhou bronzes decorated with intricate patterns, and some terra-cotta warriors taken from the Qin Shi Huang tomb. Upstairs are two more galleries. The first contains exhibits from the Han and Northern dynasties, while the second covers the Tang dynasty onward. Be sure not to miss the Tang glazed pottery pieces and the Song-era ceramics.

☎ 029 8525 3806 ◉ Mar 16–Nov 14 daily 8.30–5.30 (ticket office may close 11.30–1)

Above *The Forest of Stelae Museum in the Old City*

TERRA-COTTA WARRIORS

Unearthed in 1974 by villagers digging a well, the underground ranks of life-size terra-cotta warriors and horses in battle formation were originally created to watch over the tomb of Qin Shi Huang, the emperor responsible for uniting China in 221BC. To date more than 8,000 figures have been unearthed in three pits. The first and largest pit contains around 6,000 foot soldiers, horses and chariots. The second pit holds 1,400 cavalry and infantry, thought to be a military guard. The most recently excavated and smallest pit holds around 68 high-ranking officers and a chariot drawn by four horses. The detailing on the figures is amazing. Each warrior has a unique face, possibly modeled on a person of the time, and most would have originally held real weapons. The adjacent museum allows you to examine some of the figures up close. It also displays two horse-drawn chariots made from bronze, which were discovered near the Qin Shi Huang tomb in 1980.

☎ 029 8139 9001 🕐 Daily 8.30–5.30 💰 Adult 90RMB, child free

MORE TO SEE

BANPO NEOLITHIC VILLAGE

Excavations at Banpo Neolithic Village (Bangpo Bowuguan) have revealed evidence of human activity dating back to around 4500BC, the era of the agrarian Yangshao culture. You can see the remains of houses and kilns, as well as graves.

🕐 Daily 8–6 💰 Adult 20RMB, child free

IMPERIAL TOMBS

To the west and northwest of the city are several imperial tombs. At the Qian Tomb, burial place of the Tang Emperor Gaozong, is an impressive Imperial Way, lined with stone statues. The Zhao Tomb is notable as it is built on a mountain. With a 47m-high (154ft) mound, the Mao Tomb is the largest Han tomb.

Above *The steps up to the Little Goose Pagoda*

Below *The Tang-era Little Goose Pagoda has views over the city*

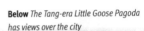

XI'AN

Explore the main sites inside the old walled city of Xi'an, including a walk through the lively Muslim Quarter.

THE WALK
Distance: 6km (3.5 miles)
Allow: 3–4 hours
Start/end: Kaiyuan Shopping Mall

HOW TO GET THERE
Take a taxi to the Kaiyuan Shopping Mall on South Street, opposite the Bell Tower.

★ The Kaiyuan Shopping Mall is one of Xi'an's largest and most modern department stores. The department store carries a wide range of brand-name goods.

Go down into the subway to cross to the Bell Tower (Zhong Lou) in the middle of the intersection in front of Kaiyuan Shopping Mall.

❶ The Bell Tower (Zhong Lou) was originally built in 1384. It was moved from the center of the city to its current location and rebuilt in 1582. The classic Ming structure, with a three-tier roof, stands in the center of the main intersection of the old city. You can climb up to the terrace for a good view across to the Drum Tower.

Head northwest across Zhonggulou Square toward the Drum Tower.

❷ The Drum Tower (Gu Lou), built in 1380, is similar in style to the Bell Tower, though smaller and rectangular rather than square. Large red traditional drums ring the main terrace. In earlier times, a drum was beaten here to mark sunset (nowadays there is a drumming show at this time of day).

Walk under the Drum Tower's massive arch to reach Beiyuanmen, the pedestrian-only street lined with trees and restored shop houses immediately to its north. Wander up and down the street and browse the stores selling calligraphy, arts and souvenirs before returning to the Drum Tower and taking the first lane on the left to the north, signposted to the mosque. Follow the street as it veers right, then turn left onto Huajue Xiang, where you'll see the entrance gate to the Great Mosque.

❸ The Great Mosque (Daqingzhen Si) was established in AD742 and is the main place of worship for Xi'an's Hui Muslim population. The buildings are Chinese in style, with upturned, green-tiled roofs, and are set amid four peaceful courtyards filled with trees and inscribed stones. It is interesting to note the Arabic calligraphy on typically Chinese panels and archways.

Return to the main entrance of the mosque and continue walking westward down Huajue Xiang. At the end of the street turn right onto Beiguangji Jie.

❹ Beiguangji Jie is one of the main streets in the Muslim Quarter (Huicheng), which stretches a few blocks north and west from the Great Mosque. As you walk through the area, you'll notice a few traditional houses as well as *halal* butchers and tea vendors catering to the local community. This is also one

of the best areas in town to sample some of the Hui delicacies such as noodles with spicy sauce and *yangrou paomo* (shredded flat bread with spicy mutton soup).

Head north along Beiguangji Jie and cross the first big intersection you reach. Then take a right after the next block onto Dapiyuan. You'll pass the top end of Beiyuanmen. Keep going until you come to Bei Dajie, the main north–south thoroughfare. Cross this road and, staying on the south side of the Xixin Jie, keep heading east for two blocks. As the road splits in front of a large administrative building, veer right until you're heading south on Nanxin Jie.

Follow this road south, across Dong Dajie, the main road heading east from the Bell Tower, and take a right down Sanxue Jie just before you reach the city wall. This will lead you to the front of the Forest of Stelae Museum.

❺ The Forest of Stelae Museum (Beilin Bowuguan) is housed in an old Confucian temple and contains a collection of Silk Road artifacts, as well as the many stone inscriptions carved in and around Xi'an, from which the museum takes its name.

Head west from the museum along Shuyuanmen, which has been restored in classic Ming and Qing

style and is now lined with art and craft vendors. This will bring you to Nan Dajie, just in front of the South Gate.

❻ Climb up the South Gate (Nan Men) for views along the massive city walls. Alternatively you can take a rickshaw or motorized buggy ride along the wall in either direction. Bring your own water if you plan to spend time up here, as the local vendors take advantage of their captive market.

When you've explored the South Gate, follow Nan Dajie north toward the Bell Tower and your starting point at the Kaiyuan Shopping Mall.

PLACES TO VISIT
THE BELL TOWER
✉ At the crossroads of Xi Dajie and Beidajie 🕐 Apr–end Oct daily 8.30–9.30; Nov–end Mar daily 8.30–5.30 💰 Adult 15–20RMB, child under 1.2m (4ft) free

THE DRUM TOWER
✉ Beiyuanmen Jie 🕐 Apr–end Oct daily 8.30–9.30; Nov–end Mar daily 8.30–5.30 💰 Adult 15–20RMB, child under 1.2m (4ft) free

FOREST OF STELAE MUSEUM
✉ 15 Sanxue Jie 🕐 Daily 8–6 💰 Adult 30RMB, child under 1.2m (4ft) free

GREAT MOSQUE
✉ Huajue Xiang 🕐 Daily 8–8.30 💰 Adult 15RMB, child under 1.2m (4ft) free

WHERE TO EAT
Many vendors in the Muslim Quarter sell kabobs and noodle dishes. For advice on buying food from street traders, ▷ 400. For Chinese fare, turn into Dong Dajie (the main road leading to the Bell Tower as you head south toward the Forest of Stelae Museum) where there is a string of good choices.

Opposite *Bell Tower Square with the Drum Tower in the background*
Left *The carved pillars at the Forest of Stelae Museum*

TOUR

QUFU HORSE-AND-CARRIAGE TOUR

Visit the Temple of Confucius (Kong Miao), the Kong Family Mansion (Kong Fu) and the Confucian Forest (Kong Lin) as well as a few other attractions around town in this trip by horse-drawn cart.

THE TOUR

Distance: 16km (9.5 miles)
Allow: 4.5–5.5 hours
Start/end: Front of Kong Family Mansion (Kong Fu)

HOW TO GET THERE

Either walk or take a taxi to the Gate of the Residence of the Saint on Queli Jie.

★ Begin in front of the Kong Family Mansion (Kong Fu; ▷ 127), by the main gate, labeled with the characters *sheng fu* (Residence of the Saint). Before starting, explore the house, which for centuries after Confucius's death was the grandest private home in China.

Leave the Mansion by the main gate and contract the services of one of the many colorful horse-drawn carts close by. You'll need to agree on a price before setting off—expect to pay around 200RMB for the cart and 150RMB for a guide (not including entrance fees along the way). Indicate that you want to head south first to Six Arts City (Liuyi Cheng). You'll go to the Drum Tower, then turn right and head out the South Gate (Nan Men). After crossing the intersection with Jingxuan Lu, you'll take a left turn down a narrow street for your first stop.

❶ A row of houses, reconstructed in traditional Qufu style, mark a former dwelling place of Confucius. The museum contains various works of art and informational placards, as well as a temple dedicated to the philosopher's ancestors.

Continue down the street, then cross diagonally across a north–south road to reach another road heading southeast. The Six Arts City is on the left.

❷ The Six Arts City (Liuyi Cheng) is an educational theme park about the life and works of Confucius, which has been developed jointly by America and China. The displays relate to the six arts mastered by Confucius, namely ritual, music,

Opposite *Strolling across a bridge in the Confucian Forest*
From left to right *Visitors at the Temple of Confucius; viewing the city on a rickshaw*

mathematics, archery, calligraphy and charioteering.

Rejoin your cart and head west until you reach the next main road. Go north along this to the southeast corner of the old city, and follow the wall westward past the South Gate (Nan Men) to the entrance to the Temple of Confucius.

❸ The Temple of Confucius (Kong Miao; ▷ 127) is definitely the highlight of Qufu and the massive complex deserves at least an hour of your time. At the heart of the building is the massive Dacheng Hall, with elegant columns decorated with carved dragons.

Leave by the South Gate where you entered to rejoin your horse and cart and indicate that you want to go to the Confucian Forest next. The driver should first head west then travel up the long west wall of the Temple of Confucius. Along the way you'll see plenty of fruit vendors. At the northern end of the wall you'll take a left and then head north through a gate in the rear walls of the temple and mansion. It's a couple of kilometers out to the Confucian Forest.

❹ The Confucian Forest (Kong Lin; ▷ 127) is the location of the Kong family tombs, including Confucius's final resting place. It is quite a large park and if you would prefer to save some time you can hop on one of the electric buggies that go round the main route inside (4RMB per person). The tomb of Confucius is a touchingly modest memorial, though there is a statue-lined Spirit Way leading to it. There are many other tombs and shrines throughout the park.

Return to the front gate and clamber back in your cart for the journey back into town. After passing through the northern city gate stop at the Yan Temple (Yan Miao) on the left.

❺ The Yan Temple (Yan Miao) was built in honor of one of Confucius's renowned disciples. Within the peaceful courtyards stand some majestic halls and elaborately carved pillars. Though less visited than the main Confucian sites, it has quite impressive architecture.

Return to your cart for the final journey down the east side of the Kong Family Mansion, taking a right at the bell tower to return to your starting point.

PLACES TO VISIT
CONFUCIAN FOREST
✉ Lindao Lu, north of town 🕐 Daily 7.30–6 ✋ Adult 40RMB, child under 1.2m (4ft) free

KONG FAMILY MANSION
✉ Queli Jie 🕐 Mar–end Nov daily 8–5.30; Dec–end Feb daily 8–5 ✋ Adult 60RMB

SIX ARTS CITY
✉ Kuiquan Lu 🕐 Daily 8–5.30 ✋ Adult 40RMB, child under 1.2m (4ft) free

TEMPLE OF CONFUCIUS
✉ Nanma Dao 🕐 Mar–end-Nov daily 8–5.30; Dec–end Feb daily 8–5 ✋ Adult 90RMB, child under 1.2m (4ft) free

YAN TEMPLE
✉ Yanmiao Jie 🕐 Daily 8–5 ✋ Adult 10RMB, child under 1.2m (4ft) free

WHAT TO DO

CHENGDE

NANYINGZI DAJIE NIGHT MARKET

Nanyingzi Dajie is the city of Chengde's main shopping street, where you'll find several department stores. In the evenings an interesting outdoor market is set up selling all kinds of souvenirs and reproduction antiques. Expect to bargain hard, but you should get better prices than at similar markets in Beijing.

✉ Nanyingzi Dajie ⏰ Evenings from 6pm onward

JINAN

DAMING HU

Daming Hu, a large lake to the north of the old city, is a popular recreational area. Activities include boating on the lake. There is also a children's playground and various trails to walk.

✉ Danming Hu Lu ☎ 0531 8611 1781 ⏰ Daily 6.30–9 ✋ Adult 30RMB, child under 1.2m (4ft) free

KAIFENG

AMUSEMENT PARKS

The area around the lakes in the northwest of the walled city contains several amusement parks with rides for children. The Longting Gongyuan park, opposite Qingming Shanghe on Longting Xilu, is one of the better ones and has a Ferris wheel.

⏰ Daily 9–8 ✋ Adult 30RMB, child under 1.2m (4ft) free

DA XIANGGUO SI SHICHANG

Next to the Temple of the Prime Minister, and housed in a grand Ming-style building, this cross between a market and a department store sells a mix of clothing and everyday items and souvenirs.

✉ Ziyou Lu ⏰ Daily 8–8

QINGMING SHANGHE PARK

A modern reconstruction of the Kaifeng of olden-times, based on a famous Chinese painting. As well as the period houses, temples and bridges, there is also an evening gala-style performance by dancers, acrobats, puppeteers, actors and musicians.

✉ 5 Longting Xilu, Kaifeng ☎ 0378 566 3633 ⏰ Park daily 8.30–6, perfomance daily 8.30pm–10pm ✋ Park 80RMB, performance 199–999RMB, child under 1.2m (4ft) free

LUOYANG

OLD CITY SHOPPING DISTRICT

Zhongzhou Donglu in the old city is one of Luoyang's major shopping districts.

Along the main stretch there are numerous plazas and department stores. But it is more interesting to wander down the smaller streets and you'll find many more traditional shops selling antiques (both genuine and reproduction) and art works.

✉ Zhongzhou Donglu, Luoyang

Above *A souvenir stall at the Imperial Summer Villa in Chengde*

QINGDAO (TSINGTAO)

CLUB NEW YORK

The resident band pumps out a stream of hits every night for the local and foreign audience at this fairly intense music club.

✉ 2F Overseas Chinese International Hotel, 41 Xianggang Zhonglu, Qingdao ☎ 0532 8573 9199 🕔 7.30pm–2am 🎫 Free entry

THE CORNER JAZZ CLUB

There's little live jazz at this popular hostelry but certainly plenty of loud music. This is one of Qingdao's premier drinking and dancing emporiums for expats and city socialites. It opens late and is a firm favorite come the weekend.

✉ 153 Minjiang Lu ☎ 0532 8575 8560 🕔 Daily 11am–late

JUSCO SHOPPING CENTRE

This large modern shopping center has two department stores and many individual retailers selling international goods. There are numerous chain restaurant branches here as well as amusement arcades and a bowling alley.

✉ 72 Xianggang Zhonglu, Eastern District, Qingdao ☎ 0532 8571 9600

LENNON CLASSIC MUSIC BAR

A Qingdao classic, the huge Lennon bar is a laidback place full of Beatles memorabillia. The bar has separate areas for dining, drinking and dancing, and has a regular line-up of live music.

✉ 20 Zhuhai Lu, Qingdao ☎ 0532 8589 3899 🕔 Daily 6pm–2am

Q BAR

The hip Q Bar is one of the trendiest places in town, with cool sounds from the resident DJ. There is an extensive menu of well-mixed cocktails and aperitifs to sup as you mix with the city's in crowd.

✉ 1st Floor, Shangri-La Hotel, 9 Xianggang Zhonglu, Qingdao ☎ 0532 8388 3838 🕔 Sun–Thu 5.30pm–1am, Fri, Sat 5.30pm–2am

SENLIN AMUSEMENT PARK

This children's amusement park is within the botanical garden at the bottom of Taipingshan Hill. There are plenty of activities within the park, including rope bridges, a toboggan ride, climbing walls and fishing ponds.

✉ 33 Yunyang Lu, South Taipingshan, Qingdao 🕔 Daily 8am–6pm 🎫 Adult 10RMB, child under 1.2m (4ft) free 🚌 Take bus 206, 310 or 370 to the Yunyuang stop

TIGER BEACH GOLF LINKS

www.tigerbeach.com

Tiger Beach feels so much like a genuine Caledonian links course that Carnoustie agreed to become a sister course, and made its Taiwanese owner and designer an honorary life member.

It's a rolling landscape of tree-less seaside scrub, pockmarked with deep bunkers and battered by sea breezes. Unlike many Chinese courses, there's no ostentatious real estate lining the fairways, or Pentagon-inspired clubhouses. The course is around one hour's drive from both Qingdao and Yantai.

✉ Fengcheng Tourist Zone, Haiyang, Shandong Province ☎ 0535 3311808 🎫 Green fees (inc caddy) Mon–Fri 800RMB, Sat, Sun and hols 1,200RMB

SHIJIAZHUANG

ZHONGSHAN XILU

Zhongshan Xilu, to the west of the railway station, is Shijiazhuang's main shopping area. There is a mix of small shops and department stores selling everyday items and souvenirs. Dongfang Shopping Centre, on the north side of the road, is a long-established and dependable store.

🕔 Shops daily 8–7

TAI'AN AND TAISHAN

HONGMEN MARKET

This bustling market sells local produce from Taishan, such as chestnuts, walnuts, ginseng and herbs, together with a wide variety of trinkets and souvenirs. There are plenty of small stone carvings of Taoist and Buddhist deities, reproduction calligraphy and paintings, as well as ceramics to choose from.

✉ Lower end of Hongmen Lu, near the Dai Temple 🕔 Daily 8.30–7

TAI'AN ANTIQUE STORE

Better organized and far more sedate than the nearby market, this sizable antiques store sells good-quality paintings and calligraphy. There's a mix of old and new items available and the staff try to help visitors find their way through the large selection.

✉ Hongmen Lu, Tai'an ☎ 0538 822 9575 🕔 Daily 8.30–6.30 (6.30 in summer)

TAI'AN SHUANGLONG SHOPPING CENTRE

This modern shopping center and entertainment complex is right in the heart of Tai'an, close to the southern gate of the Dai Temple. This is the place for luxury goods and department store shopping in pleasant air-conditioned surroundings.

✉ 11 Shengping Jie, Tai'an ☎ 0538 833 1244 🕔 Daily 9–8.30

TIANJIN

ANTIQUE MARKET

On weekends market vendors set up their stands along Shenyang Jie and down the maze of alleys on either side of the road. They sell a bewildering range of second-hand and antique items, ranging from Mao memorabilia to old ceramics and silver.

This is a popular meeting place for antiques and curio dealers, and you can still get a good deal on some very interesting items. There are also a few vendors who set up stalls during the week.

✉ Shenyang Jie and surrounding streets, Tianjin 🕔 Sat–Sun 8–3

BROADIE'S TAVERN

This American-run bar and restaurant is a cut above many of its neighbors and is a popular place among expatriates. There is live music most nights (9.30pm–2am), a wide range of drinks, and a spacious outside drinking and dining area.

✉ Bar Street, Youyi Lu, Tianjin ☎ 022 8837 0933 🕔 Daily noon–2am

GUWENHUA JIE

This is a reconstruction of a Qing dynasty street with traditional architecture. There are some cultural demonstrations to watch, though the focus is the many shops selling almost any Chinese souvenir you can imagine.

✉ Guwenhua Jie, Tianjin ⏰ Daily 8.30–5

HORSE-AND-CARRIAGE TOUR

Close to the Earthquake Monument at the intersection of Heibe Lu and Xi'an Dao you can rent a horse-and-cart to take you on a tour through the old British Concession area. It's a fun way to see some of the well-preserved architecture from this period.

✉ Intersection of Heibe Lu and Xi'an Dao, Tianjin ⏰ Daily 9–7 💰 Adult 20–30RMB for the standard tour, but be prepared to negotiate

ISETAN

You can find quality brand-name imported goods at this Tianjin branch of the prestigious Japanese department store and shopping center. Service is polite and helpful. The store is adjacent to Tianjin's main shopping streets.

✉ 108 Xiandai Cheng, Nanjing Lu, Tianjin ☎ 022 2722 1111 ⏰ Daily 9–9

SHUISHANG PARK

Tianjin's largest park is known as the Water Park as around half of its area is made up of lakes. A series of islands are linked by ornamental bridges, making this a cool and fun place to spend some time. You can also rent rowboats. There is a children's amusement park as well, with several entertaining rides.

✉ Shuishang Gongyuan Lu, Nankai, Tianjin ☎ 022 2391 6111 ⏰ Daily 8–8 💰 Adult 25RMB, child under 1.2m (4ft) free

TIANJIN WARNER INTERNATIONAL GOLF CLUB

www.warnergolfclub.com
Of more than 10 golf courses in the Tianjin area, this is the best appointed. The 18-hole, par 72 course is complemented by a floodlit driving range and a clubhouse

with full amenities, including bar, restaurant, gym, massage and accommodations. The club is in the Tianjin Economic and Development Area (TEDA) to the east of the city.

✉ 1 Nanhai Road, TEDA, Tianjin ☎ 022 2532 6009 ⏰ Course: all year. Driving range: all year 💰 Adult 420–1,150RMB depending on day of the week

WUTAISHAN

SHANXI OPERA

During the summer a traditional Shaanxi opera group puts on one or two free performances a day in the courtyard of Wanfo Temple. You can drop in mid-performance and then leave once you've had the chance to enjoy the experience.

✉ Wanfo Si, Taihuai ⏰ No fixed schedule. Ask at the temple or in town for details 💰 Free

XI'AN

THE ARTS STREET

Running between the South Gate and the Forest of Stelae Museum, this street of reconstructed Ming- and Qing-style buildings has many vendors selling craft and souvenir items. It's a good place to find calligraphy and ink paintings, as well as jade ornaments and miniature terra-cotta warrior reproductions. This street is in the heart of the tourist area so prices can be a little high unless you bargain.

✉ Shuyuanmen ⏰ Daily 9–9

DEFU XIANG

For quiet drinks in Xi'an, head to the city's answer to Beijing's Sanlitun, a small street lined with a variety of low-key bars filled with local singer-songwriters and DJs. It's an atmospheric place to grab a beer and rarely gets overly rowdy.

✉ Parallel to Nan Dajie from just north of the South Gate ⏰ Daily noon–2am

KAIYUAN SHOPPING MALL

At the Bell Tower intersection, this central store is one of the best places in Xi'an to find clothes and fashion items. The department store carries a wide range of brand-name goods, as well as more

mundane items, and the staff are knowledgable and helpful.

✉ 6 Dong Dajie ☎ 029 8723 5382 ⏰ Daily 10–9

ONE PLUS ONE (YI JIA JI)

One Plus One is very likely the Chinese hinterland's best super-club. It's a labyrinthine emporium with a variety of rooms, from intimate (and relatively quiet) lounges to a huge main dance floor, overlooked by several mezzanine levels. The music booms and the crowds heave.

✉ 285 Dong Dajie ☎ 029 872 0008 ⏰ Daily 8pm–3am

RONGSHENGZHAI TOURIST SHOPPING CENTER

This large showroom offers a comprehensive range of local handicrafts, including jade, tapestry, calligraphy, painting and furniture. The shop is attached to one of the main factories licensed to produce full-size replicas of the terra-cotta warriors so always has plenty of these for sale. They can arrange delivery worldwide and will advise on costs and formalities.

✉ 42 Chang'an Zhonglu ☎ 029 8222 9903 ⏰ Daily 8.30–6

THE TANG DYNASTY

www.xiantangdynasty.com
At this grand venue you can combine a traditional dinner with

Below *Walking through the Muslim quarter of Xi'an*

an extravaganza of song, dance, acrobatics and Chinese theater, based on Tang dynasty traditions and Buddhist legends but brought up-to-date to appeal to modern tastes. Due to the popularity of the show with tour groups you should reserve in advance. Any tour agency in town can make bookings for you.

✉ 75 Chang'an Beilu ☎ 029 8782 2222 ◉ Check the website for details or ask at a tour agency 🎫 500RMB (show and dinner), 220RMB (show only)

TANG PARADISE

This modern theme park is built around a large lake and divided into 12 zones, each celebrating a different aspect of Tang culture. You'll be able to watch a tea ceremony, calligraphy demonstrations and Chinese opera, wander through a Tang garden with statues of famous Tang poets, even enjoy a Tang banquet if you are feeling hungry. In the evenings movies are shown against a vast water screen on the lake, accompanied by fireworks and a laser show.

✉ 99 Furong Xi ☎ 029 8551 1888 ◉ Apr–end Oct daily 9am–10pm; Nov–end Mar daily 9–8.30 🎫 Adult 68RMB, child under 1.2m (4ft) free

XI'AN HUXIAN FARMER PAINTING GALLERY

www.peasantspainting.com
This gallery displays thousands of paintings by the local artisans of Huxian County, southwest of Xi'an city. The folk-art paintings are typically bold, bright and stylized depictions of traditional scenes and local people, flowers and animals. As well as the permanent displays of famous paintings in this style and a commercial section with works for sale, the gallery has an exhibition about the history of the paintings and a hands-on area where visitors can try to imitate the technique.

✉ No. 17 Building of Kaiyuan Group Corp of Jitong University, East Development Zone ☎ 029 8268 3330 ◉ Apr–end Oct daily 8.30–5.30; Nov–end Mar daily 9–5

FESTIVALS AND EVENTS

AUGUST
QINGDAO INTERNATIONAL BEER FESTIVAL

A celebration of Qingdao's most famous product, the festival includes a parade and beauty pageant, but the focus is beer drinking and partying. The main areas are Huiquan Square, Beer Street (near the old brewery) and Beer City at the Shilaoren Tourism Resort on the way to Laoshan.

✉ Qingdao ☎ 0532 888 3990 ◉ Starts 2nd weekend in Aug and runs for 2 weeks

XI'AN QUJIANG OCEAN WORLD

www.xianoceanworld.com
Opened in 2005, this modern attraction includes an underwater tunnel where you can watch sharks, rays and other sea creatures swim around and above you.

There's also a dolphin show, a fascinating exhibition on rain forests, tanks of rare fish and an interactive area where younger visitors can touch various creatures and learn about them.

✉ 1 Qujiang Er Lu ☎ 029 8553 3555 ◉ Summer daily 9–6; winter daily 9–5 🎫 Adult 100RMB, child under 1.2m (4ft) free

YANTAI
CHANGYU WINE CULTURE MUSEUM

www.changyu.com.cn
This museum documents the history of wine production in China. It was built by China's oldest commercial winery, Changyu. It's a big place with a tourist center, and auditorium and eclectic displays relating to the winery.

There is an extensive underground cellar and, of course, a store where you can sample and buy the goods.

✉ 56 Dama Lui ☎ 0535 663 2892 ◉ Daily 8–5 🎫 Adult 30–50RMB, child under 1.3m (4.3ft) free

SEPTEMBER
INTERNATIONAL CONFUCIAN FESTIVAL

Two weeks of parades, dances, theater and music celebrating China's most renowned philosopher. Most events are centered on the Temple of Confucius. The festival is a major draw for Chinese tourists.

✉ Qufu ☎ 0537 449 8881 ◉ Sep 26–Oct 10

CHAOYANGJIE

This is the heart of Yantai's loud and increasingly garish nightlife scene, with a whole street full of bars, karaoke joints and discos. It's got something of the carefree seaside atmosphere to it that keeps things fun, though. There are a few cafés along the street as well.

✉ Chaoyangjie, between Beima Lu and Yantai Hill Park ◉ Daily 11am–late

PENGLAI OCEAN AQUARIUM WORLD

This modern aquarium, built in 2004, has 14 separate exhibitions built around different ocean habitats.

✉ Penglai, 65km (39 miles) northwest of Yantai ☎ 0535 592 7666 ◉ Daily 7.30–6.30 🎫 Adult 120RMB 🚌 Buses from Yantai run throughout the day. The journey takes 1–1.5 hours

ZHENGZHOU
RENMIN PARK

This large park with trees and water features provides a pleasant respite from the city. It has a variety of fairground rides and play areas for children, including a small roller coaster. On the weekend the park gets very busy and attracts many local musicians and musical groups, who give impromptu performances.

✉ Corner of Jinshui Lu and Erqi Lu ◉ Daily 7.30am–8pm 🎫 Adult 6RMB, child under 1.2m (4ft) free

PRICES AND SYMBOLS

The restaurants are listed alphabetically. The prices are for a two-course lunch (L) and a three-course à la carte dinner (D) for one person, without drinks. The wine price is for the least expensive bottle. All the restaurants listed accept credit cards unless otherwise stated.

For a key to the symbols, ▷ 2.

CHENGDE

QIANLONG JIAOZIGUAN

This wonderful dumpling restaurant is located on Zhongxing Square (Zhongxing Guangchang). It is probably the best place in town for dumplings, but don't expect lavish surroundings. All possible types of dumplings are served, but it's worth trying either the Qianlong *shuijiao* or the game varieties.

✉ 8 Zhongxing Lu ☎ 0314 202 8559 🕐 Daily 11–2.30, 5–9 🍴 L and D 10–40RMB, Beer 6RMB

QIANYANG HOTEL

Chengde's Imperial Summer Palace has hosted lavish banquets for centuries; Emperor Kangxi regularly received groups of Mongol princes and after elaborate hunting expeditions they would attend vast feasts, usually eating the results of the hunt. The Qianyang Hotel's Chinese restaurant continues this tradition with a number of wild game dishes, including wild deer, rabbit and pheasant.

✉ 18 Pule Lu ☎ 0314 205 7188 🕐 Daily 7am–8pm 🍴 L and D 50–120RMB, Wine 70RMB

DATONG

YONGHE HONGQI MEISHICHENG

Upscale for Datong, this restaurant offers a variety of Cantonese dishes with a smattering of Sichuan, Hunan and local Shaanxi favorites. It is very popular with locals and can get really busy, and so noisy, later in the evening.

✉ 8 Yingbin Dong Lu ☎ 0352 510 0333 🕐 Daily 11–2, 6pm–2am 🍴 L and D 60RMB, Wine 60RMB

KAIFENG

DIYILOU BAOZI GUAN

Ask any local the name of their favorite dumpling restaurant and they'll probably say Diyilou. The owners know full well how good their dumplings are; Diyilou translates as Number One Restaurant. Try the *guantang xiao long bao* (pork dumpling) or *haixian xiao long bao* (seafood dumpling),

Above Locals enjoying a meal at the Night Market, Qufu

where perfectly delicate skins enclose the tasty fillings. Other specialties include an excellent *yutou huogou* (hot pot made with fish heads).

✉ 8 Sihou Jie ☎ 0378 599 8655 🕐 Daily 10.30am–10pm 🍴 L and D 40RMB, Beer 8RMB

LUOYANG

MUDAN TING

Luoyang was the capital of China for many centuries and consequently built up quite a culinary reputation. Today this is exemplified by the *Luoyang shuixi* (Water Banquet), a continuous stream of dishes, sometimes as many as 24, brought to your table one after the other. The majority of these dishes tend to be soups and dining like this can take quite a long time, so make sure you've got nothing else planned and try to go with friends. This particular hotel restaurant is a good place to start as the staff are friendly and they offer smaller banquets.

✉ Peony Hotel, 15 Zhongzhou Xilu ☎ 0379 6468 0000 🕐 Daily 7–10,

11.30–2, 5.30–9 🖐 L and D 40–100RMB, Wine 88RMB

PINGYAO

DEJUYUAN HOTEL

www.pydjy.net

If the weather is good there is no better place to eat in Pingyao than the courtyard of this delightful, traditional guest house. Even if the weather is not good, the main restaurant, with its Qing-era furnishings, is a great place to sit. Renowned for its excellent Shaanxi cuisine, the Dejuyuan serves 108 varieties of local snacks.

✉ 43 Xi Dajie ☎ 0354 568 5266
🕐 Daily 7am–11pm 🖐 L and D 40–80RMB, Wine 80RMB

TIANYUANKUI FOLK GUEST HOUSE

www.pytyk.com

This guest house has a similar set up to the Dejuyuan (▷ above), serving Pingyao snacks (cold beef, noodles with tomatoes, pickled vegetables), classic Shaanxi cuisine and a number of Western favorites. The dining area, with its Ming- and Qing-style furniture, doubles as a drinking area in the evening.

✉ 73 Nan Dajie ☎ 0354 568 0069
🕐 Daily 7am–10pm 🖐 L and D 20–40RMB, Beer 8RMB

YUNJINGCHENG BINGUAN

www.pibc.cn

An exquisite courtyard hotel and restaurant, the Yunjingcheng serves simple Shaanxi dishes including *jianbao* (fried buns stuffed with meat) and *ca ge dou* (local noodles), plus a selection of more complex meals that the rich merchants and their families might have eaten in the past. Some of the desserts, the egg custards in particular, are well worth trying.

✉ 56 Nan Dajie ☎ 0354 588 8888
🕐 Daily 11.30–2.30, 5–9.30 🖐 L and D 30–100RMB, Beer 15RMBB

QINGDAO (TSINGTAO)

CHUNHELOU FANDIAN

Reputedly the best seafood restaurant in Qingdao (quite a claim), this establishment first opened in 1891. Traditional Shandong dishes, sea cucumbers, fried sea snails and various fish platters, are served on the second floor. The first floor (open from 6am), more of a fast-food vendor than a proper restaurant, serves great steamed buns (choice of fillings) and a number of other Chinese dishes.

✉ 146 Zhongshan Lu ☎ 0532 8282 7371
🕐 Daily 9am–10pm 🖐 L 30RMB, D 80RMB, Wine 80RMB

CORNER JAZZ CLUB

Corner Jazz is one of the oldest and best clubs in Qingdao, though it is not, as the name suggests, dedicated to jazz. Regular live music, Western bar snacks (cheeseburgers, chicken wings and fries) and a laid-back vibe make it a great place to meet locals and other visitors. Make sure you try one of the club's very long list of cocktails or challenge someone to a game of foosball (table football).

✉ 153 Minjiang Lu ☎ 0532 8575 8560
🕐 Daily Sun–Thu 6pm–2am, Fri, Sat 6pm–5am 🖐 15–30RMB

HONG KONG 97

Named after the year Hong Kong was returned to Chinese rule, this restaurant serves Chinese, Japanese and Thai food, in addition to some generic western offerings, as well as a wide selection of wines, beers and traditional Chinese spirits. The red-and-black color scheme and moody lighting make a change from the usual rambunctious local dining environment and couples abound. There are heaps of after-dinner nightlife options close by.

✉ 90 Xianggang Zhong Lu ☎ 0532 8588 3388 🕐 Daily 11–2.30, 5–9.30pm
🖐 L and D 120RMB

KALINKA'S RUSSIAN RESTAURANT

Don't be deceived by the quaint, log-cabin exterior of this Russian restaurant. The raucous floor show, noisy environment buzzing from visiting Russian diners, and cholesterol-rich foods are the closest thing you'll find to eating in Moscow. Try the rich sour-cream-covered beet salad, *bitky* (meatball with onion) fried in butter or barbequed *shashlik* (kabobs). Large chunks of bread come with each meal to mop up sauces. Local and imported beers are sold, and Russian vodka is available.

✉ 52 Zhangzhou Er Lu, Shinan District, Fushan Bay area (Central Qingdao) ☎ 0532 8589 1185 🕐 Daily 11am–midnight
🖐 L and D 50–100RMB, Wine 150RMB

MURANO'S

A lavish bistro serving the very best Italian cuisine, Murano's sets the standard for all other restaurants in Qingdao. It's pricy, but worth it. Try any of the specially prepared pasta dishes and you'll not be disappointed. The Italian chef takes great pride in his pizza toppings, which, like the Sichuan spicy beef, are far from traditional.

✉ 76 Xiang Gang Zhong Lu, Crowne Plaza Hotel, ☎ 0532 8571 8888 🕐 Daily 11.30–2, 5.30–10.30 🖐 L and D 150–600RMB, Wine 270RMB

QINGDAO SEAFOOD RESTAURANT

Qingdao Seafood Restaurant has one of the best reputations for fish and seafood in the city—no mean thing in a place reputed for its seafood. Dishes are served in Shandong, Yangzhou or Cantonese styles, while large glass tanks filled with live fish, prawns and mussels are your guarantee of receiving fresh selections. Sea cucumber and conch are just a few of the exotic items on the menu. It is best to call and make reservations if you'd like a seat with an ocean view. Take a romantic stroll along the beach after feasting on the fresh seafood.

✉ 20 Qingyu Lu 🕐 Daily 10am–11pm
🖐 L and D 150RMB, Wine 90RMB

SHANGPIN KAFEI (SANPIN COFFEE)

It's no destination restaurant, but this Taiwanese coffee shop chain does a range of reliable and tasty dishes from across China. There are private rooms or alternatively opt for the open upstairs area which has a grand piano and a pleasing abundance of pot plants. Despite the coffee of the title, traditional Chinese teas are the highlight of the drinks menu.

✉ 149 Minjiang Lu ☎ 0532 8578 5626 🕐 Daily 10.30am–1.30am ✋ L 80RMB, D 100RMB, Wine 98RMB

STEVEN GAO'S INTERNATIONAL RESTAURANT

www.lennonbar.net

Sharing the same site as the Lennon Classic Music Bar (▷ 141), this popular place serves Chinese favorites and a number of fusion dishes. Particularly good is the duckling salad with orange sauce. As with the bar, the restaurant is festooned with posters; rock gods abound. It's certainly worth spending a little time studying some of the unusual memorabilia.

✉ 20 Zhuhai Lu ☎ 0532 8589 3899 🕐 Daily 10am–1am ✋ L and D 25RMB, Wine 90RMB

TIAN FU LAO MA

Decorated outside in traditional style and accented by neon lights, this large chain restaurant is a favorite with locals. Particularly good is the Sichuan-style 'mandarin duck hot pot.' If you have a hankering for seafood, the spicy crab or the fragrant red abalone are excellent. Tables and booths along the walls are separated by faux bamboo dividers giving limited privacy, while bigger tables dominate the main dining room.

✉ 54 Yun Xiao Lu, Shinan District, Fushan Bay area (Central Qingdao) ☎ 0532 8576 4906 🕐 Daily 10am–2am ✋ L and D 80–200RMB, Wine 70RMB

QUFU

QUELI HOTEL'S CONFUCIAN BANQUET

www.quelihotel.com

The Kong family created the Confucian Mansion Banquet for visitors; the royal version is said to have once included 196 courses

served over four days. The modern-day banquet and dance show is attended by a mostly Chinese crowd enjoying Shandong dishes such as Yipin bean curd.

✉ 1 Queli Jie ☎ 0537 486 6523 🕐 Daily 11–2, 5–9.30 ✋ L and D 100–150RMB, Wine 200RMB

TIANJIN

BROADIES TAVERN

A live music venue with pool tables and a cocktail list as long as your arm, Broadies serves excellent Western food, including burgers and pizzas. Depending on what night you visit, there will either be a Filipino band knocking out well-known rock, jazz and blues classics or a Chinese band doing the same. The tavern occasionally attracts some high-profile US jazz musicians and singers.

✉ 5 Bar Street, Youyi Lu ☎ 022 8837 0933 🕐 Daily 2pm–2am ✋ D 50–100RMB, Beer 25RMB

GOUBULI STUFFED BUN

This restaurant, which has been in business more than 100 years, is famed throughout the country for its baozi (steamed buns) filled with pork, chicken or shrimp, all mostly with spices. They do no less than 98 different varieties. The restaurant's first floor is dedicated to baozi, but carry on up the stairs to the second and third floors and you'll come across a wider variety of Chinese food.

✉ 77 Shandong Lu ☎ 022 2730 2540 🕐 Daily 10am–10pm ✋ L and D 60RMB, Beer 30RMB

XI'AN

DEFACHANG DUMPLING RESTAURANT

A favorite on the Xi'an tourist circuit, this huge restaurant between the Drum and Bell towers is well worth a visit. With more than 100 different varieties of jiaoze (pastry-wrapped dumplings) to pick from, the choice can be mind-boggling. Try the famed Dumpling Feast for a banquet of jiaoze, including fillings of savory chive, duck, shrimp and even sweet

walnut marzipan. A hot pot and an equally impressive number of appetizers and cold salads will come with your meal, but it is the jiaoze that are the real treat. Be careful ordering à la carte as house specials like sharks'-fin jiaoze can be very pricy.

✉ 1 Xi Dajie, Zhonggulou Guangchang ☎ 029 8721 8187 🕐 Daily 10am–midnight ✋ L and D 20–200RMB, Beer 8RMB

ENTERTAINERS PUB AND PIZZERIA

The popular Entertainers Pub doubles as a nightclub and pizzeria. Live music nightly and an excellent wine list, plus thin-crust pizza, bar snacks, a stylish bar area and snooker room, make this a good place to unwind after a busy day exploring the sights.

✉ Hyatt Regency Xi'an, 158 Dong Dajie ☎ 029 8769 1234 🕐 Daily 5.30pm–1am ✋ D 80–200RMB, Wine 200RMB

LAOSUNJIA

Yangrou paomo (mutton soup), the house specialty at this family-run establishment frequented by many in the city's Muslim community, is now a Xi'an favorite. The richly flavored soup is filled with soft mutton and glass noodles. Steamed bread should be ripped into pieces and soaked in the stew. To order, get an order form from a waitress, walk along the counter pointing at the dishes you'd like and they will be delivered to your table. Alcohol is served.

✉ 364 Dong Dajie, Beilin District ☎ 029 8721 4438 🕐 Daily 8am–9.30pm ✋ L and D 50RMB, Beer 10RMB

MUSLIM STREET

Muslim Street has market stalls during the day but really comes alive at night-time when the hawker restaurants take center stage. A range of family-run establishments stand on this tree-lined thoroughfare, conjuring Xi'an's Silk Road heritage by serving traditional Muslim dishes. Be sure to try the yang rou pao mo, a famous soup

TANG DYNASTY THEATRE RESTAURANT

www.xiantangdynasty.com
A set menu of fusion cooking is on offer at this large, well-furnished dinner theater. Imaginatively named dishes like Heart of the Dragon (crispy shrimp) and Willow's Melody (taro and water chestnut dessert) accompany an equally creative 90-minute floorshow. A Cantonese lunch buffet is available, as are tickets for show-only patrons. A schedule of show times is available on the website.

✉ 75 Chang An Lu ☎ 029 8782 2222 🕑 Daily 11–2.30, 6.30–10 ✋ L and D 200RMB, D with show 400RMB; show only 220RMB, Wine 100RMB

XI'AN RESTAURANT

Built in 1929, the restaurant is one of the city's older establishments and has hosted many famous people, including former premier and foreign minister Zhou Enlai. It is justly renowned for its first-class Shaanxi cuisine. Some of the staff speak English and they can help you in your choice, usually guiding toward the set menus—a good idea if you want to sample a number of dishes.

✉ 298 Dong Dajie ☎ 029 8768 0618 🕑 Daily 11am–10.30pm ✋ L and D 120RMB, Wine 70RMB

YANTAI
SONG DAO

It's great fun to slurp scallops at one of the simple seaside hawker joints along Binhai Lu but for a more refined seafood experience, head to Song Dao, a Korean seafood restaurant owned by Shang and Amy, a friendly Korean-American husband and wife team. It excels in mammoth Korean-styled seafood platters, but there's a good selection of rice and noodle dishes to choose from, too.

✉ 1F, Hongkou Dasha, 155 Erma Lu ☎ 0535 661 9746 🕑 Daily 9.30–2, 4.30–10 ✋ L 100RMB, D 350RMB (set-meal), Beer 5RMB

Above *A typical selection of starters available*

in which flat bread is broken into a broth and served up with slices of lamb.

✉ Huimin Jie, Xian (north of the Drum Tower) 🕑 Daily 8am–midnight ✋ L and D 10–50RMB

SHANG PALACE

A typically grand, first-class hotel restaurant, the Shang specializes in Cantonese delicacies, and a number of classic Chinese seafood dishes. There are some controversial choices—abalone, sharks' fin and bird's nest soup—but many other dishes that are not. The Shangri-La Golden Flower is one of Xi'an's finest hotels.

✉ Shangri-La Golden Flower, 8 Chang Le

Xi Lu ☎ 029 8322 1199 🕑 Daily 11.30–2, 5.30–10 ✋ L 100RMB, D 300RMB, Wine 140RMB

SHERATON FOOD STREET

Perhaps a bit cafeteria-like but none-the-less clean, this is an ideal place to dive into the city's food scene while you see how hot 'spicy' really is or learn how to eat with chopsticks without local scrutiny.

In the Sheraton Hotel complex, the all-you-can-eat Chinese hot pot is do-it-yourself, and the staff are happy to show you how to prepare your own.

✉ 262 Feng Hao Dong Lu ☎ 029 8426 1888 🕑 Daily 11–11 ✋ L and D 60RMB, Beer 16RMB

PRICES AND SYMBOLS

Prices are the starting price for a double room for one night, unless otherwise stated. Breakfast is included unless noted otherwise. All the hotels listed accept credit cards unless otherwise stated. Note that rates vary widely throughout the year.

For a key to the symbols, ▷ 2.

CHENGDE
MOUNTAIN VILLA HOTEL

www.hemvhotel.com/english
Perfectly positioned opposite the main entrance to Chengde's Imperial Summer Villa, the Mountain Villa Hotel offers exceptional value. It has a variety of rooms to suit all tastes and budgets, six restaurants, shops and business facilities.

✉ 127 Xiaonanmen Lu ☎ 0314 202 5588 🖑 180–580RMB 🛈 400 🛗 🔻

DATONG
DATONG HOTEL

www.datonghotel.com
Though renovated in 2000, the hotel's spacious rooms still maintain the air of a recent upgrade. Many have balconies overlooking the extensive landscaped gardens—request one of these rooms when making a reservation. Recreational facilities are excellent.

✉ 37 Yingbin Xilu ☎ 0352 586 8002 🖑 580–760RMB 🛈 221 🛗

JINAN
CROWNE PLAZA JINAN

www.ichotelsgroup.com
This luxury hotel is the best in town. Next to attractive Chuan Cheng Square in central Jinan, it is within easy reach of the major sights. With plenty of pale wood fixtures and fittings, large televisions and exceptionally comfortable bathrooms, each of these spacious attractive rooms boasts a broadband internet connection.

✉ 3 Tianditan Jie ☎ 0531 8602 9999 🖑 840–1070RMB 🛈 306 🛗 🔻 🏊 Indoor

KAIFENG
DONGJING HOTEL

Just inside Kaifeng's ancient southern walls, and with easy access to the bus station, the Dongjing is a good mid-range option. Set in its own garden, it is quiet, and the friendly staff speak an above-average amount of English. Facilities include a beauty salon, a few shops and a karaoke lounge.

✉ 99 Yingbin Lu ☎ 0378 398 9388 🖑 120–328RMB, excluding breakfast 🛈 230 🛗 🏊

LUOYANG
NEW FRIENDSHIP HOTEL

A favorite with tour groups, this comfortable mid-range hotel is in Luoyang's bustling business district. A tranquil, Suzhou-style garden at the back makes a pleasant place to unwind. The standard facilities include a business center, sauna, snooker room and a table tennis room.

✉ Minus 6, Xiyuan Lu ☎ 0379 6468 6666 🖑 358RMB 🛈 145 🛗 🔻

PEONY HOTEL

This above-average, mid-range hotel, with attractive, spacious rooms, is just across the road from Wangcheng Park, famous for its peonies and Zhou dynasty excavations. The restaurant is recommended for its Cantonese cuisine. Other facilities include a sauna and coffee shop.

✉ 15 Zhongzhou Xilu ☎ 0379 6468 0000 🖑 380–550RMB, excluding breakfast 🛈 178 🛗 🔻

PINGYAO
TIANYUANKUI FOLK GUEST HOUSE

www.pytyk.com
Built in 1791, this wonderful period house, with a beautiful courtyard and bright red lanterns, caters to all budgets. Dormitory beds are available, as well as a variety of comfortable, variously sized

Above *Lobby of the Sofitel Hotel, Xi'an*

standard rooms. Ming- and Qing-style furniture lend the whole place a traditional Chinese feel.

✉ 73 Nan Dajie ☎ 0354 568 0069
✋ 200–600RMB 🛏 35 ⬛

QINGDAO (TSINGTAO)
OCEANWIDE ELITE HOTEL
www.oweh.com

With views over Qingdao Bay and the attractive Zhanqiao Pier, the setting for this upscale hotel cannot be bettered. Though fairly new, the hotel is built in colonial style, fitting in perfectly with the city's German heritage. A first-class restaurant, good business facilities and well-maintained, spacious rooms make this a fine place to stay.

✉ 29 Taiping Lu ☎ 0532 8299 6699
✋ 400–800RMB 🛏 87 ⬛ 📺

QUFU
QUELI HOTEL
www.quelihotel.com

A stone's throw from the Temple of Confucius, the Queli is constructed in traditional Shandong style, allowing it to blend flawlessly with the surrounding buildings. The hotel is set in a pleasant garden with some exquisite courtyards.

✉ 1 Queli Jie ☎ 0537 486 6818
✋ 300–600RMB 🛏 174 ⬛

TAI'AN AND TAISHAN
TAISHAN HOTEL
The Taishan is the most convenient place to stay on the mountain and its helpful staff can help with most trekking and climbing queries. Rooms are simple but spacious. The hotel also has a good restaurant.

✉ 26 Hongmen Lu ☎ 0538 822 5888
✋ 300–500RMB, excluding breakfast
🛏 99 ⬛ 📺

TAIYUAN
SHAANXI GRAND HOTEL
The Shaanxi Grand is a fairly typical upscale provincial hotel; perfectly comfortable, but perhaps lacking a little charm. The amenities include a disco and a karaoke lounge.

✉ 5 Xinjian Nan Lu ☎ 0351 882 9999 ✋ 620–900RMB 🛏 166
⬛ 📺 🏊 Indoor

TIANJIN
ASTOR HOTEL
The Astor is one of Tianjin's most celebrated hotels. Built in 1863 by the British, it has hosted Puyi, the last Chinese emperor, Sun Yat-sen, father of modern China, and US President Herbert Hoover. The reception area, decorated with old English plaques and period furniture, is worth a look in itself.

✉ 33 Tai'erzhuang Lu ☎ 022 2331 1688
✋ 550–700RMB 🛏 223 ⬛ 📺

XI'AN
BELL TOWER HOTEL
This reasonably priced hotel is within walking distance of Xi'an's famed Bell Tower, the Great Mosque and Huimin Lu. Street-side rooms have some traffic noise, but the views of the Bell Tower at dusk are unparalleled. Renovations are ongoing so if the furnishings in your room aren't up to par, tell the staff as there are newly furnished rooms. In-room internet is available. Note that the Bell Tower Hotel is not the same as the rundown Bell and Drum Tower Hotel nearby.

✉ 110 Nan Da Jie ☎ 029 8760 0000
✋ 480–700RMB, plus 15 percent service charge, excluding breakfast 🛏 300 ⬛

HOWARD JOHNSON JINWA PLAZA HOTEL XI'AN
www.hojochina.com

Looming over the city's South Gate, this high-tech hotel is close to the old city. Rooms are spacious with a classy, contemporary feel. Sleek bathrooms and plush bedding, and extras like wireless internet access, make the hotel a winner. A lavish breakfast spread is on offer. Reserve in advance for nonsmoking rooms.

✉ 18 West Section, Huancheng Nan Lu
☎ 029 8842 1111 ✋ 700–1,400RMB, plus 15 percent service charge, excluding breakfast 🛏 198 ⬛ 📺 🏊 Indoor

SOFITEL HOTEL
www.sofitel.com

The Sofitel is one of the city's most luxurious hotels. Its spacious lobby oozes style but not many places to sit. Rooms are comfortably

furnished in a hip, at-home style, with all the modern conveniences you'd expect. Try the excellent Japanese restaurant for a change of Asian flavors.

✉ 319 Dongzin Jie ☎ 029 8792 8888
✋ 500–2,000RMB, excluding breakfast
🛏 432 ⬛ 📺 🏊 Indoor

HYATT REGENCY XI'AN
www.xian.regency.hyatt.com

This superb luxury hotel within the walls of the old city attracts tour groups. The grand interior and the high standards of service make it a delightful place to stay. Amenities include a fitness club, tennis, spa and wireless internet access.

✉ 158 Dong Dajie ☎ 029 8769 1234
✋ 700–1,093RMB), excluding breakfast
🛏 430 ⬛ 📺

YAN'AN
SILVER SEAS INTERNATIONAL HOTEL
www.yinhaihotel.cn

This 26-floor, upscale hotel, built in 2003, offers an array of amenities, including sauna, nightclub and karaoke lounge. Rooms are spacious and include broadband internet access. The higher up you are the better the views of the surrounding countryside.

✉ Daqiao Jie ☎ 0911 213 9999 ✋ 340–450RMB 🛏 212 ⬛ 📺 🏊 Indoor

ZHENGZHOU
CROWNE PLAZA ZHENGZHOU
www.ichotelsgroup.com

The hotel is part of a complex of three hotels with shared facilities (the other two are a Holiday Inn and an Express By Holiday Inn). The advantage of this arrangement is that you can choose a less expensive room if necessary. The vast, marble columned lobby is a great place to relax and soak up the atmosphere of this 1950s-era Russian-built hotel. Amenities are excellent and include an exceptionally helpful travel desk.

✉ 115A Jinshui Lu ☎ 0371 6595 0055 ✋ 448–808RMB 🛏 449
⬛ 📺 🏊 Indoor

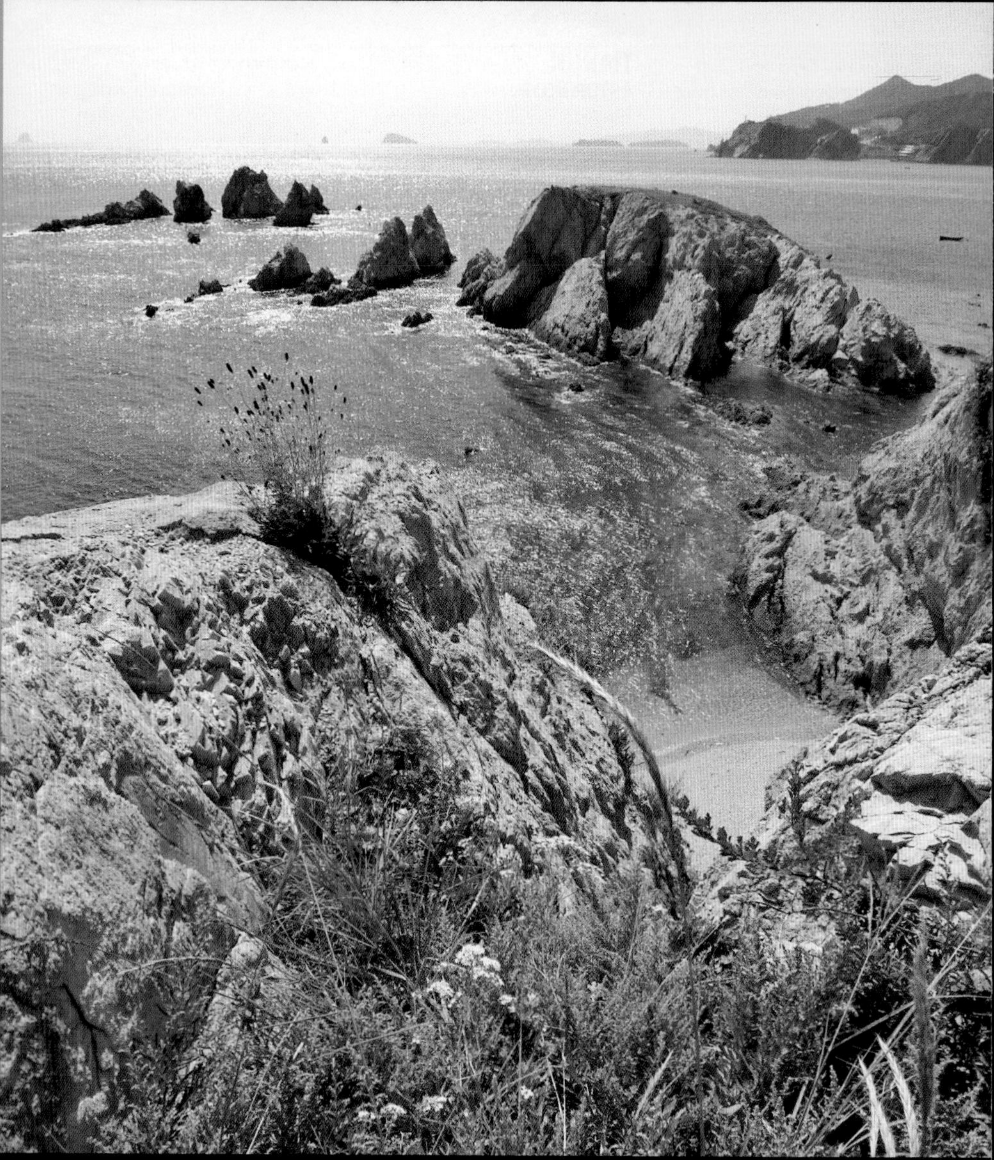

THE NORTHEAST

Northeast of Beijing are the provinces of Jilin, Liaoning and Heilongjiang. This region is best known in the West as 'Manchuria', a place of frighteningly cold winters and wild, forested landscapes. It's also China's historic industrial heartland, the first to develop heavy industry, which explains the many attempts by China's neighbors to wrest the region from its grasp. Indeed the Russian, Korean and Japanese influences evident today give this area its unique character.

This was once among the most ethnically diverse parts of the country. Ethnic Koreans still comprise a sizeable minority group. The other major group are the Manchu, descendents of Mongolian tribesmen who went on to lead China during the Qing dynasty. The Manchu now form a significant minority, but most have been assimilated into Han Chinese culture. The Manchu language is almost extinct, but many Han in Northeast China still claim Manchu ancestry.

The landscapes of the northeast are more rolling than mountainous, though the remote border with North Korea has one of China's least explored ranges, named after its highest volcanic peak, Changbaishan. Despite aggressive logging, large forested areas remain in the northern areas.

In a land where growing options are limited by Siberian weather conditions—some of the coldest on earth in winter—northeastern (dongbei) food tends to feature plenty of hearty meat dishes. This is China's wheat bowl and steamed breads and flour-wrapped dumplings are hugely popular.

CHANGBAISHAN

On the North Korean border, Changbaishan is the largest nature reserve in China at 1,965sq km (766sq miles), with deciduous and coniferous forests on its mountainous slopes, and alpine tundra at the highest elevations. At the heart of the reserve is Heaven Lake, a deep volcanic lake straddling the border and surrounded by steep peaks. The lake can be reached from the main parking area by four-wheel-drive vehicles or on foot. The climb to the lake begins at the base of the 68m-high (223ft) Changbai waterfall and takes around two hours. Along the path to the waterfall are several hot springs, where vendors cook eggs. Some of the pools are suitable for bathing.

Changbaishan can be visited on multiday organized tours from Jilin or on day trips from nearby Baihe. There are also some accommodations within the reserve, close to the parking area.

🛨 421 V5 🕓 Daily dawn–dusk 👜 Adult 100RMB, child free 🚉 Baihe Train Station. Trains to Baihe from Tonghua (7 hours). Changbaishan is accessible year-round, though the route can be difficult in winter (Nov–end Mar) due to snow 🚌 Minibuses from Baihe; buses to Baihe from Yanji

CHANGCHUN

Changchun is best known as the capital of the Japanese-controlled state of Manchukuo between 1932 and 1945. It is here that the Japanese installed Puyi as puppet emperor of the Great Manchu Empire. Changchun is today the sprawling capital of Jilin province, surprisingly attractive given the industrial nature of the area. The main draw is the Puppet Emperor's Palace (daily 8.30–5), the residence of Puyi, and the location for some of the scenes in Bernardo Bertolucci's 1987 film *The Last Emperor*. The palace has been well restored, and the private residential chambers provide an intimate insight into the life of this tragic figure. Changchun is also known, at least in China, for its car manufacturing and film

Above *The Yalu Jiang bridge links Dandong to North Korea*
Opposite *The entrance to the Puppet Emperor's Palace in Changchun*

production. Interested visitors can arrange to visit the film studios and automobile plant on organized tours.

🛨 421 U5 🚉 Changchun Train Station. Trains from Beijing (9–10 hours), Jilin (2 hours) and Harbin (3 hours) 🚌 From Beijing, and major cities in the northeast ✈ Daily flights to major cities

DALIAN
▷ 154

DANDONG

Dandong is a busy border town across the Yalu River (Yalu Jiang) from North Korea. To gaze across to China's secretive neighbor head for the park next to the one-and-a-half bridges across the river. The original Yalu River Bridge (daily 8.30–6) was dismantled by the Koreans on their side, leaving only the support pillars. You can walk out onto the remaining section of the steel bridge. Speedboats (50RMB) will take you on a quick trip close to the Korean side.

The Museum to Commemorate US Aggression (daily 8–4.30) hosts displays related to the 1950–53 conflict with the US. Although the captions are mainly in Chinese and Korean it's not hard to follow the spirit of the story that unfolds. About 20km (12 miles) northeast of Dandong, the Hushan Great Wall (daily 8.30–5) is the most easterly stretch of the wall. The restored section ends at a small museum with well-presented wall-related exhibits.

🛨 423 U6 🚉 Dandong Train Station. Trains from Beijing (14 hours), Changchun (9–10 hours), Dalian (10 hours) and Shenyang (4–5 hours) 🚌 From Dalian, Harbin, Shenyang and Tonghua

INFORMATION

⊞ 423 T7 ℹ Dalian Tourist Information hotline ☎ 0411 96181 🚆 Dalian Train Station. Rail services from major cities. Beijing is 10–12 hours 🚌 Beijing is 9 hours on the fast bus 🚢 To Yantai, Weihai and Tianjin ✈ Daily domestic flights from Beijing, Harbin, Hong Kong and Guangzhou

DALIAN

The lively, cosmopolitan port city of Dalian has great seafood and good beaches. It's a prosperous city, with plenty to offer for a relaxing vacation.

Dalian sits on the southern Liaodong Peninsula, which juts out into the Yellow Sea. It has a milder climate than most places in northeastern China, and the port is open all year round. As a result of Russian and Japanese influence, the town has some interesting architecture. But the real attraction here is the city's dynamic yet carefree atmosphere, which makes it a great place for those seeking to relax and enjoy the seaside.

TOWN CENTER

Dalian is centered around Zhongshan Square. This landscaped focal point is surrounded by the city's most important Russian and Japanese buildings, and is a popular gathering place for locals in the evening. A block to the northwest is the pedestrianized shopping area along Tianjin Jie, which leads to the underground mall at Victory Square. To the southwest is Labor Park (daily 7–7), where you'll find the giant soccer ball that seems to be the unofficial symbol of the city. There is another attractive park farther west next to People's Square.

COASTLINE

The coast running along the east and south of the peninsula has a number of fine beaches. At Donghai Park there is a pebble beach with some maritime-themed statues. Bangchuidao Scenic Area (daily 8–5), just to the south, has an excellent stretch of sand with good swimming. Along the south-facing stretch of coast are several busy beaches, with amusement parks at Tiger Beach Scenic Area, Fujiazhuang and Xianghai. Xianghai is also the location of the Sun Asia Ocean World (daily 8.30–5), a popular tunnel aquarium along the sea floor.

Below *Central Zhongshan Square*

take a river cruise (10–20RMB) to catch a glimpse of life on the other side. On Daheihe Island there's a bustling consumer goods market.
✚ 421 U2 🚂 Heihe Train Station. Connections from Harbin (12 hours) 🚌 Services from Harbin and Qiqihar

JIAMUSI

This mid-sized city in the far east of Heilongjiang province is a major port on the Songhua river as it makes its way from Harbin to the the border and Khabarovsk in Russia. It takes pride in being the first place in China to see the sun rise. There are a park and lake in town. The surrounding countryside is home to the Hezhen minority people, who are still active hunters and very skilled fishermen. They are perhaps best known for the clothing they make from fish skins.
✚ 421 V3 🚂 Jiamusi Train Station. Trains from Harbin 🚌 Services from Harbin

JILIN

Jilin is an industrial city on the Songhua River with a major chemical industry. It's a pleasant city for walking, though, with good paths along the river and in Beishan Park (daily 8–6), to the west, which has some interesting temples and pagodas. One of the major attractions is the frost-covered pine and willow trees along the

river, turning the center of the city into a splendid scene during the cold winter months. The frost is a natural phenomenon (known as rime frost) exacerbated by the flow of warm water down the river from the Fengman hydroelectric station. Century Square, just south of Jilin Bridge, is a popular place for the local people to meet and to go skating and has a small museum (daily 8.30–11.30, 1–4.30) with a collection of meteorites that landed nearby in 1976.
✚ 421 U5 ℹ CITS, 1 Chongqing Lu, ☎ 0432 244 1304 🕐 Daily 8–5 🚂 Jilin Train Station. Rail connections from Changchun, Harbin, Shenyang and Beijing 🚌 Services from Changchun, Harbin and Shenyang ✈ Flights from Beijing, Guangzhou and Shanghai

JINGPO HU

In the southwest of Heilongjiang province, close to the border with Jilin, the 50km-long (31-mile) Jingpo Lake (Jingpo Hu) is a popular destination for Chinese and Russian tourists. The lake was formed when a volcanic eruption blocked the Mudan River valley. The resort town on the northern shore acts as a base for boat trips on the lake. Other popular activities include fishing (tackle and boats are available for rent) and hiking in the forest.

The 20m-high (65ft) Diaoshuilou waterfall, which freezes over in winter, is at the northern edge of the lake. From Jingpo Lake you can take a bus or taxi to the Underground Forest (Dixia Senlin), about 50km (31 miles) away. This pristine forest grows within a series of volcanic craters and supports a diverse range of plants and animals. The forest and the lake are also accessible by minibus and taxi from Dongjing, though in the winter transportation is much less easy to find.
✚ 421 V4 🚌 Services from Mudanjiang (2 hours)

HEIHE

The border between China's northeastern Heilongjiang province and Siberia is marked for much of its length by the Heilong River (or Amur River as it is known to the Russians), from which the province takes its name. Located close to the midway point along this riverine border, the remote town of Heihe sits opposite Blagoveshchensk on the Russian side. Thanks to the establishment of a free-trade zone, border trade is significant, and the town is now reasonably prosperous. Unless you are in possession of a Russian visa (available in Beijing), you'll need to

Above *The Heilong River at Heihe marks the boundary with Siberia*
Left *The promenade along Songhua River at Jilin City is an inviting pathway for walking*

INFORMATION

✚ 421 U4 ℹ CITS, 2/F Huaqiao Hotel ✉ 72 Hongjun Jie ☎ 045 5366 1191 🕓 Mon–Sat 8–5 🚆 Harbin Main Train Station. Rail connections to Beijing (12–14 hours) and cities in the northeast 🚌 Regular buses from Jilin and Shenyang ✈ Flights to most major Chinese cities as well as international cities

Above *A concrete rendition of an ice sculpture, Sun Island Park*

INTRODUCTION

With its mix of Byzantine, Buddhist and contemporary architecture, Harbin is very distinctive. During the long, cold winters the city's spirit shows in magnificent illuminated ice and snow sculptures.

Harbin is the capital of Heilongjiang province in the far northeast, and one of the biggest cities in the region. Most of the historical attractions lie in the area between the Songhua River to the north and the railway station to the south and can be explored on foot, though, be warned, a fair amount of walking is involved. There are reasonably good bus services throughout the city, with many of the routes converging on the railway station.

Until the 1890s, Harbin was a quiet village by the Songhua River. But in 1896 the Russians were granted the right to put in a rail link to the area from Vladivostok. The Russian laborers who worked on the project were soon followed by compatriots fleeing the Bolsheviks in the early 20th century, and before long Harbin had a thriving Russian population. After World War II, Harbin developed as an industrial town. But with the increasingly free market conditions in recent decades, trade with neighboring Russia has become an important part of the local economy. Now there is also a burgeoning flow of tourists from across the Russian border.

WHAT TO SEE

DAOLIQU AND ST. SOPHIA

Most of Harbin's Russian architecture can be found in the streets of Daoliqu to the north of the railway station. The most famous example, with its distinctive green onion-shaped dome and redbrick walls, is the Church of St. Sophia (daily 9.30–5.30), completed in 1932, which houses a photographic exhibition of Harbin's Russian influence. West of the church, Zhongyang Dajie is a pedestrianized street with many well-preserved Russian buildings. Zhaolin Park, to the north of the church, is the main area for ice sculptures during the annual ice festival in January and February.

STALIN PARK

At the northern end of Zhongyang Dajie, Stalin Park (Sidalin Gongyuan) is a popular meeting place for locals. The promenade stretches for 42km (26.5 miles) along the riverbank atop the embankment built to prevent flooding. The curious Flood Control Monument stands testimony to the embankment's success. In the winter the frozen river becomes a playground for people looking to practice their skating, sledding and ice-sailing.

SUN ISLAND PARK

Across the river, and accessible by boat (5RMB) or cable car (20RMB one-way, 30RMB round-trip), the Sun Island Park (Taiyangdao Gongyuan, daily 8.30–5.30, 30RMB) combines gardens, woodland areas and a water park. In the summer it's a favorite weekend destination for the locals, while in the winter (when it can be reached on foot) an exhibition of snow sculptures is held here. About 15km (9 miles) farther north is the Siberian Tiger Park (Dongbei Hu Linyuan; daily 8–4.30), which was set up to breed these endangered animals for eventual release into the wild.

MUSEUM AND BUDDHIST TEMPLES

South of the railway station, the Provincial Museum (daily 9–4) has archeological exhibits relating to the very early habitation of the region, though there are no English captions and the presentation is lackluster. About 3km (1.5 miles) to the northeast, along Dongdazhi Jie, is a row of Buddhist sites. The Jile Temple (daily 8.30–4) is the largest Buddhist complex in the province, and was completed in 1924. By some accounts it was built to counterbalance the bad feng shui of some of the Russian buildings. Right next door, the Qiji Futu Pagoda (daily 8.30–4) is a graceful seven-tiered stone pagoda.

Below left to right *Sun Island Park is accessible by boat or cable car; the distinctive exterior of the Church of St. Sophia*

YABULI SKI RESORT

Between November and April it's possible to ski in this part of China. Yabuli Ski Resort (Yabuli Huaxue Zhongxin), around 200km (124 miles) southeast of Harbin, is the country's best-equipped resort, having hosted the Asian Games in 1996. Three chairlifts provide access to the 11 runs on Daguokui Mountain (Sanguokui Shan). The runs vary in difficulty, and all are more than 1km (0.5 miles) long, with the longest over 5km (3 miles). From Harbin you can catch a bus or train for the three-hour trip to Yabuli village where accommodations are available. Minibuses carry skiers from the village up to the resort. The resort itself (Windmill Village, tel 0451 5345 5168) also provides a range of accommodations, restaurants and night-time entertainment. Inclusive packages can be booked from agents in Harbin, although ensure your skiing is at the Windmill resort rather than one of the many lesser slopes surrounding it.

MORE TO SEE

JAPANESE GERM WARFARE EXPERIMENTAL BASE

A chilling testament to people's potential for barbarity, this museum records the atrocious experiments performed by the 731 division of the Japanese army on their Chinese and Allied prisoners of war in the name of science. The museum, which is 20km (12.5 miles) south of town, has photographic and video exhibits with captions in Chinese.

☎ 0450 8680 1556 🕐 Daily 9–11.30, 1–4 ✋ Adult 20RMB, child free 🚌 338

CHILDREN'S PARK

About 2km (1.5 miles) east of the station, this park has plenty of rides and activities for children. A miniature railway (5RMB) runs around the park.

🕐 Daily 6.30–8 ✋ Adult 2RMB, child 1RMB

Below *A city backdrop near the Provincial Museum*

From left to right *White-naped cranes in the Zhalong Nature Reserve; jasmine growing in Wudalianchi*

THE NORTHEAST • SIGHTS

MOHE

China's most northerly town also has the distinction of recording the country's lowest temperature ever (–52°C). Despite the bitter winters, Mohe draws a steady flow of visitors hoping to witness the aurora borealis, or northern lights, the colorful astronomical display visible only from northern latitudes. In the summer months the sunlight hours are long, giving plenty of time to explore the stark countryside around the town. Across the river you can see the small Russian town of Ignasino.

✛ 420 S1 🚊 Services from Gulian, which is reachable by train from Inner Mongolia

SHENYANG

▷ 160–161

WUDALIANCHI

Designated a UNESCO Biosphere Reserve in 2003, Wudalianchi is a volcanic area about 370km (230 miles) north of Harbin. Although the volcanoes here are all now dormant there is still plenty of geothermal activity. The numerous mineral springs are held in high regard for the curative properties of their waters.

Wudalianchi means 'Five Big Connected Lakes,' a name it takes from the five barrier lakes that were created during the last eruption when the Bei River was blocked by lava. The lakes and some of the 14 volcanoes around them can most easily be visited by private taxi from the town. Next to the third and largest lake is Laohei Mountain (Laohei Shan), one of the volcanoes active during the 18th-century eruptions, and the most popular spot to visit. From the parking area you can climb to the top in about 30 minutes to peer into the 140m-deep (459ft) crater or walk to the extensive adjacent lava field. The Zhongling Temple (daily 8–6), on a peak above the road between here and the town, offers good views across the rugged landscape. In the Lava Ice Cave (Rongyan Bingdong; daily 9–4.30) temperatures are low enough year round to maintain a permanent ice lantern display, with sculptures similar to those in Harbin.

✛ 421 U2 🚊 Services to Bei'an from Harbin and Qiqihar 🚌 Services from Bei'an

ZHALONG NATURE RESERVE

Zhalong Nature Reserve (Zhalong Ziran Baohuqu; daily 7–5; 20RMB) is the largest wetland reserve in China and an important stop on bird migration routes between the Arctic and Southeast Asia. The reserve, established in 1979, encompasses 2,100sq km (819sq miles) of marshlands in the Songhua and Nen river plains. More than 300 species of birds spend at least some of their lives here, with most arriving, breeding and moving on between April and September. The reserve is particularly renowned for its cranes. Six species can be found here, including the endangered red-crowned and white-naped cranes, which both breed within the reserve. Other rare birds include black and white storks and wild ibis. The area of the reserve accessible to visitors is at the far western edge. There are observation towers for spotting the birds, as well as exhibits and a video about the life and breeding habits of cranes. The unbroken vistas of the marshlands are an attraction in their own right, and boat trips out into the marshes are sometimes available. The reserve offers some limited accommodations, though it is easily accessible from Qiqihar by minibus or taxi.

✛ 421 T3 🚌 Minibuses from Qiqihar

INFORMATION
➕ 421 T6 ℹ️ CITS, 113 South Huanghe Dajie, next to Beiling Park 🕐 Daily 8.30–5 🚉 There are two stations, North and South, with connections to major cities in the northeast as well as Beijing (North or South Station, 8–10 hours), Guangzhou (South Station, 30 hours) and Shanghai (South Station, 27 hours) 🚌 Buses throughout the northeast and from Beijing (7–8 hours) ✈️ Flights from most major cities

INTRODUCTION

The first Manchu capital, Shenyang features a majestic Imperial Palace second only to that in Beijing. The well-preserved Qing Tombs are the resting place of the founders of China's last dynasty.

There's no escaping the fact that Shenyang is a large, bustling city and it can be a little intimidating to get around. The main sights are spread out, so joining an organized tour may be the least frustrating way to see what the city has to offer. That said, with a little planning, independent exploration is an option worth considering. The city is covered by a comprehensive bus network, and taxis are readily available.

Shenyang was a fairly large Mongol town during the Song era, but it was when the Manchu leader Nurhachi established his capital here in 1625 that it truly grew in importance. Although the city was the Manchu capital only until 1644 (when the newly established Qing relocated to Beijing), it continued to be an important imperial city throughout the rest of the dynasty. In the 20th century the Russians, the Japanese, the Soviets and the Chinese Nationalists controlled the city before the Communists finally captured it in October 1948. Since then Shenyang has become an industrial center.

WHAT TO SEE

IMPERIAL PALACE

Construction of the Imperial Palace (Shenyang Gugong) began in 1625, when the Manchu leader Nurhachi moved his capital to Shenyang, and was completed in 1636 by his son, the first Qing emperor, Huang Taiji. Built with Beijing's Forbidden City in mind, though incorporating Manchu and Tibetan styles, the palace has 300 rooms and 10 large courtyards. Highlights include the octagonal Dazheng Hall and the central Chongzheng Hall. After the Qing moved their capital to Beijing in 1644, this became a secondary palace, though it remained a popular retreat for the Qing emperors.

☎️ 024 2484 2215 🕐 Apr–end Oct daily 8.30–5.30; Nov–end Mar 9–4.30 🎟️ Adult 50RMB, child free

Above A rich wall decoration in the Imperial Palace

QING TOMBS

The North Tomb (daily 8.30–6), in Beiling park in the northern part of the city, is the mausoleum of Huang Taiji (or Abahai), founder of the Qing dynasty. You can see the entrance gate and pavilions, the statue-lined Spirit Way and the Hall of Eminent Favor on the way to the main burial mound. About 6km (3.5 miles) from the city on the slopes of Tianzhu Mountain (Tianzhu Shan) is the more modest East Tomb (daily 8.30–6.30), where Huang Taiji's predecessor, Nurhachi, and his wife are buried. The woodland and scenery make for a peaceful break.

18 SEPTEMBER MUSEUM

Established in 1999, this modern museum houses photography and exhibits relating to the occupation of Manchuria by the Japanese from 1931 to 1945. The 18 September Museum (Jiu Yi Ba Lishi Bowuguan) sits next to the then Japanese-owned railroad, which was bombed on September 18, 1931. This bombing was the pretext for their invasion and subsequent occupation of Shenyang, the so-called Manchuria Incident.

☎ 024 8832 0918 🕐 Daily 9–4 ✋ Free

MORE TO SEE

NORTH PAGODA

One of four pagodas that marked the city's boundaries in earlier times, the North Pagoda is by far the best preserved. It is located within the Falunsi Temple compound, which is also home to the Great Hall. Built in 1640, the hall is notable for its huge twin Buddhas. Most of the other buildings are recent recreations, but they contain some interesting paintings and statues.

🕐 Daily 8–4.30 ✋ Adult 5RMB, child free

Below *Roofs and balconies of the Imperial Palace*

HARBIN

Visit the Church of St. Sophia (Sheng Suofeiya Jiaotang), stroll among historic Russian buildings and take a ferry to the diverse gardens of Sun Island Park (Taiyangdao Gongyuan). Before returning from the island, you can detour to view a magnificent suspension bridge.

THE WALK
Distance: 4km (2.5 miles), 8km (5 miles) with detour
Allow: 4 hours, 6 hours with detour
Start/end: South end of Zhongyang Dajie

HOW TO GET THERE
Take a taxi to the southern end of pedestrian-only Zhongyang Dajie. To avoid being dropped at intersections midway along this street, ask to be taken to the Zhongda Dajiudian Hotel at its southern end. From here, walk north along Zhongyang Dajie for a few meters, looking for Toulong Jie on your right, then head

east for a few blocks until you reach the Church of St. Sophia.

★ The neo-Byzantine Church of St. Sophia was built over the span of a decade by Russian émigrés, finally opening its doors to the Russian Orthodox community for worship in 1932. Severely damaged during the Cultural Revolution, the church was used as a warehouse until being restored to its current state. Its green onion dome stands 53m (173ft) high. The church now acts as a photographic museum of Harbin's immigrant past and is

certainly worth exploring for anyone interested in history.

Leaving the church, either return to Zhongyang Dajie the way you came via Toulong Jie, or walk north until the next east–west street, Nanma Lu, taking it west to get back on to Zhongyang Dajie.

❶ Zhongyang Dajie supposedly began as a trail cut by carts hauling supplies from the river. Harbin's 'Central Avenue' was laid in 1898 and quickly became the city's most prosperous street. Lined with stone paving by a Russian architect in 1924, it became the place to buy and sell international goods. About 1.4km (1 mile) of the street is now closed to traffic, and pedestrians can soak up the European atmosphere.

Walk north along this historic avenue, being sure to make some detours down side avenues, where local vendors sell Harbin sausages and home-made ice cream. At the end of Zhongyang Dajie you'll reach the Flood Control Monument (Fanghong Shengli Jinianta).

❷ Tree-lined Stalin Park stretches along the southern bank of the Songhua River. It has numerous monuments and statues, the largest of which is the Flood Control Monument at the end of Zhongyang Dajie. Standing around 15m (49ft) tall, it was built to commemorate the citizens who stopped the river flooding, a common occurrence until the construction of the embankment in 1957.

From the north end of Zhongyang Dajie walk straight to the steps on the banks of the river, then turn right and stroll under the trees, watching for the small ferry landing on your left. Buy a one-way ticket to Sun Island Park (Taiyangdao Gongyuan) if you want to take the cable car back, or a round-trip ticket to return to the same pier, and cross to Sun Island.

❸ At 3,800ha (9,386 acres), Sun Island Park (Taiyangdao Gongyuan) is Harbin's largest recreational area, with 300,000 trees, as well as beaches, boating ponds and gardens. In summer you can enjoy the water park, while in winter there is skiing, skating and the renowned annual Ice Lantern Festival (▷ 169).

After arriving, walk north, down the main avenue next to the drop-off point, to explore some botanical gardens and Russian-theme parks.

Or rent a bicycle (single, tandem and tri-person bikes are available) for more extensive exploration. The many roadside maps on the island show your location as well as rest facilities.

Return to the river, optionally taking a detour toward the west to see the striking modern suspension bridge. Cross the river by ferry or cable car (tickets are available from the cable-car station near the river). The cable car is especially enjoyable at sunset. From the cable-car station on the south bank head west toward the Flood Control Monument. Alternatively, walk up the steps from the ferry landing point.

❹ Vendors set up shop to the west of the Flood Control Monument in the late afternoon and early evening during the summer. The food they sell reflects Harbin's varied culture—sausages, lamb and seafood barbeque, and dark beer by the mug (with a refundable deposit on the mug).

Head back down Zhongyang Dajie to return to where you started. Or stay on longer to enjoy the evening music and dancing by the Flood Control Monument.

WHERE TO EAT
There are various restaurants in Sun Island Park or you can buy snacks from the vendors who gather near the Flood Control Monument later in the afternoon. For advice on buying food from street traders, ▷ 400.

PLACE TO VISIT
THE CHURCH OF ST. SOPHIA
✉ 89 Toulong Jie 🕐 Daily 9.30–5.30
✋ Adult 25RMB, child under 1.2m (4ft) free

Below The green onion dome and roofs of the Church of St. Sophia, which now houses a photographic museum

DALIAN CITY AND SEA

Dalian is often cited as one of the best places to live in China, but visitors sometimes leave disappointed by the tidy-yet-unremarkable city center and tacky beach culture. This tour exposes Dalian's real charms—its colonial history, its modern Chinese efficiencies and its spectacular coastline, well within reach of the city center. The seaside section of the walk is long, so prepare for a full day on your feet.

THE WALK

Distance: 15km (9 miles)
Allow: 6 hours (including transport)
Start: Zhongshan Square
End: Xinghai Square

HOW TO GET THERE

Several major bus routes pass Zhongshan Square, including the Nos. 7 and 23. If you're staying downtown, the square will likely be a short taxi ride away.

★ Rise early and begin your walk in the closest thing that sprawling Dalian has to a center: Zhongshan Square. Unlike most Chinese squares, there's no real mass of concrete here. Even more confusingly, the square is in fact a circle. A total of 10 streets radiate from this central hub, and between each is an example of the city's very grandest kind of colonial-era architecture. Though the street design was first laid out by the Russians, most of the neoclassical

and Gothic buildings were built between 1910 and 1920 by the occupying Japanese forces. Today most of these buildings are home to government financial institutions, but the Dalian Hotel (Dalian Bingguan), to the south, remains open to the public and is well worth a peek.

Following signs to the Shangri-la Hotel, walk down Renmin Lu. This is 'downtown' Dalian, a wide grand boulevard that's home to Dalian's scores of multinational companies and some of its best hotels. When you meet the tram lines, turn right and follow them until you reach the tram stop up ahead. Board the 201 tram in a southerly direction (using the right-hand platform) and ride all the way to the terminus.

❶ Haizhiyun Guangchang (Song of the Sea Square) holds a group of surprisingly tasteful sculptures (the flying dragon is particularly epic)

and a large artificial waterfall mark the point at which urban, manmade Dalian magically transforms into a rugged, natural landscape. Facing the sea, look left to see the tail end of Dalian's huge port development— the third largest in China—stretching right back into the city.

Head east (bearing right) across the large concrete plaza, which soon meets a stretch of shingle, Donghai Beach. Walk along the paving or the beach to rejoin Binhai Lu.

❷ Central Dalian is located on a promontory that juts out at right angles from the large Liaoning Peninsula. Only around half of this landmass has been urbanized. The other half is refreshingly untarnished, a mixture of verdant hills and rugged coastline. Binhai Lu runs a total of 42.5km (26 miles) from Haizhiyun Square in the north, to Heishijiao, the point where the peninsula rejoins the mainland. This next section of the route runs for around 15km (9 miles), so expect to do some proper hiking, and pack plenty of water and snacks.

Shortly after passing a second beach, Binhai Bei Lu veers southward, upwards into the hills. You'll soon come to the '18 Hairpin Bend' (Shiba Pan), speckled with plastic moulds of sea creatures that have been affixed to the rocks beside the road. Head uphill, round the series of bends to eventually reach a small circular plaza on a clifftop, marked out by three fake plastic trees, from where there are views of Bangchui Dao (Bangchui Island). Continue on, walking away from the sea. After doing a U-turn back towards the sea, take the right-hand fork at the next two junctions to avoid the long sightseeing loop, designed mainly for cars.

Soon you'll leave the rugged landscape and join a large junction, surrounded by landscaped gardens. Cross the main road (Yinbin Lu) and continue onto Binhai Nan Lu (Binhai South Road). Down below to your left is the beautiful 9-hole Bangchui Island Hotel Golf Club. While the northerly section of Binhai Lu is largely set back from the sea, the southerly portion veers much closer to the water's edge and allows for closer inspection of the craggy outcrops that dot this wild, windswept portion of the peninsula.

After several kilometers you will reach Shicaotun, a small resort area at the southwestern tip of the peninsula where fishing boats bob in the harbor. There are great views up the coast to your next destination.

❸ Heading north now, continue on to reach Tiger Beach, a heavily developed resort area. Despite the impressive 'four star' rating by the China National Tourism Administration, the synthetic Tiger Beach Ocean Park theme park is unlikely to appeal to foreign tourists, particularly those who have relished

Opposite *The view looking out over Labor Park across the city of Dalian*
Above *Jetskiers enjoying the fun*

the natural landscapes of the last few hours. There is a creaking fun fair, a cable car and plastic tack everywhere. The polar aquarium is the main reason to head inside. Polar bears, walruses and penguins are among the residents.

It's possible to pick up a taxi from close to the main entrance to Tiger Park to Xinghai Square, several kilometers to the west. The journey should cost around 30RMB. To use public transportation, take No. 4 to Olympic Square and change to the Nos. 23, 801 or 901.

❹ Built to commemorate Hong Kong's return to China in 1997, Xinghai Square is reckoned to be the largest urban public space in Asia. Enjoy the salty sea air by renting a bike. Other activities include parasailing, horse-drawn carriage rides and carnival games. The bizarre fairytale castle built into the cliffs east of Xinghai Square was the Xinghai Seashell Museum until 2008, but was being converted into a five-star hotel at the time of writing.

In the south of the park, close to the seafront of the huge 20m-high (65ft) Centennial Sculpture, built to mark the anniversary of Dalian's founding in 1899 (by Russia). Its striking shape symbolically takes the form of an open book, or a pair of wings, and features the sculpted imprints of 1,000 Dalian residents' feet. On

the seafront there's a dedicated bungee-jumping tower.

South of Xinghai Square is an attractive couplet of half-moon sand beaches which make for a lovely stroll at sunset, and a great way to warm down after a long day's hike. Continue west to reach a marina and the Sun Asia World Aquarium. The polar aquarium is a little dispiriting but the 116m-long (126 yard) underwater tunnel is fun.

WHEN TO GO
The long, winding and exposed route along Binhai Lu is absolutely gorgeous on a warm sunny day. In winter, it's frightening. Optimum times are between May and October.

WHERE TO EAT
LEFT BANK WESTERN RESTAURANT (ZUO AN XI CANTING)
✉ Xinghai Xintiandi, Xinghai Square, 527-1 Binhai Xi Lu, Shahekou District ☎ 0411 8480 3188 🕓 Daily 10–9

PLACES TO VISIT
TIGER BEACH OCEAN PARK
✉ 3 Laohu Jie, Zhongshan District
☎ 0411 8239 9398 🕓 Daily 9–6 (varies slightly according to season) 🎫 15RMB park entry (100RMB to enter aquarium)

SUN ASIA WORLD AQUARIUM
✉ 608-6-8 Zhongshan Lu (west of Xinghai Square) 🕓 Daily 8.30–5 (varies slightly according to season) ☎ 0411 8458 1113 🎫 Adult 100RMB, child 50RMB

WHAT TO DO

CHANGBAISHAN

HOT SPRINGS BATHING POOLS

There are several pools at Changbaishan Hot Springs, along the route between the main parking area and the waterfall. The springs are rich in sulfur and considered very good for your health.

☎ 0433 571 2966 🕐 Daily 9–5 ✋ Adult 80RMB

JILIN CHANGBAISHAN SKI RESORT

Many Chinese athletes prefer this resort, even though it is more basic than others in the region, for both downhill and cross-country training. There is a single lift providing access to two downhill runs.

☎ 0433 574 6066, 0433 574 6077 🕐 Season runs Nov–end May ✋ Adult/child passes from 230RMB per day. Guests must first pay to enter the transit area (150RMB)

Above *Night shopping along Zhongyang Dajie, Harbin*

CHANGCHUN

JINGYUETAN NATURE RESERVE

About 18km (11 miles) east of Changchun, this nature reserve and park is around a lake surrounded by a forest. In the summer months (roughly April–September) the park is a popular destination for walking and camping, and you can go swimming, boating and waterskiing on the lake.

In the winter, a ski resort (tel 0431 0452 9399) operates in the park and there is ice-skating on the lake. Enjoyable day trips can be arranged from Changchun during the skiing season.

✉ Jingyuetan ☎ 0431 8451 8000 🕐 Mar–end Oct daily 8–5.30; Nov–end Feb 8.30–4.30. Skiing Dec–Mar ✋ Adult 30RMB, child under 1.2m (4ft) free. Skiing from US$10 per hour

MAXCOURT BOWLING CENTRE

In one of Changchun's leading hotels, this well-appointed bowling alley is popular, particularly in the cold winter months. Next to the bowling lanes is a snooker hall with well-maintained tables. Snacks and drinks are available, though at the standard hotel rates.

✉ Maxcourt Hotel, 823 Xi'an Dalu ☎ 0431 896 2688, ext. 20 🕐 Daily 10am–11pm ✋ Adult/child 10–15RMB per bowling game, 50RMB per hour for snooker

DALIAN

DALIAN FOREST ZOO

Set between the mountains and the sea, this spacious zoo has areas with animals in enclosures and also an open area. Species on show include lions and tigers, various primates, and giant and lesser red pandas. An elevated train runs through the free-range part of the zoo and it offers some great views of the surrounding park and Dalian city.

✉ Baiyunyanshui ☎ 0411 8247 2535 🕐 Daily 8.30–6 ✋ Adult 80–120RMB, child under 1.2m (4ft) free 🚌 17 and 715 stop at the zoo entrance

DAVE'S BAR (MAKEWEI JIUBA)

An old campaigner on the hard-drinking social scene in Dalian, this slightly eccentric basement bar is as popular and cheaply priced as ever. It's well liked by students at the nearby Dalian University of Foreign Languages, and tends to get packed on weekends. There's dancing at night, and an street-level outdoor area for relaxing during the day.

✉ Qiyi Jie (just north of Zhongshan Square) ☎ 0411 8264 1183 🕐 Daily 11am–late

GOLDEN PEBBLE BEACH

www.jinshitan.com

The northern terminus of Dalian's light rail line is now an extensive tourist resort, complete with a clutch of on-site hotels. Among a miscellany of paid-for attractions is a folk customs museum, a martial arts hall and a waxwork museum. Kids get a Disneyland-clone while golfers can enjoy a spectacular coastal course. The main reason to come remains the pleasant stretch of sand and stone beach (free to enter) or the National Geo-park, which offers access to a spectacular stretch of coastline (120RMB).

✉ Golden Pebble Beach National Tourist Resort ☎ 0411 8791 5807 🚆 Take the Light Rail from Dalian Railway Station.

MANDOLIN

This is a trendy bar and club with local and guest DJs playing upbeat tunes for a young and fashionable crowd. The bar serves cocktails, spirits, wines and teas. This is definitely one of the places to be seen on the Dalian nightlife circuit at the moment.

✉ 12 Tianjin Jie ☎ 0411 8259 7333 🕐 Daily 8pm–2am

NEPALESE BAR (XIXIABAMA)

An intimate and atmospheric dive bar with cheap beers and moreish pizzas. There's a couple of acoustic guitars stacked up in the corner and sing-songs occasionally break out among the mixed Chinese and overseas crowd. It is friendly and informal, especially when compared

with some of Dalian's edgier nightlife establishments.

✉ Wusi Lu (by Wansui Jie) ☎ 0411 8580 3798 🕐 Daily 6pm–2am

NUOYA FANGZHOU

A laid-back pub, Nuoya Fangzhou is popular with both expatriates and locals. The wooden interior lends the place a quiet, intimate feel. Local bands provide entertainment in the evenings (8.20pm–late), with the music tending to be fairly subdued.

✉ 32 Wusi Lu ☎ 0411 8369 2798 🕐 Daily 10.30am–2am

POLAR AQUARIUM

One of several attractions at Laohutan Leyuan (Tiger Beach Park), this polar aquarium houses a number of species from both the South and North poles. You'll be able to watch polar bears and penguins, as well as seals, walruses and beluga whales. There are dolphin performances several times each day. For children there is a separate exhibition area where it is possible to touch several different sea creatures.

✉ Laohutan Leyuan ☎ 0411 8268 6295 🕐 Daily 8.30–5.30 🎫 Adult 190RMB 🚌 2, 4, 30, 712 for Tiger Beach

SUN ASIA OCEAN WORLD

In Xinghai Gongyuan (Xinghai Park) on the south of the Dalian Peninsula, this aquarium is a popular destination and can be very busy, especially during holidays. The main feature is a 118m-long (387ft) underwater tunnel with a moving walkway. There are plenty of creatures to see, including sharks and rays.

✉ Xinghai Gongyuan ☎ 0411 8458 1113, 0411 8467 9517 🕐 Daily 8.30–5 🎫 Adult 120RMB, child under 1.3m (4.25ft) free 🚌 22, 23, 201 and 406

TIN WHISTLE PUB

This reliable Irish bar, just a short walk from the Shangri-la Hotel, is noticeably calmer and more convivial than Dalian's famously edgy music bars and after-dark meat markets. Expect to find imported stout on

tap, big-screen sports, quiz nights and expense-account holders up at the bar. The Hole in the Wall bar is just next door if the atmosphere doesn't suit.

✉ 14 Changjiang Lu, Zhongshan District ☎ 0411 8264 1443 🕐 Daily noon–2am

VICTORY PLAZA SHOPPING CENTRE

Below Shengli Guangchang (Victory Square) in front of the railroad station, this bustling shopping center goes down three levels beneath the concourse. One floor is almost entirely dedicated to food vendors, but elsewhere you'll find many small stores selling clothes, cosmetics, electronics and souvenirs. There are entrances and exits all around Victory Square.

✉ Shengli Guangchang 🕐 Daily 10–10

HARBIN

BLUE KISS

Formerly a distillery, Harbin's most famous dance club is loud, boozy and sleazy—all of which goes to explain its enduring popularity. Not one for the wallflower, Blue Kiss specializes in heavy Russian techno, vodka-shooters and post-punk dance steps. A bout of properly choreographed pole dancing is never far away.

✉ 100 Diduan Jie ☎ 0451 8468 4277 🕐 Daily 1pm–late

FLOOD CONTROL MONUMENT NIGHT MARKET

In the summer months, locals gather close to the Flood Control Monument to watch a variety of music and dance performances on a specially constructed stage. It's great for light-hearted evening entertainment and is a good place to sample another of Harbin's great attractions, the local beer.

✉ Fanghong Shengli Jinianta 🕐 May–end Sep daily 6pm–9pm

HARBIN JEWISH HISTORY AND CULTURE EXHIBITION HALL

Harbin's grandest old synagogue has been converted into an interesting memorial to the city's former Jewish inhabitants. Harbin once had the largest Jewish population in the Far East, numbering around 20,000 in the early part of the 20th century. Having played a central part in designing and building the city, most left after the Communist takeover. This newly renovated three-story temple does an admirable job of telling their story.

✉ 162 Jingwei Jie, Daoli District ☎ 0451 8763 0882 🕐 Daily 9am–5pm 🎫 Adult 10RMB 🚍 2

HONGBO SHICHANG SHOPPING CENTRE

This huge underground shopping mall, set in an old air-raid shelter, sells inexpensive fashion items, jewelry, electronics and souvenirs. The quality of the goods can vary widely, as local and Russian copies share shelf space with genuine items, so be on your guard and shop carefully. It's an entertaining place though, with plenty for everyone to buy, and in winter, a warm refuge from the bitterly cold weather.

✉ Hongbo Shichang, corner of Dongdazhi Jie and Hongjun Jie 🕐 Daily 9–9

RED LION PUB

This English theme pub with gnarled wooden fixtures and dark corners serves a good selection of drinks and bar food. It is a warm retreat when temperatures outside drop, though tends to be quiet.

✉ Holiday Inn Hotel, 90 Jingwei Jie ☎ 0451 8422 6666 🕐 Daily 5pm–2am

ZHONGYANG DAJIE

This cobbled street is not only home to some of Harbin's best-preserved Russian architecture, it also offers the city's best shopping experience (photograph, ▷ 166). There are many department stores, upscale boutiques and local vendors along the road offering everything from inexpensive Russian souvenirs to exclusive, fashionable couture.

✉ To the south of Fanghong Shengli Jinianta (Flood Control Monument) 🕐 Daily 8.30–8

JILIN
BEIDAHU SKI AREA

www.beidahuski.com

Jilin's best-appointed skiing area and host for the 6th Asian Winter Games in 2007, Beidahu has five downhill trails and a cross-country route, with grades suitable for all levels of skier. Snow machines, and the high altitude, make for a slightly longer season than at other resorts nearby. Equipment rental is available. Packages can be arranged from agents in Jilin or Changchun.

☎ 0432 420 2023 🕐 Around Dec to mid-Mar 🎫 Adult 320–400RMB per day, child under 1.4m (4.6ft) half price

BEISHAN PARK

In the western part of the city, this park encompasses Taoyuan Mountain (Taoyuan Shan) and is a good place for walking and jogging. There are some large wooded areas inside the park and well-marked footpaths. If you're heading here for exercise avoid weekends and public holidays, when it can get very busy.

✉ Densheng Lu ☎ 0432 213 2290 🕐 Daily 7–5 🎫 Adult 5RMB, child under 1.2m (4ft) free

SHENYANG
MULLIGAN'S IRISH BAR

This popular Irish theme pub is on the fifth floor of the Intercontinental Hotel. The live music in the evenings attracts a mix of locals, expatriates and tourists. The bar is well stocked and there is an extensive cocktail menu. The large televisions show major sporting events.

✉ Intercontinenal Hotel, 208 Nanjing Beilu ☎ 024 2334 1999 🕐 Daily 5pm–2am, music from 8.15 until midnight

QIANSHAN NATIONAL PARK

There are many steep peaks dotted with Buddhist and Taoist temples in this mountain park, 20km (12 miles) from Anshan city. It is a good area for hiking along the clearly marked trails, particularly on weekdays when there are not too many visitors. There are some hot springs at the base of the mountains with a bathing area.

✉ About 100km (60 miles) south of Shenyang 🕐 24 hours 🎫 Adult Apr–end Oct 50RMB, Nov–end Mar 40RMB, child under 1.2m (4ft) free 🚍 Regular buses from Shenyang (Qiche Kuaisu Keyunzhan or South Long-Distance Bus Station) to Anshan, then bus 308 from Anshan to the park. Total journey time is around 1 hour

SAN HAO STREET COMPUTER AND SOFTWARE CITY

Representing one of the largest electronic marts in northeast China, San Hao Street is a collection of high-rise blocks housing pretty much every kind of electronic goodie you can imagine. Despite efforts to crack down, counterfeit software and DVDs are also in no short supply.

✉ Sanhao Jie (west of the Wenhua Lu interchange, close to the Northeast University) 🕐 Daily 9am–5.30pm

SHENYANG BOTANICAL GARDENS

A series of lush green gardens spread along a small river and dotted with lakes, this place makes a relaxing change from the city. There's more than a 1,000 species of plants and trees here, with a section dedicated to azaleas and special displays of tulips and chrysanthemums in season.

✉ Gokan Town (20km/12 miles east of city), Dongling District ☎ 024 8803 8015 🕐 Daily 8–5 🎫 Adult 20RMB, child under 1.2m (4ft) free 🚍 330

SHENYANG STEAM EXHIBITION HALL

This museum houses more than 20 steam locomotives from China and as far afield as the US and Eastern Europe. The engines are well presented in their new exhibition hall, and there are several secondary exhibitions telling the story of steam engines and the history of steam railways in China. This is the largest museum of its kind in the country, and well worth a visit for anyone with an interest in railways.

✉ In the Shenyang Botanical Gardens, Gokan Town, Dongling District ☎ 024 8803 8014 🕐 Daily 8–5 🎫 Adult 20RMB, child under 1.2m (4ft) free 🚍 330

STROLLER'S BAR (LIU LANG ZHE JIUBA)

A convivial little watering hole that offers hearty European comfort food and mercifully familiar music to foreign tourists.

The wall-mounted memorabilia suggests a US expat bar, but most of the posters and signs are actually in German, pointing both to the nationality of Stroller's owner, and what kind of beer can be had from behind the bar.

✉ 36 Beiwujing Jie (north of Shiwei Lu) ☎ 024 2287 6677 🕓 Daily 11.30am–2am

WU AI MARKET

This sprawling market area covers several blocks on the south side of Zhong Jie and sells everything from clothing and jewelry through toys and games to household items and garden equipment. It is definitely low end compared to the department stores of Taiyuan Jie and Zhong Jie, but it is fun too, and prices are very low if you are prepared to bargain.

✉ Wu Ai Shichang, south of Zhong Jie 🕓 Daily 10–8

Below Enjoying a night out at one of the popular bars in Dalian

FESTIVALS AND EVENTS

JANUARY
JILIN ICE LANTERN FESTIVAL

Similar to the better-known event in Harbin, this festival sees local artists carve large illuminated buildings and figures out of ice.

✉ Jiangnan Park, Jilin ☎ 0432 243 5819 🕓 Mid-Jan (exact dates vary)

JANUARY–FEBRUARY
HARBIN ICE LANTERN FESTIVAL

Stunning ice sculptures can be seen throughout town, though the main areas are at the Ice and Snow World theme park across the river in Sun Island Park (▷ 157) and in Zhaolin Park close to the Flood Control Monument.

Many of the immense ice sculptures are lit from the inside, best seen at night. During the day

ZHONGHUA LU AND TAIYUAN JIE

These intersecting streets, close to the South Railroad Station, form Shenyang's most upscale shopping district. The emphasis here is on department stores, clothing shops

you can see the snow sculptures in Sun Island Park.

✉ Harbin ☎ 0451 8625 0068 🕓 Jan 5–Feb 25 (officially though it now begins in late Dec and continues until the beginning of Mar)

SEPTEMBER
DALIAN INTERNATIONAL FASHION FESTIVAL

The annual trade show attracts designers and fashion houses from across the world, but there is also a range of fashion-related events organized throughout the city, including fashion parades and sales. The city gets very busy at this time, so be sure to reserve your hotel in advance.

✉ Various venues, Dalian 🕓 Third week of Sep

and brand-name goods, though you will find some smaller vendors on the streets and in the malls too.

✉ Close to the South Railroad Station 🕓 Daily 9–9

PRICES AND SYMBOLS

The restaurants are listed alphabetically. The prices are for a two-course lunch (L) and a three-course à la carte dinner (D) for one person, without drinks. The wine price is for the least expensive bottle. All the restaurants listed accept credit cards unless otherwise stated.

For a key to the symbols, ▷ 2.

CHANGBAISHAN

CHANGBAI MOUNTAIN INTERNATIONAL TOURIST HOTEL

The Changbaishan area offers few exceptional places to eat out, although it is a good place to try infusions of healthy herbs and roots from the mountain's slopes. This comfortable, no-nonsense hotel restaurant serves standard dishes, and a few Korean possibilities. They also have a friendly bar with a moderate list of cocktails and beers,

a welcome sight after a day trekking on the mountain.

✉ Tourist Village ☎ 0433 574 6001 🕐 Daily 6am–8.30am, 11.30am–2pm, 6pm–9pm 🖐 L and D 30–50RMB, Beer 10RMB

CHANGCHUN

FRENCH BAKERY (HONG MOFANG)

An intimate European-style café in a good central location. There are French movie posters hung off the fake brick walls and an excellent range of meals, the expected breads, pastries being topped up with random selections like Malaysian favorite, *nasi goreng*. The bakery also runs a sideline selling imported foods.

✉ 1225 Guilin Lu ☎ 0431 8848 6773 🕐 Daily 8am–10.30pm 🖐 L and D 60–80RMB, Coffee from 15RMB

Above *Excellent dining is on offer in restaurants in the Northeast region of China*

DALIAN

BA BAI WAN SUSHI

Being popular with Japanese visitors, Dalian has its fair share of Japanese restaurants. Ba Bai Wan Sushi serves some of the best Japanese food in town. A sushi bar using only the freshest of seafood ingredients, it's a feast for the eyes as much as the stomach.

✉ 2 Lu Xun Lu 🕐 Daily 9.30am–10pm 🖐 L and D 100RMB

BU JIAN BU SAN

This four-level restaurant is locally famed for its lobster, but has an impressive range of fish and seafood dishes. Diners wanting to try more hearty Manchurian classics are also catered to, with dumplings and steamed breads on the menu. With its central location and 24-hour door policy, this is good place to settle the stomach if you've been out partying late in Dalian.

✉ Zhongshan Square, 2 Jiefang Lu
☎ 0411 8280 9760 🕐 24 Hours ✋ L and D 100RMB, Wine 78RMB

CUIFENG HOT POT

This wildly popular hot pot parlor is a little way outside the city center of Dalian, though a great choice for those in the vicinity of Xinghai Park. Cuifeng introduces a modicum of class to the down-at-heel hot pot industry with a brightly lit, fresh decor. Add to that great prices and you understand why diners tend to linger. Accordingly, you'll probably need to wait for a table.

✉ 650 Zhongshan Lu, Heishijiao, Shahekou District ☎ 0411 8468 9268 🕐 Daily 10am–midnight ✋ L and D 60RMB, Bottled beer from 3RMB

DALIAN NORTH PEARL RESTAURANT

Playing on Dalian's reputation as the 'Pearl of the North,' this Cantonese-style seafood restaurant is a culinary gem. With its 400sq m (4,300sq ft) dining hall, supported by 26 private dining rooms, there is always room for one more diner. Even so, wait-staff bustle among crowded tables while parties, families and visitors enjoy the food.

✉ 3 Foushou Lu 🕐 Daily 11–11
✋ L 80RMB, D 120RMB, Wine 100RMB

ECHO CAFÉ AND BOOKSHOP

Housed in a striking white villa, just west of Olympic Square, Echo Café and Bookshop attracts the city's young bohemians for long afternoons and evenings of caffeine-fueled pontificating and Wi-Fi surfing.

The books are stacked so high that step ladders are needed for top shelves, and there are weekly exhibitions, shows and events.

✉ Junction of Zhenren Jie and Jianye Jie, Xigang District ☎ 0411 8430 7899 🕐 Daily 10am–2am ✋ L and D 50RMB, Beer from 15RMB

LE CAFÉ IGOSSO

This popular, upscale Italian restaurant serves thin-crust pizzas, beef carpaccio in olive oil, and seafood pesto salad, plus seasonal seafood dishes. The wine selection is one of Dalian's best. Cheesecake or one of the other freshly made desserts is a must.

✉ 45 Nanshan Lu ☎ 0411 8265 6453
🕐 Mon–Sat 11am–1.30am, Sun 11–10
✋ L and D 40–120RMB, Wine 120RMB

PAULANER BRAUHAUS

Good German food in China is hard to come by, but the Kempinski's Paulaner Brauhaus is an exception. It's a little pricy, but the portions are large and the beer, freshly brewed at the restaurant's microbrewery, is excellent. The resident band perform jazz and pop nightly.

✉ Kempinski Hotel Dalian, 92 Jiefang Lu
☎ 0411 8259 8888 🕐 Daily 11.30am–1am ✋ L and D 100–200RMB, Beer 80RMB

TAPAS SPANISH RESTAURANT

www.tapas.com.cn

On the edge of Russian Street, this classy two-level restaurant is one of the most popular international restaurants in town. The menu offers an exhaustive list of generously portioned tapas, good for either a snack or a whole meal. Try the Parma ham on toast, or the gratin mushroom tart. The largely imported wine list features plenty of Iberian flavor, and the both the *tiramisù* and *crème brûlée* desserts are classically European. Booking ahead is essential on weekends and useful during the week.

✉ No.3, 35 Shengli Jie, Xigang District
☎ 0411 8254 0996 🕐 Daily 11am–10.30pm ✋ L 120RMB, D 180RMB, Wine 35RMB (per glass)

TIAN TIAN YU GANG

Tian Tian Yu Gang is a well-known chain of seafood restaurants. While service may vary somewhat among the 10-or-so branches throughout the city, the menu is standardized to have around 100 of the same dishes. Fresh fish, abalone, eel and shrimp are just a few of the choices

that are cooked to taste and served piping hot. Hand peel spicy crab or peppered shrimp and wash it down with fresh beer, brewed on the premises.

✉ 45 Tongtai Jie ☎ 0411 8454 9000
🕐 Daily 9–9 ✋ L and D 40–70RMB, Beer 10RMB

THE TIN WHISTLE IRISH PUB

Advertising itself as 'Dalian's only Traditional Irish Pub,' the Tin Whistle serves up pub food, a chummy atmosphere and foreign beer on tap. A regular crowd gathers to watch sport on the pub's widescreen television, and on the second Thursday night of every month you can take part in an entertaining trivia quiz. Live bands play regularly and, unlike in Ireland, smoking is permitted at the bar.

✉ 14 Changjiang Lu (behind Shangri-La hotel) 🕐 Daily 6pm–2am ✋ D 25–50RMB

DANDONG
AILILANG

This reasonably salubrious restaurant is one of the most popular of the many Korean joints that line the riverside in this city on the border of the Democratic People's Republic of Korea. Raw beef and dog are among the Korean staples on the menu. Order your own personal hot pot to ensure you retain full control over ingredients and cooking methods.

✉ Binjiang Zhong Lu ☎ 0415 212 2333 🕐 Daily 9.30–9.30 ✋ L and D 80–150RMB, Bottled beer from 4RMB

ANDONG PAVILION

Next to the Yalu River, and with the best views of North Korea other than from the middle of the old Yalu River Bridge, the classy Andong Pavilion serves a mix of Sichuanese, Cantonese and Macanese dishes. They do a very good *gongbao jiding* (Sichuan spicy chicken with peanuts) and the *tangcu paigu* (sweet-and-sour ribs) are particularly tender.

✉ Kaifalu Lu (west of Yalujiang Park)
☎ 0415 314 5801 🕐 Daily 11–9
✋ L and D 30–50RMB, Wine 98RMB

DANDONG INTERNATIONAL HOTEL

www.dd-hotel.com

This rotating hotel restaurant, 23 floors above central Dandong, serves both Chinese and Western dishes. Try some of the fish dishes, made using freshwater fish, such as *lu zi yu*, from the Yalu River. Alternatively, if you are hankering for the taste of home, the steaks and spaghetti dishes are quite good. From this high vantage point there are some wonderful views of North Korea on clear days. The self-service buffet breakfast (20RMB) is the best in town.

✉ 23rd Floor, 88 Xinan Lu ☎ 0415 281 7788 🕐 Daily 6.30am–8.30am, 11am–1pm, 5.30pm–9pm 🖐 L and D 20–60RMB, Wine 80RMB

HARBIN

ARBUCKS BAR (USA BUCKS)

Themed with cowboy and kitschy Americana, this interesting restaurant-bar attracts mostly young Chinese adults with its good cheeseburgers and pizzas. The swinging saloon doors out front are hard to miss, as is the very familiar (but slightly different) green-and-white 'Arbucks' sign. Inside you'll find wooden, high-back booths and a large wooden bar surrounded by assorted paraphernalia.

✉ 100 Zhongyang Dajie 🕐 Daily 9am–10pm 🖐 L and D 15–40RMB, Beer 16RMB

CAFÉ RUSSIA 1914

The door of this small bistro is wrapped in ivy during summer months and a look inside is warranted. Dishes like *piroshki* (savory pastries), borscht soup, beef brisket with sauerkraut and *pelmeni* (a small pasty stuffed with beef and pork minced meat, onions and occasionally potato) are served at closely set tables. Coffee, tea and cookies are also available. Old photographs and paintings on the walls tell the story of Harbin's émigré past.

✉ 57 Xi Toudao Jie (on corner of Zhongyang Dajie), Harbin ☎ 0451 8456

3207 🕐 Daily 9am–midnight 🖐 L and D 60RMB, Beer 12RMB

DONGFANG JIAOZI WANG

Easy to find while strolling along Zhongyang Dajie, this busy restaurant serves many types of *jiaozi*. Large mugs of draft beer are served cold, next to steaming dishes, soups and salads in the somewhat spartan, cafeteria-like interior. You can watch *jiaozi* being made in bulk in the kitchen at the back through a large window.

✉ 39 Zhongyang Dajie ☎ 0451 8465 3920 🕐 Daily 10–9.30 🖐 L and D 4–15RMB per order, Beer 7RMB

FRENCH BAKERY

The aroma of strong coffee wafts from this pleasant café. A full coffee menu, pastries and ice creams are listed on the chalkboard, and while a little expensive, there's nothing like a real cup of coffee.

✉ 185 Zhongyang Dajie ☎ 0451 8911 3753 🕐 Daily 8.30am–10.30pm 🖐 L and D 20RMB

HUAMEI XICANTING

Harbin's premier Russian restaurant has a long and distinguished history. Originally established in 1925, it was once a preferred haunt of White Russians escaping revolutionary Russia. Today the menu is not confined solely to Russian specialties (the beef stroganoff is delightful), but also includes a number of French and Italian dishes.

✉ 112 Zhongyang Dajie (opposite the Modern Hotel) 🕐 Daily 11–9.30 🖐 L and D 100RMB, Wine 120RMB

THE PORTMAN

The Portman bar-restaurant has a well-founded reputation for its draft beer. The mainly Western dishes on the menu include some very good steaks, grilled salmon, salads, pizzas and burgers, plus borscht and a few other Russian dishes. Most nights there is live classical music.

✉ 53 Xiqi Daojie ☎ 0451 8468 6888 🕐 7.30pm–9pm 🕐 Daily 11am–midnight 🖐 L and D 50–100RMB, Wine 68RMB

RED LION PUB

Like so many English pubs around the world, the Red Lion serves proper fish-and-chips and other pub fare, plus beer on tap. Though prices are more than for local fare, you'll know exactly what you're ordering!

✉ Holiday Inn Hotel, 90 Jingwei Jie ☎ 0451 8422 6666 🕐 Daily 5pm–2am 🖐 D 50RMB, Wine 168RMB

SHANG PALACE

Enjoy mainly Cantonese cooking of five-star quality in the Shang Palace's spacious, rosewood-appointed dining room. The Chinese-Malay chef presents his colorful dishes with the flare found in Hong Kong restaurants. Try the crispy chicken or the long bean specialty.

✉ Shangri-La Harbin Hotel, 555 You Yi Lu ☎ 0451 8485 8888, ext. 21 🕐 Daily 11–2, 5–10 🖐 L 80RMB, D 100RMB, Wine 110RMB

SHUI CHENG GUSHI SHISHANG

A smart Taiwanese-owned mini-chain in Harbin, with two outlets around the city. WiFi enabled and attracting a young, trendy crowd, this restaurant offers a smattering of familiar dishes like fried rice, sweet and sour and spring rolls in an immaculately presented format. The light and airy decor compensates for the overly tight table layout.

✉ 5F, Daoli Songlei International Commercial Building, 66 Zhongyang Da Jie, Daoli District ☎ 0451 8468 5429 🕐 Daily 9–9 🖐 L and D 100RMB, Bottled beer from 12RMB

XUEFU YIPIN JIANGGU

Specializing in succulent pork ribs (the eponymous '*jianggu*') this excellent locals' local has a point-and-order picture menu that comes filled with Northeastern favorites, dumplings and pancakes included. The atmosphere can get a touch raucous but it's lots of fun. Every table comes with a pair of throwaway plastic gloves with which to tackle the meat.

✉ 329 Tongda Jie, Daoli District ☎ 0451 8762 1288 🕐 Daily 10.30am–9.30pm 🖐 L and D 50RMB, Bottled beer from 4RMB

JILIN

LIYADE SHIFU

Jilin has a substantial Hui Muslim minority and the Liyade (Riyadh), the town's top halal restaurant, serves them well. Expect plenty of mutton dishes, including the restaurant's signature dish, *shousi yangrou* (tender strips of hand-torn lamb). Hui Muslim cooking differs substantially from the Uighur Muslim variety found in the Xinjiang region and is reminiscent of standard Han Chinese cooking, with more sauces and dips.

✉ 56 Jiefang Dalu ☎ 0432 201 7999 🕐 Daily 9–9 🍴 L and D 50RMB

SUMMER PALACE RESTAURANT

The Summer Palace is a fairly ordinary hotel restaurant serving mostly Cantonese cuisine and some regional dishes. If you've not tried *Dongbei* (northeastern) cuisine, this is an easy place to start. Try the *Dongbei dala pi* (Dongbei-style mung bean noodles) or *yuxiang rousi* (fish-flavored shredded pork), both served with noodles and pickles.

✉ Century Hotel, 77 Jilin Dajie, Jilin City ☎ 0432 216 8888 🕐 Daily 11.30–3, 4.30–10 🍴 L 100RMB, D 150RMB, Wine 80RMB

MUDANJIANG

JIN KUAIZI DAXIAN JIAOZI CUN

This wonderful dumpling restaurant's name translates as 'Golden Chopsticks Big Stuffed Dumpling' and the *jiaozi* here really are delicious. Apart from their dumplings, the restaurant serves an excellent spicy potato stew, particularly welcome on cold days in this part of the world.

✉ 5 Shizheng Lu (100km/62 miles from Jingpo Lake) ☎ 0453 622 9228 🕐 Daily 9–9 🍴 L and D 10–40RMB, Beer 3.5RMB

SHENYANG

BANANA LEAF (JIAO YE)

One of several incarnations around the country of this popular Thai-theme restaurant. The food is as authentically Thai as possible in this remote northeastern corner of China, and the atmosphere invariably lively: the friendly servers double as musicians during regular serenading sessions.

✉ 5F, Huafu Tiandi Building, 118 Ha'erbin Lu, Shenhe District ☎ 024 8862 3222 🕐 Daily 10–10 🍴 L and D 90–120RMB

CAFÉ LIDO

One of five excellent restaurants in Shenyang's finest hotel, the Café Lido serves the best Western-style buffet outside Beijing. The dessert section is especially fine—it is unusual to find the likes of Black Forest gateau or chocolate-covered profiteroles in many places in China. The hotel's Celestial Court restaurant serves good Cantonese cuisine, at a price.

✉ Sheraton Shenyang Lido Hotel, 386 Qingnian Dajie ☎ 024 2318 8888 🕐 Daily 6am–midnight 🍴 L and D 150–250RMB, Wine 178RMB

LAO BIAN DUMPLING HOUSE

Shenyang is renowned for its delicious dumplings and Lao Bian, established in 1829, is the granddaddy of the city's many noteworthy establishments. A bewildering choice of fillings includes pork and chives, chicken and turnip, and mutton and shallots.

✉ 206 Zhongjie 🕐 Daily 8am–10.30pm 🍴 L and D 10–40RMB, Beer 8RMB

MEIAHLI KOREAN BBQ

Shenyang has a number of good Korean restaurants. The Meiahli's specialties include *lengmian* (cold boiled noodles), which, though they sound unappealing, are actually very good with a plate of *kimchi* (Korean pickles) and local beer. Other standards include barbecued beef and *zaocha* (a fruity tea).

✉ 62 Kunming Beijie 🕐 Daily 10–9 🍴 L and D 30–50RMB, Beer 10RMB

MULLIGANS IRISH BAR

With authentic Irish ales on tap this is as close to the real thing as you are likely to find in northeast China. There's a generous Happy Hour period between 5pm and 7.30pm. Food is very much pub-style, chicken in the basket, fish and chips and plenty of bar snacks, plus live music Monday to Saturday from around 9pm.

✉ Intercontinental Hotel, 208 Nanjing Beilu ☎ 024 2334 1999 🕐 Daily 5pm–2am 🍴 D 40–90RMB, Beer 28RMB

Left *There's plenty of choice at stalls in Stalin Park, Harbin*

Above *The lobby of the ultramodern Traders Hotel in Shenyang*

PRICES AND SYMBOLS

Prices are the starting price for a double room for one night, unless otherwise stated. Breakfast is included unless noted otherwise. All the hotels listed accept credit cards unless otherwise stated. Note that rates vary widely throughout the year.

For a key to the symbols, ▷ 2.

CHANGBAISHAN

CHANGBAI MOUNTAIN INTERNATIONAL TOURIST HOTEL

www.cithotel.cn

The city of Changbaishan is best visited between June and September when this comfortable, upscale hotel comes into its own, with superb views of the nearby Changbai Waterfall.

✉ Tourist Village ☎ 0433 574 6001 🖐 600–800RMB 🛈 43 🕃

CHANGCHUN

SHANGRI-LA HOTEL, CHANGCHUN

www.shangri-la.com

The first (and currently only) internationally managed hotel in town is part of a hulking office-retail-apartment complex and offers travelers something of a haven in the center of this noisy, developing city. It's not quite as luxurious as other hotels in the Shangri-la family, but all the usual five-star trappings are present; tennis courts, pool and Jacuzzis included.

✉ 569 Xi'an Lu, nr People's Square ☎ 0431 8898 1818 🖐 890–1,250RMB 🛈 458 🖾 🛅 🕃

DALIAN

DALIAN HOTEL

Built in 1927 by the Japanese, this aging hotel is a good budget choice. Zhongshan Square is a two-minute walk away, while good shopping avenues and underground malls are just across the street. Ask for a quieter room near the end of the hall.

✉ 4 Zhongshan Guangchang ☎ 0411 8263 3111 🖐 450–640RMB 🛈 64 🕃

HOTEL NIKKO

www.jalhotels.com

With spectacular views of Dalian's harbor and just a short walk from Zhongshan Square, the hotel offers first-class rooms. Amenities include a floodlit tennis court, solarium, Jacuzzi and sauna. The spacious rooms all have broadband internet access, satellite television, minibar and luxurious bathrooms.

✉ 123 Changjiang Lu ☎ 0411 8252 9999 🖐 930–1,500RMB, excluding breakfast 🛈 372 🕃 🛅 🖾 Indoor

KEMPINSKI HOTEL DALIAN

www.kempinski-dalian.com

This new twin-tower five-star provides some competition to the Shangri-La at the top end of the Dalian hotel market, and still manages to offer reasonable value. Rooms have a warm, homey feel with bouncy carpets and kick-back furniture, and there are great views of Labor Park from some rooms. The food options include a Paulaner Brauhaus—the popular Bavarian-themed pub chain from Shanghai (▷ 171). The Arabian theme Oasis Spa is also excellent.

✉ 92 Jiefang Lu, Zhongshan District, Dalian ☎ 0411 8259 8888 🖐 1,000–1,200RMB 🛈 457 🖾 🛅 🕃

SHANGRI-LA DALIAN

www.shangri-la.com

Like other hotels in the Shangri-La chain, the Dalian branch has traditionally outfitted, comfortable

Chinese-style rooms. It is ideal for exploring the city.

✉ 66 Renmin Lu ☎ 0411 8252 5000 ✋ 1,750–2,300RMB 🛏 562 ♿ 📺 ≋ Indoor

DANDONG
ZHONGLIAN HOTEL
www.zlhotel.com

Overlooking the Yalu River into North Korea, this is Dandong's top hotel. It is worth paying the extra money to get a room with a view of the river and the half-destroyed Yalu River Bridge. Unusual facilities include a bowling alley and a cigar bar.

✉ 62 Binjiang Zhonglu ☎ 0415 233 3333 ✋ 757RMB 🛏 165 ♿ 📺

HARBIN
HARBIN ROMANTIC HOTEL
This mid-range hotel is only a few minutes' walk from the city's main strolling and shopping street, Zhongyang Dajie, and a sound choice for budget travelers looking for Western amenities. The heated pool is a delightful bonus for winter tourists.

✉ 178 Shangzhi Dajie ☎ 0451 8677 5555 ✋ 320–450RMB, excluding breakfast 🛏 83 ♿ ≋ Indoor

SHANGRI-LA HARBIN
www.shangri-la.com

This is by far Harbin's most luxurious hotel. The Shangri-La is on the banks of the Songhua River near Stalin Park. Though well placed for the winter Ice Lantern Festival, it is a little way from the city center. The revamped Horizon Club floors exude a hip, modern style. The service and facilities make this the perfect place for the well-heeled traveler.

✉ 555 You Yi Lu ☎ 0451 8485 8888 ✋ 980–1,500RMB 🛏 400 ♿ 📺 ≋ Indoor

SONGHUAJIANG GLORIA INN HARBIN
Next to the Flood Control Monument, this large hotel is ideal year-round. Its exterior reflects the Russian architecture along Zhongyang Dajie, while inside its

modestly appointed rooms provide a comfortable place to stay. Duplex rooms are available for families. The steamship-theme Boathouse Restaurant serves seafood to those feeling overly landlocked.

✉ 257 Zhongyang Dajie ☎ 0451 8463 8855 ✋ 280–800RMB, excluding breakfast 🛏 280 ♿

JILIN
CENTURY HOTEL
www.centuryhotel.com.cn

Jilin's finest hotel, this palace of luxury makes up for the lack of other good accommodations in the city. The bedrooms are huge and very welcoming after a day outside in winter. Facilities include squash and tennis courts, sauna, Jacuzzi and a snooker room.

✉ 77 Jilin Dajie, Jilin City ☎ 0432 216 8888 ✋ 484–850RMB 🛏 230 ♿ 📺 ≋ Indoor

JIANGCHENG HOTEL
The Jiangcheng, probably the city's best mid-range hotel, is in the heart of downtown Jilin, near the Catholic church. Rooms are comfortable and reasonably well cared for, but other facilities are lacking.

✉ 4 Jiangwan Lu ☎ 0432 216 2777 ✋ 180–210RMB 🛏 120 ♿

MUDANJIANG
GOLDEN DOME INTERNATIONAL HOTEL
www.mdjgdihotel.com

The best hotel in Mudanjiang isn't exactly five-star standard but facilities are adequate and the location is central. TVs have satellite channels and there is in-room broadband. This is the best place to stay if you plan a visit to Jingpo Lake. The ski resort of Yabuli is also nearby and can be easily reached by train.

✉ 99 Jingfu Jie ☎ 0453 893 9999 ✋ 350–500RMB 🛏 274 ♿ 📺

QIQIHAR
GUOMAI HOTEL
Within easy reach of the Zhalong Nature Reserve, 30km (18 miles) away, the Guomai is Qiqihar's

only good hotel. Rooms in this new, 28-floor high-rise are large and comfortable although a little impersonal. Facilities include a restaurant, bar, sauna, travel agency and beauty parlor.

✉ 1 Junxiao Jie ☎ 0452 241 0000 ✋ 320–700RMB 🛏 266 ♿ ≋ Indoor

SHENYANG
LIAONING HOTEL
Built in 1927 by the Japanese and superbly renovated in 2001, the interior of the Liaoning is all marble staircases, period furniture and beautiful tiled floors. It's certainly one of the most atmospheric hotels in the Northeast. All rooms have towering ceilings and tasteful furnishings. Facilities include a restaurant and bar, tennis court and sauna.

✉ 97 Zhongshan Lu ☎ 024 2383 9166 ✋ 358–500RMB 🛏 79 ♿

SHERATON SHENYANG LIDO HOTEL
Guest rooms in the Lido, undoubtedly one of China's finest hotels, are luxurious, with excellent art on the walls, luxurious bathrooms and good facilities, including internet access. Unusual amenities include a golf simulator, indoor rock-climbing wall, squash court and also some first-class restaurants.

✉ 386 Qingnian Dajie ☎ 024 2318 8888 ✋ 850–1,400RMB 🛏 590 ♿ 📺 ≋ Indoor

TRADERS HOTEL
www.shangri-la.com

This beautifully designed, ultramodern hotel (▷ picture on page 174) is well placed for the main sights and includes its own shopping mall. There is broadband internet access in every bedroom (charges apply), sauna, Jacuzzi and some of Shenyang's finest restaurants.

✉ 68 Zhonghua Lu ☎ 024 2341 2288 ✋ 550–1,700RMB 🛏 588 ♿ 📺

INNER MONGOLIA AND THE SILK ROAD

The Silk Road was ancient China's hotline to the West, a lonely desert trail that allowed the Middle Kingdom's most important ideas and innovations to spread west, and exposed the nation to Asia's great religions, Islam and Buddhism. The region remains an exotic blend of religions, races and cultures.

The Silk Road was first pioneered by China's great unifier, Qin Shihuang, after 221 BC. Business was particularly brisk during the Han (3rd century BC to the 3rd century AD) and Tang (7th to 10th centuries AD) dynasties when merchants arrived from Persia, India and the eastern fringes of Europe. Going in the opposite direction, camel-led caravans began their journey along the Hexi Corridor, a narrow strip between the Mongolian steppe and the Tibetan Plateau. This is modern-day Gansu province, officially China's poorest region but a place of desolate beauty. It's also home to one of China's most remarkable historical sites—the Mogao Caves.

Farther west, in the region now known as Xinjiang, the Silk Road forks either side of the Taklamakan Desert, converging again at Kashgar, close to the snow-capped mountains of China's western borders. In both its culture and geography, this lively Islamic market town represents China's final frontier, though Han migration is threatening to impose a new social order, here as elsewhere in Xinjiang. A railway, completed in 1999, has bought Kashi (Kashgar) that bit closer to the East, though it still remains difficult to believe it's part of the same country.

Inner Mongolia is similarly distinct. This enormous and rarely visited region shares borders with Mongolia and Russia and alternates between desert and steppe landscape. Once home to nomadic communities who roamed the vast, oceanic grassland, most of Inner Mongolia's 24 million people now live in cities.

DUNHUANG
▷ 180–181

GUYUAN

In the south of Ningxia province, Guyuan is a small town that doesn't see many foreign visitors, though it is a pleasant place with a lively night market. It is also a useful base for visiting the Buddhist grottoes of Xumishan, about 50km (30 miles) northwest of town.

The grottoes were cut into the sandstone hills during the northern Wei, Sui and Tang dynasties, when Guyuan was a gateway town on the Silk Road. The five mountains that make up the area contain more than 300 Buddha images in 132 caves. Some of the caves are still protected by temple structures, and in these some of the Buddha images still have their original paint. The largest carving here is the 19m-tall (62ft) Maitreya Buddha in Cave 5.

Getting to the caves can be somewhat challenging and time-consuming. You'll need to take a bus to the town of Sanying, about an hour north of Guyuan. From here the road to the caves branches off to the southwest, and you can take a taxi (50–60RMB round-trip) for the rest of the journey.

✚ 417 M9 🚉 Guyuan Train Station. Trains from Xi'an (8 hours), Yinchuan (4–5 hours) and Lanzhou (8 hours) 🚌 Services from Yinchuan, Lanzhou and Tianshui

BAOTOU

Developed by the Communists as an iron and steel center in the 1950s, Baotou is today a sprawling industrial city, the largest in Inner Mongolia, near the great northern bend of the Yellow River. About 70km (42 miles) northeast of the city and accessible by bus from East Baotou Long-Distance Bus Station, you'll find the Wudang Lamasery (daily 8–6). Established in 1749, the 2,500-room monastery is in traditional Tibetan style, and was formerly the residence of more than 1,000 Yellow Hat monks. The main prayer hall includes some vibrant Qing Buddhist murals, and the surrounding valley is a good place for a walk. Resonant Sand Gorge (daily 8–6), 60km (36 miles) south of the city, is a valley of sand dunes that you can walk (and slide) on. You can also take a short camel ride here.

✚ 417 P7 ✈ Flights from Beijing and Shanghai 🚉 Trains from Hohot (2 hours) and Beijing (12 hours)

DONGSHENG

Dongsheng, a small town to the south of Baotou on the road to Shaanxi, is a base for visiting Ghengis Khan's Mausoleum. The mausoleum (daily 9–5) dates back to 1954, when certain relics were brought back here from Qinghai. They had been hidden there to keep them safe from the Japanese, who had been extending their influence in the region during World War II. It's unlikely that Ghengis Khan is buried here, though the site has become an important place of pilgrimage for Mongolians and Daur people. The structure consists of three linked, vaguely yurt-like buildings with domed roofs. Inside are Mongolian artifacts, murals depicting the escapades of Ghengis Khan, and a map showing the extent of the empire he founded. The centerpiece is a 5m-high (16.5ft) statue of the leader in the main hall.

✚ 417 P7 🚌 Services from Baotou and Yulin (Shaanxi)

Clockwise from left to right *Ding incense burner at the Xumishan grottoes; the Wudang Lamasery, close to Baotou; the triple-domed mausoleum of Ghengis Khan, near Dongsheng*

INFORMATION
415 H7 CITS, 32 Mingshan Lu
0937 882 5584 Daily 8.30–5
Services from Liuyuan (2–3 hours),
Jiayuguan (5–7 hours) and Golmud
(8 hours) Flights from Beijing,
Lanzhou, Xi'an and Ürümqi Dunhuang
station has links to Lanzhou, Ürümqi,
Tulufan and Jiayuguan

Above *A pagoda near Crescent Moon Lake, with the dunes behind*

INTRODUCTION

Close to this desert oasis are the Mogao Caves, one of the world's most significant repositories of Buddhist painting and sculpture. Beyond the town the Gobi desert dunes stretch into the distance.

Dunhuang town is small enough to explore on foot, and the lake and dunes to the south of town can be reached by bicycle or taxi. To get to the Mogao Caves you can take a bus, minibus or taxi for the 30-minute journey. From the area around the central Government Guesthouse it's easy enough to find transportation. Once you reach the caves you'll be obliged to pay a guide to show you around a selection of the caves.

As commerce along the Silk Road developed, Dunhuang became an important trading oasis and resting place. For those heading west, it was the final supply station before taking the northern or southern route around the Taklamakan Desert, while for those heading the other way it marked a welcome return to the comforts of civilization. By the 1st century BC, when the town lay at the western extreme of China, it was already a heavily fortified outpost. It grew and remained prosperous under ensuing Han, Tibetan, Western Xia and Mongol rule before falling on hard times as trade on the Silk Road declined.

WHAT TO SEE
MOGAO CAVES
The earliest shrine in the Mogao Caves (Mogao Ku) dates back to AD366, when a monk requested that a follower decorate and consecrate one of the caves in the cliff-face. Over the next 1,000 years wealthy travelers and pilgrims

created more than 500 such caves, thanking or imploring the gods for safe passage through treacherous lands. At its height, the area was a major center of Buddhist scholarship and pilgrimage, with around 20 temples and 1,400 resident monks. With the decline in trade along the Silk Road in the 15th century, the caves were largely forgotten until the early 20th century.

Today only 30 of the caves are regularly open to visitors, though you'll only be allowed to see 10 on any given tour. The caves are located on several levels across a 1.5km (1-mile) span of cliff-face and are interlinked by staircases and platforms. Inside you'll see carved statues and vibrant murals depicting Buddhist legends and, to a lesser extent, the Silk Road itself. The style of the paintings changes over time, from the graceful Indian influences in the earlier northern and western Wei dynasty caves to the more robust, grandiose imagery of the later Tang dynasty caves.

🕐 Daily 8.30–5.30 👐 Adult 180RMB for the basic tour, child under 1.2m (4ft) free

WHISPERING SAND DUNE AND CRESCENT MOON LAKE
About 5km (3 miles) south of town lie Whispering Sand Dune (Mingsha Shan) and Crescent Moon Lake (Yueyaguan), marking where the oasis finishes and the desert begins. You can climb the dunes here, for spectacular views across the barren landscape. You can also arrange camel rides and paragliding. The best time to visit is in the evening, when the temperature is falling. It is an easy and pleasant bicycle ride from town. The lake is now open 24 hours. If the gates are closed, knock at the door.

☎ 0937 888 3389 🕐 Apr–end Oct daily 6am–8pm, Nov–end Mar daily 6am–6.30pm 👐 Adult 60–120RMB, child under 1.2m (4ft) free ❓ Accessible by minibus or taxi

MORE TO SEE
JADE GATE PASS AND SOUTH PASS
These fortified beacon towers 80km (48 miles) to the west of Dunhuang marked the start of the northern (Jade Gate Pass) and southern (South Pass) routes around the Taklamakan Desert, and, for a long time, the entrance to China. Long abandoned and battered by the desert sands, they are interesting mainly for their atmospheric remoteness.

👐 Jade Gate Pass: adult 30RMB, child under 1.2m (4ft) free. South Pass: 40RMB, child under 1.2m (4ft) free

Left *Some of the Mogao Caves are interlinked by staircases and ornate platforms*

INFORMATION

✚ 417 P7 🚇 Hohhot Train Station. Trains from Beijing (11 hours), Datong, Baotou, Yinchuan and Erenhot
🚌 Services from Beijing, Datong, Baotou and Dongsheng ✈ Flights from Beijing, Guangzhou and Shanghai

Above *Detail of the painted* Tree of Life *in the Da Lamasery*

HOHHOT

The capital of Inner Mongolia is a lively place, with some distinctive temples in the old city. It is also a base for trips to the most accessible grasslands.

Hohhot was founded in the 16th century by Altan Khan and developed around its lamaseries. It has been the capital of Inner Mongolia since 1952, and is today a fairly prosperous place that still retains some traces of the past in the old quarter. It is a popular base for tours into the surrounding grasslands at Xilamuren, Gegentala and Huitengxile, where you can experience the vast steppes and get a taste of traditional Mongolian ways.

TEMPLES

The Five Pagoda Temple (Wuta Si, daily 8–6) is an unusual Indian-style Buddhist temple containing 1,563 Buddha images carved into its walls. Da Lamasery (Da Zhao, daily 8–6) is the largest of the old lamaseries, dating back to 1579, with murals commemorating the visit of the Qing emperor Kangxi and a precious 3m-tall (10ft) silver Buddha statue. Across the road is Xilitu Lamasery (Xilitu Zhao), the 18th-century residence of the 11th Grand Living Buddha, though it has been restored several times over the last two centuries.

JIAYUGUAN

This small city, at the northern end of the Hexi Corridor, is best known for the nearby Jiayuguan Fort (daily 8–8), the Ming garrison at the western extreme of the Great Wall. After its construction in 1372, this fort was strategically important as the last outpost between China and Central Asia, guarding the narrow route between the Qilian Mountains (Qilian Shan) to the south and Mazong Range (Mazong Shan) to the north. It is an impressive multitier walled structure with classical Ming-style upturned eaves and 17m-high (55ft) gates.

There is a reasonable museum in the former temple. To the north of the temple is the Overhanging Wall (daily 8.30–7), a restored section of the Wall climbing a ridge.

✚ 416 J7 🚆 Jiayuguan Train Station from Lanzhou (9.5 hours), Liuyuan, Zhangye and Ürümqi (15–17 hours) 🚌 From Dunhuang, Lanzhou and Zhangye

KASHI (KASHGAR)

▷ 184–185

KIZIL

A 70km (42-mile) taxi ride from Kuqa, the Thousand Buddha Caves (Kezier Qianfo Dong) at Kizil are of interest to historians because of the almost total lack of Chinese influence in their 5th- to 8th-century frescos. Only a few of the caves are open to the public. Unfortunately most of their former magnificence has been lost.

✚ 412 D6 🕐 Daily dawn–dusk 🎫 Adult 35RMB, child under 1.2m (4ft) free

KUQA

This oasis town, mainly inhabited by Uighur people, was an independent city-state on the Silk Road, and a center of Buddhism until Islam arrived in the 9th century. The area around the Great Mosque is particularly interesting on Fridays when a busy local market is held. About 30km (18 miles) northeast of town, the ancient city of Subashi (15RMB for temple, 15RMB for city) is one of several abandoned cities in the vicinity.

✚ 412 D6 🚆 Kuqa Train Station, from Ürümqi, Tulufan and Kashi 🚌 From Ürümqi, Luntai and Kashi

LANZHOU

The first major city on the Yellow River, Lanzhou, the capital of Gansu province, is an industrial town and transportation hub. Gansu Provincial Museum (tel: 0931 234 6306; Tue– Sat 9–11.30, 2.30–5.30) has some very early neolithic finds as well as Silk Road artifacts. City parks include White Pagoda Hill Park (daily 6–6), north of the river, and the mountainous Lanshan Park (daily 8.30–6, 18RMB for chairlift) accessible from Wuquan Park (daily 6–6), south of the city. The carved Buddhist caves at Bingling Si, 90km (54 miles) southwest, run 1.5km (1 mile) along a gorge, with the earliest dating back 1,600 years. Visit on an organized tour.

✚ 417 L9 ℹ️ CITS, 11th Floor, 2 Nongmin Xiang ☎ 0931 883 5566 🕐 Mon–Fri 8.30–12, 2.30–6 🚆 Lanzhou Train Station, from Ürümqi and Xi'an and cities in between 🚌 From Dunhuang, Guiyuan, Tianshui, Xi'an. In Gansu province travelers using intercity buses must purchase local Gansu travel insurance

LINXIA

To the southwest of Lanzhou, Linxia was a rest stop on the Silk Road as it wound its way through Gansu province, and also an important place in the introduction of Islam to China. Today it remains a largely Hui Muslim town, with quite a few mosques and plenty of markets selling carpets, knives, iron goods and devotional items.

✚ 417 L9 🚌 Services from Lanzhou and Xining

Left *Snow-covered mountains beyond the roofs of Jiayuguan*
Below *The Yellow River flowing through modern Lanzhou*

INFORMATION

✚ 412 B6 🚉 Kashgar Train Station
✈ Flights from Ürümqi ❓ Trains from Ürümqi

INTRODUCTION

In Kashi (Kashgar), the last stop before the mountains on the Pakistan border, mosques and markets recall ancient times. Modern Kashi spreads over a large area. While you can best see the old town and the mosque on foot, you'll need to rent a bicycle or use a taxi to explore the rest of the city. To travel up the Karakoram Highway toward the border use a local bus or charter a suitable vehicle. Kashi's importance as a trading center dates back more than 2,000 years. As the oasis town where the northern and southern routes of the Silk Road met after skirting the Taklamakan Desert before the ascent into the mountains, it offered a welcome break for traders. Though the Chinese established an outpost here in the 1st century BC, the town changed hands frequently. Today Mao's statue looks out over the main square, but the faces in the bazaar and the city streets speak of deep Central Asian roots.

WHAT TO SEE

ID KAH MOSQUE

Originally founded in 1442, the Id Kah Mosque (Ai Tiga'er Qingzhen Si) in the old city is among the largest in China. The current 18th-century structure is in typical Central Asian style, with narrow minarets on either side of an imposing entrance gate. Behind the walls are leafy grounds and a vast prayer hall.
🕐 Daily 8.30am–10pm 💵 10RMB, child under 1.2m (4ft) free

ABAKH KHOJA TOMB

Above *The Abakh Khoja Tomb in Kashi*

In the northeastern part of town is Kashi's other great Muslim monument, the

Abakh Khoja Tomb (Xiangfeimu), final resting place of one of the city's most potent rulers, his missionary father and their family. The mausoleum is within a substantial complex of prayer halls and other buildings, and is decorated with geometric-pattern tiles. Beneath the green dome, the individual burial tombs are raised on platforms and covered with silk cloths.

🕐 Daily 8–5.30 ✋ 30RMB, child under 1.2m (4ft) free

SUNDAY MARKET

The Sunday Market (Xingqitian Shichang) across the Tuman River from the old city is a bustling, and now daily, bazaar selling a wide range of items, including clothing, silks and carpets, household items and electronic goods. A weekly livestock market is still held here on Sunday.

🕐 Daily dawn–dusk

KARAKORAM HIGHWAY

The 1,300km (780-mile) road linking Kashi with Islamabad in Pakistan, via the 4,693m-high (15,393ft) Khunjerab Pass, took almost 20 years to build. The border is the highest paved international border crossing in the world.

Prone to landslides and extreme weather, it is a remote, rough road through stunning, though harsh, terrain. The first stretch beyond Kashi crosses the Pamir Plateau heading toward Tashkurgan, the last town on the Chinese side.

MORE TO SEE

HANNUOYI

Around 35km (20 miles) northeast of Kashi, Hannuoyi was a Tang dynasty outpost finally abandoned in the 12th century. The ruins lie in the desert, the most striking visible structure being the Mu'er Pagoda.

Above *Kyrgyz carpet sellers on the Karakoram Highway*

MAIJISHAN

The haystack-shape rock formation of Maijishan rises abruptly from the forested landscape 35km (21 miles) southeast of Tianshui, in Gansu province. The sheer cliffs are covered in 194 caves and grottos linked by spiral staircases and narrow walkways. They contain Buddhist statues and paintings. The earliest statues date from the 4th century, though artists continued adding new pieces until the Qing dynasty. The most imposing carvings are the trios of Buddha images in caves 18 and 98. Most of the statues are carved from clay rather than the rockface, resulting in detailed work. Many of the caves are protected by wire mesh, so it is useful to have a flashlight to view them. The adjacent Botanical Gardens (daily 8–6) offer good views and pleasant walks.

✚ 417 M10 ☎ 0938 273 1407 ⏰ Mid-Mar to end Oct daily 7–6.30; Nov to mid-Mar 8–6 💰 Adult 54RMB, child under 1.2m (4ft) free 🚌 Minibuses from the train station in Beidao, Tianshui

MANZHOULI

This Inner Mongolian border town is the last stop on the Trans-Siberian railway before it crosses into Russia, and China's main port of entry for Russian and Eastern European goods. The primary attraction, though, is the barren grasslands that surround the town. The easiest way to visit is on an organized tour, including an overnight stay in a traditional Mongolian yurt, with local-style banqueting and entertainment. Some tours also include horseback riding. To the south of Manzhouli lies Hulun Lake (Hulun Hu, daily dawn–dusk), one of China's largest lakes, and a popular spot for watching marshland birds. The lake can be reached by taxi. Steam enthusiasts can visit the open-pit coal mine at Zalainuo'er, which has a fleet of steam locomotives and maintenance facilities for them.

✚ 420 R3 🚆 Manzhouli Train Station, from Hailar (3 hours) and Harbin (14 hours) 🚌 From Hailar

PINGLIANG

Close to the border of Gansu and Ningxia provinces, this small town is slightly rundown but surrounded by very attractive mountain scenery. In the Liupan Shan mountain range to the west of town is Mount Kongtong (Kongtong Shan, daily 8–6.30), a sacred Taoist mountain renowned in Chinese mythology as the site of a meeting between the Yellow Emperor, who according to Chinese tradition was the first emperor, and an immortal. There is a reservoir at the base of the mountain and many shrines and pagodas along the paths that wind up to the summit. You can also take a cable car (30RMB round-trip) to the top.

✚ 417 M9 🚆 Pingliang Train Station, from Lanzhou and Xi'an 🚌 From Lanzhou, Tianshui, Xi'an and Yan'an

QINGTONGXIA

From the town you can catch a minibus or taxi to the Yellow River and then take a ferry to visit the mysterious 108 Dagobas (10RMB). Little is known about the origins of this Buddhist monument, which consists of 108 pagodas in a stepped triangular arrangement overlooking the river. Historians think it is probably a Yuan dynasty construction, or possibly one of the few remaining legacies of the western Xia empire. It has been well restored and is impressive when viewed from the river. You can climb the hills on the riverbank to reach some peaceful temples with excellent views.

✚ 417 M8 ⏰ Daily 8–6 🚌 Bus from Yinchuan

Left *The imposing rockface of the Maijishan caves*
Above *The mysterious 108 Dagobas monument near Qingtongxia*

TULUFAN (TURPAN)

Tulufan (Turpan) is a Silk Road oasis town that retains much of its Uighur charm. Around the town are the ruins of ancient cities set amid stunning desert scenery. In a deep depression well below sea level, Tulufan has a long history as a significant center of trade and civilization along the northern Silk Road. Present-day Tulufan is a predominantly Uighur town, and its oasis greenery offers a relief from the intensity of the surrounding desert.

EMIN MINARET

Emin Ta, an Iranian-style brick minaret, dates from 1778. The stout, tapered structure was built on the order of the local ruler, Emin Khoja, and completed by his son Prince Suleiman. The minaret and adjacent mosque are a comfortable 2km (1.2-mile) walk from the old town.

🕐 Daily dawn–dusk 🖐 Adult 30RMB, child under 1.2m (4ft) free

JIAOHE

In a desert valley 8km (4.5 miles) west of Tulufan, Jiaohe was a Han garrison town, later part of the Gaochang Kingdom, before coming under Uighur rule and eventually being abandoned during the Yuan dynasty. There is more to see here than at most other ancient ruined cities. The streets are clearly delineated, and the mud-brick walls of various domestic buildings are still standing.

🕐 Daily dawn–dusk 🖐 Adult 40RMB, child under 1.2m (4ft) free

GAOCHANG

There is less to see at the ruins at Gaochang, 45km (27 miles) southeast of town, than at Jiaohe, though in its day this was a large and cosmopolitan city. The nearby Astana Tombs (daily dawn–dusk) have largely been emptied, though the few that are open contain mummified corpses and some Tang dynasty murals.

🖐 Adult 40RMB

INFORMATION

www.turpantravel.com

➕ 413 F5 ℹ Turpan Tourist Information Hotline ☎ 0995 868 7666; 🚌 From Ürümqi (2.5 hours) and Kashi (26 hours) 🚉 Nearest railway station is Daheyan, 58km (34.5 miles) to the north

Below *Ruins of the abandoned desert town of Jiaohe, west of Tulufan*

ÜRÜMQI (WULUMUQI)

The capital of Xinjiang province, Ürümqi (Wulumuqi) is a sprawling city with a population that is about half Han Chinese and half ethnic minorities. The Xinjiang Provincial Museum (mid-Apr to mid-Oct daily 9.30–6, tickets available only at 10am, 11am, noon; mid-Oct to mid-Apr 10.30–5, tickets available only at 10.30am, 11.30am, 12.30pm), on Xibei Lu, has interesting archeological finds from Silk Road cities, including mummified corpses. During the summer take a bus from People's Park for the three-hour journey to Tian Chi (May–end Sep daily dawn–dusk), a picturesque lake amid the scenery of the Heavenly Mountains (Tian Shan). Hike in the mountains or take a horseback ride up to the snow line, and stay overnight in Kazakh yurts by the lake.

➕ 413 F5 ℹ️ CITS, 33 Renmin Lu ☎ 0991 221 8118 🕐 Mon–Fri 9–8 🚆 Ürümqi Train Station, from Beijing (45 hours), Kashi, Kuqa, Lanzhou (25 hours), Xi'an (53 hours) and others 🚌 From Turpan, Kuqa, Kashi and Yining ✈ From major Chinese cities and some Central and South Asian capitals

YINCHUAN

From the 11th century until it fell to the Mongols in 1227, Yinchuan was the capital of the western Xia kingdom. Today it is the pleasant capital of Ningxia province. The distinctive, angular Haibao Ta (daily 8–6) stands 54m (177ft) tall. The original pagoda, built in the 5th century, fell in an earthquake and the present structure is an 18th-century reconstruction. Ningxia Provincial Museum (daily 8.30–6) has some fascinating exhibits relating to the little-known western Xia kingdom. At the Helan Mountains (Helan Shan), to the west of the city, are the crumbling burial mounds of the western Xia Tombs (daily 8–7) and the prehistoric Suyu Kou Rock Paintings (daily 8–7) in a gully close to the Twin Pagodas of Baisikou.

➕ 417 M8 🚆 Yinchuan Train Station, from Lanzhou, Xi'an, Beijing and Hohhot 🚌 From Lanzhou, Guyuan, Yan'an, Zhongwei and Xi'an ✈ Regular flights from major Chinese cities

YINING

West of Ürümqi (Wulumuqi) and close to the border with Kazakhstan, Yining is a modest town with a market and a lively riverside scene. About 5km (3 miles) south is the Ili Valley, home to the Xibe minority of Manchurian ancestry. Travel 120km (72 miles) north to visit Sayram Lake (Sailimu Hu), a large, clear lake amid the meadows and snow-covered peaks of the Heavenly Mountains (Tian Shan).

➕ 412 D5 🚌 From Ürümqi, Kuqa and Almaty (Kazakhstan) ✈ Daily flights from Ürümqi

ZHANGYE

This pleasant town at a midpoint in the Hexi Corridor is best known for the Great Buddha Temple (Mar–end Sep daily 7.30–6.30; Oct–end Feb 9–5). It was built in 1098 and contains China's largest reclining Buddha statue, 34m (111ft) in length.

➕ 416 K7 🚆 Zhangye Train Station, from Lanzhou, Liuyuan, Xi'an and Ürümqi 🚌 From Jiayuguan, Dunhuang, Lanzhou and Xining

ZHONGWEI

With its mix of Yellow River and Tengger Desert scenery, Zhongwei is an attractive destination. You can visit the Gao Miao, an unusual temple, dating from Ming times, that has served Buddhists, Taoists and Confucians—reflected in its chaotic mixture of styles and buildings. On the Yellow River, Shapotou (daily 8.30–5) is a recreation area and resort.

➕ 417 M8 🚆 Zhongwei Train Station, from Yinchuan, Lanzhou, Xi'an, Beijing and Hohhot 🚌 From Lanzhou and Yinchuan

Above *A detail of the Matisi Monastery near Zhangye*

Left *Yurts in the Heavenly Mountains*

XIAHE AND THE LABRANG MONASTERY

Xiahe is China's most important Tibetan monastery town outside Tibet. The town sits in a picturesque valley at the edge of the Tibetan plateau and is dominated by the huge Labrang Monastery.

The town stretches along the northern bank of the Daxia River at an altitude of 2,090m (6,855ft), with the Labrang Monastery at its heart. To the west is the Tibetan part of town, while to the east are Hui Muslim and Han Chinese quarters. Behind the monastery, the Dragon Mountains provide a dramatic backdrop.

LABRANG MONASTERY

Labrang Monastery (Labuleng Si), the largest monastery outside Tibet, was founded in 1709 by E'angzongzhe, the first-generation Living Buddha, and at its peak was the residence of around 4,000 monks and a major center of scholarship. You can wander through much of the extensive monastery grounds on your own to see some of the many halls and temples. Tours include visits to some of the six study halls, the huge main prayer hall, the towering golden pagoda and a small museum. A 3km (2-mile) path lined with prayer wheels runs around the perimeter of the temple, which pilgrims follow in accordance with tradition.

☎ 0941 7121 774 🕐 Daily 8.30–6 💶 Complex free; Adult 40RMB for a tour, including entry to some main buildings

GRASSLANDS

Aside from the monastery, the main attraction of a visit to Xiahe is hiking through the stunning grassland scenery near the town. About 12km (7 miles) farther up the Daxia Valley (Daxia Gu), near the town of Sangke, is an extensive pastoral area used by the Tibetans for grazing yak. A little farther away, the Ganjia grasslands are much bigger and even more barren.

INFORMATION

✚ 416 L9 🚌 Buses from Lanzhou, Linxia, Tongren and Xining

Above *Tibetan Buddhists walk the perimeter of the Labrang Monastery*

189

KASHI (KASHGAR)

Wander through the alleys of the Uighur old town of Kashi (Kashgar) to catch a glimpse of traditional life in the bazaar. Along the way visit the mosque and the city wall.

THE WALK

Distance: 4km (2.5 miles), 6km (3.5 miles) with extension to the Tomb of Yusuf Has
Allow: 2–3 hours
Start/end: Mao Statue

HOW TO GET THERE

Either walk or take a taxi from your hotel to the Mao Statue on Renmin Donglu.

★ The Mao Statue (Mao Zedong Shixiang) stands imposingly by the main square. It is one of the more identifiably Chinese icons you'll see during this tour of Kashi. From the statue head west along Renmin Donglu to the main intersection with Jiefang Lu. Turn right onto Jiefang Beilu and head north about 500m (545 yards), then cross to the square in front of the Id Kah Mosque (Ai Tiga'er Qingzhen Si).

❶ The Id Kah Mosque (Ai Tiga'er Qingzhen Si) is the center of religious life in Kashi and the steps and square out front are a popular spot for socializing. If you happen to be here at prayer time on Friday, the area can be very busy. At almost any other time you can go inside the mosque, one of the largest in China, to look around.

From the mosque, take the road that leads southwest to the left of the entrance. Follow the winding street past the food stands and the silver vendors. At the end of the street, turn right on to Shengli Lu.

❷ The Old City Walls (Laochengqiang) are almost directly opposite where you joined the main road. The thick mud walls were clearly a major fortification in the past, though almost all that remains of them now is this short stretch.

Head northeast along Shengli Lu and cross the next intersection (the road on the right heads back to the mosque) on to Seman Lu. After the next intersection you'll see the Qini Bagh Hotel on the north side of the road and, behind that, the original British Consulate building.

❸ The British Consulate building was an important outpost of British India in the early 20th century. At this time Britain and Russia vied for control over Central Asia and the resident Consul fought an intelligence war against his Russian neighbor. The Consulate provided a taste of home for intrepid explorers of the time.

Continue heading northeast along Seman Lu. At the next intersection, opposite the open-air cinema, turn right to get back on to Jiefang Beilu heading south. As the mosque comes into view take the road on the left.

❹ You're now in the heart of the Old Town (Laocheng). Along this stretch of road you'll find bazaar areas. It is easy to be drawn away from the main street to explore the alleys and markets along the way, enjoying both the products and the distinctly Central Asian atmosphere.

The main street through this section of the market curves back to head south, and that's the general direction you need to follow. After about 0.5km (0.25 miles) you'll end up back on Renmin Donglu just east of the Mao Statue. If you've walked enough, this is a suitable spot to stop.

Alternatively, continue to the Tomb of Yusuf Has (Hasihaji Nan Mu). Cross Renmin Donglu and head slightly east to the Tianan Hotel, the

turn right down Tian Nanlu. You'll pass the zoo on your right. After about 800m (872 yards) turn right onto Tiyu Lu. Look for the minarets of the mausoleum ahead of you on the left.

❺ The Tomb of Yusuf has is a fairly large mausoleum with a blue dome surrounded by minarets. It is the resting place of Yusuf Has, an 11th-century Uighur poet from Balashagun who migrated to Kashi. He was originally entombed outside the city but his remains were relocated here.

To return to the starting point, either retrace your steps to the Tianan Hotel and head east along Renmin Donglu or, if you wish to walk a little farther, continue west along Tiyu Lu. Turn right when you come to Jiefang Nanlu and keep walking past the park and hospital until you get to the main intersection in town. Turn right and you'll be back at the Mao Statue.

PLACE TO VISIT
ID KAH MOSQUE
✉ Jiefang Beilu 🕐 Daily 8.30am–10pm
✋ Adult 10RMB, child under 1.2m (4ft) free

Clockwise from left to right The imposing facade of the Id Kah Mosque; a barber shop sign on a tradtional building in Kashi; sharpening tools in the bazaar

BAOTOU

RESONANT SAND GORGE

In addition to climbing the dunes (or riding the cable car up) and sliding back down, you can go on camel or horseback rides through the desert or try karting on a sand track. Mongolian song and dance shows are performed in a Mongolian yurt. The gorge is included on tour itineraries or can be reached by taxi from Baotou (around 220RMB round-trip).

✉ 60km (36 miles) south of Baotou on the way to Dongsheng 🖐 Adult 50RMB. Camel rides are 60RMB per hour

DUNHUANG

SAND DUNES AND CRESCENT MOON LAKE

This area of desert, with several tall dunes rising above a crescent-shape lake, is best visited early morning or in the evening when the sun has gone down. You can arrange a short camel ride into the dunes and also enjoy some sand sledding. In the winter (roughly Nov–Mar) the lake is frozen and the desert can be very cold, with snow at times.

✉ 5km (3 miles) south of Dunhuang ☎ 0937 888 3389 🕐 Apr–end Nov daily 7am–8pm, Dec–end Mar daily 7am–6pm 🖐 Entrance: adult Apr–end Nov 120RMB, Dec–end Mar 60RMB, child under 1.2m (4ft) free. Camel ride: adult 60RMB, child under 1.2m (4ft) free. Sand sledding: adult 15RMB

SHAZHOU NIGHT MARKET

A great place to sample local after-dark habits in warmer months. Groups of friends sit in the main square under the stars, sipping a beer or eating from the numerous hawker stands (which open throughout the day). For shopping, head to the adjacent Fanggu Shangye Yitao Jie (Ancient Shopping Street), a long pedestrian strip that runs from Yangguan Donglu to Xinjian Lu and opens between around 5pm and midnight daily. Look out for Dunhuang's famous 'Yangguan' luminous cups.

✉ Entrance of Xinjiang Lu, close to Mingshan Lu 🕐 Daily 10am–midnight

HOHHOT

GRASSLANDS TOUR

To the north and west of Hohhot are some of Inner Mongolia's renowned grassland areas. They can easily be visited on 1–2 day tours from Hohhot. The tours typically include a visit to a yurt with a meal and local drinks, horseback riding on the steppes, and Mongolian sport displays. If staying overnight, you'll sleep in a comfortable modernized yurt after enjoying singing and dancing around a campfire. The closest, and so most visited, area is at Xilamuren. Gegentala and Huitengxile are more remote, and overall a better

Above *A camel train heads for the giant sand dunes near Dunhuang*

experience. Tour agents in Hohhot can reserve these trips.

✉ Xilamuren, Huitengxile and Gegentala grasslands 🕐 Best time to visit Jun–Sep, though trips are possible year-round 🖐 Tour prices vary depending on area and content, but expect 200–300RMB per person per day

JIAYUGUAN

JULY 1 GLACIER

The glacier (Qiyi Bingchuan) is particularly accessible and is a good place for a walk when the weather is not too cold. A trail follows the base of the glacier. To get there you can take the train from Jiayuguan to Jingtieshan (3 hours), then a taxi (130RMB round-trip) for the final 20km (12 miles). Travel agents in Jiayuguan can also arrange daytrips to the glacier.

✉ Qilian Mountains, 90km (54 miles) southwest of Jiayuguan 🕐 Glacier accessible Apr–end Oct

KASHI (KASHGAR)

CARAVAN CAFÉ

www.caravancafe.com

This café and travel agency can organize a range of mountain treks, bicycling trips and desert excursions using a combination of camels and 4-wheel-drive vehicles. Their English-speaking staff are helpful and will give you plenty of advice.

✉ 120 Seman Lu ☎ 0998 298 1864, 0998 298 2196

OLD TOWN BAZAAR
Kashi Old Town is a great area for shopping. Certain areas specialize in certain goods, such as carpets, knives, cloth and shoes, but all these areas merge into one enticing whole. You should be able to get good prices with some shrewd bargaining.

✉ Jiefang Beilu, and surrounding streets
🕐 Generally 8–6

MANZHOULI
HULUN LAKE
In the summer this lake, the largest in Inner Mongolia, is a popular sunbathing and swimming spot for Chinese and Russian tourists. Other activities on the lake include boating, fishing and birding (more than 200 species have been sighted here), as well as walking though the grasslands. Take a taxi from Manzhouli (120–150RMB round-trip).

✉ 40km (24 miles) southeast of Manzhouli on the road to Hailar ✋ Adult 5RMB, child under 1.2m (4ft) free; 10RMB for vehicles
🍽 Several restaurants on the beaches

TULUFAN (TURPAN)
TULUFAN BAZAAR
This modest bazaar may not compare in scale with those in other Xinjiang cities, but it is a rewarding enough place to wander around. There are various Uighur items for sale that may make interesting souvenirs.

✉ Laocheng Lu 🕐 Daily 8–5

TURPAN MUSEUM
Many exhibits at this odd-looking museum were taken from the nearby Astana Graves and demonstrate the amazing powers of preservation of Xinjiang's arid climate. Alongside the mummified remains of Silk Road settlers are food items more than 1,000 years old, as well as a 9m (30-foot) dinosaur skeleton. The unearthed writings feature contracts, account books and personal letters written

FESTIVALS AND EVENTS

FEBRUARY/MARCH
MONLAM FESTIVAL
The Monlam, or Great Prayer Festival, is a Tibetan Buddhist celebration that follows Tibetan New Year. It lasts several days and involves chanting, dances, sculpture displays and parades with Buddha images. It is celebrated wherever there are major Tibetan communities, including Xiahe.
🕐 Feb or Mar (date varies)

in a variety of languages Uighur, Sanskrit and Han Chinese included. The museum was undergoing renovation at the time of writing and is due to re-open in 2009.

✉ 26 Gaochang Lu 🕐 Daily 9.30–7.30
✋ Free

ÜRÜMQI (WULUMUQI)
ERDAOQIAO MARKET
The largest bazaar in Ürümqi is a reasonably good place for handicrafts, clothing and silk. Prices are competitive, but you will need to bargain. On the second floor several stores sell good-quality silk carpets.

✉ Between Jiefang Lu and Xinhua Nanlu
🕐 Daily 9–7

FUBAR
This cool bar near the People's Park, with a good selection of beers and spirits and a well-prepared Western menu, is a welcome addition to Ürümqi's (Wulumuqi) quiet night scene. It has a pool table, large televisions showing sports, and a knowledgable and friendly staff.

✉ 40 Gongyuan Beijie ☎ 0991 584 4498
🕐 Daily noon–3am

HONGSHAN PARK
The more northerly of Ürümqi's (Wulumuqi) two major parks, this has several fairground rides for younger children. You can also go boating on the lake. You can climb

JULY–AUGUST
NAADAM FESTIVAL
If you happen to be in Hohhot when the annual Naadam Festival is held then you'll be able to experience the biggest display of Mongolian sports in the area. Competitive events include wrestling, archery and horse racing, and there are also more cultural events such as singing and dancing. Venues and exact timing vary.

✉ Outskirts of Hohhot and surrounding grasslands 🕐 Mid-Jul to late Aug

the 1,391m-high (4,562ft) peak that dominates the park.

✉ Xinmin Xijie, north of Hongshan Lu
🕐 Daily 7–7 ✋ Entrance: adult 20RMB, child under 1.2m (4ft) free. Amusement rides: 3–8RMB each

XIAHE
TIBETAN GOODS AND SOUVENIR SHOPPING
The main road through Xiahe is lined with stands selling Tibetan goods and local handicrafts. Hats, shawls, silver ornaments and Buddha images are good things to buy here. You'll need to bargain, though on the whole prices are reasonable.

✉ Main Street

ZHONGWEI
SHAPOTOU
This resort lies between the mighty Yellow River and the dunes of the Tengger Desert. Various activities are available, including sand sledding, camel riding and rafting on traditional sheep-skin vessels. There's also a cable slide across the Yellow River. For a break from the activities, there are pleasant orchards and a botanic garden. Food and drinks are available.

✉ 12km (7 miles) west of Zhongwei
🕐 Daily 8.30–5 ✋ Entrance: adult 30RMB, child under 1.2m (4ft) free. Sheep-skin raft rides: 60RMB for 1 hour, 300–350RMB per day

PRICES AND SYMBOLS

The restaurants are listed alphabetically within each town. The prices are for a two-course lunch (L) and a three-course à la carte dinner (D). Prices in pubs are for a two-course lunchtime bar meal and a two-course dinner in the restaurant, unless specified otherwise. All the restaurants listed accept credit cards unless otherwise stated. For a key to the symbols, ▷ 2.

DUNHUANG

CHARLEY JOHNG'S CAFÉ

Dunhuang is home to a number of good Western-style cafés. All serve similar fare, with menus including Chinese favorites, such as *gulu rou* (sweet-and-sour pork) and *mala doufu* (spicy tofu), and Western standards: banana fritters, muesli with local fruit, large breakfasts and usually good coffee. Charley Johng's will help out with most travel inquiries, as well as bus, train and air tickets. Bicycle rental and internet access are also available.
✉ 21 Mingshan Lu ☎ 0937 883 3039 ◷ Daily 8am–10pm 🖐 L and D 15–40RMB

FENG YI TING

JOHN'S INFORMATION CAFÉ

Part of a chain, John's is owned by a Chinese entrepreneur who seems to tap effortlessly into the backpacker psyche, providing banana pancakes,

fruit smoothies, cheese omelettes, Western-style breakfasts and always excellent coffee. In addition to food, the café is a good source of travel information and they will arrange trips into the surrounding desert.
✉ 22 Mingshan Lu (beside the Feitian Hotel) ◷ Daily 9am–10pm 🖐 L and D 15–40RMB, Beer 8RMB

SILK ROAD DUNHUANG HOTEL

Hotel dining in China can be a pretty disappointing experience, but not here. *Feng Yi Ting*, meaning 'Chamber of Grandeur,' serves some excellent Cantonese and Sichuan specials. Attractive red lanterns hang from the ceiling in the spacious dining area. In the high season between July and September traditional dancers perform nightly in the courtyard next to the restaurant.
✉ Dunyue Lu ☎ 0937 888 2088 ◷ Daily 6.30am–11pm 🖐 L 50RMB, D 55RMB, Wine 120RMB

HOHHOT

MALAQIN RESTAURANT

The hot pot is particularly good at this popular, traditional Mongolian restaurant. Though the surroundings are utilitarian, the food is far from limited. If you come here with a few people, try the *kao quanyang* (whole roast goat). It takes a while to cook, but it is worth the wait. The English

Above Both Chinese and Western food is on offer at Charley Johng's Café in Dunhuang

menu includes a number of Chinese and vegetarian dishes.
✉ 34 Xinhua Dajie ☎ 0471 692 6685 ◷ Daily 11–2, 5.30–9 🖐 L 20RMB, D 40RMB, Beer 8RMB

XIN AN JU RESTAURANT

In the Phoenix Hotel, the Xin An Ju offers a fine selection of dishes from a number of different types of Chinese cookery, including local Mongolian cuisine. The chef, from Xi'an, is famed for his Shaanxi specialties, among them *yang rou pao mo* (mutton soup with pancake). The large dining room has a number of banquet tables, perfect for large groups.
✉ Phoenix Hotel, 10 Xincheng Beijie ☎ 0471 660 8888 ◷ Daily 12–1.30, 6–9.30 🖐 L 40RMB, D 100RMB, Wine 118RMB, Beer 18RMB

KASHI (KASHGAR)

JIEFANG BEILU

The stalls near the Id Kah Mosque offer a variety of Muslim cuisine, from Chinese-style noodles to Muslim lamb kebabs and boiled goats heads. The breads, in particular are delicious and Kashi's legendary fruit harvest means culinary cowards still have

plenty to chew on.
✉ Daily 5pm–midnight 🍴 D 5–20RMB

JOHN'S INFORMATION CAFÉ
www.johncafe.net
Another traveler's dream, John's offers a selection of standard Chinese dishes, tasty pancakes, apple pie, a variety of sundaes and cold beer. Just opposite the Seman Hotel, the café provides free travel information and can arrange local trips. They also provide internet access and bike rentals. Check out their excellent website for any extra information you might need before arriving.
✉ 337 Seman Lu ✪ Daily 9am–10.30pm 🍴 L and D 12–50RMB, Beer 8RMB

LAO CHAYUAN JIUDIAN
For many locals this is the best restaurant in town. It serves excellent Uighur food, including lamb shish kabobs, beef noodle soup and *polo* (a Uighur rice specialty). Unusually for Xinjiang province, dishes are attractively presented.
✉ 50 Renmin Xi Lu ☎ 0998 282 4467 ✪ Daily noon–2am 🍴 L and D 10–50RMB, Beer 5RMB

LANZHOU
FENGSHAN JIUDIAN
Bustling Nongmin Xiang, behind the Lanzhou Hotel, has a number of good, relatively inexpensive, restaurants serving local treats. Most don't have English menus, but this needn't be a problem if you're prepared to point at what you fancy. The Fengshan, close to the CITS office, serves a bewildering array of local Gansu dishes. Try some of the desserts, such as steamed lily or stuffed melon.
✉ Nongmin Xiang ✪ Daily 8.30–8 🍴 L and D 5–40RMB, Beer 8RMB

MINGDE GONG
Lanzhou is a great place to eat out, with lots of good restaurants and the best examples of the unique Gansu school of cooking: Expect some beautifully presented dishes, with elaborately carved fruit and vegetables. The town is famous

for its *niurou mian* (beef noodles), known locally as *Lanzhou lamian* (Lanzhou pulled noodles). The four-floor Mingde Gong serves a variety of Gansu dishes in lavish surroundings, each floor becoming progressively more elaborate and more expensive. Try the *jincheng baita*, a dish designed to approximate the shape of Lanzhou's famous White Pagoda (Baita).
✉ 328 Jiuquan Lu ☎ 0931 466 8588 ✪ Daily 10–2, 4.30–9.30 🍴 L and D 50–80RMB, Wine 70RMB

MANZHOULI
XINMANYUAN XICANTING
With so many Russians visiting Manzhouli, the town is home to a number of very good Russian restaurants. The Xinmanyuan is probably the liveliest of the bunch; in the evenings it doubles as a nightclub and attracts raucous groups from across the border. For a snack try the *pelmeni*, a small meat pie stuffed with beef and pork minced meat, onions and occasionally potato.
✉ 38 San Daojie ☎ 0470 622 2008 ✪ Daily 7am–1am 🍴 L and D 10–25RMB, Wine 60RMB

TULUFAN (TURPAN)
JOHN'S INFORMATION CAFÉ
One in a chain, John's Information Café provides a welcome change from the heavy, sometimes fatty, local Uighur cooking. As with the other two branches in Dunhuang and Kashi (Kashgar; ▷ left), you can expect standard Chinese and Western dishes, and free travel information and advice dispensed with a smile. You can check your email here and also rent a bicycle to see Tulufan's sights.
✉ 2 Qingnian Nanlu (in the grounds of the Turpan Hotel) ✪ Daily 9am–10.30pm 🍴 L and D 15–40RMB, Beer 7RMB

XIN SHIJI
A great place to try a Uighur banquet, the lively Xin Shiji is popular with tourists and locals alike. Staff dressed in traditional costume and nightly dance performances

make this a perfect venue to unwind after a long stint in the desert. The restaurant is well known for its cook-your-own kabobs and *sangshen jiu* (mulberry wine).
✉ Xinzhan Dingzi Lukou ✪ Daily 1.30pm–11pm 🍴 L and D 50–120RMB, Wine 60RMB

ÜRÜMQI (WULUMUQI)
KASHGARI'S
Kashgari's, in the Xinjiang Grand Hotel, serves some of the very best Uighur Muslim cuisine to be found in Ürümqi. If you are part of a group, try the Xinjiang barbecue, comprising an entire roast lamb; you need to give 24-hours' notice but it is well worth it. Other possibilities include *gang pan*, a rice dish with mutton and vegetables. Dishes are similar to those you'll find in surrounding markets, but the general quality of ingredients is better.
✉ 139 Xinhua Beilu ☎ 0991 281 8788 ✪ Daily 1–3.30, 7–10.45 🍴 L and D 50–100RMB, Wine 68RMB

YAKEXI HALAL RESTAURANT
Plump silk cushions, minaret shaped dividers and a bright, fresh salubrious dining room in which to enjoy the Central Asian cuisine at the new Sheraton, one of the best hotels in town.
✉ 699 Youhao Beilu ☎ 0991 699 9999 ✪ Daily noon–3, 6.30–11.30 🍴 L 150RMB, D 200RMB, Bottled beer 20RMB

XIAHE
SNOWLAND RESTAURANT
Since Xiahe began to receive visitors in large numbers in the 1990s, the number of appealing restaurants in the town has increased. The Snowland caters to Westerners with its desserts and good Tibetan cuisine. Try the *momo* (dumplings) and the *tsampa* (yak butter and barley), all washed down with a glass of *chang* (barley beer). They also serve some standard Chinese and Western dishes.
✉ Next to the Overseas Tibetan Hotel (▷ 197) ☎ 0941 712 2856 ✪ Daily 8am–10pm 🍴 L and D 10–40RMB, Beer 8RMB

STAYING

PRICES AND SYMBOLS
Prices are for a double room for one night, unless otherwise stated. Breakfast is included unless noted otherwise. All the hotels listed accept credit cards unless otherwise stated. Note that rates vary widely throughout the year.

For a key to the symbols, ▷ 2.

BAOTOU
SHENHUA INTERNATIONAL HOTEL
www.shenhuahotel.com
Although Baotou is a large, uninspiring industrial town, the Shenhua stands out as an oasis of calm, dignified luxury. This central, upscale high-rise contains a nightclub and sauna. Guest rooms are tastefully decorated.
✉ 1A Erding Dajie ☎ 0472 536 8888
🖐 600–800RMB 🛏 284 ⭐ 🍽
🏊 Indoor

DONGSHENG
TIANJIAO HOTEL
If you do make the journey to Ghengis Khan's Mausoleum, the Tianjiao, 60km (36 miles) away, is really the only decent place to stay in the vicinity. Facilities include a restaurant and a pool.

✉ 102 Dalate Nanlu ☎ 0477 853 3888
🖐 400–600RMB, including breakfast
🛏 110 ⭐ 🍽 🏊

DUNHUANG
GRAND SUN HOTEL
This is a friendly, welcoming place and probably the best in central Dunhuang. Rooms in the new wing are very good but are more expensive, while those in the old wing have more character but are not in such good condition.
✉ 5 Shazhou Beilu ☎ 0937 882 9998
🖐 400–6008RMB 🛏 220 ⭐ 🍽

SILK ROAD DUNHUANG HOTEL
www.the-silk-road.com
Set amid the sand dunes south of town, the hotel blends perfectly with its surroundings. All rooms are decorated in warm desert colors. The hotel offers camel riding and sand sledding, or archery. There are also nightly cultural performances.
✉ Dunyue Lu ☎ 0937 888 2088
🖐 480–830RMB, excluding breakfast
🛏 230 ⭐ 🍽

HOHHOT
HOHHOT HOLIDAY INN
www.ichotelsgroup.com
Sleek, ultramodern and close to

Above *The Silk Road Hotel in Dunhuang is the same color as the nearby sand dunes*

the attractive Qingcheng Park, the Holiday Inn represents a comfortable, central and less expensive option to Hohhot's two excellent luxury hotels. Bedrooms are large and delicately decorated. Facilities include a restaurant, bar, sauna and whirlpool. The hotel also offers a free airport shuttle bus.
✉ 33 Zhongshan Xilu ☎ 0471 635 1888
🖐 560–750RMB 🛏 198 ⭐ 🍽

INNER MONGOLIA HOTEL
www.nmghotel.com
One of Hohhot's two luxury hotels, this is decorated in grand style. Guest rooms are beautifully furnished, almost too elaborately, and bathrooms are enormous. Amenities include a pleasant tearoom and possibly the city's best restaurants.
✉ 31 Wulanchabu Xilu ☎ 0471 693 8888
🖐 600–800RMB 🛏 343 ⭐ 🍽
🏊 Indoor

XINCHENG HOTEL
www.xincheng-hotel.com.cn
Set in landscaped grounds, the Xincheng has a staggering 18

restaurants. Leisure facilities include a bowling alley, swimming pool and golf driving range.

✉ 40 Hulunbei'er Nanlu ☎ 0471 666 0320/666 0322 👣 400–680RMB 🛈 320 📶 📺 🏊 Indoor

JIAYUGUAN
GREAT WALL HOTEL
Vaguely modeled on Jiayuguan's famous fort, the hotel is an enormous complex of buildings, all renovated in 2001. Excellent facilities include a snooker room, beauty salon and sauna.

✉ 6 Jianshe Xi Lu ☎ 0937 622 6306 👣 200–480RMB, excluding breakfast 🛈 168 📶 📺

KASHI (KASHGAR)
CHINI BAGH HOTEL
Spacious and comfortable rooms hide behind the ugly exterior of this hotel, built in the gardens of the old British Consulate. This has the best dormitory accommodations in town. Facilities include a snooker room, sauna and a restaurant in the old Consulate building.

✉ 144 Seman Lu ☎ 0998 298 0671 👣 100–400RMB 🛈 340 📶 📺

QIANHAI HOTEL
This quiet, laid-back, if quite anonymous place, has a few facilities, including a couple of reasonable restaurants. Bedrooms include refrigerators, definitely a must during the hot summer months. The staff certainly try their best to impress, but service can leave rather a lot to be desired.

✉ 199 Renmin Xi Lu ☎ 0998 282 2922 👣 150–180RMB, including breakfast 🛈 140 📶

SEMAN HOTEL
www.semanhotel.com
Originally the Russian Consulate, this extensive complex offers reasonably comfortable rooms. The old Consulate building itself has the best rooms, though these are often reserved well in advance.

✉ 337 Seman Lu ☎ 0998 258 2150 👣 120–580RMB, including breakfast 🛈 212 📶 📺

LANZHOU
JJ SUN HOTEL
www.jinjianghotels.com
An excellent, 24-floor, mid-range hotel. Guest rooms are attractively furnished with dark-wood furniture and have good facilities. The hotel is surrounded by some excellent cafés and restaurants.

✉ 589 Donggang Xi Lu ☎ 0931 880 5511 👣 500–700RMB 🛈 236 📶 📺

MANZHOULI
FRIENDSHIP HOTEL
The most comfortable place in town, the Friendship offers good rooms for the price and there are even better bargains during the fall and winter. Guests enjoy friendly service and have the use of two fairly good restaurants.

✉ 26 Yi Daojie ☎ 0470 624 8881 👣 160–300RMB 🛈 100 📶 📺 🏊 Indoor

TULUFAN (TURPAN)
GRAND TURPAN HOTEL
Once a rather rundown, unattractive place, the Grand has been renovated, with a new wing added in 2001. The staff are generally very helpful and the tour desk dispenses valuable information.

The newer rooms are comfortable and spacious, with satellite television, minibar and internet access. There are also a karaoke lounge and sauna.

✉ 422 Gaochang Lu ☎ 0995 855 3868 👣 300–500RMB 🛈 154 📶

OASIS HOTEL
www.the-silk-road.com
The Oasis is another attractive hotel in the chain that stretches across much of China. There is a variety of rooms, but the special Uighur-style rooms provide *kang* beds (sleeping platforms) that originally would have been heated underneath.

Facilities include an internet café and sauna room. The Muslim restaurant serves excellent regional specialties.

✉ 815 Qingnian Lu ☎ 0995 852 2491 👣 300–500RMB, excluding breakfast 🛈 190 📶

ÜRÜMQI (WULUMUQI)
HOI TAK HOTEL
www.hoitakhotel.com
This central, 36-floor monolith is truly luxurious. Ask for a room on the upper floors as the views of the Tian Shan mountain range can be stunning. Facilities include an eight-lane bowling alley.

✉ 1 Dong Feng Lu ☎ 0991 232 2828 👣 700–850RMB 🛈 318 📶 📺 🏊 Indoor

HONGFU HOTEL
www.hongfuhotel.com
This attractive, modern high-rise is first and foremost a business hotel, but it's possible to get great bargains on what is essentially a luxury hotel. Rooms are huge and the bathrooms luxurious. The recreation center is superb.

✉ 160 Wuyi Lu ☎ 0991 588 1588 👣 458–900RMB 🛈 304 📶 📺 🏊 Indoor

XIAHE
OVERSEAS TIBETAN HOTEL
www.overseastibetanhotel.com
This hotel is within easy reach of the Labrang Monastery. Rooms are comfortable, though not all have their own bathroom.

There's a welcoming environment, with lovely Tibetan paintings and colorful carpets. Perhaps it doesn't have the facilities of the more expensive hotels, but it more than makes up for this in character.

✉ 77 Renmin Xijie ☎ 0941 712 2642 👣 160–200RMB, excluding breakfast 🛈 35 📶

YINCHUAN
RAINBOW BRIDGE HOTEL
The hotel's exterior may be unprepossessing but its interior is more inviting. Near the lovely West Pagoda, the Rainbow offers good facilities including a well-equipped gym and sauna. The smallish rooms are well-equipped.

✉ 38 Jiefang Xijie ☎ 0951 691 8888 👣 339–382RMB 🛈 339 📶 📺

SICHUAN AND THE TIBETAN PLATEAU

Tibet takes the sense of being in an alien environment, common among first-time visitors to China, and elevates it to an altogether new level. The 'Roof of the World' is a bleak but beautiful land, its culture and spirituality as unique as its geography.

Tibet is every bit as breathtaking as its 4,000m (13,000 ft) average elevation suggests. Though the Himalayas mark the region's southern border, the landscape is characterized less by soaring peaks, and more by barren, undulating plains and fathomless blue skies—China's Wild West, if you like, with an added sprinkling of snow and ice. Though immigration and tourism have begun to change ancient traditions, most Tibetans still cherish their pastoral way of life. Many Tibetans dedicate years to making peripatetic pilgrimages between the region's holy landmarks, manmade temples and long-revered lakes and mountains. In contrast to other parts of China where cultural displays can seem staged, the religious rituals observed in Tibet are chillingly passionate.

As in Xinjiang, there are fears that improved infrastructure, particularly the new Golmud-Lhasa train route, will dilute the character of Tibet. The good news is that Tibetan culture is not only confined within the borders of Tibet itself. Nearly all of Qinghai, to the north, is ethnically Tibetan. Sichuan province, to the southeast, also has strong Tibetan links, particularly in its mountainous western half.

Sichuan's eastern plains are more industrial, with dense concentrations of large Han towns and cities. The area exerts huge culinary, as well as economic influence. Sichuanese food, arguably the most spicy in the land, is popular across China but rarely better than here in its homeland. Bordering this area is Chongqing Municipality, formerly part of Sichuan province, and now one of the fastest developing areas in the world.

CHENGDU
▷ 202–204

DEGE
Tortuous roads through high mountains make for a long and difficult journey to this town on Sichuan's border with Tibet. From Garze it takes at least seven hours. Other than the spectacular scenery, its main appeal is the Bakong Scripture Printing Lamasery (opening can be irregular, but usually daily 9–12, 2–5.30). The 18th-century lamasery is among the most important for the Tibetan literary heritage it contains. There are many books and hundreds of thousands of Buddhist text printing blocks, including the last copy of a history of Indian Buddhism, carved on 555 wooden plates. The price includes a tour guide and you can see workshops where prints are handmade from printing blocks.
✛ 418 J11

EMEISHAN
▷ 205

GANDEN
One of Tibet's oldest monasteries, Ganden sits on a mountain slope just over 45km (28 miles) east of Lhasa. The head of the monastery, the *tripa*, is also head of the sect. Expanded over centuries but virtually destroyed in the Cultural Revolution, at which time there were 5,000

resident monks, it has largely been restored and reconstruction continues. Several hundred monks now live here. Highlights include the main assembly hall, which has 108 columns, and Tsongkhapa's golden tomb. Buses leave from Lhasa's Barkhor Square 7–8am each day, heading back from Ganden at 2pm. The round trip costs 40RMB.
✛ 415 F12 🚩 Daily 9–4 ✋ 45RMB

GARZE (GANZI)
A staging post for those heading to Dege or Serxu, Garze is the capital of the Ganzi Tibetan Autonomous Region in mountainous northwest Sichuan. It likes in a wide valley. The 540-year-old Ganzi Lama Monastery (Garze Gompa) stands guard above clay and wood Tibetan homes of the town's old quarter. It is worth a visit for the views of the valley and town from its roof, its many golden statues, and a giant statue of Maitreya, the Future Buddha.
✛ 418 K11

HAILUOGOU
www.hailuogou.com
China's largest glacier plunges from the flanks of Sichuan's tallest mountain. At 7,556m (24,790ft), Gongga is nearly 15km (9 miles) long and drops to its lowest point at 2,850m (9,350ft), deep in forest. It is within the Hailuogou National Glacier Forest Park, the entrance of which is close to Moxi. A cable car up to

the viewing area costs an additional 160RMB for the round trip. The glacier park, which is 320km (200 miles) northwest of Chengdu, also encompasses hot springs and takes a day to tour.
✛ 418 L12 ☎ 0836 326 6203 🕐 Daily 8–6 ✋ Adult 82RMB admission and 60RMB sightseeing bus (obligatory), child (under 1.2m/4ft) free

HUANGLONG
www.huanglong.com
A UNESCO World Heritage Site since 1992, Huanglong (Yellow Dragon Valley) is a beautiful forested limestone karst area in northwest Sichuan with snow-clad peaks and China's easternmost glaciers. The main attraction is the 3.6km (2.3-mile) stretch of travertine terraces cupping pools of vivid hues. There are also waterfalls, hot springs, caves and the long yellowish limestone slope for which the valley was named. Muni Valley has a large lake, more caves and a calcified waterfall. In the forests are giant pandas and golden snub-nosed monkeys. A new cable car makes exploring the valley easier.
✛ 419 L10 ☎ 028 8773 8076 🕐 Daily 8–dusk ✋ Adult 200RMB Apr–19 Nov; 60RMB Nov 20–end Mar, child (under 1.2m/4ft) free

Opposite *A yak at Ganden Monastery*
Below *Bright Ganden prayer flags strung out between the trees on the side of a hill*

CHENGDU

INFORMATION

www.chengdu.gov.cn/echengdu

☩ 419 M11 ☒ North Railway Station, South Railway Station ☒ Shuangliu International Airport (tel 028 8520 5333) is 20km (12.5 miles) from Chengdu

INTRODUCTION

Chengdu, the capital of Chengdu, is centrally located in Sichuan, and has good road, rail and air links, as well as being a major gateway to Tibet. The city and surrounding area have many historic and cultural attractions, and giant pandas roam bamboo-forested mountains a short distance away. Many old areas have disappeared as Chengdu has reinvented itself as a modern metropolis. But you can still find vestiges in narrow streets and alleys. Traditional teahouses, scattered throughout the city, are popular places to watch Sichuan's take on classic Chinese opera. A new metro system is due to open in 2010.

Archeological discoveries at Sangxingdui show the area around Chengdu was home to a sophisticated civilization nearly 5,000 years ago. In the third century BC the Dujiangyan Irrigation Project turned the Chengdu Plain into fertile land. Chengdu was the Chinese Nationalists' last mainland stronghold before they fled to Taiwan in 1949. Today it is China's fifth largest city.

WHAT TO SEE

DU FU'S THATCHED COTTAGE

www.dfmuseum.org.cn

Lush bamboo groves and water gardens provide a tranquil city setting for the modest thatched home (Dufu Caotang) where one of China's greatest poets lived for several years after fleeing his war-torn home region in AD759. Several statues and memorial halls honor Du Fu, as well as the cottage, rebuilt from ruins 200 years after his death and reconstructed again in 1811.

✉ 38 Qinghai Lu ☎ 028 8731 9258 ⏰ Apr–end Sep daily 7.30–7; Oct–end Mar 8–6.30
♿ Adult 60RMB, child (under 18) free 🚌 35, 47, 82, 84, 301

Above *A resident at the Giant Panda Breeding Research Base*

GIANT PANDA BREEDING RESEARCH BASE

www.panda.org.cn

Short of a day trip into the giant panda's mountain habitat, the Research Base (Daxiongmao Fanzhi Yanjiu Zhongxin) is the best place for a close encounter of the furry kind. You can see several dozen of the lovable mammals in enclosures with tree stumps and climbing frames. The panda cubs are the stars and you may be lucky enough to see a mother and newborn baby in the indoor nursery. Many pandas have been bred here over the years.

✉ 26 Xiongmao Lu ☎ 028 8351 6748 🕐 Daily 8–6 (last ticket at 5) 🖐 Adult 30RMB, child (under 1.2m/4ft) free

PEOPLE'S PARK (RENMIN GONGYUAN)

Hang out with the locals and soak up the atmosphere in this lovely central park. In between the early-morning *taiji* (tai chi) and nightly dancing classes you can go boating on the lake or take tea in the pretty lakeside teahouse. You can even have your ears cleaned by a man armed with a fearsome array of tools. Ear-cleaning is an old Chengdu profession and it is not an unpleasant experience.

✉ 12 Shaicheng Lu 🕐 Daily 6am–10pm 🖐 Free 🚌 1, 64, 302

WUHOU TEMPLE

This museum shrine is the largest set of buildings from China's Three Kingdoms period. It is steeped in Chinese history and legend and honors Shu dynasty prime minister Zhuge Liang, given the title Marquis Wu (Wuhou), and Shu founding emperor Liu Bei. The lifelike statues are the main attraction. Next-door Jin Street is a restored cobbled street with old wooden buildings and lots of snack vendors.

✉ Wohou Street ☎ 028 8555 9027 🕐 Daily 8–6 🖐 Adult 60RMB, child (under 1.4m/4.5ft) 30RMB 🚌 1, 57, 59, 334

DUJIANGYAN IRRIGATION PROJECT

China's oldest water irrigation scheme, a UNESCO World Heritage Site, is on a gargantuan scale and still functions 2,200 years after its first incarnation. To appreciate the scale of the project, walk from South Bridge past Fulong Temple, across the Anlan chain link bridge and climb the hill to Erwang Temple for a grandstand view across the area. Despite being close to the epicenter of the 2008 earthquake, Dujiangyan largely escaped damage.

✉ Dujiangyan City, 39km (about 25 miles) northwest of Chengdu ☎ 028 8729 6689 🕐 Daily 8–6 🖐 Adult 90RMB, child (under 1.4m/4.5ft) 45RMB

QINGCHENG SHAN

Taoism's mountain birthplace is jointly recognized by UNESCO with Dujiangyan, 17km (about 10 miles) away. Founder Zhang Daolin came here to preach nearly 2,000 years ago; today its wooded slopes have 11 temples and many caves. The main peak rises to 2,434m (7,985ft) and can be climbed in a day. There is also a cable car.

✉ 63km (39 miles) from Chengdu ☎ 028 8722 042 🕐 Daily 5am–dusk 🍴 🖐 Adult 90RMB, child (under 1.4m/4.5ft) 45RMB

MORE TO SEE
CHENGDU ZOO

Concrete enclosures may not appeal but the largest zoo in southwest China is strong on education and conservation, and has several giant pandas. Other exhibits include Asian elephants, Siberian tigers and golden monkeys.

✉ South Zhaojue Temple Road ☎ 028 8351 6953 🕐 Daily 8–5 🖐 Adult 12RMB, child (under 1.2m/4ft) free

Above *A group of worshipers outside a monastery in Chengdu*
Below *Detail of a dragon decoration at a Taoist temple in Chengdu*

TIPS

» The best time to see giant pandas is in the morning, when they are most active. They sleep for much of the day.

» The rainy season is from July to September, but Chengdu is notorious for its lack of sun. Locals joke that dogs bark when the sun shines because they don't recognize it.

» Escape Chengdu's traffic-choked city center by renting a bicycle for 10–15RMB a day and discovering hidden lanes.

» Air-conditioned buses are worth paying the 2RMB per journey against the 1RMB for normal buses, especially in the stifling summers.

» You can watch the sunrise from the top of Qingchengshan if you break the climb into two days and stay in a temple (15–30RMB) near the summit overnight.

WENSHU

This Tang dynasty monastery complex includes Chengdu's best-preserved Buddhist temple. It has a large teahouse and a vegetarian restaurant.
✉ 3 Duan Renmin Zhong Lu ☎ 028 8693 2375 🕐 Daily 6.30am–8pm 🖐 Adult 5RMB, child (under 1.2m/4ft) free

MONASTERY OF DIVINE LIGHT (BAOGUANGSI)

Another Tang dynasty monastery, this was rebuilt in the 17th century. Its crowning glory is a crooked 13-floor pagoda. The Arhat Hall has 500 clay Buddhist statues and there is a stone frieze of 1,000 Buddhas.
✉ 81 Baoguang Street, Xindu district ☎ 028 8399 6875 🕐 8–5 🖐 Adult 5RMB, child (under 1.2m/4ft) free

SANGXINGDUI MUSEUM

www.sxd.cn
This museum is devoted to the beautiful bronze masks and other bronze, gold, copper and jade treasures of the Sanxingdui culture unearthed since 1929.
✉ Guanghan, 40km (25 miles) north of Chengdu (taxi 100RMB) ☎ 0838 550 0349 🕐 8.30–5.30 🖐 Adult 80RMB, child (under 1.4m/4.5ft) 40RMB

EMEISHAN AND LESHAN

These jointly listed UNESCO World Heritage Sites are about 160km (100 miles) from Chengdu and 28km (17.5 miles) apart. Emeishan rises 3,099m (10,167ft) to its highest peak, Ten Thousand Buddha Summit (Wanfo Ding). Stepped paths climb forested slopes from the base. Trekking up and down usually takes three days, staying at monasteries and mountain hotels, or you can take a minibus then walk or get a cable car up to Golden Summit (Jin Ding) before taking the monorail up the final section.

SEA OF CLOUDS

Emeishan (Lofty Eyebrow Mountain) is often obscured but it may be clear at the peaks, giving an amazing view down onto a sea of clouds. And when the sun breaks through the vistas of sheer cliffs and thick forest (some trees are 1,000 years old) are truly awe-inspiring. More than 100 temples and monasteries once littered the mountain, of which about 30 remain. Baoguo Temple (daily 6.30am–8pm in summer, 7.30–7 in winter) is at its base, just above an artificial waterfall. A more natural waterfall cascades below Qingyin Pavilion, higher up.

HEAD FOR HEIGHTS

The best view of Leshan's 71m (233ft) sitting Buddha, carved out of a cliff face in the 8th century, is on a 20-minute boat trip (adult 50RMB, child under 1.2m/4ft free) on the Minjiang River. In the Grand Buddha scenic area you can look down from the high vantage points next to the giant head, if you can find a space in the crowds and have a head for heights. Long lines wait for the path down the cliff to its feet.

INFORMATION

Emeishan

www.ems517.com

✚ 419 L12 ☎ 0833 559 0111 ⓧ 24 hours 🍴 Food stands near the top, and restaurants by Leidongping bus station 💰 Adult 150RMB, child (under 1.4m/4.5ft) 80RMB 🚌 Emei Town bus station, 6.5km (4 miles) from Baoguo. Buses every 20 minutes from Chengdu 🚆 Emei Town

Leshan Grand Buddha Scenic Area

✚ 419 L12 ☎ 0833 230 2207 ⓧ Apr–early Oct daily 7.30–7.30, early Oct–end Mar 8–6 💰 Adult 70RMB, child (under 1.2m/4ft) free 🚌 Chengdu buses to and from Leshan Xiaoba Tourist Bus Station. From here take bus 3 or 13 to the gate of Leshan Grand Buddha

Opposite *Visitors at Qingyang Gong in Chengdu*
Above *The Grand Buddha at Leshan*

JIANGZI (GYANTZE)

This delightful small Tibetan town is dominated by hills surmounted by its two key attractions. The Old Fort (daily 8–8), which was captured by the British after a three-month siege in 1904, towers over the main intersection, while red walls and towers atop another hill virtually encircle the Palkhor Monastery (daily 10–7). Built in 1429, the monastery is notable for the huge Kumbum, a nine-floor pyramid-like structure consisting of a series of chapels containing numerous murals topped by a circular *chorten* (stupa). The main temple's many statues include a gilded bronze Maitreya, 8m (26ft) high. Unusually, the monastery houses monks from three different Buddhist sects.

The excellent views from the Kumbum's upper floors are surpassed by those from the fort. Get up before dawn and climb the ridge between the fort and monastery and you will enjoy a commanding vista as the rising sun sends shadows racing across the plain and lights up distant snow-capped mountains while smoke curls skyward from the waking town. A flashlight will help find the steep, narrow paths behind old houses bisected by snaking alleyways. And you can watch the townspeople go through their morning rituals as you walk back to your hotel for breakfast.

✚ 415 F12

JIUZHAIGOU
▷ 207

KANGDING

Kangding is a sizeable town straddling the fast-flowing Zheduo River in a high mountain valley. The capital of the Ganze Tibetan Autonomous Prefecture in Sichuan, the town has a population that is largely Tibetan.

The town is less than 40km (25 miles) from the mighty Gongga. Its 'house' mountain, Paomashan, is the setting for the Tibetan Walking Around the Mountain Festival in the fourth lunar month (usually May), when Tibetan people gather, put up tents, and hold events including horse races and wrestling matches. Kangding also has lamaseries worth visiting, among them Anjue and Nanwu.

✚ 418 L12

LHASA
▷ 208–210

LITANG

This quiet community on western Sichuan's high plateau grasslands comes alive every August 1–7 with the Litang Horse Festival. It attracts thousands of nomadic Tibetans from around Sichuan. The festival comprises horse races and events in which participants have to demonstrate their skills on horseback. The town is on the Sichuan–Tibet Highway and you can enter Tibet from here, with a permit, although check if there are any restrictions in force.

✚ 418 K12

LUDING

This transit point for buses from Chengdu and western Sichuan is most notable for the iron chain suspension bridge over the Dadu River, which saw one of the defining events of the Long March in 1935. Pursued by Nationalist forces, the Communists were forced to cross the Nationalist-held bridge. The popularly held account is that the bridge was captured by a heroic suicide squad under heavy fire, allowing their comrades to cross and continue the march. You can walk to the bridge from the bus station.

✚ 418 L12

JIUZHAIGOU

Until the 1960s Jiuzhaigou was a secret corner of remote northern Sichuan, its sublime natural beauty and wildlife shared only by the nine Tibetan villages for which it was named. Discovered by the logging industry, roads were driven through and many trees cut down before it was declared a reserve in 1979. UNESCO has since designated it a World Heritage Site and World Biosphere Reserve.

MASS TOURISM

From just 5,000 visitors in 1984, Jiuzhaigou now receives more than one million a year. New highways and a new airport, its runway lengthened in 2006, have dramatically improved access and many hotels have opened in nearby Zhanga. More than 220 eco-friendly buses ferry visitors—capped at 12,000 a day—from the entrance to three river valleys, with a bus interchange and 4,000-capacity restaurant and souvenir hall at the junction (Nuorilang).

WATERFALLS AND LAKES

The park covers an area of 720sq km (280sq miles). It encompasses 114 lakes, 17 groups of waterfalls and calcified terraces, and has more than 2,500 plant types, 141 bird species and 62 species of mammals. Some 47km (29 miles) of boardwalk trails, circling lakes and traversing and skirting waterfalls spread the throng. Key attractions get crowded. Several villages remain, adding cultural interest.

INFORMATION

www.jiuzhai.com
✚ 419 L10 ☎ 0837 773 9753 🕓 Apr to mid-Nov daily 7–7.30; mid-Nov to end Mar 8–5.30 💰 Adult 220RMB plus 90RMB shuttle bus, child (under 1.3m/4.3ft) free, including bus 🚌 Buses leave from the entrance and stop to drop off or pick up passengers at designated bus stops in the park 🏛 🍴 📖

TIPS

» Starting at Shuzheng and working your way up past Nuorilang will avoid the tour groups until later in the day.
» Buses leave promptly at closing time; you may be some distance from a bus stop so plan carefully.

Opposite *Candles and novices at the Nanwu temple in Kangding*
Below *The view across Arrow Bamboo Lake in Jiuzhaigou's scenic area*

Above *The Potala Palace viewed through prayer flags from Chokpur Hill*

INFORMATION

www.tibettour.org/chinatibettoursite/moban/index.asp

415 F12 China Tibet Tourism Bureau, 3 Luobulinka Lu, tel 0891 682 6247 May–end Sep daily 9–6.30; Oct–end Apr 9.30–5.30 Lhasa's new railway station is 8km (5 miles) south of the city, across the Lhasa River Gongkar Airport is 55km (34 miles) from Lhasa, now a 45-minute journey, thanks to a new tunnel

INTRODUCTION

The new railway line across the Tibetan Plateau from Qinghai is opening up Lhasa to many more Chinese and foreign visitors. Visitor numbers to Tibet were forecast to reach 5.5 million by 2010 but the violent unrest of 2008 and subsequent travel restrictions on foreign travelers may have changed the outlook somewhat. Nevertheless, the increasing traffic has put pressure on Lhasa's attractions, and limitations have been introduced. Potala Palace and the Jokhang Monastery are must-sees, but to experience the city's essence, wander around atmospheric Barkhor, mingling with pilgrims amid the markets.

Made capital of Tibet in the 7th century by warlord king Songtsen Gampo, Lhasa saw its fortunes revived with the founding of the three great Yellow Hat (Gelukpa) monasteries of Ganden, Drepung and Sera in the 15th century. In 1645 the fifth Dalai Lama began construction of Potala Palace. The Chinese invasion and occupation of Tibet led to the exile of the present Dalai Lama and many followers, and a crackdown on religious freedom. Lhasa's cultural heritage suffered much destruction in the Cultural Revolution, though some has since been rebuilt. Tourism is a recent phenomenon. Its growing impact, and the arrival of many Chinese settlers, is of major concern to exiles and others demanding a return to independence or greater autonomy.

WHAT TO SEE

POTALA PALACE

With its fortress-like walls and prominent position atop Red Mountain, this imposing UNESCO World Heritage icon radiates a spirit of power and majesty. The winter home of Dalai Lamas from the 18th century, the White Palace was the living area, the Red Palace its religious heart. It contains the main hall and chapels celebrating its founder, the fifth Dalai Lama, and housing the magnificent stupas of later Dalai Lamas. Photography inside chapels is prohibited. Visitor numbers are now capped at 2,300 a day, so gaining admission will become harder.

✉ Beijing Donglu ☎ 0891 682 4568 🕐 Daily 9–3 (but tickets must be purchased the day prior to visit at the ticket office beside the west gate) ✋ Adult 100RMB, child (under 1.2m/4ft) free

BARKHOR

This rectangle of streets around Jokhang Temple is Lhasa's historic hub and is lined with fascinating shops, restaurants and bars. Barkhor throngs with pilgrims and tourists browsing market stands. Buddhist devotees can also buy real Tibetan yak butter to put in temple candles as offerings.

JOKHANG TEMPLE

Built in the 7th century, Tibet's oldest temple is one of its holiest Buddhist shrines. It attracts large numbers of pilgrims, some taking years to reach here. They walk a continual clockwise circuit around the temple, many spinning prayer wheels and dropping to the ground to prostrate themselves. Visitors enter via a side gate in the afternoon. The small temple is significant for its gold statue of the young Sakyamuni Buddha. From the roof are great views onto Barkhor and across the city to Potala Palace.

✉ Barkhor Street ☎ 0891 633 6858 🕐 Daily 9–5 ✋ Adult 70RMB

TIPS

» Due to Lhasa's altitude, 3,650m (11,975ft), acute mountain sickness (AMS) is a risk. It affects many visitors and can last several days. Acclimatize first before tackling the strenuous long walk up to Potala Palace, and take everything slowly. Natural remedies for AMS include a special tea called Gao Yuan. It is available from shops in Lhasa and the Dunya Restaurant, 100 Beijing Donglu, where it costs 28RMB for six sachets. Take three a day.

» Wear the highest-factor sunblock and take a hat. Lhasa enjoys 3,000 hours of sun a year and the high altitude makes the ultraviolet rays much stronger.

Below *Monks working on traditional butter carvings and lamps*

NORBULINGKA (SUMMER PALACE)

The seventh Dalai Lama built his summer home in this large park in the 1750s and subsequent incumbents added their own. The New Summer Palace, built by the present Dalai Lama, the 14th, was finished in 1956. It gives a fascinating glimpse into his life prior to exile. The main meeting room contains a huge throne and the only picture of him on public display in Lhasa. A clock at the top of the stairs is stopped at 9 o'clock, the time he fled to India on March 19, 1959. The 13th Dalai Lama's palace has been undergoing major renovation. Give the small zoo a miss.

✉ Luobulinka Nanlu ☎ 0891 682 6274 🕒 May–end Oct daily 9–6; Nov–end Apr daily 9.30–6
✋ Adult 60RMB, child (under 1.1m/3.6ft) free 🚌 106, 109

DREPUNG MONASTERY

The largest monastery in Tibet and one of the key Yellow Hat sect institutions is on a mountainside 10km (6 miles) northwest of Lhasa. It was built in 1416. Its main hall has brightly decked columns and the dimly lit kitchen—a medieval throw-back complete with the odd rodent—is worth a visit; its giant cauldron fed all 10,000 monks once resident here.

☎ 0891 686 0727 🕒 Daily 9–5 ✋ Adult 50RMB

MORE TO SEE

SERA MONASTERY

Built in 1419, this is another of Tibet's three great Yellow Hat monasteries and is 5km (3 miles) north of Lhasa.

☎ 0891 638 3639 🕒 Daily 9–5 ✋ Adult 50RMB

YAMDROK TSO LAKE

The turquoise waters of this beautiful lake, 120km (75 miles) southwest of Lhasa come dramatically into view when you crest Gangbala Pass at 4,780m (15,682ft), on the old road from Lhasa to Gyantze.

NAMTSO LAKE

One of the highest lakes in the world at 4,718m (15,479ft), Lake Namtso lies 200km (125 miles) northwest of Lhasa. It measures 72km (45 miles) by 30km (19 miles) and pilgrims take more than 10 days to circle it.

Above *Norbulingka was once the summer home of the Dalai Lama*

QINGHAI

This plateau province, once part of Tibet, has been something of a tourism backwater until now, but the new railway line to Lhasa via Xining and Golmud has opened up the area to investment and new visitors. Xining, the capital, has one of northwest China's largest mosques, the 14th-century Dongguan Mosque. Northern Mountain Temple, carved into the side of a precipitous cliff, is Qinghai's oldest religious structure. There's a good market by the West Gate.

The Taer Monastery (daily 9–5), 25km (15 miles) southwest of Xining, is one of the six most important Yellow Hat sect monasteries. A few of its 30 buildings are open to visitors, and you can marvel at its extraordinary collection of yak butter sculptures and its murals. West of Xining, Qinghai Lake (Kokonor, in Tibetan) is China's largest inland saltwater lake and an important bird sanctuary.

✚ 415 H9

RONGPHU/EVEREST (QOMOLANGMA)

Rongphu is the closest most people get to spending a night on Everest (Qomolangma). At 4,980m (16,338ft), it is the highest monastery in the world but is unremarkable, with basic dorm beds. But for 25–40RMB you can wake to the majestic sight of the 8,850m (29,035ft) peak through your window. Another 8km (5 miles) farther on is Everest Base Camp (admission 20RMB), where you can sleep in a tent for 25RMB and buy postcards with an Everest postmark. Walking there takes just over two hours, compared to 15 minutes in a car. You will need a travel permit unless you are carrying on to Nepal. This area is a protected park and entry costs 65RMB per person.

In poor weather you may be within touching distance of Everest, yet never see it. April to June and September are the best months to visit; July and August are monsoon season and after October it is too cold.

✚ 414 E12

SAKYA

This important site, nearly 160km (100 miles) southwest of Xigaze (Shigatse), is two monastery complexes divided by a river, and is the seat of the Sakyapa Buddhist sect. The earlier Northern Monastery was all but destroyed in the Cultural Revolution but is being rebuilt. The impressive Southern Monastery resembles a fortress and houses important books and sutras (scriptures) as well as murals, seals, robes and crowns from the Yuan dynasty (1279–1368).

✚ 414 E12 🕐 Daily 9–12, 3–4
✋ 45RMB

SAMYE

Samye was the first monastery in Tibet, founded in the 8th century by Tibetan king Trisong Detsen at the foot of a mountain in the arid Yarlung Tsangpo (Brahmaputra) River valley. It is 30km (19 miles) west of Zetang (Tsedang). A new bridge and a new road have considerably eased the once-difficult journey. The monastery combines three architectural styles, with a Tibetan ground floor including a large assembly hall, a Chinese second floor and an Indian-style roof. It contains an ancient bell and stone sculptures, including two precious marble statues. You can take photographs in the assembly hall for 30RMB, and other rooms for 10RMB.

Tibet's first royal palace and one of its earliest buildings, Yumbalagang (daily 9–6) is perched on a hilltop about 12km (8 miles) southwest of Zetang. It is now a monastery. Closer to town is another ancient Buddhist monastery, Trandruk (daily 9–6).

✚ 415 F12 🕐 Daily 8–6 ✋ 40RMB

Below *The road to Mount Everest*, on the border of Tibet and Nepal

SONGPAN

This small town high in the mountains of northern Sichuan is a stop on tours to Jiuzhaigou, and a popular base for horse treks of the surrounding countryside.

The town has a long history of trade and commerce between the Chinese and Tibetans. It was once a walled stronghold, and several gates and sections of wall remain, as do two flamboyant covered bridges across the Min River.

✚ 419 L10

WOLONG NATURE RESERVE

Established in the 1970s and a UNESCO-designated biosphere reserve, Wolong Nature Reserve (Wolong Ziran Baohuqu) is the largest of China's 40 protected reserves set up to preserve habitats of the endangered giant panda. It is 150km (94 miles) from Chengdu and covers an area of 200,000ha (494,000 acres) of towering mountains and deep valleys. It contains 4,000 plant species, including several varieties of the pandas' staple food, bamboo.

Sadly, Wolong was one of the many casualties of the devastating earthquake that hit Sichuan in May 2008. One giant panda was killed by a collapsing wall and the majority of the panda enclosures were destroyed. In the aftermath of the disaster many giant pandas were moved to the nearby Bifengxia Panda Migration Centre, where the captive breeding program was scheduled to resume. However, it may take up to three years before Wolong is back to normal and able to welcome tourists.

✚ 418 L11 ☎ 0837 624 6773 ℹ Daily 8.30–11.45, 12.45–5 ✋ Adult 50RMB, child (under 1.1m/3.6ft) free

XIGAZE (SHIGATSE)

Tibet's second-largest town is the site of one of the foremost Yellow Hat sect monasteries, Tashilhunpo (daily 9–7). It was founded by the first Dalai Lama in 1447 and is the spiritual home of the Panchen Lama, Tibet's second most important spiritual leader. The monastery houses 900 monks today compared with 5,000 in 1959.

Key buildings are the Maitreya Chapel, with a 26m-high (85ft) gilded bronze Future Buddha statue, the Kelsang Temple, with its grand hall, the Panchen Lama's Palace and the 35m (115ft) Thangka Wall, where giant images of the Buddha are displayed on April 14 of the Tibetan lunar calendar. Photography inside each building costs 75–150RMB. Xigaze Fortress is undergoing reconstruction.

✚ 414 E12

XILING

www.xiling.cn

Xiling Snow Mountain is one of China's largest skiing and snow playground resorts. It is 120km (75 miles) from Chengdu in a scenic area below the 5,364m (17,598ft) Daxuetang mountain. The resort itself is at an altitude of 2,200m (7,218ft) and has snow from November to March. You can rent skis and protective clothing. Xiling is a year-round resort, its cable car taking visitors up to a summit reserve where pandas and golden monkeys live. The area has hot springs and many waterfalls.

✚ 419 L11 ☎ 028 8830 2010 🕑 Daily ✋ Adult 40–100RMB, child (under 1.2m/4ft) free

Below *The hillside buildings of Tashilhunpo Monastery at Xigaze*
Opposite *Young giant pandas at Wolong Nature Reserve*

EMEISHAN

Sichuan's holy Buddhist mountain rises to 3,099m (10,167ft). The easy way up is to take a minibus and cable car to Golden Summit. Stone steps lead up through thick forest and rich flora past temples and monasteries. Hardy hikers can walk the entire route, a distance of 50km (31 miles), but most walkers opt for a combination of bus and hiking.

THE WALK

Distance: About 20km (12.5 miles)
Allow: 2 days
Start/end: Baoguo bus station

HOW TO GET THERE

Baoguo bus station is next to the Teddy Bear Café and Hotel, just down the road from Baoguo Temple at the foot of Emeishan.

★ Regular buses start running up the mountain from 7am in summer and 8am in winter, although special sunrise buses operate as early as 3.30am.

Take the bus to Wannian Cable Car Station, a 40-minute journey costing 11RMB one way.

❶ Steps lead up to Wannian Temple, an hour's walk. Take the cable-car ride (40RMB one way) instead and escape the hawkers.

Wannian Temple (10RMB) has been rebuilt many times during its 1,600-year history. It is noted for its 16th-century beamless brick hall with its domed brick roof and a statue of bodhisattva Puxian (Samantabhadra), the patron of the mountain's monasteries, riding a white six-tusked elephant. The 7.85m (26ft) statue weighs 62 tons. The temple stands at 1,020m (3,346ft). There is a tourist information office and a restaurant by the cable-car station.

The path continues up past several temples to Huayan Peak at 1,900m (6,324ft), descending to meet another path from Baoguo Temple via Xianfeng Temple. It then climbs again to Elephant Bathing Pool (Xixiang Pool).

❷ The monastery at Elephant Bathing Pool has beds (30–40RMB), but facilities are very rudimentary.

The small hexagonal stone pond where Puxian is said to have washed his elephant is near the monastery, which is at 2,070m (6,791ft). The 14km (8.5-mile) trek to here takes five to seven hours. Monkeys rule the path here. They may look cute, especially the small ones, but they are Emeishan's highway robbers. These bold creatures are so used to people and to being fed that they will often come up and virtually demand food, grabbing and running off with anything not secured, and the large males can be very aggressive.

Carry on to Leidong Terrace (Leidongping), about 1.5 hours up the path.

❸ The solitude of the mountain paths will be broken when you reach Leidongping. At 2,430m (7,972ft), this is the bus terminus for the top

Summit), is on the monorail. The 10-minute ride costs 60RMB return.

6 A sign at Wanfo Ding (Ten Thousand Buddha Summit) proclaims it as 'The Toppest of Mt Emei'. A pagoda-style temple stands 21m (69ft) and has a bell at the top which brings good luck for your family if you ring it. If you are really lucky the summit will not be clouded in and you can enjoy sweeping sunlit vistas. Return to Leidong Terrace for a bus back to Baoguo (11RMB, last bus 5pm).

WHEN TO GO
Emeishan is open all year but the weather can close in at any time, bringing rain and reduced visibility. The peak averages 3°C (37°F) and in winter the topmost areas get snow.

WHERE TO EAT
The approach to Baoguo Temple is lined with simple village-style restaurants. The Teddy Bear Café, 43 Baoguo Lu, offers Chinese or western-style lunch-boxes for the climb. There are also several simple restaurants around the Leidon Terrace bus terminus, on the mountain itself.

of Emeishan and it swarms with people. Several small hotels offer basic but clean rooms, and there are a number of restaurants, as well as another tourist information office. In winter there is skiing here.

Climb the 700 steps up to the cable-car station by Jieyin Temple.

4 The path only rises 110m (361ft), but the steps are crowded with tourists from the buses and sedan-bearers pushing past with their indolent loads. Snack- and souvenir-sellers line the path. There are monkeys here, too, but staff armed with catapults keep them at bay. Overlooks provide views of misty cliffs through the trees.

If you are tired, take the cable car at Jieyin (up 40RMB, down 30RMB) to Golden Summit.

5 Golden Summit (Jin Ding) is at 3,077m (10,095ft). Its temple is undergoing major renovation, but the original had a shiny copper roof

which gave the peak its name. This area heaves with camera-toting tourists and pilgrims lighting candles in front of the temple. You can stay at the Jinding Hotel for the sunrise.

The hike here takes about 10 hours. The only way to get to the mountain's highest point, Wanfo Ding (Ten Thousand Buddha

Clockwise from left to right Pilgrims climbing to the summit of Emeishan; a cable car emerges from the cloud; a giant bell in Baoguo Monastery

CHENGDU

CHUNXI STREET

Chengdu's answer to the Champs-Elysées in Paris or London's revived Carnaby Street, this is where the trendy catch up with the latest in fashion and accessories. The pedestrian street is lined with department stores and fun boutiques stocked with brightly coloured goods.

✉ Chunxi Lu ⊙ Daily 9am–10pm

GIANT PANDA BREEDING RESEARCH BASE

www.panda.org.cn
Enclosures house adult giant pandas and cubs born and reared at this research facility-cum-zoo. In the nursery area you can look in on mothers with their newborn cubs.

✉ 26 Xiongmao Boulevard ☎ 028 8351 6748 ⊙ Daily 7–6 (last ticket at 5) ✋ Adult 30RMB, child (under 1.2m/4ft) free

LITTLE BAR

www.littlebar.com.cn (in Chinese)
A Chengdu institution in recent years, this nightspot is one of the city's liveliest. On Fridays there's live music from local rock bands.

✉ 87 Fangqin Jie ☎ 028 8556 8552 ⊙ Daily 6.30pm–2am. Live music Fridays 8.30pm–10pm ✋ Free except Fri when entry is 10RMB for local bands and 15RMB for other bands

QINGSHIQIAO MARKET

One of Chengdu's largest markets, this is also known as the flower and pets market. You will find animals from the exotic to the cuddly, and many types of fish, plus hand-crafted items and a flower section with miniature *penjing* (Chinese bonsai) plants.

✉ Xinkai and Nanfu Jie, central Chengdu ⊙ Daily 7am-8pm ✋ Free

SHU FENG YA YUN TEAHOUSE

www.shufengyayun.com
A delightful Sichuan Opera show with mask-changing, puppetry, music, fire-spitting, hand shadows, tea pouring and comedy in a historic outdoor teahouse with lanterns. Entry fee includes tea and nibbles.

✉ Chengdu Culture Park, 23 Qintai Lu ☎ 028 8776 4530 ⊙ Daily 8–9.30 ✋ Adult 180–220RMB, child (1.1–1.4m/3.6–4.5ft) half price 🍴

Z DUJIANGYAN QINGCHENG GOLF CLUB

Close to the Dujiangyan weir, and just 3km (2 miles) from Qingchengshan scenic area, this 6,422m (7,023-yard) course provides lots of water hazards on 15 of its 18 holes.

✉ Daguan Township, Dujiangyan ☎ 028 8721 3413 ⊙ Daily ✋ 18 holes 740RMB weekdays, 940RMB weekends/holidays

including caddy fee; cart 200RMB; club rental 100–260RMB; golf shoe rental 20RMB

EMEISHAN

EMEISHAN GRAND HOTEL YOGA HOT SPRING

This large complex has separate indoor and outdoor springs. Entry includes use of the fitness room. Thai and Hong Kong massages, back beating, cupping massage and herbal foot soaking are among treatments.

✉ Emeishan Grand Hotel, Baoguo Temple ☎ 0833 5595466 ⊙ Indoor spring Mon–Thu 2.30–1, Fri–Sun 1–1; outdoor spring Mon–Thu 1–1, Fri–Sun 10am–1am ✋ Admission: adult 98RMB, child (under 1.3m/4.3ft) 20RMB. Treatments: massage 68–168RMB, cupping massage 45RMB, herbal foot soaking 20RMB

JIUZHAIGOU

ETHNIC SONG AND DANCE ENSEMBLE

www.sheraton.com/jiuzhaigou
Twice-nightly shows featuring traditional Tibetan songs and dancing are performed in a 523-seat, custom-built auditorium with revolving stage, hi-fi sound system and atmospheric back-projection.

✉ Sheraton Jiuzhaigou Resort, Jiuzhaigou Scenic Area ☎ 0837 773 9988 ⊙ Shows at 7.30pm and 9.30pm, lasting 1.5 hours each ✋ 180RMB, no child reduction 🍴

FESTIVALS AND EVENTS

GODDESS LAKE

www.jiuzhaiparadisecom

Horseback riding through forest and grassland, paddling on a gentle, picturesque river and white-water rafting are on offer in this scenic area outside the Jiuzhaigou reserve. Tour buses operate from Jiuzhai Paradise Intercontinental Resort which owns and manages the area.

✉ Jiuzhaigou, Sichuan ☎ 0837 778 8296
◑ Daily ✋ Horseback riding 80–280RMB, one-hour paddling trip or 50-minute white-water rafting trip 128RMB

LESHAN

JIAJIANG TEN FU TEA GARDEN

This huge chainstore branch sells all kinds of tea, from local green tea to top-quality Tie Guanyin at 40,000RMB for 1kg (2.2lb). There's also a large museum with 10-minute ritual tea ceremonies.

✉ Jiajiang Service Area, Chengle Expressway, Qingzhouxiang ☎ 0833 591 0666 ◑ Summer daily 8am–9pm, winter daily 8.30am–8pm; museum summer daily 8–5.30, winter 8.30–6 ✋ Adult 30RMB, child (under 1.4m/4.5ft) 15RMB 🍴

LHASA

DROPENLING HANDICRAFT DEVELOPMENT CENTRE

www.dropenling.com

With most of Lhasa's tourist tat now made in Nepal, this charitable organization attempts to help the local economy by selling only locally made wares. Its gorgeous backstreet boutique showcases everything from large wall hangings and woven carpets and more pocketable gifts like handmade cushion covers and wallets. Profits are used to fund community loans within the Tibetan community.

✉ 11 Chak Tsal Gang Lu ☎ 0891 636 0558 ◑ Daily 10–5

MOUNT KAILASH TREK

www.shigatsetravels.com
www.royalmt.com.np

Treks to the sacred mountain of Kailash (Kangrinboqe), in western Tibet (▷ picture on page 216), take 12–15 days from Lhasa. You cannot climb it, but you can join pilgrims making the three-day clockwise walk around its base, camping or staying in guesthouses.

✉ Shigatse Travels, Yak Hotel, 100 Beijing Donglu ☎ 0891 633 0489 ◑ Mid Apr to end Oct ✋ About $600–700 for transportation, guide and permits, but not accommodations

WOLONG

CHINA RESEARCH AND CONSERVATION CENTRE FOR THE GIANT PANDA

China's most important panda research base was badly damaged in the devastating earthquake that hit Sichuan in May 2008. One giant panda was killed by a collapsing wall and some of the panda enclosures were destroyed. Many pandas were moved to the nearby Bifengxia Giant Panda, where the captive breeding program will resume, but it may take

FEBRUARY/MARCH

TIBETAN NEW YEAR

The most significant festival for Tibetans generally falls in February or March. Towns and villages take on a festive spirit and everyone dresses up in their finery on the first day to take gifts to friends and relatives. Singing and dancing follows over the next few days, and you may see monks joining in the festivities. The Butter Lamp Festival is halfway through the first month of the New Year and involves the display of yak butter sculptures in temples and monasteries and the lighting of butter oil lamps.

APRIL

WATER-RELEASING FESTIVAL

The building of China's historic Dujiangyan Weir more than 2,200 years ago is marked early each April during this nationwide festival with a ceremony involving cannon-firing, traditional music and masked dancers. It culminates with ropes holding logs representing the original structure being ceremonially cut, to release the waters of the Min River.

✉ Dujiangyan Irrigation System, Dujiangyan

AUGUST

LITANG HORSE FESTIVAL

This large festival each August sees Khampa (Tibetan nomads) converge on the Sichuan border town of Litang for a week of horsemanship and festivities. Highlights include riders target-shooting and picking up scarves from the ground while galloping at full speed. The women wear highly decorative costumes and have their hair braided. Horse festivals in Tibet include Nakchu Horse Race Festival, also in early August, and one at Jiangzi (Gyantze), usually in May.

✉ Litang ◑ 1–7 Aug

up to three years before things get back to normal at Wolong.

✉ Wolong Nature Reserve ☎ 0837 624 6773 ◑ Daily 8.30–11.45, 12.45–5 ✋ Adult 50RMB, child (under 1.3m/4.3ft) free

XILING

XILING SNOW MOUNTAIN

www.xiling.cn

China's largest snow park has seven pistes and 2,500 sets of rental skis plus snowmobiles, sleigh rides and, in summer and winter, hot-air balloon rides and all-terrain vehicles. Other summer activities include grass skiing and a 1.6km (1 mile) toboggan run.

✉ Dayi County ☎ 028 8830 2010 ◑ Skiing 1 Dec–end Mar daily 8–6, summer activities Apr–end Oct ✋ Skiing 120RMB for 2 hours, 400RMB per day including basic equipment; hot-air balloon ride 50RMB. Entrance: adult 120RMB, child (under 1.2m/4ft) free; cable car 60RMB

PRICES AND SYMBOLS

The restaurants are listed alphabetically within each town. The prices are for a two-course lunch (L) and a three-course à la carte dinner (D), unless specified otherwise. All the restaurants listed accept credit cards unless otherwise stated.

For a key to the symbols, ▷ 2.

CHENGDU

BAGUOBUYI

www.baguobuyi.com

Sichuan cuisine par excellence is served up in this restaurant on Chengdu's main southern artery. If you like it hot and spicy, the stir-fried pig's intestine with hot pepper should fit the bill. Other dishes of note on the menu include beancurd fish, which is fish cooked with tofu. The restaurant has an English menu. ✉ 55 Shenxianshu Nan Lu ☎ 028 8551 1999 🕙 Daily 11–9.30 🖐 L and D 80RMB, Wine 98RMB

THE BOOKWORM

www.chengdubookworm.com

This 'literary restaurant' has a collection of 8,000 books in a variety of languages and a kitchen headed up by an overseas chef. Culinary highlights include 'The Wordsworth', a plate of locally sourced grilled mixed vegetables, or 'The Popeye', spinach with bacon strips, green onions and parmesan cheese. Unusually for this part of the country, the savvy bar staff have been well trained in coffee- and cocktail-making. There's live music on Saturday evening, creative writing classes on Wednesday and regular wine nights. It's hugely popular with Chengdu's bohemian expatriate crowd. ✉ 2–7 Yujie Dong Jie, 28 Renmin Nanlu, Chengdu ☎ 028 8552 0177 🕙 Daily 9am–1am (food until 11pm) 🖐 L 75RMB, D 130RMB

CAIGEN XIANG

One of Chengdu's most popular restaurants now has outlets across the country and specializes in *pao cai* dishes, made with traditional pickled vegetables. The spare ribs, and the whole fish, which comes swimming in fiery chili cauldron, are both essential. There are several other branches in Chengdu itself. Ask at your hotel for the nearest. ✉ 3 Gaoshengqiao Dong Lu ☎ 028 8519 0501 🕙 Daily 9.30am–9pm 🖐 L and D 50–80RMB

CELESTIAL COURT

www.sheraton.com

Cantonese and Sichuan cuisine are the staple fare of this, the top eatery at the upscale Sheraton Lido Hotel and one of Chengdu's classiest restaurants, with prices to match. Among other Asian choices, if you prefer to venture beyond China's borders, are Thai steamed Mandarin fish with green chili and lemon sauce and Malaysian aloe vera or Vietnamese cendol for dessert.

✉ Sheraton Chengdu Lido, No 15, Section 1, Renmin Zhonglu ☎ 028 8676 8999 🕐 Daily 11–2.30, 5–10.30 🖐 L 88RMB, D 156RMB, Wine 198RMB (for all prices add 15 percent service charge)

CHEN MAPO BEANCURD RESTAURANT

www.chenmapo.com

The Chen Mapo bean curd, or tofu, dish popular all over China has been a Chengdu institution since 1862, when it was first cooked by Grandma Chen, after whom it was named. The traditional dish, which consists of bean curd served with a very spicy chili sauce, minced beef and dried chilies, is exported all round the world by the Chen family's eight-restaurant Chengdu chain and is the top menu item here. Other options include duck feet and sea slug bean curd. There is an English menu.

✉ 19 Tsing Hua Lu ☎ 028 8731 7216 🕐 Daily 11–9.30 🖐 L 50RMB, D 65RMB, Wine 98RMB

FIESTA THAI

A likeable Thai restaurant that goes heavy on the imported spices and provides a big-night-out ambience. Despite being Chinese owned, Fiesta Thai serves more authentic cuisine than most of Chengdu's international restaurants. The pleasant terrace is used in summer and has river views.

✉ 6 Linjiang Zhong Lu ☎ 028 8545 4530 🕐 Daily 11am–10.30pm 🖐 L and D 80–100RMB, Wine 98RMB

GRANDMA'S KITCHEN

For those tired of Sichuan's famous tea or hot pot, Grandma's Kitchen is just the ticket. Hamburgers, stuffed potato skins and chicken wings are all are among the American classics served in beautiful dining rooms that recall the feel of an

American country home. Prices are also surprisingly reasonable. A small library stocks foreign paperbacks. There's another outlet at 22 Renmin Nan Lu.

✉ 75 Kehua Bei Lu ☎ 028 8524 2835 🕐 Mon–Fri 9.30am–11.30pm, Sat–Sun 8.30am–11.30pm 🖐 L and D 60–150RMB, Wine 98RMB

GUANGHE TEAHOUSE (GUANGHE CHALOU)

A beautiful riverside teahouse with light wood fittings, rattan chairs and huge pot plants. Tea takes up a sizable chunk of the excellent English-language menu, with varieties drawn from across the country and helpful descriptions on health benefits contributing to the general salubrious vibe. The food ranges from pick-at snacks to Sichuanese stalwarts.

✉ 16 Linjiang Zhong Lu ☎ 028 8550 1688 🕐 Daily 9am–last customer leaves (normally well after midnight) 🖐 L and D 30–60RMB, Tea from 14RMB per cup

HUANG CHENG LAOMA RESTAURANT

www.hclm.net

This large, modern restaurant is part of a chain acclaimed as having Chengdu's finest hot pot restaurants. Diners can create their own meals from ingredients that pass their tables on a sushi-style conveyor belt. The building stands in an area where old neighborhoods were swept away for regeneration. The old times are recalled in a 3D tableau on a wall outside the entrance which resembles the jumble of ancient tiled roofs. Another popular branch is in Qintai Road.

✉ 20 Nan Shan Duan, Erhuan Lu ☎ 028 8513 9999 🕐 Daily 11–11 🖐 L 150RMB, D 200RMB, Wine 138RMB

KANGAROO BAR

www.freewebs.com/roobarchengdu

Known simply as the Roo Bar, this lively watering hole is run by an expat Australian and is a bonza slice of Down Under in the heart of China. Tuck into a selection of pizzas such as the Aussie Pizza,

with bacon, garlic, mozzarella and oregano, or a Great Aussie Burger, washed down by Foster's. For more substantial fare, there's Scotch fillet steak, Australian snapper, and the obligatory BBQ chicken and pork.

✉ 6 Kehua Jie Road 🕐 Daily 7pm–2am 🖐 L 40RMB, D 75RMB, Wine 80RMB

LAPIS LAZULI (ZANG LONG FANG)

A luxe Taiwanese-owned brand that has boutiques and upscale restaurants in many of China's biggest metropolises. The food is pan-European and comes in the tiny portion-oversize plate haute format, complete with immaculate presentation. The decor is glamorous with silken textures blended with wood and slate fittings to create a Zen-like vibe. This is an elegant choice, which is reflected in the prices.

✉ 12 Tongzilin Bei Lu, Wuhou District ☎ 028 8519 0208 DDaily 11am–1am 🖐 L and D 150–300RMB

LONGCHAOSHOU

This is one of Chengdu's most popular snack food restaurants. You can try many different dishes in here, including the eponymous *longchaoshou*, which is a type of dumpling filled with meat or vegetables. You can also take your pick from snacks such as *dandan* noodles, a typical Chengdu dish, and spicy, sweet and sour *zhong* dumplings.

✉ 8 Chunxi Lu ☎ 028 8666 6947 🕐 Daily 8.30am–10pm 🖐 L and D 50RMB, snacks from 5RMB per dish

QIN SHAN ZHAI RESTAURANT

A popular Sichuan cuisine restaurant, Qin Shan Zhai specializes in using many different types of herbs in its dishes. The herbs not only spice up the food, but are also a tonic said to help build up strength: A sign proclaims that if you eat herbal food in the autumn and winter you can kill a tiger in spring. Dishes include hot pot with more than 10 herb varieties. The restaurant also produces its own herbal spirits and displays bottles around the walls. A highlight is an enclosed miniature garden with a waterfall.

✉ 247 Wuhouchi Dajie ☎ 028 8505 3333 🕐 Daily 11–2, 5–9 or later 🖐 L 75RMB, D 100RMB, Wine 118RMB

SHAMROCK BAR & RESTAURANT

www.shamrockinchengdu.com
As Irish as they come, this place offers a warm welcome and cold Guinness, not to mention tasty international food. The choice ranges from pub food like sausages and mash or fish and chips to quesadilla, fajita, spaghetti, steaks and weekend BBQs. Well worth a try is the chef's special, the chicken cordon bleu (chicken stuffed with ham and cheese).

✉ No 15, Section 4, Renmin Nanlu ☎ 028 8523 6158 🕐 Daily 9.30am–2am 🖐 L 45RMB, D 80RMB, Wine 100RMB

SHUNXING OLD TEAHOUSE

Some may find the 'ancient' ambience slightly forced, but this expansive teahouse remains a great spot to enjoy the many facets of the Sichuan tea-drinking experience, of which food is a key ingredient. The wait staff pour tea from an impossibly long spout (to better ferment the flavors) while ear-cleaners wander among the crowd with intimidating metallic implements that turn out to be agents of pleasure.

✉ 3/F, Chengdu International Exhibition and Convention Centre, 258 Shawan Lu, Chengdu ☎ 028 8769 3202 🕐 Daily 9.30am–10pm 🖐 L and D 100RMB

EMEISHAN
TEDDY BEAR CAFÉ

www.teddybear.com.cn
Tuck into one of owner Andy He's generous Big Bear burger meals to give you plenty of sustenance for the grueling climb up nearby Emeishan. It comes with fries and a coffee or Coca Cola, as does the chicken sandwich. And don't forget to pick up one of his stylized hiking maps of the mountain. The house specials include sweet-and-sour

boneless chicken and fried eggplant (aubergine) with garlic and ginger. Both go down a treat.

✉ 43 Baoguo Lu, Baoguo ☎ 0833 559 0135 🕐 Daily 7am–10pm 🖐 L 25RMB, D 45RMB, Wine 60RMB

TIAN XIU RESTAURANT

One of several guesthouse restaurants by the Buddhist mountain's topmost bus station and the walkway to the summit cable car, it offers a typical menu at reasonable prices, unlike some of the mountain food stalls. The ribs with sugar and vinegar are to die for and will help hikers recover their strength for the final part of their trek. You might want to give the pig's heart and pig's head dishes a miss, though.

☎ 0833 509 8051 🕐 Daily 8–8 🖐 L 40RMB, D 55RMB, Wine 68RMB

JIANGZI (GYANTZE)
PRINCESS WENCHENG WESTERN RESTAURANT

Formerly the Yak Tibetan Restaurant, this upstairs eatery is a sister restaurant to the Songtsen in Xigaze. The staff are very friendly and welcoming, and speak English. Burning incense sticks on an altar on the far wall give off a pervading but not unpleasant aroma, while light jazz plays in the background. A liking for yak meat is an advantage here, as it features strongly on the Western, Tibetan, Nepali and Indian cuisine menu, with dishes from yak pizza to yak curry.

✉ Yingxiong Nanlu, Jiangzie (Gyantze) 🕐 Daily 8am–midnight 🖐 L 50RMB, D 65RMB, Wine 160RMB

JIUZHAIGOU
JIU ZHAI SHAN ZHUANG

This is a local Tibetan restaurant rather than one geared for tourists, so you won't find an English menu here. But they do have pictures in the menu so you can order by looks. Perhaps that is no bad thing, either. Local mushrooms are a feature of the restaurant, and one variety is called mutton intestine. Mashed potato soup is another interesting,

and unexpectedly good, option.

✉ Zhangha Town ☎ 0837 776 4918 🕐 Daily 9am–10pm 🖐 L 40RMB, D 60RMB, Wine 60RMB

PEARL RESTAURANT

www.sheraton.com/jiuzhaigou
The Tibetan essence of the region is mirrored in the blend of Sichuan and Tibetan cuisine at the top restaurant in town. The restaurant also successfully exudes an air of elegant informality, an essential ingredient for a five-star leisure resort. Starters of spicy yak stomach or braised goose feet will appeal to adventurous diners, while local wild mushrooms and fish from Jiuzhaigou's lakes and rivers are both must-tries.

✉ Sheraton Jiuzhaigou Resort, Jiuzhaigou Scenic Area ☎ 0837 773 9988 🕐 Daily 11.30–2, 6–10 🖐 L 100RMB, D 150RMB, Wine 160RMB

LHASA
HOUSE OF SHAMBHALA

The restaurant of Lhasa's first boutique hotel is charmingly intimate and exotic. Many of the Nepali-Tibetan-Chinese dishes comes with a New Age patron—try the Guru Rinpoche chicken tikka or the Heinrich Harrer schnitzel—and can be sampled either in the candlelit second-floor dining room or up on the fabulous rooftop terrace.

✉ 7 Jiri Erxiang (south of Barkhor Square) ☎ 0891 632 6533 🕐 Daily 9am–8pm 🖐 L 100RMB, D 150RMB, Beer 10RMB

MAKYE AME (MAJI A'MI)

On the southeast corner of the Barkhor circuit sits this wonderful and increasingly trendy tourist hang-out. The second floor has soft sofas and relaxing Tibetan folk music while the third-floor balcony is a great vantage point for watching the endless procession of pilgrims doing circuits around the Jokhang Temple. There are many excellent vegetarian choices, including spinach-tofu ravioli, plus more generic dhal and curry sets.

✉ Bakuo Jie (southeast corner of Jokhang Temple) ☎ 0891 632 8608 🕐 Daily

9am–midnight 🖐 L 40RMB, D 60RMB, Beer 13RMB

NORLING RESTAURANT

www.kyichuhotel.com

The rock terrace and spacious courtyard garden of the Kyichu Hotel in Lhasa's old quarter serve as outdoor extensions for its restaurant. The Tibetan and Nepali chefs rustle up a wide choice of Tibetan, Nepali and Indian food, as well as home-made pastas.

Yak is the key ingredient for dishes from traditional *momo* dumplings to burgers, tenderloin steaks and stroganoff. Curry lovers will be in seventh heaven.

✉ Kyichu Hotel, 18 Beijing Zhonglu ☎ 0891 636 6550 🕓 Daily 7.30am–10pm 🖐 L 40RMB, D 50RMB, Wine 80RMB

OLD MANDALA RESTAURANT

The gloomy interior and grubby carpet won't win prizes for appearance, but where this little restaurant in the heart of old Lhasa scores is with the variety of cuisine styles—Western, Chinese, Nepalese, Italian and Japanese. Yak variations encompass sizzler, curry and *momo* among others, and desserts include a delicious apple truffle with chocolate. It also has a small roof terrace teahouse with great views.

✉ 31 South Barkhor, Lhasa ☎ 0891 632 9645 🕓 Daily 7am–midnight 🖐 L 35RMB, D 45RMB, Wine 60RMB

TIBET LHASA KITCHEN

The sign of a good restaurant is that it is frequented by locals, and you'll see plenty in this very Tibetan second-floor establishment, including saffron-robed monks. Local staples such as Tibet cheese bread made with *tsampa*, cheese and sugar, yak butter tea, yak steak and yak *momo* dumplings are offered alongside typical Western and Chinese selections.

✉ 3 Minchi Khang Donglu ☎ 0891 634 8855 🕓 Daily 8am–10pm 🖐 L 40RMB, D 50RMB, Wine 180RMB

XIGAZE (SHIGATSE)
SHIGATSE HOTEL

The beautifully decorated Banquet Hall, depicting a rural mountain scene across one wall, is one of the few saving graces of an otherwise disappointing experience if you stay at this hotel. The food is more international than in the hotel's smaller Tibetan Restaurant, and offers unusual concoctions such as silver fungus soup and scrambled egg soup.

✉ 12 Shanghai Zhonglu ☎ 0892 882 2525 🕓 Daily 9–9 🖐 L 60RMB, D 90RMB, Wine 140RMB

Below *Pearl Restaurant at the Sheraton Resort at Jiuzhaigou*

PRICES AND SYMBOLS

Prices are for a double room for one night, unless otherwise stated. Breakfast is included unless noted otherwise. All the hotels listed accept credit cards unless otherwise stated. Note that rates vary widely throughout the year.

For a key to the symbols, ▷ 2.

CHENGDU
JINJIANG HOTEL

www.jjhotel.com

Refined elegance perfectly sums up Chengdu's grande dame. Opened in 1960 and often referred to as the Garden Hotel for its garden setting and profusion of greenery, the Jinjiang offers guests the very highest levels of comfort and service. Its showpiece restaurant is the Louvre Garden, set below a glass roof and flanked by balconies housing two of its four other restaurants.

✉ No 80, 2nd Section, Renmin Nanlu
☎ 028 8550 6666 🖐 900–1,587RMB
🛈 480 🅢 🅨 ♒

SHERATON CHENGDU LIDO

www.sheraton.com/chengdu

In the heart of Chengdu's central business district, this classy hotel will appeal to both discerning leisure guests and executives. Rooms are bright and spacious and there is 24-hour room service. Executive Floor rooms offer dedicated check-in and check-out and a lounge with free breakfast, afternoon tea and evening cocktails. Leisure facilities include a sizable indoor pool, three restaurants and a bar.

✉ No 15, Section 1, Renmin Zhonglu
☎ 028 8676 8999 🖐 838–1,200RMB
🛈 413 🅢 🅨 ♒

WEN JUN MANSION HOTEL

www.dreams-travel.com/wenjun

Built in the style of a Ming and Qing mansion, this pretty, affordable establishment claims to be the only courtyard hostel hotel in Chengdu. The good-size rooms offer free broadband internet access and are set around two courtyards off balconied corridors. All have private bathrooms except for two large dorm suites. Free pick-ups are offered from the railway station and the hotel can arrange other travel and tours.

✉ 180 Qintai Lu ☎ 028 86138884
🖐 180–680RMB, dorm suites 40–60RMB per bed. Breakfast 20RMB 🛈 39 including 4-bed and 6-bed dorm suites

EMEISHAN
EMEISHAN GRAND HOTEL

www.emshotel.cn

This four-star hotel enjoys a superb location at the foot of Emeishan mountain next to Baoguo Temple. It also has an extensive hot spring complex, with 10 hot spring pools in the outdoor Yoga Hot Spring and an indoor center with a pool, geothermal baths, saunas and fitness facilities. A lively Snack Corridor entertainment complex, mimicking ancient buildings, is a recent addition.

✉ Baoguo Temple ☎ 0833 552 6888
🖐 400–800RMB 🛈 435 🅢

HONG ZHU SHAN HOTEL

www.hzshotel.com

Another hot spring resort and business hotel close to Baoguo Temple, this is a more stylish proposition. The property is spread across a cluster of buildings and villas around a lake. One building was where Nationalist Chinese leader Chiang Kaishek lived during a stay in Emeishan. The indoor hot spring complex is on a much smaller scale than that of the Emeishan Grand but you can stay in a hot spring suite.

Opposite The exterior of the Jinjiang Hotel in Chengdu

✉ Baoguo ☎ 0833 552 5888
✋ 544–1580RMB ⓘ 508 💲 🍴 ⛱

TEDDY BEAR HOTEL

www.teddybear.com.cn
Friendly service, clean rooms and a great location (next to the Baoguo Temple bus station from where buses set off up the slopes of Emeishan) make this hostel-style hotel a popular choice for backpackers. Accommodations are in dorms and private rooms, some with bathrooms. You can store luggage and borrow walking sticks and crampons for free to help with your climb.

✉ 43 Baoguo Lu, Baoguo ☎ 0833 559 0135; 1389 068 1961 (owner Andy's mobile) ✋ 30–40RMB for a dorm bed; 80–250RMB for a room with a private bathroom ⓘ 18 including dorm rooms 💲

JIANGZI (GYANTZE)
GYANTSE HOTEL

Architecturally dull on the outside, the colorful, ornate reception desk and lobby inside are very Tibetan. A row of full-size costumed figures lines the indoor lobby courtyard, so when you sit in one of the chairs you get an uncomfortable feeling of being watched. Some rooms are Tibetan-style, but the decor is muted.

✉ 2 Yingxiong Donglu ☎ 0892 817 2222 ✋ 250–300RMB ⓘ 164 💲

GYANTSE ZONG RI HOTEL

This unassuming little hotel, close to the town's main street and just below the hilltop fort, was built in 2002 and offers clean and modern double rooms with a shower and telephone in each room
✉ 11 Wei Guo Lu ☎ 0892 817 5555 ✋ 80–150RMB ⓘ 32

JIUZHAIGOU
JIUZHAI PARADISE INTERCONTINENTAL RESORT

www.jiuzhaiparadise.com
Set in the middle of a forest and with a huge lobby capped by a glass roof enclosing trees, streams and ponds, the effect is breathtaking. There are plenty of leisure facilities in this 1,000-room resort and lots to do around it, yet its sheer size and the gaudy lighting at night leaves you with sensory overload. Special rooms are provided for guests with disabilities.

✉ Gahaizi, Zhangzha Town ☎ 0837 778 9999 ✋ 1,000–3,458RMB ⓘ 1,020 💲 🍴 ⛱

LHASA
DHOD GU HOTEL

Rich handmade Tibetan fabrics, furniture and vivid decorations adorn this intimate joint-venture hotel slap bang in the heart of old Lhasa. The rooftop bar has fabulous views of the Potala Palace and Jokhang Temple, and you will need a drink after climbing the four flights of stairs to reach it as there are no elevators. Live music serenades diners in the restaurant.

✉ 19 Beijing Zhong Lu, Trom Si Kang ☎ 0891 632 2555 🕐 Closed end Oct to mid-Apr ✋ 520–1,000RMB ⓘ 63 💲

HOUSE OF SHAMBHALA

www.houseofshambhala.com
Sister hotel to Beijing's Red Capital Residence, the House of Shambhala was the first boutique hotel to reach the Tibetan highlands. Set around a three-floor courtyard home, the 10 rooms lack natural light but make up for this in rustic charm, with antique furniture and rich, warm color schemes. There's a restaurant on site, and next door is the Tibetan spa, which uses organic and locally produced products, and a shop dedicated to local crafts, jewelry and fashions. The best part is the location, among the narrow alleys in the traditional heart of old Barkhor.

✉ 7 Jiri Erxiang (just south of Barkhor Square) ☎ 010 6402 7151 ✋ 750–1,000RMB ⓘ 10

KYICHU HOTEL

www.kyichuhotel.com
The friendy, family-run Kyichu Hotel is one of Lhasa's oldest privately run hotels. Decor is traditional Tibetan in public areas, and an art gallery gift shop allows you to buy local crafts without the hassles of the nearby market and shops. In fine weather you can relax on the large courtyard lawn and adjacent rock terrace, also used as an alfresco extension for the indoor restaurant.

✉ 149 Beijing Donglu, Lhasa ☎ 0891 6331541 ✋ 260–420RMB Apr–end Oct, 180–240RMB Nov–end Mar. Breakfast 30RMB ⓘ 50 💲

MANDALA HOTEL

Ask for a room on the Barkhor Street side if you stay in this small hotel in the heart of old Lhasa. Of its 35 rooms, 14 look out onto the street and Jokhang Temple and you can watch the pilgrims as they circle the building. The rooftop teahouse has even better views of the temple and the rest of the city.

✉ 31 South Barkhor ☎ 0891 633 8940 ✋ 200–300RMB Apr–end Sep, 180–200RMB Dec–end Mar ⓘ 35

SAMYE
SAMYE MONASTERY HOTEL

As basic as they come, this guesthouse is inside the compound of Tibet's oldest monastery, and a stay here will give you more time to see and experience it when other tourists have long returned to their city hotels. Accommodations are in dorms and rooms, with shared toilets and showers.

✉ Samye Monastery Compound ☎ 0893 790 6120 ✋ 10RMB for dorm beds, 150RMB for rooms ⓘ 53 beds

WOLONG
WOLONG HOTEL

A few miles up the mountain road, this hotel opened in 2005 and offers the convenience of walking from your room to the panda enclosures. Rattan (bamboo) is used extensively in the furniture. There's a lovely teahouse but no swimming pool as yet, although one is planned. The hotel may be closed temporarily after the earthquake in May 2008.

✉ Wolong Nature Reserve ☎ 0837 624 6888 ✋ 270–500RMB ⓘ 323 💲

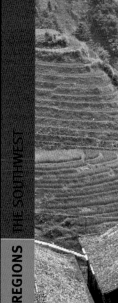

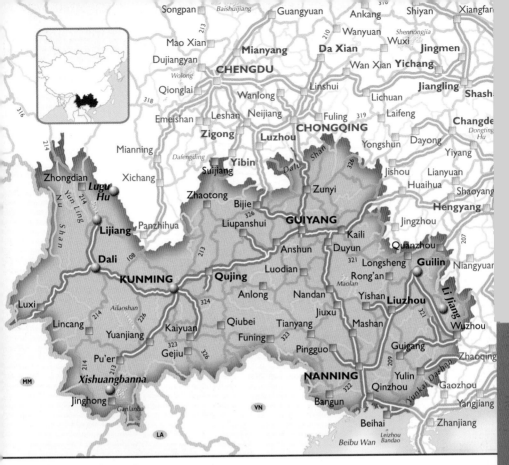

THE SOUTHWEST

Compared to the flat landscapes and homogenous culture of much of eastern China, the multicultural Southwest marks a complete change of scene. The provinces of Guangxi, Guizhou and Yunnan are not only home to spectacular gorges, lush rainforests, stacked rice terraces and snowy mountains. They also contain nearly all of China's 55 minority groups.

Guangxi has arguably China's most famous natural landscape. The northern part of the province is covered by a see-it-to-believe-it forest of conical karst mountains. In the middle is the city of Guilin, one of China's most popular tourist destinations. More than a third of the province's population is ethnically Zhuang and the area has been designated a 'Zhuang Autonomous Region'.

According to legend, Guizhou never enjoys more than three straight days without rain, and not a single square meter of flat land. These conditions explain why the province has often been labeled an irrelevant, impoverished backwater. But those same drawbacks for residents make it a spectacular find for tourists. Its mountains are raw and its rivers and waterfalls grateful for the downpours. On the downside tourism resources remain rudimentary.

Not so Yunnan, tucked away in the far southwest. This is the only part of China that enjoys a pleasant year-round climate and the landscape is stunningly diverse, ranging from rainforests in the south to the imperious Himalayas in the north. Rediscovered by backpackers in the 1990s, Yunnan has blossomed to become a firm tourist favorite both with domestic and international travelers. In terms of cultural and geographic diversity, there's nowhere to touch it in all of China.

ANSHUN

Once an important trading link on the opium route, Anshun is still a place to cut deals and barter. The goods are far more benign these days, though. This area of Guizhou province is famous for its batik fabric prints, a tradition going back to the Tang dynasty (618–907). The Sunday market in the middle of town is a good place to buy these and other local crafts. The 15th-century Wenmiao (daily 9–6), rebuilt in later times, is notable for its intricate stone carvings. Anshun is the main access point for Asia's largest waterfall, the Huangguoshu Falls (daily 8–6), in a scenic area 45km (28 miles) to the southwest. The Baishui River plunges over a series of ledges, the main cascade thundering down 73m (240ft). Windows cut into a cave behind the tumbling curtain give an excellent close-up view. Take rain gear to avoid getting wet.

The falls can be combined with a tour of the Longgong, or Dragon Palace, caves (daily 8–6) on the way. This extensive system of caves, waterfalls, streams and stalactites includes a boat ride.

✚ 419 M13

DALI

▷ 228

DEHONG

Bordering Myanmar (Burma), in the far west of Yunnan, the Dehong Dai-Jingpo Autonomous Prefecture is a rain forest-covered region of Dai and Jingpo minority towns and villages. Flights from Kunming serve regional capital Mangshi, where there are several interesting temples and pagodas. Ruili is 76km (47.5 miles) farther along the Burma Road, which links Kunming with Burma (Myanmar). It has a jade market selling Burmese jade, regarded as the world's best. Jiele Pagoda has a series of conical stepped towers— the tallest is 36m (118ft).

✚ 418 J14

DUYUN

The Bouyei and Miao Autonomous Prefecture in southern Guizhou, of which Duyun is capital, is rich in minority culture. It is called the City of Bridges because of the 100 bridges that cross the Jianjiang River here. Among them is Little Seven Holes Stone Bridge, its arches mirrored in the blue-green waters of the river. The old part of Duyun has an attractive wide pedestrian-only paved street lined with old wooden balconied buildings, all a uniform red.

✚ 419 N13

GUILIN AND LI JIANG

▷ 230–232.

GUIYANG

Guiyang is the capital of Guizhou, an often-overlooked province of beautiful limestone mountains and preserved minority villages. Qianling Park, on its outskirts, has a pleasant lake and forested mountain trails and Hongfu Temple, Guiyang's biggest, at the summit. The park's Qilin Cave, where Nationalist (Guomindang) leader Chiang Kaishek imprisoned two rebellious generals, is one of several key sites in the area associated with the Communists' Long March.

Other Guiyang landmarks include the Jiaxiu Pavilion by the Nanming River, and the early 17th-century Wenchang Pavilion. Zhijin Cave (daily 8.30–5), 160km (100 miles) west of Guiyang, is China's largest cave and impressive for its scale and extraordinary formations. The ancient town of Qingyang, 29km (18 miles) south of Guiyang, is surrounded by walls interspersed with watchtowers and forts.

✚ 419 N13

Opposite *Huangguoshu Falls is Asia's largest waterfall*
Above *The Jiaxiu Pavilion in Guiyang*

INFORMATION

⊕ 418 K14 ⓘ Dali Tourism Bureau, Longshan Administrative Area, ☎ 0872 231 6777 🚌 Long-distance bus station in Xiaguan; buses to Dali Old Town go from next to Xiaguan rail station 🚉 Xiaguan Railway Station, 12km (7.5 miles) from Dali Old Town ✈ Dali Airport, 27km (15.5 miles) from Dali Old Town

TIPS

» Experience ethnic culture in the markets of towns and villages around Dali.
» Bus number 7 runs to and from Dali Airport from Xiaguan. The taxi journey takes 45 minutes and costs around 100RMB.
» Bicycles are a good way to explore the area. They cost about 10RMB a day to rent, including a map.

Above *Boats on Erhai Lake*

DALI

This old walled backpackers' hangout has laid-back bars and good-value restaurants. Splendid pagodas, mountains and Erhai Lake all offer wider appeal. Set between Erhai Lake and the 4,000m (13,000ft) Cangshan mountain, Dali is on the road from the Yunnan capital of Kunming to Lijiang and is a great place to chill out. Trains and buses arrive in Xiaguan, otherwise known as Dali City, 12km (7.5 miles) south of the Old Town.

COBBLED STREETS

Dali Old Town's compact grid of cobbled streets is enclosed by stone walls on three sides and by four impressive Qing gates. Huguo Road, known as Foreigner Street for its café culture, encompasses surrounding roads. The cafés and bars buzz both day and night. The small Dali Museum (Fuxing Road, daily 8.30–6) has exhibits on the local Bai minority culture and marble.

THREE PAGODAS

Northwest of town, in a park with a reflecting lake, are Dali's multitiered 9th-century Three Pagodas. They are made from richly decorated local marble. Entry (daily 7–7) includes the reconstructed Chongsheng Temple.

ERHAI LAKE

A trip on the 42km (26-mile) long Erhai Lake includes a visit to the Bai fishing community on Jinshuo Island. For great views of Dali and Erhai Lake, walk or take the chairlift up Zhonghe Mountain to Zhonge Temple (daily 8–6).

KAILI

The mountains around Kaili, in eastern Guizhou, are dotted with fascinating minority villages. The Miao village of Langde, 29km (18 miles) from Kaili, enjoys state protection for its cultural heritage. Old wooden houses line paved and cobbled streets. Visitors are welcomed by women in traditional long dresses and decorative silver head-pieces, and long-robed men playing lusheng bamboo instruments. Spontaneous music and dancing can be enjoyed at the 100-plus annual festivals in villages throughout the region. Matang village's Ge minority inhabitants are noted for their embroidery, and their hard-sell techniques.

✚ 419 N13

KUNMING
▷ 233

LIJIANG
▷ 234–236

LONGSHENG

This mountainous area of minority groups, two hours north of Guilin, is renowned for the Dragon's Backbone Rice Terraces (daily, 50RMB). Virtually every scrap of hillside has been carved into terraced paddy fields across 600 years. Zhuang villagers still tend the fields, but tourism is now big business, with busloads of visitors setting off from a parking area below Ping'an village every day to climb the steep and narrow path up to its high setting. Sedan bearers carry the less mobile, but the ride can be harrowing. You can eat and stay in a family guesthouse (100–200RMB per room). Facilities are basic, but early-morning walks up deserted paths give sweeping views of the village and layered mountain, the sun glinting off the water-filled terraces like a giant kaleidoscope.

The area's Red Yao women famously have the longest hair in China. They let it down to dangle in a stream while they brush and sing in a tradition that is now a popular tourist spectacle at Hangluo village, below the terraces.

✚ 419 P14

LUGU HU (LUGU LAKE)
▷ 237

NANNING

The Guangxi province capital, Nanning is a transit hub with long-distance rail links to Beijing, Shanghai, Chengdu and Kunming. You can also take a train across the border to Vietnam, a mere 160km (100 miles) from here. Often bypassed by those heading to Guilin and Yangshuo, Nanning is a large, green city on the Yong River. Among its attractions, the Guangxi Provincial Museum (daily 9–5) traces the city's history and displays cultural items from the area's ethnic minorities.

✚ 428 N15

SHILIN

A formation of gray limestone karst rocks weathered into upright pillars and spires interspersed with trees, Shilin (Stone Forest), at 130km (81 miles) from Kunming, is a worthwhile day trip. Take an organized tour, go by bus or take a taxi (round trip 350RMB). The whole scene is very manicured. The main Major Stone Forest is encircled by a paved path. Electric buggies trundle around it with seats at 4RMB each. Tour groups swamp the main paths but the slow trek up to the viewing pavilion is rewarded with a panoramic scene. Escape the crowds by seeking smaller paths and more distant areas. The Minor Stone Forest has smaller rocks. Similar formations are at Naigu Stone Forest (daily 8–6), along with caves and a waterfall.

✚ 419 L14 ☎ 0871 771 1278 ⏰ Daily 24 hours 💷 Adult 140RMB, child (above 1.3m/4.3ft) 100RMB, child (under 1.3m/4.3ft) free 🚌 From Kunming, 43RMB round-trip 🖥

Left *The village of Ping'an is near Longsheng*

INFORMATION

www.guilin.com.cn/newenglish/index.htm

➕ 419 P14 ℹ️ Guilin Tourism Information Service Centre, 14 North Ronghu Road ☎ 800 879 3318 (toll free) 🕐 Daily 8–10 🚌 Guilin has three bus stations, the main one on South Zhongshan Lu. Yangshuo's bus station is on Pantau Lu 🚆 Guilin Railway Station (South Station) is southwest of the city and closer in than Guilin North Railway Station ✈️ Guilin International Airport is 26km (16 miles) west of Guilin

Above *A section of the Li Jiang near Elephant Trunk Hill*

INTRODUCTION

Few cities rival Guilin's dramatic skyline. Lofty limestone peaks, weathered into sharp, tooth-like formations, march right into the city. Between the mountains and through the city flows the meandering Li Jiang (Li River), a once-tranquil waterway of cormorant fishing villages, now a marine highway with a constant stream of tourist-laden cruise boats. Other than enjoying a river cruise, you can climb some of the mountains, explore numerous caves beneath them, take structured tours or go hiking and bicycling on your own to explore the astonishing scenery.

The mountains forming Guilin's beguiling backdrop are limestone sediments thrust up from the seabed 200 million years ago and shaped over eons by wind and rain erosion. Most formations lie south of Guilin. Capital of Guangxi province until Nanning replaced it in 1914, Guilin's position on the Li River has long made it an important military and trading post. The mild climate makes Guilin a year-round tourism destination, and it attracts 11 million visitors a year. The city has a population of 600,000 and the surrounding area is home to 12 ethnic minority nationalities.

WHAT TO SEE

GUILIN'S PEAK PARKS

Among Guilin city's evocatively named pinnacles, Elephant Trunk Hill (daily 7.30am–9pm) resembles an elephant drinking from the confluence of the Li and Peach Blossom rivers. Bamboo raft trips allow closer inpection. Fubo Hill, or Wave Subduing Hill (daily 7.30–6), is just along the river and features Pearl-returned Cave, Sword-testing Rock, Thousand Buddha Cave (there are actually far fewer) and rock carvings. Nearby Folded Brocade Hill (daily 7.30–6) is named because its layered rocks look like folded silk. Steps lead to the top, giving a bird's-eye view of the Li River and city.

REED FLUTE CAVE

You might need your shades for this popular attraction, Ludi Yan, in Guilin's northwest. Stalagmites and stalactites contorted into weird and wonderful shapes are illuminated in shades of bright green, blue, red and yellow. The visual effect is overwhelming, but the more subtle monotone treatment of rocks reflected in a pool at the cave's star feature, the Crystal Palace, is extremely well done.

✉ Ludi Scenic Area ☎ 0773 269 5075 🕐 Apr–end Oct daily 7.30–6, Nov–end Mar daily 8–5.30 ✋ Adult 60RMB, child (under 1.4m/4.5ft) free 🚌 3, 58 (this is a free service)

SEVEN STAR PARK

Across the Li River from the city, this park (Qixing Gongyuan) derived its name from peaks that supposedly form the star pattern of the Big Dipper constellation. Camel Hill is well-named and tour groups jostle to take photos where US president Bill Clinton gave a speech on conservation during a visit in 1998. Other attractions include a temple, a huge cauldron and stone inscriptions. A zoo houses animals in cramped pens.

✉ 1 Qixing Lu ☎ 0773 280 3000 🕐 Daily 6–7.30 ✋ 35RMB 🚌 6, 10, 11, 14, 58

TIPS

» Take a 20RMB note when you go on a Li River cruise. The scene on the back is the view looking toward Guilin when you reach the sharp bend at Xingping.

» The Yulong River valley, just to the south of Yangshuo, is as spectacular as the Li River, and far less commercial.

» You can flag down one of the electric carts that trundle up to Yangshuo's main square, but agree the price first as they charge different fares.

» September to November are the best months for warm, dry weather and when fragrant osmanthus flowers are in bloom. Spring can be wet and summers are very hot.

REGIONS

Left Riming Shuang Ta Pagodas
Below Houses and hills of Guilin from Solitary Beauty Peak

LI JIANG (LI RIVER)

A Li River boat trip (adult 470RMB, child under 1.4m/4.5ft, 235RMB, including return bus trip) gives superb views of the incredible karst landscape. Cruises start south of Guilin and take four to five hours to reach Yangshuo, 83km (52 miles) downriver. Dozens of tourist craft are filled and dispatched with military precision. Yet the convoys do not lessen the spectacle. If anything, the boats give the soaring cliffs perspective and highlight their immense scale. Western tour group boats are better appointed than Chinese ones but cost much more; in either case, the cruise includes lunch. You pass several villages where fishermen still use cormorants, although it is mostly for tourists these days. Enterprising locals punt their bamboo rafts alongside tour boats to clamber aboard and sell souvenirs. The boats return upstream empty, with visitors staying in Yangshuo or going back by bus.

YANGSHUO

This long-time backpacker's haven is the all-action base for enjoying the region's sugarloaf landscape. The surrounding countryside is more picturesque than Guilin's and there's a plethora of sightseeing, activity and adventure options. The focal point is West Street, a touristy pedestrian street when the cruise boat hordes descend, which jumps to the beat of loud music from its many bars and cafés at night. The best way to see Yangshuo's scenery and attractions is by renting a bicycle (▷ 242). You can rent from numerous locations around town for 10–20RMB a day.

MORE TO SEE

CROWN CAVE

This 12km (7.5 mile) cave is a subterranean river system through which visitors are transported by elevator, miniature train and boats. One of the area's biggest attractions, it is 29km (18 miles) south of Guilin on the Li River
☎ 0773 384 8899 ⊘ Daily 8–4.30 ✋ 60RMB

XINGPING

An ancient Li River town with extraordinary river views, Xingping is 27km (17 miles) north of Yangshuo. You can take a bus or bicycle there. A Ming dynasty fishing village close by has preserved houses with traditional carvings. Villagers still fish from bamboo rafts using fishing cormorants.

SHANGRI-LA YANGSHUO

www.niceview.cn

This recreated minority village 10 minutes north of Yangshuo on the road to Guilin is set by a lake reflecting the nearby karst mountains. Visitors are welcome to join in the dancing and other folk customs of costumed Miao, Yao, Dong and Zhuang groups.
☎ 0773 877 5666 ⊘ Daily 8.20–5.45 ✋ Adult 50RMB, child (under 1.4m/4.5ft) 25RMB

TWO RIVERS AND FOUR LAKES

Four scenic downtown lakes have been linked together with the Li and Peach Blossom rivers for a 90-minute circular boat tour. There is no English commentary. Trees surrounding the central lakes are dazzlingly lit at night, as are island pagodas in the middle, and walking the perimeter paths at night is popular.
☎ 0773 280 5098 ⊘ Daily 8.25–10.40, 1.45–4.30, 7.30–9.45 ✋ Adult 105–155RMB day and night cruises (air-conditioned boat)

Below *Market stalls in front of one of the Yangshuo's many limestone peaks*

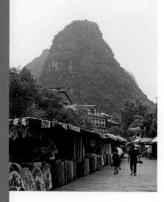

KUNMING

With a strategic position on a plateau bounded by mountains and a large lake, Kunming was a key outpost on the southern Silk Road. Occupied first by regional kingdoms, it was swept up by the Mongols 800 years ago. It was a link on the Vietnam–China railway line and was the eastern end of the Burma Road, the Allied World War II supply route. Today it is the main access point for visitors coming to see the diverse cultures of Yunnan's 26 minority groups and its scenic wonders.

RICH HISTORY

Kunming's rich history is chronicled at the Yunnan Provincial Museum (daily 9.30–5.30). In the Western Hills, 16km (10 miles) west, the tunnels and statue-filled grotto of Dragon Gate (daily 8–5.30) took 72 years to build and overlook Lake Dian. Britain's Queen Elizabeth II was entertained in one of the halls. The nearby 1,000-year-old Huating Temple (daily 8–6) has 500 Qing dynasty clay figures.

ETHNIC CULTURES

From Western Hills a cable car (daily 8–5.30) goes to the lakeside Yunnan Nationalities Village (Mon–Fri 8–6, Sat, Sun 8–7), which highlights ethnic minority cultures including Bai, Dai, Naxi and Mosuo. The Yunnan Nationalities Museum (Tue–Sun 9–5.30) is next door. In Kunming highlights include the ancient Yuantong Temple (daily 8–5.30), Bamboo Temple (daily 8–6) and hilltop Golden Temple (daily 8–6.30), although the entire building is actually made of copper, not gold. A cable car links to the World Horti Expo Garden (daily 8–6).

INFORMATION

✚ 418 L14 ℹ Kunming Tourist Information Service Centre, Honghe Hotel, ✉ 204 Chuncheng Lu ☎ 0871 310 7859 🚌 Kunming bus station, on Beijing Lu, operates long-distance buses 🚆 Kunming station, 4km (2.5 miles) south of the city. North Railway Station, 3km (1.8 miles) north ✈ Kunming Wujiaba International Airport is less than 8km (5 miles) from the city

TIPS

» Try a local dish, across-the-bridge noodle soup (*guoqiao mixian*).
» The best way to see Dragon Gate is to take the chairlift (15RMB) to the top, walk down, then take the electric shuttle (3RMB) to the entrance.

Below *The ancient Bamboo Temple in Kunming*

LIJIANG

INFORMATION

www.lijiang.cn

418 K13 Lijiang Old Town Tourist Service Center 1 Dong Dajie (East Main Street) 0888 511 6666 (8.30am–10.30pm) There are four bus stations outside the Old Town served by long-distance buses Lijiang Airport is 25km (16 miles) to the east. The 40-minute ride to town costs 15RMB

Above *Sifang Jie (Market Square) is in the Old Town*

INTRODUCTION

Lijiang's pristine 800-year-old Old Town, a UNESCO World Heritage Site, is like a time capsule. The traffic-free streets buzz with the cacophony of commerce from its many shops, ethereal *hulu si* (Naxi flute) music and the hubbub of bars and restaurants. There are many delights to discover in the winding alleys tucked away off hillside streets radiating from its main square. Stay in a Naxi-style guesthouse or small hotel in the Old Town and it is all on your doorstep. Many travel agencies offer day trips or longer tours to regional scenic and cultural attractions. Buses operate from the new town.

In the 13th century the local ruling family moved its base from Baisha and established a walled and moated new town, Dayan. Its name was later changed to that of the prefecture that it administered, Lijiang. The myriad streams, crossed by more than 350 bridges, serviced houses and acted as a sanitation system. A commercial center for the Naxi people, it has flexible wooden buildings that have helped it survive several earthquakes, most recently in 1996. Tourism is the historic town's new threat—it receives more than three million visitors a year, and a railway line being built from Kunming will boost numbers even more when it opens in 2009.

WHAT TO SEE

OLD TOWN

The sights and sounds intoxicate the senses the moment you arrive. Two giant waterwheels mark the Old Town's (Lijiang Gucheng) northern entrance. The main hub is Market Square (Sifang Jie). Everyone hangs out here: bearded men on benches smoking long pipes; women in traditional Naxi blue and white gossiping in groups; and rifle-toting, sheepskin-clad Tibetans posing with horses. Each afternoon the Naxi elders join hands to dance in circles, and anyone can join in. Xinhua Street, or Bar Street, is bisected by a stream spanned by stone bridges. At night, floating candles drift past red lanterns strung outside restaurants whose staff sing and chant in raucous rivalry. The Mu Family Mansion (daily 8.30–6) is the restored Yuan dynasty mansion of Lijiang's ruling family. High on Lion Hill (daily 7am–10pm), the wooden Wanggu Lou Pagoda looks out over the jumble of curved, tiled roofs to the mountains. The evening performances of traditional Naxi music and Dongba music and dancing (▷ 245) are recommended.

🌐 Daily ✋ Entrance to old town free. For all sights: adult 80RMB, child (under 1.2m/4ft) free

BLACK DRAGON POOL PARK

The main attraction in this park (Heilongtan Gongyuan) is the classic picture-postcard scene across the pond to an arched marble bridge and Jade Dragon Snow Mountain beyond. Springs welling up in the park feed the many water courses, which rush through the Old Town. Also here are the Ming-era Wufenglu Pavilion and the Dongba Research Institute, where English-speaking guides explain this enigmatic part of the Naxi culture. Paths lead up Elephant Hill for great Jade Dragon views.

☎ 0888 511 2968 🌐 Daily 7.30am–9pm ✋ Adult 60RMB, child (under 1.2m/4ft) free

JADE DRAGON SNOW MOUNTAIN (YULONG MOUNTAIN)

This stately mountain is 35km (22 miles) north of Lijiang. A cable car takes you up to a terrace with a 4,506m (14,783ft) marker. The 13 craggy, permanently snow-covered peaks seem touchable but actually reach 5,596m (18,359ft), while in the valley below is the world's highest and longest golf course, Jade Dragon Golf Club. Farther up the valley, chairlifts go up to Yak Meadow, where villagers tend yaks, and scenic Spruce Meadow.

☎ 0888 516 2707 🌐 Daily 24 hours; cable cars run 8–5.30 (approximately) ✋ Adult 160RMB (including 80RMB 'protection fee' for Lijiang), child (under 1.2m/4ft) free

TIPS

» Lijiang gets very crowded during the day and well into the night. If you get up early you are rewarded with streets deserted, save for shopkeepers drawing water from streams to sluice down walkways.

» Most bars and restaurants in Lijiang do not have toilets. There are a number of public toilets but they are not free, so take small change and some toilet paper.

» Oxygen bottles (30RMB) are available on Jade Dragon Snow Mountain. The high altitude can trigger acute mountain sickness.

» If you plan to hike Tiger Leaping Gorge you will need to allow an overnight stay in Qiatou or on the trail. Going by road to Walnut Garden from the entrance takes 40 minutes.

REGIONS

Below *A view of Black Dragon Pool with an arched marble bridge and Jade Dragon Snow Mountain beyond*

TIGER LEAPING GORGE

Squeezed between the towering Jade Dragon and Ha Ba mountains, 60km (37.5 miles) north of Lijiang, the Yangtze (Jinsha) River forms a dramatic, deep canyon of raging torrents, 16km (10 miles) long—Hutiao Xia. Here, according to legend, a tiger leapt across the river to escape a hunter. Busloads of tourists swarm down steep steps to a viewing platform overlooking a rock proclaiming to be where the tiger jumped, although the real spot is much farther in. A narrow path high above the gorge makes a spectacular two-day hike (▷ 240–241).

🕐 Daily 24 hours 🖐 Adult 50RMB 🚌 250RMB per group

Above Detail of decoration on the Mu Family Mansion
Below The viewing platform at Tiger Leaping Gorge

MORE TO SEE

SHU HE

A small old town close to Lijiang, this was formerly a key waypoint for the traders using the tea horse route to transport tea to Tibet and the Middle East. Restoration and development have made it a smaller clone of Lijiang, with similar cobbled streets edged by waterways and lined by growing numbers of bars, hotels and restaurants.

🕐 Daily 🖐 30RMB

BAISHA

This once-important village 8km (5 miles) north of Lijiang has several of the area's famous 500-year-old temple frescoes, the most notable at Dabaoji Palace (adult 15RMB, child under 1m/3.3ft free). Nearby is Yuhu village, where botanist and explorer Joseph Rock lived for 27 years. His house is now a small museum.

FIRST BEND OF THE YANGTZE RIVER

About 70km (44 miles) from Lijiang and a half-hour detour en route to Tiger Leaping Gorge, the fledgling Yangtze abruptly changes direction by the town of Shigu. The legendary Kublai Khan is said to have crossed the river here with his forces.

YUFENG MONASTERY

One of several Red Hat sect Buddhist monasteries around Lijiang, Yufeng is on the lower slopes of Jade Dragon Snow Mountain. The 10,000 Blossom Camellia Tree spreads its branches over a wooden canopy and is named for the number of flowers it is claimed to bear each spring.

🕐 Daily 8.30–6 🖐 Adult 15RMB

LUGU HU (LUGU LAKE)

Lugu Lake is a beautiful alpine lake, but tourists are mainly drawn to see the Mosuo people, a sub-group of the Naxi who live on its shores. Their way of life is unique in China. Women head households and couples do not marry or live together. Instead, they spend nights together but live in their respective family homes in a practice known as *axia*, or 'walking marriage.'

LUOSHUI VILLAGE

The crystal-clear lake, measuring 50sq km (19.3sq miles), lies at 2,690m (8,825ft) and is cradled by mountains. The journey from Lijiang takes five hours on twisty mountain roads. Most tourists stay in Luoshui village on the Yunnan side, where tourism is more developed. Hotels include the 31-room Daba Grand Hotel (tel 0888 588 1088), while some Mosuo farmhouses offer guest rooms.

BOAT TRIPS

Activities include boat trips to Liwubi Island, which has a small temple, or Heiwae Island, where Austro-American botanist Joseph Rock once lived. Using dugouts called *zhucao*, or pig-trough boats, the traditionally dressed girl and boy rowers sing love songs as they row. Horse rides along the lakefront cost 25RMB. Other options include excursions to Zhamei Temple (daily 8–6), Yongning town market, or the Mosuo Folk Museum (daily 8am–11pm).

INFORMATION

www.liluguhu.com.cn/cs/index.asp
Lugu Lake Scenic Area ✚ 418 K13

TIPS

» The best view of Lugu Lake is from an elevated scenic area on the way to Luoshui, with Sichuan's Gemu Goddess Mountain rising up behind the lake.
» Early mornings and evenings are the best times for taking pictures of Lugu Lake. During the middle of the day the high sun reflecting off the lake water creates harsh shadows.
» You can tell if a Mosuo girl is single or has a lover by the way she wears the pearls in her headdress.

Below *Lugu Lake is in the mountainous Yunnan Province*

Above *Women in traditional dress*

INFORMATION

http://english.xsbnly.com

➕ 418 K15 ℹ️ Xishuangbanna Dai Autonomous Prefecture Tourism Bureau, ✉️ Building 13, Nakunkang Residential Area, Jinghong ☎ 0691 213 2285 🚌 There are two bus stations: Jinghong City Bus Station and Xishuangbanna Bus Station, both in Jinghong ✈️ Jinghong Airport is 5km (3 miles) south of Jinghong

TIPS

» Avoid the tour groups at Wild Elephant Valley by starting at the back gate and watching the elephant show before taking the 40-minute forest canopy cable car ride (40RMB one-way) and leaving from the front gate.

» The best time to visit is from September to May.

XISHUANGBANNA

Yunnan's southwestern corner has a Southeast Asian feel, underlined by its minority cultures, of which the dominant Dai, closely related to the Thai, are notable for their writing style and Buddhist temples. The region has China's only tropical rain forest, threatened by expanding rubber tree plantations, developments and roads. It is a UNESCO biosphere reserve and is home to more than a dozen ethnic minorities.

MEKONG RIVER

The fascinating minority villages are easily visited from regional capital Jinghong, a pleasant, green city on the Mekong (Lancang) River. The Xishuangbanna Tropical Flowers and Plants Garden (daily 8–6), in Jinghong's Yunnan Institute of Tropical Crops, includes a rare plants section.

WILD ELEPHANTS

Just outside Jinghong, the Tropical Primeval Rainforest Park (daily 8.30–5) has several forest walks. You can take a 3km (2-mile) forest walk at Wild Elephant Valley (daily 8–5.30), 50km (31 miles) to the north. You may see the wild elephants if you stay in the valley's tree hotel (▷ 252). Beyond Menghai, west of Jinghong, is the Qing-era Octagonal Pavilion (daily 8.30–6). About 70km (43 miles) south, near the Myanmar (Burma) border, is the Manfeilong White Pagoda (daily 8.30–6) at Damenglong.

XISHUANGBANNA
▷ 238

ZHAOXING

Timeless Dong minority villages pepper the rice-terrace-etched hills of Guizhou's southeastern corner. Each has a wooden drum tower on stilts and a wind and rain bridge capped by a pavilion, where locals gather to hang out. The largest village, Zhaoxing, has five of each, the drum towers representing the village's five different clan units. Evening cultural performances of singing and *lusheng* bamboo pipe music are watched by both villagers and tourists. There is also a delightfully named Potato Service Hotel.

Tourism is in its infancy here, so villages feel less artificial than elsewhere. The area's most celebrated wind and rain bridge, at Diping, was swept away in a flash flood in 2004, but is being rebuilt using the salvaged timbers. The Miao men of Basha village, to the west, sport ponytails on their otherwise shaved heads.
✚ 419 P14

ZHONGDIAN

Known as Gyalthang by locals and called Shangri-La by authorities, who claim the area is the legendary paradise made famous by James Hilton's 1933 novel *Lost Horizon*, Zhongdian is in the autonomous Diqing Tibetan region of Yunnan's far north. Soaring snow-capped mountains cradle this upland region of fertile fields and Tibetan villages.

Balconied wooden buildings line the large square in the historic district. Every night, young and old dance in lines around a fire to blaring techno-Tibetan music in a resurrected tradition. Even uniformed policemen join the circling dancers, who sometimes carry on until midnight. A giant new prayer wheel dominates from a hill on the old town's outskirts, lit at night like a beacon. It takes three people to turn it.

The 17th-century Ganden Sumtseling (Songzanlin) Monastery (daily 8–6) stands above a village 5km (3 miles) from Zhongdian, hence its nickname, Little Potala. Its commanding location was chosen by the fifth Dalai Lama. Note-worthy features are its eight huge golden Sakyamuni Buddha statues, rare Buddhist scriptures and murals, and its dazzling gilded roofs.

A prayer flag-bedecked rural hill is the setting for modest Ringha Temple, an important pilgrimage site half an hour away. Bita Lake (daily 8–7) is in a high mountain park 25km (15.5 miles) east of Zhongdian, where black-necked cranes flock in winter. A new entrance has made access less of a high-altitude hike. Wooden boardwalks encircle the lake, where you can take a boat trip for 30RMB.
✚ 418 K13

ZUNYI

This northern Guizhou town has a pivotal place in China's history. It was here, during the Red Army's Long March in 1935, after a rout by the Nationalists (Guomindang), that the Communist Party held the pivotal three-day Zunyi Conference that changed its principles and paved the way for Mao Zedong to assume authority. The two-floor wood and brick building (daily 8–5.30) where it was held is on Hongqi Lu but is strictly for history buffs. Loushan Pass, 50km (31 miles) south of Zunyi, is another key Long March site. The Red Army's first triumph was at this strategic mountain pass in 1935.

Maotai, 60km (37.5 miles) northwest of Zunyi, is where China's eponymous national liquor is distilled. You can tour the Maotai National Liquor Culture City (daily 8.30–11.30, 2.30–6).
✚ 419 N13

Below *The position of Ganden Sumtseling Monastery was chosen by the fifth Dalai Lama*

REGIONS

239

TIGER LEAPING GORGE

Squeezed between Yunnan's towering Jade Dragon and Haba mountains, the Yangtze River has carved out one of the world's deepest river canyons. Tiger Leaping Gorge will be drowned by a lake under proposals to dam the river for hydroelectricity. In the meantime, a spectacular trail high along the gorge's edge is a popular hike, but one not to be undertaken lightly.

THE WALK

Distance: 30km (18.75 miles)
Allow: 2 days
Start: Qiaotou
End: Walnut Garden/Qiaotou

HOW TO GET THERE

Qiatou is a small town three hours north of Lijiang by road. In Qiaotou cross the river and turn right. The gorge ticket office is near the bridge and entry costs 50RMB. Shortly after the ticket office, on the left, is the Gorged Tiger Café and Guesthouse. Check there before starting the walk. The owner, Australian Margo Carter, freely offers advice on trail conditions and a map produced by her and husband, Sean, a local guide who runs a guesthouse at Walnut Garden (▷ 253). Late-comers should stay overnight in Qiaotou to allow an early start on the trail. You can store bags at Margo's.

★ The high trail climbs nearly 900m (2,953ft) in the first section. There are Naxi villages, farms and guesthouses throughout the trail, one of two routes through the gorge. The Lower Road is now sealed the entire length of the gorge and beyond. Most tourists visit by bus, only getting as far as a scenic spot 9km (6 miles) in.

About 300m (930ft) beyond the Gorged Tiger Café, look for a small stone marker on the left of the road with the number 194. An arrow points the way up a small path. This is the starting point for the high trail. Make sure you turn right at the Sunrise Guesthouse, after 20–30 minutes, otherwise you will miss the trail and could get lost on the mountainside.

❶ 24 Bends is a series of steeply rising switchbacks after about three hours on the path. Some call it 28 Bends—an hour negotiating this tough section and you will lose count as well. Above the bends the trail reaches its highest point, at 2,660m (8,727ft). Stop to catch your breath and take in the glorious scene. The gorge and Yangtze River (known locally as the Jinshu, or Golden Sands River) stretch in both directions and across the gorge is 5,596m (18,359ft) Jade Dragon Snow Mountain.

The path here is very exposed. Aim to complete this section by noon in

Opposite *Rickshaws on the path along the gorge*
Right *Legend has it that a tiger leapt across the gorge*
Below *A monument states the depth of Tiger Leaping Gorge*

summer. Alternatively, wait until late afternoon. You could also spend the night at the Naxi Family Guesthouse, about an hour before the bends.

The trail drops down through pine forest and over streams, passing the Tea Horse Guesthouse, which has a hot shower and washing machine, and the Halfway Guesthouse. About six hours from the start, it makes a good place to rest or eat.

❷ Several waterfalls send water streaming across the path, which you cross using stepping stones. With the steep canyon slope plunging on one side, vertigo sufferers might endure some anxious moments. Trust your footing and you will be fine as the stones are firm.

You descend from here to the Lower Road. The high trail continues on after branching to the left, but should only be tackled with a guide.

❸ The New Bridge is worth stopping at for pictures of the ravine it spans. Beyond it a sign points to the Sky Ladder, a vertical metal ladder on a path down to the

river near the Tiger Leaping Stone. Do not go this way. The route is very dangerous (there were three fatalities in 2005) and aggressive touts demand money to use it.

Another 15 minutes on the road brings you to Walnut Garden, about eight hours after setting off. Options for overnight accommodation include Sean's Spring Guesthouse (▷ 253). Local transportation will take you back to Qiaotou for a fee.

❹ Walnut Garden is named for its walnut trees. From here the walk down to the river and tiger leap spot takes 30–40 minutes and is hassle-free. Guided hikes go up to the Bamboo Forest and a waterfall, and to Haba mountain village, a day's hike.

WHEN TO GO
The high trail can be hiked year round, but is sometimes closed by snow in winter. It is also unsafe to hike in heavy rain and should not be tackled in the heat of the day in summer. Take plenty of water, especially in summer.

WHERE TO STAY
NAXI FAMILY GUESTHOUSE
☎ 0887 880 6928/139 8873 6431

YANGSHUO TO MOON HILL

The countryside around Yangshuo is made for exploring by bicycle. Its pointy limestone mountains rear up dramatically over the rice fields and rivers, but the terrain itself is relatively flat. There are also many roads and paths that wind between the peaks and skirt rivers, passing through old towns and villages.

THE BICYCLE TOUR

Distance: 16km (10 miles)
Allow: 4-6 hours (including visiting attractions)
Start/end: Yangshuo

HOW TO GET THERE

Yangshuo is 65km (40 mile) southeast of Guilin.

★ Begin your ride in Yangshuo. You can rent a bicycle for 10–20RMB per day from many places, including West Street and in front of the New Century Hotel, off Pantao Road.

Turn left onto Pantao Road and ride south out of the town. The road bears right before you reach a large roundabout. Continue in the same direction and the shops lining the road soon give way to paddy fields.

❶ As the road sweeps left around a karst hill you will see climbers scaling its sheer cliff. This is Golden Cat Hill, a popular local climbing spot. Tethered hot-air balloon rides are available next to it, while just beyond and across the road is Butterfly Spring, which has a spring, suspended bridge and China's largest butterfly conservatory.

Continue on the same road for about 20 minutes to reach Gongnong Bridge, spanning the Yulong River. A road bridge has opened to ease pressure on the old one. A small road off to the right just before the river leads past the Yangshuo Mountain Retreat to Yima, Baisha and Dragon Bridge, 17km (10.5 miles) upriver. This is another good bike ride.

❷ At Gongnong Bridge you can walk down to the Yulong River for photogenic views of the karst mountains reflected in the water. Bamboo raft trips operate from here down toward the Li River, and cormorant fishermen demonstrate how their birds catch fish. There is also a restaurant here.

Just past the river, a path leads off across fields to the left of the road and eventually meets another path leading to Moon Hill. This route avoids the busy road and is very picturesque, but without a guide is hard to find.

❸ At about 6km (3.75 miles) from Yangshuo is the Big Banyan Tree scenic area. The 1,400-year-old riverside tree is said to be where peasant girl Liu Sanjie and her fisherman boyfriend pledged their love to each other, celebrated in a famous Chinese film, *Liu Sanjie*, and now in a spectacular show (▷ 246).

Jianshan Temple is visible off to the left, at the foot of Yunji Hill. It is a short detour off the main road. Street traders along the main road

WHEN TO GO

Winters are cool while summers are hot and humid. Spring is a good time because of the blossom but there are frequent showers, while autumn is warm without the summer humidity or rain. The road is busy with sightseeing buses and local traffic even on weekends. Later in the day is quieter.

PLACES TO VISIT

ASSEMBLING DRAGON CAVE
🕐 Daily 8–6.30
✋ 45RMB

BIG BANYAN TREE SCENIC AREA
🕐 Daily 7–6.30
✋ 18RMB

BUDDHA CAVE
🕐 Daily 9–5.30
✋ 128RMB

BUTTERFLY SPRING
🕐 Daily 8–6
✋ 45RMB

JIANSHAN TEMPLE
🕐 Daily 8.30–5
✋ 20RMB

WATER CAVE
🕐 Daily 9–6
✋ 130RMB

WHERE TO EAT

Yangshuo's West Street has a variety of international cafés for major refuelling before or after the ride and there are several family-run restaurants en route, particularly around the Big Banyan Tree and Jianshan Temple.

Clockwise from left to right *The view from the top of Moon Hill; a boat on the river near Yangshuo; bicycling near Yangshuo*

sell a variety of fruit including *sha tian you*, or pomelo, a hard-to-peel but refreshing citrus fruit.

❹ Jianshan Temple was built in the Tang dynasty and is one of the region's oldest temples. It is also the largest temple in Guangxi and has been a place of pilgrimage for 1,200 years. The nearby Assembling Dragon Cave gets its name from the shape of the surrounding hills.

After several twists in the road, take a turning on the left, leading to Buddha Cave and, beyond it, Water Cave. The Water Cave ticket office is on the right-hand side of the main road before this turning.

❺ Both the Buddha Cave and Water Cave offer mud baths as well as swimming in underground rivers. Remember to take your swimsuit.

The road back from the caves offers the classic view of Moon Hill. Turn left at the main road and the entrance is soon after, on the right.

❻ Moon Hill has an almost perfect half-circular hole near the top, about 50m (164ft) across. For a fee of about 10RMB you can climb up to the hole and enjoy a panorama of the pinnacle-studded landscape.

CHONGZUO

CHONGZUO ECO-PARK

China's endangered white-headed langur, a monkey indigenous to Guangxi and rarer than the giant panda, is protected in this nature park about 90km (56 miles) southwest of Nanning, which has one third of the remaining 700 population. There's also a restaurant and hotel (room 150RMB per day). ✉ Chongzuo Shengtai Park, Banlixiang ☎ 0771 793 0223 ◷ Daily 7.30–6 but is open later for those staying at the hotel in the park ✋ Adult 80RMB, child (under 1.2m/4ft) 40RMB

DALI

CHINA MINORITY TRAVEL

www.china-travel.nl
Day trips and longer tours are offered to minority villages and less touristy areas of Yunnan. Day trips include a guided visit to the old Bai village of Xizhou, said to be how Dali used to be, a boat trip across Erhai Lake to Wase and a drive back via other lakeside villages. Trips to see cormorant fishermen on the lake are also available. ✉ 63 Boai Lu, Dali Old Town ☎ 0872 267 1822 ◷ Daily ✋ Erhai lake and villages day trip 420RMB, including lunch

HIGHERLAND INN

Guided hiking trips of one to four days are offered by this friendly little hotel, halfway up Cangshan mountain at 2,600m (8,530ft). Two-day hikes will take you to the summit to camp overnight and return the next day. ✉ Cangshan, Dali Old Town ☎ 0872 266 1599 ◷ Hiking all year, but on lower slopes Jan and Feb when Cangshan peak has heavy snow ✋ Hike with guide 200RMB a day. Bed 30RMB, double room 60RMB

GUILIN

DREAMLAND OF LI RIVER

Ballet, acrobatics, dance and circus acts are choreographed with music and lighting into a show of grace and fluidity in an auditorium a short walk from central Guilin. ✉ 95 Qixing Lu ☎ 0773 585 0868 ◷ Daily 7pm, show starts 8pm ✋ Adult 150–180RMB, child (under 1.4m/4.5ft) half price

ETHNICRAFTS

Locally produced sculptures and table decorations are augmented by hand-crafted silver jewelry from local minorities including the Miao, and fine embroidery from Guangxi, Guizhou and Yunnan ethnic groups such as the Yao, Miao, Zhuang and Dong. This establishment is well worth a visit. ✉ 95 Zhengyang Lu ☎ 0773 280 9777 ◷ Daily 9.30am–11pm

Above *People waiting for the ferry on the Li river, Xingping*

GUILIN HOSPITAL OF SINO-WESTERN MEDICINE

www.tcmadvisory.com
One of China's best-known hospitals offering traditional treatments and age-old herbal remedies, the Guilin Hospital has several former international heads of state among its clients, including former President George Bush senior. Tour the informative reception area before treatments, including reflexology and acupuncture. ✉ Guida Lu ☎ 0773 582 0588 ◷ Daily 9–5.30, massage till 9pm ✋ Acupuncture and reflexology 100RMB per hour, back massage 120RMB per hour. Herbal remedies available by mail order

I-FLYING HOT AIR BALLOON CLUB

Get a unique perspective of the region's beautiful limestone karst pinnacles on a short-tethered balloon trip or an hour-long free-floating flight with this well-established ballooning outfit, which also has a sister branch in Xi'an. Flights take place outside of town. ✉ 72 Dacunmen, Kaifa District ☎ 0773 882 8555/137 3739 6537 ◷ Daily 6am–7am or 5pm–6pm ✋ 150–700RMB per person

LIJIANG WATERFALL HOTEL

www.waterfallguilin.com

The nightly spectacle of the world's biggest manmade waterfall tumbling off a hotel roof by Guilin's main square is the best free show in town and draws big crowds. The cascading water pulses in synch to music.

✉ 1 Shanhu Beilu ☎ 0773 282 2881
🕐 Daily 8.30–8.45 ✋ Free

MARKETS

By day, the market stalls along and off Guilin's central pedestrian shopping street (Zhengyang Lu) are the place to bargain for knick-knacks and local handicrafts or dine out on local snacks from food stands. Come dusk, and the bigger night market on the western side of Zhongshan Lu is where the action is.

✉ Zhengyang Lu and Zhongshan Lu
🕐 Zhengyang market daily 10am–midnight, Zhongshan market daily 7pm–midnight
✋ Free

MERRYLAND

About 60km (37.5 miles) north of Guilin, this theme park complex alongside Ling Lake has four themed areas representing different parts of the world with thrill rides and attractions. There is also an on-site hotel.

✉ Xingan County 🕐 Daily 8.30–6
✋ Adult 110RMB, child (under 1.4m/4.5ft) 55RMB

KUNMING

JIXINYUAN RESTAURANT

This huge, elaborate banquet-style restaurant opposite the World Horti-Expo Garden entrance stages exotic dance revues with semi-naked girls plus stylized ethnic dance performances by a 180-strong cast. The food is an assortment of dishes from Yunnan's minority cultures.

✉ 431 Bailong Lu ☎ 0871 501 3777
🕐 Daily shows 6.30–8.20
✋ 198–568RMB, including a meal

RECREATION CENTRE, KUNMING HOTEL

Chill out with a sauna session followed by a massage any time of the day or night in this second-floor recreation area in one of Kunming's landmark hotels.

✉ 52 Dongfeng Donglu ☎ 0871 316 2063
🕐 Daily 24 hours ✋ Hour-long massage and sauna, 128RMB

SPRING CITY GOLF AND LAKE RESORT

www.springcityresort.com

This award-winning lakeside resort 36km (22.5 miles) east of Kunming, has two courses by top designers Jack Nicklaus (rated the top course in China by US golf magazine *Golf Digest*) and Robert Trent Jones Jr., plus villas and a spa.

✉ Yang Zong Hai, Kunming ☎ 0871 7671188 🕐 All year ✋ Resort guest: 18 holes 620RMB weekdays, 810RMB weekends and holidays; walk-in rate 18 holes 1,640RMB weekdays, 1,940RMB weekends and holidays. Rates include compulsory cart and one caddy shared between two golfers

WORLD HORTI-EXPO GARDEN

www.expo99km.gov.cn

Created for the 1999 World Horticultural Expo, this park has more than two dozen theme international gardens, a tropical greenhouse, tea plantation, herb garden, bamboo forest and museums. Cultural music and dance is performed through the day.

✉ Bailong Lu ☎ 0871 501 2367 🕐 Daily 8–6 ✋ Adult 100RMB, child (1.2–1.4m/4–4.5ft) 50RMB

LIJIANG

BELL SHOPS

Lijiang was on the old Yunnan–Tibet tea horse trading route and the traders would put bells on their horses to announce their arrival. The wooden beams of these two shops drip with bronze bells of all descriptions.

✉ Old Trail Bells, 34 Xian Wen Xiang, Guang Yi Jie, Lijiang Old Town ☎ 0888 510 6731 ✉ Bunong Bell, Big Old Stone Bridge, Lijiang Old Town ☎ 0888 512 6638
🕐 Daily 8.30am–midnight ✋ Prices range up to almost 2,000RMB for a 10cm (4in) bell with your name engraved on it (delivery 20–40 days)

DONGBA DANCE AND MUSIC

www.dongbagong.com

This entertaining 90-minute show is a song and dance depiction of the Naxi's Dongba religious culture, which uses a pictographic script. The Dongba shamens' highly decorative costumes are fascinating.

✉ Dongba Palace, Lijiang Old Town
☎ 0888 518 4372 🕐 Daily 8pm–9.30pm
✋ Adult 120–160RMB, child (under 1.2m/4ft) half price

JADE DRAGON SNOW MOUNTAIN GOLF CLUB

www.ljxsgolf.com (in Chinese)

Smoke your drives like the pros on the world's highest and longest golf course, nestling at the foot of the eponymous mountain. The ball flies 20 percent farther in the rarified air of the 3,100m (10,170ft) setting, helping to tame this 7,816m (8,548-yard), par-72 beast.

✉ Ganhaizi, Jade Dragon Snow Mountain, Lijiang ☎ 0888 516 3666 🕐 Daily, open all year but best May–end Oct ✋ 18 holes 1,280RMB, including caddy and cart. Cost reduced to 655RMB Mon–Fri/735RMB Sat, Sun with advance reservation. Club rental 120–400RMB, shoe rental 80RMB

LI AND RICHARD HE TRAVELLING GUIDE SERVICE

Personal guided tours off the beaten track by Li (half Naxi, half Tibetan) and Richard (half Naxi, half Bai) take you to minority villages where you can stay and eat with families. Touring and trekking trips go throughout Yunnan and Sichuan and into Tibet.

✉ 5 Long Quan Xi Yuan ☎ 135 78370587
🕐 Year round ✋ Trips cost 250-300RMB per person per day including meals, guiding and transportation

NAXI ORCHESTRA

Naxi music is played on original instruments by an orchestra of richly garbed, wispy-bearded musicians who seem as ancient as the music and venue. Leader, the venerable Xuan Ke, introduces each piece in amusing but lengthy monologues in Chinese and English. A must-see, it often sells out.

✉ Naxi Music Academy, Dong Dajie, Lijiang Old Town ☎ 0888 512 7971 🕐 Daily 8–9.30pm ✋ Adult 120RMB, 140RMB and 160RMB, child (1.2–1.4m/ 4–4.5ft) half price, under 1.2m (4ft) free

LE PETIT PARIS

French wines and food add a certain *je ne sais quoi* to this French-run bar and restaurant, at one end of Lijiang's boisterous Xinhua Street. There's international music and you can join in the singing contests, too. ✉ Xinhua Jie, Lijiang Old Town ☎ 0888 518 7379 🕐 Daily 7am–2am

SAKURA CAFÉ

This Korean-owned restaurant-bar has been pulling in the (mostly) Asian punters since 1997 and is especially lively at night-time when there are live music performances. The menu features Korean dishes as well as local Naxi meals and a bottle of local(ish) Tibetan wine costs 130RMB. This canal-dissected street is lined with bars and restaurants and there are heaps of alternatives nearby if Sakura isn't your thing. ✉ 123 Cuiwen Hutong, Old Town ☎ 0888 518 7619 🕐 Daily 7am–2am

XISHUANGBANNA

DAI GARDEN

If you can't make the annual Water Splashing Festival in April, this park, with its artificial Dai minority village, southeast of Jinghong, offers a sanitized version each afternoon in the main square. Visitors are promised they will get soaked, but leave happy. ✉ Ganlanba ☎ 0691 250 4099 🕐 24 hours, water splashing 2.30–3.10 and 4.30–5 ✋ Adult 50RMB, child (under 1.4m/ 4.5ft) 35RMB, under 1.1m (3.6ft) free

HONGJINGSHI LANCANG-MEKONG

Rafting trips on the Mekong start by Jinghong's new bridge and end at a minority village with thatched houses 18km (11 miles) downstream. The 90-minute trips include some white-water rapids and use powered rafts made of two lashed-together inflatable pontoons, on which riders sit. ✉ River Rafting, Riverside, Mekong River, Jinghong ☎ 0691 213 3588 🕐 Daily ✋ Adult 160RMB, child (under 1.2m/4ft) free

LANCANG-MEKONG RIVER SINGING AND DANCING FIRE

A Dai barbeque dinner is followed by a Chinese-narrated show with a bonfire party and singing and dancing performances by Dai and other local ethnic groups in a lakeside park setting. ✉ Evening Party, Manting Park, Manting Road, Jinghong ☎ 0691 216 0296 🕐 Park daily 8–6. 30-min shows at 10.30am and 1.30pm (30RMB). Dinner daily 6.40pm. Show 7.40– 9.40pm ✋ Adult 120RMB, 160RMB and 280RMB, child (under 1.2m/4ft) free

MARKETS

Jinghong and minority villages The villages of the Dai, Jinuo, Hani (Aini) and other minorities are noted for their markets. Ganlanba has a daily market while others worth visiting are at Menghun (Sun) and Xiding (Thu). There are nightly markets in Jinghong under the new Mekong bridge (food) and between the Crown and Sightseeing hotels (handcrafts). 🕐 Village markets usually mornings, Xiding's ends at 11am; night markets 8–11pm ✋ Free

MENGBALANAXI SHOW

If you want to see traditional minority dancing and singing, such as the famous Dai Peacock Dance, this is not the show for you. It does showcase the ethnic cultures of southern Yunnan, but in a very glitzy and slick musical production. There is no English dialogue. ✉ Mengbalanaxi Theatre, 6 Ganlan Zhonglu ☎ 0691 212 0100 🕐 Daily 8.30pm–10.10pm ✋ Adult 120RMB and 160 RMB, child (under 1.2m/4ft) free

WILD ELEPHANT VALLEY

The wild elephants may be elusive, but regular shows by resident tame Asian elephants will delight young and old, especially the soccer match. Youngsters can hand-feed the jumbos with bananas, too. There's also a butterfly house, boa house and a monkey pen. ✉ Sanchahe Nature Reserve ☎ 0691 243 1024 🕐 Daily 8–5 ✋ Adult 65RMB, child (under 1.2m/4ft) Free

YANGSHUO

BUFFALO BAR

The music at this three-floor Australian-run bar switches from laid-back chill-out during the day to mostly rock at night, with a lot of new British, Australian and Canadian material. ✉ 50 Xianqian Jie ☎ 0773 881 3644 🕐 Summer daily 8am–2am, winter 8am–2am (sometimes closes earlier if quiet)

CHINACLIMB

Yangshuo is the new Mecca for rock climbing in Asia. The vertical cliffs of its soaring limestone karst pinnacles provide China's best climbing area, with hundreds of bolted routes suitable for all levels. A half-day or full-day introductory course includes equipment, instruction, transportation and snacks. ✉ The Lizard Lounge, 45 Xianqian Jie ☎ 0773 881 1033 🕐 Daily, year-round ✋ Half-day course 200–300RMB, full-day 400–500RMB. Price depends on the number of people in the party

CORMORANT FISHING

Hour-long boat tours take you to the Li and Yulong rivers at dusk to watch cormorant fishermen hunt fish with their trained birds from their bamboo rafts by lantern light. Touristy it may be now, but it makes a fascinating and highly photogenic excursion. ✉ 42 Xi Jie ☎ 0773 882 8061 🕐 Daily 7.30–8.30 ✋ 50RMB from Yangshuo travel agencies, including Uncle Sam's Travel

IMPRESSION LIU SANJIE

www.yxlsj.com Based on a local love story legend (and major 1961 film), this spectacular 70-minute outdoor light and music show takes place at the confluence of the Li and Yulong rivers, against a backdrop of karst peaks floodlit in red and blue.

A mix of traditional and modern, it has a cast of 600 fishermen and dancers on a vast floating set. The show was choreographed by Zhang Yimou, the film director behind the spectacular Beijing Games opening and closing ceremonies.

✉ Li River Mountain-Water Theatre ☎ 0773 881 1982 ⊙ Daily 7.45pm–9pm (not in windy or wet weather) 🎫 Standard seats (2,000) 188RMB, VIP seats (200) 238–320RMB, presidential seats (35 in private boxes, including snacks and drinks) 480–680RMB.

THE LIZARD LOUNGE

One of several rock climbers' hangouts in town (another is Karst Café across the road), this bar has a bouldering wall one-and-a-half floors high, popular at night when the drinks flow. Best not to try it after downing the house special cocktail, Neptune's Nemesis, which is *baijiu* spirit infused with sea creatures and costs 5RMB a shot.

✉ 45 Xianqian Jie ☎ 0773 881 1033 ⊙ Daily 8.30am–late, typically 2am

JINGXIUGE MASSAGE CENTRE

This massage establishment is on the ground floor of the Regency Hotel and uses certified masseuses. A range of treatments is offered, from head, neck and full-body massages to herbal foot massages and pedicures.

✉ Corner of Xijie and Pantau Lu ☎ 0773 881 7988 ⊙ Daily 10am–1am 🎫 Head massage (1 hour) 40RMB, Miao minority herbal medicine foot massage (1 hour) 50RMB, pedicure and foot massage (90 min) 60RMB, Chinese body and foot massage (2 hours) 70RMB

ZHONGDIAN

ANGSANA SPA

www.angsana.com

At this intimate spa on the first floor of a Tibetan lamasery-style boutique hotel, the facilities may not be extensive but the comfortable room and personable service make it feel like you are in a cocoon of serenity.

✉ Gyalthang Dzong Hotel ☎ 0887 822 3646 ⊙ Daily 3pm–11pm 🎫 The signature Angsana massage, using palm

FESTIVALS AND EVENTS

APRIL

WATER SPLASHING FESTIVAL

http://english.xsbnly.com

The Dai people celebrate their New Year with a three-day festival involving splashing water, cleansing away the old year to bring Buddha's blessing and good fortune for the new one. Xishuangbanna's capital Jinghong is a focal point for festivities. Dragon boat races and fireworks mark the first day, while the water splashing takes place on the final day. Everyone gets wet.

✉ Xishuangbanna and Dehong ⊙ Mid-Apr (dates vary)

MARCH FAIR

This traditional Bai festival is held for a week from the 15th day of the third lunar month, usually April. Its original religious significance, celebrating a visit by Buddhist goddess Guanyin, has been lost in the huge jamboree of market stalls, horse racing and other events held at the foot of Cangshan mountain, just outside the old town walls.

✉ Dali

MAY/JUNE

ZHONGDIAN HORSE FESTIVAL

This three-day fair, in May or June, sees Tibetan nomads gather to camp and picnic on pasture land just outside Zhongdian. The festivities include displays of Tibetan horsemanship skills as well as horse races.

✉ Zhongdian

strokes and thumb pressure on key pressure points with specially formulated oil, costs 564RMB (190 min)

BANYAN TREE

www.banyantree.com

This sanctuary is on the ground floor of an ornate old Tibetan family house forming part of the luxury Banyan Tree resort, alongside a rural village. Local Tibetan therapies incorporated

JUNE/JULY

DRAGON BOAT FESTIVAL

The Miao village of Shidong, northeast of Kaili, is the setting for three days of dragon boat racing between rival villages on the Qingshui River. The racers are egged on by excited supporters on both sides of the river, the Miao women resplendent in their traditional dress and silver ornamentations.

✉ Shidong Village, Guizhou

JULY/AUGUST

TORCH FESTIVAL

This three-day Yi minority celebration, held after the 24th day of the sixth lunar month, involves music, dancing and other events, including bullfights, and culminates with a parade of torches which are thrown onto a huge bonfire. One of the largest events is held at Shilin Stone Forest, near Kunming.

✉ Central Yunnan and Guizhou

OCTOBER

NANNING INTERNATIONAL FOLK SONG FESTIVAL

www.nnsong.com

Started in 1999, this huge festival generally takes place in October, which is a traditional time of folk song celebration for minority groups in Guangxi. The five-day event now attracts music and dance performers from across China and all over the world.

✉ Nanning, various locations

into treatments include Himalayan Gui Shui hot stone massage.

✉ Spa Ringha, Hong Po Village, Jiang Tang Town ☎ 0887 828 8822 ⊙ Daily 10–8 🎫 Ringha Relief blending yoga with Chinese Tui Na and Tibetan Gui Shui massages, an Indonesian spice wrap and green tea bath 1,280RMB (150 mins); Tibetan Tiptoe herbal foot soak, reflexology and paraffin foot treatment 900RMB (120 mins)

PRICES AND SYMBOLS

The restaurants are listed alphabetically. The prices are for a two-course lunch (L) and a three-course à la carte dinner (D) for one person, without drinks. The wine price is for the least expensive bottle. All the restaurants listed accept credit cards unless otherwise stated.

For a key to the symbols, ▷ 2.

DALI

BAMBOO CAFE

There's nothing fancy about this little place, but it is a friendly gem on what is known as Dali's second Foreigner Street.

The food is a combination of local, Western and Japanese dishes, and the prices are good. The banana, honey or chocolate pancakes will leave you drooling, as will the milkshakes.

✉ 71 Renmin Lu, Dali Old Town ☎ 0872 266 3518 ◷ Daily 8am–midnight ✋ L 25RMB, D 40RMB, Wine 90RMB

CAFÉ DE JACK

A Dali institution since 1989, Jack's was one of the first restaurants to open in the Old Town and is as popular as ever. The place is very laid back by day and lively with a good mix of music on the hi-fi—live acts are promised soon—at night. You can also get travel information, swap books and chill out in the roof garden. Steaks and pizzas are the menu mainstay, but local Bai hot pot is very good.

✉ 82 Boai Lu, Dali Old Town ☎ 0872 267 1572 ◷ Daily 8am–midnight ✋ L 40RMB, D 50RMB, Wine 40RMB

JIM'S TIBETAN CAFÉ

www.china-travel.nl

Tibetan goulash made with yak meat is the house special at this friendly little café in a boutique hotel. You might be advised to resist the temptation to wash it down with a slug of Jim's No. 1 Special, however. A home-produced firewater

concoction using ingredients including ginseng, you only need one or two to knock you out and 'sleep like a baby', as Jim says. But at 10RMB a shot, it's a cheap remedy for insomnia.

✉ 13 Yuxiu Lu ☎ 0872 267 7824 ◷ Daily 7.30am–10pm ✋ L 25RMB, D 30RMB, Wine 80RMB

MARLEY'S CAFÉ

This large café proclaims itself to be the best in Dali, and judging by the constant flow of diners it seems many would agree. Among local Bai specials are fish casserole with goat's cheese and fried chicken, while Chinese dishes include sweet and sour Dai-style beef.

✉ 105 Boai Lu, Dali Old Town ☎ 0872 267 6651 ◷ Daily 8.20am–11pm ✋ L 25RMB, D 40RMB, Wine 80RMB

REGENT HOTEL WESTERN FOOD RESTAURANT

Prices are surprisingly reasonable

at this, the Western restaurant of Dali's top hotel. The large room also serves as the breakfast hall, so it is somewhat functional.

The menu is also rather less than exciting but portions are good and the food tasty enough, and the bill won't give you a nasty shock. Try the tasty pan-fried sole with tomato sauce.

✉ Regent Hotel, Yuer Lu ☎ 0872 266 6666 ⏰ Daily 6.30am–1am 🍴 L 70RMB, D 100RMB, Wine 68RMB

SISTER'S CAFÉ

www.kikuya.it.fm

Celebrating its 10th anniversary in 2006, this intimate café is known for its Japanese food, but you can also get local Dali cuisine as well as Chinese and Western dishes. Notable dishes are the fried pork, chicken stew and braised local fish in soy sauce.

Sister's Café serves wide selection of alcoholic drinks includes papaya and must wines, served from jars containing the fermented fruits. But don't miss the excellent Dali green tea, a house special.

✉ 92 Boai Lu, Dali Old Town ☎ 0872 267 6151 ⏰ Daily 8.30am–11pm 🍴 L 20RMB, D 35RMB, Wine 60RMB

TIBETAN CAFE

The place that claims to have started Dali's café culture was first established in the early 1980s by a young Tibetan on Huguo Road, which became known as Foreigner Street for the international crowd drawn by it and other cafés that followed. The lodge moved to its current premises in 2005.

Both the food and ambience are strongly Tibetan with Western and Chinese influences. On the menu are items such as yak steak, lasagne, chocolate cake and chocolate brownies. There is occasional live music in the front patio area.

✉ 58 Renmin Lu, Dali Old Town

☎ 0872 266 4177 ⏰ Daily 7.30am–midnight 🍴 L 25–30RMB, D 30–50RMB, Wine 100RMB

YUNNAN CAFÉ

A popular restaurant with groups and individuals, it recently moved to its more spacious current location next to the Tibetan Lodge. Traditional local Bai food is served alongside Chinese and Western dishes. The house special is a very filling yak steak, which comes with potatoes and mushrooms and costs 28RMB. You can surf the internet for free while you wait for the food to come, but you won't have long with the quick service.

✉ 46 Renmin Lu, Dali Old Town ☎ 0872 2661898 ⏰ Daily 8am–midnight 🍴 L 30RMB, D 40–45RMB, Wine 88RMB

GUILIN

CATHAY CHINESE RESTAURANT

Among the tempting chef's specials in this classy restaurant are braised pork dumplings with curry sauce, sautéed sliced beef with glutinous rice cake, sautéed tea-smoked duck with bamboo shoot and steamed stuffed *luffa* (gourd) with minced pork and soy sauce. Stay long enough and you could try all of them.

✉ Sheraton Guilin, 15 Bin Jiang Lu ☎ 0773 282 5588 ⏰ Daily 6.30–10, 12–2.30, 5.30–10 🍴 L 88RMB, D 108RMB, Wine 148RMB

GREAT CONGEE OF GUILIN

This popular restaurant opposite Guilin's picturesque Fir Lake specializes in *congee*, the traditional rice porridge breakfast dish. Variations on the theme include pork with eggs, while spicy chicken and steamed local Mandarin fish are among main course options. It also has a great snack food bar, with chefs rustling up tasty take-out from a stall outside. It is a good place to sate your appetite after watching the lake light shows, as it stays open very late.

✉ 3 Shan Hu Bei Lu ☎ 0773 282 8172 ⏰ 24 hours 🍴 L 60RMB, D 90RMB, Wine 90RMB

JU FU LIN

This large restaurant in a central position on Guilin's main pedestrian street has fairly basic decor but there is plenty of seating outside to people-watch over your meal. Dishes include the excellent osmanthus chicken, using flowers of the trees for which the city is famous. Pork and eggplant (aubergine) is another good option.

✉ 10 Zhengyang Pedestrian Street ☎ 0773 282 9542 ⏰ Daily 10am–1am 🍴 L 30RMB, D 50RMB, Wine 50RMB

NENGREN VEGETARIAN RESTAURANT

This two-floor vegetarian restaurant inside the Nengren Temple (daily 7.30am–9pm, free) proclaims that it uses recipes hundreds of years old for its dishes. The food is beautifully presented and the menu has pictures. Among the dishes are vegetarian chicken leg made from flour, sweet corn and carrot, and vegetarian fish, which uses taro and flour and tastes sweet and salty. Local beer is just 3RMB a bottle.

✉ Nengren Temple, 6 Lijun Lu ☎ 0773 286 8845 ⏰ Daily 9.30–2, 4.30–8 🍴 L 40RMB, D 60RMB

YIYUAN FANDIAN

A small, family-run restaurant a short walk from Elephant Trunk Hill, the food here has a great reputation. Cuisine is Sichuan-style with dishes featuring plenty of chilies. Deep-fried chicken with chilies is a good option. Early-afternoon closing means you won't be able to linger over lunch.

✉ 17 Nanhuan Lu ☎ 0773 282 0470 ⏰ Daily 11.30–2, 5.20–10.30 🍴 L 45RMB, D 85RMB, Wine 70RMB

ZHENGYANG TANG CHEN

Soups are the highlight here, although there is no English menu. Take your pick from options such as turtle, green bean and rice, wild duck and watermelon or deer and pork. If you really want to go for it, try the famous Jiu Bao, comprising turtle, deer, snake and peach. It costs 390RMB, but is for six people, so you will need a little help from some friends. Alternatively, try the local Guilin rice noodle with shredded pork and vegetables. ✉ 8 Zhengyang Pedestrian Street ☎ 0773 285 8553 ⏰ Daily 9.30am–3am, later in summer ✋ L 30RMB, D 60RMB

JINGHONG
MEI MEI CAFÉ
The most popular café in Jinghong, especially with backpackers, this is also the top choice for good, inexpensive meals. The selection of burgers, pizzas and pancakes is augmented with local Dai food such as fried beef with lemongrass. The bar is a good place to meet people from all over the world and swap stories. Owner Orchid is a mine of information and can organize tours at reasonable prices. ✉ 5 Manting Lu ☎ 0691 216 1221 ⏰ Daily 8.30am–midnight ✋ L 30RMB, D 50RMB, Wine 60RMB

KUNMING
KUNMING LAO FANGZI
Lao Fangzi means old house, and the typical wooden Qing dynasty building dates back more than 150 years, although it has only been a restaurant since 2000. A central courtyard is surrounded by galleries with private dining rooms. There's an English menu, and you may get an explanation in perfect English by old Mr Zhou, who learned it from Americans stationed in Kunming in World War II. Food is pricy but superb, one of the best dishes being the steamed chicken hot pot with *tian ma* medicinal herbs. The fried honey bees and bamboo insects (worms) are surprisingly tasty. ✉ 18–19 Ji Xiang Xiang, Jing Xing Jie, Dongfeng Xi Lu ☎ 0871 364 4555 ⏰ Daily 11.30am–9pm ✋ L 50RMB, D 70RMB, Wine 66RMB

MAMA FU'S
Sandwiches made from freshly baked bread and delicious homemade ice cream using real cream and butter help this popular little restaurant stand out from the crowd. The menu also features the

typical rice, noodle and pasta options you would expect, as well as steaks. Sister noodle restaurant Fu Mama, a few doors along the road, is also worth trying. ✉ 219 Baita Lu, Kunming ☎ 0871 311 1015 ⏰ Daily 8.30am–11pm ✋ L 50RMB, D 50–80RMB, Wine 68RMB

SALVADOR'S COFFEE HOUSE
www.salvadors.cn
Home-made ice creams and bagels, Tex-Mex dishes with fresh salsa and espresso coffee using Yunnan coffee beans are augmented by a happy hour from 4 to 8pm when gin and tonic, vodka tonic or a screwdriver cost just 10RMB a time. Buy eight ice creams or coffees, get a card stamped and the ninth one is free. ✉ 76 Wenhua Xiang, Wenlin Jie ☎ 0871 536 3525 ⏰ Daily 9am–11.30pm ✋ Breakfast 25RMB, cappuccino 16RMB, Irish coffee 26RMB

WEI'S PIZZERIA
You'll find this friendly little restaurant in a small alley just behind the Greenland Hotel. Pizzas come straight from a wood-fired oven and the pasta is also freshly made. Beyond that there are other typical Western dishes plus Mexican and

Chinese food. Diners can also use the internet, exchange books and get travel information on Kunming and its environs. ✉ 27 Xiaodong Jie ☎ 0871 316 6189 ⏰ Daily 8am–1am ✋ L 30RMB, D 50RMB, Wine 80RMB

YUNNAN FLAVOR RESTAURANT
Shows by Yunnan minority groups are staged in this grand, two-level restaurant every lunchtime and evening. The evening shows, which start at 7pm, are very popular so getting a table then can be hard. Try arriving earlier, or when the show finishes just after 8.

The set menu feasts range from three dishes to 14 and are a good way to try regional delicacies. You can also try across the bridge noodles, a local dish in which noodles continue cooking in hot broth in the bowl. ✉ 102 Dongfeng Donglu ☎ 0871 317 8508 ⏰ Daily 10am–9pm ✋ L 40RMB, D 80RMB, Wine 65RMB

LIJIANG
ALGARVE SOL CAFÉ
Food at this peaceful café next to the gurgling Jade Dragon River in

Below *Relaxing in a bar in Dali's Old Town*

the old town of Shu He has a distinct Portuguese twist. The owner comes from Macau, so dishes include popular Maconese treats such as Portuguese baked chicken. You can also try a cup of the milky Portuguese *galao* coffee for 35RMB. The restaurant is much quieter than counterparts in Lijiang's old town but with visitor numbers increasing steadily it is bound to become busier.

✉ Yan Liu Lu, Shu He ☎ 0888 513 6602 🕐 Daily 10am–11pm 🍴 L 45RMB, D 60–80RMB, Wine 100RMB

MOSUO BAR

The lovely setting next to one of Lijiang's streams is relaxing at lunchtime, but don't expect a peaceful meal at night. After all, this is Lijiang's infamous Bar Street, and staff at this and other restaurants try to outdo each other with their continuous, high-decibel chants. The staff are charming Mosuo minority girls who wear traditional costume and speak little English. The menu is in delightful Chinglish but is understandable, and includes local Naxi and Mosuo dishes such as Naxi pork, hot pot and pig's face (only for the brave).

✉ Xinhua Jie, Lijiang Old Town 🕐 Daily 9am–1am 🍴 L 40RMB, D 50RMB, Wine 108RMB

SAKURA CAFÉ

www.sakura.yn.cn

Across the stream from the Mosuo Bar, this is one of Lijiang's most popular restaurants, open since 1997 and with other branches. Korean and Japanese food is served as well as Western and local fare. Among the Korean specials are *bi bim bab* (beef cooked in a clay pot with vegetables and rice) and *kim chee* (cabbage cooked with chili sauce in a pot for 24 hours). Naxi dishes include Naxi *baba* (cake bread) with honey or ham, which tends to be dry.

✉ 123 Cuiwen Duan, Xinhua Jie, Lijiang Old Town ☎ 0888 518 7619 🕐 Daily 8am–3am 🍴 L 50RMB, D (buffet) 28RMB, Wine 98RMB

NANNING

ZHONGSHAN ROAD SNACK MARKET, ZHONGSHAN LU

The food stalls of Zhongshan Road's night market are the place to head if you want to try some of Nanning's famous snacks. They include spicy, sour-tasting lemon duck, river snails, sweet *babao* rice pudding and *laoyou* rice noodles, Nanning's most popular snack which is also known as Old Friend Noodles and said to be good for you if you have a cold. Dog meat is also served, mainly in winter.

🕐 Daily 7pm–2am

TIGER LEAPING GORGE

SEAN'S SPRING GUESTHOUSE

Sean's special Walnut Garden walnut pie is the star item on the menu, using locally grown nuts. The guesthouse serves Chinese and Western breakfast, lunch and dinner, with decent-size portions to set you up for the gorge trail and satisfy those hungry after a hard day's hike. Chocolate cake, pancakes and apple pie are alternative desserts.

✉ Walnut Garden ☎ 0887 820 2222 🕐 Daily 7am–10pm 🍴 L 25RMB, D 35RMB, Wine 70RMB

YANGSHUO

BELLEVUE CAFÉ & RESTAURANT

Views to dine for are offered at this restaurant, thanks to its elevated position on the bank of the Li River. One of the best dishes is Li River fish. Braised in beer, a local special, it is very tasty with not too many bones. Sizzling pork with curried peanuts is another dish worth a try.

✉ Binjiang Lu ☎ 0773 882 0617 🕐 Daily 7.30–midnight 🍴 L 45RMB, D 65RMB, Wine 50RMB

CAFÉ CHINA

Another restaurant with great views, this has Yangshuo's only rooftop dining terrace, as well as a ground-floor restaurant, allowing diners to watch the sun set over the karst mountains. House specials are claypot duck and beef noodle claypot, with lasagne and pizza too. The cheesecake goes down easily,

as does the fresh ground coffee or a red or white wine.

✉ 34 Xi Jie ☎ 0773 882 7744 🕐 Daily 8am–midnight, food served until 11.30pm 🍴 L 30RMB, D 70RMB, Wine 90RMB

LE VOTRE FRENCH RESTAURANT

French cuisine features strongly at this French-owned eatery with a large outdoor dining area on Yangshuo's most famous street, although deep-fried snail is as much a local treat as a Gallic one. You might find it a touch spicier than the European version! Alternatively, sink your teeth into deep-fried snake or snake and chicken soup.

The restaurant also has its own micro-brewery. All-night revelers can revive their flagging spirits with a hearty set breakfast, good value at 26RMB.

✉ 79 Xi Jie ☎ 0773 882 8040 🕐 Daily 7.30am–1am 🍴 L 70RMB, D 70–100RMB, Wine 120RMB

ZHONGDIAN

METOK PEMA RESTAURANT

www.coloursofangsana.com/gyalthang
The simple, understated decor of the main restaurant in this Tibetan lamasery-style hotel creates a calm and relaxing tone. By contrast, the Tibetan, Chinese and Western food sets the taste buds racing. Dishes include steamed mountain river carp with ginger, leek, soy and sesame sliced garlic or Tibetan hot pot, which takes an hour to prepare after ordering.

✉ Gyalthang Dzong Hotel ☎ 0887 822 7610 🕐 Daily 7am–10pm 🍴 L 70RMB, D 85RMB, Wine 200RMB

YAK CAFÉ

Tibetan porridge and fried yak are on offer at this small, no-frills restaurant close to the old town square. Korean, Japanese and Western food is also served. They don't speak English, but they have an English menu. Large portions are served.

✉ Dawa Lu (Gucheng Lu Kou), Zhongdian ☎ 0887 828 8665 🕐 Daily 8am–11.30pm 🍴 L 25RMB, D 45RMB, Wine 78RMB

PRICES AND SYMBOLS

Prices are the starting price for a double room for one night, unless otherwise stated. Breakfast is included unless noted otherwise. All the hotels listed accept credit cards unless otherwise stated. Note that rates vary widely throughout the year.

For a key to the symbols, ▷ 2.

DALI
JIM'S TIBETAN HOTEL

www.china-travel.nl

This new boutique hotel just outside the old city walls is beautifully decorated in traditional Bai and Tibetan styles with handmade furniture and wooden floors. Rooms have heated bathrooms, phone, water heater, TV, wireless internet and electric blankets in winter. Two have attached kitchens. Best of all is the roof terrace, overlooking the old city and Cangshan mountain.

✉ 13 Yuxiu Lu ☎ 0872 267 7824
🖐 350–400RMB, breakfast 25RMB ⓘ 14

REGENT HOTEL

www.regent.hotel.com

Dali's top hotel doesn't disappoint in its quality or grandeur, although perhaps it is a touch out of place in this laid-back, casual tourist haunt. The huge marble lobby, dominated by a giant pendant chandelier, makes for a breathtaking if impersonal entrance. Thankfully the rooms—there are 500 including 100 suites in Chinese, Japanese and Western styles—are more snug and intimate, with high ceilings so they don't feel claustrophobic.

✉ Yuer Lu ☎ 0872 266 6666 🖐 572–880RMB ⓘ 500 🔲 🔳 🏊 Outdoor

GUILIN
LIJIANG WATERFALL HOTEL

www.waterfallguilin.com

If you see water cascading past your window at night, it isn't rain but the world's biggest artificial waterfall tumbling from the roof of this central five-star hotel. This is a nightly spectacle. Inside, the hotel offers nearly 650 rooms, including family rooms and a presidential suite, four restaurants and a teahouse, while the leisure facilities include a rooftop fitness room.

✉ 1 Shanhu Beilu ☎ 0773 282 2881 🖐 660–1,534RMB, excluding breakfast ⓘ 646 🔲 🔳 🏊

SHERATON GUILIN

www.sheraton.com/guilin

A luxurious hotel set by the Li River and close to Guilin's bustling center, it has an intimate and friendly feel despite its 430 rooms. The airy lobby lounge's large picture windows look out over a courtyard with a restful water garden complete with waterfall and pavilion. There is also an atrium coffee shop and a restaurant.

✉ 15 Bin Jiang Lu ☎ 0773 282 5588 🖐 700–1,245RMB, excluding breakfast ⓘ 430 🔲 🔳 🏊 Outdoor

JINGHONG
SANCHAHE TREEHOUSE LODGE

The accommodations may be basic, but who cares when you can look down on wild elephants drinking and bathing in a stream directly below your perch high in the trees of a rain forest park. Huts have fans, a Western-style toilet and basin and are linked by an elevated walkway. Access is via a cable car or a long forest walk from the main entrance, where there are another 57 air-conditioned bungalows.

✉ Wild Elephant Valley, Sanchahe Nature Reserve, Xishuangbanna ☎ 0691 243 0299 🖐 240–500RMB, although rooms can be booked in Jinghong from just 100RMB ⓘ 12 lodge huts plus 57 bungalows at the park entrance 🔄 Resort bungalows only

TAI GARDEN HOTEL

www.xsbn-taigardenhotel.com
Currently the only four-star hotel in Xishuangbanna, the Tai Garden makes a very comfortable base for exploring this area of Yunnan. The hotel has plenty of leisure facilities to enjoy. Perhaps its only minus is the fact that it is on the outskirts of the city.

✉ 61 Min Hang Lu ☎ 0691 212 3888
✋ 350–800RMB. Prices increase during the annual Water Splashing Festival, April 13–15 ⓘ 238 ⬛ ⬛ Outdoor

KUNMING

CAMELLIA HOTEL

www.kmcamelliahotel.com
A long-time backpackers' choice, the Camellia offers excellent value accommodations with spacious rooms as well as dorms in the hostel section. It houses the Laos consulate—the Burmese one has moved out—and a travel desk. Don't miss the collection of historic photographs of Yunnan in the courtyard garden's Cha Ma Bar. Transportation to the airport is 5RMB per person.

✉ 96 Dongfeng Donglu ☎ 0871 316 3000 ✋ 120–200RMB; dorm beds 30RMB ⓘ 192

SAKURA HOTEL

One of the best things about this high-rise four-star hotel is its location, next to a four-floor shopping complex and close to the city's core. It also has a wide choice of venues for dining and drinking, including the Western-theme Marco Polo on the second floor and Ban Thai on the 18th floor with great views.

✉ 29 Dongfeng Donglu ☎ 0871 316 5888
✋ 450–780RMB ⓘ 235 ⬛ ⬛ ⬛

LIJIANG

GRAND LIJIANG HOTEL

This modern three-star hotel, jointly owned and managed by a Thai company, enjoys a great position on the northern edge of the old town near the famous water wheels and alongside Jade River. The lobby bar is next to the river and offers lovely views. And if you need to work, the business center is open 24 hours.

✉ Xinyi Jie ☎ 0888 512 8888
✋ 360–480RMB ⓘ 117 ⬛

SENLONG HOTEL

This architectural mish-mash has a strange front that looks more like a warehouse but opens onto a grand, marble-columned lobby. Rooms are cozy, with some accommodations in Naxi-style mansions around a pool. The hotel is close to the old town. Some rooms come with their own computers.

✉ Minzhu Lu ☎ 0888 512 0666
✋ 500–1,380RMB ⓘ 242 ⬛

XIN FU SAN CUN

This new guesthouse set back from the main street of Shu He old town has simply furnished rooms with twin beds, a Western-style toilet plus shower and basin, and a water cooler.

✉ Si Fan Jie, Shu He ☎ 0888 517 4690
✋ 60–250RMB, breakfast 5–10RMB
ⓘ 13

LONGSHENG

LI QING GUESTHOUSE

This was the first guesthouse in the Zhuang village of Ping'an, high on the terraced rice slopes. It remains one of the largest and has a sundeck looking out over the terraces. The staff speaks English, and Zhuang, Chinese and Western food is served.

✉ Ping'an village, Dragon's Backbone Rice Terraces ☎ 0773 758 3048 ✋ 60–70RMB room with bathroom, 80–100RMB air-conditioned room with bathroom. Breakfast 20RMB ⓘ 28 ⬛ Some rooms

TIGER LEAPING GORGE

SEAN'S SPRING GUESTHOUSE

www.tigerleapinggorge.com
Sean's makes an ideal stop for hikers and a good base to explore the mountainous area around Walnut Garden. A homey place run by a local mountain guide, it provides comfortable beds in 8- to 12-bed dorms and double rooms, some with en-suite facilities. There is hot water, satellite TV, internet access and bicycle rental. A new martial arts training school opened in 2008.

✉ Walnut Garden ☎ 0887 820 2222
✋ 20RMB dorm bed, 30RMB in double room without bathroom, 200RMB en-suite double room ⓘ 76 beds in 4 dorms and 19 twin-share rooms

YANGSHUO

HONG FU PALACE HOTEL

www.yangshuohongfuhotel.com
A lovely little French-run Qing dynasty-style hotel offering a quiet escape despite its central setting. Its rooms are in two buildings, the main one being over 300 years old with slightly larger rooms. All are simply furnished.

✉ 79 Xi Jie ☎ 0773 882 9489
✋ 250–400RMB ⓘ 29 ⬛

OUTSIDE INN

www.yangshuo-outside.com
A group of old mud-brick farmhouses in a village 5km (3 miles) from Yangshuo have been renovated and turned into a comfortable and friendly little guesthouse by its Dutch owner. It has a teahouse and beer garden.

✉ Chaolong village ☎ 0773 881 7109
✋ 110–150RMB. Breakfast 25RMB ⓘ 18, some with private bathroom

ZHONGDIAN

BANYAN TREE RINGHA

www.banyantree.com
Perhaps nowhere else does the Shangri-La vision of author James Hilton come so close to reality as in the beautiful rural setting of this luxury retreat alongside a Tibetan village. The 32 villas are all traditional local Tibetan farmhouses, some over 50 years old, which were reconstructed on site. Some have handmade wooden hot tubs. A range of spa treatments will soothe aches after you return from one of the treks and tours offered from the resort.

✉ Hong Po Village, Jiang Tang Town
☎ 0887 828 8822 ✋ $400–$800 (prices quoted in US dollars) ⓘ 32

SOUTH CHINA AND THE YANGTZE

The world's third-longest river divides China fairly neatly into northern and southern halves. While the north is famously dry, the south receives buckets of rain, explaining the landscape's lush covering and subtropical feel, particularly in the southerly provinces.

The area known as Jiangnan (literally, 'South of the Yangtze') straddles the provinces of Jiangsu and Zhejiang, a region famed for its picturesque water towns, which combine arched bridges, burbling brooks and distinctive whitewashed houses. These two well-developed provinces border Shanghai, and have three of China's most attractive historic cities, Hangzhou, Suzhou and Nanjing.

Slightly inland are the poorer provinces of Hunan, Anhui, Jiangxi and Hubei. They make for tougher traveling but reward the adventurous with standout natural attractions. Hunan's jewel is Zhangjiajie, a deep canyon studded with thousands of natural quartzite pillars. Anhui draws tourists to craggy Huangshan (Yellow Mountain) while southern neighbor Jiangxi lays claim to Lushan, a holy place for Buddhists and an historic favourite among painters and poets. The Three Gorges Dam is located in Hubei province, at the mid-reaches of the Yangtze. The gorges may have been kneecapped slightly since the Yangtze was finally dammed in 2003 but this natural corridor of sheer rock and towering peaks still mesmerizes.

Guangdong province is the crucible of Cantonese culture and world-famous food. Its central sections are massively industrial—an indication of why the province is the richest in mainland China—but there are several charming locales worth seeking out on the fringes. Guangdong's western neighbor Fujian may also feel oddly familiar. Most of China's emigrants of the last half millennia came from this famously outward-looking region. For China's clearest skies, head to Hainan Island, China's most southerly province and newly anointed beach-holiday hot spot, complete with a new range of luxury five-star resorts.

CHANG JIANG (YANGTZE RIVER)

Cruising China's longest river, the Yangtze, is one of the great journeys. Known locally as Chang Jiang ('Long River'), a cruise down a stretch makes a leisurly break. The riverside scene is changing due to the effects of the great Three Gorges Dam. There are superb views and you get an unforgettable glimpse of life along the banks, now threatened by the mammoth Three Gorges Dam. You can tour this turbulent mirror of a nation's history and soul, spending two to four days on a river cruise.

DOWNSTREAM THROUGH CHINA'S HEARTLAND

Cruises begin at the Chaotianmen Dock in Chongqing (▷ 258). At Fengdu, you glide past Ghost Mountain and Stone Treasure Stronghold, with its pagoda; and the relocated Zhang Fei Temple. Farther on, the former imperial capitals Fengjie and Baidicheng are now submerged.

The famous Three Gorges—Qutangxia (Bellows Gorge), Wuxia (Witches Gorge), and Xiling (West Mountain Gorge)—follow each other in majestic succession, at least until the lake created by the Three Gorges Dam drowns them. Then comes the great Yangtze dam at Sandouping, which has changed forever the character of the river. The tour ends at Yichang, Yueyang, Wuhan (▷ 269), Nanjing (▷ 266–268), or even Shanghai (▷ 286–329).

DANING RIVER SIDE-TRIP

This side-trip from Wushan down the lesser three gorges is more exciting than the main river trip. You transfer from the river cruiser to a small, powerful boat able to negotiate the rock-studded rapids on the Daning tributary.

INFORMATION

www.hikeyangtze.com

✚ 419 N12–428 T10 🛈 CITS ✉ 8th Floor, Building A, Zourong Plaza, 151 Zourong Lu, Yuzhong District ☎ 023 6287 6537 🕔 Daily 9–5 🚇 Chongqing

TIP

» Make sure your ticket indisputably includes onboard meals and any side trips. Some tour operators pocket the money for these but 'neglect' to provide the necessary proof. Take emergency rations (and bottled water) with you in case you find the shipboard food unpalatable.

Opposite *Sunrise over the Yangtze River near Qutang Gorge*

Above *Sunset in the Xiling Gorge on the Yangtze River*

CHANGZHOU

Midway between Suzhou and Nanjing, Changzhou stands on the Grand Canal and the south bank of the Chang Jiang (Yangtze River). The old heart of town is threaded by small canals crossed by stone bridges, narrow streets and alleys. Among the interesting monuments in the 2,500-year-old city is the 7th-century Temple of Heavenly Tranquillity (Tianning Si), also known as the Red Plum Pavilion for its plum-hued lacquerwork decoration (daily 8–6).

Changzhou is famed for the ornamental handmade 'White Elephant' combs that have been produced here since 1925.

✚ 425 T10 🚇 Changzhou

CHONGQING

www.hikeyangtze.com

Fewer people would visit this large port at the confluence of the Yangtze and Jialing rivers were Chongqing not the starting point for Yangtze River cruises (▷ 257). This is icing on the cake for what is, due to its location and the commercial acumen of its inhabitants, a booming city. The heart of town occupies a strikingly hilly peninsula in the shape of an inverted 'S' between the two rivers, which you can cross by way of dramatic cable-car rides.

There are places of interest to see in and around Chongqing. The city's highest point, the park (daily 6am–10pm) on Pipashan (Loquat Hill), offers tolerably fresh air and a fine view over the city. On Renmin Lu is the Three Gorges Museum (daily 8.30–5), which has mementos of the old days in Chongqing, along with dinosaur skeletons.

✚ 419 M12 🛈 CITS ✉ 8th Floor, Building A, Zourong Plaza, 151 Zourong Lu, Yuzhong District ☎ 023 6287 6537 🕓 Daily 9–5 🚇 Chongqing

DAZU

Some 100km (62 miles) northwest of burgeoning Chongqing (▷ left), Dazu is famed for the cliffside stone carvings in the area around the town. These are in two main locations and about 40 subsidiary ones. Those at Beishan (daily 8–5), 2km (1 mile) north of Dazu, date from 892 to the mid-12th century, and form an astonishing array of 264 niches with 10,000 figures. These include Buddhist ascetics, sages and divines, and everyday scenes from the Tang dynasty.

The carvings at Baodingshan (daily 8–5), 16km (10 miles) northeast of Dazu, are in clusters and were made between 1179 and 1249 under the supervision of the monk Zhao Zhifeng, who is depicted at the center of a Wheel of Life in one niche.

✚ 419 M12 🚇 Chongqing

DINGSHU

Kilns in Dingshu, on the less-populated, more rural western shore of Tai Hu (▷ 271), are the source of the unglazed purple-sand Yixing pottery teaware, which has been prized since the beginning of China's recorded history. Shops and street stalls do a brisk trade in these small and artfully plain items, and you can visit some factories. The Ceramics Museum (daily 7.30–4.30) in Yixing, in a traditional pavilion, has some of the finest historical and modern pieces.

✚ 425 T11 🚇 Dingshan

Below *The Red Plum Pavilion in Changzhou is so-named because of the color of its lacquerwork decoration*

FENGHUANG CHENG

This ancient town, also known as Phoenix Town, near Hunan's border with Guizhou is billed as a great spot to sample the traditional way of life of China's Miao minority. With tourism increasingly making its mark, Fenghuang is best seen as a remote equivalent to the popular rural tourist towns of Lijiang and Yangshuo. With traditional stilted dwellings that rise like mist from the emerald-green Tuojiang River, it's as photogenic a place as anywhere in the country. The huge Rainbow Bridge marks the center of town while a network of pretty alleys radiates outward, filled with shops, cafés and restaurants. The local specialist handicrafts include hand-made silver jewelry and tie-dyed, printed or batik cloths. Fenghuang is worth a day or two of any travelers' time but it's not particularly easy to get to.

✚ 419 P13 ✉ Near Jishou, Hunan;
✖ Nearest airport is Zhangjiajie HJishou, then 90-minute bus ride to Fenghuang.

GUANGZHOU (CANTON)
▷ 260–263

HAINAN DAO

A subtropical island province, Hainan is not quite an island paradise, though the south coast's golden sand beaches fringed by palm trees on one side and a warm azure sea on the other go far toward making it seem so. But the island is coming from a backward state economically, and its forested interior has suffered from misguided 'development.' Hainan is best reached by flying to Haikou, the provincial capital, or by a train from Guangzhou that crosses the Qiongzhou Straits aboard a ferry. Coastal tourism is expanding fast. Sanya on the south coast is the focus, with Dadonghai and Yalong Bay beaches drawing the crowds. Off the resort and pearling port of Xincun is Nanwan Monkey Island (it's a peninsula), a reserve for Guangxi macaque monkeys (daily 9–5).

✚ 428 P16–P17 ▣ Haikou

Above *Traditional lantern-maker at work using authentic materials*

HANGZHOU
▷ 264–265

HUANGSHAN

www.huangshantour.com
You might think you've stepped into a beautiful Ming-dynasty painting at Huangshan (Yellow Mountain), which is actually a range rather than a single peak.

Considered to be China's most beautiful mountain, it has craggy granite pinnacles clothed in pine trees and, usually, veiled by cloud. Tour groups swarm in to marvel at the mountain. Several summits are higher than 1,800m (5,900ft) and hiking among them can be strenuous. The hot springs near Purple Cloud Peak make a relaxing curative.

South of Huangshan, around Yixian, is a cluster of old villages—Xidi, Hongcun and Nanping—filled with well-preserved Ming-dynasty houses.

✚ 425 S11 ▣ China International Travel Service, 1 Binjiang Xilu, tel 0559 254 2110
▣ Huangshan

LUSHAN

Lushan is known as 'little Switzerland' in the heart of China. Permeated with cool, tangy air, this beauty spot drew wealthy Europeans during the 19th century and, later, Chiang Kaishek and Mao Zedong. The mountain's highest peak reaches 1,474m (4,835ft) above Poyang Lake, China's largest freshwater lake (during the summer rainy season) and an important nature reserve for Siberian, white-naped and hooded cranes. At a height of 1,200m (3,936ft), the spa town of Guling has many European-style villas.

Lushan is busy in summer as visitors head upward to escape the heat of the Yangtze plain. You won't be alone from when the azaleas blossom in spring until the first winter chills. To escape the crowds go beyond the main beauty spots, such as the Flower Path and Small Heavenly Lake, and strike out along lesser mountain paths.

✚ 424 R12 ▣ Jiujiang

SOUTH CHINA AND THE YANGTZE • SIGHTS

GUANGZHOU (CANTON)

INTRODUCTION

Guangzhou (Canton), the capital of subtropical Guangdong province, has a driving commercial energy and lively nightlife but it requires plenty of stamina to get around on foot—with the exceptions of Shamian Island, a few places where notable sights are clustered together, and inside the city's parks. The ever-expanding metro system does a good job of moving people around speedily through the heart of town and to some points beyond, but since the trains travel underground you don't get to see much. Plentiful and cheap buses and trolleybuses cover a complex network of several hundred routes that's not easy to figure out; lines that follow the main thoroughfares are the easiest to use. Taxis and motorcycle taxis are another option.

Historical evidence places Guangzhou's origins in the 9th century BC. Not until the Tang dynasty (618–907AD), however, did the city begin to blossom through trade with the East and the Arabs; the latter contacts bequeathed the city its mosques. Portuguese traders arrived in the 15th century, starting a European fascination with all things Chinese that would continue for centuries. The British and French, too, came to trade, and forced opium on the Chinese to finance it. Chinese resistance to this 'foreign mud' triggered a series of 19th-century Opium Wars that China lost, thereby forcing open Canton and other treaty ports. Guangzhou was a focal point of early 20th-century Nationalist revolts against China's Qing dynasty rulers.

WHAT TO SEE

SIX BANYAN TREE TEMPLE

Invariably busy and often resounding to the chanting of its monks, the Zen (Chan) Buddhist temple, Liurong Si, dates from the 6th century, though little survives from that time. Its most prominent structure is the graceful octagonal Flowery Pagoda, built in 1097. It stood 57m (189ft) tall and the nine tiers visible from the outside actually contain 17 interior floors. A bronze column at the top contains 1,000 Buddha images. From the top, too, you get a panoramic view over the city. The temple's name comes from the Song dynasty poet Su Shi (or Su Dongpo), who visited in 1100 and was captivated by the temple's banyan trees. He composed the inscription 'Liu Rong' (Six Banyan Trees), which is carved on a tablet at the temple entrance.

Liurong Si was associated with the Sixth Patriarch of Zen, Hui Neng (638–713), who was born in Guangzhou. A bronze statue (989) of the sage stands in the Hall of the Sixth Patriarch. In the Grand Hall are three colossal bronze Buddha statues cast in 1663.

✉ Liurong Lu ◷ Daily 9–5.30 ✋ 15RMB

TOMB OF THE KING OF SOUTHERN YUE

Discovered in 1983, the Nanyuewang Hanwu is the mausoleum of Wen Di, or Zhao Mo, the second king of the Southern Yue Kingdom during the Western Han dynasty (206BC–AD220). It contained sensational objects, including the king's burial costume, made from hundreds of small jade platelets. The on-site museum houses this and around 1,000 other items recovered from the tomb, which was built into a hillside 2,000 years ago; it stands just west of Yuexiu Park (▷ 263). There are swords, a chariot, jade ornaments, gold seals, jewelry and more—and the remains of servants and concubines who went into the afterlife with their ruler. Just west of here, on Liuha Lu, are the lakes and gardens of Liuhua Park (daily 10–6).

✉ Jiefang Bei Lu ☎ 020 3618 2920 ◷ Daily 9–5.30 ✋ Adult 12RMB, child (under 1.1m/3.6ft) free

INFORMATION

www.citsgd.com.cn
✚ 429 Q15 ℹ Guangzhou Tourist Information Center ✉ Yitai Square, 986 Jiefang Beilu ☎ 020 8335 2856 ◷ Daily 9–6 🚉 Guangzhou Huoche Zhan (Central Station); Guangzhou Dong Zhan (East Station)

Left *The Flowery Pagoda at Six Banyan Tree Temple*

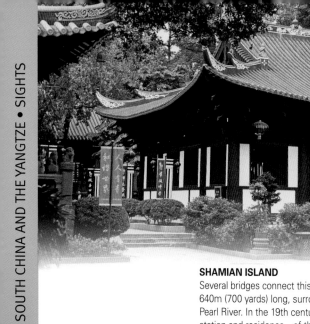

SHAMIAN ISLAND

Several bridges connect this small island, just 300m (325 yards) wide and 640m (700 yards) long, surrounded by a canal and the muddy waters of the Pearl River. In the 19th century, Shamian became a 'concession'—a trading station and residence—of the British and French, having been secured by them as part of the booty of the Opium Wars. The city has maintained the grand 19th- and early 20th-century colonial villas, banks, trading houses, churches and other period buildings, though they are mostly occupied by businesses and apartments now. The island is a pleasant place for a stroll, along streets shaded by banyan trees, through Shamian Park, and along Pearl River waterfront.
✉ South of Liu'ersan Lu

SUN YAT-SEN MEMORIAL HALL

Set in an ornamental garden that is a southern annex to Yuexiu Park (▷ below), the monumental Sun Zhongshan Jinian Tang is dedicated to the revolutionary hero Sun (1866–1925), who lived and studied for a time in Guangzhou. Words of wisdom from the revered statesman, the first president of the Republic of China, are inscribed on large urns at the entrance and there's a bronze sculpture of the great man. The extensive and ornate hall, with its blue-tiled roof, dates from 1931 and was built in a traditional Chinese architectural style. It is now used as a cultural center and as a performance venue for traditional Chinese music, theater, opera and dance.
✉ Dongfeng Zhong Lu 🕐 Daily 8.30–6 ✋ 10RMB

Above *The Bright Filial Piety Temple was founded in the 5th century*
Below *People walking through Yuexiu Park*

YUEXIU PARK

Guangzhou's largest park covers 86ha (213 acres) with open green space speckled with monuments. You can rent rowboats to cruise Beixiu Lake. In the middle of the park is the red Zhenhai Tower (1380), 28m (92ft) high, the only surviving part of the city wall. It houses the Guangzhou Museum, which covers Guangzhou's history. Just west of here is the famous Five Goats Sculpture, an emblem of the city that honors five goats who bore gods bringing gifts of rice. A nearby monument to Sun Yat-sen takes the form of an inscribed granite obelisk.

Across Jiefang Bei Lu are the pavilions, pools and bamboo groves of the Orchid Garden, built on the site of a Muslim cemetery. The best time to visit is February, when more than 10,000 orchids are in bloom, but it's delightful at any time. Here, too, is the supposed tomb of Abu Waqqas, an uncle of the Prophet Muhammad.
✉ Jiefang Bei Lu (other entrances around the park) 🕐 Daily 6am–9pm ✋ 5RMB

MORE TO SEE

BRIGHT FILIAL PIETY TEMPLE
Founded in the 5th century AD on the site of a royal palace, the Buddhist temple contains a hair relic said to be from the Sixth Patriarch of Zen, Hui Neng. Most of the carefully tended structures among the temple gardens were built in the 19th century, but a pair of pagodas date from the 10th.
✉ Guangxiao Lu ⏰ Daily 6.30–5.30 🖐 10RMB

CHEN FAMILY TEMPLE
Built during the 1890s in the traditional Guangdong architectural style, this was a memorial hall and Confucian cultural foundation for members of the Chen (Chan in Cantonese) clan. The complex, at the heart of which is the memorial tower, is rich in carvings and porcelain and today contains the Guangdong Folk Arts and Crafts Museum.
✉ Zhongshan Qilu ☎ 020 8181 4559 ⏰ Daily 8.30–5.30 🖐 10RMB

GUANGDONG PROVINCIAL MUSEUM
Part of the museum, in the old Zhongshan University building, is given over to the life of Lu Xun (1881–1936), a professor who helped modernize Chinese intellectual life. The main part is in a modern building and covers the province's natural history, jade and Chaozhu wood carvings, Shiwan ceramics from Foshan, calligraphy, and more. A new state-of-the-art museum is being built in the Pearl River New City, Tianhe District and is expected to open by 2010.
✉ Wenming Lu ☎ 020 8383 2195 ⏰ Tue–Sun 9–5 🖐 15RMB

MAUSOLEUM OF THE 72 MARTYRS
This 1918 mausoleum, surrounded by the tranquil acres of Huanghuagang Park in the northeast of Guangzhou, honors those killed in a 1911 revolt led by Dr Sun Yat-sen aimed at overthrowing the autocratic Qing dynasty. It's a somewhat strange-looking structure, built in a variety of styles, and funded by contributions from Chinese people around the world.
✉ Xianlie Lu ⏰ Daily 6.30–8.30 🖐 8RMB

Below *A colonial building on Shamian Island*

HANGZHOU

INFORMATION
➕ 425 T11 ℹ Hangzhou Tourist
Information ✉ Huangzhou Railway
Station ☎ 0571 8782 5755 🕐 Daily
8.30–9 🚇 Hangzhou

INTRODUCTION

Hangzhou's focal point for visitors is the magnificent West Lake (Xi Hu). It begins just 2km (1 mile) west of the railway station, an easily walkable distance. Around the lake, a combination of walking (or bicycling if your hotel rents out decent bicycles) and boating makes a pleasant way to get around. Beyond the lake, using city buses and taxis makes more sense.

Founded during the Sui dynasty in the 6th century AD at the southern terminus of the Grand Canal, Hangzhou waited more than 600 years for its moment of glory, when it became the Southern Song dynasty's capital. Marco Polo called it the 'City of Heaven' and the best city in the world, filled with rich palaces and fine baths. Much of this legacy was lost during the 19th-century Taiping Rebellion, but Hangzhou has since become one of China's most important tourist destinations.

WHAT TO SEE

TEMPLE OF SPIRITUAL RETREAT

The Buddhist Lingyin Si temple, with origins dating back to 326AD, stands in extensive grounds above the western shore of West Lake. It and the surrounding hills have become a popular place of escape as much as a place of worship. Yet Lingyin Si was meritorious enough to be saved from destruction during the Cultural Revolution by Prime Minister Zhou Enlai. Its highlight is a gold-filigreed camphor-wood statue of the Buddha, in the Great Hall.
One of the hills is called Feilaifeng (Peak that Flew from Afar), inscribed with hundreds of Buddhist reliefs carved by the monks over the centuries. Look out especially for the kindly Laughing Buddha dating from around 1000.
✉ Lingyin Lu 🕐 Daily 7–6 💰 Grounds 35RMB, plus temple 30RMB

WEST LAKE (XI HU)

Should you be fortunate enough to visit when the usual throngs of visitors are absent, you may get some idea why Chinese emperors considered West Lake one of their brightest jewels. Even if you must share with many other admirers, experiencing it should still be memorable. An inlet of Hangzhou Bay until its mouth silted over, the freshwater lake is 14km (9 miles) around, with hills, parks, pagodas and pavilions on three sides and downtown Hangzhou on the fourth.

Above *View of the West Lake from the Leifeng Pagoda*

A road follows the shore, and tree-lined causeways run through the northern and western reaches, but the best way to see the lake is by boat. Vessels range from small ferries to rowboats, which can be boarded or rented at several points around the lake. The most visited spots are Island of Small Seas, a cluster of dike-rimmed lotus ponds near the middle of the lake, and three nearby miniature pagodas in the water that form Three Pools Mirroring the Moon. On Solitary Hill Island, off the north shore, are the historical and art collections of the Zhejiang Provincial Museum (Tue–Sun 9–4.30, Mon 12.30–4.30).

TEMPLE AND TOMB OF GENERAL YUE FEI

Visitors come in large numbers to the temple (Yue Fei Miao) to pay their respects to the patriotic hero for whom it was named. Yue Fei was a loyal and successful military commander during the Southern Song dynasty in the 12th century, who was executed on false treason charges. A future emperor tried to make amends, setting up Yue Fei's remains on the north shore of West Lake in a handsome tomb, which in 1221 was encompassed by a temple. The tomb is reached via a small bridge and a memorial way lined with inscriptions and sculptures, and is accompanied by low-status iron statues of the general's persecutors.

✉ Beishan Lu 🕐 Daily 7–6 ✋ 25RMB

LONGJING

This hill village at the heart of Hangzhou's tea-growing district is the source of the much-esteemed Longjing Dragon Well tea. You can get the inside story on the Chinese tea ceremony and view antique teapots and crockery at the Chinese Tea Museum (daily 8–5).

✉ Longjing Lu, 3km (1.8 miles) southwest of West Lake

MORE TO SEE

SIX HARMONIES PAGODA

You get a fine view over the Qiantang River from the tower of this 10th-century hilltop pagoda (since rebuilt several times) on the river's north bank. Dedicated to the six Buddhist precepts and raised in an effort to tame the unruly river's tides, it stands some 60m (200ft) high and has more than 100 bells.

✉ Yuelin Shan 🕐 Daily 7–6 ✋ 20RMB

Left *Fat-bellied Buddha at the Temple of Spiritual Retreat*
Below *Six Harmonies Pagoda*

INTRODUCTION

Nanjing lies on the Yangtze River 270km (167 miles) northwest of Shanghai. It is large and its attractions are well spread out around busy streets, so walking between them is not much fun for the most part. Exceptions are Purple and Gold Mountain, around the shore of Xuanwu Lake, and the warren of streets around the Fuzi Miao temple. Inexpensive buses are a good alternative, and working out the principal routes is not that difficult. Taxis are generally the quickest way to get around, and motorcycle taxis are available for youthful or adventurous spirits.

    Nanjing (Southern Capital) got its first taste of life as a capital city in AD229, when it became the seat of the Kingdom of Wu. It has been the capital of some short-lived state, emperor, usurper or rebel general off and on ever since. Even its status as a fully fledged capital of China, under the first Ming dynasty emperor Zhu Yuanzhang (or Hongwu) didn't last long; his successor moved the capital to Beijing, as did the 20th-century Communists after they had defeated the Nationalists.

WHAT TO SEE

CONFUCIAN TEMPLE

Confucianism in practise seems to have been as much about behaving well as anything else. So it is interesting to find the atmospheric warren of lanes and canalsides around the Fuzi Miao temple filled with parlors, cafes and boutiques, where people are behaving, if not exactly badly, then not always with a stiff sense of due decorum. The temple originated in the 11th century but was rebuilt in the 1980s, which no doubt accounts for its pristine look and kitsch decoration. To maintain appearances, part of the complex has been given over to a museum of the imperial civil service and the examinations given to aspiring bureaucrats.

✉ Jiankang Lu 🕐 Daily 8am–9pm 🎫 20RMB

NANJING MUSEUM

At the eastern end of the Old Town, Nanjing Museum (Nanjing Bowuguan) is a modern structure built in a traditional style. It is large enough to do justice to Nanjing's long and eventful history, along with its art, folklore and handicrafts.

INFORMATION

✚ 425 S10 🛈 China International Travel Service ✉ 202 Zhongshan North Road ☎ 025 8353 8546 🕐 Mon–Fri 8.30–5, Sat, Sun 9–4 🚇 Nanjing

Opposite *People walking up the steps to the Sun Yat-sen Mausoleum*
Above *Stone elephant statues line a path near the Ming Filial tomb*

Pride of place goes to a 1,800-year-old, Han-era jade burial suit, created by using silver thread to link squares of the semiprecious stone. Nanjing played an important role in Chinese astronomy (and astrology) and there are various antique observational instruments. Other pieces include model sailing ships, ceramics, bronze sculptures, brocades and lacquerware.

The museum is close to Longshan Gate (daily 8am–10pm), a combined entranceway and fortified redoubt in the rambling, 32km (20-mile) circuit of the Ming-era city wall, much of which is still standing.

✉ Longshan Donglu 321 ☎ 025 8480 2119 🕔 Daily 9–4.30 🖐 20RMB

ZIJINSHAN

Nanjing is said to be the hottest of China's 'three furnaces'. In summertime it's virtually a survival tactic to get up onto tree-shaded Zijinshan (Purple and Gold Mountain) on the city's northeast edge and luxuriate amid cool, scented air. Named for the hues of its rocks, the scenic mountain is home to some of the city's most notable attractions. Among them is the magnificent Sun Yat-sen Mausoleum (Apr–end Nov daily 6–7; Dec–end Mar daily 6–5.30). The tomb of the founder of republican China is an extravagant construction of white Fujian marble with a blue-tiled roof, standing at the head of a mammoth stairway. East of the mausoleum is a complex of structures built around the central Linggu Temple, a Buddhist foundation. There's also the originally 14th-century Beamless Hall and the 1929 Linggu Pagoda. West of the mausoleum is another monumental tomb, the Ming Filial Tomb (Apr–end Nov daily 6.30–6.30; Dec–end Mar daily 7–6), the final resting place of the former Buddhist monk turned despotic first emperor of the Ming dynasty, Zhu Yuanzhang (known as Hongwu). Near the top of Zijinshan is a working astronomical observatory.

MORE TO SEE
DRUM TOWER

Although hemmed in by frenetic traffic arteries, the restored 14th-century Ming-era tower retains an antique atmosphere inside. It housed the ceremonial drums used on official occasions. Across the way, on Zhongyang Lu, the contemporary Bell Pavilion now houses a teahouse and a bronze bell cast in 1388 that weighs 25 tons.

✉ Beijing Xilu 🕔 Daily 8.30–5.30 🖐 5RMB

XUANWU HU GONGYUAN (XUANWU LAKE PARK)

An easy-going break from the busy city streets can be had at this large park just outside the Ming walls. It is almost entirely occupied by a lake, with a flotilla of islets connected by causeways in the middle. The best way to tour it is by boat, and various small craft are available for rent.

✉ Longpan Lu and Zhongyang Lu 🕔 Daily 7am–9pm 🖐 20RMB

Left *A golden Buddha statue at Linggu Temple*
Right *Portals in the ruins of Zhonghua Men fortifications*

NANJING

▷ 266–268

NINGBO AND PUTUOSHAN

Ningbo, 140km (87 miles) southeast of Hangzhou, is one of China's booming coastal cities, building on its legacy as a 19th-century treaty port. Despite this, Ningbo's charms are modest: There's the 16th-century Tianyige private library (daily 8–5) and the restored Tianfeng Pagoda. The main reason for visiting the city is to take the boat to Putuoshan (Potala Mountain) island, a four-hour trip. Covering just 12.5sq km (8sq miles), Putuoshan has one of China's four sacred Buddhist peaks, also called Putuoshan (300m/985ft). The island is also home to a cluster of monasteries, pagodas and shrines. The small island has decent walking trails and beaches.

✚ Ningbo 425 T11 ✚ Putuoshan 425 U11
🚇 Ningbo

SHAOXING

After the hubbub in most Chinese cities, Shaoxing, off the beaten track 50km (31 miles) southeast of Hangzhou, might seem like a breath of (almost) fresh air. You can stroll or bicycle around canal-threaded residential districts lined with old-fashioned houses.

There's the museum (daily 8–5) in the childhood home of revolutionary philosopher and writer Lu Xun (1881–1936), and the Green Vine Study (daily 8.30–4.30), the home of the artist Xu Wei (1521–93). Shaoxing is noted for its yellow rice wine, which is produced at the modern Shaoxing County Winery outside the town.

✚ 425 T11 🚇 Shaoxing

SUZHOU

▷ 270

WUHAN

A busy Yangtze River port, Wuhan is an arrival point for cruises. The city has three sections—Hankou, Hanyang and Wuchang—separated by the Yangtze and Han rivers. Each

Above *The Yellow Crane Pavilion in Snake Hill Park, Wuhan*

was once an independent entity. Hankou was a treaty port from 1861, a base for merchants and consular officials. The remnants of its colonial-era heritage can be seen along waterfront Yanjiang Lu. Wuchang has the remarkable Yellow Crane Pavilion in Snake Hill Park. Built in AD223, and rebuilt in 1981, it has yellow tiled roofs with curved eaves. Hubei Provincial Museum (daily 9–5) contains items excavated from the lavish tomb of Marquis Yi, who died in 433BC.

✚ 424 R11 🚇 Hankou, Wuchang

WULINGYUAN SCENIC RESERVE

This UNESCO-listed national park in northwest Hunan has claims on top spot in China's list of geological oddities. Thousands of rock columns rise precipitously from a deep valley, each a gravity defying compression of slate decorated in patches of lush vegetation.

The park is divided into three sections, Zhangjiajie Forest Park in the south, Tianzi Mountain in the north and Suoxi Valley in the west. Though the park can get busy, hiking trails allow visitors to get away from the crowds. Stone staircases allow fitter visitors to climb to the peaks though there are mechanized alternatives. The Bailong Lift is cited in the *Guinness Book of World Records* as the largest outdoor elevator in the world, while there are also two spectacular cable cars and a shuttle bus. The hefty 248RMB ticket buys two days' entry to the park and use of the bus network.

✚ 419 P12 ✉ Entrance 30km (18 miles) north of Zhangjiajie city, Hunan ☎ 0744 571 2595 D24 hours 🚌 Regular bus service to park entrance from railway station
🚇 Zhangjiajie Station 💰 248 RMB, cable cars and lift cost around 50 RMB for a one-way trip ✈ Zhangjiajie airport

INFORMATION

🔡 425 T11 🅘 Suzhou Tourist Centre,
✉ North Bus Station, 29 Xihui Beilu
☎ 0512 6751 6376 🕔 Daily 9–6
🚇 Suzhou

TIPS

» Visiting Suzhou and missing the
gardens makes little sense, but if the
main ones are simply too crowded to
enjoy, there are others, like the Paired
Garden, which might not be so busy.
Then there is the canal district around the
southwestern Coiled Gate area, which is
worth going out of your way for.
» The Suzhou Museum (204 Dongbei Lu,
tel 0512 6757 5666, daily 9–5) has more
than 30,000 cultural relics—including
ancient archeological finds from across
the nation—and is seen as one of eastern
China's top museums.

Above *A pavilion at the Humble
Administrator's Garden*

SUZHOU

Suzhou is noted for its genteel gardens, canals and silk, and is a pleasant place
for walking and bicycling. It is at the heart of a heavily populated region with
good connections to other cities. Too good, you might well think, since its
Ming- and Qing-era ornamental gardens are often very crowded.

SUZHOU'S VERY SPECIAL GARDENS

Fewer than 100 of the original 200 or so gardens survive and only a dozen
can be visited (most open daily from 7.30 or 8 to 5.30) and they are behind
high walls, so you need to go inside. Most are quite small and their carefully
contrived miniature vistas of rocks, pools, islets, plants, flowers, screens,
causeways, bridges and pavilions, intended to be appreciated in serenity, are
often swamped by noisy tour groups. Yet beautiful they remain. Highlights
include the rock-encrusted Forest of Stone Lions Garden, at 23 Yuanlin Lu; the
large Humble Administrator's Garden, at 178 Dong Bei Jie; Lingering Garden, at
338 Liuyuan Lu, and its giant rock from Tai Hu (▷ 271); the placid views at tiny
Master of the Nets Garden, off Shiquan Jie; Blue Wave Pavilion Garden, at 3
Canglang Ting Jie, the oldest garden; and Harmony Garden, at 343 Renmin Lu.

TIGER HILL

It's an easy excursion from the city to this scenic park on a hill 5km (3 miles)
northwest of the city (Huqiushan, daily 8–5.30), with its curious mix of
kitsch theme-park attractions and venerable temple pavilions and pagodas.
Astonishingly, the hill is artificial—a burial mound for a ruler of the Kingdom of
Wu, who died in 494BC.

WUXI AND TAI HU

Unremarkable Wuxi, though it produces silk and the Huishan porcelain figurines dubbed 'fatties,' and has some attractive old houses along its stretch of the Grand Canal, is best viewed as a stepping stone to the scenic lake. Its great days as capital of the Wu Kingdom are 3,000 years in the past.

Rimmed by hills and speckled with fishing and tour boats, Lake Tai, at 2,350sq km (907sq miles), is one of China's largest freshwater lakes, but its depth is rarely more than 2m (6ft). The lakeside near Wuxi has two fine Chinese gardens. Wormy Garden (daily 6.30–6) dates from the 1930s and has a beautiful pavilion with a lake view. At its best during the spring blossom season, nearby Plum Garden (daily 6.30–6) was laid out in 1912. Boats depart from this area to islands, beauty spots and theme parks, such as Turtle Head Peninsula, around the lake.

✚ 425 T11 🚉 Wuxi

XIAMEN

An island connected to the mainland by a causeway, Xiamen is a busy seaport and a pleasant resort, having avoided the worst of the development-induced stresses that afflict other booming coastal cities. The extensive Wanshi Botanical Gardens (daily 6.30–6.30) in the south of Xiamen Town display a multihued array of tropical and subtropical flora. South of here is 1,000-year-old Nanputuo Si (daily 6–6), a Buddhist temple with a flamboyant style (and a decent vegetarian restaurant). European merchants set up trading concessions in Xiamen in the 1840s—they called the town Amoy. Most of the foreigners actually lived on the tiny island of Gulangyu, where their villas remain. Ferries offer a 10-minute crossing from Xiamen Town. Car-free and carefree, Gulangyu has a sandy beach on the west coast and a Piano Museum (daily 9–5).

✚ 427 S14 🛈 CITS 2F, Guangda Hotel, 708 Lianqian Xilu 🚉 Xiamen

YANGZHOU

Standing on the Da Yunhe (Grand Canal) north of the Yangtze River, the birthplace of former president Jiang Zemin is a city of canals, gardens and lakes, with a cultured past going back 2,500 years. The gardens (daily 8–6) are not as large as those of Suzhou (▷ 270), a fact that makes them seem all the more crowded on weekends and other busy times. Four gardens—Xuyuan, Xiyuan, Yechunyuan and Hongyuan—are in the area of Slender West Lake, a narrow lake in the west of town. Look out here for the much-photographed 18th-century Five Pavilion Bridge. North of the lake, the Temple of Great Brightness is popular with the Japanese, who paid for the pagoda dedicated to the monk Jian Zhen, who took his Buddhist teachings to Japan in the 8th century.

✚ 425 S10 🚉 Yangzhou

ZHAOQING

On the Xijiang River, 90km (56 miles) west of Guangzhou, Zhaoqing has an old quarter surrounded by the original city walls built during the Song dynasty (960–1279), and the Plum Monastery (daily 7–6) in the west of town.

The Seven Star Crags—limestone peaks emerging from the watery setting of Qixing Yan Park (daily 7–6), north of Star Lake—form a modest substitute for the spectacular riverside scenery at Guilin (▷ 230). East of Zhaoqing, the forested Dinghu Shan mountains are a beautiful national park where 17,000 species of plants have been identified. A through-train departs daily for Hong Kong (4 hours).

✚ 429 Q15 🚉 Zhaoqing

Below *Xiamen (known as Amoy to Westerners) with Gulang Island in the foreground, on the coast of Fujian Province*

GUANGZHOU CENTRAL DISTRICT

Staying close to the Pearl River, this walk takes in the colonial-era district of Shamian Island before diverting through Guangzhou's most famous street market and an atmospheric part of the old city. It returns to the river at a point with memorable views before crossing back to Shamian Island for the final leg.

THE WALK
Distance: 3.5km (2 miles)
Allow: 2 hours
Start/end: White Swan Hotel, Shamian Island

HOW TO GET THERE
To get to the White Swan Hotel (▷ 284), walk or take a taxi from Huangsha metro station.

★ Shamian Island (▷ 262) is a piece of colonial-era Europe at the heart of modern Guangzhou. Some of the island's villas have been restored; others have been moldering for half a century or more but, together with the setting, they make this one of the most distinctive and interesting quarters of the booming city. On a hot and humid day you might well be reluctant to leave the cool confines of the White Swan. From the hotel's waterside location you have a fantastic view up and down the Pearl River and across the water

to 'Bar Street,' famous for its smart watering holes that really start to hum after dark. Turn left outside the hotel and walk a short distance along Shamian Nanjie, past the Qing-era residence of a salt trade official at No 58., and the adjacent modern customs building (the tree outside is 270 years old).

❶ Christ Church (1865), a Church of England (Anglican) church, stands on the west corner of Shamian Nanjie and Shamian Wujie. It's a functioning church and holds services in both English and Chinese. Just beyond this is the US consulate. For security reasons, Shamian Nanjie is blocked off at this point and you can go no farther.

Return to Shamian Wujie at the side of Christ Church, through a small park or garden, to Shamian Dajie, where you turn right on the far side of the street.

❷ Shamian Dajie has several interesting restored buildings. Among them are the Art 64 arts and crafts shop at No. 64; the former British Canton Club, in a restored villa with a pair of British-style sculpted lions in the garden, at No. 60; and the Taoran Teahouse (▷ 277) at No. 58. The teahouse, which is also a school for 'tea ladies,' is a treasure trove of antique and craft tea sets, teapots, crockery, silverware, calligraphy and painting, and antique musical instruments. It's also a shop, so many of the contents are for sale, and you can taste a variety of Chinese teas. Next door, at No. 56, the former Japanese Yokohama Specie Bank (1893), which also housed the old American Consulate, is fronted by neoclassical columns.

Go left into Shamian Sijie, past various souvenir shops and a wing of the Victory Hotel—famous for its dim sum. Turn right on Shamian Beijie, which faces the northern arm of the Pearl River. It's worth stopping by the Shamian Cultural Centre, at No. 61, which houses the Gallery of Original Chinese Contemporary Art, for a look at the works inside. Continue to the next bridge, Xi Qiao (West Bridge), and cross over. You're now on busy Liu'ersan Lu, which you can cross by the nearby footbridge.

❸ The Qingping Market begins at the foot of this bridge and covers several streets around Qingping Lu, on the north side of Liu'ersan Lu. It's easy to get disoriented amid this atmospheric medley of stalls selling dried herbs and spices; live animals including turtles, scorpions, snakes and fish for the cookpot; flowers and many other products.

If you take the south–north street you came in on (Qingping Lu) as your anchor, and return to it when you wander off into side streets, you shouldn't get lost, and in any case the market actually covers a fairly small area. You'll emerge at the north end of the market, on the busy shopping street Dishifu Lu, beside the Holiday Inn Hotel. Just beyond the crossroads with Xiajiu Lu is the vast and famous Guangzhou Jiujia restaurant (▷ 281), a temple of dim sum.

Take the connecting streets Shibafu Beilu and Shibafu Nanlu south from the hotel. These take you through a characteristic part of the old town. You can explore some of the side alleys, returning always to the main street. This will bring you out once again on Liu'ersan Lu. Go left (east).

❹ Cultural Park is not Guangzhou's finest park but it is a tree-shaded environment where children play on fairground attractions and visit a slightly ragged aquarium.

Come out again on Liu'ersan Lu and cross over to the large Nanfang Department Store. Take the stairs down to the right of the store. Go left (east) to the junction of Liu'ersan Lu and the main north–south road, Renmin Nanlu. Cross over to the south side.

❺ Xidi Wharf, on the north shore of the Pearl River, is a great place for a waterfront stroll westwards past the tour-boat docks (you might want to check out the departure times for an evening tour). The fine river views are part of the attraction.

Continue under the Renmin road bridge and cross over by the bridge ahead of you, back to Shamian Island.

❻ This part of Shamian Island is dominated by Shamian Park, a pleasant way to return to the White Swan Hotel.

WHEN TO GO

Guangzhou is very busy, and during summer it is hot and humid too. So doing this walk in the spring or autumn would be the best time (winter can be chilly at times). The walk begins and ends on tranquil Shamian Island, and takes in a street market, a park and a riverside promenade. Only in the central segment does it traverse a section that is defined by heavy traffic.

PLACES TO VISIT
CHRIST CHURCH
✉ Shamian Nanjie 🕐 Daily 9–6 (hours vary)

QINGPING MARKET
✉ Qingping Lu 🕐 Daily 8am–10pm (hours vary)

CULTURAL PARK
✉ Liu'ershan Lu 🕐 Daily 6am–9pm
✋ 3RMB

TOURIST INFORMATION
✉ Guangzhou Tourist Information Centre Yitai Square, 986 Jiefang Beilu
☎ 020 8666 2325 🕐 Daily 9–6

WHERE TO EAT
GUANGZHOU JIUJIA
✉ 2 Wenchang Nanlu ☎ 020 8138 0388
🕐 Daily 7am–midnight

Opposite *Shopping on Xiajiu Lu*
Left *An attractive park on Shamian Island*

THE GARDENS OF SUZHOU

This walk is an introduction to three of Suzhou's glories: gardens, silk and pagodas. Three of the city's antique ornamental gardens, conceived rather as works of landscape art than as faithful representations of nature, are the main focus of the tour.

THE WALK

Distance: 5.5km (3.5 miles)
Allow: 2 hours (not including visits. Note, it may be best to actually visit no more than three or four of the six places featured, as you will need at least an hour for each one)
Start: Suzhou Silk Museum, on Renmin Lu
End: Harmony Garden, on Renmin Lu

HOW TO GET THERE

From Suzhou Railway Station in the north of the city you reach the first stop on the itinerary by walking east (to your left, with your back to the station) about 300m (330 yards) on Chezhan Lu to its junction with the major north–south street Renmin Lu, going right to cross over the Outer Moat on the Pingmen Bridge (note the tour-boat dock off to your right), then continuing south for about 600m (660 yards) down the west side of Renmin Lu to No. 2001.

★ The Suzhou Silk Museum focuses on the city's long tradition of silk manufacture and embroidery. You can see silkworms chewing mulberry leaves and threading silken cocoons before they pupate into moths, along with weaving machines, and fine embroidered damasks and brocades.

Cross over to the east side of Renmin Lu.

❶ North Temple Pagoda (Beisi Ta) is 76m (250ft) high, dates from 1582 in its current form, and has nine surviving floors (out of 11). It is set in its own fair-sized garden. A wooden interior stairway leads to a point that gives a fine view of the city. Enjoy a cup of Suzhou's own Biluochun tea at the teahouse here.

Take the next street south, Xibei Jie, and go east (left). This street becomes Dongbei Jie after it crosses the junction with Qinmen Lu and Lindun Lu. Just beyond this intersection is Suzhou Museum (Suzhou Bowuguan), housed in a mansion where Li Xiucheng, the leader of the Taiping rebellion, lived in 1860. Pass by the uninteresting museum to No. 178.

❷ The Humble Administrator's Garden is not really so humble since it is both Suzhou's largest garden, covering 4ha (10 acres) and is considered one of the finest. From the 16th century onward, different designers made use of this extensive space to achieve varied effects. Eaved pavilions, rocks, weeping willows, and crooked bridges connecting islands set in lotus ponds are characteristic of the western half, which contains a teahouse somewhat in the shape of a boat, while the eastern half is more open.

Backtrack a short way on Dongbei Jie before crossing the canal and

Opposite A view from the Orange Pavilion at the Humble Administrator's Garden

going south on Yuanlin Lu, which leads after about 150m (165 yards) to the next garden.

❸ The Forest of Stone Lions Garden was begun in the 14th century and is considered to be the most classically Chinese of all Suzhou's gardens. Its central motif comprises large and often bizarrely shaped rocks taken from Tai Hu (▷ 271) then assembled into rock gardens. Some rocks are said to resemble lions, hence the name. Reflecting the rock gardens are pools of water lined with graceful pavilions. In the past, the garden was frequented by emperors, monks, poets and painters.

Go west to Lindun Lu, the next busy main street running north to south. This street runs south alongside a narrow canal. About two-thirds of the way down, a bridge leads west into the animated central district around pedestrianized Guanqian Jie, dubbed Suzhou Bazaar for its plethora of shops, teahouses and restaurants—among them the centuries-old Songhelou Restaurant. At the south end of Lindun Lu follow a dogleg left on Ganjiang Donglu and right, across the canal, on Fenghuang Jie, then south on this street a short way, to the small street called Dinghui Si Xian.

❹ Shuang Ta Si (Twin Pagoda Temple) is a distinctive sight thanks to its two Song-dynasty pagodas. These you can view, at least in passing, on the way through the heart of the city.

Return to Ganjiang Donglu and go west (left) to its junction with busy Renmin Lu. Cross to the west side of Renmin Lu, and walk a brief distance north.

❺ Harmony Garden, laid out during the late 19th century, is the newest of Suzhou's major classical gardens.

Above Flags lining the walkway to the North Temple Pagoda

The designer adopted and adapted some of the finest elements from earlier gardens, be it the general shape of the central pond, a pavilion or a weathered rock from Tai Hu that's meant to suggest a mountain. Look out for these little touches.

From here you can continue north on Renmin Lu back to the Suzhou Silk Museum, or to the railway station.

WHEN TO GO
The gardens that are the main feature of this tour change their character with the seasons, though not as much as you might expect because they rely on a combination of trees, water, rocks and pavilions rather than blossoming flowers for their effect. During the busiest summer months they are often too crowded to fully be appreciated.

PLACES TO VISIT
FOREST OF STONE LIONS GARDEN
✉ 23 Yuanlin Lu ☎ 0512 6727 2428

🕐 Mar–end Oct daily 7.30–5.30, Nov–end Feb daily 8–5 💰 20RMB

HUMBLE ADMINISTRATOR'S GARDEN
✉ 178 Dong Bei Jie ☎ 0512 6751 0286 🕐 Daily 7.30–5 (core hours) 💰 50–70RMB

SUZHOU SILK MUSEUM
✉ 2001 Renmin Lu ☎ 0512 6753 6538 🕐 Daily 9–5 💰 10RMB

TOURIST INFORMATION
www.citssz.com
✉ China International Travel Service, 18 Dajing Xiang ☎ 0512 6522 3783 🕐 Daily 9–5

WHERE TO EAT
SONGHELOU RESTAURANT
✉ 72 Taijian Lu (off Guanqian Jie) ☎ 0512 6727 7006 🕐 Daily 11–2, 4–9

CHANGZHOU
CHANGZHOU CHINA DINOSAUR PARK
www.china-dinosaurpark.com
China proudly calls this large open-air theme park its own 'Jurassic Park'. Although it boasts no actual living, breathing, preying giant reptiles brought back from extinction, there are 36 skeletons of dinosaurs found in China, including a top-of-the-food-chain *Tyrannosaurus rex*, and dinosaur models.
✉ 1 Hanjiang Lu, North District
☎ 05198512 0812 🕐 Daily 9–5
👆 120RMB 🚌 29

CHONGQING
CABLE CAR RIDE
Children should appreciate the sheer white-knuckle excitement of the city's unique transportation system, cable cars that cross both the Jialing River and the Yangtze River from separate points on the central peninsula just before the rivers merge. The cars swoop high above the muddy waters, giving an excellent view of the city and life on the river.
🕐 Daily 6am–11pm 👆 2RMB

DINGSHU
LONGQI CERAMICS MARKET
Handily located near the Yixing Ceramics Museum (▷ 258), the market is the largest of its kind in China. Its slightly unprepossessing shops and stalls are great for buying the famous local Yixing tea sets and other valuable ceramics.
✉ Yixing 🕐 Daily 7–10, 5–8
🚉 Dingshan Station, Dingshu

GUANGZHOU
SHANGXIAJIU
Three consecutive roads represent the most atmospheric place to shop in this increasingly mall-friendly city. Known collectively as Shangxiajiu, these partly pedestrianized streets contain a host of cheap fashion stores, housed within colonnaded 1920s buildings.

Some of Guangzhou's best markets are just north of the pedestrianized streets. For jade, head to the stalls around Changshou Lu, while antique-hunters should drop by the Xiguan Antique Market on Lizhiwan Lu.
✉ Dishifu Lu, Xiajiu Lu and Shangjiu Lu, Liwan District

GUANGZHOU (CANTON)
ELEPHANT & CASTLE PUB
With a name like this, it could only be an English-style pub. North of the city center, it has a pool table, satellite sports channel, Chinese and international beers alongside wines, cocktails, decent pub food, and a spacious outdoor terrace. Its clientele is mostly expats and visiting Westerners.
✉ 363 Huanshi Donglu ☎ 020 8359 3309
🕐 Daily 5pm–2am 👆 Free G30

HARE & MOON
www.whiteswanhotel.com
If you like your down time in a bar to be carefree—and if you are lodging on Shamian Island, car-free—the lobby bar of the White Swan should fit the bill. There's a superb view of the Pearl River.
✉ White Swan Hotel, 1 Shamian Nanjie, Shamian Dao ☎ 020 8188 6968 🕐 Daily 11am–1am 👆 Free 🚇 Huangsha

SUN YAT-SEN MEMORIAL HALL (SUN ZHONGSHAN JINIAN TANG)
Classical and modern ballet, including such repertoire standards

as *Swan Lake*, along with events like puppet theater performed by the city's own excellent Guangzhou Puppet Troupe, take place at this national cultural monument, dating from 1931.

✉ Dongfeng Zhong Lu ☎ 020 8384 6330 ⏱ Box office daily 9–5.30 J60–1,000RMB ⊕ Zhongshan Jinian Tang

TAORAN TEAHOUSE

This teahouse on Shamian Island is also a school for 'tea ladies' and a treasure trove of antique and craft tea sets, teapots, crockery, silverware, calligraphy and painting, and antique musical instruments. Much of the content is for sale, test before buying.

✉ 58 Shamian Dajie ☎ 020 8121 9888 ⏱ Daily 9.30am–11pm ⊕ Huangsha

XIANGJIANG SAFARI PARK

More than most Chinese zoos, this safari park south of Guangzhou, which is toured aboard the park's own buses, has the space to allow its 10,000 animals elbow room and the chance to move around and behave in ways that seem more natural than lying bored in a small cage. Among the 300 species that can be seen are rare white tigers, crocodiles and elephants (there are elephant rides).

✉ Yingbin Lu, Dashi, Panyu ☎ 020 8478 3333 ⏱ Daily 9–6 🖑 Adult 150RMB, child (under 1.1m/3.6ft) free

XINGHAI CONCERT HALL

www.concerthall.com.cn
Western classical music by visiting symphony and chamber orchestras, as well as by the city's own Guangzhou Symphony Orchestra, along with Chinese and other Asian classical music are performed at this ultramodern venue named after the locally born composer Xian Xinghai. As many performances are in the evening, you have the chance to view the bright lights of Guangzhou's fast-redeveloping Pearl River waterfront.

✉ 33 Qingbo Lu, Ersha Dao ☎ 020 8735 2222 ⏱ Box office daily 10–7 🖑 100–200RMB G12, 89, 194, 277

HAINAN DAO

JINGRUN PEARL DAO

Pearls are a specialty of Hainan, and this fancy store on Haikou's main shopping street has a fine selection of pearl earrings, rings, necklaces and other personal jewelry and of pearl-inlaid ornaments, in addition to items in gold, silver, and jade.

✉ Facing Wanghai Mansion 3, Haixiu Donglu, Haikou ☎ 0898 6675 0129 ⏱ Daily 9am–10pm

OCEAN BAY GOLF CLUB

A championship-level 18-hole course created by American and Japanese designers, the links runs right beside the South China Sea—four holes actually involve carries across the waves. If the golf begins to pall, you can try out the surfing on Nanyan Bay.

✉ Nanyanwan Beach, Wanning ☎ 0898 6252 5999 ⏱ Tee-off time 7am–3pm 🖑 800–1,000RMB green fee, 150RMB caddy, 260RMB cart, 100RMb for clubs, 50RMB for shoes

SANYA MARRIOTT RESORT AND SPA DIVING CENTRE

www.marriott.com
www.qianshui.cc
The unpolluted waters of the South China Sea, with a year-round temperature in the range 20–26°C (68–78°F), make an ideal setting for scuba-diving on the coral reef on Yalong Bay. The PADI-recognized courses offered here are an ideal introduction. Snorkeling is also available, for less than a third of the diving rate.

✉ Sanya Yalong Wanguojia, (Yalong Bay), Sanya ☎ 0135 1809 9286 ⏱ Daily by arrangement 🖑 580–800RMB per session

HANGZHOU

IMPRESSION WEST LAKE

The last few years have proved that China's most famous film director, Zhang Yimou, has a genius for visually dazzling mass choreography. Not only was he behind the opening and closing ceremonies for the Beijing Games, he has also created something of a franchise of outdoor stage shows, the latest of which is this mesmerizing spectacle. Staged entirely upon the lake itself, *Impression West Lake* is a elegant, costume-heavy mixture of dance, music and lighting in a stunning natural theater. If you can't get to Yangshuo and Lijiang (the other *Impression* venues), make this a must-see. Performances take place nightly.

✉ Yue Lake (northwest corner of West Lake) ☎ 0571 8796 2222 🖑 Tickets 220–10,000RMB (most hotels can help with booking)

NANJING

DANNY'S IRISH PUB

www.sheraton.com/nanjing
Nanjing's first—and so far only—Irish pub, on the fourth floor of the plush Sheraton Hotel, attracts a lively expat crowd with its cozy feel of old Ireland combined with a breezy style that takes in live music and dancing, only some of which is Irish in nature.

✉ Sheraton Nanjing Hotel, 169 Hanzhong Lu ☎ 025 8666 8888 ⏱ Daily 6pm–midnight 🖑 Free ⊕ Xinjiekou 🚌 4

HUNAN LU NIGHT MARKET

The night market, at the west end of the busy shopping street Hunan Lu, which itself is just west of Xuanwu Hu Park, is invariably sardine-packed with people rummaging for bargain-basement CDs, DVDs, game-console video games, personal ornamentation, cheap clothing, and some genuine arts and crafts.

✉ Hunan Lu (at Zhongshan Beilu) ⏱ Daily 5–11 ⊕ Xuanwumen

SANYA

JIANFENGLING PRIMEVAL TROPICAL RAINFOREST

www.jianfengling.net
Jianfengling is the most accessible fragment of Hainan's indigenous mountain rain forest. Industrial-speed deforestation of Hainan took place during China's communist heyday but the diversity of the island's wildlife remains tangible in this sprawling reserve on the west

Opposite *Early morning exercise*

coast. Some of the island's 344 varieties of birdlife and 82 kinds of mammals, including the rare black-crested gibbon, macaque and Eld's deer may be glimpsed. It's a must for hikers and wildlife enthusiasts. Trips to Jianfengling can be arranged from Sanya.

✉ Ledong County, Hainan Island ☎ 0898 8827 5161

SURFING HAINAN (CHONGLANG HAINAN)

www.surfinghainan.com
A cheaper alternative to the pricy hotel watersports in Sanya can be had at this established surfing operation on Dadonghai. It offers a selection of surf and kite boards, wetsuits, fins, and other paraphernalia for those who haven't traveled with gear. They also do lessons for beginners—in English and Chinese—and can organize individual or small group surfing trips to lesser populated parts.

✉ Room 8219, 2F Yindu Hotel, 8 Haiyun Lu, Sanya, Hainan Island ☎ 135 1980 0103 (mobile) 🖐 Day trips for 4–6 people go for 350RMB per person.

SHENZHEN
THEME PARKS

What Shenzhen lacks in traditional culture and architecture, it makes up for in US-style theme parks. Four are clustered in the Overseas Chinese Town (OCT), west of the city: **Window of the World** (Shijie Zhichuang; daily 9am–10pm), is a sort of global Lilliput which

showcases scale models of everything from Thai palaces to Japanese teahouses; **Splendid China** (Jinxiu Zhonghua; daily 9–6) has facsimile models of some of China's most famous attractions, the Terra-cotta Warriors and Great Wall included; the **China Folk Culture Village** (Minsu Wenhua Cun; daily 9am–9.30pm) recreates the homes and lifestyles of the country's ethnic minorities; **Happy Valley** (Huanle Gu: Mon–Fri 9.30am–10pm, Sat–Sun 9am–10pm) majors on rides and rollercoasters. On the opposite side of the city is **OCT East**, a 890ha (2,200-acre) site where a Swiss village has been constructed around a manmade lake, complete with ski chalets and Chinese *'fräulein'* girls in braids.

SUZHOU
HARRY'S BAR

The market leader nightlife spot for expats and cool—or just plain curious—locals has a classy downstairs bar that rocks (or folks and jazzes) to live music most nights of the week from about 9pm, and an upstairs room with pool tables. Satellite TV sports is another big draw.

✉ 70 Luogua Qiao Xia Tang, Lindun Lu ☎ 0512 6521 9319 🕐 Daily 11am–2am 🖐 Free 🚍 301, 401

PULP FICTION

Local Chinese and expat revelers and visitors with some steam to blow off, or a big televised

international sporting event to take in, head for this cosmopolitan music bar close to the Suzhou Hotel and the Master of the Nets Garden.

✉ 169 Shiquan Jie ☎ 0512 6520 8067 🕐 Daily 11am–2am 🖐 Free 🚍 4, 401

SUZHOU CIXIU YANJIUSUO (SUZHOU EMBROIDERY RESEARCH INSTITUTE)

Suzhou silk is widely considered to be among the best in China, and the city has a long tradition of silk embroidery. On the road leading west from the central stretch of Renmin Lu, this foundation is a combined factory with demonstrations of the craft and a shop.

✉ 262 Jingde Lu ☎ 0512 6522 4723 🕐 Daily 8.30–4.30 🚍 3

WUHAN
ORIENTAL LUCKY CITY

Hubei's capital is the historic home of Chinese horse racing after the British established stables and courses here in the 19th century. Sixty years after it was banned by the incoming Communist government, the success of experimental race meetings in 2008 indicates legal gambling may be about to return to the mainland at this modern racecourse. Expect the gambling process to be difficult in the short-term. Hong Kong it is not. Bi-weekly meetings were being

Below *The cable car across the river at Chongqing*

scheduled for 2009 at the time of writing. Ask at your hotel for details. ⊠ 1 Jinnan Yilu, Dongxihu District ☎ 027 8588 0008

XIAMEN

RIYUEGU HOT SPRING

www.riyuegu.com

One of China's oldest established hot spring resorts, Riyuegu has pools of most imaginable shapes, sizes, temperatures and mineral contents. These include the multi-layered 'Spring of Bliss', hot at the center and cooler toward the outer tiers. The natural spring water is used in other ways: rest on granite stones warmed by hot spring water or soothe blistered soles by strolling on the hot spring-heated beach. There is an attached resort hotel. ⊠ 1888 Fulian Lu, Haicang District ☎ 0592 631 2222 🕐 Mon–Fri noon–1am, Sat–Sun 10am–1am (times shorten in summer)

YONGDING

FOLK CULTURE VILLAGE

www.hakkatulou.com

Once mistaken for missile silos by overzealous US satellite operators, the stone and adobe Hakka roundhouses, or *tulou*, of Fujian are UNESCO World Heritage-listed. These fortified mini-villages are concentrated in photogenic clusters in mountainous Yongding. The village of Hukeng is among the best developed, and includes a 'Folk Culture Village', complete with a museum and tour guides. The more intrepid might rent a car to reach less polished settlements. ⊠ Hukeng Village, Yongding County, Longyan, Fujian ☎ 0597 5531999 ⊠ Folk Culture Village 🕐 Daily 8–6pm 🚘 Yongding can be reached by car from Longyan, which has direct rail links to Shanghai and Guangzhou. The nearest major city is Xiamen from where trips can be organized.

ZHAOQING

ZHAOQING RESORT AND GOLF CLUB

This 18-hole course, designed by South African legend Gary Player,

JANUARY/FEBRUARY

SPRING FLOWER FESTIVAL

A tradition of buying flowers for good luck that originated in Guangzhou and has spread to other parts of southern China unfolds at flower markets around the city, but is focused on the flower stalls along Binjiang Xilu, south of the Pearl River. ⊠ Binjiang Xilu, Guangzhou 🕐 Variable: first new moon after Jan 21 🚇 Shi Er Gong

FEBRUARY/MARCH

NANJING INTERNATIONAL PLUM FESTIVAL

Cultural performances take place and market stalls are set out to celebrate the spring blooming period of Nanjing's official flower, the plum blossom. Events take place on Plum Blossom Hill, traditionally the original source of plum blossom, which is close to the Ming Tombs on Purple and Gold Mountain. ⊠ Meihuashan (Plum Blossom Hill), Zijinshan (Purple and Gold Mountain), Nanjing 🕐 Variable: 4 weeks in Feb/Mar

APRIL AND JULY

WATER-SPLASHING FESTIVAL

Hainan's Dai people (and some other minorities) celebrate the second day of their New Year by splashing water on each other to ward off disease and bring luck. The island's Li and Miao peoples celebrate the event at the end of July. ⊠ Hainan Dao 🕐 Mid-Apr and end Jul

JUNE

DUANWU (DRAGON BOAT) FESTIVAL

Held to honor an upright imperial official who preferred to commit suicide by drowning to becoming corrupt, these races employ lovingly built and enthusiastically paddled boats with a dragon emblem at the bow. 🕐 Variable: the races take place on the fifth day of the fifth moon of the Chinese lunar calendar ⊠ Baie Tan, Zhujiang (Pearl River), Guangzhou 🚇 Fangcun

THREE GORGES INTERNATIONAL TOURISM FESTIVAL

A modern festival that capitalizes on the city's annual 60 million tourist visitors. The opening week sees theatrical performances, art exhibitions, food and beverage tastings, and more, at various locations around town. ⊠ Chongqing 🕐 Begins fourth week of Jun and runs throughout the summer

SEPTEMBER

XI HU SWEET OSMANTHUS FESTIVAL

Sweet osmanthus is Hangzhou's official flower. Events to celebrate the autumn blooming period take place at various locations around town, with the focus on Manjuelong on the southwest shore of West Lake. ⊠ Manjuelong, Hangzhou 🕐 Middle 10 days in Sep

is refreshingly rural. It's beautifully contoured, and fairways are lined with mature firs and dotted with challenging water features. If you want to play later in the day, nine holes can be played under floodlights and prices are far lower than other courses in more moneyed parts of China's biggest

golfing province. There are on-site accommodations for those who want to stay close to the course. ⊠ Huilong Town, Gaoyao City, Zhaoqing ☎ 0758 816 2168 🕐 Mon–Fri 6.30pm–10.30pm, Sat–Sun 6pm–10.30pm 💳 400–1,200RMB. Advance booking required. 🚘 20km south of Zhaoqing. Take taxi (90–100RMB)

PRICES AND SYMBOLS

The restaurants are listed alphabetically. The prices are for a two-course lunch (L) and a three-course à la carte dinner (D) for one person, without drinks. The wine price is for the least expensive bottle. All the restaurants listed accept credit cards unless otherwise stated.

For a key to the symbols, ▷ 2.

CHONGQING

LUOHAN SI VEGETARIAN RESTAURANT

There aren't too many sights worth visiting in Chongqing but the Luohan Si Buddhist temple is one, for its 500-plus figures of the Buddha. It stands in the heart of the central peninsula, on a direct line between the cable cars that cross the Yangtze and Jialing rivers. The temple's basic vegetarian restaurant serves up at plain tables a more-than-decent lunch of steamed and stir-fried vegetables with boiled rice, fruits, Chinese tea and soft drinks.

✉ Luohan Si Jie, off Minzu Lu ⏰ Daily 11am–3pm 👊 L 10RMB

FUZHOU

JUCHUNYUAN DAJIUDIAN

You need to pass a Kentucky Fried Chicken joint at the front of the Juchunyuan Hotel in the central Dongjiekou district before climbing to the third floor to experience the modern incarnation of a traditional hot pot restaurant founded in 1877. Taste the wonderfully named Fujianese (or Min) stew 'Buddha Jumps Over the Wall'—multiple meat and seafood ingredients simmered in Shaoxing wine—that's so tasty not even a Buddha could resist it. Other local dishes, and some Cantonese, are on the menu.

✉ 2 Dong Jie ☎ 0591 8750 2328 ⏰ Daily 9.30–1.30, 5–8.30 👊 L 100RMB, D 120RMB, Wine 180RMB

GUANGZHOU (CANTON)

1920

www.1920cn.com

Located on the riverside in Guangzhou's architecturally charming old quarter, this German restaurant serves up protein-heavy central European dishes—potato, sauerkraut and sausages feature heavily—as well as some fantastic Bavarian micro-brewed ales. It's a perfect place to kick back and watch the world go by in this famously hectic city, and turns into a lively drinking spot at night-time.

✉ 183 Yanjiang Zhong Lu ☎ 020 8333 6156 ⏰ Daily 11am–1.30am 👊 L 120RMB, D 160RMB, Beers from 30RMB

BANANA LEAF CURRY HOUSE

www.bananaleaf.com.cn

Green sets the tone in both the decor and the guiding philosophy at this restaurant north of the Memorial Garden, one of a small chain that began in Guangzhou. Primarily Thai, with notable dishes being red and green curries, the menu is buttressed by choices from India, Malaysia and Indonesia. The chefs keep the various national characteristics separate, handily avoiding any tendency to pan-Asian blandness. Impromptu song- and dance-performances by staff members set the tone for a breezy dining experience.

✉ 5/F World Trade Centre, 371–375 Huanshi Donglu ☎ 020 8776 3738 ⏰ Daily 11–11 👊 L 80RMB, D 140RMB, Wine 128RMB 🚇 Lieshi Lingyuan

BELLAGIO

Ignore the Latin-sounding name: Bellagio is one of the nation's most successful Chinese-food restaurants, serving beautifully presented dishes from across Greater China in trendy surrounds. Despite the hip decor, lounge music and careful presentation (think fried rice on oversized plates), prices are reasonable. There is

another outlet at 77 Tiyu Xi Lu in the Tianhe District.
✉ G/F Zhujiang Building, 360 Huanshi Dong Lu, Yuexiu District ☎ 020 8376 6106 🕐 Daily 11am–2am 🖐 L and D 80–100RMB, Bottled beer from 20RMB

DONGJIANG SEAFOOD RESTAURANT

One of a chain of enduringly popular, astonishingly vast and permanently crowded Cantonese restaurants, this branch fills a building and outdoor terrace in a prime location close to the riverside at Haizhu Bridge. Seafood is the main featured item, as you will quickly notice from the number of large tanks filled with all manner of live fish, along with prawns, crabs and other crawling sea creatures, but plenty of other dishes are available, too.
✉ 198 Yanjiang Zhonglu ☎ 020 8318 4901 🕐 24 hours 🖐 L 100RMB, D 140RMB, Wine 108RMB 🚇 Haizhu Guangchang

GUANGZHOU JIUJIA

www.gzr.com.cn
A rambling place on several floors built around multiple courtyards, this city institution, north of Shamian Island, is filled to bursting with diners who pile into heaps of dim sum and a variety of Cantonese delicacies like chicken's feet, crispy-skinned pork and shark's fin soup. At the busiest times you'll have to wait for a table.
✉ 2 Wenchang Nanlu ☎ 020 8138 0388 🕐 Daily 7.30am–10pm 🖐 L 50RMB, D 80RMB 🚇 Changshou Lu

HAVELI RESTAURANT AND BAR

Haveli, close to the Holiday Inn hotel, does its native cuisine justice by having it prepared by Indian chefs, who can also rustle up a decent dish or two from other lands. A clientele of residents and visiting compatriots is evidence that they are getting the homegrown stuff right. Curries of varying strengths,

tandoori dishes, thalis and more are served up in a setting that hits a romantic subcontinental design note, or in a tree-shaded garden.
✉ 2 Aiguo Lu, Overseas Chinese Village, Huanshi Donglu ☎ 020 8359 4533 🕐 Daily 10am–midnight 🖐 L 60RMB, D 80RMB, Wine 150RMB 🚌 28, 523

LAN KWAI FONG SALON

This restaurant offers a cosmopolitan dining experience built around Thai cuisine while taking in Asian fusion elements along the way—Thai curries and other rice dishes, with Indonesian lamb and Indian roti, for instance. Scenically located next to the waterfront park (and the tennis courts) on Shamian Island, it has a calm and professional mien and subdued, snug look that makes it seem like a haven when compared to the sometimes chaotic bustle of many Guangzhou eateries.
✉ 5 Shamian Nanjie, Shamian Dao ☎ 020 8121 6523 🕐 Daily 11–3, 5–10.30 🖐 L 80RMB, D 100RMB, Wine 128RMB 🚇 Huangsha

LA SEINE RESTAURANT FRANÇAIS

Being embedded at the Xinghai Concert Hall on Ersha Island makes this fine French restaurant a good option. It is popular with visiting and resident business people, both Chinese and foreign. The interior is comfortable and restrained, though there's also a chic outdoor terrace with umbrella-shaded tables and river views. Plenty of flair comes through in the nouvelle-style cuisine from a French chef and the service is discreet and professional. The Sunday lunch buffet is justifiably highly regarded.
✉ 33 Qingbo Lu, Ersha Dao ☎ 020 8735 2222, ext. 888 🕐 Daily 10am–11.30pm 🖐 L 120RMB, D 240RMB, Wine 220RMB 🚌 12, 89, 194, 277

WILBER'S BAR AND RESTAURANT

www.wilber.com.cn
The generic 'European' food is fine, but the real reason to visit is the fantastic ambience of this converted

1920s mansion, tucked up in one of the oldest parts of the city. Spread over three floors, including one which is completely non-smoking, Wilber's main dining rooms are romantically intimate, while the roof terrace and outside patio suit the balmy southern weather. The wine list includes varietals from China's most famous boutique winery, Grace Vineyards.
✉ 62 Zhusigang Erlu ☎ 020 3761 1101 🕐 Daily 3pm–2am 🖐 D 200RMB, Wine 220RMB

YONG YA SHAN FANG

By no means the most varied restaurant in town—hot pot is basically the only dish on the menu—Yong Ya Shan Fang knows what it does and does it well. Fish head is the house specialty but there is a mind-boggling choice of alternate ingredients. The patio is perfect for balmy Guangdong nights and, though the busy Huanshi Lu flyover is close, the trellises and greenery make the restaurant feel more like an extension of adjacent Yuexiu Park.
✉ Huanshi Zhong Lu (beside Yuexiu Park's North Gate) ☎ 020 8666 6626 🕐 Daily 9am–3am 🖐 L and D 60–150RMB; Bottled beer from 12RMB

HAINAN DAO
SPICE GARDEN

www.starwoodhotels.com
If lazing around all day on the white sand beaches of a tropical resort stirs your appetite, relief is close at hand in the Sheraton's breezy-looking yet refined pan-Asian restaurant. Given the coastal location, there's an emphasis on seafood, though not to the exclusion of other Malaysian, Thai and Japanese choices. The shaded tables on the outdoor balcony patio command magnificent views of the turquoise sea. The resort is 11km (7 miles) from Sanya.
✉ Sheraton Sanya Resort, Yalong Bay National Resort District, Sanya ☎ 0898 8855 8855 🕐 Daily 6pm–11pm 🖐 D 300RMB, Wine 188RMB 🚌 Sanya–Yalong Bay

HANGZHOU

HAVELI

On the east shore of West Lake, this authentic performer across a range of Indian cuisine styles delivers far more than competent curries. The mural-bedecked, slightly heavy dining room is filled with angles that are separated into snug nooks by dark-shaded drapes. A belly dancer performs every evening among the tables—an unusual feature for an Indian restaurant, but one that's popular with customers—and there's a patio for fine-weather dining outdoors.

✉ 77 Nanshan Lu ☎ 0571 8707 9677 🕙 Daily 10am–midnight ✋ L 100RMB, D 130RMB, Wine 108RMB 🚌 4, 12, 504, 809

LOUWAILOU

www.louwailou.com.cn

This traditional restaurant, in business since 1848, has a fine location on Solitary Hill Island in the northern part of West Lake. It serves up Hangzhou cuisine in a cavernous main dining room or in private rooms. Look for distinguished dishes like the lake fish in sweet-and-sour sauce, beggar's chicken (a whole chicken suffused in Shaoxing rice wine and baked in clay), and fried shrimps with *longjing* tea leaves. You will need to reserve a table with a lake view.

✉ 30 Gushan Lu, Gushan Dao ☎ 0571 8796 9023 🕙 Daily 10–2.30, 4.30–8.45 ✋ L 75RMB, D 125RMB, Wine 87RMB 🚌 K7

VA BENE ITALIAN BAR & GRILL

www.vabenewestlake.com

Sophisticated Italian dining in a restored Chinese mansion is the concept at this eatery in the Tiandi enclave on the east shore of West Lake. Only the upper floors aspire to being a cut above, with elegantly outfitted rooms where classic provincial trattoria dishes, like porcini mushroom tart in a truffle sauce, are served up by Italian chefs. On the ground floor, which has a garden terrace, the Pizza Pazza pizza parlor delivers a looser, less expensive Italian style.

✉ House 8, Xihu Tiandi, 147 Nanshan Lu ☎ 0571 8702 6333 🕙 11.30am–12.30am ✋ L 180RMB, D 380RMB, Wine 250RMB 🚌 4, 12, 809

NANJING

LAO ZHENXING

When visiting the Confucius Temple in the atmospheric Fuzi Miao district (Gongyuan Jie is also known as Fuzi Miao Lu) in the south of the Old City, take the opportunity to dine at this plain cafeteria-style eatery, one of several on the street. A vibrant place in bright primary tones, it backs onto a branch of the Qinhuai River. With Jiangsu dishes like duck's blood soup and pressed duck on the menu, it's not for the faint-hearted, but an authentic taste of China it most certainly is.

✉ 119 Gongyuan Jie 🕙 Mon–Fri 9–9, Sat, Sun 9am–10pm ✋ L 10RMB, D 15RMB 🚌 2, 4

RU SHI DONG GE

A sleek organic food restaurant that has, controversially, been built into a rebuilt chunk of what was once Nanjing's ancient city wall, close to Xuanwu Lake. Chefs have been flown in from across the country to ensure authenticity in each of China's famous eight schools of cuisine. Private two-person 'lovers' rooms are an unusual novelty.

✉ 46 Xitang Da Jie, Xuanwu District ☎ 025 5771 7777 🕙 Daily 11am–10pm ✋ L and D 120–150RMB

WANQINGLOU

This long-standing tourist favorite is the perfect place to get acquainted with the range of Nanjing specialty dishes. The basic set menu include 16 snacks, six hot dishes and a colorful fruit plate, and includes obvious classics, dumplings and spring rolls, as well as challenging concoctions like duck blood soup. Wanqinglou is located beside the Confucius Temple towards the southeast of the city.

✉ 150 Gongyuan Jie (inside Confucius Temple complex) ☎ 025 8662 6950 🕙 Daily 11am–9pm ✋ Set menus start at 108RMB

SANYA

SAND (HAI BIAN)

One of the outstanding new Ritz-Carlton Sanya's dining venues, Sand is has an idyllic alfresco setting on the white sand beachfront. There's no more romantic place to try some of Hainan's famous seafood. A bar offers an alternative venue to relax and enjoy Latin music every evening (except Tuesdays) after 8pm.

✉ Ritz-Carlton Sanya, Yalong Bay National Resort District ☎ 0898 8898 8888 🕙 Daily 11am–11pm ✋ L 400RMB D 600–800RMB

SUZHOU

GARDEN BRASSERIE

www.sheraton-suzhou.com

In the southwest corner of the city center, close to the Pan Gate, the Sheraton has done a fair job of fitting in with Suzhou's historical surroundings. This extends to its graceful brasserie, which has traditional Chinese interior design themes and overlooks the hotel's own landscaped Chinese garden. It offers a reliable dining experience with both Western and Asian fare—the latter primarily Chinese and Japanese—both à la carte and as buffets. Occasionally the dinner buffet takes in seafood.

✉ 1st Floor, Sheraton Suzhou Hotel & Towers, 259 Xinshi Lu ☎ 0512 6510 3388 🕙 Daily 6.30am–11pm ✋ L 110RMB, D 160RMB, Wine 250RMB 🚌 3

QIAN TANG CHA REN

Located on the famous Shiquan Jie pedestrian street, this wooden-textured restaurant-cum-teahouse lays its historic pretensions on thick, with antique decorations in all corners and waitresses in heavy period garb. It's undeniably charming though, and the simple Jiangsu dishes are beautifully executed.

✉ 793 Shiquan Street, Canglang District ☎ 512 6530 0001 🕙 Daily 9.30am–2pm, 5pm–2am ✋ L and D 50RMB

SONGHELOU RESTAURANT

The 'Pine and Crane,' founded in 1737, was a hit with the Qing dynasty Emperor Qianlong. While it doesn't treat today's diners like emperors, it has retained an elegantly artistic decor and is deservedly popular. On a restaurant-filled street in the heart of town, it has space for up to 2,000 diners in nine separate rooms. Suzhou's slightly sweet cuisine strikes the predominant note, based around freshwater fish—like the signature squirrel mandarin fish—vegetables and eels, and including braised duck and other meats.

✉ 72 Taijian Lu (off Guanqian Jie) ☎ 0512 6727 7006 🕐 Daily 11–2, 5–9 ✋ L 80RMB, D 150RMB, Wine 68RMB 🚌 4

WUHAN

BAOTONG SI SUCAI GUAN

The Buddhist Baotong Temple stands in Hong Shan Park in the Wuchang district, on the east side of the Yangtze River. Its primary treasures are two great bells, one of them cast around 500AD. Something of a treasure, too, is the temple's Buddhist vegetarian restaurant, and experiencing the two together makes for a worthwhile visit. Using tofu to imitate various meat and fish dishes adds a piquant touch to go with imaginative dishes of steamed and stir-fried vegetables and boiled rice.

✉ 289 Wuluo Lu ☎ 027 8787 0309 🕐 Daily 9–8.30 ✋ L 30RMB, D 50RMB 🚌 18, 25, 518, 519

XIAMEN

THE HOUSE (LAO BIESHU)

One of Xiamen's most upscale western food restaurants. The generic spaghetti bolognese and bland curries of most 'western restaurants' is replaced here with a fair effort at haute French and Italian cuisine. Even if the kitchen doesn't always pull it off, it's worth coming for the 1930s colonial ambience of this beautiful converted old villa. There's an outdoor dining deck too.

✉ 10–1 Baihe Lu, Siming District (opposite the east gate of Zhongshan Park) ☎ 0592 2044358 🕐 Daily 11–11 ✋ L and D 80–120RMB, Wine 150RMB

Above *Seafood on display at an outdoor fish restaurant*

LIYUMEN SHIFU

A destination seafood restaurant loved by locals for the sea views. Choose your fish from the tanks and enjoy a seaside stroll on the boardwalk after dinner. There are two other branches around Xiamen, including another close to the sea on Huandao Lu, near the Taiwan Folk Village.

✉ Zhenzhu Wan Huayuan; 316–322 Zengcuo'an Lu, Siming District ☎ 0592 2517779 🕐 Daily 11–11 ✋ L and D 100–150RMB, Bottled beer from 8RMB

NANPUTUO SI TEMPLE RESTAURANT

The restaurant of Xiamen's main Buddhist temple, south of Gushan Hill, serves vegetarian meals that are a cut above most such places—and pricier too. Neither the components nor their accompaniments are remarkable in themselves, but the cooks create wonderfully inventive combinations and add a heavenly

ingredient: taste. The restaurant is a convivial place, full of restrained good cheer. There are two dining rooms. Diners must first buy a meal ticket at a central office.

✉ Siming Nanlu ☎ 0592 2087 281 🕐 Daily 12–7 ✋ L 50RMB, D 80RMB

ZHAOQING

YANQIAN VILLAGE

Located on a small, scenic peninsula that juts out into Zhaoqing's Star Lake complex, this village-within-the-city has a parade of simple waterside village restaurants which allow you to sample cheap Cantonese dishes while enjoying a magnificent view of the city's famous karst crags. English is unlikely to be spoken, and picture menus may be in short supply so try bringing a Chinese-speaking helper.

✉ Yanqian Cun, Duanzhou District 🕐 Daily 11am–10pm approx ✋ L and D 40–60RMB

PRICES AND SYMBOLS
Prices are for a double room for one night, unless otherwise stated. Breakfast is included unless noted otherwise. All the hotels listed accept credit cards unless otherwise stated. Note that rates vary widely throughout the year.

For a key to the symbols, ▷ 2.

CHONGQING
DALITANG HOTEL
If the Dalitang looks familiar, that's because its central wing is modeled on Beijing's emblematic Tiantan (Temple of Heaven). The 'People's Hotel', in the north of Chongqing's central peninsula, incorporates the hall of the city's Great Hall of the People and is the lodging of choice for visiting dignitaries. Sichuan cuisine is available in one of the three restaurants. There are several wings, with rooms of varying size and quality.
✉ 173 Renmin Lu, Yuzhong, Chongqing ☎ 023 8652 7666 ⚒ 380–480RMB ⓘ 116 ⬛⬛⬛ 112, 145, 181, 609

GUANGZHOU (CANTON)
RITZ-CARLTON GUANGZHOU
www.ritzcarlton.com
The Ritz-Carlton Guangzhou takes

China's kitsch fascination for aristocratic European fittings and reapplies a bit of class. Rooms come with real wood floors and palatial marble bathrooms. There's a live string quartet to accompany afternoon tea and a bar and billiards room that resembles a Westminster gentlemen's club. Service is sublime, with heaps of homey touches like the mints that are left beside the door. The only current drawback is the location inside the Pearl River New City, a business area that's still under construction. By 2010 the building should be complete and the Ritz-Carlton can claim its title as King of Hospitality in Guangzhou.
✉ 3 Xing'an Lu, Tianhe District ☎ 020 3813 6688 ⚒ 1,088–3,088RMB ⓘ 351 ⊙ Zhujiang Xin Cheng (Pearl River New City) ⬛⬛⬛

SHAMIAN HOTEL
www.gdshamianhotel.com
A long-term favorite with the budget-conscious. Some rooms are small, but the suites are larger. All are furnished with an emphasis on bright, homey comfort, and have tiled bathrooms.
✉ 52 Shamian Nanjie, Shamian Dao

☎ 020 8121 8288 ⚒ 200–520RMB, excluding breakfast ⓘ 58 ⊙ Huangsha

UNOTEL ZUHAI
www.unotel.net.cn
The innovative Unotel group has eight small hotels in Guangzhou, all of them embedded within larger hotels that offer additional amenities. Centrally located, the Zuhai has bright modern rooms, businesslike in the sense of having no distracting frills, though a design and environmental flair lifts it out of the purely functional class.
✉ 6/F Zuhai SEZ Hotel, 11–15 Haizhu Beilu ☎ 020 6127 6888 ⚒ 300–550RMB ⓘ 16 ⊙ Gongyuanqian

WHITE SWAN HOTEL
www.whiteswanhotel.com
One of China's most famous hotels, the White Swan towers high above Shamian Island and the Pearl River. Inside, all is luxurious enough to pull in a stream of big-name guests. The lobby, with its waterfall and giant fish pool, is a study in opulent kitsch. Higher rooms are better equipped; those on the riverside have an outstanding view. There are nine restaurants to choose from.

Opposite Exterior of the Shamian Hotel on Shamian Island in Guangzhou

✉ 1 Shamian Nanjie, Shamian Dao ☎ 020 8188 6968 👋 900–1,725RMB, excluding breakfast ① 843 🈳 📺 🏊 Outdoor 🚇 Huangsha

HAINAN DAO
CROWNE PLAZA SPA RESORT HAINAN
www.crowneplazahainan.com
Nowhere in Haikou does a beach vacation better than this rambling, palatial resort hotel at Haikou. Some rooms have a sea view and some a garden view, but all are bright and breezy in a way that complements the subtropical beach setting; the upper-range suites are simply more chic in this respect. The hotel's hot-spring spa is huge.
✉ 1 Qiongshan Dadao, Haikou ☎ 0898 6596 6888 👋 580–1,600RMB; suites 1,500–3,200RMB ① 333 🈳 📺 🏊

HANGZHOU
HYATT REGENCY HANGZHOU
http://hangzhou.hyatt.regency.com
Located on the east bank of West Lake, within a recently pedestrianized zone, the Hyatt Regency exudes five-star quality, with great service, immaculate furnishings and a particularly impressive breakfast spread. Rooms at the front have some gorgeous lake views but command a much higher tariff.
✉ 28 Hubin Lu ☎ 0571 8779 1234 👋 1,400–2,600RMB ① 190 🏊 📺 🈳

SHANGRI-LA HOTEL & RESORT
www.shangri-la.com
If expense is not a consideration, there is no better place to stay in Hangzhou than at this elegant hotel on the north shore of West Lake (Xi Lu). Set in approximately 16ha (40 acres) of private, leafy grounds, it is palatial from top to bottom. The rooms—many with a lake view—are almost cluttered with tasteful paintings, vases, potted plants, and all manner of furniture and fittings. Along with a restaurant serving superb Cantonese and Hangzhou

cuisine there's a decent Italian eatery, Peppino.
✉ 78 Beishan Lu ☎ 0571 8797 7951 👋 1,500–2,500RMB; suites 2,900–3,900RMB ① 383 🈳 📺 🏊 Indoor 🚗 7

NANJING
CELEBRITY CITY HOTEL
www.yilaicch.com
Located in the northern part of the city center, in the bustling district west of Xuanwu Lake Park, this hotel opened in 2004 and is the height of modernity, with all kinds of satellite and computer gadgetry in place, and it has something of a design flair besides. Rooms cover a range of sizes and amenities and two in-house restaurants serve up Hunan and Sichuan cuisine.
✉ 30 Zhongshan Beilu ☎ 025 8312 3333 👋 838–1,400RMB; suites 1,500RMB ① 370 🈳 📺

JINLING HOTEL
www.jinlinghotel.com
Pretty plush for a government-owned institution, the Jinling covers a lot of ground, physically and in terms of the range of accommodations and amenities, such as shops and restaurants. Rooms have style as well as content, particularly those on the executive floors.
✉ 2 Hanzhong Lu, Xinjiekou ☎ 025 8471 1888 👋 580–1,500RMB; suites 2,500–3,500RMB ① 592 🈳 📺 🏊 Indoor

SOFITEL ZHONGSHAN GOLF RESORT NANJING
www.sofitel.com
Sofitel's reliably excellent standards, married with a 27-hole rural golf course designed by Gary Player, is good news for lovers of the Royal and Ancient game in China. Set amid vast swathes of green on the slopes of the Purple Mountain, the course is a welcome sight for anyone tired of the concrete urban murals of nearby Nanjing and Shanghai. With 140 luxurious rooms and suites, three quality restaurants and a Lobby Lounge with a view over the course, 19th holes don't come much more comfortable. The

distance from Nanjing may not be suitable for tourists more interested in the city's more historic attractions.
✉ Huanling Lu ☎ 025 8540 8888 👋 1,098–1,800RMB ① 140 🏊 📺 🈳

SUZHOU
BAMBOO GROVE HOTEL
www.bg-hotel.com
With its own Chinese garden and elements of traditional Chinese architecture, the bright, modern Bamboo Grove, on the next street south from the Master of the Nets Garden, fits right in with Suzhou style. The rooms, most of which are not overly large (there are larger suites), are furnished in a tolerably plush style, modern without striving to be cool.
✉ 168 Zuhui Lu ☎ 0512 6520 5601 👋 430–580RMB, excluding breakfast ① 365 🈳 📺 🏊 Indoor 🚗 2

GARDEN HOTEL SUZHOU
As a former state guesthouse and private residence of Guomindang leader Chiang Kai-shek, the Garden Hotel Suzhou has a picturesque garden setting. A massive make-over came in 2007, and prompted the reopening of a former manor house which has previously hosted visits by more than a hundred Chinese and international political leaders. There's a new spa and restaurants that take full advantage of the picturesque setting. The hotel's traditional Chinese gardens and historic remnants include Shanqing Buddha Hall, built by Qing dynasty Emperor Tongzhi in 1869, restored during the renovation.
✉ 99 Daichengqiao Lu ☎ 0512 6778 6965 👋 730–1,000RMB ① 238 📺 🈳

WUXI
GRAND PARK HOTEL WUXI
This fine hotel on the main street has a broad range of amenities for fitness and relaxation, and its restaurants are some of the most dependable in town. The rooms are furnished in an international style.
✉ 403 Zhongshan Lu ☎ 0510 8868 8688 👋 588–880RMB ① 407 🈳 📺 🏊 Indoor

REGIONS

SIGHTS 292
WALKS 310
WHAT TO DO 316
EATING 322
STAYING 328

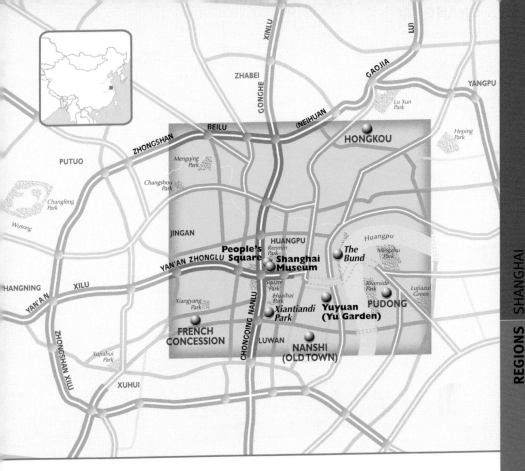

SHANGHAI

In less than a century Shanghai grew from a staid market town at the mouth of the Yangtze River to swaggering financial giant, dictating terms to the nation. The transformation was drug-fueled. Prized open by British gunships in the First Opium War, Shanghai was educated in the ways of the world by gangsters, bankers and political radicals. She was stymied by war, and then spent 30 years in Communist rehab but just as soon as she was allowed, Shanghai ditched that frumpy Mao jacket, donned a clingy *cheongsam*, and teetered up onto high heels where, you sense, she has always belonged.

The marked return of fashion is but one modern echo of Shanghai's 'swinging' heyday. As it was in the 1930s, Shanghai is a pumped-up city in permanent celebration mode after runaway economic success. Huge sums of disposable cash can be seen spilling out of wallets and into the clutches of minimum-wage bartenders at the city's endlessly trendy nightspots and restaurants. Shanghai residents' love of money and luxury is palpable. Scrap carts share the increasingly crowded roads with gleaming sports cars. So expensive are the glitzy pubs, clubs, and gated apartment complexes that they have become the exclusive preserve of the wealthy.

Since 1990, the city has flung itself into the largest urban transformation in human history, paid for by the fastest-growing economy the world has ever seen. This is a city hurtling into the future, symbolized by its remarkable architecture. The new 101-story Financial Trade Centre loiters just behind the 88-story Jinmao, and the landmark Oriental Pearl TV Tower. These three futuristic flights of fancy peer down at the colonial buildings of the Bund on the opposite riverbank—past and present, divided by the muddy Huangpu River.

SHANGHAI

M50 ART DISTRICT

Changshou Park

Shanghai International Motor Racing Circuit

CHANGSHOU

Jade Buddha Temple

JINGAN

SHANGHAI RAILWAY STATION

Shanghai Railway Station

Shanghai Railway Station

TIANMU

Hanzhong Road

Jiaotong Park

ZHONGLU

Xinzha Road

Nanjing Road (W)

Shanghai Centre

Majestic Theatre

Nanjing Road (W)

Grand Brightness Theatre

Park Hotel

New World City

People's Square

Wusha Monument

Renmin Park

Jing'an Temple

Jing'an Temple

Shanghai Exhibition Centre

Shanghai Art Museum

MOCA

Urban Planning Exhibition Hall

People's Square

Jing'an Park

YAN'AN

Shanghai Municipal People's Government

Moller Villa

Children's Art Theatre

Ruijin Theatre

Shanghai Grand Theatre

People's Square

Shanghai Museum

Square Park

People's Square

Concert Hall

YAN'AN

Square Park

Donghu Hotel

Lyceum Theatre

Jinjiang Hotel

Cathay Theatre

Huangpi Road (S)

HUAIHAI

ZHONGLU

Xiangyang Park

Changshu Road

Okura Garden Hotel

Shanxi Road (S)

HUAIHAI

Astrid Apartments

St Nicholas Church

Huaihai Park

Memorial House of the First National Congress of the Communist Party

Puxijin Monument

FRENCH CONCESSION

Shanghai Arts & Crafts Museum

Ruijin Building

Fuxing Park

Sun Yat-sen's Residence

Xiantiandi

Taipingqiao Park

Taiyuan Villa

LUWAN

White Cloud Temple

Longhua

HONGKOU

Dongbaoxing Road

Long Distance Bus Station

Baoshan Road

Children's Park

Hailun Road

CHENG QIAO

Shanghai Post Office

Huangpu Theatre

Zhongguo Theatre

Duoyunxuan Art Gallery

Nanjing Road (E)

Bank of China

Chen Yi Monument

Astor House Hotel

Monument to the People's Heroes

International Passenger Terminal

H u a n g p u

Peace Hotel

min Grand age Theatre

Yifu Theatre

HUANGPU

Metropole Hotel

BUND SIGHTSEEING TUNNEL

Shanghai Natural Wild Insect Kingdom

Shanghai International Convention Centre

Oriental Pearl Tower

Shanghai Ocean World Aquarium

Works Cultural Palace

Gong Theatre

Shanghai Museum of Natural History

YAN'AN DONGLU TUNNEL

Riverside Park

Super Brand Mall

PUDONG

Lujiazui Green

Dazhong Theatre

Shangri La Hotel

Jinmao Tower

Pudong Skyscrapers

PUDONG DADAO

Chenxiangge Nunnery

Yuyuan (Yu Garden)

LAN NI DU

Shanghai World Financial Center

Shanghai Science & Technology Museum

Cixiu Nunnery

Chenghuangmiao (Temple of the City God)

Huxinting Teahouse

Mosque of Small Peach Garden

Shilupu Passenger Terminal

Xiaotaoyuan Mosque

LAO XI MEN

Wen Miao (Confucian Temple)

NANSHI (OLD TOWN)

FUXING DONGLU TUNNEL

ZHANGYANG LU

H u a n g p u

D

E

F

SHANGHAI STREET INDEX

Street	Page	Grid
Anlan Lu	289	D5
Anqing Lu	289	D2
Anren Jie	289	E5
Anyuan Lu	288	A2
Aomen Lu	288	A1
Bansongyuan Lu	289	E1
Baochang Lu	289	D1
Baoshan Lu	289	D1
Baotong Lu	289	D1
Baoyuan Lu	289	E1
Beihai Lu	289	D4
Beihutang Lu	289	F4
Beijing Donglu	289	D3
Beijing Xilu	288	A3
Bingchangtian Lu	289	F5
Binjiang Dadao	289	E4
Bund Sightseeing Tunnel	289	E3
Chang'an Lu	288	B1
Changchun Lu	289	E1
Changhua Lu	288	A4
Changle Lu	288	A4
Changping Lu	288	A4
Changxing Lu	288	C1
Changzhi Lu	289	E3
Chengde Lu	288	C5
Chengdu Beilu	288	C3
Chenxiangge Lu	289	D4
Chongqing Beilu	288	C4
Cixi Lu	288	B3
Dagu Lu	288	B4
Dajing Lu	289	D5
Daming Lu	289	E3
Danshui Lu	288	C5
Datong Lu	288	C1
Dong Jie	289	E5
Dongbaoxing Lu	289	E1
Dongchang Lu	289	F5
Dongchangzhi Lu	289	F2
Dongdaming Lu	289	F3
Donghanyang Lu	289	F2
Donghu Lu	288	A4
Dongjiaxing Lu	289	E2
Dongmen Lu	289	E5
Dongshahonggang Lu	289	F1
Dongtai Lu	288	C5
Dongxinmin Lu	289	D2
Dongyuhang Lu	289	F2
Duolun Lu	289	E1
Emei Lu	289	E2
Fangbang Zhonglu	289	D5
Fangxie Lu	289	D5
Fenghe Lu	289	E3
Fengyang Lu	288	B3
Fenyang Lu	288	A5
Fucheng Lu	289	E4
Fujia Jie	289	E5
Fujian Beilu	289	D3
Fujian Nanlu	289	D4
Fujian Zhonglu	289	D3
Fukang Beilu	289	F5
Fumlin Lu	288	A4
Fuxing Donglu	289	D5
Fuxing Donglu Tunnel	289	E5
Fuxing Zhonglu	288	A5
Fuyou Lu	289	D4
Fuzhou Lu	289	D4
Gangu Jie	289	E5
Gansu Lu	289	D2
Gaoyang Lu	289	F2
Gaoyang Lu	289	F2
Gonghe Lu	288	B2
Gonghe Xinlu	288	C1
Gongxing Lu	289	D1
Guangdong Lu	289	D4
Guangfu Lu	288	B2
Guangqi Lu	289	E5
Guangqi Nanlu	289	E5
Guangxi Nanlu	289	D4
Guizhou Lu	289	D3
Guling Lu	288	C3
Guoqing Lu	288	C2
Ha'erbin Lu	289	E2
Haichang Lu	288	C2
Haifang Lu	288	A2
Haila'er Lu	289	F2
Hailun Lu	289	E1
Hailun Lu	289	F2
Hailun Xilu	289	E1
Haining Lu	289	D2
Hankou Lu	289	D3
Hanyang Lu	289	E2
Hanzhong Lu	288	B2
Hefei Lu	288	B5
Henan Beilu	289	D3
Henan Nanlu	289	D5
Henan Zhonglu	289	D4
Hengfeng Lu	288	B1
Hengtong Lu	288	B2
Hong Kong Lu	289	E3
Hongxing Lu	289	D1
Houjia Lu	289	D5
Huai'an Lu	288	B2
Huaihai Donglu	289	D4
Huaihai Zhonglu	288	B4
Huanghe Lu	288	C3
Huangpi Nanlu	288	C5
Huangpu Lu	289	E3
Huating Lu	288	A4
Huaxing Lu	288	D2
Huayuanshiqiao Lu	289	F4
Hubei Lu	289	D3
Huiwen Lu	289	D1
Huqiu Lu	289	E3
Hutal Lu	288	C1
Ji'an Lu	288	C5
Jiande Lu	288	B5
Jiangning Lu	288	A2
Jianguo Donglu	288	C5
Jiangxi Beilu	289	E2
Jiangxi Nanlu	289	D4
Jiangxi Zhonglu	289	D4
Jiangyin Lu	288	C3
Jiaotong Lu	288	B1
Jiaozhou Lu	288	A2
Jiashan Lu	288	A5
Jiatong Lu	289	D2
Jinan Lu	288	C5
Jingdong Lu	289	F1
Jingjiang Lu	289	C1
Jingling Zhonglu	288	C4
Jingxiu Lu	289	D5
Jinjia Fang	289	D5
Jinling Donglu	289	D4
Jinling Xilu	288	C4
Jintian Lu	289	F2
Jinyuan Lu	288	C2
Jiucang Jie	289	D4
Jiujiang Lu	289	D3
Jiulong Lu	289	E2
Jiulong Lu	289	F2
Julu Lu	288	A4
Kangding Lu	288	A2
Kongjia Long	289	D5
Kuaiji Lu	289	D5
Kunshan Lu	289	E2
Lannidu Lu	289	F5
Laoqinyang Lu	289	F1
Laotaiping Long	289	E5
Laoxin Jie	289	E5
Liaoning Lu	289	E2
Lingji Jie	289	E5
Linping Beilu	289	F1
Linping Lu	289	F1
Linshan Lu	289	D1
Lishui Lu	289	E4
Liulin Lu	288	C5
Liyang Lu	289	E2
Lufeng Lu	289	D1
Luhe Lu	289	D3
Lujiadu Lu	289	F5
Lujiazui Xilu	289	E4
Luofu Lu	289	E2
Luxiangyuan Jie	289	D5
Machang Lu	289	F2
Madang Lu	288	C5
Maoming Beilu	288	B4
Maoming Nanlu	288	B5
Meiyuan Lu	288	B2
Menggu Lu	288	C2
Menghua Jie	289	D5
Minde Lu	289	D1
Minhang Lu	289	E2
Minli Lu	288	B1
Moganshan Lu	288	B1
Nanbei Gaojia Lu	288	B5
Nanchang Lu	288	A5
Nanjing Donglu	289	D3
Nanjing Xilu	288	A3
Nansuzhou Lu	289	E3
Nanyang Lu	288	A3
Ningbo Lu	289	D3
Ninghai Donglu	289	D4
Penglai Lu	289	D5
Pengze Lu	289	E2
People's Square	288	C4
Pu'an Lu	288	C4
Pudong Dadao	289	F4
Puji Lu	288	B2
Putuo Lu	288	A1
Qinglian Jie	289	D5
Qingyang Lu	289	F1
Qipu Lu	289	D2
Qiujiang Lu	288	C1
Qiujiang Zhilu	289	C2
Qixin Lu	289	F5
Qufu Lu	289	D2
Rehe Lu	289	D2
Renhe Jie	288	A2
Renmin Dadao	288	C4
Renmin Lu	289	D5
Rongchang Lu	289	F5
Ruijin 1-Lu	288	B4
Ruijin 2-Lu	288	B5
Sanpailou Lu	289	D5
Shaanxi Beilu	288	A1
Shaanxi Beilu	288	A3
Shaanxi Nanlu	288	A5
Shahong Lu	289	F1
Shajing Lu	289	F2
Shajinggang Lu	289	F1
Shandong Zhonglu	289	D4
Shanghaiguan Lu	288	B3
Shangqiu Lu	289	F2
Shanxi Beilu	289	D3
Shanxi Nanlu	289	D3
Shaoxing Lu	288	A5
Shengze Lu	289	D4
Shiji Dadao	289	F4
Shimen 1-Lu	288	B4
Shimen 2-Lu	288	B3
Shizi Jie	289	D5
Shouning Lu	289	D5
Shunchang Lu	288	C5
Sichuan Beilu	289	E2
Sichuan Nanlu	289	E4
Sichuan Zhonglu	289	E3
Sinan Lu	288	B5
Sipailou Lu	289	E5
Siping Lu	289	F1
Songshan Lu	288	C4
Songxue Jie	289	D5
Suzhou Beilu	289	D2
Suzhou Nanlu	288	B2
Taicang Lu	288	C5
Taidong Lu	289	F3
Taixing Lu	288	B2
Taiyangshan Lu	288	C1
Taiyuan Lu	288	A5
Tanggu Lu	289	D2
Tanggu Lu	289	D2
Tangshan Lu	289	F2
Taoyuan Lu	288	C4
Tianbao Lu	289	F1
Tiande Lu	289	F1
Tianjin Lu	289	D3
Tianmu Donglu	289	D2
Tianmu Xilu	288	B1
Tianmu Zhonglu	288	C2
Tianshui Lu	289	F1
Tiantong Lu	289	D2
Tiantong'an Lu	289	D1
Tongge Lu	289	D1
Tongjia Lu	289	F1
Tongren Lu	288	A3
Tongzhou Lu	289	F2
Waibaidu Bridge	289	E3
Waima Lu	289	E5
Waixiangua Jie	289	E5
Wangjiazhai Lu	289	D2
Wangyun Lu	289	D5
Wanzhu Jie	289	D5
Weihai Lu	288	B3
Wenzhou Lu	288	C3
Wuchang Lu	288	E2
Wuding Lu	288	A2
Wuhua Lu	289	F1
Wujiang Lu	288	B3
Wujing Lu	289	E2
Wusheng Lu	288	C4
Wusong Lu	289	E2
Wutong Lu	289	E5
Wuzhen Lu	288	C2
Wuzhou Lu	289	F2
Xiamen Lu	289	D3
Xi'an Lu	289	F2
Xiangyang Beilu	288	A4
Xiangyang Nanlu	288	A5
Xicangqiao Jie	289	D5
Xikang Lu	288	A1
Xinchang Lu	288	C2
Xing'an Lu	288	C4
Xinguang Lu	289	E1
Xinhui Lu	288	A1
Xinie Lu	288	A4
Xinjian Lu	289	F2
Xinjiang Lu	288	C2
Xinma Lu	288	C2
Xinmatou Jie	289	E5
Xinzha Lu	288	A3
Xisuzhou Lu	288	B1
Xiyajie Long	289	E5
Xizang (Tibet Road) Nanlu	289	D4
Xizang (Tibet Road) Zhonglu	288	C3
Xizang Beilu	288	C2
Xueyuan Lu	289	E5
Xundao Jie	289	E5
Yaliujiang Lu	289	F2
Yan'an Donglu	289	C4
Yan'an Donglu Tunnel	289	E4
Yan'an Zhonglu	288	A4
Yandang Lu	288	B5
Yanging Lu	288	A4
Yangjiabang Lu	289	F1
Yangshou Lu	289	E5
Yaojia'an Long	289	D5
Yincheng Beilu	289	F4
Yincheng Lu	289	F4
Yincheng Nanlu	289	F4
Yingcheng Donglu Lu	289	F3
Yingcheng Zhonglu Lu	289	F5
Yongjia Lu	288	A5
Yongkang Lu	288	A5
Yongming Lu	289	E1
Yongshou Lu	289	D4
Yongxing Lu	288	C1
Yuan Mingyuan Lu	289	E3
Yuezhou Lu	289	F2
Yunnan Nanlu	289	D4
Yunnan Zhonglu	289	D3
Yuyao Lu	288	A2
Yuyingtang	288	C1
Yuyuan Lu	288	A3
Zhangyang Lu	289	F5
Zhaozhou Lu	288	C5
Zhapu Lu	289	E2
Zhejiang Beilu	289	D2
Zhejiang Nanlu	289	D4
Zhifu Lu	289	D3
Zhijiang Zhonglu	289	D1
Zhiyuan Lu	289	D1
Zhonghua Lu	289	D5
Zhonghua Xinlu	289	C1
Zhongshan Dong 1-Lu	289	E4
Zhongshan Dong 2-Lu	289	E4
Zhongxing Lu	289	C1
Zhoujiazui Lu	289	F2
Zhuangjia Jie	289	D5
Zihua Lu	289	D5
Zizhong Lu	288	C5
Zongzi Long	289	D5

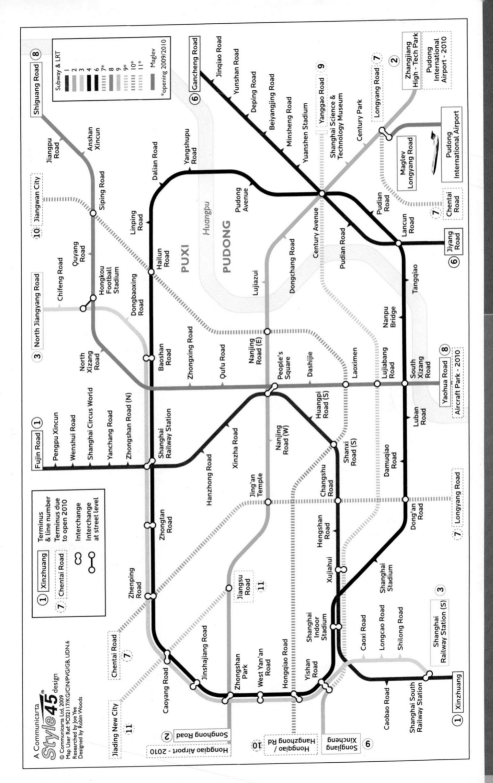

A Communicarta
Style 45® design
© Communicarta Ltd. 2009
Map User Ref: 9C02117KG/CIN/PVG/GB,UDN.6
Researched by Joe Yee
Designed by Robin Woods

Subway & LRT
1
2
3
4
6
7*
8
9
10*
11*
Maglev
*opening 2009/2010

① Xinzhuang — Terminus & line number
⑦ Chentai Road — Terminus due to open 2010
Interchange
Interchange at street level

Above *Jenson Button racing in the first Chinese Formula 1 Grand Prix*

SHANGHAI INTERNATIONAL MOTOR RACING CIRCUIT

www.icsh.sh.cn

This state-of-the-art venue was built for the first Chinese Formula 1 Grand Prix race in September 2004. Because of the marshy terrain, the track was laid on 40,000 concrete piles, each 40–80m (130–260ft) deep. Though not the world's fastest racing circuit, Shanghai is regarded by experts as one of the toughest. If you are unable to be among the 200,000 spectators at the annual Formula 1 event (held now in October), opt for one of the many other races each year, from V8 super cars and A1 to Formula 3 and MOTOGP bike races. Alternatively, SIC Management offers one-lap rides to passengers accompanied by a professional driver and track tours of the grandstands, control tower and so on. The nearby Shanghai Auto Museum has a fascinating display of 80 vehicles from across the last century.

✚ Off map 288 A1 ✉ Anting, Jiading District (30km/18 miles) northwest of Shanghai) ☎ 021 9682 6999 🚌 Tour bus 6 from Shanghai stadium, then shuttle bus 822 (shuttle services run direct on race days) ✋ Tickets from Gate 65

LONGHUA

Still an active monastery, Longhua has been much restored over the centuries. The nearby cemetery has altogether grimmer associations.

According to legend, Longhua Temple was founded in AD242 by a chieftain of the Wu Kingdom. Rebuilt many times, it retains the layout of a typical Song dynasty temple complex with ceremonial gateway, bell and drum towers, prayer halls and a freestanding wooden pagoda. Its most noteworthy features are a large bronze bell, said to bring luck if struck three times, and the general rituals of monastic life.

In the early part of the 20th century the name Longhua conjured up terror. The neighboring park, Longhua Martyrs Cemetery (daily 9–4) commemorates the 800 Communist activists who were executed here between 1928 and 1937. The Japanese turned Longhua into an internment camp and airstrip, recreated in the film adaptation of J. G. Ballard's novel *Empire of the Sun*. Though a peaceful place for a stroll, the highlight of the cemetery is the pyramid-like Memorial Museum. In contrast to almost embarrassing levels of propaganda displayed at many Shanghai museums, the memorial has several well-presented and emotionally engaging dedications and memorials to a range of 'revolutionaries', from early opponents of colonial rule in Shanghai to the early Communists who were executed in this spot in the 20s and 30s. Entrance is 5RMB.

✚ Off map 288 B5

Longhua Temple

✉ 2853 Longhua Lu, Xuhui District ☎ 021 6456 6085 🕐 Daily 7–5 🚇 Longcao Lu ✋ 10RMB

Below *The main gates to the first courtyard of Longhua Temple*

INFORMATION

✚ 288 B5

INTRODUCTION

This leafy neighborhood is perfect for a stroll. Soak up the atmosphere as you track down its architectural gems. The area also has some of Shanghai's best shopping and a lively nightlife. No longer recognized as an administrative unit, the former French Concession has been absorbed by the Luwan, Jing'an and Xuhui districts. Huaihai Zhong Lu, a busy thoroughfare running east to west and dividing the area roughly in half, is lined with shopping malls, department stores and upscale boutiques. Its three metro stops are convenient for exploring places of interest—buses, too, are plentiful and frequent.

The French first staked a claim on the territory between the old Chinese quarter and the Bund in 1844. 'French town' expanded westward until it covered an area of nearly 18sq km (7sq miles). The French created their own institutions—a *conseil municipal* directly answerable to the consul, an independent police force, churches and schools, notably the prestigious College Francais. Boulevards were laid out on the Parisian model, named after national heroes (Avenue Petain, Rue Moliere) and planted with plane trees. Ironically, there were never more than a few thousand French residents, compared with the 30,000 White Russians who turned Huaihai Lu into a 'Quartier Russe.'

Despite its genteel surroundings, by the 1930s the Concession had acquired an unsavory reputation for drug trafficking, gambling, prostitution and bloody political turf wars. The area fell into neglect after the 1949 revolution but is now enjoying a revival.

WHAT TO SEE

FUXING PARK

This hidden gem was acquired by the French community in 1909 and redesigned as a formal Parisian-style garden with sculpted flowerbeds,

Above *The gardens and terraces of the 1920's Ruijin Guesthouse*
Opposite *A couple dancing in Fuxing Park*

Above *A dress stall at busy Xiang Yang Market*

manicured lawns, decorative fountains and avenues lined with shady plane trees. Access was originally restricted to French citizens but today (especially on Sunday) people of all ages and nationalities come here to exercise, picnic, play chess or take a pre-lunch amble through the rose garden.
✚ 288 B5

ARTS AND CRAFTS MUSEUM

Part of the Shanghai Fine Arts and Crafts Institute, the museum occupies an elegant mansion designed in 1905 for a French local government official by distinguished Slovakian architect Ladislaus Hudec. Visitors enter the house from the garden and the exhibition begins on the second floor, with displays ranging from paper-cutting and lantern-making to carving in jade, ivory and bamboo. The institute's other strong suit is embroidery (third floor)—don't miss Liu Pei Zhen's needlepoint tapestry of Raphael's *Sistine Madonna* or the eye-catching Shanghai Opera costumes. Watch the artisans at work, then pop down to the basement shop, where the price tags are more reasonable than upstairs. Here you will find everything from jade birds, paper lanterns, black ceramic Buddhas, embroidered bags, ivory mirrors and woolen rugs to hand-painted T-shirts.
✉ 79 Fenyang Lu, Xuhui District ☎ 021 6431 4074 🕙 Daily 9–5 🚇 Changshu Lu ♿ Adult 8RMB, child (under 1.2m/4ft) free

CHURCHES

Christianity played an important role in the life of the French Concession right up to the Communist Revolution. Dwarfed now by the office towers and shopping malls of Xujiahui, the Roman Catholic Cathedral of St. Ignatius, completed in 1910 (Sat, Sun 1–5 and daily for services: Mon–Fri 7pm, Sat 6pm, Sun 10am) is easily identified by its twin spires and Gothic-style facade of red brick. As well as the cathedral, visitors can see the missionary school (now Xuhui Middle School), the handsome library building (part of Shanghai Public Library), the former convent (now the Old Station Restaurant) and the astronomical observatory, dating from 1872 and still in use today. Boston ivy clings to the walls of the Community Church (Sun 7.30–10, 7–8) on Hengshan Lu, a reminder that it was built by American Protestants in 1925. Around the corner is the former American School, with a design echoing Philadelphia's Independence Hall. The onion-domed Church of St. Nicholas dates from 1933 and once served the Russian community. The sympathetic caretaker who painted an icon of Chairman Mao on the wall saved the church from destruction during the Cultural Revolution. It is now on the heritage list but the future use of the building is uncertain.

HOTELS WITH A PAST

Many of Shanghai's leading citizens built imposing residences in the French Concession. The original owners of what is now the Ruijin Guesthouse were the free-spending sons of Henry Morriss, founding proprietor of the *North China Daily News*, Shanghai's first English-language newspaper. The Morrisses exercised their greyhounds on the magnificent estate before racing them at the neighboring Canidrome (dog track), to which they had private access. The equally imposing grounds of the Donghu Hotel, concealed behind a pair of wrought-iron gates, once belonged to Shanghai's most notorious gangster, Du Yuesheng, better known as 'Big-eared Du'. Du controlled the Shanghai underworld in the 1920s and 1930s and facilitated the massacre of the city's Communists in 1927. A shipping magnate, Eric Moller, built the extraordinary Moller Villa in 1936. Resembling something out of a Gothic fairy tale, it was inspired by a dream of his daughter's and was used as a set in the 2006 movie *The Painted Veil*.

THE SONG CONNECTION

The French Concession was home to members of one of the most powerful families in 20th-century China. Charlie (Chaoshu) Song was a close friend and important financial backer of the country's first president, Sun Yat-sen. The eldest of his three daughters, Ailing Song, married H. H. Kung, finance minister in the National Government. Ailing later brokered the marriage of her youngest sister Meiling to Chiang Kaishek, while the middle sister, Qingling, wed Sun Yat-sen. Charlie's son T. V. Song also served as finance minister under the Nationalists. His former home is now Sasha's, one of Shanghai's most popular nightspots. Meiling and Chiang Kaishek lived for a time behind the pebbledash frontage of Rose Cottage (now part of the Music Conservatory) at 9 Dongping Road; the next-door house (No. 11) belonged to Ailing Song and her husband. To see a typical interior of the period, visit the former home of Sun Yat-sen and Song Qingling, now an evocative museum (daily 9–4.30, 20-minute tour) on Xiangshan Lu. The couple lived in the European-style mansion from 1918 to 1924. Qingling sided with the Communists and became an active opponent of her brother-in-law, Chiang Kaishek. She lived in the house for another 12 years after Sun's death, but kept the window shutters permanently closed as she was under surveillance from Chiang's secret police. As honorary Vice President under the Communists, she served tea to visiting dignitaries in the lovely garden of her official residence (also a museum) just off Huaihai Lu (daily 9–4.30, 20-minute tour).

MORE TO SEE

OLD CHINA HAND READING ROOM

Visit the Old China Hand Reading Room to reflect on the former glories of the French Concession. Owned by photographer Deke Erh and local historian Tess Johnston, whose books, including *The Heart of the French Concession*, are on sale here, the Reading Room has a prettily furnished coffee shop selling walnut cake, cheese cake and brownies.

✉ 27 Shaoxing Lu, near Shaanxi Nanlu ☎ 021 6473 2526 🕐 Daily 10am–midnight
🚇 Shanxi Nanlu 💰 Free (no credit cards for purchases)

Below *The ornate ceiling of the Roman Catholic Cathedral of St. Ignatius*

Above *People's Park, with skyscrapers in the distance*

INFORMATION

✚ 288 C4

INTRODUCTION

This unashamedly modern square is the bustling heart of Shanghai. Attractions include three excellent museums, the Grand Theatre and People's Park, where you can hear birdsong amid the noise. The best way to negotiate People's Square (Renmin Guanchang) is to take the metro exit to Renmin Dadao (People's Avenue), which divides the square in half. All places of interest, with the exception of the Shanghai Museum, are on the north side. Following the avenue east to west will bring you to the main entrance of the Urban Planning Exhibition Centre. Continue past the city hall and the next main building is the Grand Theatre. Turn right out of the avenue and you will see the clock tower of the Art Museum and (just beyond) the entrance to People's Park. Buy a combination ticket for two, three or four sights to save time and money.

The British built the largest racecourse in the Far East here in 1862. Meetings were held twice a year and were such important events on the Shanghai social calendar that foreign banks and businesses closed early. When the Japanese occupied the city in 1941 they turned the race track into an internment camp for enemy nationals (the boy hero of J. G. Ballard's novel *Empire of the Sun* was held here briefly before being transferred to Longhua, ▷ 293). The square was redesigned in the 1990s.

WHAT TO SEE

SHANGHAI ART MUSEUM
www.sh-artmuseum.org.cn

The museum (Shanghai Meishuguan) occupies the former premises of the racecourse club, built by the British in 1933. The building is worth seeing in its own right, as many original features have survived, including the horse's head motifs on the balustrades, the original marble floors and wooden paneling, even a brick fireplace or two. The museum's collection of modern Chinese art ranges from oil paintings and pop art to calligraphy and traditional Chinese painting. Frustratingly there is little in the way of English translation, so the best times to visit are during the Shanghai Biennale or when the museum hosts exhibitions of work by international artists.

➕ 288 C3 ✉ 325 Nanjing Xilu, Huangpu District ☎ 021 6327 2829 ⏰ Daily 9–5; Biennale Sep–end Nov, even years ✋ Adult 20RMB, child (under 16) 5RMB or free if accompanied by a parent 🚇 People's Square

SHANGHAI URBAN PLANNING EXHIBITION CENTRE

This fascinating museum (Chengshi Guihua Zhanshiguan) propels visitors into the future by showing them what Shanghai might look like in the year 2020. Begin your odyssey on the mezzanine floor, where a 20-minute film takes you on a whistle-stop tour of 100 years of Shanghai history. Prepare to be bowled over by the museum's star attraction, a scale model of the city so detailed that it takes up the entire third floor. The high-tech displays on the fourth floor turn the spotlight on mammoth construction projects like the Yangshan deep-water port and the Shanghai World Expo site.

➕ 288 C3 ✉ 100 Renmin Dadao, Huangpu District (entrance on east side) ☎ 021 3306 00277 ⏰ Mon–Thu 9–5, Fri–Sun 9–6 ✋ Adult 30RMB, child (under 1.2m/4ft) free 🚇 People's Square

PEOPLE'S PARK (RENMIN PARK)

Many visitors overlook the pleasant and surprisingly tranquil green space of People's Park (Renmin Gongyuan). There are flowerbeds and manicured lawns, a Chinese-garden, a small lake and a pavilion which contains Barborossa, an excellent Moroccan-style terrace bar and restaurant. The park is popular with office workers at lunchtime but also attracts tai chi practitioners, kick-boxers and kite flying enthusiasts. If you have young children in tow, head for the play area.

➕ 288 C3 ✉ Renmin Park, Huangpu District ⏰ Daily 6–6 ✋ Free 🚇 People's Square

MORE TO SEE

SHANGHAI GRAND THEATRE
www.shgtheatre.com

China's first custom-built opera house was designed by French architect Jean-Marie Charpentier and opened to the public in 1998. The main stage is 1,700sq m (18,500sq ft) in area with a depth of 50m (164 feet) and plays host to a variety of performers, including visiting symphony orchestras. The theater is open for guided tours on Monday mornings; otherwise, visitors are allowed inside only during performances.

➕ 288 C4 ✉ 300 Renmin Dadao, Huangpu District ☎ 021 6386 8686/6372 8701 ⏰ Guided tours Monday 9–11; box office daily 9–7.30 🚇 People's Square

MOCA

The tall glass-fronted building on the south side of People's Park is MOCA (Museum of Contemporary Arts), a private foundation which hosts unusual and avant-garde exhibitions by East Asian artists.

➕ 288 C3 ✉ Gate 7, Renmin Gongyuan, Huangpu District ☎ 021 6327 9900 ⏰ Mon–Sun 10–6 (10 on Wed) ✋ Adult 20RMB, child (under 6) free

TIP
» There are fine views of the square from the glassed-in terrace of Kathleen's Five restaurant, on the fifth floor of the Art Museum, the fifth-floor viewing gallery of the Urban Planning Exhibition Centre and Art Lab, the excellent restaurant and lounge on top of the Museum of Contemporary Art (MOCA).

Below *The clock tower of Shanghai Art Museum*

XINTIANDI

www.xintiandi.com

Akin to a Shikumen theme park, Xintiandi is a successful mix of cafés, stylish restaurants, boutiques, galleries and commercial premises.

This popular shopping and entertainment complex opened in 2001. It was created by rebuilding a run-down 1930s Shikumen estate—knocking down dividing walls, refacing the brick ornaments on gateways, planting trees and making public squares in the open spaces. Only a short distance from People's Square and with a metro station close at hand, Xintiandi is great place for lunch after sightseeing.

The history of the area and the cultural significance of the buildings are explained in detail in the superb Shikumen House Museum (daily 10–10). The ground-floor exhibition provides an informative and entertaining account of the development of Shikumen housing in the city and of what daily life was like for a typical family living in Taipingqia (as Xintiandi was called) in the 1930s. The rooms are crammed with household objects and personal effects—press cuttings and movie posters, typewriters, sewing machines, radios, packing trunks, scent bottles,

even children's toys. The *tingzijia* or 'staircase room' between the first and second floors was usually rented out to students because its north-facing aspect made it cold in winter and stiflingly hot in summer. Xintiandi's other museum, the Memorial House of the First National Congress of the Communist Party of China (daily 9–4), commemorates the founding congress of the Chinese Communist Party, which took place here in July 1921.
288 C5 ✉ Huangpi Nan Lu, Luwan District ☎ 021 6311 2288 🚇 Huangpi Nan Lu 🛈 Visitor Information Center (opposite the Shikumen Museum) 🕙 Sun–Thu 10.30–10.30, Fri–Sat 11–11

NANJING LU

Famous for top-end shopping malls, luxury hotels and designer boutiques, Shanghai's most fashionable street runs all the way from the Bund to Jing'an Temple. The western section, Nanjing Xilu, is famed for its upscale boutiques and malls—Plaza 66, Citic Square

and the Westgate Mall. Farther west is the Shanghai Exhibition Centre. It dates from the 1950s, and its marble-column, chandelier-lit halls now host prestigious commercial shows.

Jing'an Temple (daily 7.30–5) has undergone countless restorations since it was founded, long before Shanghai, in AD247. Jing'an is a good place for antiques and curios, and there is a pleasant park with a café terrace across the road. Two side streets are worth investigating: Waijiang Lu for its Chinese fast food and traditional snacks; Maoming Beilu for 'Bubbling Well Road Apartments,' a model Shikumen estate from the 1930s, perfectly preserved and still very much lived in.

Nanjing Donglu (East Road) was once famous for its dance halls, restaurants and stores. The pedestrianized section is permanently packed but beware of pickpockets and scam artists.
288 A3–289 E3 🍴 3

From left to right *Nanjing Lu at night; entrance to the black-and-red Museum of First Chinese Communist Party Congress in the Xintiandi district*

SHANGHAI MUSEUM

This world-class museum showcases Chinese arts and crafts. There is no better place to discover the riches of China's artistic and cultural heritage. The building on People's Square was designed by Shanghai architect Xing Tonghe in 1994, its unusual shape inspired by an ancient bronze *ding* from the museum's signature gallery. The 120,000 exhibits are displayed to magnificent effect in spotlit and sound-proofed galleries: on the ground floor you can see haunting Buddhist sculptures; on the second, exquisite water and ink landscapes by masters from the Yuan dynasty. Vying for your attention on the third floor are gaudily painted Tibetan face masks; embroidered folk costumes representing China's 56 nationalities; jade pendants with craftsmanship so precise that a magnifying glass is needed to appreciate the detail; and supremely elegant Ming dynasty furniture.

HIGHLIGHTS FROM THE COLLECTIONS

The museum's world-famous collection of bronzes on the ground floor spans more than 2,000 years. The exhibits, used in religious ritual or by the aristocracy as status symbols include drinking vessels, food containers, weapons and musical instruments. Occupying center stage is the *ding*, a three-legged cauldron originally designed for cooking but later used to burn incense.

On the first floor is the ceramics gallery with its fabulous collection of porcelain from the workshops of Jingdezhen. By the 11th century the town's craftsmen were producing glazed porcelain of astonishing quality for the imperial court. 'Made in Jingdezhen' remained a byword for artistic excellence well into the Qing period.

INFORMATION

www.shanghaimuseum.net
➕ 288 C4 ✉ 201 Renmin Dadao, Huangpu District ☎ 021 6372 3500 🕓 Daily 9–5 (last entrance 4) 🍴 Restaurant (open 11–2, first floor); tearoom (second floor) 🖐 Free 🚇 People's Square 📖 Fact sheets and floorplan available in English and other European languages 🎧 Audioguide 40RMB plus 400RMB deposit (or leave passport)

TIP

» The museum store is one of the best places in Shanghai to buy art books. Also on sale are postcards and stationery, promotional videos, T-shirts and bags.

Below *The fountains at the Shanghai Museum at night*

Above *Traditional red-and-black buildings and shopping bazaar*

INFORMATION

✛ 289 E5 🔲 Lao Xi Men

INTRODUCTION

Yu Garden (Yuyuan) is the finest classical Chinese garden in Shanghai and the city's most popular attraction. Nearby is the lively bazaar and famous Huxinting Teahouse. The main entrance to the garden is through the bazaar (daily 8am–10pm), with exits on Fuyou Lu, Anren Jie and Fangbang Zhong Lu. The Nine Zigzag Bridge joins the two attractions and Huxinting Teahouse overlooks the lake. All sights are signposted in English. There is a visitors' information office on Jiujiaochang Lu.

Yu Garden was created for Pan Yunduan, a governor of Sichuan Province during the Ming dynasty. It took 18 years to complete (1559–77). When the family died out, the garden fell into disrepair. It was later used as a barracks during the Opium Wars and as a headquarters by members of the Small Sword Society during their 17-month occupation of Shanghai from 1852 to 1853. It opened to the public in 1961.

WHAT TO SEE

YU GARDEN

The design of Yuyuan, the 'garden of leisurely repose', is similar to the more famous private gardens of Suzhou (▷ 270; 274–275). What makes this one special is the ingenious use of a relatively confined space (2ha/5 acres) to create as many as 40 self-contained miniature landscapes, arranged in groups and partitioned by walls with view-framing windows. The Grand Rockery, near the north entrance, is a dramatic composition in stone representing towering peaks, rushing waterfalls, gorges and caverns. It used to be possible to see ships sailing on the Huangpu River from the 14m-high (46ft) summit.

The Yuhua Hall was the study of the garden's original owner, Pan Yunduan, and contains Ming furniture and porcelain as well as Pan's exquisite calligraphy set. The beams and window surrounds of the Han Bi Tower, made from Burmese nannu wood, are intricately carved with peonies, lilies and Chinese roses. In the Hall of Heralding Spring are displays of weapons and coins dating from the time of the Taiping Rebellion, when it was the headquarters of the Small Swords Society.

Don't miss the splendid 19th-century theater at the south end of the garden, its carved roof embellished with gold foil and guarded by open-mouthed dragons. The celebrated gingko tree, dating back to the time of the Ming, is as old as the garden itself.

✉ 218 Anren Jie, Huangpu District ⏰ Daily 8.30–5 (last ticket at 4.30) 🚌 11, 66, 126, 926 💰 Adult 30RMB, child (under 1.4m/4.5ft) 10RMB 🎫 Tour guides available. Plan of garden inside main entrance

HUXINTING TEAHOUSE AND NINE ZIGZAG BRIDGE

If the large building with the steeply sloping eaves looks familiar it is because it appears on the famous Blue Willow pattern dinner services. Built in 1784, it served as a counting house for cotton merchants before it was converted to a teahouse in 1855. On the walls are framed photographs of visiting dignitaries, including British monarch, Queen Elizabeth II, and President Bill Clinton. Outside, the Nine Zigzag Bridge is designed to ward off evil spirits who, it was believed, were unable to turn corners. According to tradition, feeding the carp pleases the Buddha.

✉ 257 Yuyuan Lu, Huangpu District ⏰ 8.30am–9pm

TIPS

» Yu Garden can be unbearably crowded, especially on summer weekends. The best times to visit are early in the morning or at lunchtime.

» Haggling is expected in the bazaar but you may be able to negotiate a better price in the smaller shops on Fangbang Zhonglu, once you have an idea of the going rate.

» There are ATMs at the Fangbang Zhonglu entrance to the bazaar and at the corner of Fuyou Lu and Jiujiaochang Lu.

» You can use credit cards in the teahouse and for major purchases in the bazaar.

REGIONS **SHANGHAI • SIGHTS**

Left *The exterior of the Hall of Heralding Spring*
Below *Looking down on the Nine Zigzag Bridge*

INFORMATION
✚ 289 D5

TIPS

» For the best atmosphere in the markets, come on Sunday, when Chinese bargain-hunters are out in force.

» What makes the Cang Bao building special is the third-floor flea market, with its dusty old gramaphones, Chinese musical instruments, suits of armor and assorted bric-a-brac.

» The stalls along the nearby Dongtai Lu Antiques market generally sell replica rather than genuine antiques.

Below *People outside the Shanghai Classical Hotel at Fuyou Lu in the Old Town of Shanghai*

NAN SHI

All Shanghai was once contained within the Old Town (Nan Shi), a circular area marked on modern maps by Renmin Lu and Zhonghua Lu and today the area is an enclave packed with traditional tenement houses, street markets and neighborhood temples. A small section of the 5km (3-mile) Ming dynasty wall survives as the Dajing Pavilion (daily 9–4.30), where visitors can see old photographs and paintings.

Refurbished in 2002 with American help, the Sanshan Guildhall (daily 9–4) is a must-see for its elaborately carved opera stage, dating from 1909. The side galleries form the Museum of Folk Collectibles and contain modest displays of arts and crafts from the period. Chenxiang Ge, the largest Buddhist temple in China (daily 7–4), takes its name from an eaglewood statue of the Buddha, which gives off a resinous scent in damp weather. The Temple and School of Confucius (daily 9–5), founded in the 13th century, moved to its present location on Wenmiao Lu in 1855. Inside are prayer halls, pagodas and carp ponds.

MARKETS

There are markets on many street corners in the Old Town. One of the busiest is on Dajing Lu, by Luxianghua Lu. At the Dongtai Lu antiques market (daily 9.30–6) most visitors rummage among Mao memorabilia and assorted kitsch. Don't miss the South Bund Soft Spinning Material Market (Sun–Thu 8.30–6, Fri–Sat 8.30–7) tailors can run up a Chinese *qipao* dress or linen suit in two or three days, at a fraction of the shop price.

THE BUND

The Bund's grandiose buildings, dating mostly from the 1920s, were once occupied by overseas banks, newspaper offices, consulates and shipping companies. The Communists preserved these monuments to capitalism as a reminder of hated Western exploitation. Under today's more pragmatic rulers the Bund has gained a new lease of life, as the renovated buildings are leased by art galleries, designer boutiques, smart restaurants and hotels. Bund is an Anglo-Indian word meaning 'embankment.'

IMPOSING BUILDINGS

The white-domed building at No. 12 is the former offices of the Hong Kong and Shanghai Banking Corporation (HSBC) and dates from 1923. Behind the imposing frontage, guarded by a pair of bronze lions, is an octagonal forecourt with stunning mosaic panels. Tellers still conduct their business under the lofty glass-vaulted roof of the main hall. A side entrance leads to the second-floor café, which has 1920s furnishings, including a fireplace, art deco light fittings, period photographs and maps.

Next door, the former Customs House dates from 1925–27. Above the portico, with its massive granite columns, is the clock and bell tower, known as 'Big Ching' after London's Big Ben. The mechanism was restored for the visit of Queen Elizabeth II to Shanghai in 1986, although the anthem it played was 'The East is Red.'

The art deco masterpiece with the green pyramid on the corner of Nanjing Lu, now the Peace Hotel, was the private residence and offices of the banking tycoon Victor Sassoon (his penthouse suite had the best views of the city). The building also housed the luxurious Cathay Hotel (1929). In 2007 the building closed for a massive renovation project. It is due to reopen in 2010.

INFORMATION
✚ 289 E4–E3

Above *Grand buildings of the Bund viewed from the Riverside Promenade*

PUDONG

INTRODUCTION

Pudong covers an area of more than 530sq km (200sq miles) but most visitors will not venture much farther than the financial district of Lujiazui. Getting around is straightforward as stations on metro line 2 serve major attractions such as the Oriental Pearl Tower, Shanghai Ocean Aquarium (▷ 320), the Science and Technology Museum and the Maglev train terminal. The café terraces around Lujiazui Green and Riverside Park offer a relaxing stop.

WHAT TO SEE

JINMAO TOWER

www.jinmao88.com

A Chinese pagoda inspired the design of this soaring structure, completed in 1999 and topped out at 420m (1,380ft), and on a clear day there are spectacular views from the observation deck on the 88th floor. There are shops selling souvenirs and you can send a postcard from the on-site post office. Return after dark for more views from the Cloud 9 bar on the 87th floor of the Grand Hyatt hotel.

✚ 289 F4 (Observatory 88) ✉ 2 Shiji Dadao ☎ 021 5047 0088 ⏱ Daily 8.30am–9.30pm 🎫 Adult 50RMB, child (under 1.2m/4ft) 25RMB Ⓜ Lujiazui

INFORMATION

✚ 289 F4

Opposite *Pudong's modern skyline*
Above *Looking down through the 420m-high (1,380ft) Jinmao Tower*

SHANGHAI SCIENCE AND TECHNOLOGY MUSEUM

www.sstm.org.cn

This state-of-the-art museum, the largest of its kind in Asia, opened to acclaim
in 2001. The scope of the exhibition is as ambitious as the building's futuristic
design and covers everything from biodiversity and space exploration to
design innovation and the latest in digital technology. However, the dry English
translations may dampen the enthusiasm of Western children.

🞢 Off map 289 F4 ✉ 2000 Shiji Dadao ☎ 021 6862 2000 (hotline) 🕐 Tue–Sun 9–5.15 (last
ticket 4.30). Closed Mon except for national holidays ✋ Adult 60RMB, child (under 1.2m/4ft)
20RMB. Extra charge for IMAX and IWERKS 4-D cinemas 🚇 Science and Technology Museum

ORIENTAL PEARL TOWER

This familiar 1994 landmark on the Shanghai skyline was the first major
project in Pudong to be completed. At 468m (1,536ft), it is the highest
communications tower in Asia. The 11 spheres contain shops, offices, a hotel,
a revolving restarant and observation galleries. The basement Municipal History
Museum takes visitors on a spellbinding journey through the city's tumultuous
past. The Pearl Dock is the departure point for river cruises.

🞢 289 F4 ✉ 1 Shiji Dadao ☎ 021 5879 1888 🕐 Daily 8am–9.30pm ✋ Adult from 35RMB
(Municipal History Museum) to 135RMB (three obseration galleries and museum), child under
1.2m(4ft) half price, under 0.8m (2.6ft) free 🚇 Lujiazui 🚢 Cruises 50/70RMB

MORE TO SEE

SHANGHAI WORLD FINANCIAL CENTRE

www.swfc-observatory.com

At 101 floors and 492m/1,621ft in stature, the Shanghai World Financial Centre
became the world's tallest flat-roof building when it opened in August 2008.
The building is home to scores of multinational companies, as well as the
super-exclusive Park Hyatt hotel. However the public also gets to enjoy the
view thanks to a breathtaking multilevel sightseeing facility which features a
55m-long (180ft) viewing platform on the 100th story (the highest observation
deck in the world), a glass-enclosed sky bridge on the 97th floor and a massive
observatory on 94. Three price tiers reflect access to the different levels.

🞢 289 F4 ✉ 100 Shiji Da Dao ☎ 021 5878 0101 🕐 Daily 8am–11pm (last ticket 10pm)
✋ Adult 100–150RMB, child (under 1.2m/4ft 50–75RMB) 🚇 Dongchang Lu

Right *A Maglev train*
Below *The futuristic Shanghai Science
and Technology Museum*

HONGKOU

The sights in this traditional working-class neighborhood include the former Jewish ghetto and Duolun Lu, once the haunt of radical writers.

On the eve of World War II Shanghai was one of a handful of cities in the world prepared to offer asylum to Jews fleeing Hitler's Germany. The immigrants were classed as stateless refugees by the Japanese occupying forces and confined to a ghetto in Hongkou. By 1942 there were at least 25,000 Jews living in cramped but tolerable conditions off Changyang Lu. The story of the community is told in the Jewish Refugee Memorial Hall (daily 9–4), founded in 1927 by Ashkenazi Jews fleeing persecution in Russia. Adjacent Ohel Moishe Synagogue has recently been refurbished with the help of the Israeli Consulate and is well worth a look for anyone interested in Shanghai Jewish heritage.

DUOLUN LU CULTURAL STREET

If you take the line 3 light railway to Baoxing Donglu, turn right out of the station then left on to Sichuan Beilu, you will come to Duolun after about 5 minutes' walk. This restored, pedestrian street of Shikumen houses and villas is lined with galleries, curio shops, teahouses and terrace cafés. Photograph the old brick doorways, the clock tower and the former Great Virtue Church, with its curious blend of Chinese and Western styles, or check out the exhibitions in the Duolun Museum of Modern Art (daily 9–5). Bronze statues commemorate the radical writers who met here in the 1930s. The most famous, Lu Xun, had a profound influence on Chinese literature and is still revered. Find out more about him by visiting the museum in Lu Xun Park.

INFORMATION

✠ Hongkou 289 F1 ✠ Duolun Lu 289 E1 ℹ Outside the main gate of Lu Xun Park, at the corner of Jiangwan Lu and Tian'ai Lu

TIPS

» Several local tour companies organize guided visits to the ghetto and other sights associated with Shanghai's Jewish community, at one time the largest in East Asia. If you're traveling independently, pick up the official leaflet from the Synagogue—the map will point you in the direction of other places of interest.

» Many storeowners on Duolun specialize in collectibles: Mao badges at No. 183, chopsticks at No. 191, porcelain at No. 185, while '1933' is an Aladdin's cave of period bric-a-brac.

Below *People on busy Duolun Lu*

THE FRENCH CONCESSION

Stroll back in time through the tree-lined streets of the former French Concession. The rich architectural heritage of this historic neighborhood, allowed to fall into neglect during the Cultural Revolution, has now been recognized and many of the mansions and suburban villas are being restored to their original splendor.

THE WALK
Distance: 3.5km (2 miles)
Allow: 2–2.5 hours
Start: Corner of Yandang Lu and Huaihai Zhonglu ✚ 288 C4
End: Shanxi Nanlu metro ✚ 288 A4

HOW TO GET THERE
Leave Shanxi Nanlu metro station (line 1) by the Huaihai Zhonglu exit and walk or take a bus in an easterly direction toward Yandang Lu.

★ The walk begins on busy Huaihai Zhonglu, one of Shanghai's premier shopping streets.

Turn right into Yandang Lu and walk down this street and through the parking area to Fuxing Park.

❶ Fuxing Park—the 'French Park' as it used to be known—is one of the city's most delightful green spaces. It is bordered by plane trees planted in the 1920s. Beyond the formal French gardens is a traditional Chinese lotus pond and pavilion, popular with local fishermen.

Take the right-hand path from the gate to pass Shanghai's only public monument to the founders of Communism, Marx and Engels. Tai chi enthusiasts gather here most mornings. Follow the path toward the children's playground and amusement park. The pink-and-green mansion to the right is Park 97, a haunt of Shanghai's smart set with four venues, including Upstairs at Park 97.

Leave the park here through the west gate and turn left onto Sinan Lu. The pebble-dash houses here were once the homes of wealthy residents but were taken over by ordinary Shanghainese in the Communist era. On your left, beyond Xiangshan Lu, is the former residence of the president of the first Chinese Republic, Sun Yat-sen (▷ 297).

❷ The Residence of Sun Yat-sen is open for guided tours and is well preserved, with the original wood-paneling and brick fireplaces intact. The furnishings include Sun's American gramophone, his folding desk and his priceless collection of porcelain.

Continue down Sinan Lu to Fuxing Zhonglu and turn right. About 100m (110 yards) on your left is an archway leading to lane No. 553, a 1930s housing development built

for the French Concession's half million Chinese residents. Plaques honor revolutionaries who lived in the neighborhood.

Return to Fuxing Zhonglu and continue walking to Ruijin 2-Lu. Turn left and cross the road to enter the Ruijin Guesthouse (look for the row of globe lamps on top of the wall by the gate). Walk through the extensive grounds of this former estate, where many of the 1920s villas have been converted to bars and restaurants. Take the exit on Maoming Nanlu and turn right. On the corner of Nanchang Lu are the art deco Astrid Apartments. Continue to Huaihai Zhonglu. Cross the road to the former Cathay Theater, a 1932 art deco building with a pencil-thin stone tower. Cross over Maoming Nanlu and on your left look out for the Okura Garden Hotel, which contains the former French Club, known as the Cercle Sportif Français.

❸ Cercle Sportif Français is a stunning French Renaissance-style mansion completed in 1926, when the luxurious amenities included an indoor pool, bowling alley, billiard hall, ballroom and 20 lawn tennis courts. Enter via the side entrance on Maoming Nanlu and climb the staircase to the Grand Ballroom to see some of the art deco features.

Cross over Maoming Nanlu. Near the junction with Changle Lu on your right is the Jinjiang Hotel.

❹ The north block of the Jinjiang Hotel was originally the Cathay Mansions where US President Nixon and Chinese Premier Zhou Enlai signed the 'Shanghai Communique' in 1972, the first step toward normalizing relations between the two countries.

Opposite the hotel, on Changle Lu, is the Lyceum Theatre, once the British Amateur Dramatic Club. Gilbert and Sullivan operettas are still occasionally performed here. Turn left onto Changle Lu and pass a row of silk boutiques on your way to Shaanxi Nanlu. Turn left again and walk down to Shanxi Nanlu metro station on the corner of Huaihai Zhonglu.

WHEN TO GO
Ideally do this walk in the afternoon or early evening.

PLACE TO VISIT
FUXING PARK
🕐 24 hours

WHERE TO EAT
ART DECO CAFÉ
✉ Building 3 Ruijin Guesthouse, 118 Ruijin Erlu ☎ 021 6472 5222 🕐 Daily 9am–1am

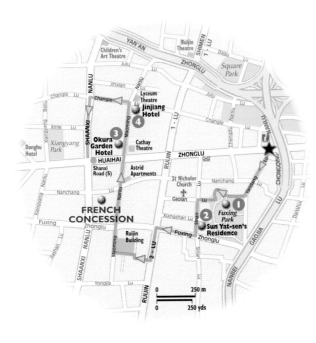

Opposite *Exterior of the former house of Zhou En Lai (once Premier and Foreign Minister)*
Above *The white Colonial-style Shanghai Arts and Crafts Museum in the French Concession*

SHANGHAI OLD TOWN

This walk guides you through the atmospheric back streets of the Old Town, taking in the remains of the Ming dynasty walls, a Taoist Temple and the famous Yu Garden (Yuyuan) and Yu Garden Bazaar (Yuyuan Bazaar).

THE WALK

Distance: 2.5km (1.5 miles)
Allow: 1.5 hours
Start/end: Dajing Lu
✚ 289 D5

HOW TO GET THERE

Take the metro to Lao Xi Men. From here it is a short walk to Dajing Lu. Head north along Zhonghua Lu which soon becomes Renmin Lu. At the old watch tower, turn right onto Dajing Lu.

★ This section of Dajing Lu is the middle of a vast building project. At the time of writing, most of the old buildings here had been cleared, with the odd ruined mansion still standing. Two buildings that were spared the wrecking ball lie on the north side of Dajing Lu. The first is the only surviving section of the Ancient City Wall (Guchengxiang Dajing Ge), which has a small exhibit on life in the Old City. Just past that is the Baiyun Daoist Temple (Baiyun Guan), which has a photogenic grand central courtyard.

Head toward the skyscrapers of Pudong, through the building project, until you meet Dajing Lu's junction with Luxianghua Lu. Here the terraces of cramped wooden homes return, along with the associated crowds. This is one of Shanghai's most famous outdoor markets and fruit and vegetables will likely be spread across the pavement, alongside the odd live turtle or duck. Continue along Dajing Lu with its cacophony of market cries and motorbike horns, until you reach Henan Nan Lu. Cross Henan Nanlu, turn right and take the next left onto Zihua Lu. Cross Houjia Lu and follow the lane to the right (Beiwang Yima Long). At the end is a white wall. Continue walking, with the wall on your right. As Beiwang Lane becomes Wangyima lane thread your way round to emerge on Chenxiangge Lu. Turn right, passing the Chenxiang Ge (▷ 304). Ahead of you is the Yuyuan Bazaar.

❶ Despite appearances, the Yuyuan Bazaar was constructed in the 1990s. This is one of the best places in Shanghai for gifts and souvenirs, though not for antiques. Street artists entertain the crowds on summer weekends, while the Yuyuan Stage puts on folk performances nightly, including excerpts from Beijing Opera.

Enter the bazaar by the lane adjoining Tong Hang Chun pharmacy, which has sold traditional Chinese medicines since 1783. Turn right onto Liangting Lu and follow the signs to the Yu Garden (left). You will come directly to a small lake with the Nine Zigzag bridge and the famous Huxinting Teahouse (▷ 303) straight ahead. Overlooking the lake

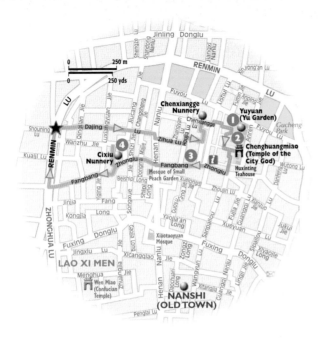

as it becomes more residential. Where it doglegs to the left, take the right fork (Zhenling Lu). When you reach the stalls selling incense sticks you will have arrived at the Cixiu Nunnery.

❹ A Buddhist temple, dating from 1869, the Cixiu Nunnery takes its name from the silk embroidery which was once a specialty of the convent.

Return to Fangbang Zhonglu and turn right. At Renmin Lu turn right and continue to the junction with Dajing Lu. From here retrace your steps to People's Square.

WHEN TO GO
It is best to do this walk in the morning, when the markets are at their busiest.

PLACES TO VISIT
TEMPLE OF THE CITY GOD
🕐 Daily 8.30–4.30 ✋ 5RMB

CIXIU NUNNERY
🕐 Daily 8.30–4.30 ✋ 10RMB

WHERE TO EAT
NAN XIANG STEAMED BUN RESTAURANT
✉ 85 Yuyuan Lu 🕐 Daily 10–9

---

to your left is Nan Xiang Steamed Bun Restaurant, where you can join the line for typical Shanghainese specialties like *xiaolongbao* (steamed meat dumplings). To visit the garden (▷ 302), cross the bridge to the entrance in the white wall beyond. Otherwise take the street to the right of the square, following the signs for Central Plaza. Turn left and ahead of you is the side entrance to the Taoist Temple.

❷ The Temple of the City God has been reconstructed more than 20 times since it was founded in 1403, but its popularity with devotees remains undiminished. The Hall of the City God is to the rear of the building, beyond the inner courtyard, where you may see red-robed trainee monks.

Leave the temple by the main gate on Fangbang Zhonglu, once a canal leading to the Old Town harbor. Turn right, passing 'Fashion Street' then continue ahead.

❸ On Fangbang Zhonglu, also known as 'Shanghai Old Street' most of the shops sell typical Chinese souvenirs and imitation antiques. Take a break at the Old Shanghai Teahouse, with its 1920s period furnishings.

Beyond the ceremonial archway cross Henan Nanlu and continue on Fangbang Zhonglu, which narrows

Opposite *Huxinting Teahouse in the Yu Garden*

Right *Vegetables for sale in the Old Town*

TWO WATERFRONTS

This walk will guide you down Shanghai's two highly contrasting waterfronts. On the one hand, the Bund embankment, its bombastic architecture redolent of the age of empires; on the other, the uncompromisingly modern skyline of Pudong with its face defiantly toward the third millennium. You will enjoy close-up views of the river traffic on the Huangpu after making the crossing via the entertaining Bund Tourist Tunnel.

THE WALK

Distance: 4km (2.5 miles)
Allow: 3 hours
Start: Nanjing Donglu
✚ 289 D3
End: Lujiazui metro station
✚ 289 F4

HOW TO GET THERE

From Nanjing Donglu metro station take Nanjing Donglu and walk east towards the river, crossing Henan Zhonglu.

★ Nanjing Donglu, partly closed to traffic, is the eastern end of Shanghai's famous shopping street.

At the bottom of Nanjing Donglu you will see the Peace Hotel on your left. Turn right onto the Bund and continue walking as far as the junction with the Yan'an Donglu.

❶ Three buildings have been instrumental in the commercial regeneration of the Bund. No. 3, No. 5 and No. 18 are now home to brand name boutiques, art galleries, bars and gourmet restaurants.

At No. 1, cross the road via the overpass and stroll back along the raised promenade, past the ferry and boat moorings.

❷ As the main customs port, this section of Shanghai's riverbank would have been crowded with cargo ships back in the colonial era. These days it is busy with an array of tourist vessels though only the largest of them—the multistory dragon boat—actually departs from here. A new dedicated pier—Shiliu Pu (Pier 16)—has been built about 1km (0.5 mile) south on Zhongshan Dong Er Lu.

Continue walking, looking to your left to appreciate the magnificent ensemble of buildings lining the Bund.

❸ The cream building (No. 6) with mock-Gothic spires and turrets dates from 1897 and was built for the Imperial Bank of China. Two doors down is a handsome salmon-pink building with a granite balcony, former offices. Four Atlases support the roof of the former offices of the *North China Daily News* at No. 17. At the end of the promenade, take the steps on the left down to Huangpu Park.

❹ There are great views of Pudong and Suzhou Creek. Under the Monument to the People's Heroes is the Bund Historical Museum with displays of old photographs of the area. Leave the park and walk back along the promenade to the entrance of the Sightseeing Tunnel, accessible from the subway beneath Zhongshan Dong Yi Lu.

❺ The tunnel, billed as a sound and light experience, entails a five-minute journey in a glass pod through 'magma chambers,' 'meteor showers' and the like, and will appeal especially to visitors with young children.

Leave the tunnel, turn right and walk as far as the river. From the viewing terrace in front of the International Convention Centre you can look across to Huangpu Park and the site of the North Bund development.

❻ Turn left and walk along the riverfront, passing a couple of bars and restaurants on the grassy slope above 'Wave View Platform,' which is occasionally flooded by summer tide water. Beyond the platform the path climbs to the Lujiazui Xilu exit and the local bus terminus. To continue the promenade walk, turn right to return to the riverfront at the former wharf of the Lixin Shipyard. From here you can walk through Riverside Park, with more terrace bars and restaurants. Plans are underway to extend the park farther down river. Return to Lujiazui Xilu and walk to the Pearl Tower. Buy a ticket for the superb Shanghai Municipal History Museum, in the base of the tower and spend 1–1.5 hours exploring the fascinating exhibits. Take exit four from the station to cross Yincheng Zhonglu to Lujiazui Green.

❼ End the walk at nearby Lujiazui metro station. If you can't face the metro's crowds just yet, take exit four to cross Yincheng Lu to Lujiazui Green. The first trees in Pudong new area were planted on what is now Lujiazui Green in 1997. The park is especially popular with local office workers who enjoy sitting in the shade of the White Sail canopy beside the lake. Return to Lujiazui metro station.

PLACES TO VISIT
BUND HISTORICAL MUSEUM
🕐 Daily 9–4 👋 Free

BUND SIGHTSEEING TUNNEL
🕐 8am–10pm (10.30 in summer) 👋 Adult one way 30RMB, round trip 40RMB, child (under 1.2m/4ft) 15RMB

SHANGHAI MUNICIPAL HISTORY MUSEUM
☎ 021 5879 8888
🕐 Daily 8am–9.30pm 👋 35RMB

WHERE TO EAT
THE KITCHEN SALVATORE CUOMO
✉ Unit D, 2967 Lujiazui Xilu ☎ 021 5054 1265 🕐 Daily 11–2.30, 6–11

Opposite *The skyscrapers of the Pudong district*
Below *The Customs House*

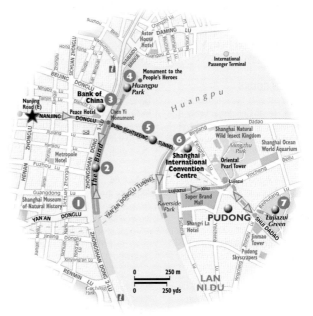

WHAT TO DO

SHOPPING

**ARTS AND CRAFTS MUSEUM
STORE (▷ 296)**

GARDEN BOOKS

This airy, well-lit bookstore in the
former French Concession sells a
wide range of imported titles, as
well as magazines and newspapers.
The other big plus is the pleasant
café and ice-cream parlor at the
front of the shop.

✉ 325 Changle Lu, Xuhui District ☎ 021
5404 8728 ⓒ Daily 10–10 ⓜ Shanxi
Nanlu

HONGQIAO INTERNATIONAL
PEARL CITY

www.hqpearl.com
Word on the grapevine is that the
prices of the fresh- and seawater
pearls in this shopping center, in the
west of the city, cannot be beaten.

Either commission your own jewelry
or buy ready-made pendants, clasps,
brooches, rings and necklaces
from one of numerous counters—
bargain hard.

✉ 3721 Hong Mei Lu, by Yan'an Xilu,
Minhang District ☎ 021 6465 0000/021
6262 6588 ⓒ Daily 10–9 🚌 911, 925, 936
to Hongqiao Lu/Hong Mei Lu crossing, then
10-min walk

PLAZA 66

Arguably the pick of the malls
lining Shanghai's main shopping
street, Plaza 66 is the place to head
if money is no object. There are
more than 100 top designer brands
represented here, from Hermès
and Ermenogildo Zegna to Bang
& Olufsen and Edinburgh Crystal.
Handy for the Shanghai Centre and
the Ritz-Carlton Hotel.

✉ 1266 Nanjing Xilu, Jing'an District

Above *People eating and drinking outside
in the garden in Sasha's in the French
Concession district*

☎ 021 6279 0910 ⓒ Daily 10–10
ⓜ Nanjing Xilu

PROPAGANDA POSTER
ART CENTRE

The private collector who runs
this store, in the basement of an
apartment building, will show you
his collection of socialist art posters
dating to the Mao era.

✉ Basement, Building B, 868 Huashan Lu,
Jing'an District ☎ 021 6211 1845 ⓒ Daily
10–4.30 🎫 Admission charge 20RMB
ⓜ Changshu Lu

RAFFLES CITY

www.rafflescity-shanghai.com
This Singaporean-owned mall
has won plaudits for being a

well-designed and comfortable place to shop. Raffles is especially good for casual clothes with chainstore names like Etam well represented. The amenities in Raffles include a cinema and a spa and fitness center on the seventh floor.

✉ Xizang Zhonglu, Huangpu District ☎ 021 6340 3600 🕐 Daily 10–10 🚇 People's Square

SILK MUSEUM

This emporium on the edge of the Yuan Bazaar sells all manner of silk, from shirts and jackets to quilts and embroidered pajamas.

✉ 125 Jiujiaochang Lu, Huangpu District ☎ 021 6355 0312 🕐 Daily 9–5.30 🚇 Nanjing Donglu

SOUTH BUND SOFT SPINNING MATERIAL MARKET

The former Dongjiadu Market moved to these new indoor premises in 2006. There is a huge selection of raw textiles to choose from (wool, silk, linen, cotton and so on)—and you should expect to pay in the region of 20–30RMB per meter. If you have a day or two to spare, go to a tailor and ask to have something made to measure, or alternatively buy off the rack. While very little English is spoken you will be amazed by how much can be understood by sign language.

✉ 399 Lujiabang Lu, Huangpu District ☎ 021 6377 2236 🕐 Daily 8.30–6 🚌 43, 64, 109, 251, 801, 928, 931

SPIN

Arguably Shanghai's most essential store, Spin sells gleefully eccentric porcelain designs—think double-spout teapots—all made using traditional methods in China's ancient ceramics capital, Jingdezhen. It's owned by the Taiwanese group behind the nearby trendsetting restaurants of People 7 and Shintori Null II, and has the same stark feel, with unadorned concrete making the shop floor feel a lot like the factory floor.

✉ Building 3, 758 Julu Lu (nr Fumin Lu) ☎ 021 6279 2545 🕐 Daily 11.30am–9pm

ENTERTAINMENT AND NIGHTLIFE

BARBAROSSA

www.barbarossa.com.cn

A restaurant by day and a nightclub after dark, Barbarossa has a fantastic location in People's Park with terrace tables overlooking the lake. DJs play chill-out, trip-hop and house music in the upstairs lounge. During happy hour, from 5 to 8, drinks are cheaper.

✉ 231 Nanjing Xilu, Huangpu District ☎ 021 6318 0220 🕐 Daily 11am–2am, lunch served 11–2 ✋ Varies; Sat, Sun brunch 88RMB 🚇 People's Square

BAR ROUGE

The stable companion of Sens & Bund (▷ 326) restaurant serves cocktails with haute cuisine tapas and finger food. The fantastic views of the river are the other attraction. The expensive cocktails and cover charge are priced for the fashionable jet-set crowd.

✉ 7F 18 Zhongshan Dong Yilu (The Bund), Huangpu District ☎ 021 6339 1199 🕐 Sun–Thu 6.30pm–2am, Fri, Sat 6.30pm–4am ✋ 150RMB 🚇 Nanjing Donglu

BLARNEY STONE

Situated in a leafy corner of the French Concession, the Blarney Stone attracts a loyal crowd of regulars who come here to chat, play pool or listen to the band that takes to the stage every night except Tuesday from 8pm. The Irish manager is very welcoming.

✉ 5A Dongping Lu, Xuhui District ☎ 021 6415 7496 🕐 Mon–Wed 4pm–1.30am, Thu–Sun 11am–1.30am 🚇 Changshu Lu/Hengshan Lu

BLUE FROG

Any bar that can rise above the sleaze on Tongren Lu—Shanghai's most thriving expat bar strip—deserves respect and admiration. So it is with the longstanding Blue Frog, a three-story bar that comes with smooth chill-out sounds and distinguished cocktails. The happy hour deals draw a good after-work crowd.

✉ 86 Tongren Lu ☎ 021 6247 0320 🕐 Daily 11am–late 🚇 Jing'an Temple

THE CATHAY THEATRE

The Cathay Theatre building is something of a landmark on Huaihai Lu, thanks largely to the building's signature art deco spire. There are more modern cinema complexes (notably in Xintiandi or the Raffles Mall) but this is a top choice for atmosphere thanks to the well-restored 1930s building.

✉ 870 Huaihai Zhonglu ☎ 021 5404 2095 🕐 Daily 12–12

CLOUD 9 BAR

www.shanghai.grand.hyatt.com

An opportunity to say you've had a drink in one of the world's highest bars, 420m (1,378ft) above street level. The surroundings are undistinguished and the drink prices exorbitant, but the views make it all worthwhile.

✉ Grand Hyatt Hotel, Jinmao Tower, 88 Shiji Dadao, Pudong District ☎ 021 5049 1234 🕐 Mon–Thu 6pm–1am, Fri 6pm–2am, Sat 11am–2am, Sun 11am–1am ✋ No cover charge, but minumum charge of 138RMB per person after 8pm 🚇 Lujiazui

COTTON'S

www.cottons-shanghai.com

Set in a sleepy corner of the French Concession, this gorgeous villa-bar offers a refreshingly friendly welcome. The building retains its residential layout, and the open hearths make it a cozy venue in winter. Eponymous owner, Cotton, also serves up spicy bar food from Hunan. Despite the posh facade, Cotton's is a down-to-earth pub and remains sociable till late.

✉ 132 Anting Lu (nr Jianguo Xilu) ☎ 021 6433 7995 🕐 Sun–Thu 11am–2am, Fri–Sat 11am–4am

ERA: INTERSECTION OF TIME

www.era-shanghai.com

Unlike the other big stage spectacles in Shanghai, everything about ERA feels fresh, from the innovative Cirque du Soleil choreography to the hi-tech auditorium in which this multimedia spectacular is held. All the usual Chinese circus tricks—hoop-jumping, magic, contortion and

balancing—are given an elegant modern arrangement. The icing on the cake is a pair of staggering, death-defying acts that end both halves of the show. This is the king of all acrobatics shows in Shanghai.
✉ 2266 Gonghexin Lu ☎ 021 6630 0000 🕐 Daily 7.30pm–9.15pm 💰 80–580RMB 🚇 Shanghai Circus World

HOUSE OF BLUES AND JAZZ
This old jazz favorite moved in 2008 to a grand new venue beside the Bund. The new furnishings recreate the glamour of the 'golden era'; there are stacked chandeliers, glossy floral wallpaper and some lovely original antique fittings. There's no cover charge to see the nightly music, but drink prices are extremely high.
✉ 60 Fuzhou Lu (nr Zhongshan Dongyilu) ☎ 021 6323 2779 🕐 Daily 11am–3am

NEW HEIGHTS
Dig deep into your pocket and enjoy this stylish bar, popular with Shanghai's beautiful people. There are fabulous views of the Pudong skyline from the indoor terrace and a drinks menu which ranges from champagne to cocktails. Music is supplied by highly professional DJs.
✉ 7F, Three on the Bund, 3 Zhongshan Donglu, Huangpu District ☎ 021 6321 0909 🕐 Daily 10am–2am 🚇 Nanjing Donglu

SASHA'S
www.sashas-shanghai.com
The main attraction of this converted villa is its garden terrace. Sasha's also serves great mojitos, one reason why the place is heaving on weekends. Pub food is served, as are John Smith's and Guinness.
✉ House 11, 9 Dongping Lu, Xuhui District ☎ 021 6474 6628 🕐 Sun–Thu 11am–1am, Fri–Sat 11am–2am 🚇 Changshu Lu/ Hengshan Lu

SHANGHAI CENTRE THEATRE
www.ashp.com
This large theater complex with the Portman-Ritz Carlton Hotel, is the home of the Shanghai Acrobatic Troupe who put on a nightly show. It's a fantastic spectacle but still feels a bit tired compared with newer shows like ERA (▷ 317).
✉ 1376 Nanjing Xilu, Jing'an District ☎ 021 6279 8948 🕐 Daily 9am–7pm 💰 70–200RMB 🚇 Jing'an Temple

SHANGHAI CIRCUS WORLD
www.circus-world.com
This modern stage in the north of the city is an alternative venue for performances by the Shanghai Acrobatic Troupe. You can also see traditional circus here, which includes animal acts.
✉ 2266 Gonghexin Lu, Zhabei District ☎ 021 5665 6622 🕐 Daily show at 7.30 💰 80–580RMB 🚇 Shanghai Circus World

SHANGHAI CONCERT HALL
www.culture.sh.cn
This handsome classical building, to the south of People's Square, was built as the Nanking Theatre in 1930. It was famously moved, brick by brick, a distance of 66m (216ft) to its present site in 2004. The 1,200-seat concert hall hosts regular performances by the Shanghai Symphony Orchestra and artists from abroad.
✉ 523 Yan'an Donglu, Huangpu District ☎ 021 5386 6666; booking hotline: 021 6217 2426/3055 🕐 Daily 9–7.30 💰 50–1,080 RMB 🚇 People's Square

SHANGHAI CONSERVATORY OF MUSIC
www.culture.sh.cn
Founded in 1927, this is China's premier nursery for musical talent. The He Luting concert hall is the venue for recitals, chamber concerts and other musical events, at lunchtimes as well as evenings.
✉ 20 Fenyang Lu, Xuhui District ☎ 021 6431 0334; booking hotline: 021 6217 2426/3055 🕐 Box office daily 9–7.30 💰 50–100RMB 🚇 Changshu Lu

SHANGHAI FILM ART CENTRE
The main venue for the Shanghai International Film Festival regularly screens new Chinese releases, as well as some foreign films.
✉ 160 Xinhua Lu, Xuhui District ☎ 021 6280 4088 🕐 Daily 💰 50–80RMB 🚇 Xujiahui

SHANGHAI GRAND THEATRE
www.shgtheatre.com (Chinese only)
The impressive glass-fronted theater dominating People's Square is famed for its acoustics and huge stage. There are several auditoriums, presenting anything from symphony concerts and chamber recitals to Western opera, ballet and musicals.
✉ 300 Renmin Dadao, Huangpu District ☎ 021 6386 8686 🕐 Box office daily 9–7.30 💰 100–1,000RMB 🚇 People's Square

SHANGHAI ORIENTAL ARTS CENTRE
www.shoac.com.cn
This enormous arts complex, designed by French architect Paul Andreu to resemble the petals of an orchid, has two concert halls, an opera house and an exhibition hall, with a total seating capacity of 3,000. The Shanghai Symphony Orchestra regularly performs here, as do visiting artists from abroad.
✉ 425 Ding Xiang Lu, Pudong District ☎ 021 3842 4800; tickets: 021 6854 1237 🕐 Box office daily 9–8 💰 30–4,000RMB 🚇 Science and Technology Museum

TIANCHAN YIFU THEATRE
www.culture.sh.cn
Head to this theater, built in 1925 and renovated in 2004, if you are interested in seeing Beijing and other forms of Chinese opera. There are evening performances most days and a Sunday matinee.
✉ 701 Fuzhou Lu, Huangpu District ☎ 021 6351 4668; booking hotline: 021 6217 2426/3055 🕐 Box office daily 9.30–8 💰 30–580RMB 🚇 People's Square

VELVET LOUNGE
Velvet Lounge has made Shanghai's sleazy Julu Lu drinking strip cool again. The mood early on has a tantric Tibetan quality though there's dancing and high jinks after midnight. With its ever-friendly lounge vibe, this is one of Shanghai's best late-night options and is equally popular with the city's high and low life. Thin-crust pizza is served till 3am.

✉ 2F, Building 3–4, 913 Julu Lu (nr Huashan Lu) ☎ 021 5403 2976 🕐 Daily Sun–Thu 5pm–3am, Fri–Sat 5pm–5am 🚇 Changshu Lu

YUYINTANG

www.yuyintang.org

This live music institution has been moved on more times than a problem beggar, thanks to rent-hikes and government restrictions. Though generally only open weekends, it remains the best place in town for Chinese rock and indie bands, and has a likeably punkish, underground feel. It's a bit out of the way in the west of town, but easy to get to on the metro.

✉ 1731 Yan'an Xi Lu (inside Tianshan Park) ☎ 021 5237 8662 🕐 Fri–Sat 8 till late 🚇 Yan'an Xilu

ZAPATAS

www.zapatas-shanghai.com

For those who like to dance and party while sipping a Margarita, Zapatas is just the place. Guest DJs play hi-decibel chart and pop while the kitchen conjures up spicy Mexican food. Happy hour is weekdays 5–7; check the website for details about other promotions.

✉ 5 Hengshan Lu, Xuhui Lu ☎ 021 6433 4104 🕐 Daily 4pm–2am 🚇 Changshu Lu/Hengshan Lu

SPORTS AND ACTIVITIES

HONGKOU STADIUM

www.sh.supertickets.com.cn

The city's top club, Shanghai Shenhua, plays its home games at Hongkou Stadium.

✉ 444 Dongjiangwan Lu, Hongkou District ☎ 021 6540 0009 🖐 20–150RMB 🚇 Hongkou Stadium (line 3)

JC MANDARIN HOTEL

Nonresidents may use the courts in the hotel; equipment is also available for rent.

✉ 1225 Nanjing Xilu, Jing'an District ☎ 021 6279 1888 🕐 Daily 6am–11pm 🖐 Tennis 60RMB 🚇 Jing'an Temple

JING'AN SPORTS CENTRE

One of the better public swimming pools, with roped-off lanes for serious swimmers who just want to swim laps. Most five-star hotels also open their swimming pools to nonguests; prices vary.

✉ 151 Kangding Lu, Jing'an District ☎ 021 6272 7277 🕐 Mon–Fri 3.30pm–9pm, Sat, Sun 1–9 🖐 25–30RMB 🚌 112

LUWAN STADIUM

This rather rundown venue houses the Shanghai Sharks, Yao Ming's former club.

✉ 128 Zhaojiabang Lu, Dapuoqiao District ☎ 021 6467 5358 🕐 Matches usually start at 7.30 🖐 From around 150RMB 🚌 17, 104

QI ZHONG TENNIS CENTRE

www.masters-cup.com
www.masters-cup.com.cn

This state-of-the-art facility with retractable roof was built with the Tennis Masters cup (November)

Above Cloud 9 Bar on the 87th floor of the Jinmao Tower

and similar events in mind. The retractable roof is a work of art as well as an architectural feat.

✉ Qi Zhong Forest Sports City Complex, Minhang District ☎ 021 6384 6601 🕐 Varies 🖐 $10–$166

SHANGHAI BINHAI GOLF CLUB

www.binhaigolf.com

The original golf course was designed by five-time British Open Champion Peter Thomson in 2000. A second 18-hole course has now been added and a third, 54-hole international standard course is in the pipeline. Binhai also has a 20-bay driving range.

✉ Binhai Resort, Dongdia Gonglu, Nanhui, Pudong District ☎ 021 5805 8888 🕐 Daily 7.30am–8pm 🖐 Non-members Mon–Fri

780RMB, Sat, Sun 1,580RMB including caddy, 150RMB cart, 200 RMB club rental 🚌 Free shuttle buses: 581 Yincheng Zhonglu, departing 7am; 1888 Wuzhong Lu, departing 7.30am; 20 Suzhou Beilu, departing 9.45am

SHANGHAI INTERNATIONAL MOTOR RACING CIRCUIT

www.icsh.sh.cn;
Formula 1 Grand Prix tickets: www.f1china.com.cn or www.f1-grandprix-tickets.com
The most important event of the year here is the Formula 1 Grand Prix at the end of September/beginning of October. Sunday is race day, but ticket prices are lower for the practice and qualifying sessions on Friday and Saturday. Sports bars throughout the city screen the event and have special promotions to entice customers.

✉ Yining Lu, Anting, Jiading District 🕐 Daily 9.30–3.30 💷 Formula One: 330RMB–3,980RMB 🚌 Buses from Shanghai Stadium during Grand Prix 🚇 Anting station under construction

SHANGHAI YINQIXING INDOOR SKIING SITE

This single ski slope is well suited to beginners, and instruction is available, as well as an on-site sauna to sooth aching muscles.
✉ 1835 Qixing Lu, Minhang District 🕐 021 6478 8666 🕐 Sun–Thu 9.30–9, Fri, Sat 9.30am–11pm 💷 Adult 98–198RMB (includes equipment rental), child 80–180RMB 🚇 Xinzhuang, then free shuttle bus 🚌 91, 92, 803, 953

TOTAL FITNESS

www.totalfitness.com.cn
Day passes are available for this gym, which has exercise machines, a sauna and solarium but no swimming pool.
✉ 5F, Zhong Chuang Building, 819 Nanjing Xilu, Jing'an District 🕐 021 6255 3535 🕐 Daily 9–9 💷 Price under review 🚇 Nanjing Xilu

HEALTH AND BEAUTY

APSARA

www.apsara.com.cn
This cozy Cambodian-theme spa may not be in the same category as the destination spas of the major five-star hotels but is the best of the affordable, street-side establishments thanks largely to the management team which imports Southeast Asian service ethos. A tea ceremony is given on arrival, along with a selection of fragrant oils to choose between. The products, like the furnishings, have been sourced from poor Cambodian villages. This is an attractive, ethical spa that won't break the bank.
✉ 457 Shanxi Beilu 🕐 021 6258 5580 🕐 Daily 10.30am–midnight 🚇 Jing'an Temple

BANYAN TREE

www.banyantreespa.com
This legendary Southeast Asian spa brand takes up residence in the five-star Westin Bund Centre hotel. There's emphasis on the five *wu xing*, or 'life forces', of earth, gold,

water, wood, and fire, both within the treatments and the design of the 13 treatment rooms, which blend traditional elements with 21st-century luxury touches. Particularly useful are the wonderfully descriptive treatment menus.
✉ 3F, The Westin, 88 Henan Zhong Lu 🕐 021 6335 188 🕐 Daily 10am–midnight 🚇 Nanjing Donglu

DRAGONFLY

www.dragonfly.net.cn
This is an ideal stress-reducer, offering a range of treatments at affordable prices. Choose from Chinese and Japanese massages and beauty treatments in the Nail Spa. There are seven other spas in Shanghai so check out the website to see if there's another spa nearer your hotel.
✉ 2F, Shanghai Kerry Centre, 1515 Nanjing Xilu, Jing'an District 🕐 021 6279 4625 🕐 Daily 1pm–10pm 💷 From 120RMB for 1 hour 🚇 Jing'an Temple

FOR CHILDREN

SHANGHAI DISCOVERY CHILDREN'S MUSEUM

www.shanghaidiscovery.org
Located in the Zhabei Youth Activity Centre, the museum offers activities based on the principle that children learn best through doing. Apart from role-play situations based around the post office, the shop, the hospital and so on, there's a prism box, a rolling ball track, a Bernoulli blower, a bubble machine and a photosensitive wall for creating frozen shadows.
✉ 61 Songyuan Lu, Changning District 🕐 021 6278 3130 🕐 Tue–Sun 8.30–4 💷 Adult 20RMB, child 15RMB 🚌 206 to terminus

SHANGHAI OCEAN AQUARIUM

www.sh-aquarium.com
There are 13,000 creatures from the deep here from 300 species, four continents and a variety of marine

Left *A young red panda sunning himself in his enclosure in the Shanghai Zoo (Shanghai Dongwuyuan), opened in 1954 in the city's western suburbs*

ecosystems. Predictably it is the sharks, penguins and spider crabs that draw the crowds, but this is a rare opportunity to see endangered Chinese species, like the sucker fish, Yangtze alligator and giant sturgeon. Another attraction is the longest glass tunnel in the world at 155m (509ft). The English-language explanations are informative while travelators keep congestion to a minimum. There is the expected souvenir shop plus a fast food restaurant that serves Asian and Western food.

✉ 158 Yincheng Beilu, Pudong District ☎ 021 5877 9988 🕙 Daily 9–6 (Jul, Aug until 9); animal feeding times around 10.30 and 3 🚇 Lujiazui 🚌 Adult 110RMB, child (0.8–1.4m/2.6–4.5ft) 70RMB

SHANGHAI WILD ANIMAL PARK
www.shwzoo.com
Located 35km (22 miles) west of town, the Shanghai Wild Animal Park offers expansive facilities and impressive stats. The park is home to more than 10,000 animals— including giraffes, lions and cheetahs—and 200 rare species, among them the white rhinoceros and the giant panda. There are two sections, one for walking and the other a drive-thru safari zone. Animal welfare standards might not be up to Western standards.

✉ 178 Naliugong Lu, Nanhui District ☎ 021 6118 0000 🚌 Adult 100RMB, child 50RMB 🚇 Zhangjiang High Technology Park (then bus)

SHANGHAI ZOO
While the conditions in which animals are kept in Chinese zoos would not be tolerated in the West, Shanghai Zoo has very pleasant wooded grounds, picnic areas, an amusement park and an indoor playground. Visit during the week if you can, as the zoo is crowded on weekends and holidays.

✉ 2381 Hongqiao Lu, Changning District ☎ 021 6268 7775 🕙 Apr–end Sep daily 6.30–5.30; Oct–end Mar daily 7–5 🚌 Adult 30RMB, child 24RMB, child under 1.2m (4ft) free 🚌 911, 925, 936

FESTIVALS AND EVENTS

JANUARY/FEBRUARY
CHINESE NEW YEAR
New Year celebrations include dragon dancing at Jing'an Temple, a firework display on the waterfront, and lantern-hanging in the Yu Garden.

✉ Jing'an Temple, Yu Garden, Bund ℹ Huangpu District Tourism Bureau, ☎ 021 6355 9999

MARCH
SHANGHAI LITERARY FESTIVAL
www.m-onthebund.com
This two-week festival was started in 2003 by Australian Michelle Garnaut, owner of M on the Bund bar, and is very popular. Internationally acclaimed Chinese and foreign writers read from and talk about their work.

✉ M on the Bund, 7/F, 5 Bund, Huangpu District ☎ 021 6350-9988 🕙 First two weeks of Mar

APRIL
LONGHUA TEMPLE FAIR
This Buddhist celebration dates back to the Ming dynasty. Dragons supposedly visit the temple to grant your wishes, but nowadays people come for the food stalls, dragon dances and other entertainment.

✉ 2853 Longhua Lu, Xuhui District ☎ 021 6456 6085 🕙 Third day of the third lunar month

JUNE
SHANGHAI INTERNATIONAL FILM FESTIVAL
www.siff.com
This star-studded annual event, attended in the past by film-makers Luc Besson and Ang Lee, actors Sigourney Weaver, Sophie Marceau, Liam Neeson and Hugh Jackman, draws huge crowds. Around 200 Chinese and foreign movies are shown during the festival and there are talks and lectures by leading directors.

✉ 11F, STV Mansions, 298 Weihai Lu, Xuhui District, Shanghai Film Art Centre

and other cinemas ☎ 021 6280 6088/021 6253 7115 🕙 Nine days in second half of Jun

SEPTEMBER–NOVEMBER
SHANGHAI BIENNALE
www.shanghaibiennale.com
Exhibitions of cutting-edge and official Chinese and foreign art are held during this six-week festival, which takes place in the elegant surroundings of the art deco museum in People's Square.

✉ Shanghai Art Museum ☎ 021 6327 4030 🕙 Even-numbered years

OCTOBER–NOVEMBER
SHANGHAI INTERNATIONAL ARTS FESTIVAL
Month-long showcase of the arts, including symphony concerts, dance, opera and drama. Other events include an arts and crafts fair, magic shows, firework displays and a carnival parade.

✉ Shanghai Museum, Shanghai Art Museum, Shanghai Grand Theatre and other venues ☎ 021 6439 1818 🕙 Oct–Nov

NOVEMBER
SHANGHAI INTERNATIONAL MARATHON
www.shmarathon.com
Some 15,000–20,000 Chinese and international runners compete in this annual event. A half-marathon and fun marathon take place on the same day.

✉ Nanjing Donglu, Huangpu District ☎ 021 6433 7109 🕙 Nov

DECEMBER
COUNTDOWN PARTY
www.xintiandi.com
Around 5,000 revelers converge on Taipingqiao Lake outside Xintiandi to listen to live pop bands and welcome in the Western new year with a firework display.

✉ Shanghai Xintiandi Information Centre, Luwan District ☎ 021 6384 9366 🕙 31 Dec

EATING

PRICES AND SYMBOLS

The restaurants are listed alphabetically. The prices are for a two-course lunch (L) and a three-course à la carte dinner (D) for one person, without drinks. The wine price is for the least expensive bottle. All the restaurants listed accept credit cards unless otherwise stated.

For a key to the symbols, ▷ 2.

100 CENTURY AVENUE

Comprising the upper stories of the Park Hyatt Hotel, located in the world's highest flat-roof building—the Shanghai World Financial Centre—100 Century Avenue claims altitude as its unique selling point. Japanese, Chinese and Western cooking is served from the various show kitchens on the 91st-floor dining area, while diners stare into the metropolitan expanse through the 25m (82 ft) high windows.
✉ 91–93F Park Hyatt Hotel, 100 Century Avenue, Pudong ☎ 021 6888 1234 ⏱ Daily 11.30–2.30, 6–10.30 ✋ L 300RMB, D 700RMB, Wine 390RMB

1221

A simple but foreigner-friendly restaurant that serves Shanghainese, Cantonese and Sichuanese dishes, reflecting both the background and culinary interests of the owner. The stylish, informal surroundings add to the appeal, making this popular with families and small groups. Unusually for a Chinese restaurant, there's a good selection of reasonably priced wines. The restaurant (a couple of blocks west of Howard Johnson Hotel) is not easily accessible by public transportation, so it's best to take a taxi.
✉ 1221 Yan'an Xilu, Changning District ☎ 021 6213 6585/2441 ⏱ Daily 11.30–2.30, 5.30–11 ✋ L 80RMB, D 130RMB, Wine 150RMB 🚌 925

ART LAB

www.mocashanghai.org
A fabulous fine dining establishment atop the Museum of Contemporary Art (MOCA). Like the art below, the conceptual 'No Borders' menu has lots of creative touches. There's a fantastic outdoor balcony at canopy level which blends views of woodland with skyscrapers. The space is divided into three: an artsy coffee and cocktail lounge with large designer sofas; a granite and glass corridor and balcony; and a dimly lit formal dining room.

Above *Traditional-Chinese meets art deco in the main corridor of the Whampoa Club on the Bund*

✉ 3F, MoCA, People's Park ☎ 021 6327 0856 ⏱ Sun–Tue, Thu 10am–midnight, Wed, Fri, Sat 10am–2am ✋ L and D 300–400RMB, Wine 228RMB 🚇 People's Square

AZUL/VIVA

Owned by Peruvian restaurateur Eduardo Vargas, Azul/Viva has become a favorite pre-clubbing destination with Shanghai's party-loving 20- and 30-somethings. They appreciate the convivial atmosphere of the downstairs bar, Azul, and the mellower ambience of Viva, the dining space on the second floor. Vargas's beautifully presented New World cuisine, with the accent on tapas, is served in both places along with pitchers of sangria. Showstoppers include lima bean and goat's cheese *salpicon*, and foie gras with banana-lentil salsa. Sunday brunch is also available.
✉ 18 Dongping Lu, Xuhui District ☎ 021 6433 1172 ⏱ Sun–Thu 11am–11.30pm, Fri–Sat 11am–12.30am ✋ L 100RMB, D 200RMB, Sangria (jug) 198RMB 🚇 Hengshan Lu

BAO LUO

You know you are in for an experience to remember the moment you climb the stairs of this 1930s neighborhood eatery near Changle Lu, usually in the company of local people waiting for a table. Bao Luo is said to offer the best Shanghainese food in town and it rates equally high on atmosphere. The voluminous menu includes such local delicacies as steamed Mandarin fish, lion's head with clams, and pot-stewed crab meat with minced pork. Reservations for lunch and dinner are strongly advised.

✉ 271 Fumin Lu, Jing'an District ☎ 021 5403 7239 🕐 Daily 11.30am–4am 🖐 L 60RMB, D 100RMB, Chinese wine 98RMB 🚇 Changshu Lu

BINJIANG ONE

www.bln.com.cn

Located at the southern extremity of the Pudong riverside promenade, the Binjiang One brings a cocktail lounge quality to a century-old former shipping office. The glassed-in dining room has obtuse views back towards the Bund and the exquisite global dishes include steaks and cakes, alongside exotic treats like the tubular lobster salad (a must-try).

✉ Fucheng Lu, Shi Bu Jie, You Long Garden, Pudong District ☎ 021 5877 7500 🕐 Daily 11.30–3, 5.30–11pm 🖐 L 150RMB, D 300RMB, Wine 65RMB (per glass) 🚇 Lujiazui (then taxi)

BUND 12 CAFÉ

A great opportunity to get a look at the inside of one of the Bund's venerable landmark buildings is to eat at Bund 12 café. Enter by the side of the building, go to the second floor and follow the wood-paneled corridor. The café is a miniature masterpiece of period refurbishment: the 1930s-style parlor has an original marble fireplace, wooden wainscoting and art deco light fittings, while old sepia photographs, books, newspapers and a 1932 map of Shanghai provide an appropriate backdrop. A balcony

with terrace tables overlooks the courtyard. The menu includes sandwiches, salads, pastas, pizzas, an assortment of cakes and fresh fruit juices.

✉ Room 226 12 Zhongshan Dongyilu (The Bund), Huangpu District ☎ 021 6329 5896 🕐 Daily 8–7 🖐 L 60RMB, D 100RMB, Wine 188RMB 🚇 Nanjing Donglu

CHARMANT

An eccentric Taiwanese-owned restaurant, Charmant blends western smoothies and onion rings with classic Chinese fried rice and tofu—all at pleasing prices. The decor is similarly schizophrenic with aqueduct-shaped arches and high-backed sofas amid the widescreen TV and giant pot plants. With a 4am closing time, this is favorite twilight stop for those partying late in the French Concession.

✉ 1414 Huaihai Lu, Luwan District ☎ 021 6431 8107 🕐 Daily 11am–4am 🖐 L 60RMB, D 100RMB, Wine 48RMB 🚇 Changshu Lu

CRYSTAL JADE

A perennial Xintiandi favorite that serves fabulous Cantonese and Shanghainese dim sum at great prices. Choose from a menu that includes such delights as steamed shrimp dumplings, pork ribs and spicy pork wonton. The food is amazingly good value, the waitstaff work well under pressure and no one goes away hungry. Booking ahead is essential or expect to wait.

✉ Unit 2F-12A & B, House 6–7 South Block Xintiandi, Lane 123 Xingye Lu, Luwan District ☎ 021 6385 8752 🕐 Mon–Sat 11–3, 5.30–11, Sun 10.30–3, 5.30–11 🖐 L 100–150RMB, D 150–200RMB, Wine 150RMB 🚇 Huangpi Nanlu

DES LYS

One of the best bistros in town, Des Lys attracts a loyal clientele who appreciate French cuisine prepared to a high standard. The specials appear daily on a chalkboard and might include soupe à l'oignon, sea bass, rabbit in mustard sauce, usually served on a bed of tagliatelle, or lamb with rosemary,

thyme and mashed potato. Red-painted walls, dark wood floors and plush furnishings create a snug yet sophisticated, setting.

✉ 178 Xinle Lu, Xuhui District ☎ 021 5404 5077 🕐 Daily 11–10.30 🖐 Set L 78–120RMB (1 course), D 170RMB, Wine 200RMB 🚇 Changshu Lu

DI SHUI DONG

Di Shui Dong has cornered the market for chili-fired home-style Hunanese food. It's proudly rustic: ruddy-cheeked waitresses wear tie-dyed dresses and observe few airs and graces; the wooden fixtures are unvarnished and brick walls unadorned, and the invariably rowdy diners eat with unreserved gusto. This chain is much loved among the expatriate population and you will need to reserve ahead. The Ziyuan spare ribs are essential eating.

✉ 2F, 56 Mao Ming Nan Lu ☎ 021 6253 2689 🕐 Daily 11–11 🖐 L 50RMB, D 80RMB, Beer 8RMB 🚇 Shanxi Nanlu

DONGBEI REN

What makes this place is the young, enthusiastic staff from Northeast China's Dongbei region, who greet you on arrival with 'Foreign friends coming in.' The restaurant is in a huge hall on the second floor with a red-and-green color scheme, wall lights decorated with paper cuts and origami birds strung from the ceiling. The easy-to-follow picture menu features duck egg yolk in sliced sausage, soy bean with pot herb mustard salad, Yalu River Mingtai fish and sautéed lamb shank. Pride of place, however, belongs to the Manchurian 'special flavor' jaozi (dumplings filled with meat or fish).

✉ 1 Shanxi Nanlu, Jing'an District ☎ 021 5228 9898 🕐 Daily 11–2, 4.30–10 🖐 L and D 100RMB, Rice wine 80RMB 🚇 Shanxi Nanlu

ELEMENT FRESH

This bright and breezy American-owned deli has proved a hit with the health conscious. The menu includes fresh bagels, wraps, inviting salads and monster gourmet sandwiches. Drinks range from coffee to juices and smoothies. Not-so-healthy brunches are served on weekends. There is terrace seating.

✉ Room 112, Shanghai Center, 1376 Nanjing Xi Lu ☎ 021 6279 8682 🕐 Mon–Thu, Sun 7am–11pm, Fri, Sat 7am–midnight 🍴 L 100RMB, D 200RMB, sandwiches from 40RMB 🚇 Jing'an Temple

FU1088

Located in an unmarked three-storey villa, Fu1088 has an exclusive, antique feel. The restaurant specializes in gourmet Shanghainese dishes, artfully presented in tiny but perfectly formed portions. There are also creative fusion options, like the tea-smoked egg with caviar. Dining is in private rooms only, so it's not the best option if you're in a small group.

✉ 375 Zhenning Lu, Jing'an District ☎ 021 5239 7878 🕐 Daily 11–2, 5.30–12 🍴 L from 158RMB (set menu), D 250RMB, Wine 188RMB 🚇 Jiangsu Lu

GUYI

This elegant restaurant in the former French Concession has a reputation for home-style Hunanese cooking. Expect mouth-searing dishes in which chilies and red peppers contend with more subtle ginger and garlic flavors. If you're feeling adventurous, try the balsam pear with smoked pork, the steamed frogs' legs, or the shredded jellyfish in a sour sauce; alternatively play safe with a hot pot. No reservations accepted after 6pm.

✉ 87 Fumin Lu, Jing'an District ☎ 021 6249 5628 🕐 Daily 11.30–11.30 🍴 L80RMB, D 120RMB, Wine 128RMB 🚇 Jing'an Temple

ISSIMO

www.issimo.cn

Residing within the city's hippest boutique accommodations, this new Italian restaurant takes the dark designer feel of the hotel proper and flicks in a few splashes of color—random scarlet leather chairs among grey seating; yellow-tinted window glass and glowing red food heaters. The menu includes lots of hearty imported meat and fish grills,

but it's the pizzas that rightly take the plaudits.

✉ 2F, JIA Shanghai, 931 Nanjing Xi Lu, Jing'an District ☎ 021 6287 9009 🕐 Daily 7–10, midday–2.30, 6.30–10.30 🍴 L 128RMB (set menu), D 250RMB, Wine 200RMB 🚇 Nanjing Xilu

JADE ON 36

French master chef Paul Pairet has created quite a stir with his tongue-in-cheek *cuisine de voyage*, a dizzying journey which takes guests to culinary heights with truffles and foie gras, then brings them abruptly down to earth with tinned sardines and Nutella chocolate spread. The surprises extend to desserts, including a lemon tart in which the reconstructed lemon has a skin made from confit. The restaurant's designer, Las Vegas veteran Adam D. Tihany, nods in the direction of Chinese culture with a ceiling that folds like an emperor's robe and a sculptural arch symbolizing a rice bowl. Excellent views of the Shanghai skyline.

✉ Floor 36, Tower 2, Pudong Shangri-La, 33 Fucheng Lu, Pudong District ☎ 021 6882 3636 🕐 Daily 6pm–12.30am 🍴 Set menus 488RMB; menu de degustation 688RMB (8 courses), Wine 500 RMB 🚇 Lujiazui

JEAN GEORGES

www.threeonthebund.com

Jean-Georges Vongerichten's only signature restaurant outside of New York is on most people's shortlist for best restaurant in town. The dining

area has a formal, stately feel and the menu has solid French foundations, though the many fusion flourishes are testament to Vongerichten's love of Asia, where he spent his formative years.

✉ 4F, Three on the Bund, 3 Zhongshan Dongyilu, Huangpu District ☎ 021 6321 7733 🕐 Mon–Fri 11.30–2.30, 6–10.30, Sat–Sun 11.30–3, 6–10.30 🍴 L 158RMB (set menu), D 300RMB, Wine 298RMB

KATHLEEN'S FIVE

The main reason people make a beeline for Kathleen Lau's restaurant in the Shanghai Art Museum is to dine out well while enjoying the views from her rooftop terrace. The owner came to China from the US, which accounts for the American slant to the international cuisine. The fish dishes can be especially recommended. These typically include crispy battered snapper fillet and seared black sea bass, or Cajun-seared scallops with potato cakes. Reservations are required.

✉ 5F, Shanghai Art Museum, 325 Nanjing Xilu, Huangpu District ☎ 021 6327 2221 🕐 Daily 11.30am–midnight 🍴 L 140RMB, D 300–350RMB, Wine 260RMB 🚇 People's Square

LAN CLUB

www.lan-global.com

Located in a colonial-era trading house back from the Bund, LAN is

Below *The modern interior of the exclusive Laris restaurant*

the most upscale venture yet from the popular Chinese South Beauty restaurant chain. The four stories of drinking and dining include a bar on the first floor, an open-plan Chinese banquet hall on two, VIP dining on three, and a super-expensive fourth floor seafood restaurant overseen by Belgian superchef, Yves Mattagne. The bar is popular among the after-work crowd on weekdays, and sees hard partying at weekends.

✉ 102 Guangdong Lu, Huangpu District ☎ 021 6323 8029 🕐 Daily 11am–10pm 🍽 L and D 400–500RMB, Wine 360RMB

LARIS

www.threeonthebund

One of the most exclusive restaurants in Shanghai in terms of price, Laris offers what is arguably the most refined dining experience. Greek-Australian master-chef David Laris relies on the freshest local and imported ingredients to create superb fusion dishes, with seafood occupying pride of place. The setting is restrained, even low-key, stark white pillars contrasting with gray marble walls and couches in mellow hues. Less expensive options than dinner include the special lunch menus or Saturday/ Sunday brunch—more opportunities to enjoy the prized views of the Pudong skyline.

✉ 6F, Three on the Bund, 3 Zhongshan Dong Yilu (The Bund), Huangpu District ☎ 021 6321 9922 🕐 Daily 11.30–2.30, 5–10.30 🍽 Mon–Fri L 158RMB (2 courses); every day D 600RMB, Wine 100RMB per glass

LI JIA CAI

This distinguished family restaurant in Huangpu Park preserves a culinary tradition going back to the Qing dynasty, and not just any culinary tradition—the present owner, now in his 80s, is a direct descendant of General Li Shunqing, Chief of the Palace Guard, whose responsibilities extended to the imperial kitchens. General Li committed numerous old recipes to memory, and his relatives eventually opened a restaurant in Beijing. This proved so

popular that this branch opened in Shanghai in 2006. The menu includes deep-fried fresh scallops with fried pickled kale, Beijing smoked pork and sweet-and-sour rib. Making a reservation in advance is essential.

✉ 1F, 500 Zhongshan Zhong Yilu, (The Bund), Huangpu District ☎ 021 5308 1919 🕐 Daily 11–2, 5.30–9.30 🍽 L set menu 400RMB, D set menu 600–1,500RMB, Wine 250RMB

LOST HEAVEN

Take tribal dishes from the southwest province of Yunnan, serve them up in an exotically decorated French Concession villa and watch the customers pile in. Lost Heaven's winning formula is given extra spice by the moody lighting, heavy incense and the folksy Asian backing music. The Dai people, who provide the culinary inspiration, are spread across Indochina and the food has similarities with Thai and Burmese cuisine. The downstairs bar is also well worth a look-in.

✉ 38 Gaoyou Lu, Luwan District ☎ 021 6433 5126 🍽 L 150RMB, D 250RMB, Wine 198RMB 🕐 Mon–Fri 11.30–3, 5.30–11, Sat–Sun 11.30am–midnight

LYNN

Lynn is one of the few upmarket Shanghainese restaurants in town. It offers both authentic staples and more modern interpretations in a gorgeously decorated, jazz-backed dining space, which glows in moody red and blue neon. The crisp white tablecloths and hardwood floors recall the more stately restaurants of the Bund, as does the excellent service, but the prices are much lower. There's also a popular weekend dim sum brunch.

✉ No. 1, 299 Xikang Lu, Jing'an District ☎ 021 6274 0101 🍽 Daily 5.30–10.30, Sat–Sun brunch 11.30–3 🕐 L 80RMB, D 120RMB, Wine 188RMB 🚇 Jing'an Temple

MEI LONG ZHEN

Opened in 1938, these sumptuous premises by Jiangning Lu (enter

through the courtyard) once belonged to the Communist Party. The gorgeous furnishings include traditional paintings and gilded reliefs, embossed ceilings, Chinese lanterns and dragon emblems, seen to best effect in the Long Feng banqueting room, where guests have included French president Jacques Chirac. The menu comprises Sichuan dishes prepared in Shanghainese style, including fried bean sprouts with winter bamboo shoots, braised yellow-fin tuna in soy sauce and smoke-dried duck. Marvel at the skill of the waiters as they pour tea from long-spouted pots without spilling a drop.

✉ 22 Lane, 1081 Nanjing Xilu, Jing'an District ☎ 021 6253 5353 🕐 Daily 11–2, 5–10 🍽 L 90RMB, D 120RMB, Chinese wine 140RMB 🚇 Nanjing Xilu

NAN XIANG (▷ 313)

NEPALI KITCHEN

Vegetarians and meat eaters are catered to in this homey Nepalese eatery in the former French Concession, where the clutter of prayer flags, tangkas and wood carvings brings to mind hippies on the Kathmandu trail in the 1960s. Most guests prefer the upstairs room, where, after removing your shoes, you sit on cushions to enjoy shabalay (deep-fried mince meat patties), sekuwa (grilled beef), curries, or momos (meat or vegetable dumplings).

✉ 4 Lane 819 Julu Lu, Jin'an District ☎ 021 5404 6281 🕐 Daily 10–2, 6–11 🍽 L 70RMB D 100RMB, wine 120RMB 🚇 Changshu Lu

OTTO

www.otto–restaurants.com

Otto plies a humble trade in standout Mediterranean dishes paired with some of the best wines in town, served from a wall-lodged wine dispenser that keeps 32 white and red varietals fresh enough to be served by the glass. The dining room has a slick, Italian designer feel and the European classics on

SHINTORI NULL II

Shintori Null II is famous for the bizarre factory feel of its industrial-size dining room which comes with an elevated open kitchen. The food is Japanese, but traditionalists might dislike the fusion ingredients on the menu, curry and foie gras included. One thing that cannot be argued with is the decor, which is unlike anything else in Shanghai.
803 Julu Lu, Luwan District ☎ 021 5404 5252 🕔 Mon–Fri 5.30–10.30, Sat–Sun 11.30–2, 5–11 ✋ L 150RMB, D 200RMB, Wine 188RMB

SIMPLY THAI

www.simplythai-sh.com
With a lovely location in the former French Concession, this stylish restaurant serves outstanding Thai food expertly prepared by native chefs. Try the *tom yum* seafood soup, the fried crispy fish slices in chili sauce or the vegetarian green curry. Alfresco dining on the patio is possible in summer. There are other branches in Xintiandi and Hong Mei Entertainment Street.
5C Dongping Lu, Xuhui District ☎ 021 6445 9551 🕔 Daily 11–11 ✋ L 130RMB, D 170RMB, Jug of frozen Margarita or mojito 150RMB 🚇 Hengshan Lu

SOUTH BEAUTY 881

Dreamed up by Japanese design house 'Hot Potato', this restaurant opposite the Shanghai Exhibition Centre (one of a small chain) has glass walls, allowing diners to enjoy lovely views of the 1930s villa and garden it overlooks. Apart from the glitzy interior, regulars comment favorably on the presentation of the Sichuanese dishes, which pull no punches in the spice department.
881 Yan'an Zhonglu, Jing'an District ☎ 021 6247 5878 🕔 Daily 11–10 ✋ L, D 250RMB, Wine 200RMB 🚇 Jing'an Temple

SOUTHERN BARBARIAN

Ensconced within a two-story art mall, this hip restaurant serves

the menu come with the odd subtle Chinese fusion flourish.
85 Fumin Lu, Jing'an District ☎ 021 6248 9186 🕔 Daily 11.30–11.30 ✋ L 120RMB, D 180RMB, Wine 208RMB

QUANJUDE

The Shanghai branch of the famous Beijing roast duck restaurant is short on atmosphere but worth a visit, as it serves the genuine article. More or less everything on the menu is duck-based, from the meat soup served with mushrooms and butter to the sautéed liver and intestines. A whole duck serves four to six people, so the set lunches (available Monday to Friday) might be a better option.
4F, 786 Huaihai Zhonglu, Luwan District ☎ 021 5404 5799 🕔 11–11 ✋ L and D 168RMB (whole duck), Wine 90RMB 🚇 Shanxi Nanlu

SECRET GARDEN

Tucked away down a narrow French Concession driveway, this unheralded restaurant specializes in beautifully prepared and presented Cantonese dishes. The food may be fantastic, but it's worth coming here for the decor alone, a dreamily ornamental fusion of floral wallpaper, creaking wooden floorboards, romantic drapes, and antique opium beds.
333 Changle Lu, Luwan District ☎ 021 5405 0789 🕔 Daily 11.30–10 ✋ L 80RMB, D 120RMB, Beer 20RMB

SENS & BUND

This star in Shanghai's culinary firmament (near the Palace Hotel) was introduced in 2004 by the French Pourcel twins, famous for creating Le Jardin de Sens restaurant in Montpellier, which was accorded the ultimate accolade of three Michelin stars. Executive Chef, Pierre Altobelli, follows the precepts of the Pourcels by appealing to the five senses with dishes like lobster terrine and duck breast with vanilla-flavored olive oil, grilled turbot with bok choy (Chinese cabbage) and goat's cheese ravioli in a coconut sauce, and fillet of beef encrusted with herbs and served with shallot confit and crispy mushrooms. The Parisian designer Imaad Rahmouni imbues Sens with an understated classical elegance.
6F, 18 Zhongshan Dong Yilu, (The Bund), Huangpu District ☎ 021 6323 9898 🕔 Daily 11.30–2.30, 6.30–10.30 ✋ L 188RMB, D 450RMB, *menu de degustation* 800RMB, Wine 100RMB per glass 🚇 Nanjing Donglu

rustic dishes from Yunnan, where folk like to indulge in deep-fried honeybees or salt-and-pepper griddled goat cheese. With a well-hidden location and minimalist decor, Southern Barbarian has a trendy feel, but the welcome is friendly and prices surprisingly reasonable. The drinks menu has a selection of imported American craft beers.

✉ 2F, Area E, Juroshine Life Arts Space, 56 Maoming Nanlu, Luwan District ☎ 021 5157 5510 🕐 Mon–Fri 11.30–2.30, 5.30–10.30, Sat–Sun 1130–10.30 ✋ L 80RMB, D 120RMB, Craft Beer from 35RMB

SUN WITH AQUA

With reasonable prices and a slick Japanese design, Sun with Aqua is the pick of the non-fine dining Bund restaurants. The wood and stone textures create a Zen vibe, but huge open kitchen bring things back to the modern era. Sun's menu will satisfy the traditionalist, as well as those used to American-inspired sushi.

✉ 2/F, 6 Bund, 6 Zhongshan Dongyilu, Huangpu District ☎ 021 6339 2779 🕐 Daily 11.30–3, 6–11 ✋ L 180RMB, D 250RMB, Beer 30RMB

T8

www.t8-shanghai.com

T8 vies with Jean Georges and Jade on 36 to be known as the best international restaurant in Shanghai. The back-lane location within Xintiandi is exclusive, with dining divided between a luxurious Balinese upstairs room and a slick, contemporary dining room at ground level that comes with a gorgeous open kitchen. The menu spans the globe, with Australian fish imports, French classics and the odd Asian detail. Dress up well though—this is about as formal as you can get in Shanghai.

✉ House 8, North Block Xintiandi, Lane 181 Taicang Lu ☎ 021 6355 8999 🕐 Mon 6.30–11, Tue–Fri 11.30–2.30, 6.30–11, Sat–Sun 11.30–4 (brunch), 6.30–11 ✋ L 150RMB (set lunch on weekends), D 300RMB, Wine 288RMB 🚇 Huangpi Nan Lu

VUE

This hotel restaurant distinguishes itself on three fronts: superb pan-European dishes that are cooked in front of guests; awesome views from the Hyatt on the Bund's privileged perch north of the river bend; and a truly funky interior design by Japanese studio Super Potato. Reserve a window seat.

✉ 30–31/F, West Tower, Hyatt on the Bund, 199 Huangpu Lu, Hongkou District ☎ 021 6393 1234 (ext. 6328) 🕐 Daily 11.30–2.30, 6–11 ✋ L 200RMB, D 300RMB, Wine 200RMB

WHAMPOA CLUB

www.threeonthebund.com

One of Asia's youngest and most exciting master chefs, Hong Kong-born Jereme Leung's mission statement is to breathe new life into traditional Shanghainese cuisine. Leung researched his subject for more than six months, in the process reviving and reinventing previously forgotten dishes of the Yangtze Delta region. The results are spectacular, with signature dishes such as drunken chicken with Shaoxing wine, shaved ice and house-smoked tea eggs, served with a sprig of parsley and a knob of caviar. Whampoa Club was designed by another Hong Kong native, Alan Chan, and might be described as traditional-Chinese-meets-modern-art-deco, a reflection of the founding chef's culinary ambitions.

✉ 5F, 3 Zhongshan Dongyilu (The Bund), Huangpu District ☎ 021 6321 3737 🕐 Daily 11.30–2.30, 5.30–10 ✋ D 458RMB; tasting menus L 188RMB (6 courses), D 588RMB (7 courses), Wine 288RMB

XIAO NAN GUO

www.xnggroup.com

'Little South Country' is a Shanghai chain widely respected locally for its fantastic cooking and meticulous attention to detail. The setting is formal: a row of waitresses dressed in silk qipaos greet you on arrival, and meals are served at large round tables intended for group dining. Don't be put off though, enjoy the

authentic Shanghai dishes, covering everything from spring onion pancakes to seafood claypots. This branch, in the grounds of the Ruijin Guesthouse, has a garden setting. Other branches are at 214–216 Huanghe Lu and 1398 Nanjing Xilu. Reservations are advised.

✉ Building 2, Ruijin Guesthouse, 118 Ruijin Erlu, Xuhui District ☎ 021 3208 9777 (reservations for all branches) 🕐 Daily 11–2, 5–9.30 ✋ L, D 150RMB, Wine 200RMB 🚇 Shanxi Nanlu

YIN

No restaurant better evokes the colonial Shanghai of the 1930s than Yin, with its wooden ceilings, art deco lamps, folding Chinese screens and traditional jazz soundtracks. Waitresses glide about the place dressed in traditional silk qipaos while serving first-rate Chinese regional cuisine. The chef is particularly strong on Shanghai and Hangzhou specialties like beef fillet stir-fried with spicy peppers, spicy fried tarot balls and drunken chicken strips soaked in Shaoxing wine. Oolong, Longjing and other quality teas are served. There is a specialist Japanese restaurant upstairs serving simple fishermen's dishes from the island of Shikoku.

✉ Gate 2, Jinjiang Hotel, 59 Maoming Nanlu, Luwan District ☎ 021 5466 5070/5078 🕐 Daily 12–2, 6–12 ✋ L 80RMB, D 120RMB, Wine 150RMB 🚇 Shanxi Nanlu

ZAPATAS (▷ 319)

ZENTRAL

Describing itself, accurately enough, as a 'health eatery,' this bright and airy chain restaurant specializes in light meals such as salads, pastas, wraps and sandwiches. You should definitely try Mango Madness or one of the other smoothies on the extensive menu.

✉ 567 Huangpi Nanlu, Luwan District ☎ 021 6374 5815 🕐 Mon–Thu 10–10, Fri 10am–midnight, Sat 9am–midnight, Sun 9am–10pm ✋ L 40RMB, D 60RMB, Wine 128RMB 🚇 Huangpi Nanlu

PRICES AND SYMBOLS

Prices are for a double room for one night, unless otherwise stated. Breakfast is included unless noted otherwise. All the hotels listed accept credit cards unless otherwise stated. Note that rates vary widely throughout the year.

For a key to the symbols, ▷ 2.

CAPTAIN HOSTEL

www.captainhostel.com.cn
Just a stone's throw from the Bund, Nanjing Lu and People's Square, this friendly and efficient hostel in a 1920s art deco building has a location that can hardly be bettered. The price below is for a 'first-class cabin' with en suite bathroom, but accommodations range from dormitory to suite. Services include laundry, bicycle rental and internet access.
✉ 37 Fuzhou Lu, Huangpu District ☎ 021 6323 5053 ⚡ 450–860RMB, excluding breakfast ⒤ 21 🅢 🄜 Nanjing Donglu

CITY HOTEL

www.cityhotelshanghai.com
What this 1980s tower lacks in character it makes up for in location, near Jing'an Temple and the Shanghai Exhibition Centre and within striking distance of the former French Concession. You should be able to negotiate a rate reduction of up to 30 percent outside high season. Rooms are pleasant, airy and tastefully furnished and the staff are courteous and attentive. Facilities include a business center, Western-style and Shanghainese restaurants, billiard room, sauna and gym.
✉ 5–7 Shanxi Nanlu, Jing'an District ☎ 021 6255 1133 ⚡ 698–955RMB ⒤ 270, 64 nonsmoking 🅢 🄥 🄬 Indoor 🄜 Shanxi Nanlu

GRAND HYATT

www.shanghai.hyatt.com
Spectacular views are the special preserve of the Hyatt, on the top 34 floors of the Jinmao Tower. All rooms have floor-to-ceiling windows, and those facing the river cost an additional 300RMB a night. Other 'highs' are the 87th-floor Cloud 9, pool (▷ picture above) and laundry chute (!). If you're not staying, take a dizzying look up from the atrium at the 33 floors of spiraling galleries.
✉ 88 Century Boulevard/Shiji Dadao, Pudong District ☎ 021 5049 1234 ⚡ 2,700–3,200RMB (weekends) ⒤ 555 🅢 🄬 🄥 🄬 🄜 Lujiazui

HOME INN

One of the few genuine budget options in Shanghai, this inn is a mere 10-minute walk from Xujiahui metro station and very convenient for shopping and the sights of Jing'an District and the former French Concession. Rooms are small but brightly painted, clean and comfortable. There's a Chinese restaurant, and services include laundry and internet access.
✉ 400 Tianyaoqiao Lu, Xuhui District ☎ 021 5425 0077, ext 9 ⚡ 285–520RMB, excluding breakfast ⒤ 140 🅢 🄜 Xujiahui

JIA SHANGHAI

www.jiashanghai.com
Fom the art-installation lobby, through the low-lit corridors and into the embrace of the kick-back comfy rooms with their pop-art fittings, designer fingerprints are all over this gorgeous boutique hotel. Loads of cool touches are to be found like the in-room Cambridge hi-fi and room service that gives you the pick from a long list of local restaurants. While the interiors are über-trendy, the hotel's facade has a colonial grandeur, while Shanghai's best malls are a stone's throw away

Left *The superb marble-surrounded swimming pool at the Grand Hyatt*

on Nanjing Xilu. Italian restaurant, Issimo, is one of the best in the city.

✉ 931 Nanjing Xilu, Jing'an District
☎ 021 6217 9000 🖐 1,800–3,200RMB
ℹ 55 🍽 🈁 🚇 Nanjing Xilu

THE MANSION

www.chinamansionhotel.com

This impressive but expensive new hotel was fashioned from the shell of a French villa that was once part of the estate of gangster, Du Yuesheng. The gorgeous lobby is busy with antiques and alive with crackly jazz while the generously sized rooms are more luxurious than anything that can be found at Shanghai's scores of locally managed heritage hotels. They come with bouncy carpets, large flatscreen TVs, and bathroom Jacuzzis. The rooftop has been renovated into a bar, which has a gorgeous outdoor balcony.

✉ 82 Xinle Lu, Luwan District ☎ 021 5403 9888 🖐 2,200–3,400RMB ℹ 30 🈁

OLD HOUSE INN

Be transported back to the Shanghai of the 1930s and stay in this quaint, beautifully renovated lane house in the French Concession. All 12 rooms are discreetly furnished in Ming dynasty style with canopy beds, carved wooden cabinets and fine-silk drapes. The restaurant serves Shanghainese cuisine and drinks are served in the courtyard garden. All in all, it's excellent value.

✉ 16, Lane 351, Huashan Lu, Jing'an District ☎ 021 6248 6118 🖐 720–1,420RMB ℹ 12 🈁 🚇 Jing'an Temple

PACIFIC HOTEL

This eye-catching neoclassical building dates from 1926 and has an unbeatable location overlooking People's Square. The public areas are spectacular and retain much of the original Italianate decoration, with lashings of marble, stucco and oak paneling. Of the rooms, only the deluxe suite matches this opulence, however, and to have a view of

People's Square you'll have to pay more than double the basic rate. The restaurants serve Chinese regional specialties and a limited number of Western dishes.

✉ 108 Nanjing Xilu, Jing'an District
☎ 021 6327 6226 🖐 560–1,500RMB, excluding breakfast ℹ 180 🈁
🚇 People's Square

PORTMAN RITZ CARLTON

www.ritzcarlton.com

Luxury and convenience are the main advantages of staying in this well-established hotel on Shanghai's most exclusive shopping street. The 50-floor tower block is part of the Shanghai Centre, with all its facilities. Palladio is the pick of the hotel's restaurants, serving refined Italian cuisine. Rooms are spacious and facilities are top-notch.

✉ Shanghai Centre, 1376 Nanjing Xilu
☎ 021 6279 8888/6279 8800 🖐 1,780–2,560RMB, excluding breakfast ℹ 610
🈁 🏊 Indoor 🎾 and spa 🚇 Jing'an Temple

PUDI BOUTIQUE HOTEL

www.boutiquehotel.cc

Whether a hotel owned by a major French hotel chain (Accor) can be considered 'boutique' is debatable, but the Pudi has a hi-tech flair that sets it apart. The building is a giant black cube on what is an otherwise sleepy French Concession street. The cool, whiz-kid vibe continues into the lobby, with its electronica soundtrack, neon-colored fish tanks, and a door girl who dresses like a fashion model. The rooms and bathrooms are huge, while the pillow menu and remote-control blinds add yet more layers of novelty. The views across low French Concession rooftops are particularly good from north-facing rooms. Xintiandi and Huaihai are both a short stroll away. A top spot.

✉ 99 Yandang Lu, Luwan District
☎ 021 5158 5888 🖐 1,200–1,960RMB
ℹ 52 🈁

PUDONG SHANGRI-LA

Close neighbor and rival of the Grand Hyatt, the Shangri-La has

a prime site in the heart of the Lujiazui Financial District. Only premier rooms and suites have Bund and river views, DVD and plasma TV on bathtubs. Packages also include a session in CHI Spa'. Other pluses are one of Shanghai's most innovative restaurants (Jade on 36), and Yi Café, with the now obligatory show kitchens.

✉ 33 Fucheng Lu, Pudong District ☎ 021 6882 8888 🖐 2,250–2,800RMB excluding breakfast ℹ 931 (545 nonsmoking)
🈁 🏊 Indoor 🎾 Tennis courts
🚇 Lujiazui

RADISSON XINGGUO PLAZA

www.radisson.com

Set amid 7 hectares (17 acres) of Shanghai's greenest parkland in the west of the French Concession, this likable Radisson is one of the most family-friendly places in town. Owing to the private ambience, it's also popular with business high-rollers and politicians; look out for black limos parked out front. The rooms feel like they should be bigger, given the expansive locale, but they are really comfortable, and warmly decorated. Highly recommended for those planning to linger around the French Concession.

✉ 78 Xingguo Lu, Luwan District ☎ 021 6212 9998 🖐 1,200–2,500RMB ℹ 190
🏊 🎾 🈁

RUIJIN GUESTHOUSE

The accommodations comprise five redbrick villas—mostly dating from the 1920s—in extensive grounds. The setting is simply stunning: Within a walled enclosure shut off from the bustle of Shanghai are a Japanese garden, a small lake and manicured lawns. All rooms are tastefully decorated and some have balconies overlooking the garden. Also on the estate is one of the city's best bars (Face) and a leading Shanghainese restaurant (Xiao Nan Guo).

✉ 118 Ruijin Erlu, Luwan District ☎ 021 6472 5222 🖐 1,200–2,300RMB ℹ 62
🈁 🚇 Shanxi Nanlu

HONG KONG AND MACAU

Like Shanghai, Hong Kong owes its 21st-century status to the grubby 19th-century drugs trade when the British seized the territory as a spoil of the First Opium War. Under colonial rule Hong Kong developed into a vibrant, cultured and wealthy port city and has continued to prosper under Communist patronage since 1997.

Colonial fingerprints remain all over Hong Kong. This is the only place in China where English is widely spoken and where British queuing etiquette is observed. Democracy is still on hold but, then again, the British weren't overly generous in that respect either. Hong Kong remains the quintessential entrepot, attracting self-starters from across Asia who relish one of the freest economies on earth. This collision of entrepreneurial energy and macho capitalism has created a land of gleaming skyscrapers and its natural offshoots: designer shops, posh restaurants and throbbing nightclubs.

Hong Kong's real charm for the visitor is in the blend of chic modernity and ancient religion, claustrophobic backstreets and wild, mountainous countryside. The region actually comprises several mountainous islands and a chunk of 'mainland' peninsula. Hong Kong Island is the most densely populated part of the city, famed for its stunning harbor skyline. In contrast, parts of the Outlying Islands and New Territories offer rugged wilderness.

The former Portuguese trading enclave of Macau is a short boat ride across the Pearl River Estuary from Hong Kong. It's several centuries older than Hong Kong, and far smaller and more relaxed than its nouveau-riche neighbor, Thanks to the liberalization of the casino industry, this tiny territory has been crowned the undisputed Las Vegas of the Far East. The Chinese, as you'll notice here, like a flutter.

HONG KONG ISLAND

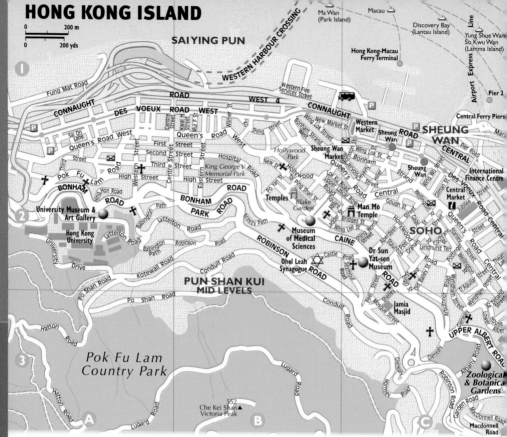

SAIYING PUN

Pok Fu Lam Country Park

552 Che Kei Shan ▲ Victoria Peak

PUN SHAN KUI MID LEVELS

HONG KONG ISLAND STREET INDEX

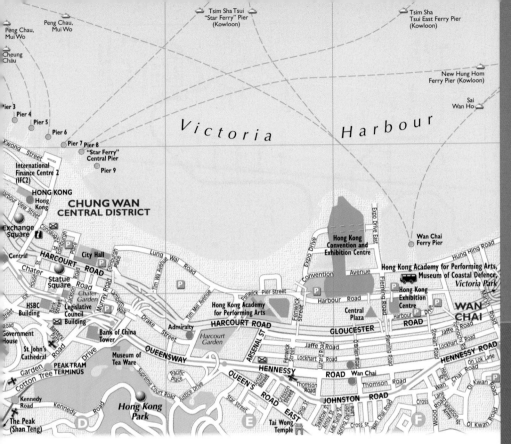

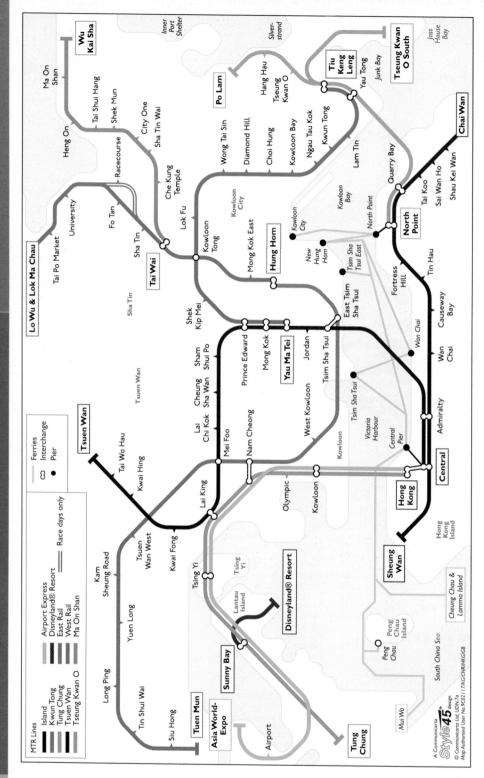

MTR Lines

- Island
- Kwun Tong
- Tung Chung
- Tsuen Wan
- Tseung Kwan O
- Airport Express
- Disneyland® Resort
- East Rail
- West Rail
- Ma On Shan
- Race days only

- Ferries
- Interchange
- Pier

A Communicarta
Style45 design
© Communicarta Ltd, UDN.7a
Map Authorised User No.9C021/7/KG/CNR/HKGGB

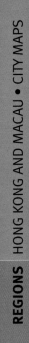

PH

INTRODUCTION

Cosmopolitan, wealthy 'Hong Kong Side' is the heart of the former colony. The Victoria Harbour Waterfront with ferry docks dwarfed by towers, is one of the world's most emblematic cityscapes.

MTR metro trains serve stations all along the densely urbanized north shore of Hong Kong Island and stations also have connections to and from Kowloon, the New Territories, Lantau Island and Hong Kong International Airport. Elsewhere, Hong Kong Island is a patchwork of mountains, forest, streams, seaside resorts and isolated beaches.

WHAT TO SEE

ABERDEEN

A busy South Side fishing port, Aberdeen has experienced a gradual reduction in the number of moored junks used as houseboats by fishing families. Celebrations (April/May) remain brisk, however, at Aberdeen's Tin Hau Temple (1851), dedicated to the goddess of the sea.

The harbor, a natural typhoon shelter, supports fleets of fishing boats, sampans (small boats that act as mini tour-boats), and fancy yachts and powerboats. After dark, life on the water picks up speed, as diners pile aboard the giant Jumbo Kingdom Floating Restaurant (▷ 363) and others like it. You can stroll along waterfront Praya Road, or go by boat or across the bridge to Apleichau (Duck's Tongue) Island, just offshore. Children will enjoy a visit to nearby Ocean Park (▷ 357).

➕ 347 R15 🚍 7, 70 from Central

DR SUN YAT-SEN MUSEUM

The arrival of a Sun Yat-Sen museum in Hong Kong is firm confirmation that Hong Kong is back in mainland hands. The revered nationalist leader (▷ 31,32) has museums dedicated to him in almost every major Chinese city, but this one really stands out, both in terms of the architecture, and the two excellent permanent exhibitions. It's housed in the 1914 Kom Tong Hall, a stunning four-story mansion which mixes stained-glass windows, and floral filigree balustrades with subtle Chinese touches. There's a range of fascinating artifacts for the history buff and educational videos for the amateur. It's well worth a look if you are around the Mid-Levels.

➕ 332 C2 ✉ 7 Castle Road (Mid-Levels, Central) ☎ (00852) 2367 6373 🕐 Mon–Wed, Fri–Sat 10–6, Sun 10–7 👆 Adult HK$10, child HK$5 🚍 12, 13, 23, 40 and 103 from Central

HONG KONG PARK

This modern park covers 8ha (20 acres), and though hemmed in by high-rise buildings, is a welcome oasis in a busy financial district. Water is a key motif, in fountains, artificial waterfalls and pools. You get a good view of the steeply sloping park from a central observation tower. An aviary (daily 8–5) that has both walk-through and caged areas houses 800 tropical birds. In the nearby conservatory (daily 8–5) are 2,000 plant species.

Hong Kong's oldest colonial building, the white Greek Revival-style Flagstaff House, dates from 1846 and was home to the British garrison commander until 1932. Since 1984 it has housed the Museum of Tea Ware (tel (00852) 2869 0690; Wed–Mon 10–5), which extends into the neighboring KS Lo Gallery. This infusion of knowledge and antique objects from centuries of Chinese tea culture includes beautiful handmade ceramic Yixing teapots.

➕ 333 D3 ✉ Main entrance on Supreme Court Road, Chung Wan (Central) ☎ (00852) 2521 5041 🕐 Daily 6am–11pm 👆 Free 🚇 Admiralty MTR

INFORMATION

www.discoverhongkong.com
➕ 347 R15 🚉 Causeway Bay MTR Station ✉ Hennessey Road and Yee Wo Street, near Exit F at Kai Chiu Road, Tung Lo Wan (Causeway Bay) ☎ (00852) 2508 1234 (line open daily 8–6) 🕐 Daily 8–8. 🚉 Hong Kong International Airport, ✉ Transfer Area E2 and Buffer Halls A and B, Arrivals Level ☎ (00852) 2508 1234 🕐 Daily 7am–11pm; Arrival Hall, 2nd Floor, Lo Wu Terminal Building 🚉 Lo Wu border railway station ☎ (00852) 2508 1234 🕐 Daily 8–6 🚇 Causeway Bay

Opposite *Looking down on the formal gardens of Hong Kong Park*

TIPS

» To simplify getting around in Hong Kong and gain a discount on MTR rides, purchase an Octopus Card costing HK$150 (less for students, seniors and children, and including HK$100 of travel credit and a deposit of HK$50 repayable when you return the card) from MTR customer service centers. You can use this smart card on most modes of public transportation (and at some shops and other businesses). The amount is automatically deducted by electronic readers and the remaining balance tallied. When the money runs out, you can reload it at other machines. A variant that's useful for short-stay visitors is the Airport Express Tourist Octopus 3-Day Hong Kong Transport Pass. The card costs HK$220 and HK$300, for Airport Express one-way and round-trip respectively, and allows three days of free MTR travel and HK$20 of other travel. For more information, tel (00852) 2266 2222; or visit www.octopuscards.com

» It's useful to remember that Hong Kong Island is far more than the north shore's skyscraper-laden urban jungle. A great place to get away from it all is at the surf-pounded white sands of Shek O beach resort in the southeast corner of the island, reachable by bus No. 9 from Shau Kei Wan.

» To telephone Hong Kong from outside the SAR, use the international access code (00 from China) followed by 852, then the number (▷ 383).

Below *Repulse Bay has a popular beach*

MAN MO TEMPLE

The pen—or rather the calligraphy brush—and the sword are celebrated in unlikely harmony at this Taoist temple dedicated to Man Cheong (God of Literature) and Mo (also known as Kuan Ti, God of War). Dating from the early colonial period, in the 1840s, it is surrounded by shops and apartments. Statues of the two gods are clothed in embroidered costumes, and images of other deities can be seen, while fragrant incense smoke suffuses the air.

⊞ 332 C2 ✉ Hollywood Road, Sheung Wan ◷ Daily 8–6 ✋ Free ⓜ Sheung Wan MTR, or Central MTR then Central–Mid Levels Escalator

THE PEAK

Riding the Peak Tram (daily 7am–12am), a funicular built in 1888 that now employs modern cars to transport 120 people per trip on its steeply angled track, is the most dramatic way to ascend The Peak, which reaches up to the Victoria Peak summit, 552m (1,299ft) above Victoria Harbour. The tram stops at the Peak Tower, at 396m (1,286ft) elevation. In this entertainment-and-dining complex you can see waxworks figures at Madame Tussaud's (daily 11–8); strange-but-true phenomena at Ripley's Believe it or Not! Odditorium (daily 10–10); motion simulation at the Peak Explorer (daily 10–10); or dine at restaurants in the wok-shape upper level. From its viewing deck—cloud permitting—you drink in a city view that is among the most breathtaking on earth. The 3.5km (2.2-mile) Peak Circle Walk pathway encircles the mountainside from near the Peak Tower and higher up is Victoria Peak Garden.

⊞ Off map 333 D3 🍴 Peak Café 🚋 Peak Tram funicular from the Lower Terminus, Garden Road 🚌 15, 15B, 15C, 515

STANLEY

Famed for its street market (▷ 358), Stanley (Chek Chu) has an extensive beach and a burgeoning restaurant scene. Its Maritime Museum (tel 00852 2813 2322; Tue–Sun 10–6), on the west shore of Stanley Bay, recounts the history of Hong Kong's ties with the sea through paintings, models, objects and interactive displays. The museum is in Murray House, a colonnaded colonial mansion dating from 1846, which until 1982 stood where the Bank of China building (▷ below) now stands, before it was dismantled and rebuilt here in 1998. The 1770s Tin Hau Temple on Stanley Main Street is dedicated to the Taoist goddess of the sea. From Stanley, you can go by ferry to Po Toi island.

⊞ 347 R15 🚌 6, 6A, 6X, 66, 260

STATUE SQUARE

Traces of the British heritage endure at this once graceful colonial square—even though the statue of the square's name, Queen Victoria's, has been banished to Victoria Park (▷ 339). Here are the Legislative Council Building and the Cenotaph British war memorial. Just beyond the adjoining Chater Garden is Japanese-American architect I. M. Pei's Bank of China Building (1990), which dwarfs the old Bank of China building (1950) on the square itself.

⊞ 333 D2 ✉ Chung Wan (Central) ⓜ Central MTR 🚋 Trams to Des Voeux Road Central

UNIVERSITY MUSEUM AND ART GALLERY

The museum, which showcases 5,000 years of Chinese arts and crafts, occupies the Fung Ping Shan Building, which dates from the 1930s and is connected by a bridge to the 1990s art gallery annex in the T. T. Tsui Building. Highlights of the collection—from ancient through antique to modern pieces—are Yuan dynasty bronze Nestorian crosses; domestic and funerary ceramics; calligraphy; paintings on canvas and silk; and furnishings. Take a break over a traditional Chinese tea served from a Yixing teapot at the Tea Gallery.

⊞ 332 A2 ✉ 94 Bonham Road, Pun Shan Kui (Mid Levels) ☎ (00852) 2241 5500 ◷ Mon–Sat 9.30–6, Sun 1–6 ✋ Free ⓜ Sheung Wan MTR 🚌 3B, 23, 40, 40M, 103 🍽 Tea Gallery

ZOOLOGICAL AND BOTANICAL GARDENS

Covering 5.6ha (14 acres) on the lower slopes of Victoria Peak, the gardens date from 1864. Though small, they have an international reputation in conservation and breeding. Tai chi aficionados add to their restful air.

Mammals and reptiles are in the Old Garden, west of Albany Road; the aviary, greenhouse and Fountain Terrace are on the east side. Specialized gardens, like the Herb Garden and Magnolia Garden, are dotted around. More than 1,000 tropical and subtropical plant species grace the gardens and the greenhouse, while animals and birds include Bornean orangutans, jaguars, American flamingos and Burmese pythons.

➕ 332 C3 ✉ Albany Road, Chung Wan (Central) ☎ (00852) 2530 0154 🕐 Daily 6am–10pm (some parts to 7pm; Greenhouse 9–4.30) ✋ Free 🚇 Central MTR 🚌 3B, 12, 13 from Central

MORE TO SEE

EXCHANGE SQUARE

Just off the Victoria Harbour waterfront, this bustling square sits behind the International Financial Centre, an extravagant construction of towers that includes the 88-floor 'IFC 2' at 420m (1,378ft) Hong Kong's tallest building. The 55th floor is dedicated to a public exhibition of the Hong Kong Monetary Authority (Mon–Fri 10–6, Sat 10–1). The square is enlivened by fountains and sculptures that include two full-size bronze water buffalo, a larger-than-life tai chi practitioner, and Henry Moore's abstract *Oval With Points*.

➕ 333 D2 ✉ Chung Wan (Central) 🚇 Central MTR

MUSEUM OF MEDICAL SCIENCES

Hong Kong is an interface between Chinese and Western medicine, and this museum takes a harmonious, yin-yang look at personalities, equipment and processes from both traditions, from the British colonial period to today's SAR (Special Administrative Region). Housed in the old Pathological Institute laboratory, a listed building dating from 1906, it includes a herbal garden.

➕ 332 B2 ✉ 2 Caine Lane, Pun Shan Kui (Mid Levels) ☎ (00852) 2549 5123 🕐 Tue–Sat 10–5, Sun 10–1 ✋ Adult HK$10, child free 🚇 Sheung Wan MTR, or Central MTR then Central–Mid Levels Escalator

TAI TAM COUNTRY PARK

One of Hong Kong Island's five country parks, all connected by footpaths, Tai Tam in the eastern sector of the island covers 15sq km (6sq miles).

➕ 347 R15 ☎ (00852) 2812 1576 🚇 Chai Wan MTR then minibus 16M G6, 61, 66 to Repulse Bay

MUSEUM OF COASTAL DEFENCE

Housed in Lei Yue Mun fortress, the museum covers 600 years of military history, from Ming dynasty works through Britain's Royal Navy to the Chinese People's Liberation Army. Children can scramble over the installations.

➕ Off map 333 F3 ✉ 175 Tung Hei Road, Shau Kei Wan ☎ (00852) 2569 1500 🕐 Fri–Wed 10–5 ✋ HK$10 adult, HK$5 child 🚇 Shau Kei Wan MTR, then north and east on the coast road

REPULSE BAY

Home to a superb sandy strand and some elegant shopping and dining. The beach is the busiest on Hong Kong Island.

➕ 347 R15 🚌 6, 6A, 6X, 260

VICTORIA PARK

This park adjacent to Causeway Bay typhoon shelter is popular for outdoor activities. On the typhoon shelter shore, the Noonday Gun is fired every day.

➕ Off map 333 F3 ✉ Tung Lo Wan (Causeway Bay) 🕐 24 hours 🚇 Tin Hau MTR 🚋 Trams from Wan Chai and Central

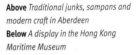

Above *Traditional junks, sampans and modern craft in Aberdeen*
Below *A display in the Hong Kong Maritime Museum*

KOWLOON

INFORMATION
➕ 347 R15 ℹ Star Ferry Concourse, Tsim Sha Tsui ☎ (00852) 2508 1234 (line open daily 8–6) 🕐 Daily 8–8 🚇 Tsim Sha Tsui and other MTR stations 🚢 Star Ferry 🚆 Hung Hom

INTRODUCTION

The best way to get from Hong Kong Island to Kowloon (and vice versa) is by the Star Ferry (▷ 342). Once on Kowloon side, you have an extensive choice of metro options: Seven lines operate here. Probably the most useful is the MTR Tsuen Wan line (the red line on MTR network maps), which bisects the Kowloon Peninsula from south to north. A dense network of buses and minibuses operates to just about all points, and many of them depart from outside the Star Ferry Concourse in Tsim Sha Tsui. Going on foot is also possible, though crowds and traffic can make this tiring.

Great Britain took control of the southern tip of the Kowloon Peninsula in 1860 through the treaty ending the Second Opium War. Over the years, Kowloon shared in Hong Kong's economic and population boom, and is now even more densely urbanized than the northern strip of Hong Kong Island.

WHAT TO SEE

HONG KONG MUSEUM OF ART

Housed in a striking modern building on the Tsim Sha Tsui waterfront, a brief hop by Star Ferry from Hong Kong Island, the museum has an extensive collection of ancient and modern Chinese arts and crafts, and covers Western art and culture as part of its special temporary exhibitions. There are striking views of Victoria Harbour from several vantage points in the interior, including the café.

Five galleries are devoted to the permanent collection and two to temporary exhibitions. Highlights of the antiquities gallery are bamboo carvings and Shiwan pottery. One gallery has modern Chinese painting and calligraphy, mostly from the 20th century. A key element of the collection is the fine art from Hong Kong, Macau and Guangzhou, mostly paintings and drawings but also photographs and maps, from the 18th century to the present time. These include fascinating paintings of Hong Kong in the 1850s, when it was almost entirely rural and was called Victoria by the British.

➕ 343 B3 ✉ 10 Salisbury Road, Tsim Sha Tsui ☎ (00852) 2721 0116 🕐 Fri–Wed 10–6, Sat 10–8 ✋ Adult HK$10, senior and child HK$5; Wed free 🚇 Tsim Sha Tsui MTR 🚢 Star Ferry ☕ Café

HONG KONG MUSEUM OF HISTORY

The museum, which opened in 2001, takes what you might call the long view of Hong Kong's history—beginning around 400 million years ago, which trumps even the most ancient Chinese dynasty by a long way. From this point

Above *The Symphony of Lights on Victoria Harbour, Hong Kong*

in geological time it moves forward to human history, beginning with the Neolithic period, proceeding through the houseboat culture of Hong Kong's indigenous Tanka people, and working up to Hong Kong's present-day status as a constituent of the People's Republic. The British colonial era, interrupted by a short but traumatic Japanese occupation during World War II, takes up a sizable amount of space, through which you can follow the burgeoning of the colony.

Much of the collection is not presented dully in glass cases, but in imaginative and at times hands-on dioramas and reconstructions of environments and scenes, both historical and modern. This helps to make the museum particulary appealing to children.

Across the piazza is the Hong Kong Science Museum.

➕ 343 C2 ✉ 100 Chatham Road South, Tsim Sha Tsui ☎ (00852) 2724 9042 🕐 Mon, Wed–Sat 10–6, Sun 10–7 ✋ Adult HK$10, child HK$5; Wed free 🚇 Tsim Sha Tsui MTR

HONG KONG SCIENCE MUSEUM

Likely to be a big hit with children—there are exhibits aimed at kids as young as three—this museum across the piazza from the History Museum uncovers the world of science (and technology). It does so imaginatively, entertainingly and, as far as possible, in an interactive and hands-on way. The Energy Machine, 22m (72ft) high, is the literal highlight of the tour.

➕ 343 C2 ✉ 2 Science Museum Road, Tsim Sha Tsui East ☎ (00852) 2732 3232 🕐 Mon–Wed, Fri 1–9, Sat, Sun 10–9 ✋ Adult HK$25, child HK$12.50; Wed free 🚇 Tsim Sha Tsui MTR

HONG KONG SPACE MUSEUM

The exhibits in the Hall of Space Science and the Hall of Astronomy—among them the Aurora 7 capsule from the 1960s US Mercury project—should be fascinating to anyone with an interest in space research.

Even better are the Sky Shows and Omnimax Shows at the combined planetarium and space theater, which sits inside the domed building (extra charge). These include films from outstanding places on earth, such as Australia's Great Barrier Reef, and astronomy presentations.

➕ 343 B3 ✉ 10 Salisbury Road, Tsim Sha Tsui ☎ (00852) 2721 0226 🕐 Mon–Wed, Fri 1–9, Sat, Sun 10–9 ✋ Adult HK$10, child HK$5; Wed free ❓ Children under 3 not admitted to Space Theatre 🚇 Tsim Sha Tsui MTR ⛴ Star Ferry

KOWLOON PARK

More than 'merely' affording a breath of fresh air in relentlessly urban Kowloon, this park is a rainbow palette of gentle hues. If you are going up or down the Kowloon peninsula, there's no better way to sidestep the din than by detouring through the park, which covers 14ha (35 acres). Park attractions include an aviary, a Chinese garden, a sculpture garden and a swimming pool.

➕ 343 B2 ✉ Nathan Road, Tsim Sha Tsui 🕐 Daily 5am–midnight ✋ Free 🚇 Tsim Sha Tsui MTR

KOWLOON WALLED CITY PARK

Once a slum and lair of organized crime, Kowloon Walled City was demolished during the 1990s. In its place is this delicate, fragrant recreation of an early Qing dynasty garden. Originally a coastal defense fortress, Kowloon Walled City entered legal limbo after Britain gained its lease on the New Territories in 1898. Remnants of the old fort remain, among them the Old South Gate and the restored Yamen, the fort mandarin's office and residence. It's pleasant to stroll through the park taking in pavilions, pools and fountains, floral walks, and a cluster of giant chessboards.

➕ Off map 343 C1 ✉ Tung Tau Road (at Junction Road), Wong Tai Sin 🕐 6.30am–11pm ✋ Free 🚇 Lok Fu MTR

HARD LANDING

Many a nervous passenger flying into Hong Kong prior to 1998 swore they could watch the televisions in Kowloon's high-rise apartments as they zipped past, before the pilot hung a hard right to land at the now disused Kai Tak Airport. The runway still sticks out into Kowloon Bay and is due to be redeveloped.

GROWING PAINS

The squat shape of the Kowloon Peninsula is a relatively recent phenomenon. The peninsula was originally much thinner, as you will see if you look back at old maps. Extensive and ongoing land reclamation, most recently in Yau Ma Tei and Hung Hom, has fattened it at the expense of Victoria Harbour and Kowloon Bay.

Below *Learning about electricity in the Hong Kong Science Museum*

TIPS

» Kowloon is the logical place from where to do a side trip to the Chinese mainland border city of Shenzhen or to Guangzhou (▷ 260–263), since the easiest way to get there is by the MTR's East Rail Line. Through-trains to Guangzhou depart from Hung Hom station on the Kowloon peninsula, while the pedestrian border crossing at Lo Wu can be reached from any of the stations along the East Rail route.

» The famed Peninsula Hotel (▷ 369) is by no means a budget option, but you can enjoy a more affordable taste of colonial Hong Kong by indulging in the institution of afternoon tea and buttered scones at the hotel's genteel Lobby Lounge.

Below *Tsim Sha Tsui Promenade, with its wonderful views*

LEI CHENG UK HAN TOMB MUSEUM

Discovered by chance in 1955, this chambered tomb is Hong Kong's oldest-known historical structure, dating from between AD25 and 220. It provides evidence of human activity in the Hong Kong area during China's Han dynasty. No human remains were found, and calligraphic inscriptions written on bricks are enigmatic. Visitors cannot enter the tomb itself, but can view it from behind glass. The small on-site museum displays pottery and bronze items from the tomb and there's an exhibition on Han culture.

✚ Off map 343 C1 ✉ 41 Tonkin Street, Sham Shui Po ☎ (00852) 2386 2863 🕐 Mon–Wed, Fri, Sat 10–6, Sun 1–6 ✋ Free 🚇 Cheung Sha Wan MTR

TSIM SHA TSUI PROMENADE

Few views in Hong Kong are better than the one from the pedestrian promenade fringing the Kowloon Peninsula's southern rim. The narrow channel of Victoria Harbour between here and Hong Kong Island's north shore is alive with vessels: the Star Ferry (▷ below), boats, tugboats, cruise ships, a Chinese Navy Ma'anshan-class guided-missile frigate, and lots more. On the west side, at Kowloon Public Pier, you can watch ferries shuttling back and forth, before passing the Clock Tower, the sole surviving fixture of the old Kowloon–Canton Railway station that once stood here. Now you pass the vast Hong Kong Cultural Centre (▷ 358) and the Hong Kong Museum of Art (▷ 340).

✚ 343 B3 ✉ Kowloon Public Pier; Avenue of Stars, Tsim Sha Tsui 🚇 Tsim Sha Tsui MTR 🚢 Star Ferry

WONG TAI SIN TEMPLE

Although towered over by high-rise housing, this large temple is the soul of popular religious practice in Hong Kong. Founded in 1921, it encompasses Taoist, Buddhist and Confucian beliefs and contains notable examples of traditional-style Chinese architecture and garden art. The temple is dedicated to Wong Chuping, who learned to transmute cinnabar (a mercury sulphide ore) to cure illness. He is revered now as Wong Tai Sin.

✚ Off map 343 C1 ✉ Off Lung Cheung Road, Wong Tai Sin 🕐 Daily 7–5.30 ✋ Free, donations welcome 🚇 Wong Tai Sin MTR

MORE TO SEE
CHI LIN NUNNERY

Although it only dates from the 1990s, this tranquil temple was built in Tang dynasty (AD618–906) style, using traditional wooden joints instead of iron nails. It covers 3ha (7.5 acres) with a blend of pavilions, rock gardens and the extensive Lotus Pond Garden.

✚ Off map 343 C1 ✉ 5 Chi Lin Drive, Tsuen Shek Shan (Diamond Hill) ☎ (00852) 2354 1789 🕐 Convent: daily 9–4; Lotus Pond Garden: 7am–9pm ✋ Donation 🚇 Diamond Hill MTR

NATHAN ROAD

If you like shopping, this dedicated 3.5km (2-mile) shopping street might seem like heaven. Nonshoppers are more likely to see one of the inner circles of hell straightened out into a long line of torment. The farther north you go, the more pronounced is the Chinese character of the shops.

✚ 343 B1–3 ✉ Between Salisbury Road and Boundary Street 🚇 Tsim Sha Tsui, Jordan, Yau Ma Tei, Mong Kok and Prince Edward MTR

STAR FERRY

The astounding view you get of Hong Kong Island and the Kowloon Peninsula from these vessels makes the short journey across Victoria Harbour—9 minutes—one of the world's most memorable 'sea voyages.' A must for any visit to this fascinating city.

✚ 343 A3 ✉ Kowloon Public Pier, Tsim Sha Tsui 🚇 Tsim Sha Tsui MTR

SYMPHONY OF LIGHTS

Kitsch perhaps, but this performance attracts crowds of onlookers. Every evening at 8pm, buildings along Hong Kong Island's Victoria Harbour waterfront are bathed in light and sound for 18 minutes. The best place to view the spectacle is from Kowloon's Tsim Sha Tsui waterfront promenade.

🔆 343 B3 ✉ Victoria Harbour waterfront, Tsim Sha Tsui 🚇 Tsim Sha Tsui MTR
⛴ Star Ferry

TIN HAU TEMPLE

All but submerged by a surrounding commercial district, the busy little temple to the goddess of the sea manages to project an air of calm. This is enhanced by its setting, beside a small park.

🔆 343 B1 ✉ Market Street, Yau Ma Tei 🕐 Daily 8–6 ✋ Donation appreciated 🚇 Yau Ma Tei MTR

YUEN PO STREET BIRD GARDEN

This bird market is an attraction in its own right. The constant twittering of beautiful song birds in bamboo cages replaces the more usual urban cacophony of Kowloon.

🔆 Off map 343 B1 ✉ Prince Edward Road West, Mong Kok 🕐 Daily 7am–8pm ✋ Free
🚇 Prince Edward MTR

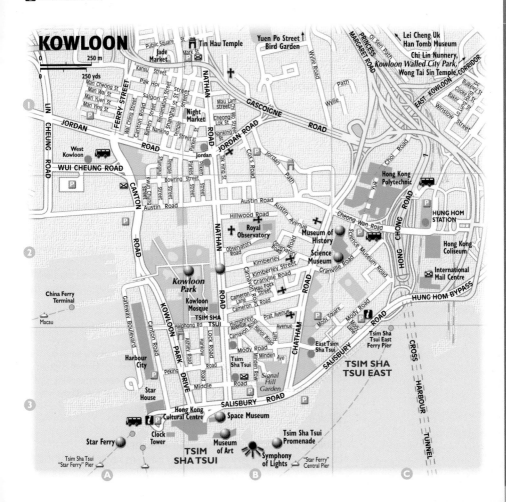

INFORMATION

🔢 346–347 R15 ℹ️ See tourist information offices on Hong Kong Island (▷ 337) and in Kowloon (▷ 340) 🚇 Tsuen Wan Line, Kwun Tong Line and the Tseung Kwan O Line serve destinations in the New Territories. In addition, the East Rail Line, West Rail Line and new Ma On Shan Line serve more remote areas; MTR Tung Chung Line serves Lantau Island 🚢 Ferries from the Outlying Islands Terminal, Central (Hong Kong Island), serve Cheung Chau, Lamma and Lantau islands

INTRODUCTION

The New Territories are a great place to relax. They cover a far-flung area stretching from the northern edge of Kowloon to the border with mainland China. Reaching the main towns and attractions takes time but there are transportation links. To explore the back country you'll need a car, a bicycle or hiking boots. A soft alternative is Hong Kong Tourist Board's The Land Between guided tour. For the islands, the only way to go is by boat (though Lantau also has a metro link). There are plenty of ferries, and the voyage, brief as it is, can be an attraction in itself.

Great Britain acquired the New Territories and their associated islands in 1898, the final territorial addition to Hong Kong. Unlike Hong Kong Island and Kowloon, which were acquired 'in perpetuity,' the New Territories were leased for 99 years. During most of that time they were Hong Kong's forgotten corner, useful mainly for affording defense against any invasion from the mainland. With the lease due to expire in 1997, the realization that this would leave only Hong Kong Island and Kowloon persuaded the British to begin negotiations for the return of the entire colony.

WHAT TO SEE

CHEUNG CHAU ISLAND

Once a haunt of pirates, Cheung Chau—'Long Island'—is actually small at just 2.5sq km (1sq mile). Ferries nose past junks and fishing boats to dock at Cheung Chau town's waterfront, which is crowded with open-air eateries. Car-free, the island is a good place for hikes along the coast and through the hilly interior. Windsurfing conditions are good and the beaches are pleasant.

🔢 346 R15 🚢 Outlying Islands ferry from Central

CHINESE UNIVERSITY OF HONG KONG ART MUSEUM

Founded in 1971 this museum appropriately maintains a tight focus on Chinese fine arts and applied arts, from ancient times until the pre-modern period. You

Above *Cheung Chau Island*

can view pottery, calligraphy, seals and other carvings, jade ornaments, fans, snuff bottles, paintings and more from all periods of recorded Chinese history. The university lies near the east coast of the New Territories, north of Sha Tin new town and west of the broad bay of Tolo Harbour.

➕ 347 R15 ✉ Chinese University, Sha Tin ☎ (00852) 2609 7416 🕐 Mon–Sat 10–4.45, Sun 12.30–5.30 ✋ Free 🚉 University East Rail Line station, then shuttle bus to university

LAMMA ISLAND

Car-free, carefree Lamma is Hong Kong's third-largest island. A good way to view it is to hike the moderately strenuous, scenic hiking trail connecting the island's two villages, arriving by ferry at one and departing from the other. You can soak up Yung Shue Wan's bohemian air, then shake it off on the trail before kicking back at one of Sok Kwu Wan's alfresco waterfront seafood restaurants. By way of a bonus, the trail intersects two of Lamma's finest beaches, Hung Shing Yeh and Lo So Shing (although the best is Mo Tat Wan on the east coast).

➕ 347 R15 ⛴ Outlying Islands ferry from Central to Yung Shue Wan or Sok Kwu Wan; or ferry from Aberdeen

LANTAU ISLAND

Sparsely populated Lantau is Hong Kong's largest island. Its natural appeal, created by forests and mountains including the 934m (3,064ft) Lantau Peak, has suffered since the new international airport opened in 1998 just off its north coast. Airport Express trains now zip across the 2.2km (1.4-mile) Tsing Ma Bridge from Kowloon. Yet wilderness abounds and Lantau's central attraction remains the Po Lin (Precious Lotus) Monastery's giant hilltop Tian Tan Buddha ('Big Buddha'; 1993), at 26m (85ft) the world's tallest seated outdoor bronze Buddha statue (monastery daily 9–6; statue 10–5.30). Buses from Mui Wo and Tung Chung stop at the monastery and you can get there by the new Skyrail cable car from Tung Chung. Also worth visiting is Tai O, a waterside fishing village on stilts, on Lantau's northwest coast.

➕ 346 R15 🚇 Tung Chung MTR ⛴ Ferry from Central to Mui Wo (Silvermine Bay)

SAI KUNG PENINSULA

The bare hills of this rugged, scenic peninsula are protected landscapes. Sai Kung Country Park covers 76sq km (29sq miles) in two sections, East and West, which meet at the Pak Tam Chung Visitor Centre. Beyond here begins the MacLehose Trail, a hiking trail 100km (60 miles) long, that snakes across the New Territories. The far less taxing Sheung Yiu Family Walk, a mere 1.8km (1.1 miles), takes in the Sheung Yiu Folk Museum (Wed–Mon 9–4), an abandoned village of the indigenous Hakka people dating from the 19th century. Try to make time for waterfront dining at a seafood restaurant on Sai Kung town's colorful Hoi Pong Square.

➕ 347 R15 ℹ Sai Kung Country Park Visitor Centre ☎ (00852) 2792 7365 🕐 Wed–Mon 9.30–4.30 ✋ Free 🚌 Green minibus 101M from Hang Hau MTR, or 1A from Choi Hung MTR to Sai Kung town then bus 94 or green minibus 7 or 9 to the Country Park

MAN FAT SZE MONASTERY

The 10,000 Buddhas of the temple's name refers to an astonishing array of small Buddha statues in the main hall. It actually understates their number by about 3,000. Founded by the scholar monk Yuet Kai in 1957, the monastery stands on a hillside west of Sha Tin new town rail station. You reach it by climbing a 431-step, statue-lined stairway (or taking an escalator) to a courtyard in which stand pavilions and a pagoda. Yuet Kai's body, covered in gold leaf, occupies a temple farther up the hillside.

➕ 347 R15 ✉ Off Pai Tau Street, Sha Tin 🕐 Daily 9–5 ✋ Free 🚉 Sha Tin East Rail Line station, then follow signs to the temple

TIP

» Visitors should be respectful to worshipers and dress appropriately when visiting Chinese temples and other places of worship. Do not touch religious objects, nor step on the threshold, nor sit with the soles of your feet pointing toward an image of the Buddha.

NEW TERRITORIES AND ISLANDS

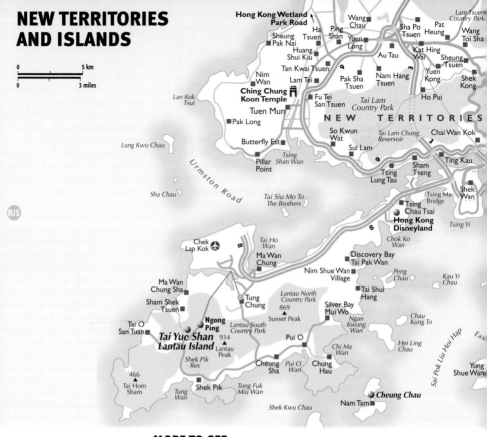

0 ——— 5 km
0 ——— 3 miles

Map labels: Hong Kong Wetland Park Road, Wang Chau, Ha Ping Shan, Sheung Pak Nai, Ha Tsuen, Yuen Long, Sha Po Tsuen, Pat Heung, Lam Tsuen Country Park, Wang Toi Shan, Au Tau, Kat Hing Wai, Sheung Tsuen, Huang Shui Kiu, Nim Wan, Tan Kwai Tsuen, Lam Tei, Pak Sha Tsuen, Nam Hang Tsuen, Yuen Kong, Shek Kong, Ching Chung Koon Temple, Fu Tei San Tsuen, Tai Lam Country Park, Ho Pui, Lan Kok Tsui, Tuen Mun, Pak Long, So Kwun Wat, Tai Lam Chung Reservoir, Chai Wan Kok, NEW TERRITORIES, Lung Kwu Chau, Butterfly Est, Sui Lam, Tsing Shan Wan, Sham Tseng, Ting Kau, Pillar Point, Tsing Lung Tau, Tsing Ma Bridge, Shek Wan, Tsing Yi, Sha Chau, Urmston Road, Tai Siu Mo To The Brothers, Tsing Chau Tsai, Hong Kong Disneyland, Chek Lap Kok, Tai Ho Wan, Chok Ko Wan, Ma Wan Chung, Discovery Bay Tai Pak Wan, Peng Chau, Kau Yi Chau, Nim Shue Wan Village, Ma Wan Chung Sha, Tung Chung, Lantau North Country Park 869, Silver Bay Mui Wo, Tai Shui Hang, Sham Shek Tsuen, Sunset Peak, Ngan Kwong Wan, Chau Kung To, Tai O San Tuan, Ngong Ping, Lantau South Country Park, Tai Yue Shan Lantau Island 934 Lantau Peak, Pui O, Chi Ma Wan, Hei Ling Chau, Sai Pok Liu Hoi Hap, Yung Shue Wan, Shek Pik Res, 466 Tai Hom Sham, Cheung Sha, Pui O Wan, Chung Hau, Tung Wan, Shek Pik, Tong Fuk Miu Wan, Nam Tam, Cheung Chau, Shek Kwu Chau

---

MORE TO SEE

CHING CHUNG KOON TEMPLE (TUEN MUN)

Despite the poetic name, which means 'Evergreen Pine Tree,' this Taoist temple is in the middle of housing in Tuen Mun new town. It is still a restful place with its pavilions, towers, arches, gardens and other ornamental features.
✚ 346 R15 ✉ Tsing Chung Path, Tsing Chung Koon Road, Tuen Mun ◷ Daily 8–6 ✋ Free
🚇 Kwai Fong MTR, then bus 58M

Below *The pathway to the Man Fat Sze Monastery at Sha Tin*

HONG KONG DISNEYLAND

www.hongkongdisneyland.com
Located on yet more reclaimed land toward Lantau's eastern tip is Hong Kong Disneyland. Opened in September 2005, the US$3.2 billion park has been closely modeled on the original 1950s Disneyland theme park and has virtually identical attractions to those found in California, Space Mountain included. There have been a few concessions to local culture though: ill-fortune is staved off by omitting the 'unlucky' number four in the resort's two huge hotels.
✚ 346 R15 ✉ Chok Ko Wan (Penny's Bay), Lantau Island ☎ (00852) 1830 1830 ◷ Daily 10–8 (times vary slightly throughout the year) 🚇 Disneyland Resort ✋ Mon–Fri adult HK$295, child HK$210, Sat–Sun adult HK$350, child HK$250

HONG KONG WETLAND PARK ROAD

www.wetlandpark.com
Set beside the huge Tin Shui Wai new town, this excellent nature park acts as buffer between urban Hong Kong and the extensive Mao Po Marshes. The reserve's most famous resident is Pui Pui, a celebrity crocodile who caused a scare when he was spotted wild in 2003 and prompted a hunt that lasted

months. Other inhabitants include a wide variety of bird, insect and butterfly species. Four boardwalks trace a path through the mangroves and provide binoculars and telescopes for close inspection of the wildlife.

🕂 346 R15 ✉ Wetland Park Road, Tin Shui Wai ☎ (00852) 2708 8885 🕐 Mon, Wed–Fri 10–5 🚇 Tin Shui Wai, then light rail to Wetland Park Station 👆 Adult HK$30, child HK$15

NGONG PING

www.np360.com.hk

The highlight of this multifaceted mass-market tourist attraction is the 5.7-km (3.5 miles) Ngong Ping Skyrail. It makes for an exhilarating journey over Lantau's mountainous landscape and alongside Chek Lap Kok Airport, and is the best way to reach the Tian Tan 'Big' Buddha. Ngong Ping Village, at the cableway's upper terminus, contains coffee- and souvenir-shops. Paying homage to the nearby Po Lin Monastery and its famous Buddhist monument, Ngong Ping has two Buddhist-influenced attractions: Walking with Buddha is an innovative multimedia exhibition detailing the story of Buddha and the spread of the religion around the globe. Kids will enjoy the Monkey's Tale Theater, with computer-generated animation and special effects.

🕂 346 R15 ✉ Po Lin Monastery, Lantau Island ☎ (00852) 2109 9898 🕐 Mon–Fri 10–6, Sat 10–6.30, Sun 9–6.30 🚇 Tung Chung 👆 Adult HK$58 one way, child HK$28 one way

TAI MO SHAN

At 958m (3,142ft), Hong Kong's highest mountain is embedded in the Tai Mo Shan Country Park, which covers 14.4sq km (5.6sq miles).

🕂 347 R15 ✉ Country Park Visitor Centre ☎ (00852) 2498 9326 🕐 Sat, Sun and holidays 9.30–4.30 👆 Free 🚌 KMB bus 51 from Tsuen Wan

Below *Fishing craft at the inner harbor; Cheung Chau*

INTRODUCTION

Macau lies on the west side of the Pearl River estuary, some 64km (40 miles) west of Hong Kong. It consists of the Macau peninsula and the small outlying islands of Taipa and Coloane, which have now been joined together by land reclamation. Covering just 27sq km (10.5sq miles), Macau is heavily urbanized on the main peninsula, less so on Taipa and Coloane. Its size makes walking a viable way for getting around, at least in part, though a multitude of bus and minibus routes covers most points. There are jetfoil connections with Hong Kong, and Macau has its own international airport on an artificial island off Taipa.

The Portuguese first arrived on Macau in about 1535. They were given permission by the Chinese government to set up a trading and missionary outpost at the sheltered harbor in 1557, and this is considered the foundation year of the Portuguese colony. It was named Amaçáo after the temple to the sea goddess A-Ma (▷ below) that stood beside the harbor. Macau flourished as a trading station and Portuguese sovereignty was recognized in 1887. In 1999 Macau was handed back to China as (like Hong Kong) a Special Administrative Region of the People's Republic, its constitution and social and economic systems guaranteed for 50 years.

WHAT TO SEE

A-MA TEMPLE

Dating from the 16th century, Macau's oldest temple stands on the southwest edge of the peninsula, below Barra Hill and, appropriately enough, next to the Inner Harbour and the Maritime Museum (Wed–Mon 10–5.30). It is dedicated to A-Ma, the Taoist goddess of the sea and sailors, and three of its pavilions honor this goddess. That leaves a fourth pavilion, dedicated to the Buddhist goddess of mercy, Kun Iam. Between the pavilions, connected by a pathway and separated by arched gates, worshipers find space, and opportunity for prayers and offerings. A carved, painted image of a junk at the entrance recalls the legend of A-Ma's safe landfall in Macau during a typhoon.

✉ Rua de Sao Tiago da Barra ⏰ Daily 8–5 ▨ Free

COLOANE

The southernmost island of Macau, green and hilly Coloane is no longer really an island, now that it has been joined to Taipa not merely by a road causeway but also by a thick waist of reclaimed land—yet it remains insular. People come here to get away from it all at the beaches of Cheoc Van in the south and Hác Sá in the east. Coloane (Lo Wan) Village also has fine restaurants and cafés and the lovely Chapel of St. Francis Xavier (1928). A white marble statue of the goddess A-Ma, just shy of 20m (65ft) tall, crowns the summit of the island's highest hill, the Alto de Coloane, which peaks at 170m (558ft). Mainland China is just across a narrow waterway from the village.

🚌 15, 21, 21A, 25, 26, 26A

KUN IAM TEMPLE

Macau's largest temple, dedicated to the Buddhist goddess of mercy, Kun Iam, stands just north of the busy town center, but a garden and lotus pond in the grounds add a tranquil aspect. A statue of Kun Iam, clothed in silk, wearing a crown and flanked by 18 male retainers, occupies the main hall. The various halls, built in a traditional style, date from the 1620s, though the temple was founded in the 14th century. In 1844 it was the somewhat surprising setting for a milestone in international relations when it hosted the signing of the first

INFORMATION

www.macautourism.gov.mo

✚ 429 R15 ℹ Alameda Dr Carlos d'Assumpção, 335–341 Hot Line Building, 12th Floor (postal address: PO Box 3006, Macau) ☎ (00853) 2831 556 ⏰ Mon–Fri 9–5 ℹ Macau International Airport, Arrival Hall ☎ (00853) 2886 1436 ⏰ Daily 9–1.30, 2.15–7.30, 8.15–10; Macau Ferry Terminal, Outer Harbour ☎ (00853) 2872 6416 ⏰ Daily 9am–10pm; also information desks at Largo do Senado, Guia Lighthouse, St. Paul's Church and the Frontier Post

Opposite *A-Ma Temple is dedicated to the goddess of the sea*
Below *Incense coils burn at the Kun Iam Temple*

TIPS

» Stretch out your resources by purchasing the Museum Pass. This costs MOP$25 for adults and MOP$12 for seniors and children, and allows entry within a five-day period to the Museum of Macau, the Maritime Museum, the Museum of Art, the Wine Museum, the Grand Prix Museum and the Lin Zexu Museum.

» To telephone Macau from outside the SAR, use the international access code (00 from China) followed by 853, then the number (▷ 383).

trade and friendship treaty between the United States and China. In the temple garden you can see the round granite table on which the accord was inked.

✉ Avenida do Coronel Mesquita ⏰ Apr–end Oct daily 8–6; Nov–end Mar daily 8–5 💲 Free 🚌 12, 17, 18, 19, 22, 23, 28C

LARGO DO SENADO

Macau's main square (Senate Square) is a handsome cocktail of pastel-hued colonial architecture surrounding a pedestrianized core marked out with a wave-pattern mosaic sidewalk. It stands at the midpoint of Avenida Alemeida Ribeiro, which connects the Inner Harbour with the Outer Harbour. Trees provide a measure of shade, and there's a fountain, benches and a café. The square's most prominent building is the Leal Senado (Loyal Senate; daily 9–9), the former seat of the Portuguese administration and now that of the Municipal Council. Built in 1784, but with a 19th-century facade, it has a sober neoclassical aspect. Behind this, there's a walled inner garden, walls tiled in blue-and-white faience, a graceful 1920s library and an art gallery (closed Mon).

🚌 2, 3, 3A, 5, 7, 10, 10A, 11, 18, 21A, 26A, 33

MUSEUM OF MACAU (MUSEU DE MACAU)

www.macaumuseum.gov.mo

Housed among the galleries of the hilltop Monte Fort, built by the Jesuits and completed in 1626, this fascinating museum covers Macanese history from the arrival of the Portuguese to the present day, along with its folklore and other traditions, and local arts and crafts. It does so in part by way of imaginative recreations of places and scenes. Two of the museum's three floors are below ground.

From trapezoidal Monte Fort's stout ramparts, still 'defended' by batteries of bronze cannon—though the fort only once saw serious action, during the Dutch naval assault of 1622—you get a fine view over the city and the Pearl River estuary. The fort was badly damaged by the 1835 fire that destroyed São Paulo Church .

Above *The view of the city from Guia Hill*

✉ Monte Fort (Fortaleza do Monte), Praceta do Museu de Macau 112; you can reach the fort by elevator from the ruins of São Paulo Church ☎ (00852) 2835 7911 🕐 Tue–Sun 10–6 ✋ Adult MOP$15, child MOP$8; free 15th of month

MORE TO SEE

LUÍS DE CAMOES GARDEN AND GROTTO
In the 18th century this hilly, tree-shaded garden (Jardín e Gruta de Luís de Camoes) belonged to the British East India Company. A bust of the 16th-century Portuguese poet Luís de Camoes, for whom the park is named, stands in a grotto. In the Casa Villa mansion on the grounds is a small museum of Chinese fine arts and crafts (daily 9–6).
✉ Praça Luís de Camoes 🕐 Daily dawn–dusk ✋ Free 🚌 8A, 17, 18, 19, 26

SÃO PAULO CHURCH
Little more than the baroque stone facade of the 17th-century Jesuit church, and the broad stairway leading to it, survive. The timber remainder went up in smoke in the fire of 1835, yet it remains the signature image of colonial Macau. A museum in the grounds has objects from onsite excavations and of sacred art (daily 9–6).
✉ Rua de São Paulo ☎ (00853) 2835 8444 🕐 Permanently ✋ Free

GUIA HILL
A park covers this hill (Collina da Guia) overlooking the Outer Harbour waterfront. As Macau's highest point, it was a natural place for a defensive work, hence the 1630s Guia Fortress (Fortaleza da Guia), and the 1835 lighthouse. The small chapel (daily 9–5.30) is dedicated to Our Lady of Guia.
✉ Guia Hill Municipal Park (Parque Municipal do Colina da Guia) 🕐 Daily 9–5.30 ✋ Free
🚌 6, 28C 🚋 Cable car from Flora Garden (Jardim da Flora)

Above *Largo do Senado*
Below *The facade is about all that remains of São Paulo Church*

SHEUNG WAN

Giving an insight into the multiple faces of Hong Kong Island's north shore, this tour begins at the waterfront, moves through a mixed governmental and financial district to a chic cosmopolitan area, then a traditional Chinese one, and ends up at a busy shopping zone.

THE WALK

Distance: 3.5km (2 miles)
Allow: 2 hours (not including diversions and visits)
Start: Star Ferry Pier, Central
✚ 333 D2
End: Western Market, Des Voeux Road Central ✚ 332 C1

HOW TO GET THERE

The Star Ferry Pier is where the Star Ferry (▷ 342) from Kowloon arrives. The nearby bus terminal and Central MTR station make it easy to get to and from most places on the north shore of Hong Kong Island.

★ The Star Ferry Dock sits alongside the other outlying island piers in front of the 88-floor 'Two IFC' tower.

Head south, following signs for the Central MTR station. Take the pedestrian tunnel outside the General Post Office. This brings you

safely out on the far side of busy Connaught Road Central.

❶ A few steps to your left after you exit the tunnel is the bustling Statue Square (▷ 338); the Cenotaph British War Memorial still stands there. The square is divided by Chater Road, on the far side of which is Hong Kong's Legislative Council (Legco) Building.

Leave from the west side of the square (to your right) and take Ice House Street. This is named after the former 1890 cold storage warehouse that you'll find at the point where the ascending Ice House Street joins Lower Albert Road and that now hosts the Fringe Club and a contemporary arts center. At the end of the street, turn right into Wyndham Street.

❷ Lan Kwai Fong, the area to the right, between Wyndham Street and

D'Aguilar Street, is filled with bars, nightclubs and restaurants. You pass the Hotel LKF at 33 Wyndham Street and the elegant antiques of the Tibetan Gallery at No. 55.

As Wyndham Street curves right then left, you pass the Pottinger Street Stairway to your right and the neoclassical 1864 Central Police Station to your left.

❸ You are entering Hollywood Road, renowned for its antiques shops. A little way along, at the junction with Cochrane Street, you can join the Central–Mid-Levels Escalator, which has been ascending on an increasingly steep trajectory from Des Voeux Central and the Central Market. Boarding the escalator and continuing upward gives you a chance to explore fashionable Soho. Go as far up the escalator as you want on Shelley Street.

Re-descending Shelley Street, using a mixture of stairs, covered walkways and the street itself, takes you back to Hollywood Road, where you turn left. Continue along the road, crossing Aberdeen Street and Shing Wong Street.

❹ The Man Mo Temple (▷ 338), which comes up now on your left, makes a good place for a break.

Just beyond the temple descend the stairs of Ladder Street, to your right. From here go left at the next junction, into Upper Lascar Row (known as Cat Street), laden with antiques shops, although their stock comes closer to bric-a-brac. Keep going to Station Street, where you turn left, then recross Hollywood Road.

❺ In Tai Ping Shan Street, the next street up, the tiny temples are scarcely distinguishable from shops at first glance.

Drop again to Hollywood Road, and go left.

❻ Hollywood Road Park is another good point for taking a break.

Retrace your steps a short way to Possession Street, and turn left. The bottom of this street used to be the Hong Kong Island waterfront. This is where the British raised their flag in 1841 to claim the island for the Crown. The distance from here to today's waterfront gives you an idea of how extensive land reclamation has been. Cross over Queen's Road West.

❼ Bonham Strand and the adjacent Bonham Strand West and Wing Lok Street West are noted for shops selling ginseng and bird's nests for soup. Also around here, Ko Shing Street is noted for herbal medicines and Des Voeux Road West for dried seafood.

Cross over to New Market Street.

❽ The building that houses the Western Market dates from 1906. Market stalls lost their place here in 1989 but the two-floor building has been restored and outfitted with bijou boutiques and cafés.

Go east a short way on Des Voeux Road Central to the Sheung Wan MTR station for quick transfer back to the Star Ferry Pier via Central MTR station.

WHERE TO EAT
STAUNTON'S WINE BAR AND CAFÉ
✉ 10–12 Staunton Street ☎ (00852) 2973 6611 🕐 Daily 8am–2am

TOURIST INFORMATION
www.discoverhongkong.com
✉ Hong Kong Tourist Board, Causeway Bay MTR Station ☎ (00852) 2508 1234
🕐 Daily 8–8

Opposite *The idyllic Hollywood Road Park*
Above *Gods in the Man Mo temple*

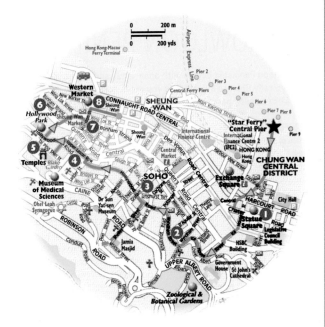

THE KOWLOON PENINSULA

The Kowloon Peninsula begins with open vistas and cosmopolitan allure at its southern end, and acquires a more typically Chinese character as you move north. This walk provides a taste of both and offers a breath of fresh air in a shady park along the way.

THE WALK

Distance: 3km (1.8 miles)
Allow: 2 hours (not including visits and shopping)
Start: Star Ferry Pier, Tsim Sha Tsui
✚ 343 A3
End: Tin Hau Temple, Nathan Road
✚ 343 B1

HOW TO GET THERE

The Star Ferry Pier is where the Star Ferry (▷ 348) from Hong Kong Island arrives. The bus terminal just outside makes it easy to get to and from most places in Kowloon.

★ Hong Kong Tourist Board has an office here, where you can pick up maps and brochures. Bear right on the concourse outside the dock.

❶ The Clock Tower, ahead on Kowloon Public Pier recalls the old Kowloon–Canton Railway Station that stood here until 1975, when it was demolished except for this graceful tower. Just behind the tower is the fortress-like Hong Kong Cultural Centre (▷ 358), where classical music, dance and Chinese opera are performed.

Go east along the water's edge for 100m (110 yards) or so, to admire the view.

❷ You enter the Hong Kong Museum of Art (▷ 340) from the landward side. The museum is best known for its wide-ranging collection of ancient and modern Chinese arts and crafts, but there is likely to be an interesting temporary exhibition on, too.

Exit the museum and walk straight ahead.

❸ You can't easily miss the Hong Kong Space Museum (▷ 341), only a few steps away, thanks to the distinctive dome housing a planetarium and space theater, as well as a capsule from a 1960s US Mercury spaceship. Go through the small shaded garden on the east side of the Space Museum. You cross over Salisbury Road by the underpass on the north side of the museum. Follow the signposted route to Nathan Road and you'll emerge beside the Peninsula Hotel (▷ 369), which is a good, if pricy, place to stop for tea and buttered scones.

❹ Nathan Road (▷ 342), Hong Kong's inimitable shopping street, begins on the east side of the Peninsula Hotel.

Go north past the Tsim Sha Tsui MTR station, then left on Haiphong Road, passing the Jamia Masjid Mosque and Islamic Centre, at the junction of Haiphong Road and Nathan Road.

❺ A short way along Haiphong Road is the southern entrance to Kowloon Park (▷ 341). Going north along the park's central axis makes it hard to lose your way and gives you a look at a rose garden, the Hong Kong Heritage Discovery Centre, a Chinese garden, an aviary, pools, fountains, and more. At the northern exit is a swim center.

This is a good place to quit the tour. Go east on Austin Road to Nathan Road, and any southbound bus to Star Ferry to return to the start.

If you're up for more, cross over Austin Road and go left along it for a few blocks to Temple Street, and go right.

❻ Temple Street Market doesn't really get going until 7pm. But at whatever time, this atmospheric street is worth visiting.

On the way to the end of Temple Street, pass the Bowring Street Market and cross over Jordan Road. At the end go west on Kansu Street, across Shanghai Street and Reclamation Street.

❼ The covered Jade Market on the right is a great place to buy jade, but not necessarily a place to buy great jade: caveat emptor.

Go back east on Kansu Street then turn left on the continuation of Temple Street.

❽ The Tin Hau Temple (▷ 343), a Chinese landmark, makes a fitting end to the tour.

Cross over to the east side of Nathan Road and go left to a group of bus stops. Take a bus with 'Star Ferry' as its destination back to the start.

WHEN TO GO
You can do this tour at any time of the day or evening.

WHERE TO EAT
THE LOBBY
✉ Peninsula Hotel ☎ (00852) 2920 2888
🕐 Daily 2–7

TOURIST INFORMATION
HONG KONG TOURIST BOARD
www.discoverhongkong.com
✉ Star Ferry Concourse ☎ (00852) 2508 1234 🕐 Daily 8–8

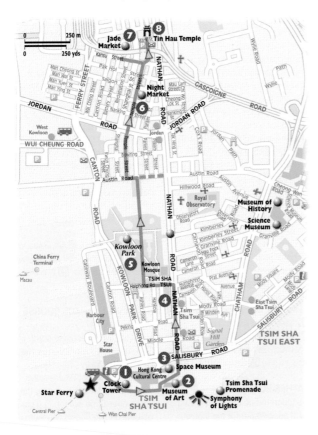

REGIONS HONG KONG AND MACAU • WALK

Opposite *The Hong Kong Cultural Centre*

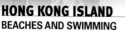

HONG KONG ISLAND

BEACHES AND SWIMMING

Beaches on the south coast of Hong Kong Island can get very crowded at peak times, such as weekends from spring to autumn and in summer. At other times they are likely to be quieter. Those listed here are sandy beaches with anti-shark nets (despite the nets, beaches are occasionally closed for shark alerts) and lifeguards on duty from April to the end of September.

✉ Deep Water Bay, between Aberdeen and Stanley 🚌 7 from Central to Aberdeen, then 73 ✉ Repulse Bay, between Deep Water Bay and Stanley 🚌 6, 6A, 6X, 66, 260 from Central ✉ Shek O, southeast corner of Hong Kong Island 🚌 9 from Shau Kei Wan ✉ Stanley, southeast Hong Kong Island 🚌 6, 6A, 6X, 66, 260 from Central

BONHAM STRAND WEST

Stretching westward from the Western Market, this street is noted for its many shops selling ginseng, a root that many Chinese consider a sovereign cure for all their ailments. Neighboring Wing Lok Street is equally noted for shops selling birds' nests (for soup), herbs and spices.

✉ Bonham Strand West, Sheung Wan ⏰ Shop hours vary; many are open daily

8am–10pm or later 🚇 Sheung Wan MTR 🚋 Trams to Western Market

CLUB 97

www.ninetysevengroup.com

An evergreen lounge-bar with dance floor that puts on a broad range of musical entertainment: gay shows, salsa and reggae nights, and more. Happy hour varies from two to four hours, depending on the night.

✉ 9 Lan Kwai Fong, Central ☎ (00852) 2816 1897 ⏰ Mon–Thu 6pm–2am, Fri 6pm–4am, Sat, Sun 8pm–late ✋ Free 🚇 Central MTR

DRAGFRINGE CLUB

www.hkfringeclub.com

This is the place for alternative and cutting-edge action—drama (in English and Cantonese), dance music and other events—generally using local performers and artists. The club occupies a protected building that dates from 1890.

✉ 2 Lower Albert Road, Central ☎ (00852) 2521 7251 ⏰ Mon–Thu 12–12, Fri, Sun noon–2am ✋ HK$100–160 (some events are free) 🚇 Central MTR 🖥 🍷

FEATHER BOA

This tough-to-find Soho bar is well worth seeking out for the fabulous

retro furnishings, decadent party ambience and—most of all—famous chocolate-sprinkled strawberry daiquiris. The tiny space creates a house-party mood and is great for making new friends.

✉ G/F, 38 Staunton Street, Central ☎ (00852) 2857 2586 ⏰ Daily 9.30am–midnight 🚇 Central

GOETHE INSTITUTE

www.goethe.de/hongkong

Although the emphasis here is on events that in one way or another touch German culture, many items on the agenda, such as art exhibitions, music and dance, either cross the language barrier or don't intersect it at all.

✉ 14th Floor, Hong Kong Arts Centre, Wan Chai ☎ (00852) 2802 0088 ⏰ Times vary ✋ Most events are free 🚇 Wan Chai MTR 🚌

HAPPY VALLEY RACE COURSE

www.hkjc.com

The attractive racecourse south of Causeway Bay is operated by the Hong Kong Jockey Club. There are meetings most Wednesdays (occasionally Tuesdays) during the September–June season. You can visit the on-site Racing Museum.

Opposite Stanley Market has become well known for its bargains in clothes, toys, ornaments, souvenirs, and Chinese arts and crafts

✉ Wong Nai Chung Road, Pau Ma Tei ☎ (00852) 2966 8111 🕐 7.15–11. Racing Museum: Tue–Sun 10–5 💷 HK$10; HK$100–150 for Members' Enclosure 🚇 Causeway Bay MTR
🍴 💻 🏪

HONG KONG ACADEMY FOR PERFORMING ARTS
www.hkapa.edu
The academy students relish the prospect of putting into practise some of what they are learning in the fields of music, theater and dance, and visiting performers help to fill out the bill. Some performances are open-air.
✉ 1 Gloucester Road, Wan Chai ☎ (00852) 2584 8500 🕐 Times vary 💷 Some events free; others HK$60–320 (reduced rates for students) 🚇 Wan Chai MTR 💻

HONG KONG ARTS CENTRE
www.hkac.org.hk
A waterfront venue on reclaimed land, with multiple auditoriums for performing arts, visual arts, and film and video arts. A busy schedule encompasses both local and visiting talent.
✉ 2 Harbour Road, Wan Chai ☎ (00852) 2582 0200 🕐 Box office daily 10–6 💷 Some events free; others HK$100–300 🚇 Wan Chai MTR 🕐 💻

HONG KONG GOLF CLUB
www.hkgolfclub.org
Close to the sea on the island's south coast, midway between Aberdeen and Repulse Bay, the handsome course is only a nine-hole affair, but you can always go around twice.
✉ 19 Island Road, Deep Water Bay ☎ (00852) 2812 7070 🕐 Visitors Mon–Fri 9–2 💷 HK$450 🚌 6A, 6X, 260 🍴 🏪

INSOMNIA
A stalwart of the late-night scene in Central, Insomnia goes until 6am every day of the week and

has a happy hour that lasts all day (8am–9pm). There are two bars and live music after 10.30pm. Things tend to get going after midnight.
✉ Ho Lee Commercial Building, 34–44 D'Aguilar Street, Central ☎ (00852) 2525 0957 🕐 Daily 8am–6am 🚇 Central

JOE BANANAS
Laid-back and beach-club-style 'JB's,' Hong Kong's premier party and pick-up scene, manages its transitions gracefully, going from stylish lunch venue to happy hour drinks emporium, to music and dance as the evening wears on.
✉ 23 Luard Road, Wan Chai ☎ (00852) 2529 1811 🕐 Mon–Thu 4pm–4am, Fri, Sat 4pm–5am, Sun 3pm–4am 💷 Usually free; Fri, Sat evening HK$100 🚇 Wan Chai MTR

MUSEUM OF COASTAL DEFENCE (▷ 339)

OCEAN PARK
www.oceanpark.com.hk
Dolphins, sea lions and seals perform at this large, multi-dimensional aquarium and theme park, and sharks can be seen in a special walk-through tank. Giant pandas Le Le and Ying Ying be seen, too. Thrilling rides and attractions for little kids are legion, and you enter by way of a cable-car ride.
✉ Deep Water Bay, Aberdeen ☎ (00852) 2552 0291 🕐 Daily 10–6 💷 Adult HK$208, child HK$103 🚌 629 💻 Seaview Café and Middle Kingdom restaurant

ON-I
www.dragon-i.com.hk
A cool place for daytime dining that thaws out during the 3pm–9pm happy hour and really heats up after midnight, when there's dance music from a mix of local and guest DJs.
✉ UG/F, The Centrium, 60 Wyndham Street, Central ☎ (00852) 3110 1222 🕐 Daily 12–3am. Restaurant 12–2.30pm, 6pm–10pm 💷 Usually free; HK$150 for special DJ nights 🚇 Central MTR

ORIENTAL SPA
www.mandarinoriental.com
For the lap of luxury, from the

fitness room, via aromatherapy and a Moroccan rasul steam bath, to the multiple-hands-on massage, this is the market leader in soothing the stressed while lightening their pocketbooks.
✉ 5th Floor, Landmark Mandarin Oriental hotel, 15 Queen's Road Central, Central ☎ (00852) 2132 0011 🕐 Daily 10am–11pm 💷 Group yoga class HK$180, deep tissue massage HK$850, four hands massage HK$2,000 🚇 Central MTR 💻

THE PEAK (▷ 338)

POKFULAM PUBLIC RIDING SCHOOL
www.hkjcridingschools.com
Beautifully located on the edge of a large country park in the southwest of the island, this large and busy riding school caters to all ages and abilities. Call ahead for information on courses.
✉ 75 Pok Fu Lam Reservoir Road, Pok Fu Lam ☎ (00852) 2550 1359 🕐 Tue–Sun 9–12, 2–6 💷 Adult HK$450 per hour, child HK$360 per 45 minutes 🚌 4, 7, 40, 40M

PROPAGANDA
Other contenders for the crown of Hong Kong's hottest gay disco come and go, but Propaganda endures. There's a separate bar that's not totally drowned in noise. Straights are not discouraged. The place doesn't really get going until after midnight.
✉ Basement, 1 Hollywood Road, Central ☎ (00852) 2868 1316 🕐 Sun–Thu 9pm–4am, Fri, Sat 9pm–5am 💷 Sun–Thu free; Fri, Sat HK$100–150 🚇 Central MTR

STANLEY MARKET
Aimed more at tourists than most other markets in Hong Kong, the street market in this south-coast resort town covers clothes for casual and office wear, silk and linen, leather goods, arts and crafts, and souvenirs and curios.
✉ Stanley 🕐 Daily 10–7 🚌 6, 6A, 6X, 66, 260

STAR FERRY (▷ 342)

TIMES SQUARE

www.timessquare.com.hk

Times Square's twin towers rise to 46 and 39 stories, the bottom 16 of which house a combination of international chains and local dealers. The stores are neatly organized by type. There are four stories of restaurants and a huge cinema complex, making it a popular all-round leisure destination.

✉ 1 Matheson Street, Causeway Bay ☎ (00852) 2118 8900 🕓 Daily 10–10 🚇 Causeway Bay

WESTERN MARKET

Dating from 1906, this elegant two-floor building housed a fresh-food market until 1989. It was preserved and restored and is now home to various souvenir shops, arts and crafts stores and boutiques, along with cafés.

✉ New Market Street, Sheung Wan 🕓 Daily 10–7 🚇 Sheung Wan MTR 🚋 Trams to Western Market

KOWLOON

AQUA SPIRIT

www.aqua.com.hk

Located on a mezzanine above two of Kowloon's trendiest restaurants, Aqua Spirit packs a major wow-factor punch thanks to the jaw-dropping widescreen views of Hong Kong Island, across the water. It's a particular favorite among expatriates when family or friends come to stay, and there's a well-dressed, yuppyish atmosphere. It may be supremely expensive but there's no better place to kick-off a big night.

✉ 29/F, 1 Peking Road, Tsim Sha Tsui, Kowloon ☎ (00852) 3427 2288 🕓 Daily 6pm–1am 🚇 Tsim Sha Tsui

BIRD MARKET

Hong Kong's men are especially fond of songbirds and they come here in numbers to buy new birds, along with cages, bird seed and other paraphernalia. There are also larger birds for sale, such as parrots. A visit here makes an entertaining outing for children.

✉ Yuen Po Street Bird Garden, Mong Kok 🕓 Daily 7am–8pm 🚇 Mong Kok MTR

FLOWER MARKET

The market fills the street with the fragrant scent and colorful sight of masses of cut flowers and potted plants from around the world, ranging from inexpensive bunches to elegant and expensive bonsais, along with accessories like pots and vases.

✉ Flower Market Road, Mong Kok 🕓 Daily 9–6 🚇 Prince Edward MTR

HELISERVICES FLIGHTSEEING TOURS

www.heliservices.com.hk

Seeing the city of Hong Kong from the air is a memorable, if by no means inexpensive, experience. Several standard tours are available and custom-designed ones can be arranged. The company's heliport may revert to Hong Kong Island once land-reclamation work there finishes.

✉ Heliport: Peninsula Hotel Helipad, Salisbury Road, Tsim Sha Tsui ☎ (00852) 2802 0200 🕓 By arrangement 🖐 HK$6,600–20,000 per helicopter, from 15 minutes to 1 hour 🚇 Tsim Sha Tsui MTR

HONG KONG COLISEUM

www.lcsd.gov.hk

Used for concerts of rock and pop music and jazz, along with sports events, conventions, and various kinds of spectacles, this modern venue lies between the Kowloon waterfront and the Kowloon and Canton Railway (KCR) station.

✉ 9 Cheong Wan Road, Hung Hom ☎ (00852) 2355 7261 🕓 Box office Mon–Fri 9–1, 2–5.45 🖐 Some events free; others HK$50–900 🚇 KCR Hung Hom ▣

HONG KONG CULTURAL CENTRE

www.lcsd.gov.hk

The fortress-like HKCC, standing just back from the Victoria Harbour waterfront, is Hong Kong's leading venue for both Western and Chinese orchestral music—it is the home base of the highly regarded Hong Kong Philharmonic Orchestra and the Hong Kong Chinese Orchestra—and for ballet and theater. The center has the flexibility to host events both large and small.

✉ 10 Salisbury Road, Tsim Sha Tsui ☎ (00852) 2734 9009 🕓 Box office daily 10–9.30 🖐 Some events free; others HK$40–900 🚇 Tsim Sha Tsui MTR 🚇 ▣

HONG KONG SPACE MUSEUM (▷ 341)

JADE MARKET

The enclosed market is the home of dozens of stalls which together have for sale thousands of jade items, ranging from cheap trinkets to expensive antiques (it is not always easy for a non-expert to tell which is which, or even what is real and what is fake).

✉ Junction of Kansu Street and Battery Street, Tsim Sha Tsui 🕓 Daily 10–4 🚇 Jordan MTR

KNUTSFORD TERRACE

It's not as expensive or as gentrified as its Hong Kong Island equivalent, Lan Kwai Fong, but the Knutsford Terrace enclave parties equally as hard and goes equally as late. This short Tsim Sha Tsui street is home to a parade of late-night bars and live music venues which attracts a mixture of foreigners and locals.

✉ Tsim Sha Tsui 🕓 Daily 5pm–5am 🚇 Tsim Sha Tsui MTR

LADIES MARKET

The stalls of this busy market cater to more than the ladies of its name, although it still does a big business in cheap underwear and other items of female apparel and accessories like belts and handbags.

✉ Tung Choi Street, Mong Kok 🕓 Daily 12–10 🚇 Mong Kok MTR

RAJA FASHIONS

www.raja-fashions.com

There are many Asian tailors in Hong Kong—men who are incessantly accosted on the street by their sales reps might conclude there are too many in fact. Few if any of them can match the standards of this quality family-owned business's handmade suits, shirts, and overcoats.

✉ 34C Cameron Road, Tsim Sha Tsui ☎ (00852) 2311 5612 🕓 Mon–Sat 9–9, Sun 11–6 🚇 Tsim Sha Tsui MTR

RELAX FOOT REFLEXOLOGY

Reflexology, acupuncture, aromamassage and several other treatments are available at this plain but welcoming studio next to the busy shops, hotels and restaurants in Knutsford Terrace and Kimberley Road.

✉ Unit B Basement, 68 Kimberley Road, Tsim Sha Tsui ☎ (00852) 2317 7786 🕐 Daily 12.30pm–2.30am ✋ Foot reflexology massage HK$98, aroma body massage HK$185, acupuncture points body massage HK$248 🚇 Tsim Sha Tsui MTR

SYMPHONY OF LIGHTS

Any position along the waterfront or on the water is fine for viewing this kitsch but fascinating light show. The high buildings on the Hong Kong Island shore are illuminated in a choreographed display that is sometimes enlivened with pyrotechnics.

✉ Victoria Harbour waterfront, Tsim Sha Tsui 🕐 Daily 8–8.20pm ✋ Free 🚇 Tsim Sha Tsui MTR ⛴ Star Ferry

TEMPLE STREET MARKET

The street's famous night market, retailing cheap clothes, leather items and all kinds of bric-a-brac, doesn't really get going until around 7pm, although some stalls have already been in business for several hours by then. In adjacent streets, market stalls are in business from morning.

✉ Temple Street, Kansu Street and Reclamation Street, Tsim Sha Tsui 🕐 Daily 8am–11pm 🚇 Jordan MTR

MACAU

CANIDROME (CANIDROMO)

www.macauyydog.com

Greyhound racing takes place at a modern track in the north of Macau town. There are generally 15 or 16 races per meeting and the atmosphere is more serious about gambling than the horse racing.

✉ Avenida do Almirante Lacerda, Macau Town ☎ (00853) 2833 3399 🕐 Mon, Thu–Sun from 7.30pm ✋ Public stand MOP$10 (can be used for betting); boxes MOP$80– MOP$120 🚌 1, 1A, 3, 4, 5, 7, 9, 9A, 23, 25, 26, 26A, 32, 33, 34 🍴 🛍 🚻

MACAU GRAND PRIX

www.macau.grandprix.gov.mo

The Guia Circuit winds Monaco-style through the ordinary streets of Macau Town, below the Guia Hill and along the Outer Harbour. The Formula 3 race is the premier event of the annual auto and motorcycle races held here.

✉ Guia Circuit, Macau Town ☎ (00853) 2855 5555 🕐 4 days mid-Nov ✋ Practice days MOP$50; race days MOP$200–900 🚌 1A, 3, 3A, 28A, 28B, 28BX, 28C, 32, AP1 🍴 🛍 🚻

MACAU JOCKEY CLUB (JOCKEY CLUBE DE MACAU)

www.mjc.mo

Horse racing takes place at the club's large and ultramodern racecourse, which has two lakes and a golfing area in the middle, in the southwest of Taipa. The grandstand is air-conditioned, and you can watch the action on a giant video screen.

✉ Estrada Governador Albano da Oliveira, Taipa Island ☎ (00853) 2882 0868 🕐 Sep–Jul Tue or Wed and Sat or Sun, 2 and 7.15pm ✋ Outdoor areas free; grandstand MOP$20 🚌 11, 15, 22, 28A, 30, 33, 34, 35, AP1 🍴 🛍 🚻

MACAU TOWER

www.macautower.com.mo

The 338m (1,100ft) structure has a variety of heart-stopping adventure rides. For the real adrenaline junkie there is a traditional bungee jump,

Below *Sharks circle above the visitor walkway at Ocean Park*

Left *A side-street market near the center of Hong Kong*

beach, at more than 3km (2 miles), is Hong Kong's longest. The beaches have anti-shark nets (even so, beaches are occasionally closed for shark alerts) and lifeguards may be present from April to end September.

✉ Cheung Sha, Lantau Island ⛴ Lantau ferry from Outlying Islands Ferry Pier, Central, then bus from Mui Wo (Silvermine Bay) ✉ Lo So Shing, Sok Kwu Wan, Lamma Island ⛴ Lamma Island Sok Kwu Wan ferry from Outlying Islands Ferry Pier, Central ✉ Hung Shing Yeh, Yung Shue Wan ⛴ Lamma Island Yung Shue Wan ferry from Outlying Islands Ferry Pier, Central ✉ Silverstrand, Sai Kung Peninsula, eastern New Territories Ⓗ Hang Hau MTR

DISCOVERY BAY GOLF CLUB
It's a long trek out here by boat for a round of golf—unless you can afford the helicopter fare—but playing on an island has its own charms, in addition to those of a challenging 18-hole course.

✉ Valley Road, Discovery Bay, Lantau Island ☎ (00852) 2987 7273 🕐 Daily 10–5.30 💲 HK$600–900 ⛴ Discovery Bay Ferry from Outlying Islands Ferry Pier

HONG KONG DISNEYLAND
www.hongkongdisneyland.com
Mickey and Minnie Mouse have set up home close to Lantau Island's northern tip, along with many other Disney characters and enough magical rides and attractions to keep most young children happy.

✉ Chok Ko Wan (Penny's Bay), Lantau Island ☎ (00852) 1830 1830 🕐 Wed–Fri 10–7, Sat–Tue 10–9 💲 Adult HK$295–350, child HK$210–250 Ⓜ Disneyland Resort MTR (change at Sunny Bay MTR) 🍴 🛍

HONG KONG GOLF CLUB
www.hkgolfclub.org
A taxi ride of less than 5 minutes takes you from the railroad station to this large complex of three 18-hole courses and a driving range in the north of the New Territories.

✉ Lot No. 1, Fan Kam Road, Fanling, New Territories ☎ (00852) 2670

as well as an innovative Skyjump, where the freefall is slowed down slightly. If this still sounds too much, try the Skywalk, a handrail-free stroll around the outside of the tower at an altitude of 223m (730ft). The tower also features an outdoor observation deck on the 61st floor, and a café and restaurant, each with stunning views.

✉ Largo da Torre de Macau ☎ (00853) 8988 8656 🕐 Mon–Fri 10–9, Sat–Sun 9–9 💲 MOP$388–1,388 (plus MOP$85 entry to Observation Deck)

SEAC PAI VAN PARK (PARQUE DE SEAC PAI VAN)
A visit to this park on the west coast of Coloane would be welcome enough as an escape from busy Macau Town. For children it has the additional attraction of a small zoo—more like a children's farm really—containing farm animals and monkeys, and an aviary. There's also the Museum of Nature and Agriculture (Tue–Sun 10.30–4.30).

✉ Coloane Island 🕐 Tue–Sun 9–6 💲 Free 🚌 21A, 25, 26, 26A 🛍

THE VENETIAN
www.venetianmacau.com
This new mega-casino trumps even Las Vegas for size and excess. There's a perennial cacophony of slot machines and sliding chips in the world's largest gambling den, all 46ha (114 acres) of it. The 1,000 slot machines and more than 600 gaming tables are open 24 hours, and served by a veritable army of croupiers and waitresses. Above is the largest hotel structure in all of China, while global celebrities wander by to perform in the 15,000-seat arena.

✉ Estrada da Baía de N. Senhora da Esperança, Taipa ☎ (00853) 2882 8888 🕐 Daily 24 hours ❓ Free shuttle buses from all of Macau's major entry points

NEW TERRITORIES AND ISLANDS
BEACHES AND SWIMMING
Being harder to get to, the sandy beaches on Lantau and Lamma islands and in the New Territories are usually quieter than those on Hong Kong Island. Cheung Sha

1211 ⊙ Visitors Mon–Fri 7am–8pm
💺 HK$1,400 🚇 Sheung Shui East Rail
Line 🍴 🍺

JOCKEY CLUB KAU SAI CHAU GOLF CLUB

www.kscgolf.com

Gary Player designed the two 18-hole courses at Hong Kong's only public golf club, in a scenic location on an island off the south coast of the Sai Kung Peninsula.

✉ Kau Sai Chau Island, Sai Kung, New Territories ☎ (00852) 2791 3380 ⊙ Daily 7am–8pm 💺 HK$400–900 🚇 Choi Hung MTR, then bus 92 to Sai Kung Bus Terminal; at the waterfront you take the golf club's own ferry to the course 🍴 🍺 🍺

NGONG PING SKYRAIL

www.np360.com.hk

Encapsulating that ancient travel cliché, the Ngong Ping Skyrail makes the journey more important than the destination. In a sense it's the easiest way to get to the famous Tiantan 'Big' Buddha of Lantau—one of Hong Kong's most popular tourist attractions—but it's also the world's longest cable-car ride and makes for an exhilarating journey over Hong Kong's most splendid natural landscape.

✉ Tung Chun/Po Lin Monastery, Lantau Island ☎ (00852) 2109 9898 ⊙ Mon–Fri 10–6, Sat 10–6.30, Sun 9–6.30 💺 Adult HK$58 one-way, child HK$28 (cable car combo prices available for joint entry with other attractions) 🚇 Tung Chung

SHA TIN RACE COURSE

www.hkjc.com

This ultramodern racecourse, with a giant video screen, is operated by the Hong Kong Jockey Club. Penfold Park, one of Hong Kong's largest parks, is part of the complex and is an attraction in itself even when there's no racing.

✉ Fo Tan, Sha Tin, New Territories ☎ (00852) 2966 8111 ⊙ 1–6. Racing generally takes place on Sunday afternoons (occasionally Saturdays). 💺 HK$10; HK$100–150 for Members' Enclosure 🚇 East Rail Line 🍴 🍺 🍺

Right *New Year celebrations*

JANUARY/FEBRUARY
CHINESE NEW YEAR

The three-day celebrations to mark the start of the new lunar year are marked in both Hong Kong and Macau with colorful processions and fireworks. Aside from these public displays, most Chinese celebrate with family and friends, decorate their homes, and engage in activities that ensure good fortune for the coming year.

✉ Hong Kong and Macau ⊙ Variable: first moon of the Chinese lunar calendar

APRIL/MAY
CHEUNG CHAU BUN FESTIVAL

Sleepy Cheung Chau wakes up with a jolt for its week-long 'moment' of fame when it becomes the place to be. There are parades and towers of traditional sweet 'lucky' buns.

✉ Praya (waterfront), Cheung, Chau Island ⊙ Variable: fourth moon of the Chinese lunar calendar 🚢 Outlying Islands ferry from Central

JUNE
DRAGON BOAT RACES

Held to honor an upright imperial official who preferred suicide by drowning to becoming corrupt, these races of lovingly built and enthusiastically paddled boats sport a dragon emblem at the bow.

✉ Various waterfront locations in both Hong Kong and Macau ⊙ Variable: The races begin on the fifth day of the fifth moon of the Chinese lunar calendar and run over two weekends

SEPTEMBER/OCTOBER
MID-AUTUMN FESTIVAL

Lanterns illuminate the night sky in a beautiful and symbolic display when Chinese people celebrate the harvest moon, and consume specially baked moon cakes.

✉ Parks, beaches and other public spaces in both Hong Kong and Macau ⊙ Variable: fifteenth day of the eighth moon of the Chinese lunar calendar

PRICES AND SYMBOLS

The restaurants are listed alphabetically. The prices are for a two-course lunch (L) and a three-course à la carte dinner (D) for one person, without drinks. The wine price is for the least expensive bottle. All the restaurants listed accept credit cards unless otherwise stated.

For a key to the symbols, ▷ 2

HONG KONG ISLAND

BACI (AND BACI PIZZA)

www.lankwaifong.com

Baci's ultramodern sleek lines and limpid tones, and windows overlooking the hip Lan Kwai Fong street scene, accompany food that celebrates national pride while appealing to a younger set. State-of-the-art thin-crust pizza and home-made pasta are joined by fine

dishes like savory escalope with Marsala sauce. The pizzeria below the main restaurant has equally good thin-crust pizza and costs quite a bit less.

✉ 1 Lan Kwai Fong, Central ☎ (00852) 2801 5885 🕓 Mon–Thu 12–2.30, 7–11, Fri, Sat 12–2.30, 7–11.30, Sun 12–2.30, 6.30–10.30 🍴 L HK$150, D HK$350, Wine HK$200 🚇 Central MTR

CLIPPER LOUNGE

www.mandarinoriental.com

Modeled on the lounge of a private yacht, the Clipper takes the English afternoon tea ceremony and wraps it up in a smooth setting of mahogany and brass. A dozen different tea varieties (no teabags here!)—and coffee for those who prefer it—are accompanied by scones with fresh cream and jam, cake, tarts and other

necessaries of the tearoom genre.

✉ Mandarin Oriental Hotel, 5 Connaught Road, Central ☎ (00852) 2522 0111 🕓 Daily 7–10 🍴 Afternoon tea HK$208 plus 10% 🚇 Central MTR

COCOCABANA

www.toptables.com.hk

On Hong Kong Island's south shore, this tranquil fount of laid-back continental chic serves up Mediterranean dishes supported by fine tastes from the Caribbean, Goa, Thailand and other beach locales from around the world—piri piri prawns and grilled Mediterranean sardine with rosemary butter, Moroccan grill, bouillabaisse. The tree-fringed alfresco deck has tables overlooking the bay and is a good spot for a sundowner sangria. Jazz and reggae accompany the splash of the waves and the plangent cries of seabirds.

✉ 2nd Floor, Beach Building, Island Road, Deep Water Bay ☎ (00852) 2812 2226 🕐 Mon–Fri 12.30–3, 6.30–11, Sat, Sun 12.30–11 🖐 L HK$200, D HK$380, Wine HK$300 🚌 6A, 6X, 260

EL CID CARAMAR

www.kingparrot.com

The best way to experience this Spanish restaurant is to dine on the balcony with a fine view of the sea, an appropriately Mediterranean-style setting for tucking into tapas from a list that includes spicy chorizo sausage, accompanied by Spanish wine or sangria. There's paella, or you can go the whole hog with roast suckling pig. Colonnaded, stone-built Murray House even looks Spanish. Inside, the checkerboard pattern floor and a dark-wood atmosphere create a pleasing Spanish effect.

✉ 102 Murray House, Stanley Plaza, Stanley ☎ (00852) 2899 0858 🕐 Mon–Fri 12–12, Sat, Sun 11–midnight 🖐 L HK$200, D HK$350, Wine HK$2600 🚌 6, 6A, 6X, 66, 260

HUNAN GARDEN

The highly spiced, sour cuisine of Hunan (Mao Zedong's home province) doesn't get as much play as it might in Hong Kong. This central restaurant goes some way toward compensating by being a worthy standard-bearer. Sophisticated and subdued despite being invariably crowded, all pink and green tones and lotus-theme images, it looks out on Exchange Square from its big picture windows. The chili-sprinkled chicken and fish dishes are what a primarily business clientele enjoy.

✉ 3rd Floor, The Forum, Exchange Square, 8 Connaught Place, Central ☎ (00852) 2868 2880 🕐 Daily 11.30–3, 5.30–11.30 🖐 L HK$180, D HK$200, Wine HK$180 🚇 Central MTR

INDOCHINE 1929

Although Vietnamese cuisine does not by any means need a

francophone fillip, the aim here is to take you back in spirit to Indochina's days of French rule. A location inside an office building uphill from Central MTR station may seem unpromising, but colonial-era fixtures and fittings set the scene and the staff are dressed in fine silk traditional Vietnamese costume. Delicate, fragrant food does the rest.

✉ 2nd Floor, California Tower, 30–32 D'Aguilar Street, Lan Kwai Fong, Central ☎ (00852) 2869 7399 🕐 Mon–Fri 12–2.30, 6.30–11, Sat 6.30–11 🖐 L HK$175, D HK275, Wine HK$170 🚇 Central MTR

JUMBO KINGDOM FLOATING RESTAURANT

www.jumbo.com.hk

Despite a liberal serving of tourist hokum, this floating eatery in Aberdeen Harbour, reached by boat, has been a 'must do' ever since it opened in 1976. The seafood-based Cantonese style of its main dining area, heavy on lobster and fried rice, enlivened by flamed drunken shrimp, is now a little passé—not that this fazes the tour groups who pile in for the ambience, the glitz and the experience. Look for classier dining in the separate Top Deck restaurant.

✉ Shum Wan Pier Drive, Wong Chuk Hang, Aberdeen ☎ (00852) 2553 9111 🕐 Mon–Sat 11–4.30, 5.30–11.30; Sun 7–4.30, 5.30–11.30 🖐 L HK$400, D HK$600, Wine HK$160 🚌 70, 75 (then by Jumbo's free private ferry)

KHANA KHAZANA

Two blocks from the Wan Chai MTR station, this pure vegetarian Indian restaurant attracts expat and visiting Indian diners to its relaxed, family-friendly upstairs dining room. It also has Chinese on the menu, but this doesn't detract from the authentic Indian dishes, like the thalis, (or from the Bollywood hit movies on the widescreen TV). The lunchtime buffet is good value for the money, especially if you load up enough to make dinner superfluous.

✉ 1st Floor, Dannies House, 20 Luard Road, Wan Chai ☎ (00852) 2520 5308

🕐 Mon–Fri noon–3, 5–10.45; Sat, Sun 12–10.45 JL HK$98, D HK$200, Wine HK$280 🚇 Wan Chai MTR

LOON WAI RESTAURANT

Any night-time visit to Causeway Bay should include a trip to this fantastic diner. Popular with young groups of friends, it specializes in mixed-grill hot plates that include more meat than seems economically possible for less than HK$40. It's very much a local's local kind of place: loud, steamy and loads of fun. There's no English on the sign, so look out for the street number on the shop sign.

✉ 54–58 Jardine Street, Causeway Bay ☎ (00852) 2576 6609 🕐 Daily 7am–midnight 🖐 L and D HK$38 🚇 Causeway Bay

LUK YU TEAHOUSE

This Cantonese teahouse, a few blocks southwest of the Central MTR station, has lightened up since the days when smiles from its famously grumpy waiters for anyone they didn't recognize were as rare as free tables. Some regular customers seem to have been occupying their seats at Luk Yu since it opened in 1933. But the pay-off for persistence is a taste of old Hong Kong—ceiling fans, private booths, brass spittoons—combined with unrivalled dim sum. The traditional wheeled dim sum trolleys give way to a menu around lunchtime.

✉ 24–26 Stanley Street, Central ☎ (00852) 2523 5464 🕐 Daily 7am–11pm 🖐 L HK$120, D HK$240 🚇 Central MTR

M AT THE FRINGE

www.m-atthefringe.com

One of Hong Kong's most celebrated fine-dining restaurants, 'Michelle's' is above the colonial-era Fringe Club (itself on the 'fringe' of the Lan Kwai Fong partying district). The contemporary cuisine is pan-Mediterranean, taking in Italian, French, Middle Eastern and North African flavors, while the dining room has a comfy, bohemian-chic feel. Getting a seat will require pre-booking as this place remains wildly

popular, 20 years after opening.
✉ 1/F, South Block, Dairy Farm Builing, 2 Lower Albert Road, Central ☎ (00852) 2877 4000 🕐 Mon–Fri 12–2.30, 7–10.30, Sat, Sun 7–10.30 🍴 D HK$450, Wine HK$240 🚇 Central

STAUNTON'S WINE BAR & CAFE
www.stauntonsgroup.com
A wine bar with an extensive wine cellar *should* be as handily placed as this one, within a few stumbling steps of the Central–Mid-Levels Escalator, in the heart of Soho, and long a prime mover of the district's trendy reputation. The ground floor is great for people-watching and casual continental dining, with the emphasis on Mediterranean cuisines. Upstairs is a touch more formal, and there is an outdoor balcony, affording a different angle for observing the passing scene.
✉ 10–12 Staunton Street, SoHo, Central ☎ (00852) 2973 6611 🕐 Mon–Fri 10am–2am, Sat, Sun 8am–2am 🍴 L HK$150, D HK$200, Wine HK$240 🚇 Central or Hong Kong MTR, then Central–Mid-Levels Escalator

TAI PING KOON
Causeway Bay is famous for its 'soy sauce restaurants,' a Hong Kong culinary sub-genre that sees Western food prepared in a quintessentially Cantonese way. Founded in 1860, Tai Ping Koon is one of the oldest surviving restaurants in all of China, and does dishes like eggs'n'curry, or soy sauce soaked steak, served by old-time waiters sporting white blazers and black ties. It's one to do for the experience rather than the quality of the food.
✉ 6 Pak Sha Road, Causeway Bay ☎ (00852) 2576 9161 🕐 Daily 11am–11.45pm 🍴 L HK$150 D HK$200 🚇 Causeway Bay MTR

TOTT'S ASIAN GRILL & BAR
www.mandarinoriental.com/excelsior
The panoramic view of Hong Kong's towers and harbor from the big windows of the 'Talk of the Town' looks like a view of the galactic capital Coruscant from *Star Wars*,

and a major renovation in 2007 has created a swish space from which to enjoy it. A tightly constructed, eclectic menu mixes and matches from China, Thailand, India, Europe and the US—everything from tandoori salmon to Aberdeen Angus beef with grilled Boston lobster. The exuberant Sunday Bubbly Brunch has become a legend in its own brunchtime.
✉ 34F, Excelsior Hotel, 281 Gloucester Road, Causeway Bay ☎ (00852) 2837 6786 🕐 Mon–Fri 12–3, 6.30–10, Sat 6.30–11, Sun 11.30–3, 6.30–10 🍴 L HK$200, D HK$400, Wine HK$200 🚇 Causeway Bay MTR

THE VERANDAH
www.therepulsebay.com
The restaurant of the tiny Repulse Bay residential community has a magnificent view across carefully tended lawns and the beach, to Lamma Island and beyond. Inside, palm trees and ceiling fans hark back to colonial days. Fine European dining takes in oysters, caviar, rack of lamb, beef stroganoff, and much more. Reserve ahead for the silver-service Sunday champagne brunch, an opulent way to pass some hours, which features classical jazz from a live combo. And do drop by for afternoon tea.
✉ South Wing, The Repulse Bay, 109 Repulse Bay Road, Repulse Bay ☎ (00852) 2812 2722 🕐 Tue–Sat 12–2.30, 6.30–10.30, Sun 11–2.30 🍴 L HK$250, D HK$450, Wine HK$250 🚌 6, 6A, 6X, 260

KOWLOON
AQUA ROMA & AQUA TOKYO
www.aqua.com.hk
Located on the top floor of TST's tallest harbour-front tower (1 Peking Road), Aqua Roma combines Italian cuisine with panoramic views over Victoria Harbour. On the other side, Aqua Tokyo has a long teppanyaki bar and several booths overlooking Kowloon's gritty cityscape. The Aqua Spirit cocktail bar—the source of the Buddha Bar-style beats—is just above on the mezzanine floor. All three venues are expensive, but

they make for an essential Hong Kong experience.
✉ 29/F, 1 Peking Road, Tsim Sha Tsui, Kowloon ☎ (00852) 3427 2288 🕐 Mon–Sat 12–3, 6–11; Sun 12–4, 6–11 🍴 L HK$300, D HK$500, Cocktails HK$90 🚇 Tsim Sha Tsui MTR

CITY CHIU CHOW RESTAURANT
Chiu Chow cuisine, a variant of Cantonese cooking based on the spicy, tangy-sauce recipes of the coastal cities of Chaozhou and Shantou, is highly fashionable in Hong Kong. Seafood leads the way, with duck dishes close behind, at this fine practitioner of the style. A cavernous place close to the Science Museum, with big tables populated by local family and business groups, it has won awards for dishes like the honey-flavored smoked duck breast.
✉ 1st Floor, East Ocean Centre, 98 Granville Road, Tsim Sha Tsui East ☎ (00852) 2723 6226 🕐 11am–midnight 🍴 L HK$100, D HK$250, Wine HK$150 🚇 Tsim Sha Tsui MTR

FOOK LAM MOON
www.fooklammoon-grp.com
Though perhaps a little too full of its own sense of importance, to the extent of a barely concealed scorn for diners who stumble on their way around the menu, this most traditional of Cantonese restaurants, both in its looks and in its presentation, unarguably delivers on the plate. Shark's fin, bird's nest soup and abalone are the elite performers, supported by a cast that includes deep-fried crispy chicken, baked stuffed crab meat and onion in the shell, and pan-fried lobster.
✉ 8 Luna Court, 53–59 Kimberley Road, Tsim Sha Tsui ☎ (00852) 2366 0286 🕐 Daily 11.30–3, 6–11 🍴 L HK$250, D HK$600, Wine HK$800 🚇 Tsim Sha Tsui or Jordan MTR

GAYLORD
Unlike the many local Indian restaurants that wear their ethnic origins on their sleeves, this personable place is cool and

restrained. A block south of Kowloon Park, on a busy but otherwise nondescript side street, it covers a range of subcontinent cuisine styles, with the major focus being on north Indian. Succulent tandooris, glowing vindaloos and nicely done fish dishes emerge from the kitchen.

✉ 1st Floor, Ashley Centre, 23–25 Ashley Road, Tsim Sha Tsui ☎ (00852) 2376 1001 🕐 Daily 12–2.30, 6–11 ✋ L HK$120, D HK$180, Wine HK$160 🚇 Tsim Sha Tsui MTR

HIBIKI

www.mhihk.com

Proof that Japanese dining doesn't have to be costly is afforded by this place, popular with Japanese expats and visitors—it's also a *sake* bar—upstairs in an enclave of international eateries off Nathan Road. The interior aims at a cool, brown-on-black style but ends up by being mainly dimly lit. They do, however, serve a decent sashimi, sushi and tempura. Other dishes include an acceptable, if rather mild, beef curry.

✉ 2nd Floor, 8 Obervatory Court ☎ (00852) 2316 2884 🕐 Daily 6pm–1am ✋ D HK$300–400, Wine HK$400 🚇 Tsim Sha Tsui or Jordan MTR

PENINSULA HOTEL LOBBY

www.peninsula.com

Hong Kong's gilded years as a British Crown Colony seem to live on among the high classical columns of the lavish, palm tree-bedecked lobby tearoom in this emblematic colonial-era hotel. Classical music from a palm court orchestra soothes the air and smoothes the way for cream tea, scones and cake, accompanied

by what tradition mandates should be civilized conversation.

✉ Peninsula Hotel, Salisbury Road, Tsim Sha Tsui ☎ (00852) 2920 2888 🕐 Daily 2–7 ✋ Afternoon tea HK$268 🚇 Tsim Sha Tsui MTR

SANTA LUCIA RESTAURANT AND LOUNGE

www.hotelpanorama.com.hk

Located on the 38th floor of the brand new Hotel Panorama, this excellent restaurant has magnificent Victoria Harbour views and a warm, intimate environment. Come for a cocktail at dusk, or enjoy the global cuisine after dark when the city sparkles. Whatever you do, request a window seat.

✉ 38F, Hotel Panorama, 8A Hart Avenue, Tsim Sha Tsui ☎ (00852) 3550 0262 🕐 Sun–Thu 6am–2am, Fri, Sat 6am–3am ✋ L HK$300, D HK$500 🚇 Tsim Sha Tsui

SHANG PALACE

www.shangri-la.com/ hongkong/kowloon
Imperial Chinese red and gold tones glow in the interior of this palatial restaurant just east of the Tsim Sha Tsui waterfront promenade. Although dishes from around China are available, the chefs seem most proficient at Cantonese cooking, with lots of dim sum, shark's fins and bird's nests doing their duty. The tables are set among Chinese wall paintings and gracefully carved lacquer screens, and the service is discreet and professional.

✉ Kowloon Shangri-La Hotel, 64 Mody Road, Kowloon East ☎ (00852) 2733 8754 🕐 Mon–Sat 12–3, 6.30–11, Sun 10.30–3, 6.30–11 ✋ L HK$200, D HK$350, Wine HK$210 🚇 Tsim Sha Tsui MTR

T'ANG COURT

http://hongkong.langhamhotels.com
The august memory of the Tang dynasty is well-served at this restaurant just south of Kowloon Park, which majors on excellent variants of those Cantonese luminaries: shark's fin, bird's nest

Left *A Western-style bar on Knutsford Terrace, Kowloon*

and abalone. Yet the chefs have a few experimental tricks up their sleeves, like the tangy stir-fried lobster with spring onion, red onion and shallots, and the sautéed prawns and crab roe. All are served in a hushed, elegant setting of red and gold.

✉ Langham Hotel, 8 Peking Road, Tsim Sha Tsui ☎ (00852) 2375 1133 ⏰ Mon–Sat 12–3, 6–11, Sun 11–3, 6–11 🍴 L HK$220, D HK$500, Wine HK$420 🚇 Tsim Sha Tsui MTR

MACAU

A LORCHA

Named after a type of square-rigged Chinese sailing-vessel once used for trading along the Pearl River, the family-run restaurant stands a block behind the Inner Harbour. You dine in a homey, tiled Portuguese setting at plain tables with green-and-white check tablecloths. The cuisine is Portuguese with Macanese touches: dishes like *bacalhau* (dried salted cod) and *feijoada* (pork and cabbage stew), and meat and prawn dishes that emerge from a charcoal grill.

✉ 289 Rua do Almirante Sérgio, Macau Town ☎ (00853) 2831 3193 ⏰ Wed–Mon 12.30–3, 6.30–11 🍴 L MOPS$90, D MOPS$200–250, Wine MOPS$85 🚌 1, 1A, 2, 5, 6, 7, 9, 10, 10A, 11, 18, 21, 21A, 26, 34

COZINHA PINOCCHIO

In an arched, brick former warehouse with a stone floor and wooden doors, close to Taipa village's municipal market and fire station, this family-owned restaurant is popular with locals and with day-trippers from Hong Kong. The cuisine is primarily Portuguese with Macanese influences and emphasizes seafood dishes, such as the garlicky and spicy baked mussels, tangy salted prawns with garlic, and sardines cooked on the charcoal grill. Roast quail is among the non-seafood highlights.

✉ 4 Rua do Sol, Taipa Village, Taipa Island ☎ (00853) 2882 7128 ⏰ Daily 11.45am– 12am 🍴 L MOP$100, D MOP$160, Wine MOP$100 🚌 11, 15, 22, 28A, 30, 33, 34

FERNANDO'S

With the downhome style of a family-run eatery in the Algarve, this indelibly Portuguese beachside restaurant is invariably busy, especially on weekends. Its decor is pretty much limited to red-and-white check tablecloths under the ceiling fans in the vine-fringed back room. You can dine outside in good weather. Spicy barbecued chicken, roast suckling pig, grilled sardines, clams in an ultra-peppery sauce from Fernando's own secret recipe, salads and more are accompanied by Portuguese wines.

✉ 9 Praia de Hác Sá, Coloane Island ☎ (00853) 2888 2264 ⏰ Daily 12–10.30 🍴 L MOPS$120, D MOPS$180, Wine MOPS$100 🚌 15, 21, 21A, 25, 26, 26A

HENRI'S GALLEY

www.henrisgalley.com.mo

In business since 1976, the Galley occupies a setting decked out in shipboard themes, on the waterfront between the Nam Van Lakes and Sai Van Lake. Owner/chef Henri rustles up spicy African chicken, Portuguese baked chicken, prawn piri piri, curried crab, stir-fried clams and many other delights of Macanese and Portuguese cuisine. Diners can kick back with a jug of sangria outdoors under the shade of umbrellas and banyan trees.

✉ 4 Avenida da República, Macau Town ☎ (00853) 2855 6251 ⏰ Daily 12–10 🍴 L and D MOPS$250–300, Wine MOPS$150 🚌 6, 9, 16, 28B

LONG KEI

Macau's elegant colonial-era main square seems an unlikely setting for a plain, café-style Cantonese eatery, yet it is certainly convenient and there should be few if any complaints about the food. Excellent dim sum, available in multiple choices, is a big draw. On a menu with more than 300 items, these are ably supported by egg noodles, both in soup and stir-fried combinations, and seafood dishes.

✉ 7B Largo do Senado, Macau Town ☎ (00853) 2858 9508 ⏰ Daily 11.30–3, 6–11 🍴 L MOP$75, D MOP$150,

Wine MOP$100 🚌 2, 3, 3A, 5, 7, 10, 10A, 11, 18, 21A, 26A, 33

ROBUCHON A GALERA

www.hotelisboa.com

Celebrated French master chef Joël Robuchon directs proceedings in this top-flight restaurant from his seat in France, appearing in person occasionally to supervise the menu and presentation. In his absence, things in the belle époque-style dining room purr along smoothly enough. The cuisine is classical French with Portuguese and Asian accents, complemented by an abundant wine list heavy with the best of Bordeaux but with room for other good wines.

✉ Hotel Lisboa, Avenida da Amizade, Macau Town ☎ (00853) 2857 7666 ⏰ Daily 12–2.30, 6.30–10.30 🍴 L MOPS$400–600, D MOPS$1000, Wine MOPS$250 🚌 3, 3A, 10A, 28B

NEW TERRITORIES AND ISLANDS

BOOKWORM CAFÉ

www.bookwormcafe.com.hk

To fit right in with Lamma's trademark alternative lifestyle, settle down at this vegetarian/vegan café-restaurant—plus second-hand bookstore, community meeting-place and performance venue. When coming from the ferry pier, it's near the far end of Yung Shue Wan, on the way to Hung Shing Yeh beach. Amid a warm, one-world ambience, or at outside tables, you dine on snacks and main dishes such as goat's cheese sandwiches, veggie burgers and organic falafel, from a large selection.

✉ 79 Main Street, Yung Shue Wan, Lamma Island ☎ (00852) 2982 4838 ⏰ Mon–Fri 10–9, Sat 9am–10pm, Sun 9–9 🍴 L HK$75, D HK$125, Organic wine HK$220 ⛴ Lamma Island Yung Shue Wan ferry from Outlying Islands Ferry Pier, Central

CHUEN KEE SEAFOOD RESTAURANT

Seafood gourmets, Cantonese cuisine fans, celebs and ordinary folk all pile in here for the large selection of seafood, the focused cooking and the raucous ambience of Sai Kung's waterfront. An aroma of garlic, chilies, ginger, sautéed shallots, steamed fish and much more suffuses the air. What you see is what you get when you point to the live fish or crustacean, floating in one of several large tanks, that is to have the dubious honor of gracing your plate in about 10 minutes. ✉ 51–53 Hoi Pong Street, Sai Kung Town ☎ (00852) 2791 1195 🕐 Daily 10.30–10.30 ✋ L HK$200, D HK$300, Wine HK$98 🚇 Diamond Hill MTR, then bus 92 to Sai Kung terminus

NEW BACCARAT RESTAURANT

A big tradition on little Chung Cheu Island is breezing in on the ferry and dining at one of the restaurants heaped up along the waterfront Praya. Oddly named, but an even performer in its field, this seafood restaurant is about 500m (550 yards) north of the ferry dock. Whether steamed, boiled, grilled, fried or baked, the seafood is fresh from the restaurant's own tanks—the steamed grouper and deep-fried squid are especially good. You can sit out front with a view of the bay or in the plain interior. ✉ 9a Pak She Praya, Cheung Chau 🕐 Daily 11–11 ✋ L HK$180, D HK$260, Wine HK$170 ⛴ Cheung Chau ferry from Outlying Islands Ferry Pier, Central

PO LIN MONASTERY VEGETARIAN RESTAURANT

The choice at the vegetarian restaurant of Lantau Island's Buddhist monastery is simple enough: Take it or leave it. There's an ordinary and a deluxe meal. Both are substantial and pretty basic, composed of fixed ingredients, and appear as soon as you sit down at your plain table. Look for rice with various steamed vegetables and spring rolls, accompanied by Chinese tea and soft drinks. Be it ever so unworldly, the food has an ineffable quality imparted by location, fragrant air and home-style cooking. ✉ Ngong Ping, Lantau Island ☎ (00852) 2985 5248 🕐 Daily 11.30–4.30 ✋ L, D HK$60 or HK$100 ⛴ Lantau Island Mui Wo (Silvermine Bay) ferry from Outlying Islands Ferry Pier, Central, then bus 2 to monastery

TUNG KEE SEAFOOD RESTAURANT

This popular Sai Kung restaurant is directly on the promenade and has plenty of outdoor tables for seaside dining on balmy evenings. It does great set meals for groups of more than two. There's a second outlet on Hoi Pong Square. ✉ 96–102, Man Nin Street, Sai Kung ☎ (00852) 2792 7453 🕐 Daily 9am–11pm ✋ L and D HK$150 🚇 Diamond Hill (then minibus 92)

Below *An outdoor dim sum restaurant on Lamma Island*

PRICES AND SYMBOLS

Prices are for a double room for one night, unless otherwise stated. Breakfast is included unless noted otherwise. All the hotels listed accept credit cards unless otherwise stated. Note that rates vary widely throughout the year.

For a key to the symbols, ▷ 2.

HONG KONG ISLAND

ALISAN GUEST HOUSE

http://home.hkstar.com/~alisangh/
Friendly owner Tommy Hou provides convincing proof that not all lodgings on Hong Kong Island have to cost an arm and a leg to be decent. The rooms in his pleasant guesthouse, close to Victoria Park, may be on the diminutive side of small, but they are clean and the furnishings are plain but new. Although there is no in-house restaurant, a nearby 24-hour supermarket and plenty of local eateries means there should be no problem.

✉ Flat A, 5th Floor, Hoito Court, 275 Gloucester Road, Causeway Bay ☎ (00852) 2838 0762 or 2574 8068 🖐 HK$280–390 ① 21 ⊙ ⊙ Causeway Bay MTR

BISHOP LEI INTERNATIONAL HOUSE

www.bishopleihtl.com.hk
This lodging, owned by Hong Kong's Catholic diocese, offers a heavenly touch, not least because of its location on the slopes of Victoria Peak. One way to reach it is by taking the Mid-Levels Escalator to the top and then walking east on Robinson Road. The rooms vary greatly in size and level of amenities, so it's worth looking and comparing if possible. Many, but not all, command city and harbor views, and there's even a great view from the outdoor swimming pool.

✉ 4 Robinson Road, Mid-Levels ☎ (00852) 2868 0828 🖐 HK$600–1,200; suites HK$800–2,400 ① 203 ⊙ ⊡ ⊠ Outdoor ⊙ Central MTR

ISLAND SHANGRI-LA HOTEL HONG KONG

www.shangri-la.com
Everything about the Shangri-La is big, from the world's largest Chinese silk painting in the vast atrium, through its 56 floors, to the king-size beds in the bedrooms. Here, however, big is beautiful, and the hotel is considered to be state-of-the-art for luxury and amenities. Set in the tiny Pacific Place mall, the view at the front is to the harbor.

✉ Pacific Place, Supreme Court Road, Central ☎ (00852) 2877 3838 🖐 HK$2,400–4,000; suites HK$6,000 upward ① 565 ⊙ ⊡ ⊠ Outdoor ⊙ Admiralty MTR

JIA HONG KONG
www.jiahongkong.com

This chic Philippe Starck-designed boutique hotel was the first of its kind in Hong Kong. JIA shoots up like a blade of grass from the commercial mêlée in Causeway Bay and, despite the unremarkable residential public facade, wows guests with gorgeous designer interiors. 'Jia' means 'home' in Mandarin and the hotel is true to its word with a well-stocked kitchen, a DVD player and an audiophile-friendly hi-fi system installed in every room. This is the perfect hotel for those to whom staying in is the new going out.

✉ 1–5 Irving Street, Causeway Bay ✋ HK$2,500–6,000 🛏 54 🚇 Causeway Bay ♿

LANDMARK MANDARIN ORIENTAL
www.mandarinoriental.com/landmark

The Landmark Mandarin Oriental occupies prime real estate in the middle of Central's moneyed financial district. It's directly connected to one of Hong Kong's most upscale malls, the Landmark, and is encircled by designer names. The hotel represents a sanctuary from this spending temptation. Dressed in off-white and ebony tones, rooms are homey, with flatscreen TVs built into the crescent wall that wraps around the spectacular circular bathtub. A contemporary feel is clinched by the socket that connects your iPod to the stereo system. It's savvy, and easily as chic as those nearby boutiques.

✉ 15 Queen's Road, Central ✋ HK$3,500–5,000 🛏 113 🚇 Central MTR

HOTEL LKF
www.hotel-lkf.com.hk

Despite regarding itself as a boutique hotel, Hotel LKF has a straightforward contemporary swishness. The lobby is dominated by smooth curves and a debonair combination of russet brown and sapphire blue, while the rooms—similarly attired—are unusually large for this high-density part of Hong Kong, starting at 45 sq m (480sq feet).

Head up to the two-story restaurant and bar on the 29th and 30th floor to be wowed by a spectacular urban vista. The LKF stands for 'Lan Kwai Fong'—Hong Kong wildest partying block—which is just around the corner.

✉ 33 Wyndham Street, Central ✋ HK$3,000–5,000 🛏 95 🚇 Central ♿

KOWLOON

EATON HOTEL
www.eaton-hotel.com

Shoppers might well consider this to be the ideal Kowloon hotel, with a position at about the midpoint on Nathan Road, the shopaholic's primary artery. Although not luxurious, the rooms have comfortable beds and decent facilities. There is a rooftop pool with terrace.

✉ 380 Nathan Road, Yau Ma Tei ☎ (00852) 2782 1818 ✋ HK$1,800–2,600 🛏 468 ♿ 🚻 🏊 Outdoor 🚇 Jordan MTR

THE LUXE MANOR
www.theluxemanor.com

The studded wooden entrance to this designer hotel is redolent of imperial Beijing but leads the way to a surreal world of droopy chandeliers, copper mosaics and scarlet leather furniture. The glam manor-house-style is sprinkled through the 159-rooms and, true to its name, the hotel goes into luxury overdrive with the six suites. Travelers overwhelmed by Hong Kong's urbanity might consider switching to the Safari suite. It comes with rustic wooden floorboards and ceiling lights that twinkle like Savannah stars above the bed.

✉ 39 Kimberley Road, Tsim Sha Tsui ✋ HK$1,600–2,200 🛏 159 🚇 Tsim Sha Tsui MTR 🚻 ♿

MINGLE PLACE
http://ming.mingleplace.com

This self-professed 'techotel' takes the traditionally cramped layout of an old TST residential block and injects a miraculous sense of space thanks to a clever interplay of glass, mirrors and metallic surfaces. The style is pure sci-fi. There's fingerprint access to lifts and rooms, tablet PCs with which to check-in, TVs built into the shower, and a computer system that monitors guests' lighting, temperature and music preferences. Wi-Fi can be taken as given. Mingle Place has a quiet, backstreet location, but is only a few steps from the Knutsford Terrace nightlife hub. Solo travelers will appreciate the dedicated single rooms—and the (relatively) cheap tariffs.

✉ 8 Observatory Court, Tsim Sha Tsui, Kowloon ✋ HK$1,180–2,080 ♿ 🚇 Tsim Sha Tsui MTR

PENINSULA HOTEL
www.peninsula.com

There's nowhere quite like the Peninsula—standing at the tip of the Kowloon Peninsula—for its ever-so-slightly updated, but still stuffy take on the colonial era, despite the opulent wellness spa. The rooms are the last word in plush. Guests can be shuttled around town by Rolls-Royce and they have an advantage when it comes to securing a table for the afternoon tea ceremony in the lobby.

✉ Salisbury Road, Tsim Sha Tsui ☎ (00852) 2920 2888 ✋ HK$3,200–4,600; suites HK$5,600–42,000 🛏 300 ♿ 🚻 🏊 Indoor 🚇 Tsim Sha Tsui MTR

SALISBURY YMCA
www.ymcahk.org.hk

This unusual YMCA has a desirable location, overlooking Victoria Harbour. There are a few singles, dormitories and family suites, but the majority of rooms are doubles and twins, plainly furnished but with plenty of amenities.

✉ 41 Salisbury Road, Tsim Sha Tsui ☎ (00852) 2268 7888 ✋ HK$700–1,100; suites HK$1,400 🛏 368 ♿ 🚻 🏊 Indoor 🚇 Tsim Sha Tsui MTR

MACAU

POUSADA DE COLÔANE

www.hotelpcoloane.com.mo

This small and friendly inn overlooking the beach from a hilltop on the southernmost tip of tranquil Coloane recalls the Algarve. Azulejo tiles decorate the Portuguese restaurant. The rooms combine bright decor and fittings with rustic Portuguese-style furnishings. All of them have a sea view and a balcony.

✉ Estrada de Cheoc Van, Coloane Island ☎ (00853) 2888 2143 💵 MOP$750–880 🕐 30 🛗 🏊 Outdoor 🚌 21A, 25, 26A

POUSADA DE SAO TIAGO

www.saotiago.com.mo

An exclusive and expensive experience is offered at this recently refurbished inn on the grounds of the Barra Fortress. It's a suite-only affair: One offers a traditional Portuguese guesthouse feel, but the others are super-modern with a huge Bang and Olufsen flatscreen TV and stereo, a Jacuzzi with Hermes toiletries and spectacular harbor views.

✉ Fortaleza de Sao Tiago de Barra, Avenida da Republica, Macau Town ☎ 00853 2837 8111 💵 MOP3,000–3,680 🕐 12 🏊 🛗 🚌 28B

THE VENETIAN MACAU RESORT HOTEL

www.venetianmacau.com

Asia's largest resort—and one of the world's biggest hotel buildings—confirms Macau's burgeoning reputation as the Vegas of the East. It's a sister hotel to the Venetian Las Vegas and shares the same sense of wanton excess: accommodations are in one of 3,000 suites; there's a huge indoor recreation of Venice, complete with a boutique-lined canal; A resident Cirque du Soleil team put on nightly shows; a 15,000 seat arena is home to pop concerts; and then there's the largest casino in the world. Located on reclaimed land between Taipa and Coloane,

Right *Hotel Lisboa in Macau has a 24-hour casino*

it's not the best spot for those interested in Macau's historic sights.
✉ Estrada da Baía de N. Senhora da Esperança, Taipa ☎ (00853) 2882 8888 💵 HK$1,800–5,000 🕐 3,000 suites
❓ Free shuttle buses from all of Macau's major entry points

NEW TERRITORIES AND ISLANDS

CONCERTO INN

www.concertoinn.com.hk

Standing just back from one of Lamma's two lifeguard-supervised beaches, about 1km (0.5 miles) south of the Yung Shue Wan ferry dock, this neat and friendly little inn has appropriately bright and breezy rooms, half of them with a sea view, and a café-restaurant in the garden.

✉ 28 Hung Shing Yeh Beach, Yung Shue Wan, Lamma Island ☎ (00852) 2982 1668 💵 HK£400–800 🕐 20 🛗 🚢 Outlying Islands ferry from Central

SILVERMINE BEACH HOTEL

www.resort.com.hk

This tranquil, low-rise hotel is a short walk from the ferry dock. The tree-shaded beach is outside the front door. The rooms are bright and clean, decently outfitted with modern furnishings, and there's a fine outdoor restaurant.

✉ 648 Silvermine Bay, Mui Wo, Lantau Island ☎ (00852) 2984 8295 💵 HK$980–1,480 🕐 128 🛗 🚽 🏊 Outdoor 🚢 Outlying Islands ferry from Central

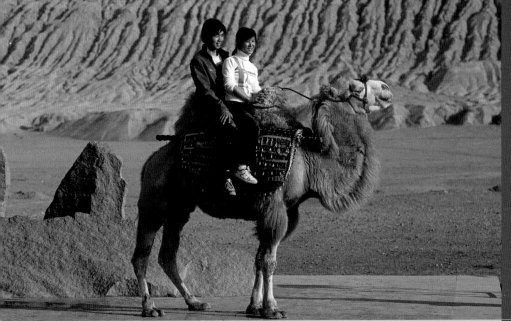

PRACTICALITIES

Practicalities gives you all the important practical information you will need during your visit from money matters to emergency phone numbers.

WEATHER

CLIMATE

» China has a huge diversity of climates encompassing everything from tropical on Hainan Island and the far south to frigid winters in the northeast, arid desert conditions from Inner Mongolia across the north to the westernmost borders and the harsh mountain climate of the Tibetan Plateau.

» Winter is very long and bitter in the north and on the Tibetan Plateau. January daytime highs in Harbin, Heilongjiang, average −12°C (10°F), with average lows at −26°C (−15°F). By contrast, the southern Hainan resort of Sanya has January temperatures of 18–26°C (64–78°F) and subtropical Hong Kong sees 14–18°C (57–64°F) then.

» Winters on the Tibetan Plateau can last into April and May, and snow squalls can block highways in June. Beijing's winters are cold, as low as −10°C (13°F) in January, but can bring clear, blue skies. Mid-September to mid-November is the best time to see Beijing bathed in sunshine. Skiing is possible from early December until April in some mountain resorts.

» Summer brings high temperatures across China. Beijing's average high is 30°C (87°F), but can top 40°C (104°F) from June to August.

Shanghai's average high in July and August is 32°C (90°F). Even Lhasa basks in average daily highs of 23°C (74°F) in June. Southern and eastern coastal areas and cities along the Yangtze (notably Chongqing, Wuhan and Nanjing) can get very hot and humid. The Turpan Basin, close

BEIJING

TEMPERATURE

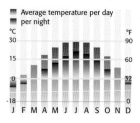

RAINFALL

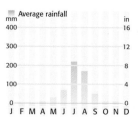

CUSTOMS ALLOWANCES

Visitors are allowed to bring the following into China:

» Two bottles (0.75 litres each) of alcoholic drinks
» 400 cigarettes
» 50g (2oz) of gold or silver
» Money: There is no limit on currency coming into China
» Reasonable amount of perfume for personal use
» One camera, one video camera and one laptop computer

All receipts for valuable articles bought in China should be kept for checking when you leave.
You are only allowed to take 300RMB worth of Chinese herbs and medicines out of the country, half that if you are going to Hong Kong or Macau. Antiques are not allowed to leave China without an official certificate for exporting cultural relics.

to the Taklamakan Desert in the northwest, is the hottest place in China and July temperatures can top 50°C (122°F). Summer is also when most rain falls in China. The south and east see most rain, due to the seasonal monsoons. For Shanghai and Hong Kong, June to August are the wettest months. May and June are wettest for Guilin, and July and August for Chengdu and Beijing.

» Tropical cyclones are a threat in the south and east from May to November.

» Sandstorms (Sha Chen Bao) are an acute problem for Beijing in late winter and spring.

WEBSITES AND WEATHER INFORMATION

» Short-range forecasts and other weather information for mainland China are available on the official Chinese internet information portal, http://weather.china.org.cn/English. The Hong Kong Observatory has more extensive information and longer forecasts on its site, at www.weather.gov.hk. It also includes tropical storm and cyclone warnings.

» For weather forecasts check www.weather.com.

» TV forecasts are broadcast by international news channels, which are accessible in many hotels.

» Hong Kong has a Dial-a-Weather service, in English as well as Cantonese and Mandarin, tel (00852) 1878 200. Severe weather and tropical cyclone warnings are issued if they pose a threat to Hong Kong. They are broadcast on local TV and radio stations.

INOCULATIONS

» No vaccinations are required for travel to China, although a yellow fever vaccination certificate is required for those arriving from infected areas. However, vaccinations are often recommended for protection against typhoid (10 days before travel), hepatitis A (two weeks), diphtheria (three months) and rabies (one month). Check with your doctor. Tetanus and polio vaccinations should be up to date.

» Malaria is a risk on Hainan and in southern Yunnan, including chloroquine- and sulfadoxine-pyrimethamine-resistant strains. As well as taking preventative medication (start up to two months before your trip), visitors should take precautions against mosquito bites. These include wearing long-sleeved clothing, long trousers and socks between dusk and dawn, using creams or sprays (those containing over 30 percent DEET are effective), spraying your room with an insecticide at night, and using a treated net over your bed.

CITY	TIME DIFFERENCE	TIME AT 12 NOON IN BEIJING
Amsterdam	−7	5am
Auckland	+4	4pm
Berlin	−7	5am
Brussels	−7	5am
Chicago	−14	10pm*
Dublin	−8	4am
London	−8	4am
Madrid	−7	5am
New York	−13	11pm*
Paris	−7	5am
Perth, Australia	0	Noon
Rome	−7	5am
San Francisco	−16	8pm*
Sydney	+3	3pm
Tokyo	+1	1pm
* = the previous day		

SHANGHAI
TEMPERATURE

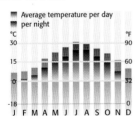

RAINFALL

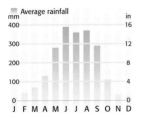

HONG KONG
TEMPERATURE

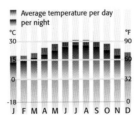

RAINFALL

LHASA
TEMPERATURE

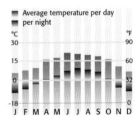

RAINFALL

CHINESE EMBASSIES AND CONSULATES ABROAD

COUNTRY	ADDRESS	TELEPHONE
Australia	15 Coronation Drive, Yarralumla, ACT 2600, Canberra; tel 02 6273 4780	http://au.china-embassy.org
Canada	515 St. Patrick Street, Ottawa, Ontario K1N 5H3; tel 613 789 3434	www.chinaembassycanada.org
Republic of Ireland	40 Ailesbury Road, Dublin 4; tel 1 269 1707	http://ie.china-embassy.org
UK	49–51 Portland Place, London W1B 1JL; tel 020 7299 4049	www.chinese-embassy.org.uk
US	2300 Connecticut Avenue NW, Washington, DC 20008; tel 202 328 2500/01/02	www.china-embassy.org

» Information on vaccination requirements and health risks is available on the World Health Organization website, at www.who.int/ith/en. In the US, the Centers for Disease Control and Prevention (tel +1 877 394 8747; www.cdc.gov) gives up-to-date advice. In the UK, get information from the websites of the Department of Health (www.dh.gov.uk), Foreign and Commonwealth Office (www.fco.gov.uk) and the National Travel Health Network and Centre (www.nathnac.org/travel/index.htm).

WHAT TO TAKE

» Many items, such as Western medicines, contact lens solution, insect repellent and sunscreen, may only be available at airports or from pharmacies in big cities. Some may not be available at all, so pack essential items. Deodorant can be hard to find.

» Summers are hot and may be humid, and ultraviolet rays are much stronger at high altitude. Take loose natural-fiber clothes, a wide-brimmed hat, good sunglasses and high-factor sunscreen.

» Don't pack clothes that are provocative or might offend. Take tops with sleeves and don't wear short shorts or skirts when visiting temples and monasteries. Otherwise casual clothes, including T-shirts, are fine. Casual or smart-casual are the norm for eating out, although fine-dining restaurants and some hotels expect smart dress.

» If you plan to hike in mountainous areas bring lightweight layers, sturdy walking boots and waterproof tops.

» A sweater and jacket should be packed for travel outside summer. If you are going up mountains take a waterproof and insulated jacket.

» Digital memory cards are cheap across China but there are lots of counterfeit cards which may not work in all machines. It is better to buy in Hong Kong or bring your own.

» Bring photocopies of all important documents (passport, visa, travel tickets) and keep them separate from the originals.

DOCUMENTS

PASSPORTS AND VISAS

» All visitors must carry a passport, which must be valid for six months from the date of your return trip. There must be at least one blank page for the visa.

» Most visitors do not need a visa to enter Hong Kong, but all visitors need a visa to enter China other than those from Brunei, Japan and Singapore for stays of up to 15 days. Obtain visas in advance but not more than three months before the entry date.

» Passport/visa regulations became much tougher before the Olympics. Tourist visitors may need to prove return flights before being granted a visa, and picking up a long-stay visa in Hong Kong may not be as easy as it once was. Check with your nearest Chinese consulate before travelling as regulations can change.

» A visa-on-arrival system usually works at Sanya International Airport and Haikou's airport for visitors to Hainan Island. It's also possible to make a visa-free trip to Shenzhen from Hong Kong. However, both these systems were suspended ahead of the Beijing Games and, at the time of writing, have not returned. Check ahead.

» Single- and double-entry visas are valid for 30 days. Visitors going to Hong Kong and Macau from mainland China and re-entering China need a double-entry visa. Multiple-entry visas for business visitors and long-stay work/ study visas are also issued.

» All foreigners must register with the Public Security Bureau, the local police. This is often done by hotels. You may be able to extend your visa by applying to the local PSB.

» A Tibet Permit is required for entry to Tibet. Individual visitors must be on a tour, although you can choose to go your own way on arrival there. Permits are issued in China. Local travel agencies can arrange one, although restrictions imposed after the March 2008 riots in Lhasa may make this process more complicated.

» Lost passports must be reported immediately to the local PSB. Embassies cannot issue replacements without a police report.

TRAVEL INSURANCE

» Full travel insurance is essential. Cover should include medical evacuation by air ambulance and you certainly need medical and personal effects insurance.

» Check that your policy covers all the activities you may do, such as rock climbing.

» Theft is commonplace in tourist areas and on public transportation. Report stolen items to the PSB and obtain a signed, dated and stamped statement.

PLAN AHEAD

» Before you set off, undergo any necessary dental work.

» If you have a long-standing medical condition, arrange a check-up with your doctor before you go.

» For more health information, ▷ 376–378.

MONEY

LOCAL CURRENCY

» The Chinese currency is the Renminbi (RMB), or people's currency, also known as the yuan (¥). Prices may be shown as either, and also in Chinese characters. Locally, it is often referred to as *kuai* literally 'piece'. One RMB is divided into 10 jiao (often called *mao*), and one jiao is divided into 10 *fen*. Notes are 1, 2 and 5 jiao (0.5RMB), 1RMB, 2RMB, 5RMB, 10RMB, 20RMB, 50RMB and 100RMB. Coins available are 1RMB, 5 jiao, 1 jiao (0.1RMB), 5 *fen* (0.05RMB), 2 *fen* and 1 *fen*. There are two types of 1 jiao coin in circulation.

» Hong Kong uses the Hong Kong dollar (HK$). It is divided into 100 cents. Notes are HK$10, HK$20, HK$50, HK$100, HK$500 and HK$1,000. Coins available are HK$10, HK$5, HK$2, HK$1, 50 cents, 20 cents and 10 cents.

» Macau uses the *pataca* (MOP$ or MOP), which is divided into 100 *avos*. Notes are 5, 10, 20, 50, 100 and 500 *patacas*. Coins in use are 5 and 1 *patacas*, and 50, 20 and 10 *avos*. Hong Kong dollars are widely accepted.

» Since the RMB became the strongest currency in Greater China, it is possible to use RMB in Macau and Hong Kong.

» Visitors are allowed to bring in or take out up to 6,000RMB in Chinese currency, and foreign currency up to the value of $5,000. To convert RMB back into your own currency you need the exchange or the ATM slip given when you changed the currency or traveler's checks into Chinese currency.

» Never change money on streets or give large notes to market traders in return for change. You may end up with counterfeit notes. Fake 50RMB and 100RMB notes are common.

BEFORE YOU GO

» Carry funds in several forms, including RMB cash, dollars in cash and traveler's checks, debit cards for ATMs and credit cards. Don't carry much cash at one time.

Below *Withdrawing cash at an automated teller machine*

CREDIT CARDS

» International credit cards are generally accepted in larger hotels and a few restaurants and department stores in major cities, but rarely otherwise.

» Cards that are accepted include Visa, MasterCard, American Express, Diners Club, and JCB.

» Credit cards can be used to withdraw money from ATMs, but a charge is usually applied and sometimes higher interest charges. Debit cards are a better option.

TRAVELER'S CHECKS

» These can be exchanged in banks in most towns and at major hotels, but it takes time to cash them and commission may be high.

» They can be used as payment in some hotels.

» There is an efficient system of replacement if checks are lost or stolen.

» Keep a full record of the serial numbers and value of your checks, and always keep them and receipts separate from the checks.

» The most widely recognized traveler's checks are those issued by American Express. Others include Thomas Cook, MasterCard and Interpayment Visa.

» The best currency for traveler's checks is US dollars, but banks will accept them in sterling, euros, Canadian and Australian dollars.

ATMS

» An ATM is the cheapest and most convenient way of obtaining funds.

» ATMs are widely available in major cities, but less so in rural areas. Chinese banks with ATMs that accept international cards include the Bank of China, the Industrial and Commercial Bank of China (ICBC) and China Merchants Bank. Cards can also be used in ATMs of foreign banks with branches in China and/ or Hong Kong and Macau. ATMs bearing VisaPlus, Cirrus and JCB logos work with Visa, MasterCard, American Express, Diners Club, JCB cards and others.

» Instructions are in Chinese and English. Maximum amounts you can withdraw at one time vary, while daily limits are set by issuing banks. Some go up to 10,000RMB.

» Chinese cards use six-digit PINs. Entering a four-digit PIN for an international card may work, but if not, it will usually do so if you add 00 at the beginning or end of the number.

BANKS/BUREAUX DE CHANGE

» All main banks provide foreign exchange services for a fee and there are foreign exchange outlets in major airports.

» You can also change money at the foreign exchange desks of major hotels.

EXCHANGE RATES

» For up-to-the-minute exchange rates, go to www.xe.com

WIRING MONEY

» Money can be wired to China with Western Union (tel 021 3310 4699; www.westernunion.com). Local RMB currency and US dollars are available at locations of China Post (maximum $10,000) and Agricultural Bank of China (maximum $20,000), which act as agents. Take valid identification.

» Funds can also be transferred to China and picked up at VisaPlus ATM machines using iKobo (www.ikobo.com). The recipient is sent a re-loadable Visa debit card with a PIN when they are first sent money.

TAXES

» An airports tax, also called airport construction fee, is levied on all flights within and out of China. The tax is included in ticket prices. For domestic flights the tax is 50RMB and for international flights it is 90RMB. Tax for flights from Hong Kong is HK$120.

» Hotels usually add a 15 percent service charge.

TIPPING

» Tipping is not customary in China but is becoming more widely accepted (▷ 381, 400).

HEALTH

BEFORE YOU GO

» See your doctor or travel clinic at least eight weeks before your departure in case you need anti-malaria tablets or vaccinations. Your doctor can also give advice on travel risks.

» Make sure you have full travel insurance and that it covers you for treatment in China and, if necessary, repatriation.

» Air ambulance evacuations from China are extremely expensive and can cost $50,000.

» Have a dental check.

» Take a spare pair of glasses with you in case yours get broken.

» Make sure you know your own blood group.

» If you suffer from a long-term condition, wear a MedicAlert bracelet/necklace.

HEALTH SERVICES

» China's expertise in traditional herbal medicine is legendary. It also has large hospitals where Western medical technology and treatments are used. But its health service is under severe pressure from rising costs and cutbacks in funding. Medical treatment, even for Chinese people, is increasingly expensive.

» Hospital conditions are often very basic.

» In major cities, hospitals have VIP wards with much better facilities and English-speaking medical staff where foreigners are treated. Top-class hospitals, clinics and emergency centers have also been set up in main cities through foreign investment.

IF YOU NEED TREATMENT

» The telephone number to call an ambulance is 120. However, ambulance staff are unlikely to have had any medical training and ambulances are poorly equipped. You may be better off taking a taxi to the nearest major hospital.

» Getting hold of medical records from Chinese hospitals can be hard for patients wanting a second opinion or needing them for follow-

MEDICALERT

Tel 888/633 4298 (US), 0800 581420 (UK)

www.medicalert.org

TRADITIONAL CHINESE MEDICINE

Guilin Hospital of Sino-Western Medicine offers herbal remedies, traditional treatments and Western medicine.

Tel 0773 582 0588

www.tcmadvisory.com

INTERNATIONAL CLINICS AND EMERGENCY MEDICAL ASSISTANCE

SOS International has clinics in several cities, including 24-hour 'alarm centers' in Beijing and Hong Kong.

Tel 010 6462 9100 (Beijing)

Tel (00852) 2528 9900 (Hong Kong)

www.internationalsos.com

Global Doctor has clinics in Beijing, Chengdu, Shenyang, Changsha, Guangzhou and Chongqing and an emergency assistance service.

Tel 010 5131 6222 (emergency service)

www.globaldoctor.com.au

United Family Hospitals & Clinics has facilities in several cities and 24-hour emergency rooms in Beijing and Shanghai.

Tel 010 5927 7120 (Beijing)

Tel 021 5133 1999 (Shanghai)

www.unitedfamilyhospitals.com

DENTISTS

DDS Dental Care has clinics in Shanghai with English-speaking staff. Tel 135 0163 5171

www.ddsdentalcare.com

Arrail Dental is a Beijing clinic affiliated with the University of Pennsylvania School of Dental Medicine.

Tel 400 880 1900

www.arrail-dental.com

up treatment or insurance claims back home.

» Check with your insurers to see if you are covered before treatment as it can be expensive.

» In rural areas, medical facilities are few and far between. They are also not equipped to deal with serious medical emergencies.

» If you need to travel to a major city for treatment call your insurance company or contact a private medical service provider.

FINDING A DOCTOR

» Pharmacies often have a doctor on staff, especially in larger towns and cities.

» Four- and five-star hotels may also have a clinic and in-house doctor, or one on call, and all hotels will be able to refer guests to external medical help.

» Private institutions with English-speaking staff have been set up by foreign companies in major cities, charging prices higher than local facilities. For more information, ▷ panel right.

WATER

» Tap water is not drinkable anywhere in China, and though standards may be higher in Hong Kong, boiling is still recommended.

» Bottled water is widely available, but ensure the seal is intact before drinking.

» Avoid ice in drinks unless you know it was made with bottled or boiled water.

SEASONAL HAZARDS

» Be careful of sunburn and heat exhaustion in summer. Drink plenty of water and don't over-exert yourself in the heat of summer.

» High humidity along the coasts and in the 'furnace cities' along the Yangtze River exacerbates the heat and can be very uncomfortable.

» Ultraviolet levels are much higher in the mountains of western China and Tibet, so high-factor sunblock should be used.

» Always wear a hat in warm or sunny weather.

» Acute mountain sickness afflicts many visitors to Tibet because of the

high altitude (▷ 209). Take things easy for the first few days. You can buy oxygen in bottles. Herbal remedies include Gao Yuan tea, sold in shops in Lhasa.

» Heavy pollution in cities and damp winters leads to many chest-related illnesses, such as colds, flu and respiratory tract infections.

» Most of China is malaria-free. However, Hainan Island and southern parts of Yunnan do have malaria. Anti-malaria medications are advised and precautions should be taken to avoid being bitten (▷ 373).

» Snack food is very popular in China, especially in cities such as

Chengdu, Beijing and Nanning. Hygiene standards of street food (▷ 400) stands sometimes leave a lot to be desired, and bugs breed and are easily transmitted in hot weather. The high heat at which Chinese food is cooked often mitigates the problem, but pack diarrhea treatments just in case.

» Avian flu cases have occurred in China as in other parts of Asia. So far outbreaks have been contained but there are fears it could spread to humans and mutate. As yet, effective drugs are not readily available.

OPTICIANS

» Glasses with pre-fitted lenses in a range of diopter values are available cheaply in many shops. High-class opticians in big cities sell smart frames which they will fit prescription lenses to, at prices well below those in the West. Go to smaller towns and cities and prices are cheaper still, although it may require trial and error to get the right lenses.

» You can also get eye tests and prescription glasses from qualified optometrists in major cities.

ALTERNATIVE MEDICINE

» Herbal remedies have been used to treat every imaginable ailment in China for thousands of years. Every city, town and village has its own pharmacies or medicine shops selling extracts of plants or animals.

» In some areas you will find shops selling medicines from jars of alcohol-infused snakes and dried snake parts. Guangzhou's Qingping market has stands selling exotic items including dried starfish, ants and deer antlers.

» Herbs are often used in conjunction with therapies such as reflexology (foot massage), acupuncture, massage and tai chi in classic Chinese medicine.

» You will find many people doing tai chi exercises, notably early in the morning in parks and other open spaces.

» Massage is available everywhere and is usually inexpensive, from as little as 20RMB for an hour and typically 50RMB. Be aware that prices can be considerably more in hotel spas. Some of the best practitioners are blind.

» The Chinese use different herbs to treat a range of problems. Gingko biloba is used to treat cardiovascular diseases, while ginseng is used to invigorate the body's yin and yang (opposing agents caused by emotions, heat and cold and other influences).

» The Chinese believe that when these are in balance, diseases can be prevented and cured.

» Tibetan herbal remedies are very different to classic Chinese ones. They are based on herbs that grow high in the high mountains, as opposed to plants often found in lush areas of the country.

PHARMACIES

» Pharmacists in China dispense Western medicines as well as traditional herbal remedies.

» You need a doctor's prescription to be able to buy antibiotics.

» Note that information on the label of domestic brands may not be in English.

DENTISTS

» China has very few dentists compared to other countries. In 2004, there were 38,000 registered practitioners—one for every 33,000 people—and overall dental hygiene standards are poor.

» Chinese dentists tend not to use painkillers.

» There are state-owned dental hospitals, and major cities have private clinics geared toward foreigners. More dental clinics are being built.

HEALTHY FLYING

» Visitors to China from as far as the US, Canada, the UK or Western Europe may be concerned about the effect of long-haul flights on their health. The most widely publicized concern is Deep Vein Thrombosis, or DVT. Misleadingly called 'economy class syndrome', DVT is the forming of a blood clot in the body's deep veins, particularly in the legs. The clot can move around the bloodstream and could be fatal.

» Those most at risk include the elderly, pregnant women and those using the contraceptive pill, smokers and the overweight. If you are at increased risk of DVT, see your doctor before departing. Flying increases the likelihood of DVT because passengers are often seated in a cramped position for long periods of time and may become dehydrated.

To minimize risk:

Drink water (not alcohol)
Don't stay immobile for hours at a time
Stretch and exercise your legs periodically
Do wear elastic flight socks, which support veins and reduce the chances of a clot forming

Exercises

1. ankle rotations	2. calf stretches	3. knee lifts
Lift feet off the floor. Draw a circle with the toes, moving one foot clockwise and the other counterclockwise	Start with heel on the floor and point foot upward as high as you can. Then lift heels high keeping balls of feet on the floor	Lift leg with knee bent while contracting your thigh muscle. Then straighten leg pressing foot flat to the floor

Other health hazards for flyers are airborne diseases and bugs spread by the plane's air-conditioning system. These are largely unavoidable, but seek advice from a doctor before flying if you have a serious medical condition.

BASICS

CHILDREN

» The Chinese adore kids and are fascinated by Western children, who will be welcomed everywhere.

» There are lots of attractions for young children, including rides or amusement areas in parks. Cheap toys sold everywhere will keep them amused on journeys. China's rich history and culture should keep older ones fascinated. There are many zoos (although conditions often leave a lot to be desired), and children will love seeing giant pandas close up in Chengdu (▷ 202–204).

» Hotel rooms do not usually have children's TV channels, but larger hotels will often have a games or entertainment area. There are few babysitting services.

» Some train journeys can take up to 50 hours, so you may need to be creative to keep them occupied.

» Restaurants generally do not have children's meals or provide high chairs. Larger cities have branches of KFC, McDonald's and Pizza Hut.

» Toilets are frequently rudimentary at best. Pack anti-bacterial wipes to wipe your children's hands.

» Crowded attractions, railway stations, airports and streets can be a danger for parents with youngsters who might wander off. Ensure they carry a note written in Chinese and English with a contact telephone number and address of where you are staying and your mobile phone number. Be careful with children crossing busy roads, especially where there are a lot of bicyclists.

» For travel with infants, few places other than major international airports have baby-changing facilities. You can find formula, baby food, wipes and diapers (nappies) in supermarkets, although they may be hard to get in rural areas.

» In September 2008 nearly all of China's major dairy producers were caught up in a countrywide health scare. In particular, tainted formula milk powder was found to have poisoned thousands—and killed several—babies. Bring your own milk powder, if at all possible.

ELECTRICITY

» Current is 220V, AC, at 50 cycles per second.

» Plugs may have three-pronged flat-angled pins as in Australia, two flat pins similar to those in America, or two round pins as in continental Europe. Sockets in hotels often have a combination of two or more. Hong Kong uses three-pronged flat pins similar to those in the UK.

» Adaptors are generally available in large hotels and at major airports, but it is still advisable to bring one from home.

» Bring a flashlight (torch) for use in rural areas.

GAY AND LESBIAN VISITORS

» For much of China's recent past, homosexuality has been a taboo subject. It was effectively a criminal act until 1997.

» The gay scene includes many bars, restaurants, nightclubs and other establishments in cities such as Hong Kong, Beijing, Shanghai and Guangzhou. But gay and lesbian visitors should exercise discretion.

Homosexuality is tolerated if you don't flaunt it.

» An excellent source of information on gay travel to China is Utopia Asia. It produces the Utopia Guide to China, available from booksellers, and has a detailed section on its website (www.utopia-asia.com/tipschin.htm).

LAUNDRY

» Most hotels offer overnight laundry services, and some will do it in a few hours for an extra charge. However, prices are very high compared to other costs. You can often find local laundries near hotels. They are usually very cheap and will press and fold clothes for you.

LOCAL WAYS

» Wherever you go you will hear people loudly clearing their throats and spitting on the ground. Beijing clamped down on public spitting ahead of the 2008 Olympics, with police patrolling the streets, issuing offenders with fines; CCTV is also being used.

» Locals may stare at foreign visitors in rural areas or smaller towns and cities. Even in larger cities they will often call out hello and try to talk to

you. It is usually so they can practise their English, but it can also be used as a sales ploy.

» While many Chinese people do not mind having their photograph taken, some people, especially rural minorities, may be unwilling to do so. Respect their wishes and do not take pictures without asking, even if you can only do so with hand gestures. Many locals in tourist hotspots now demand money before they pose. Temples and monasteries usually prohibit photographs during services, or in certain parts of buildings. Others allow photography, but charge a fee.

» Respect for elders is inherent in Chinese society. Discounts are often given on admission prices to attractions and sights.

MEASUREMENTS

» China uses the metric system. See the conversion chart, left.
» Temperatures are given in degrees Celsius (centigrade).
» Clothing sizes are in metric. Chinese people are usually more petite than Westerners, so clothes for any given size may come up smaller.

CONVERSION CHART

From	To	Multiply by
Inches	Centimetres	2.54
Centimetres	Inches	0.3937
Feet	Metres	0.3048
Metres	Feet	3.2810
Yards	Metres	0.9144
Metres	Yards	1.0940
Miles	Kilometres	1.6090
Kilometres	Miles	0.6214
Acres	Hectares	0.4047
Hectares	Acres	2.4710
Gallons	Litres	4.5460
Litres	Gallons	0.2200
Ounces	Grams	28.35
Grams	Ounces	0.0353
Pounds	Grams	453.6
Grams	Pounds	0.0022
Pounds	Kilograms	0.4536
Kilograms	Pounds	2.205
Tons	Tonnes	1.0160
Tonnes	Tons	0.9842

NATIONAL HOLIDAYS

» China has two week-long holidays at Spring Festival (Chinese New Year) in January or February, and National Day, from October 1 to 7. There are five single-day national holidays: New Year's Day (January 1), Labor Day on May 1 and Qing Ming (Grave Sweeping Day) on April 5, plus two events dictated by the lunar calendar, Dragon Boat Festival in June (occasionally May), and Mid-Autumn Festival in September (occasionally October).

» Crowding is common at many tourist attractions, on buses, trains and rail stations, especially around national holidays and in the height of summer. Expect a lot of buffeting.

PLACES OF WORSHIP

» After suppression and the destruction of temples and monasteries during the Cultural Revolution, China has adopted a more tolerant attitude towards religion and religious freedom.

» Although an atheist country, China's Protestant population numbers more than 15 million. It also has more than 50,000 churches or meeting places.

TIPPING GUIDE	
Hotel restaurants	10–15 percent (included as service charge)
Other restaurants	No tip necessary, but in good restaurants leave 10–15 percent
Tour guides	10RMB per person per day; up to 50RMB if an individual tour
Drivers	5RMB per person per day; 25–50RMB if an individual tour
Hairdressers	No tip necessary
Taxi drivers	No tip necessary
Chambermaids	No tip expected, but you may wish to leave a small gift to show appreciation in luxury hotels
Porters	8RMB per person for groups; 5–10RMB per bag for individuals

10 EVERYDAY ITEMS AND HOW MUCH THEY COST	
Bottle of water	2RMB
Burger for eating out	12RMB
Cup of tea/coffee	20–35RMB
Glass of wine	40–60RMB
Pint of beer	30–75RMB
Daily newspaper	1RMB
Roll of camera film	20RMB
20 cigarettes	5–15RMB
Ice cream	5–25RMB
5-mile (8km) taxi ride	20–28RMB

» Churches in major cities have separate services for Chinese and foreigners. You must show your passport before entering the Church.

» China has a large Muslim population, mostly in the north. The largest mosque in China is the Id Kah mosque, in Kashi (Kashgar). It can hold nearly 10,000 worshipers.

SMOKING

» China is resolutely addicted to nicotine. Almost three-quarters of Chinese men smoke, and some 350 million Chinese are smokers. It creates a smoke-filled fug in restaurants, buildings and on public transportation.

» Authorities have tried to ban smoking in some public areas, but 'no smoking' signs are flouted other than on aircraft.

» The temporary smoking restrictions that applied during the Beijing Olympics may have marked the beginning of a cultural shift. Some restaurants, shops and public areas in cities no longer allow smoking but rules are still ignored frequently.

TIME

» Despite spanning several time zones, all of China is officially on the same time: 8 hours ahead of Greenwich Mean Time. There is no daylight saving time (▷ 373).

TOILETS

» China's toilets can fall below Western standards. Most places still have traditional squat toilets. In rural areas, roadside toilets often consist of a simple hole in the floor. Facilities in some major tourist attractions are not good. Beijing has been building new, 'four-star' amenities.

» Toilets often do not provide paper so you need to take your own. There may also be no washing facilities, unless there is an attendant. These facilities usually charge a small fee.

» Hotel lobbies and shopping malls usually have better facilities. Some restaurants and bars in old towns may not have toilets.

» Monasteries and temples rarely have toilets for visitors.

VISITORS WITH DISABILITIES

» Facilities are improving for visitors with disabilities, but other than major airports and large hotels the provision of services or amenities ranges from patchy to nonexistent.

» Beijing has installed tactile paths, wheelchair ramps and easy-access toilets, and added wheelchair-accessible escalators at many subway stations.

» Hong Kong's facilities include Rehabus buses, specially adapted to carrying wheelchairs (www. rehabsociety.org.hk). A detailed access guide for visitors with disabilities is available online from the Hong Kong Council of Social Services (www.hkcss.org.hk/rh/ accessguide/default.htm). More information on access is provided by the Hong Kong Tourism Board on its website (www.discoverhongkong. com/eng/travelneeds/disabled/index. jhtml) and on the World Institute on Disability's webzine, Disability World (www.disabilityworld.org).

» Information and links on disability travel are provided in the UK by national disability network RADAR (tel 00 44 207 250 3222; www.radar. org.uk) and in the US by the Society for Accessible Travel and Hospitality (SATH, tel 00 1 212 447 7284; www. sath.org).

残 疾 人 设 施
FACILITIES FOR DISABLED PERSON

COMMUNICATION

China has an efficient telephone network, extensive mobile telephone coverage and a reliable mail system. There are also many internet cafés in cities and towns.

TELEPHONES

» To call China from abroad, dial the international access code (011 from the US and Canada; 00 from most other countries), followed by China's country code, 86, then the area or city code omitting the first 0, then the number. The country code for Hong Kong is 852 and for Macau it is 853; neither has any area codes.
» Dial the number without the city code when calling within the same

USEFUL TELEPHONE NUMBERS	
MAINLAND CHINA	
Police	110
Fire	119
Ambulance	120
Directory enquiries	114, 2689
	0114 (English)
HONG KONG	
Police, Fire and Ambulance	999
Directory enquiries	1081

city. Local calls are usually free, but hotels add a surcharge. Numbers starting with 800 are toll-free.
» To call abroad, dial the international access code (00 from China and Macau; 001 from Hong Kong), followed by the country code (▷ 383), then the area or city code omitting the first 0, then the number. Hotels charge up to 20 percent extra on international calls, which cost about 8RMB per minute.
» There are many public telephone kiosks. Most take IC prepaid phone cards. They can be bought from post offices, stores and street vendors and start at 20RMB. Insert them into the slot and follow the instructions, which are in English and Chinese.
» Long-distance calling cards, known as IP cards, allow you to make international calls from any phone, although you still need an IC card to use payphones. Values range from 20RMB to 100RMB, but can be bought for half the face value. Scratch a panel to reveal the PIN number and follow the instructions.
» A 100RMB card gives about 37 minutes' call time to the US and 27 minutes to the UK and Europe.

AREA CODES IN CHINA	
Beijing	010
Chengdu	028
Guangzhou	020
Guilin	0773
Hong Kong	00 852*
Kunming	0871
Lhasa	0891
Shanghai	021
Suzhou	0512
Xi'an	029
* = country code	

MOBILE PHONES

» Buy a prepaid Chinese sim card to put in your GSM tri-band mobile (cell) phone so you can make calls within and outside China.
» You can buy an assigned number from a store or choose one from a street vendor. Due to Chinese superstitions, numbers with lots of 3s and 8s cost more; those with more 4s are cheaper.
» A 150RMB sim card will cost 120–170RMB and have some included credit. Top-up cards cost 50–300RMB.
» International calls cost about 8RMB per minute with a local connection, typically 0.6RMB per

minute, on top. You also pay to receive calls.

» Mobile numbers in China have 11 digits, the first three of which range from 130 to 139.

» China has more than 400 million mobile phone users, and signals can be picked up in many areas, even up mountains.

» Mobile phones can be rented in China from companies including Pandaphone. Phones can be delivered in the US or picked up in China.

MAIL

» China Post (www.chinapost.gov. cn) has more than 82,000 post offices. They display a green sign. Mail boxes are outside them and in many other locations. Mail is also collected from many hotels. Hongkong Post (hotline tel 00852 2912 2222; www.hongkongpost. com) has post offices in many areas and also operates temporary mobile branches in different locations.

» Airmail is reliable. A letter or postcard normally takes 5–10 days to reach its overseas destination. Stamps can be bought at post offices, hotels and some shops. They need sticking on with glue.

» Parcels can be sent by China Post and Hongkong Post. China's postal

service also offers EMS international express delivery and courier services are operated by UPS, DHL, TNT, Fedex and others.

INTERNET

» By 2008, China had nearly 220 million internet users. Public dial-up access is available throughout China very cheaply using local access numbers (96163 is widely used), although broadband is becoming much more commonplace.

» Many hotels now have a broadband/ADSL internet connection, and an increasing number have wireless.

» Internet access in China is controled by the state. Sites seen as subversive or anti-China are prevented from being accessed by what is dubbed the Great Firewall of China. Formerly the BBC and Wikipedia were blocked by China until just prior to the 2008 Olympic Games.

» There are cybercafés in towns and cities across the country, and access

typically costs 2–10RMB per hour. Hotels often have a computer in the lobby for guests to freely access the internet. Some cafés also provide free access.

LAPTOPS

» You will need a plug socket adaptor and an adaptor for the phone socket to connect to the telephone or a cable for the high-speed link where it is offered. Hotels will provide cables but may ask for a deposit.

» Be wary of downloading anything to your laptop or onto memory sticks, CDs or DVDs. Anti-virus protection is generally nonexistent.

INTERNATIONAL DIALLING CODES

To call home from China, dial the international access code (▷ 382) followed by the country code (see below), the area code (omitting the 0), then the number:

Australia	61
Belgium	32
Canada	1
China	86
France	33
Germany	49
Holland	31
Ireland	353
New Zealand	64
Spain	34
Sweden	46
UK	44
US	1

FINDING HELP

China is one of the safest countries to travel in, thanks to its ever-present police and the generally law-abiding nature of its people. However, petty crimes such as theft are common. Sensible precautions will help ensure your stay is not marred by you becoming a victim of crime.

PERSONAL SAFETY

» Never carry more cash than you need. Leave valuables in the hotel safe or your in-room safe.

» Pickpockets operate in crowded places such as markets, stations and major tourist attractions. Do not keep items such as your passport, travel documents and tickets, credit cards or purse in a bag slung over your shoulder. Ensure bags are zipped up and wear a money belt for cash and credit cards.

» Always keep bags in sight. In busy places, hold the straps or loop one around your leg if sitting.

» China is a photographer's dream, but don't advertise all your equipment.

» Be careful when using ATMs. Avoid machines in poorly lit locations at night, and never show your money openly when you get it.

» Do not get into an argument with locals. Disputes can escalate.

LOSS OF PASSPORT

» Keep a note of your passport number and photocopies of the pages with your photo and personal information and your China visa. Keep them separate from your passport and leave copies at home. Scan the pages before you leave and email them to yourself using a web-based mail system (such as Hotmail, Googlemail or Yahoo).

» Report lost passports immediately to the Public Security Bureau (police) and contact your embassy or consulate (▷ below).

POLICE

» In an emergency dial call 110, but you will probably need someone to help translate for you. Your hotel can help contact the police.

» All towns and cities have PSB stations, usually in key locations. Cities have several.

LOST PROPERTY

» Report stolen items of value immediately to the PSB. You should complete a statement, get it signed and stamped with an incident number and ask for a copy, which will need translating for your insurance company. Your guide can help. Notify your insurers as soon as possible.

» Formalities can take a long time in China, so be prepared for that.

» If traveler's checks are lost or stolen, notify the issuing company immediately. Keep a note of the numbers and denominations separately from the checks.

HEALTH ISSUES

» Take appropriate precautions to avoid illness and incidents. China's extreme temperatures and the height and remoteness of some areas mean you need to take particular care. Seek help from local doctors. In emergencies, go to the nearest major hospital or find a clinic or emergency center catering to foreigners. You may need to travel from remote areas to a city for treatment; ▷ 376–378 for further details.

TOURIST INFORMATION

China has few tourist information facilities, other than in key cities and some tourist destinations.

» Hong Kong has a good tourist office with an informative website, visitor hotline and information offices at Hong Kong International Airport, on Hong Kong Island and in Kowloon.

» Macau's tourist office also provides visitor information counters at several locations.

» Beijing's tourist office has opened tourist information offices in the city, offering information and leaflets. It has a tourist information hotline

TOURIST OFFICES AND TRAVEL AGENTS

MAIN TOURIST OFFICES

China National Tourism Administration	Tel 010 6520 1114	www.cnta.org.cn
Hong Kong Tourism Board	Tel (00852) 2508 1234	www.discoverhongkong.com
Macau Government Tourist Office	Tel (00853) 2833 3000	www.macautourism.gov.mo
China Tibet Tourism Bureau	Tel 0891 683 4315	www.tibettour.org
Beijing Municipal Bureau of Tourism	Tel 010 6513 0828	www.bjta.gov.cn
Shanghai Municipal Tourism Administrative Commission	Tourist hotline: tel 021 962020	http://lyw.sh.gov.cn

TRAVEL AGENCIES

China International Travel Service (CITS)	Tel 010 6522 2991	www.cits.net
China Travel International Ltd	Tel 010 5137 9823	www.ctiol.com
China Merchants International Travel	Tel 0571 8723 2012	www.goaroundchina.com.cn

EMBASSIES AND CONSULATES IN BEIJING

Australia	21 Dongzhimenwai Dajie, Beijing 100600
	tel 010 5140 4111 (Mon–Fri 8.30–4.50)
Canada	19 Dongzhimenwai Dajie, Beijing 100600
	tel 010 5139 4000 (Mon–Thu 9–11, 1.30–3; Fri 9–12)
Ireland	3 Ritan Donglu, Beijing 100600
	tel 010 6532 2691 (Mon–Fri 9–12.30, 2–5)
New Zealand	1 Ritan Dongerjie, Chaoyang District, Beijing 100600
	tel 010 8532 7000 (Mon–Fri 8.30–5)
UK (consular section)	Floor 21, North Tower, Kerry Centre, 1 Guanghua Lu,
	tel 010 8529 6600 (Mon–Fri 8.30–12, 1–3.30)
US	3 Xiushui Beijie, Beijing 100600
	tel 010 6532 3831 (Mon–Fri 8–5)

and there are counters at Capital International Airport.

» Shanghai has several tourist information and service centers providing information, multimedia self-help, transportation information, ticket and room reservations.

» Accommodations reservations and tour booking services are available at major airports.

» Travel agencies can organize transportation and accommodations as well as permits to visit Tibet.

OPENING TIMES AND TICKETS

SHOPS

» Opening times vary, but are typically 8–8 seven days a week. Shops in cities may not open until 9 or 10 but stay open until 10pm. Supermarkets in cities open 10–10. In Hong Kong, shops open daily from 10 or 11 until 7.30, staying open until 10pm in main shopping areas. Bargain for everything unless in a shop with fixed prices.

BANKS

» Bank hours vary widely. In mainland China banks generally open Mon–Fri 9–5. Banks in Hong Kong open Mon–Fri 9–4.30, Sat 9–12.30. Macau banks open Mon–Fri 9–5.

POST OFFICES

» Mainland China post offices open Mon–Fri 9–5, although times are not uniform. Larger branches may open from 8 to 6.30 or 7 and some open Sat and Sun. Post offices in Hong Kong are open Mon–Fri 9–5, Sat 9–1. Macau post offices generally open Mon–Fri 9 to 5.30 or 6.

OFFICES

» Office hours in China, Hong Kong and Macau are usually Mon–Fri 9–5. Government offices may open from 8.30am and close from 12–2.30.

MUSEUMS AND GALLERIES

Museums, galleries and other institutions generally open daily 9–5. Monasteries in Tibet usually close for lunch, from 12 to 2 or later.

» In 2007 China began gradually rolling out a policy of free museum entry. Though this may help the travel budget it may also affect your travel itinerary. Increased visitor demand means that numbers are now more strictly controled and you may well be forced to wait in line and show photo ID in order to gain entry to a museum. If you are banking on a long, leisurely look around any major Chinese museum, arrive as early as possible and bring along your passport.

RESTAURANTS AND BARS

» Small restaurants open for breakfast from 6.30am. Mealtimes are early. Lunch is usually served 11.30–2 and dinner is generally from 5.30 to 9.30 or 10, although it is best to arrive before 8pm (▷ 399).

» Food, one of China's cultural treasures, breaks down into different schools or types of cuisine. Among the most celebrated are Shandong, Sichuan, Jiangsu (Huaiyang) and Guangdong (Cantonese), but Fujian, Zhejiang, Hunan, Beijing, Shanghai and Dongbei are also famous food regions. Rice, noodles, dumplings and tofu (bean curd) feature heavily, with *congee* rice soup and fried dough sticks a breakfast staple.

» Tibetan food is also very distinct, using local herbs, yak meat and tsampa barley bread. Macau's food is Portuguese-influenced.

» Bars tend to stay open until 2–3am in cities and major tourist destinations.

DISCOUNTS AND CONCESSIONS

» Airlines charge 10 percent of adult fares for children under two not occupying a seat (one adult per infant), and 50 percent of the adult fare for children over two but under 12. Under-12s do not pay the airport construction fee of 50RMB for domestic flights and 90 RMB for international flights.

» On trains, children below 1.1m (3ft 8in) travel free, those 1.1m (3ft 8in–4ft 6in) go half price, and over 1.4m (4ft 6in) pay full fare.

» Reductions for children at tourist attractions are based on height. Typically, children under 1.1m (3ft 8in) do not pay and those 1.1m–1.4m (3ft 8in–4ft 6in) pay half price. Monasteries and temples often do not give reductions.

» Students holding an International Student Identity Card (ISIC) may get discounts on admission to a number of museums and cultural sites, in some shops and restaurants, and on some transportation.

WEBSITES

DOCUMENTATION

www.fco.gov.uk
Advice and information on overseas travel from the UK Foreign and Commonwealth Office.

www.travel.state.gov
Travel and visa information from the US Department of State.

HEALTH

www.cdc.gov/travel
US government website with detailed advice on travel health.

www.doh.gov.uk
Useful information and travel advice from the UK Department of Health.

www.thehtd.org
Health advice for international destinations from the Hospital for Tropical Diseases in London.

www.who.int
This is the World Health Organization official website, detailing health risks and precautions.

www.china-aids.org
Informative English website of the independent, non-commercial group China Aids Info, with advice on Aids and HIV, and useful links.

CULTURE

www.chinaculture.org
Cultural and historical information about China on a Chinese and English site.

http://whc.unesco.org
UNESCO's official website listing World Heritage Sites, with China's 37 listed sites.

TOURIST INFORMATION

www.cnta.org.cn
English website of the China National Tourism Adminstration, China's national tourist office, giving information and tourism news about the country.

WEATHER

http://weather.china.org.cn/ English
Current weather information and forecasts for all of China from the China Internet Information Center, in English.

www.weather.gov.hk
Website for the Hong Kong Observatory, with detailed forecasts and weather warnings.

NEWS

www.china.org.cn
China's official news and information gateway, in English.

http://english.peopledaily.com.cn
English website with daily news from China's leading national newspaper.

www.xinhuanet.com/english
Online Chinese and international news in English.

http://en.tibet.cn/
Comprehensive news and information on Tibet in English from the Beijing-controlled China Tibet Information Center.

EVENTS

http://gz2010.cn
Website for the 2010 Asian Games in Guangzhou/

www.expo2010china.com
Official website for the 2010 World Expo in Shanghai.

SIGHT/TOWN	WEBSITE	PAGE
Beijing	www.beijingpage.com	60–95
Chang Jiang (Yangtze River)	www.hikeyangtze.com	257
Chengdu	www.chengdu.gov.cn/echengdu	202–204
Guilin and Li Jiang	www.guilin.com.cn/newenglish/index.htm	230–232
Guangzhou	www.citsgd.com.cn	260–263
Hong Kong	www.discoverhongkong.com	336–339
Jiuzhaigou	www.jowong.com in English	207
Lhasa	www.tibettour.org/chinatibettoursite/moban/index.asp	208–210
Lijiang	www.lijiang.cn (Chinese only)	234–236
Lugu Hu	www.ljluguhu.com.cn/cs/index.asp	237
Macau	www.macautourism.gov.mo	348–351
Shanghai	www.smartshanghai.com	292–309
Shanghai Museum	www.shanghaimuseum.net	301
Suzhou	www.citssz.com	270
Xishuangbanna	http://english.xsbnly.com	238

KEY SIGHTS QUICK WEBSITE FINDER

MEDIA, BOOKS AND FILMS

NEWSPAPERS

» The press in China is strictly monitored and regulated. *The People's Daily* is the official paper of the Communist Party of China. The largest-circulation English-language paper is *China Daily*. It has a Hong Kong edition and its stable also includes *China Business Weekly* and the *Shanghai Star*, both English-language papers.

» Another English-language paper is the *Shanghai Daily*.

» Hong Kong's two English-language daily newspapers are the *South China Morning Post* and the newer business paper *The Standard*.

» The main Chinese-only papers are Communist Party mouthpieces *Guangming Daily* and *Economic Daily*. The *Xinmin Evening News*, run by Shanghai's municipal government, is one of the larger regionals. The *Financial Times* publishes a Chinese edition, while international publications, including the *FT*'s English version, the *International Herald Tribune*, *Newsweek*, *CNN Traveler* and *Asian Wall Street Journal*, are available.

MAGAZINES

» China's main cities are awash with free listings magazines, some with feature content. Beijing and Shanghai have the bi-weekly *City Weekend*, monthly *That's Beijing* and *That's Shanghai*, (another edition covers Guangzhou and Shenzhen). Shanghai also has *Shanghai Talk*, and *SH* (Hong Kong's version is HK) and Beijing has *Beijing Today*, *Beijing Talk* and *The Beijinger*.

» English-language business magazines include *China International Business*, *China Economic Review* and regional offering *Shanghai Business Review*.

» International magazines published in Chinese include *FHM China*, *Elle China* and *Newsweek*. The glossy *Hong Kong Tatler* is in English.

NEWS AGENCIES AND ONLINE NEWS

» National news agency Xinhua supplies many China papers, including the *People's Daily*. It owns many papers and has a website (www.xinhuanet.com/English), as does China News Service (www.chinanews.cn).

» Media corporation Sina and broadcaster China Radio International (CRI) have online news sites in English and Chinese, at www.sina.com.cn and www.crienglish.com.

» China's English-language papers all have online news. Most are freely accessible, although the *South China Morning Post* requires subscription.

RADIO

» China Radio International (CRI) has English programs covering news, music and children's offerings.

» Local stations with English content include Radio Shanghai. Radio Beijing Corporation's Radio 774 was the first English service established by a city radio station in China. It spans news, talk shows, entertainment and culture. Of the capital's Chinese stations, the most popular is Beijing Music Radio.

» National broadcaster China National Radio operates eight radio stations, mostly in Mandarin but also in Mongolian, Tibetan, Uygur, Kazak, Cantonese and minority languages.

» Hong Kong has two English radio stations.

Celebrity traffic assistant

TELEVISION

» China's national TV broadcaster, China Central Television (CCTV), has 16 channels. Each focuses on different topics, from news to opera, sport and art. CCTV-9, also called CCTV International, is in English and blends propaganda news and serious chat shows with travelogues.

» Many hotels have international satellite TV. Services include Asian-based Star TV, which has several channels, BBC World, ESPN and CNN.

» Hong Kong has English channels provided by Asia Television and TVB.

BOOKS

China's literary heritage has a long and noble history, from the documented sayings of Confucius 2,500 years ago, through classical fantasies such as *Three Kingdom*s and *Outlaws of the Marsh*, to works of authors who have achieved international acclaim. Some of China's best-known books include:

Fiction

» *Waiting*, by Ha Jin, winner of the US National Book Award, is about an army doctor caught between the woman he loves and the illiterate wife he cannot divorce.

» *Three Kingdoms*, by Guanzhong Luo; *Outlaws of the Marsh*, by Shi Nai'An; *Journey to the West*, by Cheng'en Wu; and *A Dream of Red Mansions*, by Cao Xueqin, are four of China's most celebrated classics and are still entertaining.

» *Raise the Red Lantern*, by Su Tong, covers a woman's slide into insanity after being forced to become a concubine.

Autobiographical and non-fiction

» *The Analects of Confucius*, sayings of the great sage, are often still relevant today.

» *Wild Swans: Three Daughters of China*, by Jung Chang, traces the lives of three generations of her family.

» *The Travels of Marco Polo*, by Marco Polo, is a descriptive narrative of the explorer's extraordinary journey 800 years ago.

» *Red Dust*, by Ma Jian, is a deeply personal account of a haphazard journey across 1980s China. Written by a rebellious Beijing artist, it paints a beautiful picture of a country on the precipice of enormous change.

FILMS

Many Chinese films are global box office hits. These are some of the successes:

» *Raise the Red Lantern* (1990), directed by Zhang Yimou, is a powerful adaptation of the book about a young woman forced to marry a nobleman with three other wives.

» *Farewell My Concubine* (1993), directed by Chen Kaige, is the Oscar-nominated film of the book about two life-long actor friends and the woman who comes between them.

» *Crouching Tiger, Hidden Dragon* (1999), directed by Ang Lee, is a beautifully filmed *wuxia* (martial arts fantasy) film which won worldwide acclaim.

» *House of Flying Daggers* (2005), directed by Zhang Yimou, is another martial arts epic with exquisite scenery and breathtaking sequences, but more of an action love story.

» *Lust, Caution* (2007), directed by Ang Lee, provoked almost as many gasps of admiration around the world as it did scowls of outrage in China. Set in World War II Shanghai, the film tells the story of a young woman caught up in political espionage, and is far more than the sum of its famously racy sex scenes.

SHOPPING

Since the late 1990s China has experienced a shopping revolution, with mega malls and hypermarkets replacing traditional department stores and the emergence of shops catering exclusively to foreign tourists. Shopping hours are increasingly open-ended—many shops are open seven days a week until 8 or 9pm, with smaller retailers in popular tourist destinations closing even later. Credit cards are widely accepted in major cities but service charges can be as high as 5 percent. Prices in Shanghai, Beijing and Hong Kong are close to European and US levels, but you will be pleasantly surprised by how far your money goes outside the large conurbations. VAT is levied at 17 percent and is not refundable.

HOW TO HAGGLE
Few prices in China are fixed. When haggling, be courteous but firm. Never offer more than one-third of the asking price and aim to settle for around half. Communication is no problem as most traders have a calculator on hand for you to key in suggested sums. If there is a particular item you have your eye on, do not make it look too obvious—the dealer may notice and dig his heels in. If you are not satisfied with his 'final offer,' walk away—the chances are you'll get a better price. Beware of the 'switch,' when the trader substitutes an inferior product for the one you have set your mind on. You can often negotiate a small discount in stores with marked prices if you are buying a relatively expensive item.

COUNTERFEIT GOODS
By some calculations, 90 percent of all copyrighted products have been illegally copied in China, resulting in a loss of revenue to Europe, the US and Japan of approximately $60 billion. The Chinese government has expressed a determination to enforce IPR (Intellectual Property Right) and there have been some highly publicized cases. However, bootleg goods find a way into even respectable-looking stores so look out for unrealistic prices, obvious defects, or fuzzily printed labels and misspeled information on CDs, DVDs and computer software. The only way to guarantee you are getting the originals is to buy from brand-name stores and boutiques or recognized Western shops such as HMV.

DUTY-FREE SHOPPING
There are more than 150 duty-free stores in 90 mainland cities, including Beijing, Shanghai, Qingdao and Dalian. Since China joined the

World Trade Organization in 2001 these stores have lost some of their competitive edge as import tariffs have fallen substantially. Purchases do not come with an international warranty and there is no 30-day money-back guarantee. That said, the government is committed to duty-free stores and improvements in product lines, conditions of sale and overall competitiveness are anticipated.

CHOPS

Carved seals engraved with the owner's initials have been used for thousands of years to authenticate documents, sign works of art, or as trademarks. Seal carving is still regarded as an art, on a par with poetry, calligraphy and painting. Seals come in a variety of shapes, sizes and materials—jade, marble, wood, crystal, even plastic. *Jixueshi* ('chicken blood stone') from Zhejiang province is especially prized and can cost up to $1,000 per *chop*. Buy from arts and crafts stores or reputable dealers. The design may also include the owner's astrological sign (dog, snake etc). Don't leave without your pad and red ink paste.

TEA

China's national drink and most valuable agricultural export has a history going back to the Zhou dynasty. During the Tang golden age, poets waxed lyrical about its merits—one writer, Lu Yu (AD733–804), spent 20 years compiling a three-volume treatise on the subject. Tea (*cha* in Chinese) was thought to be beneficial to health and modern scientific research has tended to bear this out—apart from raising energy levels and combating fatigue, certain teas are thought to be effective in protecting against cancer and heart disease. There are three main types: green tea (*lu cha*), the most common and by far the most popular; black tea (confusingly called *hong cha*–red tea), grown from the same plant but left for a period of oxidation; and oolong (*wulong*), semi-oxidized. Tea can also be scented with flowers or fruit (*hua cha*), jasmine is the best known. Certain regions are associated with particular teas—Fujian with oolong, Yunnan with *puer* (famous for its medicinal properties), Shaoxing with pearl tea. Like wine, a classic tea improves with age—250g (8oz) of a vintage *puer* have been known to fetch 180,000RMB (US$26,000) at auction. Before buying your tea, visit a traditional teahouse and try a number of varieties to see which types you like. Every shop offers tastings, while major chains like Ten Fu have staff on hand to explain the intricacies of the tea ceremony.

ANTIQUES

Laws on the export of antiques are strict. No item made before 1795 may be sold or exported under any circumstances, while those dating from 1795–1949 are defined as 'cultural relics' and may not be taken out of the country without an official red wax seal and an export license issued by the State Cultural Relics Bureau in Beijing. Note that a seal does not necessarily guarantee a genuine antique.

These laws do not apply to Hong Kong, although the Chinese government has protested vigorously in the past when Chinese antiques have been put up for auction there. In fact, genuine antiques are increasingly hard to come by on the mainland. What you will find instead are high-quality reproductions of Ming and Qing dynasty furniture, porcelain and objets d'art.

In cities with a colonial past there are countless dealers specializing in curios and memorabilia dating mainly from the 1920s and 1930s. Here you can find anything from advertising posters and mahjong sets to gramophones, glassware, painted mirrors and electric fans. Mao-era memorabilia are also popular collectibles.

JEWELRY

For more than 7,000 years, jade has been appreciated for its esthetic qualities and as a symbol of power and wealth. Today it is as highly prized a commodity as ever and market values are soaring.

The best Chinese jade is found in Xinjiang Autonomous Region, near the border with Pakistan and Afghanistan.

When buying jade, make sure you are not being offered another hard stone, such as agate or quartz; only nephrite (soft, oily and fibrous) or jadeite (hard, waxy and glasslike) qualify as jade.

Colors vary—generally though white, pale green and dark red stones are the most valuable. When held to the light, jade should be translucent, even-hued and without blemishes or scratches. If you are paying a lot of money, make sure you are given a certificate of assay guaranteeing authenticity.

China is a major source of freshwater pearls, farmed mainly in the south of the country and the lakes and rivers around Shanghai. The only natural hues are white, pink, peach or lavender.

Pearls may be sold loose or (more commonly) on strands. Check for luster, a clear color and that there are no cracks, chips or blemishes. Roll the pearls on a flat surface to make sure they are even and of equal size, shape and shade. It is important not to be pressured into making a purchase and bargain hard over the price. While pearl-growing areas may offer the best selection and quality, the markets in Beijing are said to have the best bargains.

SOUVENIR SHOPPING BY REGION

BEIJING AND THE NORTH
Good-value buys include handwoven carpets and rugs, leather puppets originally made for shadow shows, Beijing lacquerware and ink stones. Also look out for traditional Chinese crafts such as lanterns and kites. Specialty items in Xi'an include models of the terra-cotta warriors; in Beijing, bronze lions, dragons and cranes, replicating the sculptures in the Forbidden City and the Summer Palace.

THE NORTHEAST
Seashell sculptures are popular souvenirs in coastal cities like Dalian, while the mountains of the Changbaishan nature reserve are a source of ingredients you'll find in traditional medicine shops. In Tianjin look out for clay figurines representing characters from classic folk tales.

INNER MONGOLIA AND THE SILK ROAD
The tough nomadic lifestyle of the Mongolian peoples is reflected in the region's specialties, which include knives, boots, saddles, warm lambswool clothing and handwoven rugs.

At Kashi's Sunday Market you'll find hand-carved wooden spoons and dishes, as well as colorful ethnic clothing. In Dunhuang visit the night market for replica statues and painting from the Mogao Caves.

SICHUAN AND TIBET
Chengdu has been associated with quality brocade for more than 2,000 years and the craft market sells hand-painted lacquerware and bamboo items.

In Lhasa, head for the market stalls of the Barkhor for handwoven cloth, carpets, turquoise jewelry, Tibetan bells and cotton light shades, or pick up religious objects such as incense sticks and prayer wheels. *Tangkas* (Buddhist paintings on scrolls or woven hangings) are expensive, but make beautiful souvenirs.

THE SOUTHWEST
Dali's shopping street, Fuxing Lu, is a colorful tapestry of cotton tie-dye, a specialty of the local Bai people. In the marble market they sell animal figurines and other items made from the local gray stone.

Lijiang's cobbled streets are crammed with craft and souvenir shops selling regional specialties including wood carving, copperware, Naxi handmade paper and *puer* black tea. Also look out for batik skirts, scarves and bedcovers. If your budget doesn't run to a traditional Miao silver crown or medallion, there is plenty of affordable jewelry on offer.

In Ruili, near the border with Myanmar (Burma), there is everything from mango jam and limes to gemstones and sarongs.

SOUTH CHINA
Shop on Hainan Island for its world-famous black tea, as well as shells, pearls and Sanya brocade. Shaoxing is known for its sweet rice wine, often used in cooking; less well known is the red *nu'er hong*. Guilin's university students sell watercolor paintings of the famous limestone karsts, Fuzhou is good for lacquerware, while Jingdezhen has produced exquisite porcelain for nearly 2,000 years.

Sandalwood fans may take your fancy in Suzhou, as well as silk clothing, bedding and embroidery. Silk umbrellas mounted on bamboo frames are a specialty of Hangzhou.

Opposite *Soapstone name stamps on sale at souvenir stalls in the market at Qufu*
Left *Curios and antiques displayed for sale on Dazhalan Jie in Beijing*

ENTERTAINMENT AND NIGHTLIFE

China has a great deal to offer those interested in the performing arts. In a typical week in Shanghai or Beijing choices might include a Western classical ballet, a Beijing opera, a symphony concert, a traditional Chinese *cantata*, a cello recital by a virtuoso of world renown, or a Kung Fu exhibition.

In major cities the main sources of information are English-language newspapers or the growing number of listings magazines. Buying tickets at the box office is better than by phone or online, unless you speak Chinese. Nightlife in the Western sense is relatively new on mainland China but the country is making up for lost time. Leading the way are cities like Shanghai, Beijing and Hong Kong, with a heady mix of bars, pubs, cocktail lounges and nightclubs. Other big cities, including Guangzhou, Xi'an, Kunming and Nanjing, still have a way to go before catching up.

CHINESE OPERA

Chinese opera has its origins in the traveling players of the Song and Yuan dynasties. At the end of the 18th century a distinctive Beijing Opera emerged from hundreds of regional styles and flourished under imperial patronage.

Performances are highly stylized and include singing, dance, mime and acrobatics, to a musical accompaniment. Plots are based on historical events, legends and folklore. Traditionally all roles are played by men and character traits are revealed by make up (red representing courage, white treachery and so on). There are few props and no changes of scenery.

While Beijing Opera is easy on the eye, it can be hard on the ears of the uninitiated and almost impossible to follow unless you know Chinese. Visitor-friendly shows comprising opera extracts, usually with a bit of martial arts thrown in, are advertised in hotels. Performances last around 90 minutes and tea and snacks are served during the intermissions.

ACROBATICS

The skill, agility and stamina of Chinese acrobats, whose art is rooted in a 2,000-year-old tradition, invariably impress visitors to China. The shows mix circus, gymnastics and vaudeville, with performances by contortionists, trapeze artists, tightrope walkers and the like. The two leading companies are the China Acrobatic Troupe, based in Beijing, and the Shanghai Acrobatic Troupe, which performs in the Shanghai Centre Theatre. Shows are widely advertised—making reservations through your hotel can work out less expensive than buying tickets directly or online.

FOLK PERFORMANCES

On your travels around China you will have many opportunities to sample the music and dance of the country's national minorities. Major festivals include the Nanning International Folksong Festival (October), the Xi'an Ancient Arts Festival (September) and the Qinghai 'Double Six' Folksong Fair, held in Xining in early July. Visitors to Lijiang can hear traditional music of the Naxi people, dating back to the Song dynasty and performed on traditional instruments such as the *pipa* (lute), *guqin* (zither) and *erhu* (fiddle). Guilin also showcases folk performances by its ethnic minorities—in April look out for the Red Dress Fair in Longshang. In towns or major cities organized, or impromptu, concerts take place during temple fairs and in teahouses, Chinese gardens, parks and hotels.

CLASSICAL MUSIC, BALLET AND DANCE

Introduced by Jesuit missionaries in the 17th century, Western classical music is alive and well in China. Beijing, Shanghai, Guangzhou and Hong Kong have resident symphony orchestras, while the China Philharmonic represents the country as a whole. Students and teachers at the Shanghai and Beijing conservatories also give concerts. Guest appearances by artists of international renown like Placido Domingo or the Berlin Philharmonic are increasingly frequent and generate enormous interest. State-of-the-art venues like Beijing's National Grand Theatre and the Shanghai Oriental Arts Centre stage opera and classical concerts. The Beijing International Music Festival (October) showcases homegrown talent and also attracts international stars. The repertoire of China's National Ballet ranges from *Swan Lake* to pieces from the

Maoist era. Fans of contemporary dance too will not be disappointed. Most of the action revolves around Jin Xing, who studied in New York with Martha Graham and Merce Cunningham. After founding the Beijing Modern Dance Company, she moved to Shanghai to form the Jin Xing Modern Dance Company. Guangzhou's modern dance festival is another Jin Xing initiative.

CINEMA

In 2005 the Chinese movie industry celebrated its 100th anniversary, an event marked by a retrospective of Chinese cinema at the Venice Film Festival. The story of modern Chinese film begins with an explosion of new talent in the early 1980s. Since then Beijing Film Academy graduates Chen Kaige, whose movies include *Yellow Earth* (1984) and *Farewell My Concubine* (1993), and Zhang Yimou, noted for *Red Sorghum* (1987) and *To Live* (1994), have won international acclaim for their work; stars like Zhang Ziyi (*Memoirs of a Geisha*) and Gong Li (*Hannibal Rising*) are seen regularly at international film festivals; while movies like Feng Xiaogang's *A World Without Thieves* (2004), Stephen Chow's *Kung Fu Hustle* (2005) and Xiaoshuai Wang's *Shanghai Dreams* (2005), which won the Cannes Jury Prize in 2005, have all been commercial successes, too.

Catch up with the latest Chinese movies (as well as some A-list celebrities) at June's Shanghai International Film Festival. Failing that, a number of cinemas in China's main cities show homegrown movies with English subtitles (▷ listings).

BARS

Most bars are run on Western lines and you can save money by taking advantage of 'happy hours' or theme-night promotions. On terraces you may be asked to pay after each round, otherwise the custom is to pick up the tab at the end of the evening. Food is available just about everywhere until around

10pm. Pubs usually offer billiards, pool, darts and occasional quiz nights, while many downtown bars resemble nightclubs with dancing and a regular DJ. Karaoke is also popular, especially with Asian businessmen but also increasingly with young Chinese people with money to burn. Drinks in these bars, known locally as KTV or 'partner bars,' can be pricy. Hostesses will expect you to pay for their drinks; if you do not want company, just politely refuse.

LIVE ENTERTAINMENT

China is no longer off-limits to top bands, singers and DJs, who are increasingly including Shanghai and Beijing as stops on their world tours. DJs from the UK, Ibiza, Canada and the US make guest appearances in the classier nightclubs. There are relatively few jazz venues and the majority of the musicians come from outside China. Indigenous music comes in all forms, from rock-and-roll and mando-pop to punk and hip-hop, but is often criticized for being derivative. China's most happening pop festival is the Midi Music Festival, held in October in Beijing.

HOW TO FIND OUT MORE

One or two Chinese newspapers publish English-language editions with listings for the major cities. A better bet are the listings magazines that have saturated the publishing markets in Beijing and Shanghai and have even spread as far as Jianjin, Qingdao and Chengdu. Most are free and available from hotel lobbies, expatriate bars and Western restaurants.

GENERAL INFORMATION

Opening times vary—bars open at around 4pm and close at 2am, while nightclubs open roughly from 8pm to 2am. There are few restrictions on smoking. Gambling is prohibited on mainland China; casinos are confined to Macao, though Hong Kong loves its horse racing. While attitudes are changing, tolerance should not be taken for granted.

SPORTS AND ACTIVITIES

The successful 2008 Olympic Games have given a tremendous boost to Chinese sport, which looks set to benefit from the huge generation of interest nationwide, and from the massive investment in new stadiums and other facilities in the six host cities (Beijing, Shanghai, Qingdao, Shenyang, Qinhuangdao and Tianjin). The injection of cash has been more than welcome, as many sports have suffered from underfunding in the past, while others, golf and skiing for example, are comparatively new to China. The best sources of information on spectator and participatory sports are listings magazines and websites, a growing number of which are translated into English.

GOLF

For evidence of China's golfing boom you only have to look at the growing number of shops selling clubs and equipment. It is difficult to believe that in 1984 there wasn't a single golf course in China; today there are nearly 400 courses with scores more due for completion in the next few years. The designers include Gary Player and six-time US Open winner Jack Nicklaus. Nonmembers are welcome at some golf clubs in Beijing and Shanghai, though access may be restricted on weekends. Course fees are steep—around 750RMB for 18 holes during the week and 1,250RMB on weekends, when reservations are essential. The Hong Kong Jockey Club owns one of the country's finest public courses, with scenery to match. There is more chance of getting a game here during the week.

RACKET SPORTS

There are few public tennis courts in China and where they exist demand is very high. In major cities, visitors wishing to play tennis or squash will do better to contact one of the many private tennis clubs where nonmembers are welcome. Book ahead if you can. Otherwise the best bet is the nearest five-star hotel. Fans of table tennis may get to see some of China's international stars in competitions and exhibition matches.

WINTER SPORTS

There are around a dozen ski resorts in the mountains north of Beijing, the nearest barely 30km (18 miles) from the capital. There are few really challenging slopes and there's a heavy reliance on artificial snow even in deepest winter. However, facilities are improving and resorts now offer snowboarding and tobogganing. You can rent skiing equipment at the resorts, though unless you have small feet, you may need to bring your own boots. Since 2006 it has been possible to get some ski practice in at the Qiaobo Ice and Snow World indoor resort at Shunyi, near Beijing. Ice-skating enthusiasts can use the public skating rinks in the main cities.

WALKING AND HIKING

China's stunning countryside offers wonderful opportunities for walkers. In Beijing, contact one of the many hiking associations that organize treks through local villages and along sections of the Great Wall. One of China's most popular hiking destinations is Tiger Leaping Gorge (Hutiao Xia) in Yunnan province. Visit China's holy mountains such as Wutaishan, where you can admire the spectacular scenery in the company of Buddhist pilgrims, or the peaks of Taishan, where walkers follow in the footsteps of emperors. There are numerous opportunities for less taxing walks. Trails are usually clearly signposted and there are plenty of places to stop off on the way for something to eat and drink. If do you get tired of climbing, there may well be a cable car or chairlift. Remember to come equipped—wear strong shoes and warm clothing in winter and a hat in summer, when you will also need sun block and plenty of water. Getting information on hiking trails is difficult although Hong Kong has several well-mapped routes.

GYMS AND FITNESS CENTERS

Any city with a sizable expat community will have fully equipped private gyms, fitness centers and health clubs with sauna, Jacuzzi, steam rooms and other facilities. Check first that you can pay for a single visit (the charge will be in the region of 150RMB), as many gyms expect you to sign up for at least a month or a minimum number of visits. Health clubs or hotel pools (often open to nonresidents) are also the best places to swim.

SOCCER

Soccer is a popular spectator sport with an enthusiastic TV following. But the professional sport is still in its infancy and fan bases, though growing, are still relatively small. The Chinese Football Association runs the country's professional Super League, comprising 18 clubs from around the country. Among the best

known are Dalian Shide, Shanghai Shenhua and Beijing Xiandai. During the season (Apr–end Nov) matches usually take place on Saturday or Sunday evenings. Tickets— sold at the stadium about half an hour before kick-off—are easy to come by and cost around 50RMB. In summer there are also opportunities to see top foreign teams playing pre-season friendlies and exhibition matches. Numerous sports bars in major cities show televised European League matches.

BASKETBALL

China's hottest sporting property, Yao Ming (▷ 21), now with the Houston Rockets in the US, has helped to raise the profile of basketball in China. You can see his former club, the Shanghai Sharks, play at Shanghai's Luwan Stadium. Tickets are sold at the gates.

BICYCLING

Bicycling is not just a pastime in China but a popular mode of transportation. That said, bicycle lanes are on the decrease, with more Chinese people using cars and the roads becoming increasingly congested. For these reasons, and because motorists have scant regard for bicyclists in general, it is not advisable to take to the road on a bicycle alone in big cities. For a safe ride in the capital, Cycle China arranges supervised guided tours of the *hutong* and excursions to the Great Wall and the Summer Palace. Outside the major cities, bicycling is a thoroughly enjoyable way of seeing the countryside. In tourist-friendly areas, cafés, shops and hotels have a range of bicycles to rent, from mountain bikes to tandems. The cost of a day's bicycling is around 20–50RMB, though you will be asked for a deposit of 100–200RMB against loss or damage. The better-organized outlets will supply a sketch map. Some of the best areas for a leisurely ride are Dali and Lijiang, the lakes at Yangzhou and Suzhou and the countryside around Yangshuo.

MARTIAL ARTS

The spiritual home of Chinese martial arts (*wuxu*) is the temple at Shaolin in Henan province. The best time to visit is in October, during the International Wuxu Championships, which attract competitors from all over the world. (For more information see www. shaolingongfu.com/en) At other times you can see the monks and nuns here practising their moves, while the masters give occasional demonstrations. Wudang Shan, home of Wudang boxing, is the other major center of martial arts. There are qualified instructors all over the country, including Beijing and Shanghai, while local martial arts centers offer courses, often with a free introductory class. If you do not have the time for this, check out the listing magazines for exciting martial arts performances by the Shaolin Kung Fu troupe of Shaolin Temple, who tour the country from time to time.

MAJOR EVENTS IN THE SPORTING CALENDAR

China's rising profile in world sport has led to successful bids for a host of major international sporting events, including the Olympic Games and the Special Games in Beijing and Shanghai respectively. The Formula 1 auto racing Grand Prix is held at the Shanghai International Motor Racing Circuit at Anting in October. Shanghai's Qi Zhong Tennis Center hosts the Tennis Masters Cup in November. The Shanghai Tennis Open (September) also attracts international stars. Tiger Woods has appeared at the HSBC Golfing Champion's Tournament in Shanghai (November). Rugby fans will not want to miss the International Sevens tournament, held in Hong Kong around Easter. The Beijing Marathon (mid-October) is acknowledged to be China's premier long-distance running event. Shanghai's Marathon is in November, Hong Kong's in February or March.

HEALTH AND BEAUTY

China's booming economy has created an unprecedented demand for health and beauty treatments. Spas, health clubs, beauty salons, nail boutiques and exclusive retreats are all on the increase. They offer a range of exotic treatments: Balinese massage, hydrotherapy, body scrubs, antioxidant treatments, facials, waxing, pedicures, Japanese *shiatsu*, you name it. You can start by checking out what's offered at the nearest five-star hotel.

TRADITIONAL CHINESE MASSAGE

Pampering yourself needn't cost an arm or a leg. For the price of a couple of drinks you can introduce your body to the wonders of TCM (Traditional Chinese Medicine) at a local massage parlor. The ancient art of Chinese medicinal massage, or *tuina*, aims to reduce tension, improve circulation and ensure the uninterrupted flow of *qi*, the energy of life force. Masseurs use fingers, elbows and the balls of the hands to roll and knead the muscles—this can be uncomfortable at first; so if you are experiencing pain, say '*bu shufu*' (not comfortable).

There are massage parlors on virtually every street corner (look for a barber's pole with a red stripe or a signboard with an acupuncture map of a foot). Avoid businesses which do not have a price list prominently displayed.

You may see 'Blind man's massage' advertised. Blind people are said to have a particularly acute sense of touch, but you will have to judge for yourself.

FOR CHILDREN

The Chinese love children and enjoy fussing over them, so kids can expect a warm welcome. Child-minding, though, is usually the preserve of grandparents—if you need a baby-sitting service make sure you stay in a Western five-star hotel. Eating out presents few problems. Chains like KFC, McDonald's and Starbucks already have a strong presence in the big cities and a growing number of provincial towns, while the number of independent, child-friendly restaurants is on the increase.

THINGS TO DO

In the major cities you will find every kind of attraction, from theme and amusement parks to zoos, wildlife parks, aquariums and state-of-the-art museums like Sony's ExploraScience in Beijing. Many offer concessions for children under 1.2m (4ft) or 1.4m (4ft 6in), while kids under 0.8m (2ft 6in) get in for free.

City parks invariably have play areas and often merry-go-rounds, boating lakes and other amusements. Kite flying is also a popular pastime in Chinese parks. What China is lacking in beaches it more than makes up for in the great outdoors. Bicycling is an option definitely worth considering, while hiking will appeal to older children, who relish the challenge and sense of adventure. Remember that summers are hot, so make sure your child is wearing a head covering and plenty of sun block, even on cloudy days.

FESTIVALS AND EVENTS

The hardworking Chinese people welcome any opportunity to relax and let their hair down. Apart from several national festivals and public holidays, the seasons are marked by a host of other celebrations, from music and folk dancing festivals to temple fairs and martial arts extravaganzas.

Western influence can be seen in the vogue for celebrating Christmas and Valentine's Day in big cities, likewise in festivals built around sporting events or fashion shows. Traditional Chinese holidays are based on the lunar calendar, so dates can vary each year by as much as a month.

CHINESE NEW YEAR

Spring Festival, or *Chunjie* as it is known in China, is far and away the most important event on the calendar and lasts for two weeks. This is the season for family get-togethers, for catching up with friends and for counting on better times ahead. For the authorities it is a logistical nightmare, as literally tens of millions of people leave the cities and head for home.

Celebrations begin on New Year's Eve with a first-rate meal—typical dishes include *jiaozi* (dumplings), clams and a glutinous rice pudding known as *niangao*. Children are given presents, while the adults exchange the traditional *hongbao* (a red envelope containing money) to bring good luck.

After dinner everyone gathers in front of the television to watch the annual New Year variety show as the night air explodes with the sound of firecrackers (to scare off evil spirits).

In southern China, New Year is especially lively, with lion and dragon dancers parading through the streets, bringing luck wherever they go. The New Year festivities conclude with the Lantern Festival, when red paper lanterns are carried through the streets to guide the Taoist god of heaven as he pays his annual visit to earth.

OTHER MAJOR FESTIVALS

The Dragon Boat Festival in June recalls the 3rd-century administrator and poet, Qu Yuan, who drowned himself to protest against corruption at court. Dragon Boat races commemorate the event.

During the Mid-Autumn or Moon Festival, families gather outdoors to eat moon cakes—a sticky delicacy made from red bean paste, egg yolk, walnut kernels and duck eggs. This festival, dedicated to the moon goddess, was originally for women only.

At the Clear Brightness Festival in April relatives pay their respects to their ancestors by sweeping their tombs and laying flowers. Those unhappy spirits without relatives to care for them must be appeased with food offerings and religious rituals during the Hungry Ghost Festival in August. Most Chinese put off moving house or changing jobs until this inauspicious time has passed.

China is a vast country with culinary traditions going back thousands of years. Climate, history, geography and culture have all influenced the way in which food is prepared and cooked, creating a richness and diversity of cooking styles. Food really matters to the Chinese—even today when meeting a friend, a person might say *chi fan le ma?*, literally meaning 'have you eaten yet?'

A QUICK GUIDE TO CHINESE FOOD

NORTHERN CHINA

Hearty, nourishing and warming dishes are the norm in a part of the country that endures extremely cold winters. The staple is not rice but wheat and millet, used to make steamed bread, pancakes, noodles and dumplings. Flavors are robust with lashings of garlic, scallion, peppers and soy sauce. There is a heavy reliance on preserved vegetables, especially salted, pickled cabbage. The most famous regional dish, Beijing Duck, was not invented until the 19th century (▷ 402); Mongolian lamb hot pot (▷ 402) has an older pedigree.

EASTERN CHINA

The proximity of the coastal provinces to the sea, the Yangtze Delta and a number of freshwater lakes account for the popularity of fish and seafood dishes. The most famous local delicacy, hairy crab, is seasonal and available only from early October to the end of November. 'Red cooking,' whereby pork and other meat is slowly simmered in dark, heavily sugared soy sauce until it acquires a rich red hue, is also typical of the region. Rice is the staple in the southern part of the region, wheat in the north, hence the popularity of *mantou* (steamed buns) and *xiao long bao* (dumplings) in the Shanghai area.

WESTERN CHINA

The mountainous western provinces of Sichuan and Hunan are home to some of China's fieriest dishes. Buddhist monks traveling along the Silk Road from India brought spices, while missionaries from Spain and Portugal introduced the red chili in the 17th century. Sichuanese stir-fries rely more on the use of strongly flavored vegetables, especially garlic, than rich sauces. The region's most famous dish is *mapo doufu* (spicy bean curd) but a typical menu will also include palate-numbing hot pots, and hot-and-sour soup.

SOUTHERN CHINA

Known in the west as Cantonese cuisine, the cooking of Guangdong and Hong Kong is renowned for its delicacy, inventiveness and variety of flavors. Most dishes are steamed in water or stir-fried in a wok to seal in the flavor and retain freshness. Abalone and other shellfish are popular, as is shark fin, served stewed or as a soup. Breakfast and lunch menus invariably include dim sum, steamed miniature dumplings and savory pastries containing a variety of meat and vegetable fillings. Less appealing to Western palates might be the more exotic local delicacies, which include dog, cat, monkey and lizard.

OTHER REGIONS

Travelers in northwestern China will encounter Uighur cooking, influenced by the culinary traditions of Central Asia. Mutton and lamb stews figure prominently, as do skewered meats, spicy salads, nan bread and thick noodles, usually served with red peppers, tomato, eggplant and garlic. In Tibet to the south specialties include yak meat, butter tea, a noodle-based soup known as *thukpa* and dairy products including cheese and yogurt.

WHEN TO EAT

Breakfast is taken early in China, often on the way to work, and most restaurants are open by 7.30am. The traditional breakfast dish is *congee* (rice porridge), though some prefer a hearty bowl of meat and noodle soup. Street food is also popular at this time of day, especially steamed buns, pancakes or the elongated, crispy fried donuts known as *youtiao*. Restaurants in large hotels serve buffet breakfasts to nonresidents as well as guests. Alternatively, head for the nearest pub or café, or buy from one of the growing number of Western-style bakeries and patisseries if you want

take-out. By around 11am lunch service will begin, again usually a simple affair of one or two courses. Chinese restaurants tend to close around 2.30pm; Western eateries, on the other hand, stay open all day, many serving set lunches or local specialties on their menus. Dinner, the main meal of the day, can begin as early as 5pm. If you arrive in a restaurant much after 8pm the waitstaff will be scowling at you or sweeping around your feet while you eat. Popular places fill up quickly and if you haven't made a reservation by around 6pm, you may have to wait in line, though not usually for long—people tend to leave as soon as they have finished eating.

WHERE TO EAT
RESTAURANTS

There is a restaurant of some description on virtually every street corner. They can range from gastronomic temples serving up dishes created for the imperial court to hole-in-the wall canteens with tables spilling out on to the sidewalk and vats of noodles bubbling permanently on the stove. For family gatherings and more formal occasions, the Chinese favor palatial establishments with marble walls and gilded columns. Despite these outward trappings, dinners are noisy, relaxed and convivial affairs.

When you arrive at a restaurant you will be greeted at the door with a cry of *huanying* (welcome) before being shown to your table. Tea will be served while you are consulting the menu, which is usually divided into cold and hot appetizers, meat, vegetable and fish dishes, rice and soups. Desserts feature too but are very much an afterthought. In China it is customary to order dishes to share, so choose a number of items from different parts of the menu. The food should arrive fairly promptly. Serve yourself from the communal dish using your chopsticks. Eat from the small plate in front of you—the bowl is for rice or soup, which arrives toward the end of the meal.

Your place setting will usually include a flannel in a plastic wrapping for wiping your mouth and hands, and a packet of toothpicks. If you are eating out with friends and are unable to finish all the dishes you have ordered, ask for a doggy bag.

CAFÉS AND TEAHOUSES

While traditionally China does not have a café culture, relaxed, Western-style cafés are emerging in cities like Shanghai. Cafés invariably sell reasonably priced snacks and light meals, starting with breakfast. Coffee shops too are growing in number as Chinese businesses begin to emulate the success of Western chains like Starbucks, which has branches in all the main cities. Backpacker cafés with internet access, local information, book swaps and tour arranging have emerged in popular tourist areas like Dali, Lijiang and Yangshuo. Those wishing to experience something more authentically Chinese should spend an hour or two relaxing in a teahouse. Huxinting, in Shanghai's Yu Garden, is perhaps the most famous but it's the less touristy places in Sichuan province that best convey the teahouse's traditional role as a meeting place. Bear in mind that, outside the far south, where dim sum is often served with tea, snacks and sweetmeats will be the only edibles on offer.

PUBS AND BARS

Most pubs and bars open around 11am and close between midnight and 2am. They sell a wide range of local and international (draught and bottled) beers, a limited selection of wines, and spirits. Pub food is universally available, with English-language menus offering a choice of Western and Chinese dishes. Many sell cut-price drinks during 'happy hour' (usually 5–8pm). The legal age for consuming alcohol in China is 18, but this is rarely enforced. Children accompanied by an adult are welcome in many pubs and there are sometimes gardens for them to let off steam.

INTERNATIONAL RESTAURANTS

Western restaurants abound in China's big cities, offering cuisines from most parts of the world. How good the food is depends partly on how much you are willing to spend, but also on whether there is a native chef directing the kitchen. Even in top restaurants, celebrity chefs are not always in residence year-round and standards have been known to slip. Outside the big cities 'Western restaurant' usually means exclusively Chinese kitchen staff serving up a mix of Chinese and Western standards, such as pizza, pastas and steaks.

FAST FOOD

There are branches of Western chains like KFC, McDonald's and Pizza Hut in most major Chinese cities. Chinese and Indian take-outs are also on the increase, as are homegrown fast-food restaurants. Even the neighborhood kwik-e-marts/24–7 supermarket will have tofu or sausages simmering on heaters by the checkout along with hot water for your pot noodles.

STREET FOOD

Chinese street food is renowned for being filling, flavorsome and easy on the pocket, but visitors should tread warily. While the government is collaborating with the World Health Organization (WHO) to improve hygiene standards, many street vendors continue to trade without a license and remain ignorant of even the most basic health requirements. Only buy from stands with a fast turnover—that way you can at least be sure the food has been freshly cooked. Some of the best places to look for street food are the night markets of China's big cities. Each region has its own specialties: toasted goat's cheese in Yunnan, *Xian bing* (crispy pancakes with vegetable or meat filling) in Beijing, *baozi* (steamed buns) in Shanghai. You will also see skewered kabobs, fishballs, crawfish, quail and ducks' eggs and sausages, as well as more exotic items like grasshoppers.

VEGETARIANS

Vegetarian restaurants are still uncommon, even in cities like Shanghai. On the other hand, most pubs, cafés and fast-food outlets will include vegetarian dishes on the menu. Another possibility is to check out the nearest Buddhist temple—some canteens are open to the public, although you may have difficulty making yourself understood. When eating out, bear in mind that some dishes not specifying a meat content may contain lard or meat stock.

PAYMENT

Although the use of credit cards is increasingly widespread, China is still basically a cash economy, so don't rely on the restaurant taking plastic. A service charge of 10–15 percent may be included. This does not go to the waiters, so if the service has been good, you may like to leave a tip (a few RMB will suffice), though tips are by no means expected.

PRICES

Eating out in Chinese restaurants is good value and, even in the big cities, you will pay considerably less

than you would in Europe or the US for a similar meal. Drinks are usually less expensive in local restaurants than in ones serving international cuisine, especially if you order the local beer and give mineral water a miss.

DRESS CODE
Informal dress is acceptable in all but the most exclusive restaurants.

WHAT TO DRINK
ALCOHOLIC DRINKS
Beer is by far and away the most popular alcoholic drink, especially among young men. Most regions promote their own brands of highly palatable, medium-strength pilsner lager. Tsingtao beer (from Qingdao) is widely available throughout the country, either bottled or on draft. Imported beers, sold mainly in bars and nightclubs will likely be more expensive though many brands, San Miguel, Budweiser and Heineken included, are now brewed locally.

Though China can hardly be called a great wine-producing country, there are commercial vineyards, concentrated mainly in the north and northwest (Xinjiang produces the best wines). Great Wall and Dynasty are the most common brands and crop up on virtually every restaurant menu. Reds are generally more palatable than whites. Expect to pay around 80RMB for a bottle of table wine—restaurants on Shanghai's Bund have been known to charge five times that for a 1992 vintage Great Wall. Traditional Chinese wines are sweet and have a low alcohol content. You may also come across *fanjiu* (rice wine), which is sometimes flavored with ginger juice or wolf berries, and *changjiu*, a yellow wine native to Shanghai, usually served warm. Foreign wines, especially French, Australian and Californian, are available in Western restaurants but are expensive by Chinese standards. Prices start at around 150RMB a bottle.

Baijou ('white alcohol'), made from rice and sorghum, is the most famous spirit. Quality brands include Maotai and Wuliangye. Today, *baijou* is usually reserved for weddings and other celebrations, when guests customarily drain the glass in one go. Visitors should tread more warily, given that the alcohol content can be as high as 45 percent.

NONALCOHOLIC DRINKS
Soft drinks are sold widely but be aware that the sugar content of Chinese carbonated drinks is high. Fresh fruit juices appear on most menus. Tea is always served in Chinese restaurants. Freshly brewed coffee is harder to come by and may come with sugar added. Mineral water is widely available, though some restaurants overcharge for Western brands. Water served in restaurants is safe to drink.

ETIQUETTE
The Chinese are commendably tolerant of Western foibles and ignorance of local eating customs. However, it may help to bear a few points in mind:

» When you have finished eating, place your chopsticks on the cradle provided; do not use them to gesture or point, nor should you leave them planted in food—this is considered unlucky.

» When offered rice, take the bowl with both hands and hold it up to your mouth when eating.

» If the teapot is close at hand, serve others first. If tea is offered to you, tap the table with your fingers to convey gratitude.

» If using a toothpick, cover your mouth with your left hand.

» The Chinese toast by clinking glasses. The word for cheers is *ganbei*, though this means 'bottoms up' so be wary of getting yourself into an accidental drinking contest.

» If your host offers, allow him or her to pay, otherwise they may lose face.

SMOKING
There are few, if any, restrictions on smoking in bars, cafés, restaurants or other public buildings. Even where there are designated nonsmoking areas these are often honored more in the breach than the observance. Asking for a nonsmoking table in a restaurant will often be met by a bemused stare. Exceptions are Western chains like Starbucks.

Baiguo Dun Laoya (Gingko stewed with old duck): Gingko leaves are a common ingredient in traditional Chinese medicine. Here they are served in a nourishing meat stew in a dish that originated in Guilin.

Beijing Kaoya (Beijing duck): Invented in 1864 by Qianmen fruit shop owner, Yang Quanren, who used pear and apricot wood for roasting duck. The skin, which should be thin and crispy, is at least as important as the succulent meat in this famous dish, served with honey or plum sauce, thinly sliced scallion, cucumber and wheat pancakes.

Chaye Dan (Tea eggs): Popular at Chinese New Year, this dish is also served as a breakfast snack. The eggs are boiled and mixed with black tea, soy sauce, star anise and cinnamon, then left to cool.

Da Zha Xie (Hairy crab): This Shanghai delicacy is only available in the fall. The crabs, from freshwater lakes and rivers, are steamed in bamboo baskets with ginger, herbs and vinegar. The Chinese will eat the intestines but you may want to give them a miss.

Dian Xian (Dim sum): Sweet and savory snacks eaten for breakfast or lunch in Guangdong and Hong Kong. Guangzhou cookbooks list around 2,000 varieties.

Di San Xian (Earth's three fairies): This simple dish from northeastern China mixes eggplant (aubergines), green peppers and chopped potato in a rich brown sauce.

Dong Po Rou (Dong Po Pork): Named after an 11th-century governor of Hangzhou who was also a celebrated poet, this fatty dish is made with pork belly braised in soy sauce to give it its distinctive red color.

Huoguo (Hot pot): This northern dish is said to have been invented by Mongolian soldiers who used their helmets to heat the stew, traditionally made with mutton. The meat and a variety of vegetables are dipped in boiling broth until cooked, then eaten with soy and other sauces. Sichuan is famous for its spicy variation.

Jiaohua Ji (Beggar's chicken): Baked whole chicken flavored with sesame and Shaoxing rice wine, wrapped in lotus leaves and then clay to keep it moist. The dish originates in eastern China.

Jiaozi: (Dumplings): These famous northern morsels are served in a flour wrap and soaked in vinegar, and usually served with hand-pulled noodles or pan-fried savory pancakes.

Kou Shui Ji (Mouth-watering chicken): Sichuanese cold appetizer made with poached chicken in a rich sauce of peanuts, garlic, root ginger, scallion and red chili oil.

Mapo Doufu (Mapo tofu): Named after the 'pock-marked grandmother' who supposedly invented the dish, this Sichuan specialty is made with tofu, ground pork, red chilis and tongue-numbing Sichuan peppercorns.

Mayi Shang Shu (Ants climbing a tree): A typically spicy dish from western China, made with stir-fried glass noodles and ground pork with chili, bean paste and ginger.

Shizi Tou (Lion's head meatballs): Succulent meatballs made with pork and braised in a sand clay pot. Served with a 'lion's mane' of *bai cai* (bok choy), a slightly bitter-tasting Chinese cabbage.

Suanla Tang (Hot-and-sour soup): This spicy winter-warmer from Sichuan (where else?) is made from Chinese pickled vegetables, mushrooms, scallion, root ginger, tofu, chili and rice wine.

Yangrou Pao Mo (Baked bun soaked in mutton soup): Popular Xi'an dish made with unleavened bread. The bread is brought to your table for you to break into small pieces, then returned to the kitchen to be cooked in the stew.

Yangzhou Chaofan (Yangzhou fried rice): Long grain rice, flavored with chicken stock, Shaoxing rice wine and a light soy sauce, mixed with shrimps, peas, onions, root ginger, tomato and scrambled egg.

Yu Chi Tang (Sharkfin soup): Eaten more for its medicinal properties than its flavor. Sharks' fins are dried

and bleached, then cooked very slowly in a chicken stock.

Xiao Long Bao (Little dragon bun): These small, steamed, pork-filled dumplings are dipped in a sauce made from ginger and brown vinegar and served, piping hot, in bamboo baskets. Originally a specialty of Shanghai, *xiao long bao* has become popular dim sum and is encountered all over China.

Xiechuang (Sea cucumber): Also known as the sea slug, this marine animal has a glutinous texture. In itself rather flavorless, it is served with strong sauces. An ancient cooking ingredient, there are many regional variations. In Shanghai, for example, sea cucumber is braised with shrimp roe, while in Shandong it is combined with crab eggs.

Xihu Cuyu (West Lake poached fish): Traditional Hangzhou dish made with poached carp, marinaded with a distinctive sweet-and-sour sauce of Zhenjiang black vinegar, sugar and ginger.

There is a wide range of accommodations in China, from luxury hotels conforming to the highest international standards to youth hostels and homestays. The bias toward top-end hotels is now being addressed, with many chains committed to building more mid-range and budget properties in anticipation of a huge increase in foreign visitors. China National Tourism Administration awards hotels between one and five stars, and a new platinum tier was added in 2007. However, there are considerable variations in quality and value for money.

PRICES
Expect to pay around the same for a room in eastern China as you would in Europe and the US—and remember that prices are rising generally throughout the country. You can save money by traveling in the low season (December through April), by taking advantage of hotel promotions, and by bargaining hard over rates (you can nearly always get a discount on advertised prices).

Rates quoted are usually for a person sharing a double room—in China this is usually called a 'twin' and has two single beds. A service charge of 15 percent may be added to your account.

Breakfast is not usually included in the quoted price.

Note that rooms are often hugely overpriced and customers who book with the hotel directly are expected to ask for a discount. You should rarely, if ever, pay the listed price.

FINDING SOMEWHERE TO STAY
The following travel companies offer online hotel reservations for a range of destinations, with considerable reductions on published prices:

Chinaetravel
www.chinaetravel.com
China Travel www.chinatravel.com
Ctrip http://english.ctrip.com
ELong, Inc
www.elong.com/www.elong.net
Sinohotel www.sinohotel.com
Note that most of the top international 5-star hotels offer 'best-rate' deals on their own websites and do not always co-operate with these kinds of aggregators. Alternatively, contact the nearest branch of the China International Travel Service (CITS) once you arrive.

If you are looking for somewhere to stay once you have arrived in China, always insist on seeing the room first. When considering a Chinese-run hotel with a three-star rating or less, first check that the hotel has official permission to accept foreign guests. Bear in mind that the desk staff will probably speak little English and may be unable to provide much in the way of information about the destination. If there is a restaurant, the menu may be in Chinese only.

RESERVATIONS

Advance reservations are essential during the peak season (June to end September) and are advisable at other times. Many hotels take block reservations for business conventions and conferences, and there is a high occupancy rate for most of the year in cities like Shanghai and Hong Kong. You will also have difficulty finding a room during major public holidays (▷ 380) unless you reserve well in advance.

Online reservations (▷ 404) are the easiest way to secure a room, as desk staff in anything other than four- or five-star hotels are unlikely to speak good English and misunderstandings can easily occur on the phone. If you are making a reservation by fax, insist on a detailed confirmation.

CHECKING IN AND OUT

In reception you may be given a form to fill in with your personal details. You will be expected to pay for the room in advance and will have to leave a deposit to cover minibar and phone bills and other expenses. This is refundable but you must produce the receipt. You must vacate your room by midday but can leave your luggage at the hotel until you are ready to leave. Allow plenty of time for checking out.

HOSTELS

The International Youth Hostel Association has dormitory-style accommodations in Beijing, Shanghai, Hong Kong and a growing number of other cities including Yangshuo, Guilin, Macau and Guangzhou. For details, contact: www.yhachina.com/english or email yha_china@hotmail.com; tel 020 8751 3733 (main office in China).

PRIVATE GUEST HOUSES

Private guest houses are on the increase, especially in areas that are popular with backpackers. They offer Western-style meals and will often arrange tours, continuing travel and bicycle rental. The owners are usually well informed.

HOMESTAYS

Homestays, where you stay with a Chinese family, are suited to people wishing to learn the language and local customs. The following organizations interview all prospective families, inspect premises and ensure that locations are convenient:
www.homestay.com.cn
www.chinahomestay.org

Opposite *Shanghai*
Left *The White Swan Hotel*, *Shamian Island*
Below *Door greeter*

Chinese is a written language that has given rise to several dialect groups including Mandarin, Cantonese and Hakka. Despite using the same written script, these dialects sound so different that they are usually considered distinct languages. Mandarin is the official spoken language in China and is understood by most people. Having only a small pool of syllables, Mandarin relies on tones to help users communicate clearly. There are four main tones (plus a neutral tone) and every syllable must be pronounced in the correct tone for any sentence to be quickly understood.

TONES

– =	The first tone is high and flat
/ =	The second tone rises from the middle to the top
v =	The third tone curves from low to lower and then rises slightly
\ =	The fourth tone falls from high to low
	The neutral tone has no accent

Note: If you have two 'tone three' (v) words together, the first word becomes 'tone two' (/).

Pinyin is a system of Romanization which uses the Roman alphabet to guide pronunciation of Mandarin. 'Pin' means 'spell' and 'yin' means 'sound'. Pinyin pronunciation is composed of an initial, a final and the tone. Vowels are pronounced in a similar way to those of the Romance languages, while consonants are pronounced in a similar way to English.

PINYIN PRONUNCIATION GUIDE
INITIALS

b	as **p** in s**p**eak
p	as **p** in **p**ark
m	as **m** in **m**um
f	as **f** in **f**ather
d	as **t** in s**t**ay
t	as **t** in **t**ag
n	as **n** in **n**urse
l	as **l** in **l**ay
g	as **g** in **g**irl
k	as **k** in **k**angaroo
h	as **h** in **h**e
j	as **j** in **j**eep
q	as **ch** in **ch**eap
x	as **sh** in **sh**eep
zh	as **j** in **j**erk
ch	as **ch** in **ch**urch
sh	as **sh** in **sh**ip
z	as **ds** in bea**ds**
c	as **ts** in coa**ts**
s	as **s** in **s**ee
y	as **y** in **h**ymn
w	as **w** in **w**ater

FINALS

a	as **ar** in c**ar**
o	as **ar** in w**ar**
e	as **e** in h**er**
i	as **e** in **E**nglish
u	as **oo** in b**oo**k
er	as **are** in **are**
ai	as **y** in sk**y**
ei	as **ay** in pl**ay**
ao	as **ow** in c**ow**
ou	as **o** in s**o**
an	as **an** in c**an**
en	as **un** in **un**der
ang	as **ang** in cl**ang**
ong	as **ong** in l**ong**

in	as **in** in **in**
ing	as **ing** in s**ing**
ie	as **ye** in **ye**s
ia	as **ya** in **ya**rd
ian	as **yen** in **yen**
iu	as **eo** in L**eo**
un	as **on** in w**on**
uo	as **ar** in w**ar**

USEFUL WORDS

yes
shì
no
bù
please
qǐng
thank you
xiè xie
you're welcome
bú kè qi
excuse me!
Duì bu qǐ
where
Zài nǎ lǐ
here
zhè
there
nà
when
shén me shí hou
why
wèi shén me
who
shéi
may I/can I
Wǒ kě yǐ/wǒ néng

CONVERSATION

I don't speak Chinese
Wǒ bú huì shuō hàn yǔ
Do you speak English?
Nǐ huì shuō yǐng yǔ ma?
I don't understand
Wǒ bù míng bai
Please speak more slowly
Qǐng shuō màn diānr
My name is ...
Wǒ jiào...
What's your name?
Nǐ jiào shén me míng zi?
Hello, pleased to meet you
Nǐ hǎo, hěn gāo xìng jiàn dào nǐ
**This is my wife/husband/
daughter/son/friend**
Zhè shì wǒ qī zi/zhàng fu/nǔr ěr/ér zi/
péng you

Where do you live?
Nǐ zhù nǎr?
I live in...
Wǒ zhù zài...
Good morning
Zǎo shàng hǎo
Good afternoon/evening
Xià wǔhǎo/wǎn shàng hǎo
Goodbye
Zài jiàn
How are you?
Nǐ hǎo ma?
Fine, thank you
Wǒ hěn hǎo, xiè xiè
I'm sorry
Duì bu qǐ
That's alright
Méi guān xi

GETTING AROUND

Where is the train (bus) station?
Huǒ chē zhàn (qì chē zhàn) zài nǎr?
Does this train (bus) go to...?
Zhè liàng huǒ chē (gōng gòng qì chē)
dào... ma?
Please stop at the next stop
Qǐng zài xià yí zhàn tíng
Where can I buy a ticket?
Wǒ zài nǎr mǎi piào?
Is this seat taken?
Zhè yǒu rén zuò ma?
Where can I reserve a seat?
Wǒ zài nǎr kě yǐ yù dìng zuò wèi?
**Please can I have a one-way
(round-trip) ticket to...**
Qǐng mǎi yì zhāng dào...de dān
chéng piào (wǎng fǎn piào)
When is the first (last) bus to...?
Dì yī (zuì hòu yí) liàng gōng gòng qì
chē dào ... shì shén me shí hou?
**I would like a hard (soft) seat
ticket to...**
Wǒ mǎi yì zhāng yìng zuò (ruǎn zuò)
de piào dào...
Where is the timetable?
Shí kè biǎo zài nǎr?
Do you have a metro (bus) map?
Nǐ yǒu dì tiě (gōng gòng qì chē) tú
ma?
Where can I find a taxi (rank)?
Wǒ zài nǎr kě yǐ dǎ chū zū chē?
Please take me to...
Qǐng dài wǒ dào...
How much is the journey?
Duō shao qián chē fèi?
Please turn on the meter
Qǐng dǎ kāi lǐ chéng biǎo

I'd like to get out here please
Qǐng ràng wǒ zài zhèr xià chē
Could you wait for me, please?
Qǐng děng wǒ, hǎo ma?
Excuse me, I think I am lost
Duì bu qǐ, wǒ mí lù le

IN TROUBLE

Help!
jiù mìng!
Stop, thief!
Zhuā zéi!
Can you help me, please?
Nǐ néng bāng wǒ ma?
**Call the (fire brigade/police/an
ambulance)**
Qǐng jiào (jiù huǒ chē/jǐng chá/jiù
hù chē
**I have lost my passport/wallet/
purse/handbag**
Wǒ diū le wǒ de hù zhào/qián jiá/
qián bāo/shǒu tí bāo
Is there a lost property office?
Yǒu méi yǒu shī wù zhāo lǐng chù?
I have been robbed
Wǒ bèi qiāng jié le
I have had an accident
Wǒ chū shì gù le
**I need information for my
insurance company**
Wǒ yào gěi wǒ de bǎo xiǎn gōng
sī xìn xī

ILLNESS

I don't feel well
wǒ gǎn jué bù hǎo
I need to see a doctor (dentist)
Wǒ xū yào kàn yī shēng (yá yī)
Where is the hospital?
Yī yuàn zài nǎr?
I feel sick
Wǒ bù shū fu
I am allergic to...
Wǒ duì...guò mǐn
I am diabetic
Wǒ yǒu táng niào bìng
I'm asthmatic
Wǒ yǒu xiāo chuǎn bìng
Can I have a painkiller?
Nǐ yǒu qù tòng piàn ma?
**How many tablets a day should
I take?**
Wǒ yì tiān yào chī duō shao piàn
yào?

SHOPPING

How much is this?
Zhè gè duō shao qián?
I'm looking for...
Wǒ mǎi...
Where can I buy...?
Wǒ zài nǎr kě yǐ mǎi...?
I'm just looking, thank you
Wǒ zhǐ shì kàn kan, xiè xie
I'll take this
Wǒ yào zhè gè
Do you accept credit cards?
Nǐ jiē shòu xìn yòng kǎ ma?
Can you measure me, please?
Qǐng gěi wǒ liáng yí xià?
Do you have this in (color)...?
Nǐ yǒu...de zhè gè ma?

POST AND TELEPHONES

**Where is the nearest post office/
mail box?**
Zuì jìn de yóu jú/yóu xiāng zài nǎr?
One stamp, please
Qǐng mǎi yì zhāng yóu piào
**Can you direct me to a public
phone?**
Nǐ néng gào sù wǒ gōng yòng diàn
huà zài nǎr ma?
Where can I buy a phone card?
Wǒ zài nǎ kě yǐ mǎi dào diàn huà kǎ?
**What is the number for directory
assistance?**
Diàn huà chá xún hào mǎ shì duō
shao?

MONEY

**Is there a bank (currency exchange
office) nearby?**
Fù jìn yǒu yín háng (wài huì duì huàn
diàn) ma?
Can I cash this here?
Wǒ kě yǐ duì huàn xiàn jīn ma?
**I'd like to change sterling (dollars)
into Chinese Yuan**
Wǒ xiǎng bǎ yīng bàng (měi yuán)
duì huàn chéng rén mín bì...
**Can I use my credit card to
withdraw cash?**
Wǒ kě yǐ yòng xìn yòng kǎ qǔ xiàn
jīn ma?
What is the exchange rate today?
Jīn tiān de huì lǜ shì duō shao?
I'd like to cash this traveler's check
Wǒ xiǎng bǎ lǚ xíng zhī piào huàn
chéng xiàn jīn

HOTELS

Do you have a room?
Yǒu kòng fáng ma?
**I have made a reservation for...
nights**
Wǒ yù dìng le...wǎn de fáng jiān
How much per night?
Duō shao qián yì wǎn?
Double/single room
Shuāng rén jiān/dān rén jiān
Twin room
Tào fáng
With bath/shower
Dài yù gāng/lín yù
May I see the room?
Wǒ kě yǐ kàn kan fáng jiān ma?
I'll take this room
Wǒ yào zhè jiān fáng
**Are the rooms air-conditioned
(heated)?**
Yǒu dài kōng tiáo (nuǎn qì) de fáng
jiān ma?
Is breakfast included in the price?
Zhè gè jià gé bāo kuò zǎo cān ma?
When is breakfast served?
Zǎo cān jǐ diǎn kāi shǐ?
The room is too hot/too cold/dirty
Zhè fáng jiān tài rè/tài lěng/tài zāng
Please can I pay the check (bill)?
Wǒ kě yǐ jié zhàng ma?

RESTAURANTS

waiter/waitress
nán zhāo dài/nǚ zhāo dài
A table for ..., please
Qǐng yào yì zhāng...wèi de zhuō zi
Could we sit there?
Wǒ men kě yǐ zuò nà ma?
Where are the toilets?
Cè suǒ zài nǎr?
Do you have the menu in English?
Nǐ yǒu yīng yǔ de cài dān ma?
**I can't eat wheat/sugar/salt/
pork/beef/dairy**
Wǒ bù chī miàn/táng/yán/zhū ròu/niú
ròu/nǎi zhì pǐn
I am a vegetarian
Wǒ shì sù shí zhě
I'd like...
Wǒ yào...
**Could I have bottled still
(sparkling) water?**
Wǒ kě yǐ yào píng zhuāng de shuǐ (qì
shuǐ) ma?
The food is cold
Shí wù lěng le

The meat is overcooked/too rare
Zhè gè ròu zhǔ guò le/bàn shóu
This is not what I ordered
Zhè bú shì wǒ diǎn de
Can I have the check (bill), please?
Wǒ kě yǐ mǎi dān ma?
Is service included?
Fú wù fèi bāo kuò zài nèi ma?
The check (bill) is not right
Zhàng dān bú duì
We didn't have this
Wǒ men méi yǒu zhè ge

TOURIST INFORMATION

**Where is the tourist information
office (tourist information desk),
please?**
Qǐng wèn, yóu kè xìn xī bàn zhōng
xīn(xìn xī tái) zài nǎr?
Do you have a city map?
Nǐ yǒu chéng shì dì tú ma?
What is the admission price?
Mén piào duō shao qián?
**Is there an English-speaking
guide?**
Yǒu shuō yīng yǔ de dǎo yóu ma?
**Do you have a brochure in
English?**
Nǐ yǒu yīng yǔ de lǚ yóu zhǐ nán ma?
Are there guided tours?
Yǒu dài dǎo yóu de lǚ xíng tuán ma?
Are there organized excursions?
Yǒu zhǔ zhǐ de yuán zú ma?
Are there boat trips?
Yǒu yóu chuán ma?
Can we make reservations here?
Wǒ men kě yǐ yù dìng ma?

IN THE TOWN

on/to the right
zài/dào yòu biān
on/to the left
zài/dào zuǒ biān
opposite
duì miàn
north
běi
south
nán
east
dōng
west
xī
toilets – men/women
cè suǒ – nán/nǚ

free
miăn fèi

donation
juān kuān

open
kāi

closed
guān bì

church
jiào táng

museum
bó wù guăn

monument
jì niàn bēi

palace
gōng diàn

town
chéng zhèn

road
lu

street
jiē dào

bridge
qiáo

no entry
bù kě rù nèi

NUMBERS

0	líng
1	yī
2	èr
3	sān
4	sì
5	wŭ
6	liù
7	qī
8	bā
9	jiŭ
10	shí
11	shí yī
12	shí èr
13	shí sān
14	shí sì
15	shí wŭ
16	shí liù
17	shí qī
18	shí bā
19	shí jiŭ
20	èr shí
21	èr shí yī
30	sān shí
40	sì shí
50	wŭ shí
60	liù shí
70	qī shí
80	bā shí
90	jiŭ shí

100	yì băi
1,000	yì qiān
million	băi wàn
quarter	sì fēn zhī yī
half	bàn

TIME/DAYS/MONTHS/HOLIDAYS

Monday	Xīng qī yī
Tuesday	Xīng qī èr
Wednesday	Xīng qī sān
Thursday	Xīng qī sì
Friday	Xīng qī wŭ
Saturday	Xīng qī liù
Sunday	Xīng qī tiān(rì)
morning	zăo shàng
afternoon	xià wŭ
evening	wăn shang
night	yè wăn
day	rì
month	yuè
year	nián
today	jīn tiān
yesterday	zuó tiān
tomorrow	míng tiān
January	yī yuè
February	èr yuè
March	sān yuè
April	sì yuè
May	wŭ yuè

June	liù yuè
July	qī yuè
August	bā yuè
September	jiŭ yuè
October	shí yuè
November	shí yī yuè
December	shí èr yuè
Easter	fù huó jié
National Holiday	guó dìng jià rì
Christmas	shèng dàn jié
New Year's Eve	chú xī
New Year's Day	yuán dàn

COLOURS

black	hēi sè
brown	hè sè zong sè
	(straight line over the 'o')
pink	fěn hóng sè
red	hóng sè
orange	jú sè chéng sè
yellow	huáng sè
green	lü sè
blue	lán sè
purple	zĭ sè
white	bái sè
gold	jīn sè
silver	yín sè
gray	huī sè
turquoise	qī ān lán sè

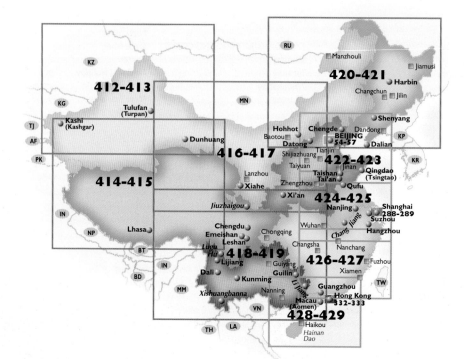

412-413

KZ

KG

TJ

AF

PK

IN

NP

Kashi (Kashgar)

Tulufan (Turpan)

Dunhuang

414-415

Lhasa

BT

IN

BD

MM

416-417

MN

Hohhot
Baotou
Datong
Shijiazhuang
Lanzhou
Taiyuan
Xiahe
Zhengzhou
Xi'an

Jiuzhaigou

Chengdu
Emeishan
Leshan
Lugu Hu
Lijiang
Dali
Kunming

Xishuangbanna

VN

TH   LA

RU

Manzhouli
Jiamusi

420-421

Changchun   Jilin

Harbin

Shenyang

Chengde   Dandong
BEIJING
54-57
Tianjin
Dalian
KP

KR

422-423
Jinan
Taishan   Qingdao
Tai'an   (Tsingtao)
Qufu

424-425
Nanjing   Shanghai
288-289
Wuhan   Suzhou
Chang Jiang   Hangzhou

Chongqing

Changsha   Nanchang

426-427   Fuzhou
Guiyang   Xiamen
Guilin   Li Jiang
Nanning   TW
Guangzhou
Macau   Hong Kong
(Aomen)   332-333
428-429
Haikou
Hainan Dao

412-421
0 — 150 km
0 — 100 miles

422-429
0 — 100 km
0 — 50 miles

▬▬▬	Motorway (Expressway)	National park
▬▬▬	National road	● Featured place of interest
▬▬▬	Regional road	ᴖᴖᴖ Great Wall of China
------	Railway	🌳 Natural place of interest
▦▦▦	International boundary	✈ Airport
▦ ▦	Undefined international boundary	621 ▲ Height in metres
--- ---	Province / Administrative region boundary	▬ Mountain pass
■	City / Town	⌂— Port / Ferry route

MAPS

Map references for the sights refer to the atlas pages within this section or to the individual town plans within the regions. For example, Harbin has the reference ✚ 421 U4, indicating the page on which the map is found (421) and the grid square in which Harbin sits (U4).

I — A B C D E

A Öskemen Ust'-Kamenogorsk

Kalbinskij toglari

Büktyrma bögeni

2

Zaïsan

KZ

Ataköl

3

Tacheng

Emin He Emin
Yumin 2540
2923 Toli
Miaoergou

Žongar Alatauy 4442
Taldykorǵan 4370 Bole
Alataw Shankou
Žongar Kakpasy
Dzungarian Gate
Ebinur Hu Tachakou

4 A353 312 Jinghe Shaquanzi 217
Korgas Huocheng 312 *B o r o h o r o S h a n*
Yining Nilka Usu Kuytun
Biškek Almaty 218 2082 5500

Gongliu *Kax He*
Zhaosu Tekes Xinyuan *Künes He*

Ysyk-Köl Xiatai
6995 Bayanbulak Adunkur Daban
KG 7439 Hantengri Feng 5068 4553 217
Ženis č *H a l k e S h a n* 4224

5 5982 *T i a n*
5108 Turugart Shankou Baicheng *Kaidu He*
4960 Dankova č *Toxkan He* Karayulgun Kizil
Akqi Wushi Xinhe Kuqa
4556 3075 Aksu 314 Xayar Luntai 314
Uluggat 2641 2723 1032 *Tarim He*
Erkeč-Tam Wuqia Artux Sugun 314 Sanchakou Awat
6 6146 Shufu 2103 Shangyou
5747 Kashi Bachu Yichang
pik Karasak (Kashgar) *Kaxgar He* Mazar Tag
Bulunkol Tazgun Yopurga 1181
7719 Serikbuya *Yarkant He*
7546 Kongur Shan 1560
Muztagata 5062 Markit *T a r i m P e n d i*
TJ Taheman Shache
Taxkorgan Zepu 414 *T a k l i m a k a n S h a m o*
Yecheng 1635 Mazartag
AF (Kargilik) Tongguzbasti
7 315 Pishan Mishaleyi
314 (Guma)
Yarkant He Sagan
5419 Moyu Tungaztarim 1253 315
35 K Akmeqit (Karakax) Shudanzhuang Qiemo
7783 Khunjerab 6482 Sanchakou Hotan 1363 Andir (Qarqan)
PK A Taturgou B Kangkir Lop C Qira D Yawatongguzlangar E Hadilik
Mazarwala Mazar 5466 *Qarqan He*
Xaidulla

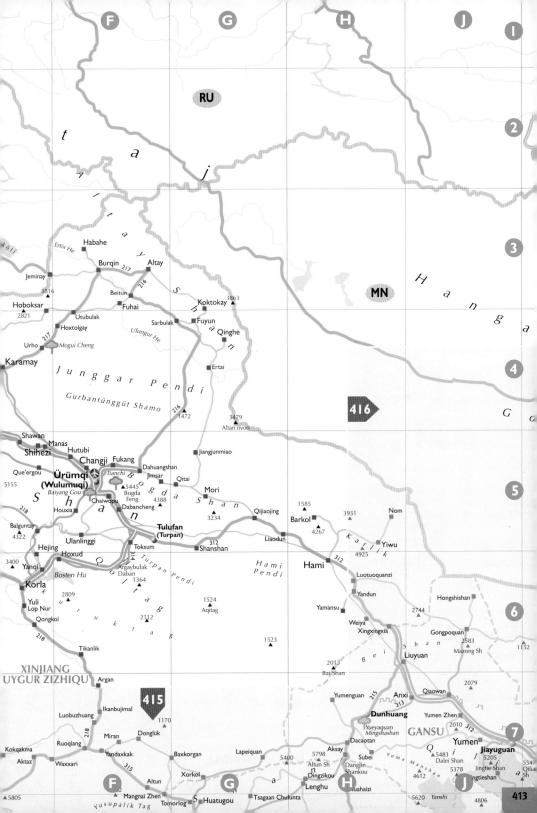

Tianshui · Wei He · Qianyang · Fengxiang · Xianyang · Weinan · Yangling · Weishi
Joné · Min Xian · Li Xian · Sanyuan · Huashan · Luoning · Yichuan · Ruzhou · Fugou · HENAN
Têwo · Dangchang · Maijishan · Feng Xian · Mei Xian · Taibai · Zhouzhi · Huangchi · Lintong · Lushi · 2094 · Song Xian · Baofeng · Pingdingshan · Xuchang
Jiangluo · Zhuqu · Cheng Xian · Taibai · Foping · Zhouzhi · 3015 · Linchang · Luonan · Luanchuan · Heyu · Lushan · Xiaofeng
Lianghekou · Lueyang · Liuba · Foping · Jingyu · Nao 2076 · Shangzhou · Danfeng · 2153 · Nanzhao · Ye Xian · Wuyang · Fangcheng · Luohe
Wudu · Wangziguan · Mian Xian · Chenggu · Zhen'an · Ningshan · Shiquan · 1444 · Xiaohe · Yun Xian · Shiyan · Danjiangkou · Laohekou · Xinyang
Nanping · Wen Xian · Bikou · Ningqiang · Hanzhong · Xixiang · Hanyin · Ziyang · Ankang · Wudangkou · Zaoyang · Xiangfan · Suizhou · Guangshui · Dawu · Anlu
Songpan · 5588 · Xuebao Ding · Qingchuan · 108 · Zhenba · Daba Shan · 2017 · Zhenping · Zhuxi · Zhushan · Fang Xian · Baokang · Nanzhang · Yicheng · Hongshan · Ringba · Zhongxiang · Jingshan · Yingcheng
Mao Xian · Beichuan · Jiangyou · Cangxi · Bazhong · Pingchang · 1253 · Qishu · Wuxi · Daninghe · 3105 · Xingshan · Hehua · Jingmen · WUHAN
Dujiangyan · Mianyang · Deyang · Nanbu · Lishan · Xuanhan · Kai Xian · Jiangkou · 1586 · Wushan · Badong · Zigui · Yuquanshan · Tianmen · Xiantao
CHENGDU · Suining · Yuechi · Changle · Guang'an · Liangping · Wufeng · Jiangling · Shashi · Tonghaiko · Honghu
Leshan · Zigong · Neijiang · Longchang · Jiangjin · Enshi · Xuan'en · Hefeng · Guandiping · Cili · Linli · Yueyang · Tongcheng
Yibin · Hejiang · Chishui · Xishui · Zheng'an · Dejian · Xiushan · Huayuan · Jishou · Luxi · HUNAN · CHANGSHA
Zunyi · Bijie · Dafang · Renhuai · Suiyang · Meitan · Sinan · Tongren · Huaihua · Shaoyang · Loudi · Lianyuan · Shuangfeng · You Xian · Hengyang
GUIYANG · Kaili · Duyun · Huangping · Jianhe · Jinping · Huitong · Suining · Tongdao · Ziyuan · Quanzhou · Guiyang · Chenzhou · Zixing
Anshun · Guanling · Ziyun · Luodian · Dushan · Congjiang · Rong'an · Guilin · Yangshuo · Lianshan · Lian Xian · Yangshan · Yingde
Qujing · Xingren · Anlong · Ceheng · Wangmo · Hechi · Luocheng · Liuzhou · Lipu · Liangtang · GUANGDONG
Lunan · Luxi · Bama · Bose · Yishan · Liujiang · Mengshan · Zhaoping · Huaiji · Qingyuan · Fogan
Kaiyuan · Mengzi · Yanshan · Funing · Tiandong · Pingguo · Wuming · NANNING · Guigang · Pingnan · Wuzhou · Zhaoqing · Foshan
Maguan · Napo · Debao · Jingxi · Longzhou · Ningming · Qinzhou · Hepu · Huazhou · Maoming · Yangjiang
VN · HÀ NỘI · Fangcheng Gang · Beihai · Zhanjiang · Leizhou Bandao · Houhai
CHONGQING · Jiulongpo · Nanchuan · Wulong · Pengshui · Youyang · Dayong · Changde · Yiyang · Xiangtan · Zhuzhou · Liling · Pingxia

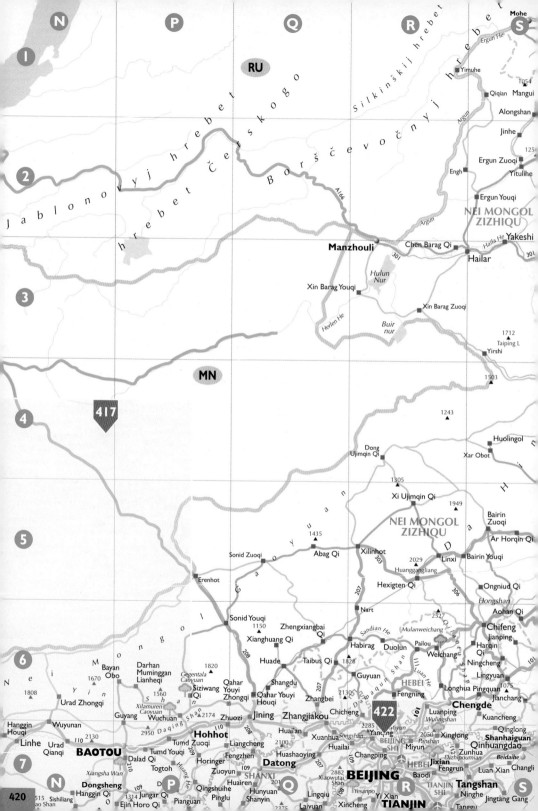

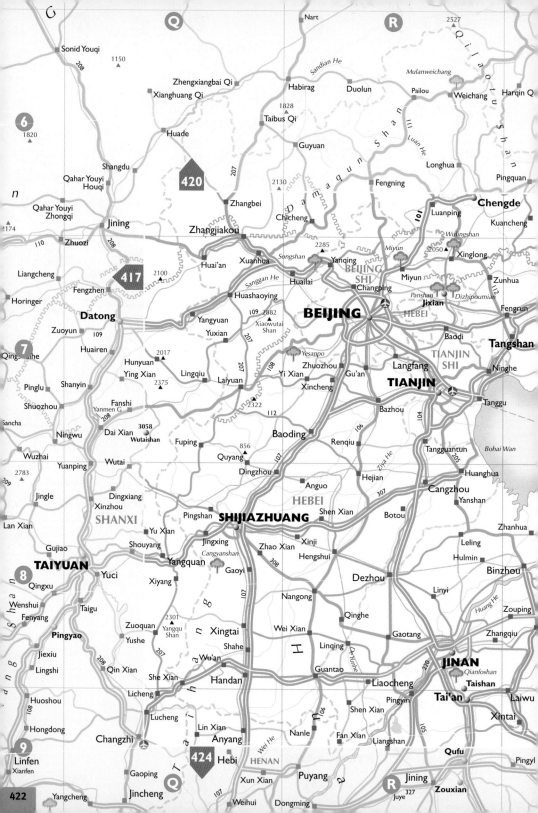

Hongshan

S

Aohan Qi

Chifeng

Baoguolao

Jianping

Ningcheng

Chaoyang

101

Lingyuan

1075

Jianchang

306

Qinglong

1306

Changli

Luan Xian

Jingtang Gang

Bo Hai

Beipiao

Yi Xian

Rishi

Yiwulüshan

Fuxin

Beizhen

Jinzhou

Goubangzi

Panjin

Jinxi

Shuangtaihekou

Xingcheng

Xiongyuecheng

Suizhong

Liaodong
Wan

202

Fuzhouzhen

Xinjin

Shanhaiguan

Qinhuangdao

Beidaihe

Xinmin

T

Liao

SHENYANG

Liaozhong

Dawa

305

421

Yingkou
(Dashiqiao)

Gai Xian

1131

Buyun
Shan

Fushun

202

Yongling

Xinbin

1335

201

U

LIAONING

Huajianzi

1325

Huanren

Baishilazi

Benxi Shuidong

Fenghuangshan

Annok Gang

Kuandian

6

Benxi

Liaoyang

Anshan

Caohekou

Qianshan

Haicheng

Qian Shan

1110

Fengcheng

304

Xiuyan

Dagushan

305

Dandong

Sinŭiju

KP

Donggou

Sinmi-do

Sŏjosŏn-man

Wafangdian

Zhuanghe

Liaodong Bandao

Changshan Qundao

Laotieshan
Shedao

Jinzhou

Dalian

Lüshun

Bohai Haixia

Miaodao Qundao

7

Ch'o-do

Baegnyeongdo

Wuhao Zhuang

Huanghe Kou

Dongying Qu

Dongying

Laizhou Wan

220

Guangrao

309

Zibo

Qingzhou

Weifang

Linqu

Anqiu

1098

Lushan

SHANDONG

Yiyuan

Fei Xian

327

Junan

Linyi

S

Penglai

Longkou

818

204

Qixia

Laizhou

309

Pingdu

Laixi

Jiaozhou

1158

Laoshan

Qingdao
(Tsingtao)

Zhucheng

Jiaonan

206

Yishui

Mengyin

Ju Xian

515

Rizhao

Haizhou
Wan

T

Bajiao Qu

Yantai

923

Wendeng

Rushan

Laiyang

Haiyang

425

Weihai

Rongcheng

Shidao

H u a n g   H a i

8

9

U

423

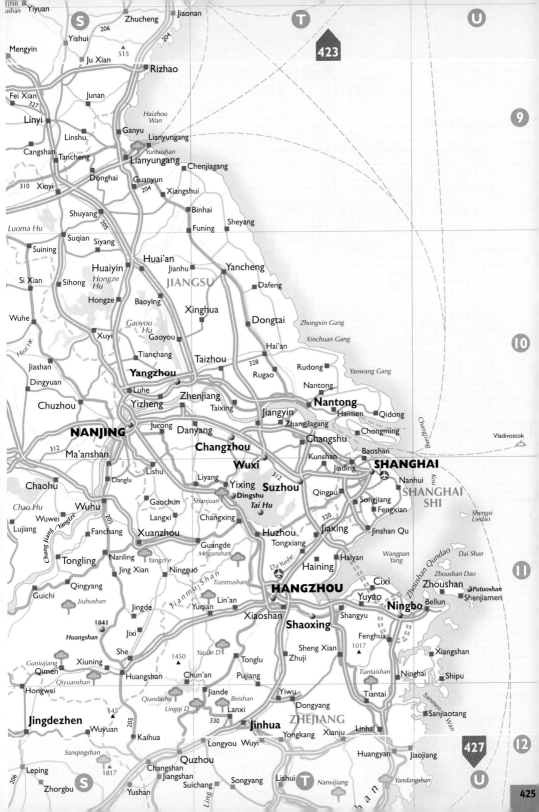

1098
ushan   Yiyuan
Zhucheng   Jiaonan

Yishui
206

Mengyin   Ju Xian
515

Rizhao

Fei Xian
327
Junan
Linyi
Linshu   Ganyu
Haizhou
Wan
Cangshan   Tancheng
Lianyungang
Yuntaishan
Donghai   Chenjiagang
310   Xinyi
Guanyun
204
Shuyang   Xiangshui
205
Luoma Hu   Binhai
Suqian   Siyang
Suining   Funing   Sheyang
Si Xian   Sihong   Huaiyin   Huai'an
Hongze   Jianhu
Hu   JIANGSU   Yancheng
Wuhe   Hongze   Dafeng
Baoying
Jiashan   Xuyi   Gaoyou   Xinghua
Huai He   Hu   Dongtai
Dingyuan   Gaoyou   Zhongxin Gang
Tianchang   Hai'an   Xinchuan Gang
Chuzhou   Taizhou   328   Rudong
Yangzhou   Rugao   Yaowang Gang
Luhe   Nantong
NANJING   Yizheng   Zhenjiang
312   Jurong   Danyang   Taixing   Jiangyin   Nantong
Ma'anshan   Changzhou   Zhangjiagang   Haimen   Qidong
Danglu   Lishu   Wuxi   Changshu   Chongming
Chaohu   Liyang   Yixing   Kunshan   Baoshan
Wuhu   Gaochun   Yixing   Suzhou   Jiading   SHANGHAI
Wuwei   Langxi   Dingshu   Qingpu   Nanhui
Lujiang   Fanchang   Changxing   Tai Hu   Songjiang   SHANGHAI SHI
Chang Jiang / Yangtze   Xuanzhou   Huzhou   Jiaxing   Fengxian
Tongling   Nanling   Guangde   Tongxiang   Jinshan Qu   Shengsi Liedao
Qingyang   Jing Xian   Ningguo   Moganshan   320
Guichi   Jiuhushan   Da Yunhe   Haiyan   Wangpan Yang
Jingde   Lin'an   Haining   Cixi   Zhoushan   Dai Shan
1841   Yuqian   HANGZHOU   Yuyao   Zhoushan Dao
Huangshan   Jixi   Xiaoshan   Shangyu   Ningbo   Bellun   Putuoshan
She   1450   Shaoxing   Shangyu   Shenjiamen
Qimen   Xiuning   Yaolin D   Tonglu   Sheng Xian   Fenghua   Xiangshan
Guniujiang   Huangshan   Chun'an   Pujiang   Zhuji   1017   Shipu
Qiyuanshan   Tiantaishan   Ninghai
Hongwei   Qiandashu   Beishan   Tiantai
Jingdezhen   Lingqi D   Jiande   Lanxi   Yiwu   Dongyang   Sanjiaotang
145   Wuyuan   330   Jinhua   Xianju   Linhai
Kaihua   Yongkang   Sanmen Wan
Longyou   Wuyi   ZHEJIANG   Huangyan   Jiaojiang
Sanqingshan   1817   Quzhou   Lishui   Yandangshan
Leping   Changshan   Jiangshan   Songyang   Nanxijiang
Zhorgbu   Yushan   Suichang   Ling

Vladivostok   Changjiang   Kou

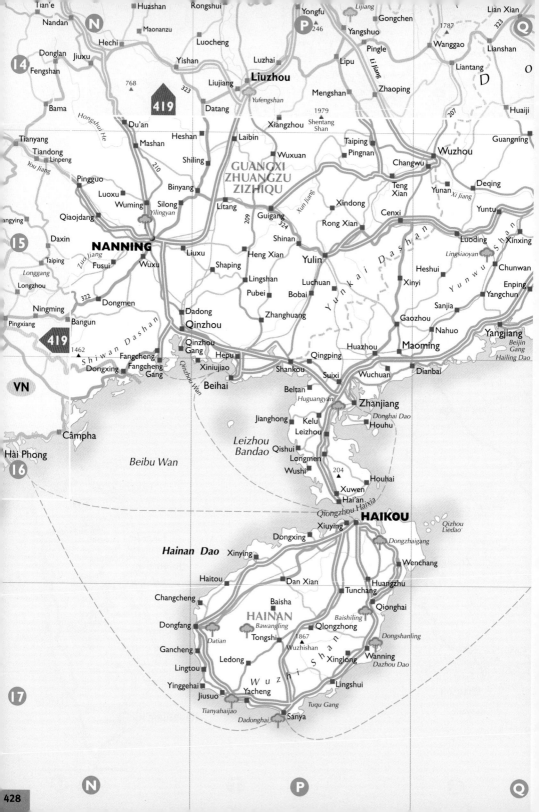

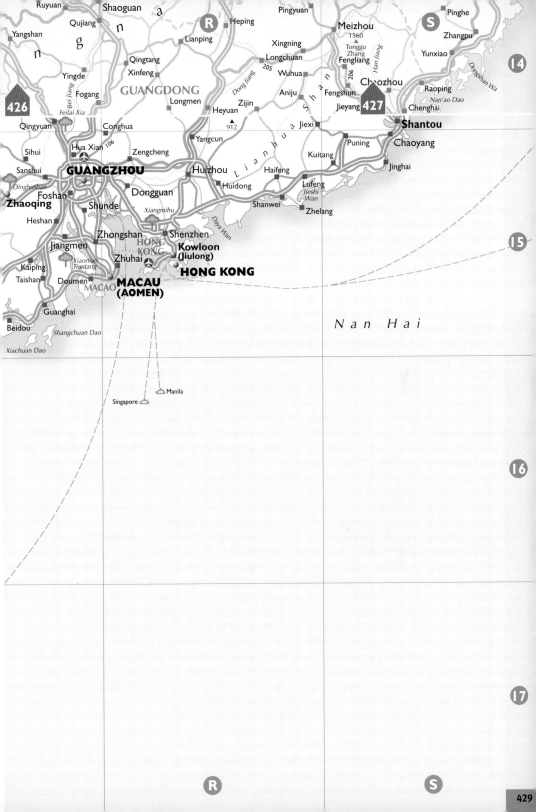

Ruyuan
Shaoguan
n a
Pingyuan
Pinghe

R
Heping
Meizhou
1560
S
Zhangpu

Qujiang
Lianping
Xingning
Tonggu
Zhang
Yunxiao

Yangshan
g
Longchuan
Fengliang
Zhangpu

n
Qingtang
Wuhua
206
Choozhou
Raoping
Nan'ao Dao

Yingde
Xinfeng
Aniju
Fengshun
Chenghai
Dongshan Wa

GUANGDONG
Longmen
Zijin
Jieyang
427
Shantou

426
Fogang
Heyuan
Jiexi

Bei Jiang
Feilai Xia
912
Yangcun

Qingyuan
Conghua
Puning
Chaoyang

Sihui
Hua Xian
106
Zengcheng
Kuitang
Jinghai

Sanshui
GUANGZHOU
Huizhou
Haifeng
Lufeng

Dinghushan
Huidong
Jieshi
Wan

Foshan
Dongguan
Shanwei
Zhelang

Zhaoqing
Shunde
Xiangmihu

Heshan
Zhongshan
Shenzhen
Daya Wan

Jiangmen
HONG
KONG
Kowloon
(Jiulong)

Kaiping
Xiaomao
Tiantang
Zhuhai

Taishan
HONG KONG

Doumen
MACAU
(AOMEN)

Guanghai
MACAO

Beidou
Shangchuan Dao
N a n   H a i

Xiachuan Dao

Manila

Singapore

14
15
16
17

L i a n h u a   S h a n
Dong Jiang
205
Han Jiang
Dongshan Wa

R
S

Name	Pg	Grid	Name	Pg	Grid	Name	Pg	Grid	Name	Pg	Grid
Aba	418	L10	Bayan	417	M7	Chaoyang	429	S15	Dawu	424	Q11
Abag Qi	420	Q5	Bayan	421	U3	Chaoyang	421	S6	Da Xian	419	N11
Acheng	421	U4	Bayanbulak	412	E5	Chaozhou	427	S14	Daxin	419	N15
Akmeqit	414	B7	Bayan Obo	417	P6	Chen Barag Qi	420	R3	Dayangshu	421	T2
Akqi	412	C6	Bayan Olji	417	M7	Chengbu	419	P13	Dayao	418	K14
Aksay	415	H7	Bayizhen	415	H12	Chengcheng	417	P9	Dayi	419	L11
Aksu	412	C6	Bazhong	419	N11	Chengde	422	R6	Dayong	419	P12
Aktaz	414	E7	Bazhou	422	R7	Chengdu	419	M11	Dayu	426	R14
Alongshan	420	S1	Bei'an	421	U3	Chenggong	418	L14	Dazhu	419	N11
Altay	413	F3	Beichuan	419	M11	Chenggu	419	N10	Dazu	419	M12
Altun	415	F7	Beidou	429	Q15	Chenghai	427	S14	De'an	426	R12
Alxa Youqi	416	L7	Beihai	428	P16	Chengjiang	418	L14	Debao	419	N15
Alxa Zuoqi	417	M8	Beijing	422	R7	Chengwu	424	R9	Dechang	418	L13
Amdo	415	G10	Beipiao	421	S6	Cheng Xian	417	M10	Dege	418	J11
Anda	421	T4	Beitun	413	F3	Chenjiagang	425	S9	Dehua	427	S13
Andirlangar	414	D7	Beizhen	421	T6	Chenxi	419	N12	Dehui	421	U4
Anfu	426	R13	Bellun	425	U11	Chenzhou	426	Q13	Dejian	419	N12
Anguo	422	R8	Beltan	428	P16	Chicheng	422	R6	Delingha	416	J8
Anhua	419	P12	Bengbu	424	S10	Chifeng	420	S6	Dengfeng	417	Q10
Aniju	426	R14	Benxi	421	T6	Chinmen	427	S14	Dengkou	417	N7
Ankang	419	N10	Benzilan	418	K13	Chishui	419	M12	Dêngqên	415	H11
Anlong	419	M14	Bijie	419	M13	Chishuihe	419	M13	Dengyuan	419	M12
Anlu	424	Q11	Bikou	419	M10	Chongming	425	T10	Dengzhou	419	Q10
Anqing	424	S11	Binhai	425	S9	Chongqing	419	L11	Dêqên	415	F11
Anqiu	423	S8	Bin Xian	417	N9	Chongqing	419	N12	Dêqên	418	J12
Ansai	417	N8	Bin Xian	421	U4	Chongren	426	R12	Deqing	428	Q15
Anshan	421	T6	Binyang	428	P15	Chongyang	424	Q12	Detuo	418	L12
Anshun	419	M13	Binzhou	422	S8	Chongyi	426	R13	Deyang	419	M11
Antu	421	V5	Biru	415	G11	Chun'an	425	S11	Dezhou	422	R8
Anxi	416	J7	Bishan	419	M12	Chunwan	428	Q15	Dianbai	428	Q16
Anxi	426	R12	Biyang	424	Q10	Chuxiong	418	K14	Ding'an	419	M14
An Xian	419	M11	Bobai	428	P15	Chuzhou	425	S10	Dingbian	417	N8
Anyang	422	Q9	Bole	412	D4	Cili	419	P12	Dinggye	414	E12
Anyuan	426	R14	Boli	421	V3	Cixi	425	T11	Dingnan	426	R14
Anyue	419	M12	Bomi	415	H12	Cona	415	G12	Dingtao	424	R9
Aohan Qi	420	S6	Boqên	415	H11	Conghua	429	R15	Dingxi	417	M9
Aqqan	414	E8	Bose	414	D8	Congjiang	419	N14	Dingxiang	417	Q8
Argan	413	F7	Bostan	414	D8	Coqên	414	D11	Dingxiao	419	M14
Ar Horqin Qi	420	S5	Botou	422	R8				Dingyuan	425	S10
Artux	412	B6	Boyang	426	S12	Da'an	421	T4	Dingzhou	422	Q8
Arun Qi	421	T3	Bozhou	424	R10	Dabancheng	413	F5	Dingzikou	415	H7
Atas Gompa	415	G11	Budongquan	415	H9	Dacaotan	415	H7	Ditang	419	N12
Awat	412	C6	Bugt	421	S3	Dadong	428	N15	Doba	415	F11
			Bulanghe	417	N8	Dafang	419	M13	Dobzha	414	E12
Babao	419	M15	Bulunkol	412	A6	Dafanpu	417	P7	Domar	414	C9
Bachu	412	B6	Burang	414	B11	Dafeng	425	T10	Donfeng	421	U5
Badong	419	P11	Burqin	413	F3	Daglung	415	F12	Dong'an	419	P13
Badu	426	R13	Butuo	418	L13	Daguan	419	L13	Dongchuan	419	L13
Baicheng	412	D5				Daguan	419	M12	Dongco	414	D10
Baicheng	421	T4	Caiyuan	418	L14	Dagushan	423	T6	Dongfang	419	P12
Baihe	419	P10	Caka	416	K8	Dagzhuka	415	F12	Dongfang	428	P17
Baihe	421	V5	Cangshan	425	S9	Daheba	416	K9	Donggou	423	U7
Baila	414	E12	Cangxi	419	M11	Dahequ	416	L8	Dongguan	418	K15
Bailang	419	N14	Cangyuan	418	J15	Dahongliutan	414	B8	Dongguan	429	R15
Baima	418	K10	Cangzhou	422	R8	Dahuangshan	413	F5	Donghai	425	S9
Baingoin	415	F11	Canmang	419	P12	Dai Xian	417	Q7	Dongjingcheng	421	V4
Baiquan	421	U3	Caohekou	421	T6	Dajing	417	L8	Dongkeng	427	T12
Bairin Youqi	420	R5	Caojian	418	J14	Dajiuba	415	F8	Dongkou	419	P13
Bairin Zuoqi	420	S5	Cao Xian	424	R9	Dakelangsi	414	F11	Donglan	419	N14
Baisha	419	M12	Ceheng	419	M14	Dakeshi	414	F12	Donglük	415	F7
Baisha	428	P17	Cenxi	428	P15	Dalad Qi	417	P7	Dongmen	428	N15
Baishan	421	U5	Cerwa	416	K10	Dali	418	K14	Dongming	424	R9
Baishui	417	P9	Cêtar	416	K8	Dali	417	P9	Dongning	421	W4
Baiyin	417	M9	Cha'anpu	419	P12	Dalian	423	T7	Dongpo	414	B10
Bajiao Qu	423	T8	Chaiwopu	413	F5	Dalu	417	M9	Dongqiao	415	F10
Bajie	419	M14	Chalengkou	415	H8	Damenglong	418	K16	Dongsheng	417	P7
Balguntay	413	E5	Chaling	426	Q13	Damtang	414	C9	Dongtai	425	T10
Balong	416	J9	Changbai	421	V6	Damxung	415	F11	Dong Ujimqin Qi	420	R4
Bama	419	N14	Changcheng	428	P17	Danba	418	L11	Dongxiang	426	S12
Banbar	415	H11	Changchun	421	U5	Dandong	423	U6	Dongxing	428	P16
Bangda	418	J11	Changde	419	Q12	Danfeng	417	P10	Dongxing	428	P16
Bangun	428	N15	Changfeng	424	S10	Dangchang	417	M10	Dongyang	425	T10
Banjia	418	J15	Changji	413	F5	Danglu	425	S11	Dongying	423	S8
Baode	417	P7	Changle	419	M11	Dangshan	424	R9	Dongying Qu	423	S8
Baodi	422	R7	Changle	427	T13	Dangyang	419	Q11	Dongzhi	424	S11
Baoding	422	R7	Changli	423	S7	Daning	417	P9	Dorbod	421	T3
Baofeng	417	Q10	Changling	421	T4	Danjiangkou	419	P10	Dougmuge	419	L15
Baofeng	424	Q10	Changning	418	K14	Dan Xian	428	P16	Doumen	429	Q15
Baoguolao	421	S6	Changning	419	M12	Danyang	425	T10	Douqing	419	M13
Baoji	417	N10	Changning	426	Q13	Daotanghe	416	K9	Du'an	428	N14
Baojing	419	P12	Changping	422	R7	Daozhen	419	N12	Duansban	419	N14
Baokang	419	P11	Changsha	426	Q12	Dapuchaihe	421	V5	Dujiangyan	419	L11
Baoqing	421	W3	Changshan	427	S12	Da Qaidam	415	H8	Dulan	416	J9
Baoshan	418	J14	Changshu	425	T10	Daqiao	419	L13	Dunhua	421	V5
Baoshan	425	T10	Changshun	419	M14	Daqing	421	T3	Dunhuang	415	H7
Baotou	417	P7	Changtai	427	S14	Darhan Muminggan Lianheqi	417	P6	Duolun	420	R6
Baoxing	418	L12	Changting	426	S13	Darlag	416	K10	Dushan	419	N14
Baoying	425	S10	Changtu	421	T5	Dashuiking	417	N8	Duyun	419	N13
Barga	414	C10	Changwu	420	Q15	Datang	419	P14			
Barkam	418	L11	Changxing	425	T11	Datian	427	S13	Ebian	419	L12
Barkol	413	H5	Changyang	419	M13	Dating	419	N14	Ejin Horo Qi	417	P7
Basaguke	414	D11	Changyuan	424	Q9	Datong	416	L8	Ejin Qi	416	K6
Batang	418	K12	Changzhi	417	Q9	Datong	417	Q7	Emeishan	419	L12
Baxkorgan	415	G7	Changzhou	425	T10	Dawa	421	T6	Emin	412	E3
Baxol	418	J12	Chaohu	425	S11	Dawu	425	S11	Enda	418	J11

Name	Page	Grid
Engh	420	R2
Enping	428	Q15
Enshi	419	P12
Erdaobaihe	421	V5
Erenhot	420	P5
Ergun Youqi	420	S2
Ergun Zuoqi	420	S2
Ertai	413	G4
Eshan	418	L14
Ezhou	424	R11
Fa'er	419	M13
Faku	421	T5
Fanchang	425	S11
Fangcheng	428	N15
Fangcheng	424	Q10
Fangcheng Gang	428	N16
Fang Xian	419	P11
Fangzheng	421	V4
Fanshi	417	Q7
Fan Xian	422	R9
Fanxue	417	N8
Fei Xian	425	S9
Fengcheng	426	R12
Fengcheng	421	U6
Fengdu	419	N12
Fenggang	419	N13
Fenghua	425	T11
Fenghuang	419	P13
Fengjie	419	P11
Fengliang	426	S14
Fengning	420	R6
Fengpo	418	K15
Fengqiu	424	Q9
Fengrun	422	S7
Fengshan	419	N14
Fengshun	426	S14
Feng Xian	417	M10
Fengxian	425	T11
Fengxiang	417	N10
Fengxin	426	R12
Fengzhen	417	Q7
Fenyang	417	P8
Fogang	426	Q14
Foping	417	N10
Foshan	429	Q15
Fuding	427	T12
Fufeng	417	N10
Fugong	418	J13
Fugou	424	Q10
Fugu	417	P7
Fuhai	413	F3
Fujin	421	W3
Fukang	413	F5
Fuling	419	N12
Funing	419	M15
Funing	425	S9
Fuping	417	N9
Fuping	422	Q7
Fuqing	427	T13
Fushun	421	T6
Fusong	421	V5
Fusui	428	N15
Fu Xian	417	N9
Fuxin	421	T6
Fuyang	424	R10
Fuyu	421	T3
Fuyu	421	T4
Fuyuan	419	M14
Fuyuan	421	W2
Fuyun	413	G4
Fuzhou	427	T13
Fuzhouzhen	423	T7
Gai Xian	423	T6
Gala	414	F12
Gamba	414	E12
Gancheng	428	P17
Gangca	416	K8
Gangchang	419	N11
Ganhe	421	S2
Ganluo	418	L12
Gannan	421	T3
Gansen	415	G8
Ganquan	417	N9
Gantang	417	M8
Ganxi	419	P12
Ganyu	425	S9
Ganzhou	426	R13
Gao'an	426	R12
Gaochun	425	S11
Gaojiabu	417	P8
Gaolan	417	L9
Gaoping	417	Q9
Gaotai	416	K7
Gaotang	422	R8
Gao Xian	419	M12
Gaoyi	422	Q8
Gaoyou	425	S10
Gaozhou	428	P15
Gar Xincun	414	B10
Garyarsa (Gartok)	414	B10
Garzê	418	K11
Gashunchaka	415	H8
Gawa Obo	416	J9
Gê'gyai	414	C10
Gebituolatuo	415	G8
Gejiu	419	L15
Gengma	418	K15
Gêrzê	414	D10
Golmud	415	H9
Golog Maqên	416	K10
Gong'an	419	Q12
Gongbo'gyamda	415	G12
Gongchen	419	P14
Gonggar	415	F12
Gonghe	416	K9
Gongliu	412	D5
Gongpoquan	416	J6
Gongshan	418	J13
Gong Xian	419	M12
Gongyi	417	Q9
Gongzhuling	421	U5
Goubangzi	421	T6
Gu'an	422	R7
Guandiping	419	P12
Guang'an	419	N11
Guangchang	426	S13
Guangde	425	T11
Guanghai	429	Q15
Guangning	428	Q14
Guangrao	423	S8
Guangshui	424	Q11
Guangxuan	419	M11
Guangze	427	S13
Guangzhou	429	Q15
Guanling	419	M14
Guanqiao	417	M9
Guantao	422	R8
Guanyun	425	S9
Gudong	418	J14
Guichi	425	S11
Guiding	419	N13
Guidong	426	R13
Guigang	428	P15
Guihua	419	M11
Guilin	419	P14
Guixi	427	S12
Guiyang	419	N13
Guiyang	426	R12
Gujiao	417	P8
Gulang	416	L8
Gulian	421	S1
Günsang	414	C11
Guocheng	417	M9
Guoyang	424	R10
Guru	414	F12
Gushi	418	H11
Gushi	424	R10
Gutian	427	T13
Gutsuo	412	D12
Guyang	417	P6
Guyuan	417	M9
Guyuan	420	R6
Guzhen	427	T13
Gyaca	415	G12
Gyirong	414	D12
Gyitang	418	J11
Handan	422	Q8
Hanggin Houqi	417	N7
Hanggin Qi	417	N7
Hanglong	419	N14
Hangzhou	425	T11
Hanyin	419	N10
Hanyuan	418	L12
Hanzhong	419	N10
Haotan	417	N8
Harbin	421	U4
Harqin Qi	420	S6
Haya'er	415	G8
Hebi	424	Q9
Hechi	419	N14
Hechuan	419	M12
Hefei	424	S10
Hefeng	419	P12
Hegang	421	V3
Hehelek	414	C8
Hehua	419	P11
Heihe	421	U2
Heimahe	416	K9
Hejiang	422	R8
Hejiang	419	M12
Hejin	417	P9
Hejing	413	E5
Hekou	417	L9
Helan	417	M8
Helong	421	V5
Hengshan	426	Q13
Hengshui	422	R8
Heng Xian	428	P15
Hengyang	426	Q13
Heping	426	R14
Hepu	428	P15
Heqing	418	K13
Heshan	428	P15
Heshan	429	Q15
Heshui	428	Q15
Hexigten Qi	420	R5
Heyang	417	P9
Heyu	417	P10
Heyuan	426	R14
Heze	424	R9
Hezhang	419	M13
Hezuozhen	416	L9
Hoboksar	413	E3
Hohhot	417	P7
Hong'an	424	R11
Hongde	417	N8
Hongdong	417	P9
Hongguqu	416	L9
Honghu	424	Q12
Hongjiang	419	P13
Hong Kong	429	R15
Hongliuyuan	416	K7
Hongshan	424	Q11
Hongshishan	416	J6
Hongwei	425	S12
Hongya	417	M9
Hongyuan	424	R10
Hongze	425	S10
Horinger	417	P7
Horqin Youji Zhongqi	421	S4
Horqin Zuoyi Houqi	421	T5
Horqin Zuoyi Zhongqi	421	T5
Horra	415	F11
Hotan	414	C7
Houhai	428	P16
Houhu	428	P16
Houma	417	P9
Houxia	413	F5
Hoxtolgay	413	F4
Hoxud	413	F6
Hua'an	427	S14
Huachi	417	N9
Huade	420	Q6
Huadian	421	U5
Huahaizi	415	H7
Huai'an	422	Q7
Huai'an	425	S10
Huaibei	424	R10
Huaibin	424	R10
Huaihua	419	P13
Huaiji	426	Q14
Huailai	422	R7
Huairen	417	Q7
Huaiyin	425	S10
Huaiyuan	424	S10
Huajianzi	421	U6
Hualong	416	L9
Huanan	421	V3
Huangchuan	424	Q11
Huanggang	424	R11
Huanghua	422	R8
Huangling	417	N9
Huanglong	417	P9
Huangmei	424	R11
Huangpi	424	R11
Huangping	419	N13
Huangsha	427	T13
Huangshan	425	S11
Huangshi	424	R11
Huangyan	427	T12
Huangyuan	416	K9
Huangzhong	416	L9
Huangzhu	428	P16
Huaning	418	L14
Huanren	421	U6
Huan Xian	417	N9
Huaping	418	K13
Huarong	419	Q12
Huashan	419	N14
Huashaoying	422	Q7
Huatugou	415	G8
Hua Xian	429	Q15
Huaying	419	N11
Huaying	417	P9
Huayuan	419	P12
Huazhou	428	P15
Huguo	419	M12
Hui'an	427	T14
Hui'anpu	417	M8
Huichang	426	R13
Huichuan	417	L9
Huidong	418	L13
Huidong	429	R15
Huili	418	L13
Huinan	421	U5
Huining	417	M9
Huinong	417	M7
Huitong	419	P13
Huize	419	L13
Huizhou	429	R15
Hukou	424	R12
Hulan	421	U4
Hulin	421	W3
Hulmin	422	R8
Huma	421	T1
Hunchun	421	W5
Hunjiang	421	U5
Hunyuan	422	Q7
Huocheng	412	D4
Huolingol	420	S4
Huoqiu	424	R10
Huoshan	424	R11
Huoshou	417	P9
Hure Qi	421	T5
Hutou	421	W3
Hutubi	413	F5
Huxi Xincun	416	K7
Huzhou	425	T11
Huzhu Tuzu Zizhixian	416	L8
Ikanbujimal	415	F7
Iqe	415	H8
Jagdaqi	421	T2
Jaggang	414	B9
Jalaid Qi	421	T4
Jarud Qi	421	S5
Jeminay	413	E3
Ji'an	426	R13
Ji'an	421	U6
Jiading	425	T11
Jiahe	426	Q14
Jiamusi	421	V3
Jian'ou	427	S13
Jianchang	420	S6
Jianchang	423	S6
Jianchuan	418	K13
Jiande	425	T12
Jiangbai	418	L15
Jiangcheng	418	L15
Jiange	419	M11
Jianghong	428	P16
Jianghua	419	Q14
Jiangjin	419	M12
Jiangjunmiao	413	G5
Jiangkou	419	N11
Jiangkou	419	N13
Jiangle	427	S13
Jiangling	419	Q11
Jiangluo	419	M10
Jiangmen	429	Q15
Jiangshan	427	S12
Jiangyin	425	T10
Jiangyong	419	Q14

Name	Pg	Ref	Name	Pg	Ref	Name	Pg	Ref	Name	Pg	Ref
Mengshan	419	P14	Ningan	418	L13	Putian	427	T13	Raba	418	K11
Mengxing	418	K15	Ningbo	425	T11	Pu Xian	417	P9	Radzi	418	J11
Mengyin	423	S9	Ningcheng	420	S6	Puyang	424	R9	Raka	414	D11
Mengzhou	417	Q9	Ningde	427	T13				Raohe	421	W3
Mengzi	419	L15	Ningdu	426	R13	Qab	417	N8	Raoping	427	S14
Menyuan	416	L8	Ningguo	425	S11	Qagan Nur	417	N7	Rasha	418	K11
Mianning	418	L12	Ninghai	425	T11	Qagan Tohoi	415	H9	Rawu	418	J12
Mian Xian	419	N10	Ninghe	422	R7	Qagcaka	414	C10	Renhe	419	N12
Mianyang	419	M11	Ninghua	427	S13	Qahar Youyi Houqi	420	Q6	Renhua	426	R14
Mianzhu	419	M11	Ningming	419	N15	Qahar Youyi Zhongqi	417	P6	Renhuai	419	M13
Miaoergou	412	E4	Ningqiang	419	M10	Qamdo	418	J11	Renmei	418	K11
Miaozu	419	M14	Ningshan	419	N10	Qarhan	415	H8	Renqiu	422	R7
Midu	418	K14	Ningwu	417	P7	Qian'an	421	T4	Renshi	419	N11
Mile	419	L14	Ning Xian	417	N9	Qianheshangyuan	417	N9	Renshou	419	M12
Miluo	426	Q12	Ningxiang	426	Q12	Qianjiang	419	N12	Ringba	424	Q11
Minfeng	414	D8	Nishi	419	P12	Qianjiang	424	Q11	Riwoqê	418	J11
Minggang	424	Q10	Niuchang	419	M14	Qianwei	419	L12	Rizhao	425	S9
Mingshui	421	U3	Nom	416	H5	Qianxi	419	M13	Rong'an	419	P14
Mingxi	427	S13	Nomhon	416	J9	Qianyang	417	N9	Rongcheng	423	T8
Minle	416	K8	Nong'an	421	U4	Qianyang	419	P13	Rongjiang	419	N14
Minqin	417	L8	Nongchang	417	N8	Qiaochuan	417	N9	Rongjiang	419	P14
Minqing	427	T13	Norba	418	J11	Qiaojdang	428	N15	Rongxar	414	E12
Minquan	424	R9	Nyainrong	415	G10	Qiaojia	418	L13	Rong Xian	419	M12
Min Xian	417	L10	Nyalam	414	D12	Qiaowan	416	J7	Rong Xian	428	P15
Miran	415	F7	Nyima	414	E10	Qiaozhen	417	N9	Rucheng	426	Q14
Mirong	418	L15	Nyingchi	415	H12	Qichun	424	R11	Rudong	425	T10
Mishaleyi	414	C7				Qidong	425	T10	Rugao	425	T10
Mishan	421	W3	Obo	416	K8	Qidugou	415	H9	Rui'an	427	T12
Miyi	418	L13	Oma	414	C10	Qiemo (Qarqan)	414	E7	Ruichang	424	R12
Miyun	422	R7	Ongniud Qi	420	S5	Qijiang	419	N12	Ruicheng	417	P9
Mizhi	417	P8	Oroqen Zizhiqi	421	T2	Qijiaojing	413	G5	Ruijin	426	R13
Moerkesung	414	D11	Otog Qi	417	N7	Qilian	416	K8	Ruili	418	J14
Mohe	420	S1	Otog Qian Qi	417	N8	Qimen	425	S11	Runan	424	Q10
Moincêr	414	B10	Ouchi	419	Q12	Qin'an	417	M9	Ruoqiang	415	F7
Mojiang	418	K15				Qing'an	421	U3	Rushan	423	T8
Mongotong	418	J12	Pagri	414	E12	Qingchuan	419	M10	Rutog	414	B9
Monza	415	G10	Pailou	420	R6	Qingdao (Tsingtao)	423	T8	Ruyuan	426	Q14
Mori	413	G5	Pangu	421	T1	Qinggang	421	U3	Ruzhou	417	Q10
Morin Dawa	421	T3	Pangzula	418	K12	Qinghe	413	G4			
Moyu (Karakax)	414	C7	Panjin	421	T6	Qinghe	422	R8	Saga	414	D11
Mubo	417	N9	Panlong	419	M11	Qingjian	417	P8	Sagan	414	B7
Muchuan	419	L12	Panshi	421	U5	Qingkou	419	N13	Saihan Toroi	416	K6
Mudanjiang	421	V4	Pan Xian	419	M14	Qinglong	423	S7	Sali	418	J13
Mugang	419	M15	Panzhihua	418	L13	Qingping	428	P15	Samsang	414	C11
Mulan	421	U3	Paryang	414	C11	Qingpu	425	T11	Sanba	418	K12
Muling	421	V4	Pei Xian	424	R9	Qingshui	424	R9	Sanbei Yangchang	417	N7
			Pemgze	424	R11	Qingshuihe	416	J10	Sancha	417	P7
Nagarzê	415	F12	Peng'an	419	M11	Qingtang	417	P7	Sanchakou	412	B6
Naggu	415	G11	Pengkou	427	S13	Qingtian	427	T12	Sangsang	414	E11
Nahuo	428	Q15	Penglai	423	T8	Qingtongxia	417	M8	Sangzhi	419	P12
Naij Tal	415	H9	Pengshan	419	L12	Qingxu	417	P8	Sanjia	428	Q15
Naiman Qi	421	S5	Pengshui	419	N12	Qingyang	417	N9	Sanjiang	419	P14
Namco	415	F11	Pianguan	417	P7	Qingyang	425	S11	Sanjiangtang	425	U12
Namling	414	E11	Ping'an	416	L9	Qingyuan	429	Q14	Sanmenxia	417	P9
Namru	414	B10	Pingchang	419	N11	Qingyuan	421	U5	Sanming	427	S13
Nanbu	419	M11	Pingdingshan	424	Q10	Qingzhen	419	M13	Sanshui	429	Q15
Nanchang	426	R12	Pingdu	423	S8	Qingzhou	423	S8	Sansui	419	N13
Nancheng	426	S13	Pingguo	428	N15	Qinhuangdao	423	S7	Santai	419	M11
Nanchong	419	M11	Pinghe	427	S14	Qinshizoi	416	L8	Sanya	428	P17
Nanchuan	419	N12	Pingjiang	426	Q12	Qin Xian	417	Q8	Sanying	417	M9
Nandan	419	N14	Pingle	419	P14	Qinyang	417	Q9	Sanyuan	417	N9
Nanfeng	426	S13	Pingliang	417	M9	Qinzhou	428	N15	Sarbulak	413	G4
Nangong	422	R8	Pinglu	417	P7	Qinzhou Gang	428	N15	Serca	415	H11
Nanggên	418	J11	Pingluo	417	M8	Qionghai	428	P17	Serikbuya	412	B6
Nang Xian	415	G12	Pingnan	428	P15	Qionglai	419	L11	Sêrtar	418	K11
Nanhua	418	K14	Pingnan	427	T13	Qiqian	420	S1	Sêrxü	418	J10
Nanhui	425	T11	Pingquan	420	S6	Qiqihar	421	T3	Shache	414	B7
Nanjian	418	K14	Pingshan	422	Q8	Qira	414	C8	Shadao	419	P12
Nanjiang	419	N11	Pingshan	421	U4	Qishu	419	N11	Shahe	422	Q8
Nanjing	425	S10	Pingshi	426	Q14	Qishui	428	P16	Shandan	416	K8
Nankang	426	R13	Pingtang	419	N14	Qitai	413	G5	Shangcai	424	Q10
Nanle	422	R9	Pingwu	419	M11	Qitaihe	421	V3	Shangcheng	424	R11
Nanling	425	S11	Pingxiang	419	N15	Qiubei	419	M14	Shangdu	420	Q6
Nanning	428	N15	Pingxiang	426	Q13	Qixia	423	T8	Shanggao	426	R12
Nanping	419	M10	Pingyang	427	T12	Qiyang	419	Q13	Shanghai	425	T11
Nanping	419	Q12	Pingyao	417	P8	Qlongzhong	428	P17	Shanghang	426	S14
Nanping	427	S13	Pingyin	422	R9	Qonggyai	415	G12	Shangqiu	424	R9
Nantong	425	T10	Pingyi	424	S9	Qongkol	413	E6	Shangrao	427	S12
Nan Xian	419	Q12	Pingyuan	426	R14	Quanzhou	419	P13	Shangying	419	N15
Nanxiong	426	R14	Pingwuanjie	419	L15	Quanzhou	427	T14	Shangyou Yichang	412	C6
Nanxu	419	P14	Pishan (Guma)	414	B7	Quanzijing	417	M7	Shangyu	425	T11
Nanyang	419	Q10	Pi Xian	419	L11	Que'erguo	413	E5	Shangzhi	421	U4
Nanzhang	419	Q11	Po	418	J12	Qufu	424	R9	Shangzhou	417	P10
Nanzhao	417	Q10	Pogranicnyj	421	W4	Quidong	419	Q13	Shanhaiguan	423	S7
Napo	419	M15	Pu'an	419	M14	Qujiang	426	Q14	Shanhetun	421	U4
Narin Nur	417	N7	Pu'er	418	K15	Qujing	419	L14	Shankou	428	P16
Nart	420	R6	Pubei	428	P15	Qumar Heyan	415	G9	Shanshan	413	G5
Nehe	421	T3	Pucheng	417	P9	Qumarlêb	415	H10	Shantou	429	S14
Neijiang	419	M12	Pucheng	427	S12	Qungtag	414	E11	Shanwei	429	R15
Neixiang	419	P10	Puge	418	L13	Qusum	415	G12	Shan Xian	424	R9
Nenjiang	421	T2	Pujiang	419	L12	Qu Xian	419	N11	Shanyang	417	P10
Ngamring	414	E12	Pujiang	425	T11	Qüxü	415	F12	Shanyin	417	Q7
Niangyuan	419	Q14	Pulu	414	C8	Quyang	422	Q7	Shaodong	419	Q13
Nilka	412	D5	Puning	429	S15	Quzhou	427	S12	Shaoguan	426	Q14
Ning'an	421	V4	Puqi	424	Q12				Shaowu	427	S13

Name			Name			Name			Name		
Shaoxing	425	T11	Suijiang	419	L12	Tongde	416	K9	Wu'an	422	Q8
Shaoyang	419	P13	Suileng	421	U3	Tonggu	426	R12	Wuchang	424	R11
Shaoyang	419	Q13	Suining	419	M11	Tongguzbasti	414	C7	Wuchang	421	U4
Shaping	428	P15	Suining	419	P13	Tonghai	418	L14	Wuchuan	419	N12
Shaquanzi	412	D4	Suining	425	S10	Tonghaiko	424	Q11	Wuchuan	428	P16
Shashi	419	Q11	Suixi	428	P16	Tonghe	421	V3	Wuchuan	417	P6
Shawan	413	E5	Suiyang	419	N13	Tonghua	421	U6	Wuda	417	M7
She	425	S11	Suiyang	421	W4	Tongjiang	419	N11	Wudalianchi	421	U2
Shehong	419	M11	Suizhong	423	S6	Tongjiang	421	W2	Wudaogou	421	U2
Shengli	421	U4	Suizhou	424	Q11	Tongliang	419	M12	Wuding	418	L14
Sheng Xian	425	T11	Sumxi	414	C9	Tongliao	421	T5	Wudu	419	M10
Shenjiamen	425	U11	Sunan	416	K8	Tongling	425	S11	Wufeng	419	P12
Shenmu	417	P8	Sunwu	421	U2	Tonglu	425	T11	Wugang	419	P13
Shen Xian	422	R8	Suqian	425	S10	Tongnan	419	M12	Wuhai	417	M7
Shen Xian	422	R9	Suzhou	424	R10	Tongren	416	L9	Wuhan	424	R11
Shenyang	421	T6	Suzhou	425	T11	Tongren	419	P13	Wuhao Zhuang	423	S8
Shenzhen	429	R15				Tongshan	424	R12	Wuhe	425	S10
She Xian	422	Q8	Tachakou	412	E4	Tongshi	428	P17	Wuhu	425	S11
Sheyang	425	T9	Tacheng	412	E3	Tongwei	417	M9	Wuhua	426	R14
Shibing	419	N13	Tagelajiabo	414	E10	Tongxiang	425	T11	Wüjang	414	B9
Shicheng	426	S13	Tahe	421	T1	Tongxin	417	M8	Wuli	415	G9
Shidao	423	T8	Taheman	412	A7	Tongyu	421	T4	Wulong	419	N12
Shihezi	413	E5	Tai'an	422	R9	Tongzi	419	N13	Wuming	428	N15
Shijiazhuang	422	Q8	Taibai	417	N10	Toramarkog	418	J10	Wuning	426	R12
Shiling	428	P15	Taibus Qi	420	Q6	Tsagaan Chulunta	415	G8	Wuping	426	S14
Shilipu	419	Q11	Taigu	417	Q8	Tucheng	419	M14	Wuqi	417	N8
Shimen	419	P12	Taihe	424	R10	Tug	417	N7	Wuqia	412	A6
Shimian	418	L12	Taihe	426	R13	Tukola Tolha	415	H10	Wushan	417	M9
Shinan	428	P15	Taihu	424	R11	Tulufan (Turpan)	413	F5	Wushan	419	P11
Shiping	418	L15	Taikang	424	R10	Tumd Youqi	417	P7	Wushi	412	C6
Shipu	425	U11	Tailai	421	T4	Tumd Zuoqi	417	P7	Wushi	428	P16
Shiqian	419	N13	Taining	427	S13	Tumen	421	V5	Wutai	417	Q8
Shiquan	419	N10	Taiping	419	N15	Tunchang	428	P17	Wutan	419	Q12
Shiquanhe	414	B10	Taiping	428	P15	Tungaztarim	414	D7	Wuwei	416	L8
Shishi	427	T14	Taipingchuan	421	T4	Tuotuo Heyan	415	G9	Wuwei	425	S11
Shishou	419	Q12	Taishan	429	Q15	Tuquan	421	S4	Wuxi	419	P11
Shiwulidun	417	M8	Taishan	422	R8	Tura	414	E8	Wuxi	425	T11
Shixing	426	R14	Taishun	427	T12				Wuxu	428	N15
Shiyan	419	P10	Taixing	425	T10	Ulan	416	J8	Wuxuan	428	P15
Shizhu	419	N12	Taiyuan	417	Q8	Ulanhot	421	S4	Wuxue	424	R11
Shizong	419	L14	Taizhou	425	T10	Ulanlinggi	413	F5	Wuyang	424	Q10
Shizuishan Qu	417	M7	Tancheng	425	S9	Ulan Tohoi	416	L7	Wuyi	418	L13
Shizuishan Shi	417	M8	Tanggu	422	R7	Uluggat	412	A6	Wuyi	427	T12
Shou Xian	424	R10	Tangguantun	422	R7	Urad Houqi	417	N6	Wuyiling	421	V2
Shouyang	417	Q8	Tanghe	419	Q10	Urad Qianqi	417	N7	Wuyishan	427	S12
Shuajingsi	418	L11	Tangjiatai	417	M9	Urad Zhongqi	417	N6	Wuyuan	425	S12
Shuangcheng	421	U4	Tangmai	415	H11	Urho	413	E4	Wuyuan	417	N7
Shuangfeng	419	Q13	Tangshan	422	S7	Ürümqi (Wulumuqi)	413	F5	Wuzhai	417	P7
Shuangjiang	418	K15	Tangyuan	421	V3	Usu	412	E4	Wuzhong	417	M8
Shuangpai	419	Q13	Taojiang	419	Q12	Utubulak	413	F4	Wuzhou	428	Q15
Shuangyang	421	U5	Taonan	421	T4	Uxin Ju	417	N7			
Shuanya-shan	421	V3	Taoyuan	419	P12	Uxin Qi	417	N8	Xagquka	415	G11
Shucheng	424	S11	Taturgou	414	A7				Xaidulla	414	B8
Shudanzhuang	414	D7	Taxi	421	U2	Wafangdian	423	T7	Xainza	414	E11
Shufu	412	A6	Taxkorgan	412	A7	Wanding	418	J14	Xarlag	417	N8
Shuiba	419	P12	Tazgun	412	B6	Wangcang	419	M11	Xar Obot	420	S4
Shulan	421	U4	Tekes	412	D5	Wangcheng	426	Q12	Xayar	412	D6
Shunchang	427	S13	Tengchong	418	J14	Wanggao	419	Q14	Xebert	421	T5
Shunde	429	Q15	Teng Xian	428	P15	Wangjiang	424	R11	Xeitongmoin	414	E12
Shuozhou	417	P7	Tengzhou	424	R9	Wangjie	418	K15	Xi'an	417	N10
Shuyang	425	S9	Têwo	417	L10	Wangmo	419	M14	Xiabande	421	T4
Sihong	425	S10	Tian'e	419	N14	Wangziguan	419	M10	Xiahe	416	L9
Sihui	429	Q15	Tianbanjie	424	S12	Wanlong	419	M12	Xiamen	427	S14
Siling	414	D12	Tianchang	425	S10	Wanning	428	P17	Xianfen	417	P9
Silong	428	N15	Tiandong	419	N15	Wanqing	421	V5	Xianfeng	419	P12
Simao	418	K15	Tianjin	422	R7	Wan Xian	419	N11	Xiangcheng	418	K12
Sinan	419	N13	Tianjun	416	K8	Wanyuan	419	N11	Xiangcheng	424	Q10
Siping	421	T5	Tianlin	419	M14	Wanzai	426	R12	Xiangfan	419	Q11
Sirong	419	P14	Tianmen	424	Q11	Waxxari	414	E7	Xianghuang Qi	420	Q6
Sishiliang	417	N7	Tiansheng	419	N11	Weichang	420	R6	Xiangning	417	P9
Sitang	416	L8	Tianshui	417	M10	Weifang	423	S8	Xiangshan	425	U11
Si Xian	425	S10	Tianshuihai	414	B8	Weihai	423	T8	Xiangshui	425	S9
Siyang	425	S10	Tiantai	425	T12	Weihui	424	Q9	Xiangtan	426	Q13
Siziwang Qi	420	P6	Tianyang	419	N15	Weinan	417	P10	Xiangxiang	426	Q13
Sog Xian	415	G11	Tianzhu	417	L8	Weining	419	M13	Xiangyun	418	K14
Solon	421	S4	Tianzhu	419	P13	Weishi	424	Q9	Xiangzhou	428	P14
Songjiang	425	T11	Tiefa	421	T5	Weitou	427	T14	Xianju	427	T12
Songjiang	421	V5	Tieli	421	U3	Weixi	418	K13	Xianning	424	R12
Songkou	427	T13	Tieling	421	T5	Wei Xian	422	R8	Xiantao	424	Q11
Songming	418	L14	Tielong	414	B8	Weiya	419	M13	Xianyang	417	N10
Songpan	419	L10	Tikanlik	413	F6	Weiya	416	H6	Xianyou	427	T13
Song Xian	417	Q10	Tingri	414	D12	Weiyuan	417	M9	Xiaogan	424	Q11
Songyang	427	T12	Tingri Xêgar	414	E12	Wenchang	419	M11	Xiaohe	419	N10
Songzi	419	Q11	Toba	418	J11	Wenchang	428	P16	Xiaojiahe	421	W3
Sonid Youqi	420	P6	Togtoh	417	P7	Wencheng	427	T12	Xiaojin	418	L11
Sonid Zuoqi	420	Q5	Toksum	413	F5	Wenchuan	419	L11	Xiaonanchuan	415	H9
Subei	415	H7	Toli	412	E4	Wendeng	423	T8	Xiaoshan	425	T11
Sugun	412	B6	Tomorlog	415	G8	Weng'an	419	N13	Xiao Xian	424	R9
Suhait	417	M7	Tong'an	427	S14	Wenquan	415	G10	Xiapu	427	T13
Suibin	421	W3	Tong'guan	417	P10	Wenquan	416	K9	Xiasi	419	N14
Suichang	427	T12	Tongbai	424	Q10	Wenshan	419	M15	Xiatai	412	C5
Suichuan	426	R13	Tongcheng	426	Q12	Wenshui	417	P8	Xiazhai	419	M14
Suide	417	P8	Tongcheng	424	S11	Wenxi	417	P9	Xiazi	419	N13
Suihua	421	U3	Tongchuan	417	P9	Wen Xian	419	M10	Xichang	418	L13
			Tongdao	419	P13	Wenzhou	427	T12	Xichou	419	M15

PICTURES

The Automobile Association wishes to thank the following photographers and organisations for their assistance in the preparation of this book.

Abbreviations for the picture credits are as follows – (t) top; (b) bottom; (l) left; (r) right; (c) centre; (AA) AA World Travel Library

2 AA/I Morejohn;
3i AA/D Henley;
3ii AA/I Morejohn;
3iii AA/I Morejohn;
3iv AA/A Mockford & N Bonetti;
4 AA/D Henley;
5 AA/D Henley;
6 AA/D Henley;
7 AA/B Bachman;
9 AA/D Henley;
10 AA/A Mockford & N Bonetti;
11t AA/B Madison;
11bl AA/A Mockford & N Bonetti;
11br AA/B Madison;
12t AA/J Goodman;
12b AA/I Morejohn;
13t AA/B Bachman;
13b AA/B Bachman;
14t AA/D Henley;
14b AA/N Hicks;
15 AA/D Henley;
16 Blue Jean Images/Getty Images;
17t Saulier Didier/Sunset/Rex Features;
17b ChinaFotoPress/Getty Images;
18 AA/B Bachman;
19l AA/D Henley;
19r AFP/Getty Images;
20 Top Photo Group/Rex Features;
21 AA/A Kouprianoff;
22 AA/I Morejohn;
23t AA/A Mockford & N Bonetti;

23b AA/A Mockford & N Bonetti;
24 AA/A Mockford & N Bonetti;
25 AA/B Bachman;
26 AA/B Madison;
27t AA/D Henley;
27b AA/A Mockford & N Bonetti;
28 The Art Archive/Bibliothèque Nationale Paris;
29bl AA/D Henley;
29br AA/W Guanmin;
30 AA/B Bachman;
31tl AA/A Mockford & N Bonetti;
31tr AA/A Mockford & N Bonetti;
32 AA/A Mockford & N Bonetti;
33bl Illustrated London News;
33br Keystone/Getty Images;
34 Forrest Anderson/Time Life Pictures/Getty Images;
35 AA/T Kaewdungdee;
37 AA/D Henley;
38 AA/B Bachman;
39 AA/D Henley;
40 AA/B Bachman;
41 AA/B Bachman;
42 Photodisc;
43 AA/A Mockford & N Bonetti;
44 AA/B Bachman;
45 AA/D Henley;
46 AA/A Mockford & N Bonetti;
47 AA/A Mockford & N Bonetti;
48 AA/D Henley;
49 AA/B Madison;
50 AA/A Mockford & N Bonetti;
51 AA/A Mockford & N Bonetti;
52 AA/A Mockford & N Bonetti;
60 AA/G Clements;
61 AA/A Mockford & N Bonetti;
62 AA/A Mockford & N Bonetti;
63 AA/A Mockford & N Bonetti;
64 AA/A Mockford & N Bonetti;
65 AA/A Mockford & N Bonetti;
66 AA/G Clements;
67 AA/A Mockford & N Bonetti;
68 AA/A Mockford & N Bonetti;
69l AA/A Mockford & N Bonetti;

69r AA/A Mockford & N Bonetti;
70 AA/A Mockford & N Bonetti;
71 AA/G Clements;
72l AA/A Mockford & N Bonetti;
72r AA/G Clements;
73 AA/G Clements;
74l AA/A Mockford & N Bonetti;
74r AA/G Clements;
75 AA/A Mockford & N Bonetti;
76 AA/A Mockford & N Bonetti;
78 AA/A Mockford & N Bonetti;
79l AA/G Clements;
79r AA/G Clements;
80 AA/A Mockford & N Bonetti;
81 AA/A Mockford & N Bonetti;
82 AA/A Mockford & N Bonetti;
83 AA/A Mockford & N Bonetti;
84 AA/A Mockford & N Bonetti;
85 AA/A Mockford & N Bonetti;
86 AA/G Clements;
87 AA/A Mockford & N Bonetti;
88 AA/A Kouprianoff;
89 AA/A Mockford & N Bonetti;
90 AA/A Mockford & N Bonetti;
91 AA/A Mockford & N Bonetti;
92 Asia Images/OTHK/Getty Images;
93 AA/A Mockford & N Bonetti;
94 AA/A Mockford & N Bonetti;
95 AA/A Mockford & N Bonetti;
96 AA/A Mockford & N Bonetti;
98 AA/A Mockford & N Bonetti;
99 AA/A Mockford & N Bonetti;
100 AA/A Mockford & N Bonetti;
101 AA/A Mockford & N Bonetti;
102 AA/A Mockford & N Bonetti;
105 AA/A Mockford & N Bonetti;
108 AA/A Mockford & N Bonetti;
111 AA/A Mockford & N Bonetti;
112 AA/A Mockford & N Bonetti;
114 AA/I Morejohn;
117 AA/A Mockford & N Bonetti;
118 AA/I Morejohn;
120 AA/I Morejohn;
121 Photolibrary Group;
122 AA/D Henley;

ACKNOWLEDGMENTS CHINA

123 AA/D Henley;
124 AA/I Morejohn;
125t Jon Arnold Images Ltd/Alamy;
125b Keren Su/China Span/Getty Images;
126 AA/I Morejohn;
127 AA/T Kaewdungdee;
128 AA/I Morejohn;
129 AA/I Morejohn;
130 Liu Liqun/Corbis;
131 AA/I Morejohn;
132 AA/B Madison;
133 AA/B Madison;
134 AA/B Madison;
135t AA/B Madison;
135b AA/B Madison;
136 AA/B Madison;
137 AA/B Madison;
138 AA/T Kaewdungdee;
139t AA/T Kaewdungdee;
139b AA/T Kaewdungdee;
140 AA/D Henley;
142 AA/B Madison;
144 AA/T Kaewdungdee;
147 AA/T Kaewdungdee;
148 AA/B Madison;
150 AA/B Madison;
152 dk/Alamy;
153 Redlink/Corbis;
154 AA/B Madison;
155t Juliet Butler/Alamy;
155b Dennis Cox/Alamy;
156 AA/B Madison;
157l AA/B Madison;
157r AA/B Madison;
158 AA/B Madison;
159l Nigel Hicks/Alamy;
159r Linda Reinink-Smith/Alamy;
160 AA/I Morejohn;
161 AA/I Morejohn;
162 AA/B Madison;
163 AA/B Madison;
164 AA/B Madison;
165 AA/B Madison;
166 AA/B Madison;
169 AA/B Madison;
170 AA/B Madison;

173 AA/B Madison;
174 Traders Hotel;
176 AA/D Henley;
178 Eddie Gerald/Alamy;
179t AA/I Morejohn;
179b AA/I Morejohn;
180 AA/D Henley;
181 AA/D Henley;
182 AA/I Morejohn;
183l AA/I Morejohn;
183r AA/I Morejohn;
184 AA/D Henley;
185 AA/D Henley;
186t Eddie Gerald/Alamy;
186b AA/I Morejohn;
187 AA/D Henley;
188t Adams Picture Library t/a apl/Alamy;
188b Doug Traverso/Robert Harding;
189 Jose Fuste Raga/Corbis;
190 AA/D Henley;
191t AA/D Henley;
191b AA/D Henley;
192 AA/D Henley;
194 AA/D Henley;
196 AA/D Henley;
198 AA/D Henley;
200 Ethel Davies/Robert Harding;
201 AA/I Morejohn;
202 AA/D Henley;
203t AA/A Kouprianoff;
203b AA/D Henley;
204 AA/D Henley;
205 AA/D Henley;
206 Rod Porteous/Robert Harding;
207 Dennis Cox/Alamy;
208 AA/I Morejohn;
209 AA/L K Stow;
210 AA/L K Stow;
211 AA/L K Stow;
212 AA/I Morejohn;
213 Dennis Cox/Alamy;
214 AA/D Henley;
215t AA/D Henley;
215b AA/D Henley;
216 Royal Mountain Travel, Kathmandu www.royal-mt-trek.com;

218 AA/D Henley;
221 Sheraton Jiuzhaigou;
222 AA/D Henley;
224 AA/D Henley;
226 Photolibrary Group;
227 Best View Stock/Alamy;
228 AA/D Henley;
229 AA/D Henley;
230 AA/D Henley;
231bl AA/D Henley;
231br AA/D Henley;
232 AA/D Henley;
233 AA/A Kouprianoff;
234 AA/D Henley;
235 AA/D Henley;
236t AA/D Henley;
236b AA/D Henley;
237 AA/J Goodman;
238 AA/I Morejohn;
239 Neil McAllister/Alamy;
240 AA/D Henley;
241t AA/D Henley;
241b AA/D Henley;
242 AA/D Henley;
243t AA/D Henley;
243b AA/D Henley 244 AA/D Henley;
248 AA/D Henley;
250 AA/D Henley;
252 AA/D Henley;
254 AA/B Bachman;
256 AA/D Henley;
257 AA/D Henley;
258 AA/I Morejohn;
259 AA/I Morejohn;
260 AA/D Henley;
262t AA/D Henley;
262b AA/D Henley;
263 AA/I Morejohn;
264 AA/D Henley;
265bl AA/I Morejohn;
265br AA/D Henley;
266 AA/D Henley;
267 AA/D Henley;
268bl AA/D Henley;
268br AA/D Henley;
269 AA/I Morejohn;

270 AA/A Mockford & N Bonetti;
271 Liu Liqun/Corbis;
272 AA/D Henley;
273 AA/D Henley;
274 AA/A Mockford & N Bonetti;
275 AA/A Mockford & N Bonetti;
276 AA/D Henley;
278 AA/D Henley;
280 AA/D Henley ;
283 AA/I Morejohn;
284 AA/D Henley;
286 AA/A Mockford & N Bonetti;
292 AA/A Mockford & N Bonetti;
293t Rex Features;
293b AA/G Clements;
294 AA/A Mockford & N Bonetti;
295 AA/A Mockford & N Bonetti;
296 AA/A Mockford & N Bonetti;
297 AA/G Clements;
298 AA/A Mockford & N Bonetti;
299 AA/A Mockford & N Bonetti;
300tl AA/A Mockford & N Bonetti;
300tr AA/A Mockford & N Bonetti;
301 AA/A Mockford & N Bonetti;
302 AA/A Mockford & N Bonetti;
303c AA/A Mockford & N Bonetti;
303r AA/A Mockford & N Bonetti;
304 AA/A Mockford & N Bonetti;
305 AA/A Mockford & N Bonetti;
306 AA/A Mockford & N Bonetti;
307 AA/A Mockford & N Bonetti;
308l AA/A Mockford & N Bonetti;
308r AA/A Mockford & N Bonetti;
309 AA/A Mockford & N Bonetti;
310 AA/A Mockford & N Bonetti;
311 AA/A Mockford & N Bonetti;
312 AA/G Clements;
313 AA/A Mockford & N Bonetti;
314 AA/A Mockford & N Bonetti;
315 AA/A Mockford & N Bonetti;
316 AA/A Mockford & N Bonetti;
319 AA/A Mockford & N Bonetti;
320 AA/G Clements;
322 Whampoa Club/Three on the Bund;
324 Three on the Bund;
326 AA/A Mockford & N Bonetti;

328 Grand Hyatt Shanghai;
330 AA/D Henley;
335 AA/D Henley;
336 AA/A Kouprianoff;
338 AA/B Bachman;
339t AA/A Kouprianoff;
339b AA/B Bachman;
340 Hong Kong Tourism Board;
341 AA/B Bachman;
342 AA/N Hicks;
344 Hong Kong Tourism Board;
346 AA/B Bachman;
347 AA/B Bachman;
348 AA/D Henley;
349 AA/D Henley;
350 AA/D Henley;
351t AA/D Henley;
351b AA/D Henley;
352 AA/A Kouprianoff;
353 AA/D Henley;
354 AA/A Kouprianoff;
356 AA/B Bachman;
359 Ocean Park Hong Kong;
360 AA/N Hicks;
361 AA/B Bachman;
362 Hong Kong Tourism Board;
365 AA/B Bachman;
367 AA/N Hicks;
368 AA/D Henley;
370 AA/D Henley;
371 AA/D Henley;
372 AA/A Mockford & N Bonetti;
375 AA/A Mockford & N Bonetti;
377 AA/D Henley;
379 Gordon D R Clements;
380 AA/A Mockford & N Bonetti;
381 AA/A Mockford & N Bonetti;
382 AA/B Bachman;
383 AA/B Bachman;
385 AA/A Mockford & N Bonetti;
386 AA/B Madison;
387 AA/A Mockford & N Bonetti;
388 AA/A Mockford & N Bonetti;
389 AA/A Mockford & N Bonetti;
390 AA/T Kaewdungdee;
391 AA/A Mockford & N Bonetti;
392 Andrew Oxenham/China Heaven

Creation;
394 John Gollings/ATP;
396 AA/B Madison;
397 Hong Kong Tourism Board;
398 AA/A Mockford & N Bonetti;
399 AA/A Mockford & N Bonetti;
400 AA/B Madison;
401l AA/A Mockford & N Bonetti;
401r AA/A Mockford & N Bonetti;
402 AA/A Mockford & N Bonetti;
403 AA/A Mockford & N Bonetti;
404 Grand Hyatt Shanghai;
405l AA/D Henley;
405r AA/A Mockford & N Bonetti;
406 AA/B Bachman;
409 AA/B Bachman;
411 AA/D Henley.

Every effort has been made to trace the copyright holders, and we apologise in advance for any accidental errors. We would be happy to apply any corrections in the following edition of this publication.

CHINA

ACKNOWLEDGMENTS

CREDITS

Managing editor
Sheila Hawkins

Project editor
Claire Strange

Design
Drew Jones, pentacorbig, Nick Otway

Cover design
Chie Ushio

Picture research
Vivien Little

Image retouching and repro
Sarah Montgomery

Main contributors
CPA Media, Peter Ellegard, George McDonald,
Christopher and Melanie Rice

Updater
Graham Bond

Indexer
Marie Lorimer

Production
Karen Gibson

See It China
ISBN 978-1-4000-0386-0
Second Edition

Published in the United States by Fodor's Travel and simultaneously in Canada by Random House of Canada Limited, Toronto.
Published in the United Kingdom by AA Publishing.
Fodor's is a registered trademark of Random House, Inc., and Fodor's See It is a trademark of Random House, Inc.
Fodor's Travel is a division of Random House, Inc.

Color separation by Keenes, Andover, UK
Printed and bound by Sirivatana, Thailand
10 9 8 7 6 5 4 3 2 1

Special Sales: This book is available for special discounts for bulk purchases for sales promotions or premiums. Special editions, including personalized covers, excerpts of existing books, and corporate imprints, can be created in large quantities for special needs.
For more information, write to Special Markets/Premium Sales, 1745 Broadway, MD 6-2, New York, NY 10019
or e-mail specialmarkets@randomhouse.com
Important Note: Time inevitably brings changes, so always confirm prices, travel facts, and other perishable information when it matters. Although Fodor's cannot accept responsibility for errors, you can use this guide in the confidence that we have taken every care to ensure its accuracy.

A03807
Maps in this title produced from mapping © MAIRDUMONT / Falk Verlag 2009
Transport maps © Communicarta Ltd, UK
Weather chart statistics supplied by Weatherbase © Copyright 2006 Canty and Associates, LLC.

Dear Traveler,

From buying a plane ticket to booking a
room and seeing the sights, a trip goes much
more smoothly when you have a good travel
guide. Dozens of writers, editors, designers,
and cartographers have worked hard to
make the book you hold in your hands a
good one. Was it everything you expected?
Were our descriptions accurate? Were our
recommendations on target? And did you find
our tips and practical advice helpful? Your
ideas and experiences matter to us. If we have
missed or misstated something, we'd love
to hear about it. Fill out our survey at www.
fodors.com/books/feedback/, or e-mail us at
seeit@fodors.com. Or you can snail mail to the
See It Editor at Fodor's, 1745 Broadway, New
York, New York 10019. We'll look forward to
hearing from you.

Tim Jarrell
Publisher

Unleash the Possibilities
of Travel With Fodor's

Read before you get there, navigate your picks while you're there – make your trip unforgettable with Fodor's guidebooks. Fodor's offers the assurance of our expertise, the guarantee of selectivity, and the choice details that truly define a destination. Our books are written by local authors, so it's like having a friend wherever you travel.

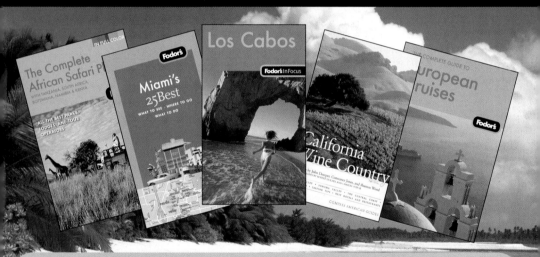

With more than 10 different types of guidebooks to more than 150 destinations around the world, Fodor's has choices to meet every traveler's needs.

Visit **www.fodors.com** to find the guidebooks and connect with a like-minded community of selective travelers – living, learning, and traveling on their terms.

Fodor's For Choice Travel Experiences